AMNESTY INTERNATIONAL REPORT

1990

This report
covers the period
January to December
1989

Amnesty International Publications
1 Easton Street, London WC1X 8DJ
United Kingdom

First published 1990
by Amnesty International Publications
1 Easton Street, London WC1X 8DJ, United Kingdom

© Copyright Amnesty International Publications 1990

ISBN 0 86210 177 8
AI Index: POL 10/03/90
Original Language: English

Typeset by: Fingerprint Graphics Limited

Printed by: The Bath Press, Lower Bristol Road, Bath

Cover design: Tessa Pellow

This report documents Amnesty International's work and its concerns throughout the world during 1989. The absence of an entry in this report on a particular country does not imply that no human rights violations of concern to Amnesty International have taken place there during the year. Nor is the length of a country entry any basis for a comparison of the extent and depth of Amnesty International's concerns in a country. Regional maps have been included in this report to indicate the location of countries and territories cited in the text and for that purpose only. It is not possible on the small scale used to show precise political boundaries, nor should the maps be taken as indicating any view on the status of disputed territory. Amnesty International takes no position on territorial questions. Disputed boundaries and cease-fire lines are shown, where possible, by broken lines. Areas whose disputed status is a matter of unresolved concern before the relevant bodies of the United Nations have been indicated by striping.

CONTENTS

APPENDICES

INTRODUCTION

Thousands of people were imprisoned, tortured and killed in 1989 by governments seeking to repress or control ethnic and nationalist tensions in their country. The repressive measures have, in many cases, served to entrench bitter conflicts, dimmed prospects for dialogue and added to the toll of suffering and death.

Peaceful protesters in many countries were arbitrarily arrested in vast numbers. Many were held for months without charge or trial. In countless cases, state torture was the price citizens paid for being identified as sympathizers with ethnic or nationalist movements.

Around the world, particularly where the tensions erupted into violence, tens of thousands of people became victims of security operations resulting in "disappearances" and extrajudicial executions.

The conflicts ranged from local disputes over the cultural rights of distinctive ethnic groups through to full-scale confrontation over demands for autonomy or secession. Often the demands were supported solely by non-violent campaigns of pressure and protest. But in many instances, violent attacks or armed insurgency became dominant features of the conflicts.

Amnesty International is aware of the social, political and economic complexities confronting governments. Conflict with armed opposition groups, intercommunal violence or economic crises are factors that cannot be ignored. In many countries, serious human rights abuses are carried out by non-governmental entities — including the torture and killing of prisoners, actions which Amnesty International condemns as a matter of principle, whoever the perpetrator. However, none of these factors can ever justify or excuse a government violating the basic human rights of any of its citizens or of those over whom it exercises control.

Many of the world's ethnic and nationalist tensions are rooted in the movement and dislocation of people in the past: the mass migrations of people fleeing oppression or seeking economic survival, and the redrawing of national borders by colonial powers or in the aftermath of wars. The result is that many of today's nation-states encompass different population groups, each with an identity and a history of its own.

This combination of people of different ethnic or national origins does not always lead to conflict or human rights violations by the authorities. Where conflicts have arisen, the causes and intensities have varied greatly. Demands to end economic or political privilege of one group, pressure for equal treatment before the law or to express a culture freely, movements to end discrimination in jobs, the armed forces or education — all these can lead to tensions and sometimes open conflict between different ethnic or national groups.

These tensions have often been exacerbated by governments pursuing policies which intensify the demands or, in some cases, result in persistent abuses against people of particular ethnic or national origin. In many countries,

2

movements have arisen promoting the aspirations of these groups.

The response of governments to such challenges is often to target individual citizens or entire local communities with measures that deprive them of the very civil and political rights they need to pursue peacefully their social and cultural rights. In some countries repressive measures such as the denial of free speech, free association and free assembly are clearly linked to an official policy aimed at the domination or forcible assimilation of ethnic groups in the nation or the destruction of distinctive features of national groups. In other countries such measures may be introduced in the interests of public order at a time of intense internal division.

Neither the existence of social unrest, nor a desire to control it, lessens the obligation upon any government to respect fundamental human rights. Rather, it is a government's responsibility to ensure that social divisions, whether or not based on ethnic or national differences, do not lead to situations in which human rights are violated.

Amnesty International does not take sides in conflicts over national independence, cultural or regional autonomy, or territorial disputes. It simply demands that international human rights standards are not violated by governments or government-like entities, irrespective of the circumstances.

In Somalia, gross human rights violations have occurred against a background of clan-related tensions. The Somali National Movement (SNM), whose membership is mainly from one northern clan, has been fighting the government since 1980. Members of the clan — the Issaq — have been targeted for arrest, torture and extrajudicial execution either in reprisal for SNM activities or on suspicion of having links with the organization. Many Issaq areas, including the northern capital of Hargeisa, have been devastated by intensified fighting since 1988. Hundreds of thousands of people have fled to Ethiopia and Djibouti to seek refuge from reprisals by the Somali army, which is dominated by other clans. Many Issaqs have been imprisoned for criticizing the government's policies towards the north or for simply being Issaq. Most were released in a general amnesty declared in early 1989 but further arrests took place later in the year. Some 46 prisoners in Mogadishu, all of them Issaq and including children, were massacred by soldiers in July. A rebellion by Ogadeni clan members in the army led to similar reprisals against Ogadeni in the southwest in late 1989. In addition, Somalis living in neighbouring Kenya were also targeted for arbitrary arrest by the Kenyan authorities in late 1989 on account of their ethnic origin.

In Ethiopia, there has been armed opposition in several parts of the country for the past three decades by groups fighting for territorial independence or against the central government on the basis of regional or ethnic identity. Many people from these areas, particularly those from Eritrea, Tigray, Wollega and Hararghe, have been imprisoned and often tortured on suspicion of having links with the Eritrean People's Liberation Front or other Eritrean groups, the Tigray People's Liberation Front or the Oromo Liberation Front. Some have been adopted as prisoners of conscience as they were imprisoned for their regional or ethnic origin and not for any proven advocacy of armed opposition. Several were released in 1989 after many years in detention without trial, but others remained in prison.

In Sudan, members of ethnic groups from the south have been tortured and killed by members of the armed forces and government-backed militias. The government has responded to the activities of the Sudan People's Liberation Army (SPLA), which draws most of its support from southern ethnic groups, by supporting several tribal militias from other ethnic groups loyal to the government. After a lull in mid-1989 due to a cease-fire, killings of villagers by government soldiers and militia increased in October, while government officials continued to dismiss raids on civilians as "tribal fighting". Members of the Dinka, Nuber, Nuer and Shilluk communities, displaced by fighting in the south, have been victims of gross human rights violations solely because of their ethnic origin. In July, three weeks after a new military government took power, at least 34 Dinka and Luo people were killed by soldiers in the southern town of Wau, apparently as a reprisal after a soldier was injured. Southerners living in the north have also been targeted. In October soldiers reportedly took some 42 Dinka and Nuba people from police custody in Khartoum and extrajudicially executed them. Troops and militias have extrajudicially executed thousands of men, women and children from Dinka and other non-Arab ethnic groups since the outbreak of civil war in 1983.

In Sri Lanka, reports of "disappearances", extrajudicial executions, arbitrary arrests and torture escalated in the 1980s against a background of an armed Tamil secessionist movement based in the northeast. Human rights violations continued in the northeast after July 1987 when Indian forces took over responsibility for security in the area. In the south, opposition to the government increased among the majority Sinhalese following the Indo-Sri Lanka accord, and since mid-1987 a militant Sinhalese group has engaged in extensive killings of civilians. New legislation and special emergency powers adopted in the early 1980s to combat Tamil secessionist movements have been used since 1987 against the Sinhalese militants in the south, where Sri Lankan security forces have committed widespread human rights violations. The legislation allows long-term incommunicado detention without charge or trial and throughout 1989 provided for security forces to dispose of bodies without post-mortem or inquest, facilitating extrajudicial executions by enabling security forces to kill with effective impunity. In 1989 thousands of people were reported to have "disappeared" following arrest or to have been extrajudicially executed by the regular Sri Lankan security forces or paramilitary forces believed to be associated with them.

In the state of Punjab in India, hundreds of non-combatant Sikh civilians have been victims of human rights abuses since armed conflict between Sikh groups and government forces escalated in 1984. "Encounter killings" — deliberate extrajudicial executions in so-called confrontations staged by the police — have continued to be reported in the region. Elderly people and children have been among those subjected to arbitrary arrest, particularly in the

4 Batala District, in apparent attempts by the authorities to intimidate the population. Government forces have also beaten village elders in public and women have been raped by the police. Civilian detainees have been tortured by police and paramilitary forces. Most reports of torture have been received from the three western districts bordering Pakistan. Several Sikhs have "disappeared" from detention.

In Myanmar (formerly Burma), army units on counter-insurgency duties have executed and tortured indigenous peasants in remote and mountainous areas where armed opposition groups are active. The peasants living in areas controlled by the insurgents, and the members of the principal insurgent groups themselves, are not ethnic Bamans (Burmans); they are members of a variety of ethnic groups such as the Kayin, Shan and Mon. The opposition groups have been waging a guerrilla war against the central government since the country gained independence from the United Kingdom (UK) in 1948.

Since 1975, when Indonesian forces invaded East Timor and claimed it as Indonesia's 27th province, there have been repeated reports of serious human rights violations against the East Timorese, who are predominantly of Malay and Melanesian origin. In 1989, despite a heavily publicized "opening" of the island to tourism and commerce, reports of unfair trials, torture in police and military custody, political killings and "disappearances" continued to emerge.

In the UK, armed groups from both the minority Catholic and majority Protestant communities in Northern Ireland have continued to resort to violence in support of their demands. In attempting to deal with perpetrators of politically motivated violent acts, the UK Government has failed to allay public concern that its agents have operated outside the rule of law. A series of fatal shootings by security forces has given rise to serious allegations of an official policy allowing suspected members of armed groups, mainly the Catholic-based Irish Republican Army (IRA), to be deliberately killed rather than arrested. The official procedures for investigating such killings have failed to clarify fully the facts of these cases, and the government has rejected calls for an independent judicial inquiry. In two separate cases involving bomb attacks carried out in 1974 by the IRA in England, people were sentenced to life imprisonment mainly or solely on the basis of uncorroborated confessions which the prisoners claimed had been obtained through threats and ill-treatment while they were held incommunicado. The "Guildford Four", convicted in 1975 for bomb attacks, were released in October 1989 after new evidence emerged that the police had lied to the courts about the confession statements. The "Birmingham Six", convicted in 1975 for bomb attacks, remained in prison at the end of the year.

But even in countries where movements have expressed nationalist or ethnic aspirations using mainly peaceful methods, people have been subjected to human rights abuses.

In the USSR, for example, there was a dramatic upsurge of unrest and political organization among national groups in 1989. In some cases the Soviet authorities responded with the forcible dispersal of non-violent demonstrations, the banning of meetings and the arrest of organizers, who were then held for up to several months before being released. Such incidents were reported in Armenia, Azerbaidzhan, Byelorussia and Moldavia. In April, 20 people died when special troops broke up a peaceful demonstration in the Georgian capital Tbilisi. Around 3,000 were said to have been injured, most by the effects of gas. In October an unarmed crowd of about 1,000 people in the western Ukraine was charged repeatedly by police and special troops, who allegedly beat and kicked children and adults indiscriminately. The crowd was protesting against police disruption of a folk festival. Several dozen of the injured needed hospital treatment.

In Yugoslavia, troops were sent into Kosovo province in February 1989 in response to a general strike by ethnic Albanians who were protesting against constitutional changes limiting the province's autonomy. Clashes led to at least 24 deaths, and several hundred ethnic Albanians were administratively detained for up to four months without charge or trial. Many later alleged that they had been savagely beaten while held incommunicado. Over 1,000 others were summarily sentenced to up to two months' imprisonment; others were held for trial on charges of "counter-revolutionary activities".

In China, demonstrations by Tibetans demanding independence were broken up in March 1989 by Chinese troops and martial law was imposed in the Tibetan capital Lhasa. Tens of Tibetan demonstrators were believed to have been shot dead during the violent confrontations and more than 1,000 were subsequently arrested. There were many reports of Tibetans being tortured in detention, including severe beating, electric shocks and suspension by the arms for long periods.

If tensions between different groups degenerate into intercommunal violence, the duty of the authorities is to keep the peace. All too often, however, governments themselves abandon the rule of law and instead of maintaining order, resort to trampling on the human rights of a section of their citizens.

In Burundi, tension between the ruling minority Tutsi and the Hutu, who make up 80 per cent of the population, erupted into intercommunal fighting in mid-1988 with many Tutsi killed by Hutu. Thousands of unarmed Hutu were subsequently massacred by the Tutsi-dominated armed forces. By the end of 1989 the massacres had not been investigated and more than 40 Hutu arrested in mid-1988 had not been brought to trial.

Intercommunal violence was also the context for government security forces committing human rights abuses in Mauritania. In the wake of disturbances between Senegalese and Mauritanians in April 1989, which led to hundreds of deaths in Mauritanian and Senegalese cities, thousands of black Mauritanians were expelled to neighbouring Senegal. In the process of these expulsions, the predominantly Beïdane (Arabic-speaking) Mauritanian police and army arbitrarily detained, tortured or killed many black Mauritanians. The Mauritanian Government rejected Amnesty International's concern about these abuses and accused the organization of taking Senegal's side.

In several countries, it has been stated official policy to deprive certain ethnic

6 or national groups of their civil and political rights. The most extreme example of this has been the *apartheid* system in South Africa, where the Constitution itself has denied the black majority population political rights and the state has persistently abused its powers to maintain a society based on racial inequality. Widespread opposition to *apartheid* has been met by emergency powers, first introduced on a nationwide scale in June 1986 and renewed annually since then. These have been used to detain many thousands of government opponents without charge or trial. Prisoners have frequently been ill-treated in detention and hundreds of political opponents of the government have been placed under restriction orders, sometimes including house arrest. Judicial death sentences have been imposed disproportionately on the black population by an almost entirely white judiciary: 97 per cent of the 1,070 people hanged in the country between 1980 and 1988 were black. In 1989 at least 60 people were executed; two of them were white.

Populations living under occupation by a foreign power are particularly liable to human rights abuses. In addition to the existence of human rights standards, there is a separate body of international law designed specifically to regulate the conduct of occupying powers. However, as has been shown in the Israeli-Occupied Territories, governments do not always respect these standards and laws.

Israel occupied the West Bank and Gaza Strip — areas populated by Palestinian Arabs — in 1967. In the two years since December 1987, when an uprising against the occupation and in support of an independent Palestinian state began, hundreds of Palestinians have been killed by Israeli forces, including possible victims of extrajudicial executions and some who may have died as a result of torture. Thousands have been beaten and about 9,000 have been administratively detained without charge or trial.

Ethnic minorities or national groups have faced varying degrees of human rights abuses in other parts of the world. In Chad, members of the Hadjeraï ethnic group have been persecuted. More than 180 Hadjeraïs were believed to have been held in secret detention since mid-1987: reportedly many of them have been tortured and some may have died. At least 200 members of the Zaghawa ethnic group were detained after April 1989. Many of those held were arrested arbitrarily because of their ethnic origin.

Kurds have faced extreme and widespread human rights violations. The Kurds were denied a state of their own by the European colonial powers after the break-up of the Ottoman Empire in the 1920s. The territory heavily populated by Kurds is now divided between Iraq, Iran, Turkey, Syria and the USSR.

In Iraq, Kurds have been systematically subjected to human rights abuses. In 1988 Kurdish towns and villages were attacked from the air with chemical weapons and bombs and whole communities were rounded up and shot. Tens of thousands of Kurds fled the country. Members of Kurdish opposition groups were among thousands of political prisoners, including possible prisoners of conscience, who remained in detention throughout 1989 without charge or trial, or after summary trials. They were also among those reportedly tortured while in detention. Of the thousands of detainees who had "disappeared" in previous years, 8,000 Barzani Kurds remained unaccounted for. Information was received in October 1989 of the "disappearance" of 353 Kurds after their arrest in 1988 in Duhok Province following chemical weapons attacks in the area by Iraqi Government forces. The majority were civilians, mainly farmers, and included 52 children. In the same month, reports were received about the "disappearance" of several Kurds from Bahark resettlement camp outside Arbil city. In addition, seven Kurds who gave themselves up to the authorities after an amnesty had been declared in February were executed in April 1989.

In Iran, hundreds of members of opposition groups fighting for Kurdish autonomy have been among thousands of political prisoners subjected to unfair trials, torture and execution since the 1979 revolution. In a wave of secret executions that began in August 1988 and continued until January 1989, over 2,000 political prisoners were executed. Among the victims were members of Kurdish opposition parties.

In Turkey, the government's policy has been to deny the existence of Kurds as an ethnic minority. It has also refused them the right to pursue their own culture. Several thousand members of Kurdish organizations have been imprisoned, among them many prisoners of conscience. One was sentenced in 1988 to seven years' imprisonment for speaking in Kurdish when defending himself in court. Kurds have also figured prominently in reports of torture in Turkish police stations and jails, in accounts of unfair political trials, and in lists of prisoners on death row.

In neighbouring Bulgaria, the pattern was similar, although the target was the Turkish minority. Until December the government denied Turks their ethnic identity and forbade the use of the Turkish language. Hundreds of ethnic Turks were imprisoned or banished for resisting the policy, and large numbers remained in prison in 1989. In May 1989 security forces killed several ethnic Turks during and after peaceful demonstrations protesting the assimilation campaign. Others died as a result of beatings, which were reportedly widespread and indiscriminate.

Suppression of cultural rights has also led to widespread abuses in Guatemala. When a council of indigenous communities was set up in 1988 to campaign for the rights of Indian communities, the people involved quickly became the target of death threats, "disappearances" and extrajudicial executions. Overwhelming evidence linked members of the official security forces with the abuses, acting either in uniform or clandestinely in the guise of "death squads". In April 1989 uniformed soldiers seized four men from their homes apparently because of their membership of the council. Their whereabouts were unknown at the end of 1989.

In several countries, ethnic groups are treated as less than equal and their rights as more expendable than those of others. Neither law enforcement agencies nor the judicial system give them adequate protection under the law. In Brazil, many members of indigenous communities — Indians — have been

8 killed trying to defend their land and communities from incursions by ranchers and mining and timber companies, often with the acquiescence or collusion of local governmental authorities. Indians are theoretically offered greater protection under the law than peasants, but in practice, as with peasants, the authorities have persistently failed to guarantee their legal rights or adequately investigate violent assaults on them and bring those responsible to justice. No progress had been made in bringing to trial non-Indian settlers accused of ambushing and killing 14 members of the Ticuna tribe in 1988. Several Yanomami men, women and children have been killed by miners since the incursion into their lands began in 1986. Ill-treatment by military police of Indians, such as the Macuxi in Roraima and Ticuna in Amazonas state, has also been reported.

A pattern of abuse of members of underprivileged groups also continued in India, where many victims of torture were members of tribal communities or scheduled castes (known as "harijans" or, formerly, "untouchables"). Although India's Constitution gives these people special protection, in practice they are particularly vulnerable to ill-treatment at the hands of the police. For example, many victims of torture and rape in police custody belong to these communities, particularly in the state of Bihar. In early 1989, 20 members of the Pardhi tribal community were held for several weeks in Maharashtra in unacknowledged detention. As in other cases, a local magistrate refused to hear their complaints of torture and one of them died in custody. Over 50 people died in police custody in India in 1989 in suspicious circumstances: a similar figure to that recorded in previous years. Most were poor and many were members of such underprivileged groups. Relatives and others alleged that they had been tortured to death. Those responsible were not known to have been brought to justice.

In 1989 Amnesty International campaigned against the death penalty and executions throughout the world. This terrible and final punishment tends to be inflicted mostly on the vulnerable members of a society — including members of racial or ethnic minorities. In the United States of America, evidence suggested that the death penalty continued to be used in a racially biased manner, with death sentences being more often imposed in cases where the murder victim was white.

It is not Amnesty International's role to take a position on the difficult and vexed questions of national independence, regional and cultural autonomy, and territorial integrity, nor does it take sides in any of the complex disputes which form the background to the human suffering described in this report. The organization sees its role as constantly reminding governments and public opinion that there are international standards set for the protection of human rights which all governments are bound to observe, irrespective of the circumstances. Where governments or government-like bodies fail to respect these standards, Amnesty International will do all that it can to bring the human rights violations to world attention and to prevent further abuses from occurring.

AMNESTY INTERNATIONAL — A WORLDWIDE CAMPAIGN

"Hello Amnesty International, I'm...from Karl-Marx-Stadt, German Democratic Republic. Amnesty International is a very sensible organization. I find it right that an organization stands up for human rights, an important matter in the world. I do not know enough about your organization. That is why I want material about Amnesty International. Please! Give me the possibility. Thank you."

This is one of the many letters which arrive every day at the International Secretariat of Amnesty International in London. They come from around the world, from women and men who simply want to do something about human rights for other people. Countless others contact their local Amnesty International offices.

In 1989 increasing numbers of people sent letters from Eastern Europe, all of them requesting information and many asking to take part in Amnesty International's work. Since April these people have been able to become "international members" — people in countries without an Amnesty International structure who regularly receive information about human rights and wherever possible participate in actions initiated by the International Secretariat. By the end of the year, over 200 people had become international members worldwide including, for the first time, in Hungary, Poland and Yugoslavia. People also joined for the first time in the island of Antigua in the Caribbean, Malaysia, the People's Republic of Mongolia, Taiwan and Viet Nam. In some of these countries international members began to form groups, meeting on a regular basis.

Although new to Amnesty International, they already have a great deal in common with more than 700,000 ordinary women and men in about 150 countries around the world who are members of the movement and subscribers. They are all inspired by the United Nations Universal Declaration of Human Rights, which forms the basis of Amnesty International's work. They share an understanding that human rights know no frontiers and are an international responsibility. They are committed to doing something about human rights violations wherever they occur and as quickly as possible, and are determined to maintain pressure on governments on behalf of prisoners of conscience for as long as it takes to free them.

As methods of communication become more advanced, news of human rights violations spreads faster and to a wider audience. This gives Amnesty International the opportunity to speed up its responses, as was made necessary in mid-1989 by events in China. Millions of television viewers worldwide were shocked when they saw for themselves government troops in Beijing firing on unarmed civilians. Within hours of the military intervention, the organization had collated information about wide-ranging human rights violations and had begun mobilizing its membership to try to prevent further abuses. Amnesty International estimates that it organized 250,000 letters and telegrams to be sent in the first five days after 4 June when the killings and arrests began. By mid-September the total had risen to well over three million.

Information about killings and arrests in China came through to the International Secretariat from many sources in the days and weeks following the military crackdown. After coordinating and cross-checking the information, the International Secretariat sent a daily stream of calls for action to Amnesty International offices and members around the world. Some actions called for urgent protest against the widespread killings. Others called for appeals on behalf of individuals arrested for their alleged part in the demonstrations. In mid-June the first of many death sentences were passed in China for activities related to the pro-democracy movement. All followed trials which, by internationally accepted standards, were grossly unfair. Amnesty International members then called for the commutation of these sentences. Amnesty International volunteers and staff, and members of the public who had perhaps never heard of the organization before, joined a massive wave of appeals.

In many countries, Amnesty International organized or joined public protests. The organization's members met representatives of their own governments to urge that diplomatic pressure be added to the wave of public outrage. Many also tried to meet Chinese embassy officials in their own country.

Although it is the International Secretariat in London which researches, analyses and makes available Amnesty International's information about human rights violations, suggesting and coordinating specific activities, it is the Amnesty International membership across the world whose actions have the greatest impact. This was highlighted in 1989 by the emergency campaign on China. In many countries, posters and postcards were printed with a message in Chinese ready for signing and sending to the authorities in China. In the Federal Republic of Germany a candlelit procession formed the Chinese characters for the phrase "human rights". In Peru a congress of the mayors of 24 Latin American cities was lobbied. Letters were sent by Dutch police and military personnel and by thousands of French medical workers. There was a three-day letter-writing marathon in Japan, and public information and telegram-sending stalls were set up in shopping centres in Canada. In Chile a protest was held at the Chinese embassy and in Mauritius there was a demonstration with street theatre. These were just a few of the hundreds of activities organized by Amnesty International members in June.

It is still too early to be able to assess the impact of this international pressure. The immediate reaction of the Chinese authorities was to dismiss all criticism from abroad as interference in China's internal affairs. However, Amnesty International knows from experience that sustained international concern about human rights violations can bring results. In South Africa, for example, the authorities seemed determined to execute the "Sharpeville Six". All possible judicial appeals against their death sentences had failed. But the sentences were eventually commuted after international public opinion had been mobilized, including by Amnesty International.

Human rights emergencies on a smaller scale are happening all the time.

Often, when Amnesty International learns of an arrest or a "disappearance" and fears that the person may be tortured or is facing execution, or where there is a concern about a political prisoner's health — in fact, any situation covered by Amnesty International's mandate which needs immediate intervention — an Urgent Action is issued. This calls for telegrams and letters to be sent and telephone calls to be made, as soon as possible, to the authorities responsible. Most result in thousands of appeals and Amnesty International knows of some improvement in the prisoner's situation in just over one-third of all cases taken up in this way. In 1989 more Urgent Actions were issued than in any previous year — a total of 577, taking up the cases of 2,886 individuals in 87 countries.

There are still some countries about which little is known abroad as the government prefers to exclude the outside world. On the basis of the little information that does leak out, Amnesty International fears that serious human rights violations are being committed.

The Research Department at the International Secretariat investigates possible human rights violations in all countries. This involves careful cross-checking and corroboration of the wealth of information that is available about some countries, asking uncomfortable questions of those governments which present an image of openness while concealing the full reality of their human rights record, or exploring every possible avenue to find more information about "closed" countries. The results of this research are published in different ways, including major reports, country briefings and a monthly newsletter.

The human rights situation in a country is often such that Amnesty International believes that an increased and focussed pressure from the international community could be effective. In 1989 Amnesty International organized such a focus on about 30 countries, including Bulgaria, Cambodia, Colombia, the German Democratic Republic, Egypt, Iraq, Israel, Jamaica, Malawi, Mauritania, Peru, South Korea, Sri Lanka, Sudan, Turkey, Uganda, the United Kingdom and Yugoslavia. In some, Amnesty International was concerned about deliberate killings of unarmed civilians — sometimes including children — by government security forces. In others, the concern was the pattern of unfair trials for political offences or systematic torture and ill-treatment of prisoners. The organization also worked to secure the immediate and unconditional release of prisoners of conscience — people detained for their beliefs, colour, sex, ethnic origin, language or religion who have not used or advocated violence.

Since Amnesty International was founded in 1961, its groups of members have always worked for the release of prisoners of conscience. A group usually consists of five to 20 individuals who live or work in the same locality and meet on a regular basis. Each group "adopts" one or more such prisoners and works on behalf of that prisoner until he or she is released, often a period of several years. Chia Thye Poh, who was imprisoned in Singapore for almost 23 years until 1989, was one of the longest serving political detainees in the world. He had been held under a succession of two-year detention orders which can be renewed indefinitely. Amnesty International concluded that he had been

12 detained for peacefully exercising his rights to freedom of expression and association because of the leading role he played in a parliamentary opposition party in the 1960s. The organization adopted him as a prisoner of conscience. Shortly after his partial and conditional release in May 1989 he wrote to the Amnesty International group in Canada which is working on his behalf:

"I received your letter and giant card in late August. They came as a great surprise. You all are really wonderful people with such a kind golden heart. It is your untiring efforts that give helpless people a ray of hope, just like crystal-clear drops of water, so sweet and so refreshing for those journeying through unending deserts.

"I am most grateful to you and your friends. My partial release onto Sentosa is the result of collective efforts, and your continued concerns during the past 10 years certainly have helped a lot.... I hope with the continued support of the people in Singapore and abroad I could achieve my complete freedom one day and then we could celebrate and taste muffins and durians together. Again, many thanks to you and your friends. Yours sincerely, Chia Thye Poh."

Working for a prisoner can mean many things, including writing letters directly to the prisoner and their family as a means of support, writing letters to the government and local and prison authorities in the country where they are held, publicizing the case at home and asking for help from members of parliament and other prominent public figures. In order to protect Amnesty International's impartiality and independence, none of the organization's groups may work for prisoners held in their own country or on human rights violations in their own country, except in relation to the death penalty. In 1989 Amnesty International groups were working on behalf of 3,376 prisoner cases held in 83 countries. At least 1,143 were released during the year, many of them as a result of government amnesties in Benin, Bulgaria, Czechoslovakia, the German Democratic Republic, Ethiopia and Somalia.

Local groups also tackle instances and longer term patterns of torture, "disappearance", extrajudicial execution and other matters covered by Amnesty International's mandate. For this they can join one of the 19 Regional Action Networks, which between them cover nearly every country in the world. A group is ready to respond promptly to a call for action on any matter in any of the cluster of countries covered by their network. Half of the organization's 4,149 groups are now active in one of these networks, which put out 288 calls for action on behalf of victims of human rights violations in 70 countries in 1989.

Some groups are composed of members of a profession, such as lawyers or medical staff, and apply their specialist knowledge in the service of human rights. For example, they may make appeals in cases where there is a strong medical or legal concern or write to lawyers or medical bodies in the country concerned. Medical groups intervened in about 100 special appeals in 1989.

Every year Amnesty International sets aside a week in October for its members and groups to focus their activities on behalf of a specific category of victims of human rights violation. In 1989 it drew attention to the plight of children: some had been imprisoned since infancy with their mothers, some had been killed because of their parents' peaceful political activities or beliefs, others were victims in their own right. Amnesty International members throughout the world campaigned on behalf of such children.

The 1980s saw the continuing growth of Amnesty International as an international movement. In Central and South America, there are groups or members in 19 countries as well as supporters and information subscribers in a further 10. The most recently created "section" — an organized structure of groups — is in Uruguay. It began in 1985 following the end of a period of military rule characterized by brutal and widespread human rights violations.

In the Middle East and North Africa, the movement continued to consolidate and expand, with members now active in eight countries. Amnesty International publications were exhibited at both the Kuwait Book Fair and at the Cairo Book Fair. In the Sudan, however, members have been forced by the actions of a new government to scale down their activities.

In Asia, the organization has established membership structures in five countries, with less formal groupings in a further nine, including Pakistan and Nepal where renewed interest was experienced in 1989.

In Sub-Saharan Africa, Amnesty International now has membership structures in five countries with groups in a further three. In 1989 members organized the printing and distribution of 100,000 copies of the African Charter of Human and Peoples' Rights — the human rights charter of the Organization of African Unity.

In Eastern Europe, the organization attracted a new and keen membership. By the end of the year several Amnesty International groups were forming in the region: in December the group in Slovenia, Yugoslavia, was the first to be officially recognized by the organization. In addition, Amnesty International was able for the first time to have an information stall at the Moscow Book Fair.

All this growth came in addition to the membership structures in areas where Amnesty International first became known — most strongly represented in Western Europe and North America. This poses the movement with one of its greatest challenges — communicating effectively in the many languages of its members. Already, the *Amnesty International Report* and the monthly *Amnesty International Newsletter* appear in the movement's official languages: Arabic, English, French and Spanish. Many research papers on individual countries and other publications are published in additional languages when appropriate, such as Portuguese, German, Chinese, Russian, Swahili, Farsi and Turkish. However, much more of the organization's vast output of reports, papers, campaign documents, video and audio material needs to be translated than is possible at present in order to make information about human rights more widely accessible.

Abolition of the Death Penalty

Amnesty International is opposed to the death penalty in all cases and under all circumstances. The issue was highlighted by the organization in 1989 through

14 its Campaign for the Abolition of the Death Penalty, launched in April with the publication of *When the State Kills...The death penalty v. human rights*, a survey of the death penalty in 180 countries. The report showed that the arguments used to justify the penalty fail the tests of logic and experience. It also identified signs of a worldwide movement towards abolition, with nearly half of all countries having abolished the death penalty in law or practice.

The campaign was one of the most ambitious and carefully planned ever launched by Amnesty International. It ran until the end of the year and included a "Week of Action Against Executions" in September as well as the production and distribution of several videos and films. Forty-one countries were highlighted, chosen either because the death penalty was widely used or because there were indications that the country was slowly moving towards abolition. Almost every member and group of members participated at some point during the campaign. People marched, joined vigils, wrote letters, collected petitions and passed resolutions to publicize that the death penalty is not a valid punishment, but a human rights violation in itself.

The campaign won encouraging support from international and national political parties, trades union organizations, religious bodies and professional associations. Over 100 leading statesmen and stateswomen from 26 countries signed an appeal to end executions. Several prominent advocates of the abolition of the death penalty toured different countries giving lectures about why, from their experience and beliefs, the death penalty must be abolished. They included a Nigerian former Chief Judge, a US mother of a murder victim, a Tunisian physician and a Canadian/Egyptian professor of criminology.

Achieving a world without executions will take many years and it will be particularly difficult to eradicate the death penalty in countries where it is used extensively. However, Amnesty International was encouraged by some significant developments during the campaign. Cambodia and New Zealand, and Romania at the very end of the year, abolished the penalty for all crimes; Nepal and Hungary abolished it for crimes against the state; and debate on the issue continued to have a high profile in the USSR and South Africa. By the end of 1989, 38 countries had abolished the death penalty for all offences and 17 for all but exceptional offences such as wartime crimes. A further 30 countries, which retained the penalty in law, had not carried out any executions for the past 10 years.

Despite the encouraging trends, 2,229 prisoners are known to have been executed in 34 countries in 1989 and 2,826 people were sentenced to death in 62 countries. These are only the cases known to Amnesty International; the true figures are certainly higher.

Refugees

Amnesty International opposes the forcible return of any person to a country where he or she might reasonably be expected to be imprisoned as a prisoner of conscience, tortured or executed. It calls on governments to ensure that refugee determination procedures are fair and that asylum-seekers have effective access to them.

If a government imposes a visa or takes some other measure restricting entry, Amnesty International calls on that government to demonstrate that this measure does not obstruct asylum-seekers in need of protection from gaining access to that country's refugee determination procedures. If the government cannot so demonstrate, Amnesty International opposes the measure.

Amnesty International calls on governments to demonstrate that in any case where asylum-seekers are detained, such detention is lawful according to international standards. If a government cannot so demonstrate, Amnesty International opposes that detention practice.

A large part of Amnesty International's work on behalf of asylum-seekers is done by the Amnesty International sections in the countries where those individuals seek asylum. Because of this, the work is not fully reflected in this report, which covers the activities of the International Secretariat.

Relief
During 1989 the International Secretariat of Amnesty International distributed £247,283 in relief payments to help prisoners of conscience and their families and to assist the rehabilitation of torture victims. Amnesty International sections and groups sent probably as much again to many thousands of prisoners and their families. This relief program is not a substitute for the primary objectives of securing freedom for prisoners of conscience and an end to the use of torture and executions. It aims only to alleviate some of the suffering caused by human rights violations. When relief payments are distributed by bodies outside Amnesty International or through individual intermediaries, the organization takes care to stipulate the precise purpose of the payments. Amnesty International's relief accounts, like its general accounts, are audited annually; information on this is included in the financial supplement which is available from the International Secretariat.

Amnesty International's Decision-making and Funding
Major organizational and program policies are determined by Amnesty International's Council, the movement's highest decision-making body. Delegates selected by each section meet biennially to establish policy. The Council also elects members of the International Executive Committee, responsible for implementing Council decisions and overseeing the work of the International Secretariat.

Amnesty International's funding reflects the movement's independence and its reliance on broad public support. No money is sought or accepted from governments. The hundreds of thousands of donations that sustain the organization's work come from the pockets of its members and the public. Fund-raising is a responsibility of the movement's groups and sections; there is no central fund-raising program.

A person who joins Amnesty International pays an annual membership fee varying from country to country. Some members also make regular monthly or yearly donations to support the work. In addition, each member personally pays the cost of the many letters, telegrams and, in some instances, parcels that he or she sends on behalf of prisoners throughout the year.

16

Even major fund-raising drives rely overwhelmingly on the cumulative effect of small donations. Amnesty International members organize street collections in their localities. They arrange film screenings, concerts and other public events that help increase public support and bring in further contributions. Some sections sell promotional items such as key-rings, T-shirts and badges.

A major source of funding in some countries has been found in direct mail programs organized by the sections, whereby literally thousands of people throughout the country are informed of the movement's work and urged to make contributions to Amnesty International.

Increasingly, Amnesty International sections are organizing major events for publicity and fund-raising. These events take the movement's message to large audiences and dramatically broaden the base of financial support.

Other sources of income include donations from foundations and corporations. To preclude the possibility of donors exerting pressure of any kind on the organization, Amnesty International has adopted several basic rules. The first is that no one can make a donation earmarked to support activity on a particular country; donations can only be made to support the work of the organization as a whole or for a broad category of its work, such as its humanitarian relief program. A second rule precludes any part of the organization, such as a group or section, from accepting a donation likely to exceed five per cent of its anticipated income in any year without prior approval by a higher governing body in the movement. This rule applies to all donations, regardless of their source.

The movement's central bodies and activities rely on income pledged by its sections. The funds to be contributed towards the central budget are determined every two years by the movement's International Council. Amnesty International's budget represents roughly one third of the estimated income likely to be raised by the sections in that year. The funds voted by the section for the budget are supplemented by additional voluntary contributions made by sections which have been particularly successful in their fund-raising.

The international budget is administered under the control of the International Executive Committee. The budget covers the cost of all international initiatives undertaken by Amnesty International, such as sending delegations to individual countries, research into human rights violations, the planning and coordination of global campaign activities, addressing the United Nations and other intergovernmental organizations, the publication of reports in various languages, an international relief program and the administration and coordination of the movement as a worldwide membership body.

The accounts are audited annually by a firm of internationally known auditors and are subjected to further scrutiny throughout the year by an elected Financial Control Committee that reports to the International Council. Anyone wishing to study the audited accounts for 1989 may obtain a copy free of charge either from the section of Amnesty International in their country or from the International Secretariat.

WORK WITH INTERNATIONAL ORGANIZATIONS

The highlight of 1989 was the adoption by the United Nations (UN) of the Second Optional Protocol to the International Covenant on Civil and Political Rights (ICCPR) Aiming at the Abolition of the Death Penalty (see Appendix IX). By Resolution 44/128, the UN General Assembly approved on 15 December the text of a draft that the UN Commission on Human Rights had agreed by consensus to send to the UN Economic and Social Council (ECOSOC). This is the world's first treaty of universal scope envisaging the legal abolition of the death penalty and confirming that the issue of the death penalty is one of human rights. Now any State Party to the ICCPR (see Appendix VI) can ratify or accede to the Protocol, thereby committing itself under international law not to carry out any execution and to take "all necessary measures" to abolish the death penalty. Provision is made for states to make reservations at the time they adhere to the Protocol allowing them to carry out executions "for a most serious crime of a military nature committed during wartime". Such a state would be obliged to notify the UN of the existence and termination of any relevant state of war. In an oral statement to the Commission on Human Rights in February in support of the Second Optional Protocol, Amnesty International had urged the Commission to transmit the text to the General Assembly. The organization welcomed its adoption and called for all Parties to the ICCPR to adhere to the Protocol, which will come into force after it has been adhered to by 10 states.

In a separate death penalty-related development, ECOSOC, on recommendation of the UN Committee on Crime Prevention and Control (see *Amnesty International Report 1989*, Introduction), extended the range of safeguards for those facing the death penalty (see *Amnesty International Report 1985*, Appendix VI). By Resolution 1989/64 adopted on 24 May, it recommended mandatory appeals or review in capital cases, the establishment of a maximum age limit for the death penalty and elimination of the death penalty for "persons suffering from mental retardation or extremely limited mental competence". The General Assembly endorsed this resolution by its Resolution 44/162 of 15 December 1989.

Another major UN standard-setting achievement was the adoption by ECOSOC of Resolution 1989/65 on 24 May containing Principles on the Effective Prevention and Investigation of Extra-Legal, Arbitrary and Summary Executions. The Principles, which were endorsed by the General Assembly in Resolution 44/162, contain numerous provisions aimed at curbing what Amnesty International calls extrajudicial executions. The Principles lay down standards for "thorough, prompt and impartial investigation of all suspected cases" of extrajudicial executions as well as for an "adequate autopsy". They provide for such executions to be punishable as crimes, with offenders being brought to justice wherever they may be found, unless they are extradited to another country for that purpose. Families and dependants of victims of extrajudicial executions are entitled to fair and adequate compensation. Superior orders are no defence

18

and "blanket immunity" from prosecution may not be granted. Law enforcement officials have "the right and the duty to defy orders" to commit extrajudicial executions. The UN Committee on Crime Prevention and Control had finalized the draft in 1988 and sent it on to ECOSOC (see *Amnesty International Report 1989*, Introduction).

On 20 November the UN General Assembly adopted by Resolution 44/25 the Convention on the Rights of the Child (see Appendix XI). This treaty covers a wide range of civil, political, economic and social rights, including rights contained in other UN instruments applicable to all people as well as new measures of protection. It thus confirms that the death penalty should not be imposed on people under 18 years old, and adds that they should not be sentenced to life imprisonment. Indeed, any official deprivation of liberty may only be used as a measure of last resort. A Committee of 10 individual experts will be appointed by States Parties to the Convention, which will come into force after 20 states adhere to it. The Committee will review periodic reports to be submitted by States Parties.

The UN Sub-Commission on Prevention of Discrimination and Protection of Minorities continued work on a draft declaration against "disappearances". Amnesty International and other non-governmental organizations (NGOs) worked to ensure that appropriate obligations on states contained in the UN Convention against Torture and in the above-mentioned Principles on extra-legal executions, as well as other means of protecting people from "disappearing", would be reflected in the eventual declaration. These included effective investigation of cases of "disappearance", the bringing to justice of perpetrators on the basis of universal jurisdiction, compensation to victims and dependants, the prohibition of secret detention and the maintenance of centralized registers of detained people.

As in 1988, progress was disappointing with regard to ratification of key international human rights treaties aimed at giving clear legal force to provisions of the Universal Declaration of Human Rights (see Appendix VI). Two states — Algeria and Ireland — acceded to the International Covenant on Economic, Social and Cultural Rights (ICESCR) and to the ICCPR, bringing the number of ratifications to 94 and 89, respectively. More positively, five states — Algeria, Ireland, Libya, New Zealand and the Philippines — acceded to the Optional Protocol to the ICCPR, which allows individuals to bring complaints under the ICCPR, bringing the total to 48. Ten states — Algeria, Australia, Brazil, Finland, Guinea, Italy, Libya, New Zealand, Poland and Portugal — ratified or acceded to the Convention against Torture and Other Cruel, Inhuman or Degrading Treatment or Punishment, bringing the total to 49. During 1989 Amnesty International continued to encourage governments to ratify international and regional human rights instruments.

A notable development in the UN's work against violations of human rights in specific countries was the adoption by the Sub-Commission on Prevention of Discrimination and Protection of Minorities of a resolution on the situation in the People's Republic of China. Prompted by the testimonies of several NGOs, including an oral statement by Amnesty International, relating to the June events in Tiananmen Square as well as the subsequent arrests and executions, the Sub-Commission appealed for clemency in these cases. It also asked the UN Secretariat to prepare a report for the 1990 session of the Commission on Human Rights. The Chinese Government described the resolution, which it deemed "illegal and null and void", as "brazenly" interfering in China's internal affairs.

The UN also took up the country situations of Romania (before the overthrow of President Ceausescu's government) and Myanmar (formerly Burma), going against the recent tendency to reduce the number of such situations it was concerned with (see *Amnesty International Report 1989*, Introduction). The Commission on Human Rights decided to appoint a Special Rapporteur on the human rights situation in Romania, largely as a result of concern about the proposed forcible relocation of the country's Hungarian minority. It did not go as far as regards Myanmar. Expressing concern at the reports of violations of human rights in 1988, the Commission confined itself to encouraging the Myanmar authorities "to assure fundamental freedoms, with a view to enhancing the prospects for democracy" and to urging them to implement their undertaking to "organize free and fair multiparty democratic elections with a view to assuring the human rights and fundamental freedoms" of the citizens.

Amnesty International and other NGOs also provided the Commission and Sub-Commission with extensive information on the grave human rights situation in Iraq, including the torture and killing of children. However, both bodies decided, by four votes, to take no action on the situation. The Sub-Commission's decision came only after Iraq had endorsed an invitation extended by its semi-official Iraqi Human Rights Association to members of the Sub-Commission to visit the country.

Amnesty International's concerns in Iraq were included in an oral statement to the Commission, which described certain problems that arise from governments' attempts to conceal their actions and evade their own and their officials' responsibility. Other countries cited in this statement were Colombia, El Salvador, Ethiopia, Myanmar and Peru.

In another oral statement to the Commission, referring to China, Guatemala, India, Iran, the Philippines, Somalia, South Africa, Syria and Turkey, Amnesty International pointed out that governments can stop human rights abuses such as "disappearances", torture and summary or arbitrary executions by measures already required under international law.

Amnesty International delivered a further oral statement on its continuing concerns relating to the human rights situation in the Israeli-Occupied Territories. It also submitted a written statement on its continuing concerns in Iran.

The Commission adopted resolutions or decisions on Afghanistan, Albania, Chile, Cuba, Equatorial Guinea, El Salvador, Guatemala, Haiti, Iran, the Israeli-Occupied Territories, Myanmar, Namibia, Romania and South Africa.

In addition to its oral statement to the Sub-Commission addressing the situations in China and Iraq referred to above, Amnesty International also presented

20   an oral statement on states of emergency. It drew the Sub-Commission's attention to current situations in Colombia, Egypt, Jordan, Peru, South Africa, Sri Lanka and Syria, where the existence of emergency provisions facilitated the occurrence of extrajudicial executions, "disappearances" or torture and ill-treatment.

In another statement to the Sub-Commission, on administrative detention, Amnesty International provided examples of abuses typically associated with a system of administrative detention by reference to Benin, Brunei Darussalam, Chad, Ethiopia, the Israeli-Occupied Territories, Malaysia, Singapore and Viet Nam.

The organization also made oral statements to two Sub-Commission working groups. A statement to the Working Group on Indigenous Populations drew attention to the torture, "disappearance" and killings of Indians in Brazil, the Zenu Indian community in Colombia, Indian peasants in Guatemala and members of the Scheduled Castes and Scheduled Tribes in India.

The other statement, made to the Working Group on Detention, drew attention to the execution of young offenders. Although international standards clearly prohibit the use of the death penalty on those aged under 18 at the time of the commission of the offence, the statement noted the execution in the past decade of considerable numbers of juvenile offenders in Iran and Iraq; at least eight others in Bangladesh (although the government disputed the age of the person concerned), Barbados, Pakistan and the United States of America (USA); and at least one person believed to be under the age of 18 at the time of the offence in Nigeria.

The Sub-Commission adopted resolutions on China, East Timor, El Salvador, Guatemala, Iran, the Israeli-Occupied Territories, Lebanon and South Africa. The resolution on East Timor was the first in several years from a UN body expressing concern about the human rights situation there.

Amnesty International submitted information on nine countries to the UN procedure established by ECOSOC Resolutions 728F and 1503: Brunei Darussalam, Chad, Colombia, Ethiopia, the German Democratic Republic, Myanmar, Peru, Somalia and Turkey. Resolution 728F authorizes the UN to receive communications about human rights violations and to bring them to the attention of the government concerned. Under Resolution 1503 the UN examines communications in confidential proceedings to determine whether there is evidence of a "consistent pattern of gross violations of human rights" in a country.

During 1989 Amnesty International brought to the attention of the UN's Working Group on Enforced or Involuntary Disappearances information on cases from 19 countries, including Chile, Colombia, East Timor, Ecuador, El Salvador, Guatemala, Haiti, Honduras, India, Mexico, Morocco, Peru, the Philippines, Sri Lanka, Syria, Uganda and Zimbabwe. It submitted to the Special Rapporteur on summary or arbitrary executions information on cases of possible extrajudicial execution from 29 countries — Argentina, Benin, Brazil, Bulgaria, Chad, China, Colombia, East Timor, El Salvador, Guatemala, Haiti, Honduras, India, the Israeli-Occupied Territories, Malawi, Mauritania, Myanmar, Nicaragua, Peru, the Philippines, Romania, Saudi Arabia, Somalia, Sri Lanka, Sudan, Turkey, Uganda, the United Kingdom (UK) and Venezuela. It also reported on situations where death sentences were imposed in apparent violation of international minimum **21** standards in 17 countries — the Bahamas, Burkina Faso, Cameroon, China (including Tibet), Ghana, India, Iran, Iraq, Jamaica, Maldives, Myanmar, Nigeria, Somalia, South Africa, Sudan, the USA and the USSR. Information on cases from 47 countries, including Benin, Chad, Chile, Colombia, Egypt, Hong Kong, India, Iran, Malawi, Mauritania, Peru, Saudi Arabia, Somalia, South Africa, Sri Lanka, Turkey, the United Arab Emirates, the Yemen Arab Republic and Zaire, was submitted to the Special Rapporteur on torture.

Amnesty International continued to submit relevant information to the UN Special Rapporteurs on Afghanistan, Chile and Romania; the Special Representatives on El Salvador and Iran; the Experts concerned with advisory services to Equatorial Guinea, Guatemala and Haiti; the Special Committee on Israeli Practices; and the Commission's *Ad Hoc* Working Group of Experts on southern Africa before which it also testified during the Working Group's regular hearings held in August.

In August Amnesty International made a statement on East Timor to the UN Special Committee on Decolonization. It welcomed the recent "opening" of East Timor but stressed that it continued to receive reports of grave human rights violations in the territory, including mass arrests, torture, extrajudicial executions and "disappearances".

Amnesty International continued to submit information to the Committee on Conventions and Recommendations set up by the United Nations Educational, Scientific and Cultural Organization (UNESCO), which examines human rights violations against writers, teachers and others within UNESCO's mandate. Amnesty International brought to the Committee's attention new cases from Jordan, the Republic of Korea, Morocco, Romania and the USSR.

As in past years, Amnesty International attended the International Labour Conference of the International Labour Organisation (ILO) in Geneva as an observer and followed the proceedings of the Conference Committee on the Application of Conventions and Recommendations. This Committee is part of the ILO's supervisory mechanism for the implementation of its conventions. Amnesty International raised concerns about human rights violations against workers or trade unionists in Colombia, the Philippines and Romania, and against the Indian community in Brazil.

Three member states of the Organization of African Unity (OAU) ratified the African Charter on Human and Peoples' Rights during the year — Burundi, Cameroon and Ghana. The African Commission — the monitoring body established under the African Charter — continued its regular sessions during the year, meeting in Libya in April and in Gambia in October. The African Commission's new headquarters in Banjul, Gambia, were inaugurated in June, the Commission's first permanent base since its establishment in 1987. Amnesty International continued to follow the activities of the African Commission, with which it has observer status. Amnesty International attended in May the 19th annual meeting, held in Ghana, of the OAU's Coordinating Committee on Assistance to Refugees in Africa, of which the organization is a member. It

22

delivered a statement stressing the need to address human rights violations which give rise to many refugee situations. It also highlighted Amnesty International's recent activities with regard to refugees in the African context.

In January 1989 the Inter-American Court of Human Rights handed down its second decision in respect of four "disappearance" cases in Honduras, which represented the first "contentious cases" before the Court. The Court, established under the American Convention on Human Rights, found the Honduran Government responsible for violations of the rights to life, personal freedom and humane treatment under Articles 5, 4 and 7 of the Convention in the case of Saúl Godínez Cruz, and ordered the government to pay compensation to his family. It had earlier reached a similar decision in the case of Angel Manfredo Velásquez Rodríguez (see *Amnesty International Report 1989*). In the two other outstanding cases, concerning the "disappearances" of Francisco Fairén Garbi and Yolanda Solís Corrales, a Costa Rican couple, the Court concluded that "numerous and insoluble difficulties" prevented it from establishing whether the "disappearances" occurred in Honduras and could definitely be attributed to the Honduran Government, although it noted that the government had apparently presented obstacles to the case's clarification.

Amnesty International continued its practice of bringing its concerns in member states of the Organization of American States (OAS) to the attention of the Inter-American Commission on Human Rights (IACHR), particularly with regard to Colombia and Peru. As in past years, Amnesty International attended the General Assembly of the OAS as a "special guest". Prior to the Assembly it sent a letter to all member states, expressing the hope that the draft optional protocol to the American Convention on Human Rights on abolition of the death penalty being prepared by the Permanent Council would be adopted in 1989. It also welcomed the decision of the 1988 Assembly to draft an Inter-American Convention on Forced Disappearance of Persons. It suggested points for inclusion in the text, such as provisions for protection of witnesses and complainants to forced "disappearances", universal jurisdiction over alleged perpetrators and compensation to victims, and prevention of pre-trial measures exonerating those accused of forced "disappearances" of criminal liability. The letter also urged the OAS to examine urgently the problem of "death squad" activities in the region. Unfortunately, as no text had been completed, consideration of the draft optional protocol was deferred until 1990. Similarly, because few government responses to the draft "disappearances" convention prepared by the IACHR had been received, it was decided to defer consideration of the text until the next Assembly. The Assembly also took no action on the question of "death squad" activity in the region.

In July the European Court of Human Rights delivered an important judgment in the case of Jens Soering, who was facing extradition to the USA (Commonwealth of Virginia) from the United Kingdom (UK) on a capital murder charge. In its unanimous decision, the Court held that if the UK were to extradite Soering it would violate its obligations under Article 3 of the European Convention on Human Rights, which prohibits torture and inhuman or degrading treatment or punishment. Although the Court did not find that the application of the death penalty was in itself a violation of the European Convention, it held that the circumstances in which it is imposed can give rise to issues under Article 3. In the Soering case, it found that a combination of factors relating to the "death row phenomenon", including the applicant's youth (he was 18 at the time of the offence), the long period between sentence and execution and the severity of conditions on death row in Virginia, would amount to a violation of Article 3. In April Amnesty International had submitted a third party intervention to the Court in connection with this case asking the Court to rule that, in the light of evolving European standards, the death penalty itself amounted to a violation of the European Convention. It also provided information about the "death row phenomenon" as a form of inhuman or degrading treatment.

The European Convention for the Prevention of Torture and Inhuman or Degrading Treatment or Punishment adopted by the Council of Europe in 1987 came into force on 1 February. Six member states of the Council of Europe ratified this convention during 1989 — Austria, Cyprus, Denmark, France, Norway and Spain — bringing the total number of ratifications to 15. In September, 14 members of the European Committee established under this Convention were elected. The Committee, which meets in confidential session, held its first meeting in November.

In May Finland joined the Council of Europe as the 23rd member state. In March San Marino, which joined in 1988, ratified the European Convention for the Protection of Human Rights and Fundamental Freedoms. Cyprus and San Marino recognized for the first time the right of individual petition under Article 25 of the Convention. Two member states — the Federal Republic of Germany and San Marino — also ratified Protocol No. 6 to the European Convention concerning abolition of the death penalty, bringing the total number of ratifications of this protocol to 14.

Amnesty International continued to attend as an observer the biannual meetings of the Council of Europe's Steering Committee for Human Rights. The organization also attended a hearing of the Legal Affairs Committee of the Parliamentary Assembly on the harmonization in Europe of rules concerning autopsies. It delivered a statement in support of the elaboration of European standards as a contribution to the further development of international norms in this area. Representatives of Amnesty International continued to attend the regular meetings of the parliamentary Committee on Migration, Refugees and Demography.

In April the European Parliament (EP) adopted a Declaration concerning fundamental rights and freedoms while continuing to press for the preparation of a legally binding European Community (EC) instrument on human rights. In June a new EP was elected for a five-year term. Amnesty International approached candidates and members of the EP both before and after these elections to urge renewed attention to human rights concerns in its new program. During the year resolutions were passed by the EP concerning human rights violations in a wide range of countries, including Brazil, China, East Timor, El Salvador, Iran, Morocco, Panama, Romania, South Africa, Turkey and Yugoslavia. Resolutions

24 against the imposition of death sentences in Indonesia and Myanmar, and against the execution of minors in the USA, were also adopted by the new EP. In October it adopted a resolution on conscientious objection for the first time in six years, reaffirming the EP's call for the right of conscientious objection to be respected in all EC member states. The resolution included a number of new provisions relating to alternative service.

In January the third major Follow-Up Meeting of the Conference on Security and Cooperation in Europe (CSCE) concluded in Vienna. The Concluding Document contained a number of significant new commitments in the field of human rights, including the establishment of a mechanism under which a CSCE participating state can raise human rights questions, even concerning specific cases, with other CSCE states on a bilateral and eventually a multilateral basis. It was also agreed to hold a Conference on the Human Dimension of the CSCE in Paris (1989), Copenhagen (1990) and Moscow (1991).

Amnesty International did not attend the Paris human rights conference, which opened on 30 May. Access for NGOs was granted only on the direct invitation of a participating government and the organization considered that accepting such an invitation would be incompatible with its impartiality and independence. However, prior to the conference, Amnesty International contacted all the participating states and raised a number of human rights concerns in CSCE countries. It also urged that greater participation by NGOs in the CSCE process should be allowed and, in particular, that such organizations should be permitted to attend future CSCE human rights conferences in their own right.

Amnesty International highlighted its concerns about continuing human rights violations in participating states at two major intergovernmental meetings — the summit meeting of francophone countries (*"la Francophonie"*) held in Senegal in May, and the biennial Commonwealth Heads of Government Meeting in Malaysia in October. At the latter it was agreed to request the new Secretary-General, Chief Emeka Anyaoku (Nigeria), to convene a governmental working group of experts on human rights to review existing cooperation on human rights and to recommend future avenues for action, in areas such as education, training and technical assistance. Amnesty International also approached members of parliament attending the Commonwealth Parliamentary Association meeting in Barbados in October to raise its concerns about the death penalty and, in particular, the execution of minors.

The Inter-Parliamentary Union (IPU), a non-governmental organization composed of members of parliament from 111 countries, maintains a special committee to investigate reported violations of the human rights of members of parliament. During 1989 Amnesty International sent the committee information on the situation of members or former members of parliament in Honduras, Indonesia, Malaysia, Somalia and Sudan. Amnesty International delegations observed the March session of the IPU's Inter-Parliamentary Conference in Budapest, Hungary, and the September session in London, the UK.

COUNTRY
ENTRIES

AFGHANISTAN

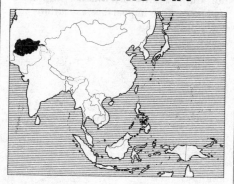

Thousands of political prisoners were believed to be imprisoned, including some possible prisoners of conscience. Torture and ill-treatment of prisoners, particularly during interrogation, continued to be reported, although on a lesser scale than in previous years.

Despite the completion of the withdrawal of Soviet troops in February, the conflict between government forces and armed opposition groups — the Mujahideen — continued; arms were supplied to the government by the USSR, and to the Mujahideen by the USA and Pakistan. It was difficult to obtain and corroborate information about human rights violations due to the war and social dislocation. However, there were several reports of Mujahideen forces carrying out extrajudicial executions of prisoners and civilians.

In February the authorities at Kabul's Pul-e-Charkhi Prison said they were holding 2,165 political prisoners; definite information about prisoners of conscience was available in only a few cases. Maulavi Abdul Rauf Logari, the Imam of the Wazir Akbar Khan Mosque in Kabul, was detained in March after preaching at the mosque in the presence of President Najibullah. He reportedly recited a Persian verse which seemed to be directed at the President: "You have done nothing for your Creator, so you cannot do anything for His creatures." He did not advocate violence during the sermon and was considered to be a prisoner of conscience. He was released from Pul-e-Charkhi Prison later in the year.

Among possible prisoners of conscience believed still held at the end of the year was Amin Yusufzai. He had been detained at Kabul airport in January 1986, reportedly because he was found carrying a picture of his brother, a member of the Mujahideen. He was not known to have been charged or tried.

There was no new information about two other possible prisoners of conscience, Syed Abdul Samad and Mohammad Nazar. Both Afghans, they were tried and convicted of spying in January 1988 after they had entered the country illegally with Alain Guillo, a French journalist (see *Amnesty International Report 1989*). They were sentenced to 16 years' imprisonment and were believed to be held at Pul-e-Charkhi Prison.

Dr Mohammad Younis Akbari, a nuclear physicist sentenced to death in 1984 (see *Amnesty International Report 1985*), was also believed to be still imprisoned, although his whereabouts were unknown. Information was received in January that seven members of the *Afghan Mellat*, the Afghan Social Democratic Party, held since 1983, had been released in 1988 (see *Amnesty International Report 1989*).

Torture and ill-treatment of prisoners, particularly during interrogation, by the security police and the military continued to be reported. In one case, a member of the Mujahideen captured in combat at Deh-e-Sabz village in January was released in May after he had become deranged reportedly as a result of torture. He was still suffering from its effects when he was admitted to a psychiatric clinic in Pakistan in July.

There was no new information about people who had reportedly "disappeared" in detention in previous years, such as Zia-ul-Haq, who had "disappeared" in early 1983 (see *Amnesty International Report 1989*).

Mujahideen forces were reported to have carried out extrajudicial executions of captured government soldiers and civilians, including children, in areas which they effectively controlled. In one case, a Mujahideen force which included Wahabi Arab volunteers was reported to have summarily killed an unspecified number of government soldiers and at least 20 unarmed civilians on 13 and 14 January after taking control of the village of Kuna Deh, in the Khewa district of Nangarhar province. In March and April, journalists reported that Mujahideen groups besieging the city of Jalalabad had shot dead government soldiers after they had surrendered.

28

In March Amnesty International made an appeal jointly to the Afghan Government and the leaders of the seven Mujahideen groups based in Peshawar, Pakistan. It urged them to take all possible measures to ensure full protection of basic human rights for all prisoners and non-combatants on both sides of the Afghan conflict. The organization also appealed to the governments of the USSR, the USA and Pakistan to use their influence with the main parties to the conflict to ensure respect for human rights. Three Mujahideen groups — *Mahaz-e Melli-e Islami Afghanistan*, led by Sayed Ahmad Gailani; *Jamiat-e-Islami Afghanistan*, led by Burhanuddin Rabbani; and *Jebha-e Nejat-e Melli Afghanistan*, led by Sibghatullah Mojaddedi — responded to Amnesty International's appeal, saying that their organizations treated prisoners humanely and would continue to do so. The Pakistan Foreign Ministry responded to the appeal by referring to the Pakistan Government's role in arranging for the International Committee of the Red Cross to visit prisoners held by Mujahideen groups in Afghanistan and in helping to arrange meetings between the USSR and the Mujahideen for an exchange of prisoners.

During the year, Amnesty International repeatedly wrote to the Afghan authorities asking for the release of Maulavi Abdul Rauf Logari. It also asked for information about Amin Yusufzai, Syed Abdul Samad, Mohammad Nazar, Mohammad Younis Akbari and Zia-ul-Haq. In November the authorities informed Amnesty International that Maulavi Logari had been released.

ALBANIA

An unknown number of prisoners of conscience were held in prison or corrective labour camps under legislation which severely restricted certain human rights. People who attempted to exercise their right to freedom of expression or freedom of movement were liable to harsh punishment. A 14-year-old boy allegedly died after he was arrested for attempting to leave the country without official permission. Legal safeguards for political detainees were inadequate and prison conditions harsh. A large number of offences, including all but one of the

political offences defined in the criminal code, were punishable by death. It was not known, however, whether any death sentences were imposed or executions carried out in 1989.

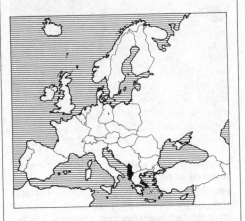

Information about political prisoners and the death penalty was limited as a result of strict official censorship and restrictions on freedom of movement.

On 13 November the Presidium of the People's Assembly decreed a "general pardon", but this meant release for only a few categories of political prisoners: those aged over 60 and convicted of either "anti-state agitation and propaganda" or attempting to leave the country without permission, and those convicted of the same offences who had one year or less of their sentence left to serve. In addition, all prisoners under 18 years old and all women serving sentences of up to 15 years' imprisonment, including political prisoners, were released. The sentences for other categories of political prisoners were reduced by one quarter.

The pardon decree confirmed that since the pardon of January 1986 the authorities had continued to imprison people for exercising their rights to freedom of movement and expression. The state restricted travel abroad. People who left or attempted to leave without permission were liable to prosecution for "flight from the state" under Article 47, paragraph 11, of the criminal code. This offence is punishable by 10 to 25 years' imprisonment or death. Among those reportedly serving long prison sentences for attempting to leave the country without permission was Mihali Kosta from Erseke. In mid-1989 Amnesty International learned that he was serving a 25-year prison sentence, his second term of imprisonment for this offence.

In December refugees from Albania who reached Greece reported that four members of Albania's Greek minority had been arrested on 11 October while attempting to cross into Greece without official permission. According to the refugees' account, four brothers from the Prasos family were arrested and then dragged behind a tractor through streets while the public was encouraged to beat them. This brutality allegedly led to the death of the youngest brother, Odysseas, aged 14. The refugees did not know the fate of the other three brothers. The Albanian authorities denied that these events took place.

People who criticized political or economic conditions in Albania or who publicly expressed or propagated their religious convictions were liable to imprisonment for "anti-state agitation and propaganda" under Article 55 of the criminal code. This article proscribes, among other things, "propaganda" considered to be "religious" or "anti-socialist". It provides for a punishment of three to 10 years' imprisonment, or death in cases of "especially serious consequences". Ethnic Albanian sources in Yugoslavia claimed that in early December demonstrators in the town of Shkoder were arrested after protesting against economic hardship and restrictions on human rights. The Albanian authorities denied these reports.

In 1967 all organized or public forms of worship were made illegal. In the following years there were many reports of clergy being sent into internal exile, usually to collective farms, or imprisoned.

In August Mother Teresa of Calcutta, who is of Albanian origin and the founder of the Missionaries of Charity religious order, visited Albania. However, official attitudes towards organized religion within the country appeared to remain unchanged. In March the Foreign Minister had reportedly told the French newspaper Le Monde: "In our country there is no place for religion". There was no further information during 1989 about Father Ndoc Luli (see Amnesty International Report 1985), a Roman Catholic priest reportedly imprisoned for celebrating religious services.

People continued to be punished with internal exile, without charge or trial, because their relatives had left the country without permission. The law provides internal exile for unspecified periods, by administrative order and without recourse to courts, for "members of the family of fugitives" and people regarded as a danger to the country's social system. Petros Babis, a refugee who arrived in Greece in November, said that after his brother left Albania without permission in 1987, he and his family were exiled from their home in Sarande and sent to work on a state farm.

Legal safeguards for political detainees under investigation or on trial remained extremely limited. Under the Code of Criminal Procedure, they have no right while under investigation to visits from relatives. They also have no right to legal advice during investigation or trial unless the court "deems it necessary". In 1967 the institution of legal advocacy was abolished and lawyers lost their legal status.

Former political prisoners reported harsh conditions of imprisonment, including poor food and inadequate medical care. Political prisoners reportedly faced long hours of heavy labour with minimal industrial protection in corrective labour camps such as that at Qafe e Barit, where prisoners mine pyrites. Some prisoners of conscience were held at Burrel Prison, where detainees included former government officials and others regarded as particularly dangerous.

A refugee alleged during the year that three young border guards had been executed in January 1988 after they failed to prevent a high-ranking officer and his family from defecting to Yugoslavia. Unconfirmed reports were received that in the previous two years four men had been executed after being convicted of economic crimes.

Amnesty International called on the authorities for an independent and impartial investigation into allegations of torture of the Prasos brothers and the death of Odysseas Prasos. The organization urged the release of all prisoners of conscience and called on the government to ratify or accede to the international covenants on human rights.

ALGERIA

Fifteen political prisoners, including possible prisoners of conscience, remained in prison pending a retrial after the original verdict was quashed. They had been sentenced in 1987 after an unfair trial. Hundreds of demonstrators were arrested during the year and scores were allegedly ill-treated. Most were released within a few days. At least two people were executed.

The government of President Chadli Benjedid introduced a number of reforms after widespread civil unrest which occurred in October 1988 (see *Amnesty International Report 1989*). In January a national referendum approved a new constitution which guarantees fundamental human rights, including the rights to freedom of conscience, opinion, expression, association and assembly. The Constitution also reinforces safeguards relating to *garde à vue* detention, during which detainees are held incommunicado in police custody, and prohibits all forms of physical and mental ill-treatment. In April the *Assemblée populaire nationale*, National Assembly, abolished the *Cour de sûreté de l'Etat*, State Security Court. This court had previously tried political prisoners under procedures that did not satisfy international standards for fair trial. Legislation introduced in July by the ruling *Front de libération national* (FLN), National Liberation Front, permits the creation of new political parties, at least 12 of which were officially recognized by the end of 1989.

In September Algeria either ratified or acceded to major human rights treaties: the International Covenant on Civil and Political Rights and its Optional Protocol; the International Covenant on Economic, Social and Cultural Rights; and the United Nations Convention against Torture and Other Cruel, Inhuman or Degrading Treatment or Punishment.

Fifteen Islamic activists, who were among 188 people convicted in July 1987 after an unfair trial before the State Security Court, had their convictions and sentences quashed early in the year on technical grounds. However, all remained in prison awaiting retrial at the end of the year. The charges against them included plotting to overthrow the government, murder, sabotage, armed robbery and membership of armed gangs (see *Amnesty International Report 1989*). Twelve of them had been serving sentences of up to life imprisonment. The three others — Mansouri Milyani, Abdelkader Chbouti and Mohamed A'mamrah — had received death sentences. The case of the 15 was referred in October to the Court of Assizes in Blida. However, it was ruled that this court was not competent to hear the case, which was then returned to the State Prosecutor.

Some of the 188 had been arrested in 1985 in connection with violent incidents and clashes with security forces resulting in deaths. Others may have been prisoners of conscience, arrested for their non-violent political activity. Most of the 188 defendants alleged that police or military security agents had tortured them. Fourteen of those convicted at the July 1987 trial were freed by presidential decree in July and 51 others in November. The remaining prisoners had completed their sentences before the year began and had been released, leaving only the 15 political prisoners in custody pending retrial.

Two alleged members of the *Mouvement pour la démocratie en Algérie* (MDA), the Movement for Democracy in Algeria, were released after completing their prison sentences. They were among 22 people convicted in June 1987 on charges including distributing subversive leaflets and violating currency regulations after an unfair trial before the State Security Court (see *Amnesty International Report 1989*). The 20 others convicted in this trial had been released previously.

Hundreds of people were detained in 1989 in connection with strikes and demonstrations, mostly about alleged unfair distribution of housing. Some detainees were reportedly assaulted in police custody; all were apparently released within 48 hours of their arrest.

The government took no known steps to initiate investigations into the widespread torture following detentions in October 1988, or to bring those responsible to justice. However, press reports suggested that some police and army personnel had been disciplined. In late November 1988 the President had publicly acknowledged the use of torture and stated that those responsible would be punished.

In December two men were reportedly executed after having exhausted all legal appeals. Criminal courts had sentenced them to death in March 1986. One was convicted of murder, the other of murder and gross indecency with violence.

In May Amnesty International wrote to President Chadli Benjedid welcoming Algeria's ratification of international human rights treaties and its adoption of new constitutional guarantees of fundamental human rights. The organization expressed concern, however, at the continued imprisonment of a number of political prisoners sentenced after unfair trials before the State Security Court. Amnesty International recommended that they be retried in accordance with international standards, or released.

ANGOLA

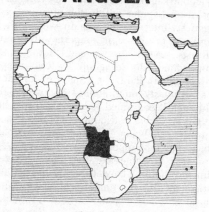

Hundreds of people suspected of supporting an armed opposition organization were imprisoned, some of whom may have been prisoners of conscience. The prisoners included people arrested in previous years who remained in detention without charge or trial. More than 700 prisoners were freed during the year in an amnesty. Over 20 people were tried and convicted, including possible prisoners of conscience. Two people were sentenced

to death but 50 death sentences imposed in previous years were commuted. No executions were reported. Namibians released from imprisonment in Angola said they had been tortured while in custody. More than 260 Namibians reportedly imprisoned in Angola could not be accounted for.

Fighting continued between government forces and the opposition *União Nacional para a Independência Total de Angola* (UNITA), National Union for the Total Independence of Angola, despite diplomatic efforts to obtain a peace settlement and direct talks between President José Eduardo dos Santos and UNITA's leader, Jonas Savimbi. As a result of the continuing conflict, hundreds of thousands of civilians were forced to abandon their homes and there were acute food shortages. Each side accused the other of deliberately killing civilians and both held prisoners. UNITA reportedly captured hundreds of civilians and forced them to serve in its ranks.

During the year more than half of the 50,000 Cuban troops based in Angola left the country as part of an international agreement to bring about Namibia's independence.

An amnesty law promulgated in 1988 under the government's policy of "Clemency and National Harmonization" came into force in February. This granted amnesty or clemency to all government opponents who agreed to renounce violence and comply with the Constitution, including those who had been detained or convicted. Such an agreement implied recognizing the legitimacy of a one-party state.

More than 700 political prisoners, including detainees held without trial, were released in mid-1989 under the February amnesty law.

The government-controlled media reported the capture of hundreds of UNITA combatants in many parts of the country. Other sources said hundreds of civilians were also arrested on suspicion of supporting, sheltering or supplying information to UNITA. Some of those arrested may have been prisoners of conscience, held on account of their non-violent views or activities, although few details were available about individual prisoners. One man was reportedly arrested for possessing a cassette recording of a UNITA radio broadcast, but it

32

was not clear whether he was charged or brought to trial.

An unknown number of suspected UNITA members or supporters arrested in previous years continued to be detained without charge or trial in Luanda and other towns, and in rural detention camps such as Bentiaba in Namibe Province. Detailed information about these prisoners could not be obtained.

Two people imprisoned for criticizing senior government figures may have been prisoners of conscience. Elizabeth Maria dos Reis Fançony, a brewery worker, was serving a two-year sentence imposed in December 1988 by the People's Revolutionary Court in Luanda. The charges against her apparently stemmed from a critical reference to a senior security police official which she made after one of her colleagues was arrested in connection with another matter. José Manuel Simeão Miranda, an accountant, was sentenced to one year's imprisonment in August. He had been arrested in November 1988 and convicted of making a defamatory remark about President dos Santos. He was released in October, apparently because his period of pre-trial detention was deducted from his sentence.

The trial of 30 members of the Church of Jesus Christ on Earth, known as the Tocoist Church, which began in Luanda in November 1988, ended in February. The People's Revolutionary Tribunal convicted 19 defendants of crimes against state security and homicide, and sentenced them to between five and 19 years' imprisonment. The 11 other defendants were acquitted. Most of the defendants were believed to have been arrested after clashes, resulting in several deaths, between factions of the sect in late 1986 and early 1987 (see Amnesty International Report 1989). After the clashes, government officials claimed that supporters of one faction sought to destabilize the government. Precise details of the charges on which the defendants were convicted were not published. Those convicted reportedly had no right to appeal against their conviction and sentence.

Political detainees were reportedly subjected to severe beatings or other forms of torture shortly after their arrest, particularly in Luanda and in Benguela and Namibe provinces. Although few details were available, some reports indicated that detainees held at the security prison in Luanda, known as the Catete Road Prison, were tortured with electric shocks.

The death sentences imposed on 50 people by courts between 1981 and 1987 were commuted in June under the Clemency and National Harmonization policy. None of these death sentences, imposed for crimes allegedly linked to UNITA activities, had previously been reported publicly. The announcement of their commutation indicated that death sentences were imposed more extensively in Angola during recent years than was officially acknowledged. It was not known how many prisoners remained under sentence of death.

Death sentences were imposed in July on Captain Humberto Campos Abrantes, an air force pilot, and Captain Francisco José Jorge Setas Ferreira, a helicopter pilot. The People's Revolutionary Court in Luanda convicted them on charges of passing military secrets to South Africa. Their death sentences were subject to automatic review by a special Appeals Court, the findings of which had not been announced by the end of the year.

In March UNITA publicly denied allegations that several of its senior officials had been killed and some of its members had been burned to death in previous years as a result of disputes within the organization. Amnesty International was unable to either confirm or discount reports of these killings. UNITA also denied that it had imprisoned Tito Chingunji, its former representative in the United States of America (see Amnesty International Report 1989), although it continued to be alleged that he might be under restriction at UNITA'S headquarters at Jamba in southeast Angola. Jonas Savimbi reportedly said at a UNITA congress in September that the organization was holding between 8,000 and 10,000 prisoners. It was unclear, however, who these prisoners were and whether, in addition to captured government soldiers, they included civilian supporters of the government or UNITA dissidents.

More than 500 Namibians who had been held in Angola by the South West African People's Organisation (SWAPO) were released during the year, mostly in May, in accordance with a United Nations (UN) plan for Namibian independence. Upon returning to Namibia, those freed said they had been tortured in Angola and that other Namibians were still held in Angola. In

September a UN delegation appointed to investigate the fate of more than 1,000 prisoners reportedly held by SWAPO visited 22 SWAPO bases in Angola. The delegation found no evidence that SWAPO was still holding prisoners but noted that 123 detainees had reportedly died in SWAPO custody and that 263 others could not be accounted for (see Namibia).

Amnesty International welcomed the release of political prisoners and investigated the cases of two convicted prisoners who may have been prisoners of conscience. The organization also welcomed the commutation of 50 death sentences and urged the commutation of the two death sentences known to have been imposed in 1989. In March Amnesty International submitted to the Angolan Government lists of Namibian prisoners reportedly held in Angola by SWAPO and qualifying for release and repatriation under the UN plan for Namibian independence. The organization later expressed concern about reports that many of these prisoners had been tortured and urged the Angolan authorities to investigate the fate of others who apparently "disappeared" while held in Angola. In December the Procurator General replied that all SWAPO's prisoners had been released but did not provide information about detainees who had "disappeared".

ANTIGUA AND BARBUDA

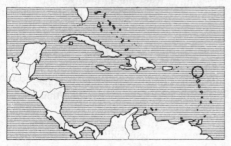

One person was executed. This followed an execution in 1988, which was the first to be carried out for nine years.

Eardley Browne was hanged on 13 June. He had been sentenced to death for a murder committed in 1988. His appeal to the Eastern Caribbean Court of Appeal had been dismissed earlier in the year. However, at the time of his execution he had apparently not petitioned the Judicial Committee of the Privy Council (JCPC) in London, Antigua's final court of appeal. There were no prisoners under sentence of death at the end of the year.

Amnesty International wrote to Prime Minister Vere C. Bird Sr in July asking whether Eardley Browne had had the opportunity to appeal to the JCPC and, if not, the reasons for his execution before he had been able to pursue fully all legal procedures for review of his sentence. No reply had been received by the end of the year.

ARGENTINA

Members of a left-wing group, who had attacked a military barracks in January, were allegedly tortured after surrendering. There was evidence that two of them may have been summarily executed after surrendering and that three others "disappeared". Following the declaration of a state of siege there were a number of short-term arrests of members of left-wing political parties, accused of inciting riots in May. A pre-trial presidential pardon in October for senior military officers further curtailed hopes that past gross human rights violations would be investigated.

The year was marked by social unrest and political violence. In January members of a left-wing group, *Movimiento Todos Por la Patria* (MTP), All For the Fatherland Movement, attacked a military barracks at La Tablada in the province of Buenos Aires. Thirty-nine people died in the attack, 11 of whom were police or military personnel.

Presidential and congressional elections were held in May, which were won by the

34

Justicialista (Peronist) party. At the end of May hyperinflation and spiralling food prices provoked a series of attacks on supermarkets in the cities of Rosario and Córdoba, which were accompanied by violent clashes between looters and police forces. The government accused left-wing political parties of inciting the riots. President Raúl Alfonsín's government imposed a 30-day state of siege, but looting spread to other regions. About 15 people were killed in the rioting, approximately 100 were injured and more than 2,000 were detained. Most of those detained were charged with looting and other public order offences, but at least 28 people, including trade unionists and members of left-wing political parties, were detained under the state of siege provisions. At the end of June, the state of siege was suspended and President Alfonsín stepped down five months early in favour of the President-elect, Carlos Menem. In October President Menem, faced with continuing military pressure over human rights trials, issued pre-trial pardons for 39 senior military officers.

An armed attack by members of the MTP on the Third Infantry Regiment barracks at La Tablada in Buenos Aires province in January resulted in the death of nine soldiers, two police officers and 28 MTP members. There was evidence that two of the MTP members listed as dead may have been summarily executed after having surrendered and that three others "disappeared" after having been captured. It was also reported that detainees were tortured while in military custody after surrendering, and that some were subjected to further torture while in incommunicado detention under the supervision of the Federal Police and prison service personnel. All were reportedly held by the police in conditions which amounted to cruel, inhuman or degrading treatment.

In April the Attorney General said that judicial inquiries had been opened into the alleged violations of human rights of the MTP members. By the end of the year the inquiry had been completed in only one case. It concerned alleged assaults by police and prison officers on five MTP prisoners in the main courthouse cells in Buenos Aires on 28 January. Official medical examinations ordered by a judge revealed a substantial increase in injuries compared with those registered four days

earlier, after the prisoners' surrender. Sebastian Joaquín Ramos, for example, had three injuries when first taken into custody and 45 injuries on 28 January. The judge accepted that illegal force had been used against some of the defendants. However, he dismissed the case on the grounds that the evidence implicating police and prison service officials was insufficient. An appeal was lodged against the ruling.

In October, 20 MTP defendants involved in the attack on La Tablada barracks were found guilty of aggravated illicit association, rebellion, 11 counts of homicide, 12 counts of attempted homicide and other charges. They were given sentences ranging from 10 years to life imprisonment. Since all the defendants had been charged with illicit association, special summary procedures were applied under Law 23.077 on the Protection of Constitutional Order. The trial was heard before the Federal Appeals Court of San Martín; under Law 23.077 appeals to the Supreme Court in such trials are limited to constitutional matters. In December the Federal Appeals Court of San Martín refused the defendants leave to appeal to the Supreme Court, ruling that the grounds for appeal were insufficient.

Amnesty International's subsequent report on the events at La Tablada reflected the organization's concern that the judicial inquiries had failed to obtain important evidence from the barracks that would have helped ascertain the time, place and manner of death of all of the 39 who died. It also commented on the fact that autopsy procedures were not of a sufficiently high standard to help determine whether particular deaths had occurred in combat or were the result of extrajudicial executions after surrender. Amnesty International concluded that there was evidence to support the allegations that two MTP members had been extrajudicially executed and that three others had "disappeared" after surrendering. Amnesty International believed that the delays in investigating the related complaints of torture and ill-treatment could not be justified. These delays amounted to a denial of the right of all detainees to have such complaints promptly, impartially and effectively investigated.

In June a judge ordered a raid on the headquarters of the *Partido Obrero* (PO), Workers' Party, in Buenos Aires and the arrest of five of its leaders. They were charged with "seeking to impose their ideas by force or fear" because of leaflets they had distributed urging workers to demonstrate. By the end of June the PO leaders had been freed and charges against them had been dropped.

In July Fermín Angel Núñez, who had been detained in 1975, was granted parole. Amnesty International believed that Fermín Núñez had received an unfair trial when convicted in 1979 of politically motivated crimes of violence (see *Amnesty International Report 1989*). Fermín Núñez was among a group of 64 alleged former guerrillas pardoned by President Menem in October.

On 6 October President Menem pardoned 39 senior military officers, who were to have been tried by civilian courts for crimes perpetrated between 1976 and 1983 during the Argentine Armed Forces' "dirty war" against alleged subversives. Two federal public prosecutors faced disciplinary hearings and risked dismissal when they challenged the constitutionality of the pre-trial pardons, despite instructions from the Attorney General not to do so. These pardons brought to a standstill all but one of the criminal proceedings into past human rights violations including "disappearance", torture and extrajudicial execution. By the end of the year only one trial was continuing, that of the former Commander of the First Army Corps, Guillermo Suárez Mason. In separate decrees President Menem pardoned military officers charged with rebellion after military uprisings in late 1987, early 1988 and late 1988.

Human rights organizations expressed concern about undue delays by juvenile courts in the identification of children born to women held in secret detention centres during the 1970s, who were then allegedly given to police or military families. In May twin 13-year-old boys and an Argentine couple, (a former police sergeant and his wife), were extradited from Paraguay to Argentina. The couple had claimed they were the parents of the children. In 1985 a juvenile court, acting on behalf of a former political exile who believed they were his children, ordered blood tests but the couple fled with the twins. On their return to Argentina the couple were charged with falsifying the children's birth certificates and concealing their identities. The twins were placed with foster parents. In October blood tests proved that the boys were not the children of the original plain-tiff but of another couple, María Rosa Ana Tolosa and Juan Enrique Reggiardo, who had "disappeared" in 1977. The judge then freed the former police officer and his wife, and returned the boys to their custody. By December the court had still not ruled on four petitions lodged by the boys' maternal grandfather to be accepted as a plaintiff in the case and to be granted custody of the children.

In June Amnesty International wrote to both President Alfonsín and President-elect Menem reiterating the principle that all human rights violations should be independently investigated, notwithstanding a change of government. It said that any law which granted immunity from prosecution to people charged with criminal responsibility for violations of human rights ran the risk of being seen as encouraging or facilitating future abuses. Amnesty International delegates observed sessions of the MTP trial in September and October, and sought information about the judicial inquiries into the alleged violations of the rights of the MTP detainees.

AUSTRALIA

At least nine Aboriginals died in custody in 1989, despite the endorsement in February by federal and state Aboriginal affairs ministers of recommendations to prevent such deaths made by a Royal Commission of Inquiry in December 1988. The commission was established in 1987 in response to widespread concern about the pattern and high incidence of Aboriginal deaths in custody and the fears expressed by several deceased prisoners' families that some deaths may have resulted from ill-treatment by police or prison officials.

The federal Minister for Justice announced in early May that the Royal

36 Commission would not inquire into any deaths occurring after the end of that month. The commission had already recommended improved procedures at police lock-ups, better training for police and prison officers, better medical care for prisoners and the decriminalizing of drunkenness. Federal and state officials met in May to discuss ways of monitoring implementation of the recommendations.

A coroner's inquest recorded an open verdict in March on the death of Edward Cameron, a 23-year-old Aboriginal football player, who was found hanged by a single bootlace in a police cell in the small Western Australian town of Geraldton in July 1988. This meant the inquest was unable to determine the precise circumstances of his death.

The coroner found "...that the failure of individual police officers to understand the importance of frequent checks on persons detained in custody, after the publicity given to the several deaths in custody that had already occurred in this state and elsewhere, is almost beyond comprehension. This failure indicates an attitude of mind which must be overcome if deaths in custody are to be minimized. The construction of 'suicide proof' cells will not be sufficient on its own. It is not the physical surroundings of custody but the care exercised by the custodians which will have the most influence on the problem."

There was no new information about the circumstances of the death of Graham Walley, a 21-year-old Aboriginal, who was found in October 1988 hanged by his belt in a cell of Greenough Regional Prison, also in Geraldton. Amnesty International had expressed concern to the authorities about the reported circumstances leading to the deaths of both Graham Walley and Edward Cameron shortly after they occurred (see *Amnesty International Report 1989*).

In May an Amnesty International representative met Prime Minister Bob Hawke, Federal Aboriginal Affairs Minister Gerry Hand and Peter Dowding, the Premier of Western Australia, the state with the highest incidence of Aboriginal deaths in custody, and urged the speedy implementation of safeguards against further deaths in custody. All three government ministers expressed their commitment to the prevention of such deaths.

AUSTRIA

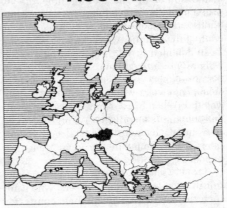

Regular and consistent reports of ill-treatment in police custody continued in 1989. In some cases the incidents described were severe enough to amount to torture. People who complained about ill-treatment ran a high risk of criminal prosecution or investigation after lodging their complaint.

In January Austria ratified the European Convention for the Prevention of Torture and Inhuman or Degrading Treatment or Punishment.

In July the Interior Minister stated that between 1986 and 1988, 530 criminal complaints of "inadmissible use of force" were lodged against the police. Eight police officers had been convicted, three of whom were transferred to different posts. The minister also provided statistics which showed that, in those regions for which statistics were available, 45 per cent of those lodging such a criminal complaint had been investigated by the police or prosecuted as a result of their complaints.

A number of alleged victims of ill-treatment stated to Amnesty International that they were reluctant to make complaints or allow their names to be published for fear of prosecution for "defamation". As a result it was difficult to assess accurately the number of cases of ill-treatment which occurred.

One alleged victim of torture said that he was held for two days in March in the offices of the Vienna Special Branch. He was allegedly questioned by six police officers who repeatedly held his head under water until he agreed to sign a statement confessing to a number of crimes. He asked Amnesty International not to reveal his name as he had met someone in prison who had been prosecuted for "defamation" and given an additional prison sentence after making a complaint about ill-treatment.

In March Mustafa Ali and Fatahi Ali were stopped in Vienna and fined by two police officers who said that they had crossed the road when a pedestrian signal was red. When Mustafa Ali refused to pay, the police officers allegedly used insulting and racist language. Mustafa Ali was arrested and handcuffed — allegedly as a result of resisting the police officers' attempts to push him towards a deep pit on a building site. Fatahi Ali and Mustafa Ali alleged that more police officers arrived and beat them with truncheons, continuing to do so even when Mustafa Ali fell to the ground.

Mustafa Ali was taken to the Leopoldstadt police station where allegedly he was again beaten until he lost consciousness after being pushed against a pane of glass. He was transferred to the Lorenz Böhler Hospital where concussion, facial wounds, bruising and tenderness below the eyes and on the cheekbone were established. He was released from the hospital two days later.

In May Mustafa Ali made a complaint about his ill-treatment to the Constitutional Court. It had not been heard by the end of the year.

During a trial in May at the Vienna Provincial Court a witness, Miroslav Stojic, said that as a result of being beaten by police officers in February 1988 he had been forced to make a statement that the defendant had helped him break into a tobacconist's shop. The defendant was acquitted of this offence. A police doctor had examined Miroslav Stojic immediately after the alleged beating and had found, *inter alia*, that his left eye had been completely closed through recently caused bruising. Investigations into Miroslav Stojic's allegations were stopped in April 1988 under Article 412 of the Code of Penal Procedure, which allows this in cases where it has proved impossible to establish the identity of the perpetrators. The Public Procurator warned Miroslav Stojic in court that if it was proved that he had falsely accused the police officers he should expect a charge of defamation.

In July, at the Graz Provincial Court, the first hearing took place in a case brought by the Graz Public Procurator against Wilhelm Sommer (see *Amnesty International Report 1989*). Wilhelm Sommer was accused of defamation as a result of complaining that in September 1988 he had been physically assaulted by the police while handcuffed. The criminal complaint against the police officers had been dismissed by the Graz Public Procurator. An Amnesty International delegate observed the hearing. In December Wilhelm Sommer was acquitted.

Amnesty International sent the Austrian Government a memorandum and a detailed report about its concerns in March and December respectively. These included the lack of an adequate procedure for complaints about ill-treatment, the need for more practical and legislative safeguards against ill-treatment, and the need to ensure that genuine complainants are not discouraged from making a complaint about police ill-treatment through fear of being charged with a criminal offence. In August, in their reply to the memorandum, the authorities pointed to steps already taken to prevent ill-treatment, such as changes to the Administrative Offences Code (see *Amnesty International Report 1989*). They said that further measures were planned, such as a decree to the courts and public procurators on the implementation of Article 15 of the United Nations Convention against Torture and Other Cruel, Inhuman or Degrading Treatment or Punishment. Article 15 prohibits evidence produced through torture from being used in court against the victim.

BAHAMAS

Seven prisoners were scheduled for execution but all were granted stays. Four death sentences were commuted. At the end of the year 19 people were under sentence of death. No executions were carried out in 1989: none had been carried out since early 1986.

The seven had been convicted of murder between 1985 and 1988: the Bahamas Court of Appeal had dismissed their appeals between 1986 and 1989. However, at the time warrants were issued for their executions, none of them had appealed to the Judicial Committee of the Privy Council

38 (JCPC) in London, which acts as the final court of appeal for the Bahamas.

In two cases where Amnesty International had advance information about scheduled executions, the organization wrote to the authorities reiterating its opposition to the death penalty and stressing the importance of prisoners under sentence of death being able to pursue fully all means of appeal in view of the severity and finality of the death penalty.

In November Amnesty International received a reply from the government saying that in no case would a death sentence be carried out if an appeal was pending. The letter added that in the case of Stafford Clarke, application for leave to appeal to the JCPC was made only after the date for execution had been set. Consequently, a stay was granted according to law.

BAHRAIN

Dozens of people, including possible prisoners of conscience, were detained without charge or trial. Over 100 other prisoners were serving prison terms imposed after unfair trials for alleged political offences. There were reports of political detainees being tortured, particularly during pre-trial incommunicado detention, apparently to force them to confess to political offences. An alleged death from torture was categorically denied by the government.

Most of those detained were from Bahrain's majority Shi'a community and were suspected of involvement with illegal revolutionary groups based outside Bahrain, particularly in Iran and Syria.

The authorities used wide-ranging powers of detention, available under the 1974 Decree Law on State Security

Measures, to imprison suspected government opponents. These permit administrative detention without charge or trial for up to three years by order of the Minister of the Interior. Judicial review in such cases, which takes place *in camera*, is only available three months after the date of detention, at the prisoner's request, and at six-monthly intervals thereafter. However, it is rarely used, possibly as a result of detainees not being informed about the procedure.

The 1974 Decree Law, through an amendment to Article 79 of the Code of Criminal Procedure, also allows detainees to be held in unlimited pre-trial detention if they are suspected of involvement in illegal activities threatening state security. Detainees are denied access to lawyers and are not informed of the reasons for their detention. Under this procedure there is no opportunity for judicial review. The broad formulation of these powers appears to allow the detention of those expressing their political or other conscientiously held beliefs in a non-violent manner.

In early February approximately 30 people were detained under the 1974 Decree Law in and around Bani Jamra in northwest Bahrain. Among them was a well-known religious teacher, 'Omran Hussein 'Omran, one of 12 of those held who remained in incommunicado detention in 'Adliya Prison at the end of the year. Among the 12 were four youths. At least 30 other members of the Shi'a community were arrested in May and June and were still detained at the end of 1989.

All cases involving charges against the internal or external security of the state are tried by the Civil Supreme Court of Appeal. Procedures before this court fail to comply with international standards for a fair trial. In particular, the court is empowered to convict defendants solely on the basis of confessions, which are admissible as evidence even if they are contained only in police or prosecution documents and unsupported by corroborating evidence, including witness evidence. Effectively unlimited pre-trial incommunicado detention increases the risk that prisoners may be tortured to force them to confess to crimes they may not have committed. The Civil Supreme Court of Appeal sits as a court of first instance in political cases; there is no right of appeal.

At least two political trials began before the court in 1989 and were still in progress at the end of the year. In June, nine people who were detained in September 1988 (see *Amnesty International Report 1989*) appeared on charges related to membership of an illegal political organization and incitement against the government. They included Muhammad Jamil 'Abdul 'Amir al-Jamri and 'Abdul Jalil Khalil Ibrahim Hassan, respectively the son and son-in-law of Sheikh 'Abdul 'Amir al-Jamri, a prominent religious leader whose brief detention in 1988 had caused unrest in the Shi'a community. In September three men arrested in November 1987 appeared before the court on charges of planning to sabotage oil installations (see *Amnesty International Report 1988*).

Over 100 political prisoners sentenced after unfair trials before the Civil Supreme Court of Appeal remained in prison. They included 14 alleged supporters of the banned Bahrain National Liberation Front, who were convicted in October 1987; 18 alleged supporters of the illegal Islamic Enlightenment Society, who were convicted in 1984; and nine alleged members of the outlawed Islamic Front for the Liberation of Bahrain, who were convicted in 1988 (see *Amnesty International Report 1989*). Approximately 70 others sentenced in connection with an alleged coup attempt in 1981 also remained in prison.

Several defendants in political trials were alleged to have been tortured to force them to make confessions prior to their appearance in court. Mirza 'Abdulkhaliq, who came before the court in September accused of attempted sabotage, alleged that he had been tied by rope to a car and dragged across stony ground. Interrogators also allegedly threatened to rape prisoners' wives or their female relatives. Other methods of torture reportedly included beating and suspension by the wrists.

In February the body of Muhammad Mansour Hassan, whose brother is a former political prisoner in Bahrain now living in exile, was found lying on waste ground. There were contradictory explanations of how he met his death. Opposition groups alleged that he had died in police custody as a result of torture after being detained at Bahrain International Airport on 25 January. The Minister of the Interior denied that Muhammad Mansour Hassan had ever been in police custody and told Amnesty International that there were no suspicious circumstances surrounding his death, which the ministry attributed to natural causes.

Amnesty International called for the fair trial or release of uncharged political detainees arrested in February, May and June. It continued to seek information about prisoners sentenced after unfair trials by the Civil Supreme Court of Appeal, urging that they should be retried in accordance with international standards, or released.

In May Amnesty International received comments from the government on the Bahrain entry in *Amnesty International Report 1988*. These stated that any allegations of torture can be presented to the courts and that allegations of torture and prohibiting family visits and access to lawyers are "baseless". The organization responded by bringing to the government's attention its detailed recommendations regarding the implementation of human rights safeguards in its December 1988 document, *Concerns in the State of Bahrain*. No reply had been received by the end of the year.

BANGLADESH

Many Hindus held without charge or trial for up to six months in connection with a separatist movement were released, but several others were arrested. Reports of torture in police custody continued to be received. At least 13 people were sentenced to death but it is not known if there were any executions. Over 30 tribal villagers in the Chittagong Hill Tracts were reportedly killed in apparent extrajudicial executions by members of a civil defence unit and other non-tribal settlers.

The government of President Hossain Mohammad Ershad introduced new legislation in February providing for elected

40

councils with tribal majorities to be established in the Rangamati, Khagrachari and Bandarban districts of the Chittagong Hill Tracts. The government declared an amnesty from 23 April, granting immunity against prosecution to members of the armed tribal opposition group, the *Shanti Bahini* (Peace Forces), who surrendered prior to the council elections on 25 June; there was very little response. The *Jana Samhati Samiti* (JSS), People's Solidarity Association, the political wing of the *Shanti Bahini*, opposed the new administrative arrangements and boycotted the June elections. The *Shanti Bahini* was blamed for scores of killings, including the murder of 13 non-tribal people in Kaptai sub-district in April. It continued its violent opposition to the government, and attacks on non-combatant civilians in the area, after the elections. Twelve people (including eight tribal people) were killed when a bomb exploded on a passenger boat in Naniarchar sub-district in August in an attack attributed to the *Shanti Bahini*.

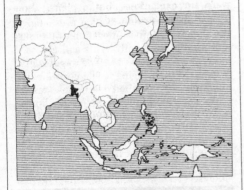

Several people were reportedly arrested in the southwest for alleged involvement in a Hindu separatist movement based in India. Over 100 others, including possible prisoners of conscience, had been arrested for similar reasons in December 1988 (see *Amnesty International Report 1989*): some of them were released on the order of Dhaka High Court after spending up to six months in detention without charge or trial. They included Chittaranjan Ghose, secretary of the Faridpur district National Awami Party, and Bipul Kumar Ghose, Joint Secretary of the Faridpur district Awami League. In February the Home Minister said 40 people were in detention under the Special Powers Act (SPA) of 1974 for involvement in the separatist move-

ment; in June, 26 people were acknowledged to be in detention. It was not known how many remained in detention at the end of the year.

People alleged to have committed a "prejudicial act" likely to "endanger public safety or the maintenance of public order" can be detained without charge or trial under the SPA for up to 30 days; the District Magistrate can renew detention orders indefinitely with the approval of the Ministry of Home Affairs. In June the Home Minister said that 2,436 prisoners had been detained under the SPA from January 1988 to April 1989. It was not known how many of them were political prisoners and whether they included any prisoners of conscience.

In August five leaders of the Bangladesh Agricultural Workers Association, including Habibur Rahman Hira, were reportedly detained without charge or trial under the SPA. They had organized protests around agricultural workers' grievances and against the arrests of four agricultural workers on what they said were false charges. They had been released by November.

The torture of criminal suspects by police continued to be reported. Two sisters were reportedly raped by police officers in Chittagong in August when they went to the police station to file a complaint. Several criminal suspects died in custody, allegedly as a result of torture. In one reported case a murder suspect named Ofazuddin was admitted to hospital in June with head and other injuries apparently sustained when he was interrogated at Dhamrai police station, Dhamrai district. He died in hospital one month later. A local human rights organization brought charges against a police officer accused of causing his death but the case had not been heard by the end of the year. In another case, Shahidul Islam reportedly had extensive injuries and was unable to speak when he was taken to hospital from Katwali police station, Jessore district, in June. He died the next day. A judicial inquiry was not known to have been held into his death. A police officer in Jessore was sentenced to seven years' rigorous imprisonment in February for causing a prisoner's death through torture.

Police severely beat several people during strikes and some arrested demonstrators were reportedly tortured. Nurul Islam Chotan, a leader of the left-wing five-party alliance, was arrested during a strike called by the alliance in August. He suffered a fractured leg and hand allegedly as a result of severe beatings inflicted while he was in custody. A private prosecution was brought against the six police officers allegedly involved, but the outcome was not known by the end of the year.

At least 13 people were sentenced to death for murder, but the true figure was probably higher. It was not known if there were any executions.

In May at least 36 tribal villagers in the Chittagong Hill Tracts were reportedly killed by Village Defence Party (VDP) members and other non-tribal settlers. The VDPs are local civil defence units recruited, armed and trained by the police to protect their localities at night. The killings were apparently in reprisal for the murder of the non-tribal chairperson of Langadu council, allegedly by the *Shanti Bahini*: between six and 11 villages were reportedly attacked. Survivors were said to have fled to the hills and forests for refuge, and thousands crossed the border into Tripura in India, joining tens of thousands of refugees who remained in India from previous years.

After the Langadu killings, tribal leader Raja Debashish Roy was placed under house arrest for three days, preventing him from attending a Buddhist ceremony to commemorate the dead. The day before his arrest he and 21 other tribal leaders had submitted a memorandum to the authorities demanding action against the perpetrators of the killings.

The government informed Amnesty International in June that it had investigated the killings and found that 16 tribal people had been killed by an "unruly mob". It said that over 30 people had been arrested on suspicion of involvement in rioting; the precise charges were not made known. It suggested that the attack was a spontaneous outburst by non-tribal people reacting to the killing of the Langadu council chairperson, which the security forces had immediately attempted to contain. However, it did not provide full details of the inquiry, the findings of which conflict with reports Amnesty International received from other sources. No trials were known to have taken place by the end of the year in connection with these killings.

Amnesty International sought information about detainees held under the SPA.

It called on the government to prohibit the execution of minors and reduce the number of offences punishable by death as steps towards abolition.

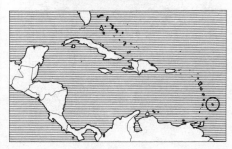

BARBADOS

Eight death sentences were commuted during the year, including those of two juvenile offenders. Legislation was approved raising to 18 the minimum age for imposition of the death penalty. There were no executions, but at least three people were sentenced to death. Nine people remained on death row at the end of the year.

The death sentences of Patrick Greaves and Michael Taylor were commuted to life imprisonment on 20 November. At the time of the crime they were 17 years old.

On 21 November the House of Assembly voted unanimously to prohibit the execution of people aged under 18 years at the time of the crime. In December the Senate approved this amendment to the Juvenile Offenders Act, bringing Barbados' law into line with international standards. Barbados had been one of only five countries in the world known to have executed during the past decade someone aged under 18 at the time of the offence: Martin Marsh was executed in 1982 for a crime committed when he was 17 years old.

In December Amnesty International wrote to the government welcoming the commutations granted during the year, including those of Patrick Greaves and Michael Taylor. Amnesty International had made numerous appeals on behalf of Greaves and Taylor and had called for the commutation of all death sentences. The organization also welcomed the legislation abolishing the death penalty for juveniles and urged the government to take steps towards the total abolition of the penalty.

BENIN

At least 80 prisoners of conscience arrested in previous years were still held at the beginning of the year and a further 50 were arrested during 1989 in connection with demonstrations and strikes. However, they were all released in an amnesty declared in August. Further arrests of prisoners of conscience took place in November. Two groups of prisoners accused of plotting to overthrow the government in 1988 remained in detention: some were not brought to trial, others were tried before the State Security Court, whose procedures did not meet international standards for fair trial. Reports that political detainees were tortured included the cases of three people who died as a result. A government order to shoot demonstrators on sight resulted in other deaths. Twelve opponents of the Government of the Central African Republic were arrested in July and forcibly repatriated.

Major demonstrations against the government of President Mathieu Kérékou occurred at the beginning and end of the year. During strikes in Porto Novo in January and February, the security forces were empowered to shoot demonstrators on sight, even those using no violence. Two people were killed and many were injured in March when troops opened fire on strikers at a sugar factory in Savé in the south of the country. The strikers were protesting at not being paid and against threatened redundancies. Some of those injured reportedly died later in hospital.

In December striking workers in various towns demonstrated for democratic free-

doms and payment of their salaries. The security forces shot one demonstrator dead in Lokossa and another in Abomey: it remained unclear whether demonstrators in either town had resorted to violence. There were no official inquiries into any of the killings. The security forces' immunity from prosecution was also evident in the case of Boko Crespin, a neighbour of a suspected opposition activist, Simon Fanou. In what appeared to be a case of mistaken identity, soldiers surrounded Boko Crespin's house in March and shot him dead when he shouted for help. There was no official investigation into his death.

The government took some steps to protect human rights. In February the President instructed the security forces and prosecuting authorities to abide by a Code of Penal Procedure requirement to bring detainees before a magistrate within a few days of their arrest, or release them. However, this requirement was not observed in political cases and political detainees continued to be held for indefinite periods without referral to the procuracy.

In April the National Revolutionary Assembly enacted legislation to establish a National Human Rights Commission. Members of the commission, which is empowered to investigate complaints and propose legislative changes, are to include government appointees and elected representatives of the country's non-governmental organizations. The commission had not been convened by the end of the year.

More than 50 suspected supporters of the banned *Parti communiste du Dahomey* (PCD), Communist Party of Dahomey (Benin's former name), and other alleged government opponents were arrested in January and February. The arrests followed strikes and demonstrations by teachers, students and others protesting the government's failure to pay their salaries and grants. The detainees included Tiamiou Adjibadé, a former government minister and leading figure in the Porto Novo area, who was arrested on suspicion of using his influence to raise support for strike action. He and some of the other detainees were soon released, while at least 50 others were held for periods of up to several months. Those who remained in detention were apparently arrested for opposing the government rather than for participating in demonstrations. Some of them were forcibly conscripted into the army. All of the conscripts and some of the remaining detainees were released in April. The others were released in the August amnesty.

Other suspected government opponents were arrested between February and May. Jonas Gninmagnon, a human rights activist, was held incommunicado and without charge at Abomey-Calavi gendarmerie post until his release in the August amnesty. He chairs the *Comité des parents et épouses des détenus d'opinion*, Committee of Relatives and Wives of Prisoners of Conscience, which was formed in 1986 to campaign for the release of political prisoners.

About 50 untried political detainees, all prisoners of conscience, were released in April. Most had been detained because of their alleged links with the PCD and some had remained in custody since 1984 or 1985. In 1988 they had appealed to the head of state for clemency in connection with their political activities. Detainees who refused to seek clemency were not freed until late August, when the government announced an amnesty for 192 of its political opponents. The amnesty was also intended to allow the return of government opponents living abroad who feared prosecution in Benin. Sixty prisoners of conscience were freed, including Raymond Adékambi, a civil engineer held since October 1985, and Mathias Finoundé, a health technician held since April 1985. Also freed were prisoners convicted of involvement in the 1975 and 1977 coup attempts.

Several former prisoners of conscience were rearrested in November. Two students, released in the August amnesty after four years' detention without trial, were detained for a few days in Natitingou. Following a public meeting at which they had criticized government policies, they were apparently found in possession of political tracts. Emile Ahossi, a medical doctor, was arrested at a road-block as he returned from a political meeting. He too was apparently carrying documents which the authorities considered to be political tracts. He was released on 8 December.

Two trials took place before the State Security Court. The court, established in April 1988 to try people accused of offences against the security of the state (see *Amnesty International Report 1989*),

had not previously been used. Both trials failed to meet international standards for fair trial. The first concluded in February with the conviction of four people charged with attempting to assassinate the head of state in June 1988. Some of the judges and other senior court officials were members of the armed forces or of the central committee of Benin's ruling party. Some defence witnesses, such as a presidential adviser, did not appear because the court refused to summon them. Two of the defendants were sentenced to 20 years' imprisonment, one to 10 years and one to five years. At least 11 other people arrested with the four defendants remained in custody without charge or trial at the end of the year. They included Marcellin Atindehou, a military officer, and Michel Bamenou Toko, a former minister of justice. In July the State Security Court announced the conviction *in absentia* of Moudachirou Dourossimi, who was also charged in connection with the June 1988 coup attempt. His case had not been examined in the February hearings, and he was sentenced to life imprisonment.

A second trial opened before the State Security Court in July. Nineteen people, four of whom were tried *in absentia*, were charged with attempting to overthrow the government in March 1988. Defence lawyers requested postponement to allow medical treatment for the accused and to obtain medical evidence of torture. The lawyers also protested that the notes of earlier investigations had not been included in their legal dossiers. The hearings, postponed several times, had not taken place by the end of the year.

Political detainees were reportedly tortured at the Camp PLM Aledjo military post in Cotonou and at other locations. Prisoners were severely beaten and some were buried up to their necks, according to reports, then beaten again about the head. One prisoner lost the hearing in one ear as a result of this treatment.

Three untried political detainees reportedly died in custody after they were tortured. Serge Gnimadi, an 18-year-old school student who was detained in January, died in police custody in Porto Novo the following month. Parfait Agbalé, a journalist, was apparently detained in March because of his inquiries into the student's death. Parfait Agbalé was released without charge after about three weeks'

44

detention. Christophe Hounmenou, an army sergeant held since 1988 for alleged involvement in the March 1988 coup attempt, died in April after transfer from Bembéréké military camp to hospital in Parakou. He was reportedly seriously ill as a result of harsh conditions and ill-treatment at Bembéréké. Luc Togbadja, a student arrested in April for possessing anti-government tracts, died in May after repeated interrogation at the *Petit Palais*, Small Palace, headquarters of the national security service in Cotonou.

No official investigations into the three deaths were reported, despite a legal requirement of judicial investigation into all deaths in custody. The authorities said that they had investigated the case of Rémy Glélé Akpokpo, who died in custody in 1988 (see *Amnesty International Report 1989*). While stating that torture was not the cause of death, they issued no further details.

In July, 12 people from the Central African Republic were arrested and detained incommunicado at Camp PLM Aledjo. All were members of political groups opposed to the Government of the Central African Republic. Although they had lived in Benin for several years, they had not formally sought asylum. Without any court hearing or legal procedures, they were forcibly repatriated in August to the Central African Republic, where they were detained on arrival.

Amnesty International delegates visited Benin in April and met President Kérékou and government ministers. The President said that torture was not used in Benin and that no prisoners of conscience or other political prisoners were in custody, although he acknowledged the detention of about 100 suspected left-wing activists. He said that Amnesty International observers could attend their trial if and when it took place. The authorities said that security officials had written instructions forbidding the use of torture and that the Procurator General had recently visited several places of detention to ensure that all detainees were well treated. However, it was clear that representatives of the procuracy were not allowed to visit detention centres where political detainees were held.

Amnesty International appealed for the release of all prisoners of conscience and called on the authorities either to grant

political detainees fair and prompt trials, or to release them. The organization also urged the authorities to take steps to halt the use of torture and to investigate torture allegations and all deaths in detention, with a view to prosecuting those responsible if torture had occurred. Amnesty International also expressed its concern about the order given to security forces to shoot demonstrators on sight: this order permitted the shooting of people peacefully exercising their rights to assembly and association, as well as demonstrators resorting to life-threatening violence.

In August Amnesty International reported its concerns about administrative detention in a statement circulated to the United Nations Sub-Commission on Prevention of Discrimination and Protection of Minorities.

BERMUDA

The only prisoner under sentence of death had his sentence commuted to life imprisonment. No executions had been carried out for 12 years.

Troy Shorter had been sentenced to death in 1987 for premeditated murder. In February the Judicial Committee of the Privy Council in London, which acts as Bermuda's final court of appeal, rejected Troy Shorter's petition for leave to appeal. However, in March the Governor, Sir Desmond Langley, commuted the death sentence.

On 10 March a parliamentary bill was introduced to abolish the death penalty for all crimes. On 28 April parliament decided to postpone the vote for six months. On 3 June it passed an act providing for a public referendum to take place within the following six months on the issue of "whether or not capital punishment for premeditated murder is favoured in Bermuda". The referendum would not be binding on parliament, which would be free to debate the issue again. Neither the referendum nor the postponed parliamentary vote had taken place by the end of the year.

Amnesty International wrote to Bermuda's Governor General in March welcoming the decision to commute Troy Shorter's death sentence. In April the organization wrote to Prime Minister John Swan welcoming the future debate in parliament on the death penalty and urging that parliament take the decisive step of abolishing the penalty.

BHUTAN

A government critic was imprisoned as a prisoner of conscience.

In May the government of King Druk Gyalpo Jigme Singye Wangchuck reportedly decreed that Bhutanese who did not wear national dress in public could be imprisoned for one week or fined.

Ratan Gazmere, a teacher, author of pamphlets and campaigner on behalf of minority rights, was arrested in October for "anti-national activities", an offence punishable with death. He was still held without trial at the end of the year.

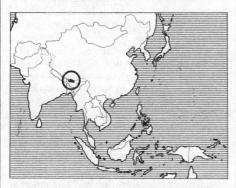

Amnesty International expressed its concern to the Bhutanese Government that Ratan Gazmere had been arrested simply because he had written and distributed literature on minority rights. In response, the government stated that Ratan Gazmere had been arrested not solely for his writings, but also for "anti-national activities". The government said Ratan Gazmere would receive a fair trial.

BOLIVIA

About 200 people were arrested in November after the government declared a state of siege. Most were members of striking teachers' unions. Other groups of detainees were reportedly tortured and ill-treated by intelligence officials and the police. Inmates of police-run reformatories were reported to have been tortured and ill-treated: one reformatory was closed pending an investigation into alleged torture, extrajudicial executions and secret burials.

In August President Victor Paz Estenssoro of the *Movimiento Nacional Revolucionario* (MNR), National Revolutionary Movement, was succeeded by Jaime Paz Zamora of the *Movimiento de la Izquierda Revolucionaria* (MIR), Revolutionary Left Movement. The new President headed a coalition government — *Unidad Nacional*, National Unity — which included the party led by General Hugo Banzer, the *Acción Democrática Nacionalista* (ADN), Nationalist Democratic Action. The MNR government had reduced inflation by cutting the health and education budgets and by dismissing 23,000 miners from the state mining company, COMIBOL. The austerity measures led to numerous trade union protest actions, including public hunger-strikes and symbolic "crucifixions".

In September President Paz Zamora said he would try to accelerate proceedings against General Luís García Meza, the former president, who had been on trial with 54 co-defendants since 1984. They faced charges of violating the Constitution, sedition, and killing and torturing opponents between 1980 and 1982 (see *Amnesty*

46 *International Reports 1981* to *1983*).

On 15 November about 200 people were arrested after the government declared a 90-day state of siege. Most were members of the urban and rural teachers' unions, who had been on hunger-strike for three weeks in support of a salary increase. Many of those detained were sent briefly into internal exile. By the end of the year, all those detained had been released.

In May two Mormon missionaries from the United States of America (USA) were killed in La Paz. Shortly afterwards officials from the Ministry of the Interior detained dozens of people, mainly students. Most were released after a few days, but four people were kept in detention and charged with the killings: Nelson and Felix Encinas Laguna, and Constantino Yurja, three students from the *Universidad Mayor de San Andrés*, and Gabriel Rojas, a medical doctor. They were accused of belonging to a little-known organization, *Fuerzas Armadas de Liberación Zarate Willka* (FAL-ZW), the Zarate Willka Armed Liberation Forces, which had claimed responsibility for the killings and other assaults. The four were reportedly held incommunicado for 10 days after their arrest. Three of them later alleged that intelligence agents had tortured them at a secret interrogation centre in La Paz. All denied involvement in the killings. Their defence lawyers complained of undue government pressure on the trial. They noted that after the investigating magistrate dismissed the charges for lack of evidence and ordered the case closed, the public prosecutor's office successfully petitioned La Paz District Court to remove the judge from the case. The succeeding judge was also removed, allegedly for expressing a premature opinion on the case by supporting the previous judge's ruling. No official investigation appeared to have been opened into the detainees' allegations of ill-treatment.

Torture and ill-treatment of detainees at remote police-run reformatories were frequently reported. Inmates were held under the vagrancy provisions of the Police Law of 1886, which permit detention without charge or trial for up to one year of those considered a "potential danger to society", such as drug addicts or suspected petty criminals. Although minors are specifically excluded from the provisions of this law, they were regularly interned at these reformatories.

In recent years former inmates have repeatedly claimed that some inmates have died as a result of beatings and that police have deliberately killed others. Evidence substantiating some of these allegations emerged in October during a judicial investigation into alleged secret burials at the *Granja de Espejos* reformatory in Santa Cruz de la Sierra. Forensic pathologists from Argentina and the USA assisting in the investigation estimated that one burial site held over 40 bodies. The Police Governor of the *Granja de Espejos* claimed that the inmates had died of natural causes or had been shot while trying to escape. The forensic scientists exhumed the remains of four people who had died in the past five years and found that three had met violent deaths: one had apparently been beaten to death. The fourth body was that of a 14 or 15-year-old youth. The *Granja de Espejos* was closed in late October and its governor and three police officers were arrested and charged in connection with the killing and torture of inmates. The three police officers immediately escaped in unexplained circumstances; two had been rearrested by December.

Although the Constitution prohibits detention without charge for more than 48 hours, numerous detentions exceeded this limit. Placido Mamani, aged 18, was arrested in May during a police raid on a poor district of La Paz. He was held incommunicado for 32 days in the Criminal Investigations Department, where police allegedly beat him. He was then transferred to a hospital. He discharged himself after two days but collapsed and died on his way home. Although the official cause of death was pulmonary infection, evidence indicated that the alleged ill-treatment may have contributed to Placido Mamani's death.

An Amnesty International delegate visited the *Granja de Espejos* reformatory in early October and observed the judicial inspection of the secret graves. The organization informed the government of its concerns about reported human rights violations at reformatories. Ministry of the Interior officials told Amnesty International that the government was seeking to improve conditions in the prison system.

In November Amnesty International called on the new President to ensure the humane treatment of detainees held under the state of siege, urging that they be released immediately, or charged with a recognizably criminal offence.

Amnesty International called on the government to investigate the alleged torture of the detainees accused of killing two Mormon missionaries. The organization expressed concern about reports that judges had been improperly dismissed from the case and called for assurances that the defendants would receive a fair trial conforming to international standards.

Amnesty International also urged the government to take steps to prevent torture, ill-treatment and extrajudicial killings by ensuring that all detainees are under judicial supervision and have access to legal counsel and their relatives.

In December Amnesty International expressed concern to the government about the continual delays in the investigation into gross human rights violations committed during the García Meza administration. In particular, it noted that the government had impeded the trial's progress by removing from the jurisdiction of the Bolivian courts one of the principal defendants in the trial, Luís Arce Gómez, the former Minister of the Interior. Charges against him included the murder of eight political leaders in 1981. He had remained in hiding until December, when he was arrested and immediately handed over to the USA authorities for trial on a drugs offence.

BRAZIL

Peasants involved in land disputes were arbitrarily detained in growing numbers. The detainees were often ill-treated or tortured. Torture of criminal suspects and prisoners continued to be widespread, in many cases leading to deaths in custody. The circumstances of some deaths in custody were suggestive of extrajudicial killings. In urban areas, killings increased of suspected petty criminals and juvenile offenders by "death squads" allegedly made up of police personnel. In rural areas, trade unionists and campaigners for agrarian reform continued to receive threats and more than 50 were killed: the state authorities persistently failed to bring to justice those responsible for these crimes or for assaults on members of indigenous communities.

The first direct presidential elections since 1960 were held in two rounds in November and December. The successful candidate, Fernando Collor de Mello of the National Reconstruction Party, was due to take office in March 1990. During the year Brazil ratified the United Nations (UN) Convention against Torture and Other Cruel, Inhuman or Degrading Treatment or Punishment and the Inter-American Convention to Prevent and Punish Torture.

There was an increase in detention without warrant of peasants involved in land disputes and further reports of their being tortured and ill-treated in short-term custody. On 11 March battalions of the *Brigada Militar*, Military Police, from Rio Grande do Sul expelled a group of some 600 peasant families from land they had recently occupied in Salto do Jacuí. After sealing off the encampment and spraying it with tear-gas, members of the *Brigada Militar* allegedly fired into the crowd. Five police officers and 400 peasants were reported to have been wounded in the eviction, and 14 peasants were treated for bullet wounds. The police reportedly beat many peasants taken into custody, and five detainees were allegedly staked to ant-hills after arrest.

Ivan Brito de Assis, a leader of the *Movimento Dos Trabalhadores Rurais Sem Terra* (MST), Landless Rural Workers' Movement, was one of 11 MST members detained without warrant for a day on 29 August in the state of Alagoas. Ivan Brito de Assis said afterwards that he had been repeatedly beaten and threatened with summary execution. He said that a rope had been tied around his testicles and that he had been tortured with electricity while

48

hung from an iron bar (called the *pau de arara*, parrot's perch). He alleged he had been tortured in order to make him give information to police and landowners about the MST, a legal organization. A medical examination the day after his release found that he had multiple bruising and swellings consistent with his testimony.

There were continued reports of the widespread use of torture and ill-treatment of criminal prisoners and suspects. In March a joint commission of Brazilian human rights organizations visited a prison in São Paulo, the *Casa de Detenção*. The commission interviewed prisoners there following allegations that over 1,000 of them had been beaten after an escape attempt by two inmates in which a prison guard was killed. According to the commission's report, military police stationed at the prison removed prisoners from their cells and made them strip and kneel against the wall so that they could not see their assailants. Prison guards then cut them with knives or beat them with pieces of wood, iron bars, cables and rubber truncheons. The commission noted many fractures of legs, arms and ribs in addition to bruising on the prisoners interviewed. Medical assistance had apparently not been given for some days after the incident. The results of a judicial inquiry into the allegations had not been made public by the end of the year. A number of prisoners also testified to the commission about continuing torture, including the use of electric shocks and beatings with iron bars, in Pavilion 6 of the *Casa de Detenção* (see *Amnesty International Report 1988*).

On 5 February, 18 prisoners died of asphyxiation in the 42nd police precinct of São Paulo. They had been sealed with 33 other inmates in a punishment cell which measured 1.4 metres by 3.6 metres with no air vent. According to survivors, the incident followed an escape attempt which had been foiled by guards. After the prisoners had been brought under control, they were stripped naked and beaten by a column of military and civil police. Fifty-one of them were then forced into the cell. Despite cries that prisoners were dying, the cell was not opened for over two hours. Civil and military police inquiries were opened, but by the end of the year little progress had been made in bringing judicial proceedings against the 21 police officers charged with aggravated homicide for the ill-treatment

and deaths. After 30 days' suspension, two of the three civil police agents who were charged were transferred to active duty at the Police Disciplinary Board, which was investigating the case. Eighteen military police officers also charged with aggravated homicide, whose case was to be heard by a military tribunal, were not suspended from active duty.

Prisoners were killed following escape attempts in other states in circumstances suggestive of extrajudicial executions. Ten military and three civil police were charged with the killing in February of seven detainees at the Vila Aurora police station in Rondonopolis, Mato Grosso state. The detainees had been dragged out of their cells and then stabbed and shot by hooded men, identified by survivors as military police officers. Prisoners were also killed in custody following three other prison disturbances: 11 were killed in Cuiabá, Mato Grosso, in March; eight were killed in Curitiba, Paraná state, in November; and five were killed in Rio de Janeiro state in December. In all these cases there were allegations that prisoners had been assaulted by the authorities after they had surrendered.

"Death squads" were reported to have increased their activities against suspected petty criminals and juvenile offenders in major cities. "Extermination groups" made up of civilian vigilantes and members of the civil and military police were reportedly responsible for hundreds of killings. The Rio de Janeiro State Police Commission of Inquiry into Extermination Groups, established in 1983, continued its investigation, but the level of crimes attributed to "extermination groups" with police participation did not fall. A study of official police statistics and newspaper reports in Rio de Janeiro state by a joint commission of local human rights groups recorded 1,175 homicides in seven municipalities in the state in the first six months of 1989. Press reports asserted that many of these killings had been committed by "extermination groups". In a number of cases, witnesses had reported uniformed police among the assailants.

In Recife, Pernambuco, the *Gabinete de Assessoria Juridico Popular*, Popular Legal Advice Bureau, reported 212 killings attributed to "death squads" in the city during 1988 and 88 such killings in the first three months of 1989. Victims were mainly suspected petty criminals, predominantly youths between the ages of 18 and 25. Bodies were usually riddled with bullets. Some had marks of handcuffs on them or the hands were tied with nylon rope. In July the Governor of Amazonas state disbanded the entire state civil police force following evidence of substantial civil police involvement in "death squads" in the capital, Manaus.

Investigations into "extermination groups" were hampered by intimidation of witnesses and threats or attacks on those denouncing the killings. In March Luis Tenderini, President of the Justice and Peace Commission of Recife, was abducted, beaten and burned with cigarettes by men who warned him not to investigate "death squad" activities in the city. The Justice and Peace Commission had urged the authorities to prosecute police found responsible for the killings. Some military police officers were being officially investigated for involvement in "death squad" activities. In July Dom Mauro Morelli, the Bishop of Duque de Caxias, Rio de Janeiro state, received death threats after he had denounced police involvement in "extermination groups".

In rural areas there was no significant progress in bringing to justice those responsible for killing peasant leaders involved in land or labour disputes. Gunmen allegedly hired by landowners and land claimants continued to carry out such killings with impunity throughout the year. Amnesty International believed that the persistent failure to prosecute in such cases suggested acquiescence by the state authorities in these crimes. In spite of the notorious, widespread and persistent nature of these killings, the Brazilian authorities failed at every level to take effective measures to stop them.

A number of trade unionists and community leaders supporting the actions of peasants were killed in Espirito Santo state. Killings increased following a violent confrontation in June during which squatter peasants linked to the MST allegedly killed a landowner and a plainclothes police officer who were attempting to expel them from land they had recently occupied near the town of Pedro Canario.

On 6 June, 13 peasants were arrested and allegedly tortured by state police seeking information incriminating other members of the community. The 13 were released the following day, but a series of further arrests followed. Among those detained was Verino Sossai, President of the Rural Workers' Trade Union of Montanha, who was arrested on 6 July and accused of sheltering one of the principal suspects. He was released after a few days, but was assassinated two weeks later. A month earlier the treasurer of the Workers' Party in Linhares, Paulo Damião Tristão, had been killed. He had previously denounced state complicity in what he believed to be a campaign of violence against peasants and human rights activists sponsored by a landowners' organization, the União Democratica Ruralista (UDR), Democratic Ruralists' Union. By the end of July federal police were reported to be investigating connections between these two killings and the July killing of a newspaper columnist, Maria Nilce Magalhaes, who was reportedly planning to publish material on local corruption.

In August attempts were made on the lives of Vilmar Schneider, a Lutheran pastor from Linhares, and Osmar Barcelos do Nascimento, a human rights lawyer. Church workers in Espirito Santo, including the Bishop of Mateus and several members of the Comissão Pastoral da Terra (CPT), Church Land Commission, received death threats. In September Valdernicio Barbosa dos Santos, a leader of the Rural Workers' Trade Union of Pedro Canário, was shot dead, reportedly with a police-issue weapon. In December a French priest, Father Gabriel Maire, was shot dead as he drove back to his parish in the city of Vitoria. Before his death Father Maire had made a statement to the local Justice and Peace Commission about death threats he had allegedly received from police officers because of his work in support of the landless poor. By the end of the year a former civil police chief had been charged with commissioning the murder of Maria Nilce Magalhaes. The public prosecution service had not yet brought charges for the other killings of trade unionists and community leaders supporting peasants in Espirito Santo.

In July two men were indicted for the murder of rubber tappers' trade union leader Francisco Alves Mendes Filho, known as Chico Mendes, who was killed in December 1988 in Acre state (see Amnesty International Report 1989). They were appealing against the indictment.

50 Two other men charged with the killing had not yet been arrested.

There was very little progress during the year in bringing to trial those responsible for scores of other killings studied by Amnesty International.

The authorities failed to take effective measures to prevent further attacks on members of indigenous communities. Scant progress was made in bringing any-one to trial for the March 1988 killings of 14 Ticuna Indians in Amazonas state (see *Amnesty International Report 1989*). Gold prospectors were reported to have killed Yanomami Indians in Roraima state, but there was no news of the outcome of police inquiries into these incidents. In one case in August, two women and a child were killed at an illegal airstrip near the Surucucus Indian post. While the author-ities did not prevent gold miners entering Yanomami lands, they maintained their ban on anthropologists and health workers. This hindered the effective reporting of incidents and made it impossible to deter-mine the circumstances and extent of killings in Yanomami areas.

Amnesty International asked the Brazilian authorities about investigations into allegations of torture in detention cen-tres and prisons. The allegations referred both to peasants detained in the context of land disputes and to ordinary criminal prisoners. Following the deaths in custody through asphyxiation in São Paulo in February, Amnesty International raised with judicial authorities their role in the protection and promotion of human rights in the state. In March Amnesty Inter-national sent a medical delegation to Rio Grande do Sul to examine prisoners detained following the expulsion of some 600 peasant families. The delegation con-firmed the existence of injuries consistent with the prisoners' allegations of ill-treat-ment. Following reports of alleged extraju-dicial executions and death threats, the organization appealed to the authorities to investigate these incidents fully and bring those responsible to justice.

In August Amnesty International expressed concern to the UN Sub-Commission on the Prevention of Dis-crimination and Protection of Minorities about the Brazilian Government's failure to protect indigenous people from violent assault, or to prosecute those responsible for the killing of Indians.

BRUNEI DARUSSALAM

Seven prisoners of conscience, four of whom have been held continuously for 27 years and one for more than 13 years, remained in detention without charge or trial. Criminal offenders continued to be sentenced to mandatory whippings, which constitute cruel, inhuman or degrading punishment.

Five prisoners of conscience were held at the Jerudong Place of Detention outside the capital, Bandar Seri Bagawan, under Emergency Orders which provide for indefinite detention without charge or trial. Such orders, which can be imposed for an unlimited number of two-year periods, have effect while Brunei remains under a state of emergency. This has been continuously in force since its imposition in 1962 following an abortive rebellion by the *Partai Rakyat Brunei* (PRB), Brunei People's Party. Sarponin bin Sarpo, Suhaili bin Badas, Tinggal bin Muhammad and Baha bin Mohammed were arrested in December 1962 on account of their links with the PRB but have never been charged or brought to trial. Amnesty International considered that they had been kept in detention and denied judicial review of their cases as a deterrent to other political activists. Sheikh Nikman bin Sheikh Mahmud, the brother of the PRB President in exile, has also been detained without charge or trial under an Emergency Order since 1975. He was arrested soon after the revolt although he was not a member of the PRB. He was later released but redetained in 1975 apparently on account of his family links with the PRB.

Abdul Latif Hamid and Abdul Latif

Chuchu, respectively the President and Secretary-General of the Brunei National Democratic Party (BNDP), also remained in detention without charge or trial following their arrest in January 1988 (see *Amnesty International Report 1989*). They were held under the Internal Security Enactment of 1982, which permits the Minister of Home Affairs to authorize the indefinite detention without charge or trial of anyone "acting in a manner prejudicial to the security of the state". The two BNDP leaders had advocated parliamentary democracy under a constitutional monarchy prior to their arrest.

In May some Hong Kong judges said they might decline to sit in the Brunei High Court as a matter of conscience following a September 1988 amendment to the Brunei Penal Code, which made whipping mandatory for 42 criminal offences (see *Amnesty International Report 1989*). Hong Kong provides judges for Brunei's High Court and Appeal Court under a 1964 Treaty of Friendship between the United Kingdom and Brunei. However, the Brunei High Court continued to impose whipping in addition to a jail sentence for specified criminal offences. In June, for example, a man was sentenced to 12 lashes and 14 years' imprisonment for a drugs-related offence.

In May Amnesty International submitted information about the prolonged imprisonment without trial of prisoners of conscience in Brunei Darussalam for United Nations review under a procedure, established by Economic and Social Council Resolutions 728F/1503, for confidential consideration of communications about human rights violations. It wrote to the government requesting its comments on the submission but received no response.

BULGARIA

At least 18 prisoners of conscience, and probably many more, were detained for the non-violent exercise of their right to freedom of expression or religion. Dozens of ethnic Turks remained imprisoned in connection with their resistance to the enforced assimilation of the ethnic Turkish minority, which began in 1984. Five human rights activists were detained without charge or trial for nearly four **months before being released on bail. At least seven ethnic Turks were killed and scores beaten during and immediately after demonstrations protesting against the continuing assimilation campaign. At least four people were sentenced to death and executed.**

Important political changes, which began in November with the resignation of Todor Zhivkov, Chairman of the State Council, brought about the relaxation of censorship laws and the growth of independent groups. The new government, headed by former Foreign Minister Petar Mladenov, announced in November the abolition of Article 273 of the Criminal Code and declared an amnesty for all those detained under its provisions. Earlier in the year many prisoners of conscience had been imprisoned under Article 273 for "spreading untrue allegations" leading to "dissatisfaction with the government" or "confusion within society". In December, 60 prisoners of conscience were released in an amnesty for all those detained under Article 108 of the Criminal Code, which deals with "anti-state agitation and propaganda"; Article 109, which deals with the formation of anti-government groups; and a number of other articles. Article 108 was amended to make it apply only to those advocating "fascism or other anti-democratic ideologies" or violence. In late December the government announced an end to key aspects of the official policy of assimilating ethnic Turks. It reinstated the right of ethnic Turks to choose their own names, speak Turkish and practise the Islamic religion (see *Amnesty International Report 1988* and *1989*).

Until December the Bulgarian authorities

52

continued to impose strict censorship on information concerning the Turkish ethnic minority. Because of the difficulty in obtaining reliable information, it was not clear how many imprisoned ethnic Turks were prisoners of conscience. However, it appeared that at least some convicted of offences such as "terrorism" or "hooliganism" might have been imprisoned for their non-violent activities in opposition to the assimilation campaign.

Following large-scale demonstrations in May against the assimilation campaign, many ethnic Turkish activists were expelled from the country. Subsequently, more than 300,000 ethnic Turks were permitted to leave for Turkey. New passport laws easing restrictions on travel abroad were introduced in September.

There were reports of prisoners of conscience jailed for human rights activities. Ali Topalov and Shukri Sherifov, both from Varna, were sentenced in August to six months' and 10 months' imprisonment respectively under Article 273 of the Criminal Code. The basis of the charge was a letter they had sent to the government in May, calling for ethnic Turks to be granted full religious, cultural and civil rights. The letter was broadcast by foreign radio stations. Shukri Sherifov's sentence was reduced to six months' imprisonment on appeal in September. Both men were released in the November amnesty. Kostadin Ivanov, a factory worker from Mihailovgrad, was sentenced to 22 months' imprisonment in October under Articles 148 ("slandering a public official") and 273 of the Criminal Code, reportedly in connection with the distribution of leaflets and posters concerning the unofficial Independent Association for the Defence of Human Rights. In November Yanko Yankov, a jurist from Sofia, was released from prison after completing a five-year sentence for his human rights activities (see *Amnesty International Report 1989*).

After the May demonstrations many ethnic Turks were detained and charged with offences against public and state order, some for the peaceful exercise of their rights to freedom of expression and assembly. For example, Fidan Demirov Goranov, who took part in a demonstration in Shumen on 27 May, was subsequently sentenced to 18 months' imprisonment under Article 273 of the Criminal Code. He was released in the November amnesty.

Five prisoners of conscience were held without charge or trial for nearly four months in Sofia. Anton Zapryanov, Nikolay Kolev, Konstantin Trenchev, Hristofor Sabev and Todor Gagalov, all leading members of unofficial human rights organizations, were detained at the end of May and early June after publicly supporting the demands of the ethnic Turkish minority for an end to the assimilation campaign. They were released on bail at the beginning of September and all charges were later dropped.

During the year further information was received about Asen Fedaliev Aliev (Bulgarian name Asen Filipov Stoyanov – see *Amnesty International Report 1989*). Asen Fedaliev Aliev, an ethnic Turk, was detained in 1988 after staging a hunger-strike in protest at the authorities' refusal to allow him to emigrate. He was sentenced in June 1988 to 42 months' imprisonment for "slandering a public official" (Article 148 of the Criminal Code) and "hooliganism" (Article 325, paragraph 1, of the Criminal Code). The authorities stated that while in a state of intoxication Asen Fedaliev Aliev assaulted a restaurant manager in the village of Oborishte in February 1988. Other reports stated that Aliev was assaulted by security agents in the restaurant and that the charges against him were false.

Reports were received of killings and beatings of ethnic Turks by the security forces during and immediately after the May demonstrations. The official death toll was seven, but unofficial sources said many more had died. Hasan Aliev Arnaudov, Mehmed Lom and Mehmed Saliev Rushudov died in Todor Ikonomovo, near Kaolinovo, on or around 21 May when troops opened fire into a crowd of reportedly peaceful demonstrators. On 23 or 24 May soldiers fired into a crowd of reportedly peaceful demonstrators in Ezerche in northeast Bulgaria near Razgrad and killed Ahmet Burukov and 18-year-old Sezgin Saliev Karaomerov. Myumyun Fehimov, a radio technician from Momchilgrad, died on 30 May, reportedly from wounds received when he was beaten in the street by security forces on 25 May. Particularly severe beatings in Dzhebel in the south were reported between 22 and 25 May – troops were alleged to have gone from house to house on 22 May indiscriminately beating the occupants.

In September the official Bulgarian

news agency reported that three men, sentenced to death in 1988 for murdering a woman during a robbery, had been executed. In November it reported that a man, sentenced to death in 1988 for murdering three people during robberies committed between July and November, had been executed.

Throughout the year Amnesty International urged the authorities to release prisoners of conscience and to provide further information on a large number of prisoners – most of whom were ethnic Turks – who may have been prisoners of conscience. In February the organization published a report, *Bulgaria: Imprisonment of Ethnic Turks and Human Rights Activists*. The Bulgarian Government made some information available to Amnesty International in response to allegations referred to in the report, but the organization requested further details on a number of cases. In June Amnesty International wrote to the government calling for full and impartial investigations into reports of killings and beatings of ethnic Turks by the security forces during the second half of May.

BURKINA FASO

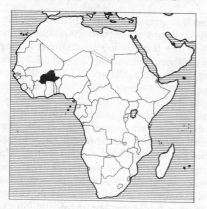

Twenty political prisoners detained without charge or trial since 1987 were freed in August. Four people accused of planning to overthrow the government were executed in September without any form of trial. The government denied that prisoners arrested in December, accused of conspiring against the government, had been executed, but some were reported to have been tortured. There were uncon-

firmed reports in January of five other executions. Seven people were sentenced to death for criminal offences in March but had not been executed by the end of the year.

Twenty people associated with the former president, Thomas Sankara, who was killed in the October 1987 military coup which brought President Blaise Compaoré to power, remained in detention without charge or trial until August, when they were freed in an amnesty. Most had been held at the headquarters of the *Gendarmerie nationale* in the capital, Ouagadougou. One had been held at the *Conseil de l'Entente* building and two had been held under house arrest (see *Amnesty International Report 1989*). The amnesty for political prisoners was declared on 3 August by President Compaoré to mark the sixth anniversary of the 1983 coup which had brought President Sankara to power.

Two military officers who had played leading roles in the governments of both President Sankara and President Compaoré were summarily executed together with two other soldiers within hours of their arrest on 18 September. The authorities claimed that Commander Jean-Baptiste Lingani, the Minister of Defence and Security, and Captain Henri Zongo, the Minister for Economic Promotion, had planned to detain President Compaoré at Ouagadougou airport on his return from a visit abroad, and then seize power. They and two others – Captain Koundaba and Warrant Officer Gnignin – were not formally charged or given any form of trial. All four were summarily executed by firing squad. Alleged confessions by Commander Lingani and Captain Zongo were broadcast by the official radio station two days after their execution. President Compaoré told journalists that the executions had taken place without his express authorization. However, his government took no action against those who ordered and carried out the killings.

Several people were reported to have been arrested in connection with the alleged coup attempt. They were said to have included Jean Yado Toé, the Secretary of State for Mines, and Soumaila Keita, a teacher. The government denied the reports and said that others who had been arrested, including Hamidou Ouedraogo, were released uncharged after questioning.

A leading trade unionist, Soumane

54

Touré, was arrested on 19 September. This was apparently not related to the alleged coup attempt but to an open letter he addressed to President Compaoré complaining about restrictions on trade union activity since June 1987. He was released uncharged after two days.

At least five of those released in August, including Mousbila Sankara, a close relative of President Sankara, were among some 30 civilians and soldiers arrested in late December after it was announced that a conspiracy against the government had been uncovered. The government denied international news reports that seven people had been executed. There were also reports that some of those arrested were tortured and that one person might have died as a result. The government publicly stated that those accused of complicity in the alleged conspiracy would be tried according to the law. Most of those arrested had been closely associated with President Sankara: Raymond Train Poda, a former minister of justice, and Guillaume Sessouma, a university teacher, were members of the *Union de lutte communiste-reconstruite* (ULC-R), Union of Communist Struggle-Reconstructed, a political group which had participated in the Sankara government.

In January there were unofficial reports that five soldiers had been executed at Kamboinsin military camp, 12 kilometres from Ouagadougou. The reports were neither confirmed nor denied by the government. In March seven men were sentenced to death in two separate trials at the Criminal Court in Ouagadougou: four for attacking a group of tourists, one of whom died; and three for aggravated theft. These were the first death sentences known to have been passed by civilian courts for more than five years, although at least 14 people were sentenced to death by military courts and executed between August 1983, when President Sankara came to power, and the beginning of 1989. All seven defendants were sentenced under Article 381 of the Penal Code, which provides for the death penalty if one or more of those found guilty of robbery was armed at the time the offence was committed. The seven men lodged appeals to a higher court and had not been executed by the end of the year.

Amnesty International continued to appeal for the fair trial or release of those arrested after the coup in 1987 and wel-

comed their release in August. Amnesty International protested to the government about the summary executions of four people in September and urged that no further executions take place. It also sought information, without response, about others arrested at the same time, urging that they receive a fair trial if accused of committing an offence. Earlier, Amnesty International had expressed concern about the executions of seven soldiers in December 1988 and appealed for commutation of the seven death sentences passed in March.

BURUNDI

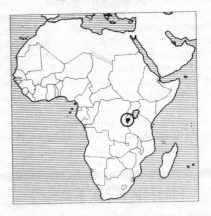

Several prisoners of conscience were released, but more than 40 people arrested at the time of intercommunal killings in northern Burundi in August 1988 were detained without charge or trial throughout 1989. Some of those detained appeared to have played no role in the killings. About 15 people accused of conspiring against the security of the state were arrested in March: no formal charges were brought against them during the year. Some 20 Jehovah's Witnesses were reportedly detained on account of their religious beliefs. At least 30 prisoners were under sentence of death. No executions were reported.

In May a commission appointed by the government in October 1988 to study the question of national unity issued a report on the origins of conflict between the country's majority Hutu and minority Tutsi ethnic groups and proposed various remedial measures. In June President Pierre Buyoya asked the commission to prepare a "charter for national unity" to define each citizen's responsibilities in relation to national unity and rights to security and equality. In July Burundi ratified the African Charter on Human and Peoples' Rights.

In January the government released at least 10 Hutu who had been detained without charge or trial since September 1988, including six prisoners of conscience – all signatories to an open letter to President Pierre Buyoya which blamed government soldiers for the August 1988 killings and called for greater participation of Hutu in national affairs (see Amnesty International Report 1989). The six included three university teachers: Aloys Habonimana, Léonce Ndikumana and Augustin Nsanze.

At least 40 other Hutu prisoners were said by the government in June to be awaiting possible prosecution on murder charges arising from the August 1988 killings. However, none had been formally charged or brought to trial by the end of the year. Most were held either at Mpimba prison in the capital Bujumbura, or at Rumonge prison in southwest Burundi. It appeared that some were imprisoned on account of their leading role in their community, not because of any direct involvement in the intercommunal killings of August 1988. For example, Marc Ntahondereye, a development project director and leader in Kirundo province of the ruling Union pour le progrès national (UPRONA), Union for National Progress, appeared to be held because of his social and political prominence among the Hutu. The authorities reportedly said that he was held because the development project with which he was involved had distributed machetes to local villagers. However, this apparently occurred several months before the intercommunal killings and there appeared to be no evidence that the machetes were intended for anything other than agricultural use.

Another Hutu, Emmanuel Habintore, was arrested in September 1988 in Bujumbura apparently because he was suspected of organizing civil unrest in Ntega district. However, there appeared to be no evidence to substantiate this and he remained in detention without charge or trial at the end of 1989.

Manara Elonga Nsamba, a Zairian national employed by the Burundi Government, was arrested in June in Bujumbura. The authorities claimed that he had been found in possession of "anti-Burundi" tracts, the contents of which were not revealed. He was still held without charge or trial at the end of the year.

About 15 soldiers and civilians were arrested in March and accused of conspiring against the government. Despite reports that they were being held incommunicado in poorly lit isolation cells without any bedding, the government refused to reveal their identities or the places of their detention. No formal charges were known to have been brought against them by the end of the year.

Jehovah's Witnesses were reported to have been imprisoned in a number of provinces on account of their religious beliefs. At least 20 were reportedly arrested in June and held in prisons in Gitega and Muramvya. Most of them were reported to have been released without charge by the end of the year. In August a government representative sought to justify official action against Jehovah's Witnesses in a speech to the United Nations Sub-Commission on the Prevention of Discrimination and Protection of Minorities. He said Jehovah's Witnesses had been "rejected" by the people of Burundi and were considered unpatriotic because they would not salute the national flag, recognize state authority, or work on days of prayer.

Three former government ministers imprisoned for corruption after the coup which brought President Buyoya to power in September 1987, and three other prisoners, were reportedly kept in isolation cells without any bedding for long periods and refused regular contact with their families. Isidore Nyaboya, one of the former ministers, was said to have been accused by the authorities of masterminding from his prison cell the conspiracy which the government said it had uncovered in March. Another former minister, Albert Muganga, was reportedly in danger of losing his sight owing to the poor conditions in which he was held.

Kabongo Ntambwe, a Zairian recognized as a refugee by the United Nations High Commissioner for Refugees, was reported to have been forcibly repatriated in April to Zaire, where he was secretly detained until October and subsequently restricted to a hotel in Kinshasa. The Burundi authorities admitted detaining him briefly in November 1988 but denied any involvement in his repatriation to Zaire.

At least 30 prisoners convicted of

56

murder and other crimes were under sentence of death in mid-1989. One new death sentence was imposed in December by the Bujumbura Criminal Court on a man convicted of murder. The total number of death sentences passed by the courts during the year was not made public. Most of those sentenced to death had apparently not been assisted by legal counsel at their trials. The last known executions in Burundi took place in 1980.

Amnesty International welcomed the releases of prisoners of conscience and other untried political detainees at the beginning of the year. It urged the government to release Jehovah's Witnesses imprisoned on account of their religious beliefs and to review the cases of other political detainees and either bring them to trial promptly on recognizably criminal charges or release them. Amnesty International also called on the government to investigate the circumstances of Kabongo Ntambwe's alleged forcible repatriation to Zaire.

In June an Amnesty International delegation visited Burundi and met President Buyoya, Prime Minister Adrien Sibomana, the Ministers of Justice, the Interior and External Relations and Cooperation, other officials and members of the judiciary and the security service. Amnesty International urged the government to ratify major international and regional human rights instruments and expressed concern at the government's refusal to investigate reports of thousands of extrajudicial executions by government security forces in August 1988. It also raised other outstanding concerns, including prisoner cases.

CAMBODIA (KAMPUCHEA)

Hundreds of people were reportedly arrested for alleged involvement in armed opposition activities amid continued armed conflict on the western fringes of the country and scattered guerrilla activity elsewhere: they were apparently detained without charge or trial. One political trial was reported. The death penalty was abolished.

The Government of the State of Cambodia, headed by Chairperson of the Council of Ministers Hun Sen, faced continued armed opposition from the forces of the exiled Coalition Government of Democratic Kampuchea (CGDK) whose nominal head was Prince Norodom Sihanouk. The CGDK, which continued to represent Cambodia at the United Nations, included the *Partie* of Democratic Kampuchea, known as the "Khmer Rouge", whose guerrilla forces were mainly active in areas adjoining the border with Thailand. They mounted new attacks following the reported September withdrawal of Vietnamese troops, which had supported the government of Hun Sen. Widespread kidnappings and deliberate killings of non-combatant villagers and local administrators by guerrilla forces, particularly those of the "Khmer Rouge", were reported but could not be independently confirmed. International efforts aiming at a peace settlement continued.

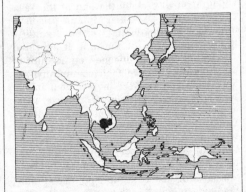

In April an amended constitution was promulgated which abolished the death penalty and changed the name of the country from "People's Republic of Kampuchea" to "State of Cambodia". The Constitution also strengthened safeguards against torture and incorporated formal provisions for fair trials. However, the implementation of these measures was difficult to gauge as international human rights investigators were not permitted to visit the country and the difficulty of obtaining detailed information about human rights continued.

In June the Public Prosecutor General disclosed that over 534 political prisoners had been released since the central government initiated a review of their cases in December 1987. Those freed had apparently all been held without charge or trial or after unfair political trials. However, the identities of those released were not known, nor was it clear how many were freed during the year.

Hundreds of people were reportedly arrested, suspected of supporting the CGDK. The official radio, *Voice of the Cambodian People* (VOCP), said in August that in the first three months of the year police had arrested 517 "covert enemy elements" who had been "hiding among the population in various localities". In June the VOCP reported that "implanted agents of the enemy" had been arrested by the Batdambang provincial armed forces between December 1988 and April 1989. Three "enemy agents" were also said to have been arrested by the Kampung Thom provincial armed forces in May. Thirty-one others, officially described as "enemy agents" who formed parts of "hidden enemy networks", were reportedly arrested in September by armed forces of the Fourth Military Region, believed to comprise Siem Reap-Utdar Meanchey, Banteay Meanchey and Batdambang provinces. None of those arrested was known to have been brought to trial.

Suspected opponents of the government continued to be subjected to arbitrary arrest and detention. A report submitted to the National Assembly by the Public Prosecutor General in June stated that local authorities were arresting political suspects without obtaining proper legal authorization and detaining them for longer periods than permitted by law. In particular, they were failing to observe a requirement under Decree-Law 27 D-L that the Council of Ministers' approval should be obtained before anyone can be detained without charge or for more than 12 months. The report also noted that despite unlawfully long periods of "temporary detention", there was "an incapacity to build up dossiers for presentation to the courts for trials". This resulted in the widespread detention without trial of people accused of criminal offences. The National Assembly was also informed in June that the Supreme People's Court had been unable to commence hearing appeal cases owing to lack of resources and other problems. This implied that tried and convicted political prisoners might effectively be denied an opportunity to appeal against conviction and sentence. However, a new Code of Criminal Procedure, passed on 16 July, stated that prisoners were entitled to file a "suit of contest" before the People's Supreme Court if they were "unwilling to accept the verdict" of lower courts.

One political trial was reported: in March the official news agency announced that 15 CGDK guerrilla fighters belonging to the Sihanoukist National Army had been sentenced to prison terms of three to 20 years. All 15, apparently arrested in Kampot province in November 1988, reportedly pleaded guilty to establishing "clandestine forces" inside Cambodia, moving weapons into the country from Thailand and preparing to fire rockets into the capital, Phnum Penh. There was insufficient information to indicate whether their trial satisfied international fair trial standards.

Amnesty International continued to seek information from the government and other sources about political prisoners. In March the organization published the names of 343 political prisoners reportedly arrested between 1979 and 1986 and since held without charge or trial; it asked the authorities to clarify their current status. No reply was obtained during the year.

Amnesty International welcomed the abolition of the death penalty and other new constitutional measures to protect human rights. It wrote several times to the government to suggest that an Amnesty International delegation should visit Cambodia to discuss human rights, but no response had been received by the end of the year.

CAMEROON

Five prisoners of conscience arrested in previous years and held without trial were released. At least 110 other political prisoners, including prisoners of conscience, were still held at the end of the year for reasons including religious belief and alleged involvement in a 1984 coup attempt. One new arrest of a possible prisoner of conscience was reported. Two political prisoners died, allegedly as a result of torture and medical neglect. Prison conditions were reported to be harsh. At least one death sentence was imposed but no executions were known to have been carried out.

In September Cameroon ratified the African Charter on Human and Peoples' Rights.

58

One prisoner of conscience, Albert Mukong, a writer who had also been a prisoner of conscience in the 1970s, was released unconditionally in May. He had been held since June 1988 (see *Amnesty International Report 1989*), when he was arrested for criticizing both the government and its predecessor in radio interviews with the British Broadcasting Corporation (BBC). He was charged with using subversive language detrimental to the government and to the Head of State, an offence punishable by up to five years' imprisonment. His trial before a military court was repeatedly adjourned in early 1989 and in May the charge was withdrawn.

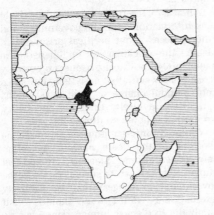

Frédéric Batoum, a prisoner of conscience, was released from Yoko prison in July. He and Samuel Zézé, another prisoner of conscience who reportedly remained in detention without charge or trial, had been among 14 people arrested in December 1985. Those arrested had distributed literature on behalf of the *Union des populations du Cameroun* (UPC), Union of Cameroonian Peoples, an opposition party which is not permitted to engage in any activities although it has not been banned by law. The 14 were released without charge in August 1986, but Frédéric Batoum and Samuel Zézé were redetained in November 1986 and again held without charge or trial.

Other prisoners of conscience included five members of the Jehovah's Witnesses, which has been banned since 1970. Olivier Nwana, arrested in February 1982, and three other Jehovah's Witnesses detained since May 1988, were believed still held without charge or trial at the end of 1989. One Jehovah's Witness was known to be serving a prison sentence: Augustine Kong was jailed for two years in June 1987 for practising a banned religion. It was not known whether he had been released during 1989. One of a number of Jehovah's Witnesses arrested in late 1988 was released in early 1989, and it appeared that those arrested with him were released later in the year.

The legal basis for detaining Jehovah's Witnesses and others without charge or trial remained unclear, although emergency legislation provides for administrative detention without charge or trial on grounds of national security in certain parts of the country. Political detainees have no opportunity for judicial appeal to establish the reason for, or the legal basis or likely duration of, their detention.

Possible prisoners of conscience arrested in previous years and believed still held without trial at the end of the year included Mohamed Lawane Krama, who was arrested on his return to Cameroon from abroad in January 1984; and Georges Yopa and his sister, Nicole Ngakou, detained since January 1987 although reportedly acquitted in October 1987 on charges of possessing subversive documents. Djeukam Tchameni Dominique, a computer company director arrested in November 1988 on suspicion of importing subversive material, was also in custody throughout the year. Initially held incommunicado by the military in harsh conditions, he was transferred in July to the headquarters of the *Brigade mixte mobile*, the paramilitary police. In October he was transferred to hospital suffering from angina, where he remained at the end of the year. Amadou Bakary, a senior official, was reportedly arrested in February on suspicion of communicating with an exiled government opponent and was believed to be still held at the end of 1989.

More than 100 people arrested in connection with a failed coup attempt in April 1984 were reportedly still held at the end of the year. At least 78 had been sentenced after trials before military courts which did not conform to international standards of fairness. At least eight others were believed to have remained in detention despite their acquittal by military courts. At least eight prisoners were held after expiry of their sentences and at least 10 were detained without charge or trial (see *Amnesty International Reports 1985* to *1989*).

Some of those still held appeared to be prisoners of conscience, detained despite the absence of evidence linking them to the coup attempt. They were apparently arrested because of family or other connections with former president Ahmadou Ahidjo, who died in 1989, or with others suspected of plotting to overthrow the government. They included Suzanne Lecaille and Oumarou Aman, who remained in detention, despite their acquittal in 1984 on charges connected with the coup attempt. Abdoulaye Mazou, a judge and former senior civil servant, was still held after his five-year sentence expired during the year. Habouba Moussa, an airline employee, and Roger Bolimo, a customs inspector, remained in detention without charge or trial.

In March Cameroon's Ambassador to France stated publicly that those still held in connection with the 1984 coup attempt were military personnel convicted of criminal, not political, offences after fair trials. He said that those still imprisoned after completing their sentences were held in administrative detention without charge or trial because they had not repented and posed a continuing threat to public safety.

Four prisoners held in connection with the 1984 coup attempt were reportedly released. Information received during the year confirmed the release of Rose Zia, a bank employee, who may have been freed in 1987 after being acquitted by a military tribunal in 1984. Alain Touffic Othman, who was redetained in January 1985 after being acquitted by a military tribunal in 1984, was released in July. Jean Ngogang and Christophe Zangbou, electricians who had been detained without charge or trial since April 1984, apparently for criticizing the government, were also released in July.

Two political prisoners died in December at the Central Prison (known as Nkondengui prison) in the capital, Yaoundé, allegedly as a result of torture or ill-treatment followed by medical neglect. Both were believed to be held in connection with the 1984 coup attempt: one of them, former Captain Madam Dogo Aboubakar, had been sentenced to life imprisonment. They and some 30 other political prisoners were reportedly tortured and severely beaten after they were found with religious and other personal items prohibited to prisoners.

New information was received about harsh conditions in police cells and prisons, particularly the Nkondengui prison, where some 5,000 prisoners were reportedly held. As many as four or five prisoners allegedly died there each day during periods in 1987 and 1988 due to malnutrition, medical neglect and gross overcrowding.

No executions were reported but at least one person received a death sentence. Augustin Bandin was convicted of breaking into a bar and stealing musical equipment. The death penalty is mandatory for "aggravated theft", a broadly defined offence which includes any theft accompanied by forcible entry.

In November the National Assembly passed a law introducing the death penalty for the illegal importation, production, stocking, transportation or transit of toxic or dangerous wastes.

Amnesty International continued to appeal for the release of prisoners of conscience and for either the fair trial or release of political detainees. The organization also appealed on behalf of prisoners sentenced after unfair trials by military courts in 1984, calling for retrials in accordance with international fair trial standards. Amnesty International urgently appealed for improvements in prison conditions and urged abolition of the death penalty.

CENTRAL AFRICAN REPUBLIC

Two prisoners of conscience were released after serving prison sentences, but one was later rearrested. An untried political detainee arrested in 1987 remained in

60 custody throughout the year. Twelve government opponents were detained after being forcibly repatriated from Benin; they were still held without charge or trial at the end of the year. Three prisoners remained under sentence of death; no new death sentences or executions were reported.

Two prisoners of conscience — Thomas Koazo, a journalist, and Jeanne-Marie Ruth Rolland, a former president of the national Red Cross Society — were released. Both had been sentenced in August 1987 to three-year prison terms by the Special Tribunal in separate trials (see *Amnesty International Report 1989*). Thomas Koazo was convicted of insulting the Head of State by reporting — falsely, according to the authorities — that President André Kolingba had secretly met former Emperor Jean-Bedel Bokassa shortly after the latter had returned to the country and been detained. In July and August, prior to his release in September, Thomas Koazo was reportedly held in chains at the Seventh District Police Station in the capital, Bangui. Jeanne-Marie Ruth Rolland was convicted of inciting people to disobey and insult the authorities; she had publicly criticized government officials for confiscating a diamond which she had found. She was released from Ngaragba Prison in Bangui in September and was rearrested in December after refusing to move out of the way of a government motorcade.

One untried political detainee, who also appeared to be a prisoner of conscience, remained in prison throughout the year. Jacques Ngoli, a civil aviation authority employee, was arrested in May 1987. He had apparently helped an army officer to draft a tract which urged the government to respect democratic freedoms and criticized what were described as the arbitrary powers of the country's leaders. No charges had been brought against him by the end of 1989. He was said to be held at Ngaragba Prison, where he was reportedly beaten by guards and kept naked in chains for a few days in 1988.

Confirmation was received during 1989 that 12 students arrested in September 1988, at least four of whom had appeared to be still held at the end of 1988 (see *Amnesty International Report 1989*), had all been released in November 1988. Seven were acquitted and five received suspended sentences after they were tried by Bangui's Criminal Court on charges of inciting people to strike and preventing others from exercising their freedom to work.

Twelve opponents of the government were arrested in August after they were forcibly repatriated to the Central African Republic from Benin. They included General François Bozize, a former Minister of Information who had sought refuge abroad after he was accused of involvement in an unsuccessful coup attempt in March 1982 (see *Amnesty International Report 1983*), and five of his supporters. The six others were said to be members of the opposition *Front patriotique ouban-guien-Parti du travail* (FPO-PT), Oubangui Patriotic Front-Labour Party, an illegal organization under the Central African Republic's one-party constitution. Although the repatriations took place in August, the detention of the 12 was only acknowledged by the authorities in October. They said that the 12 had planned to sabotage fuel and electric installations and carry out a series of assassinations, but none of them had been charged or brought to trial by the end of 1989. They were all held incommunicado in military custody in Bangui: François Bozize was detained at Roux military camp, the others at Kassaï military camp.

Three people convicted by the Special Tribunal in 1982 of placing explosives with intent to cause an explosion at a French military base remained under sentence of death. No new death sentences or executions were reported in 1989.

Two Zairian university students, Fariala and Mwamba, who had been seeking asylum in the Central African Republic, were reportedly arrested in Bangui and forcibly repatriated in June to Zaire, where they were immediately detained. They had left Zaire following the violent suppression of student demonstrations in February 1989. The two students were still held without charge or trial in Zaire at the end of 1989.

Amnesty International appealed for the release of the two prisoners of conscience and investigated the case of Jacques Ngoli as a possible prisoner of conscience, urging his trial or release. Amnesty International also sought information about those detained following their forcible repatriation from Benin and pressed the authorities to bring them to trial on recognizably criminal charges, or release them. Amnesty

International urged the Head of State to commute the three death sentences outstanding since 1982.

CHAD

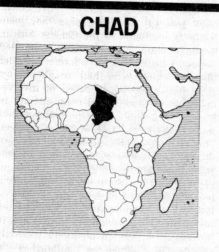

Several hundred political prisoners, including prisoners of conscience, were held throughout the year. Over 150 others were released, including four women prisoners of conscience. None of more than 200 political detainees arrested during the year was brought to trial. They were held in secret detention centres where conditions were harsh and torture was reportedly common. The fate of numerous prisoners arrested in previous years was still unknown.

The government faced armed opposition in the southeastern prefecture of Guéra and fighting broke out in eastern Chad near the Sudan border after the arrests in April of several hundred members of the Zaghawa ethnic group. The arrests followed an alleged coup attempt. However, the government of President Hissein Habré continued its process of reconciliation with other political groups and several former opposition leaders were appointed as ministers in March. In August a peace agreement was signed with neighbouring Libya, although Libyan prisoners of war remained imprisoned in Chad.

A new constitution was approved by referendum in December and took immediate effect. It contained important human rights guarantees, including prohibitions against arbitrary arrest, torture, or inhuman or degrading treatment. It also provided for freedom of expression and association, although in practice only the political party established by the President in 1984 was allowed to function.

In April the government said it had thwarted a coup attempt led by Ibrahim Mahamat Itno, the Interior Minister; Hassane Djamous, the army commander; and Idriss Déby, a former army commander acting as adviser to the President.

The minister was arrested along with his brother and others. The two former army commanders evaded arrest and left the capital, N'Djamena, in a military convoy. Most members of the convoy were soldiers who supported the commanders and belonged to the Zaghawa ethnic group. Government troops pursued them and clashes occurred in eastern Chad and across the frontier in neighbouring Sudan's Darfur region. Hassane Djamous was wounded and captured by government troops. He reportedly died in a military hospital in N'Djamena on 21 April. It was not known how many others were captured. Several thousand Zaghawa were displaced by the fighting and crossed into Sudan to seek asylum. Further clashes between government troops and Zaghawa rebels were reported in October.

More than 200 Zaghawa were arrested in N'Djamena and northeast Chad in connection with the alleged coup attempt. Few details about the detainees were available and their whereabouts were unknown at the end of the year. None was charged or brought to trial. Unconfirmed reports suggested that some were secretly killed or had died in custody. It appeared that some detainees were held because of their ethnic origin or their family connections with those allegedly involved in the conspiracy.

Those arrested included Mahamat Abdoulaye, a university professor, and six brothers of Sidik Fadoul, who had been detained since June 1988. One of the six, Dr Zakania Fadoul, was held only briefly but the other five were apparently still held incommunicado at the end of the year.

In March the government announced the release of 116 political detainees. Those freed included four women prisoners of conscience. Mabrouka Houni Rahil and her daughter, Mardié Ibrahim, had been held since the mid-1980s, and Hadja Merami and her daughter, Azzina Sako, since February 1986. A further 45 political prisoners were released in December. They included Mokhtar Bachar Mokhtar, who was a member of the government when

62 arrested in July 1988 for criticizing the President. Most of the other prisoners released in March and December had been detained for reasons which were not disclosed.

More than 200 people held without charge or trial in previous years were believed still held in secret detention. Although Chad's Code of Penal Procedure provides for all prisoners to be brought before the judicial authorities within a few days of arrest, in practice these political detainees were held outside the framework of the law. Unofficial sources suggested that some had been killed while in the custody of the national security service, the *Direction de la documentation et de la sécurité* (DDS), Directorate for Documentation and Security. Those held included over 180 members of the Hadjeraï ethnic group arrested in N'Djamena and in the Guéra prefecture between May and July 1987 (see *Amnesty International Report 1988* and *1989*). The Hadjeraï were apparently suspected of supporting the armed opposition *Mouvement du salut national du Tchad* (MOSANAT), Movement for the National Salvation of Chad, which is composed primarily of Hadjeraï. Some Hadjeraï detainees appeared to be prisoners of conscience held because of their ethnic origin. Those reportedly remaining in custody at the end of the year included Ahmat Dadji, the director of a state-owned company; Hissein Manga (nicknamed "Michelin"), a businessman; and Dimanche Seli, a secondary school student.

At least 20 people associated with former President Goukouni Oueddeï, including three of his relatives, also remained in secret detention at the end of 1989 (see *Amnesty International Report 1989*). They were arrested in mid-1988, shortly after returning to Chad from abroad.

Political detainees were reportedly tortured and ill-treated. The DDS in particular allegedly subjected detainees to severe beatings, electric shocks and harsh conditions. Reports were received in early 1989 that Asseila Ibrahim, a Hadjeraï mother of four, had been tortured and had died soon after her release in late 1988. She had been detained in November 1988 after trying to leave the country to join her husband, a suspected government opponent. The authorities did not confirm her death and no investigation into its circumstances was known to have been carried out.

Amnesty International appealed for the release of prisoners of conscience and investigated the cases of people who may have been prisoners of conscience. The organization urged the government to try other political detainees or release them. Amnesty International pressed the government to end secret detentions, to take measures to prevent torture and to clarify the whereabouts of all political prisoners.

In May Amnesty International submitted information about its concerns in Chad for United Nations review under a procedure, established by Economic and Social Council Resolutions 728F/1503, for confidential consideration of communications about human rights violations.

In August the government issued a public statement denying the "disappearance", torture or extrajudicial execution of prisoners. The statement acknowledged, however, the "exceptional detentions" of government opponents involved in armed opposition. It suggested that such prisoners were detained outside the framework of the law and that their participation in armed opposition justified their being subjected to "exceptional treatment", although the precise meaning of this term was not indicated.

CHILE

Investigations into more than 100 "disappearance" cases were closed before they had been completed. There was limited progress in some judicial investigations into past human rights violations, but most cases remained unclarified. Approximately 450 prisoners remained in prison facing legal proceedings for politically motivated offences, most of whom were denied proper guarantees for a fair and impartial hearing. Reports of torture, although fewer than in previous years, continued. There were fewer cases of abduction and torture by clandestine groups believed to have links with the security forces. However, these groups continued to harass critics of the military government, and a politician was assassinated in September. Two political prisoners were sentenced to death and the prosecution recommended death sentences in a further 17 cases.

The first presidential and congressional elections since the military coup that brought General Augusto Pinochet to power in 1973 were held in December. Patricio Aylwin, leader of the 17-party *Concertación de Partidos por la Democracia*, Coalition of Parties for Democracy, was elected President. The opposition coalition gained 22 of the 38 elected seats in the Senate. However, this was not enough to achieve an overall majority, because of a constitutional provision enabling the Pinochet administration to appoint nine senators. In the House of Deputies the opposition gained 72 of the 120 seats. The civilian government was scheduled to take office in March 1990.

The transition towards an elected government resulted in greater opportunities for political activity. The election campaign was, for the most part, peaceful, although some violent incidents were reported and a number of political activists were allegedly harassed. About 20 *carabineros* (uniformed police officers) were reportedly arrested for beating a demonstrator to death in the aftermath of the elections. At the end of the year the case was pending before a military court.

As part of the transition process, a plebiscite was held in July in which voters approved 54 amendments to the 1980 Constitution. These included: an end to the president's power to dissolve Congress, censor the media during states of exception, and send into exile or ban Chileans from entering the country; a prohibition of any suspension of *amparo* (the right to challenge one's detention before a court, similar to *habeas corpus*) during states of exception; and the repeal of Article 8, which had been used to ban the Communist Party and other parties. A new clause stipulates that state institutions have

to respect and promote human rights instruments ratified by Chile.

After years of campaigning by local human rights groups, in April the International Covenant on Civil and Political Rights was incorporated into Chilean law. It had been ratified by Chile in 1972.

Attacks by members of armed opposition groups were reported during the year. The *Frente Patriótico Manuel Rodríguez* (FPMR), Manuel Rodríguez Patriotic Front, said it was responsible for killing Roberto Fuentes Morrison in June. He was a former member of the security forces who had been accused of participating in serious human rights violations, including "disappearances", during the 1970s. A group calling itself the *Movimiento Juvenil Lautaro*, Lautaro Youth Movement, claimed responsibility for the deaths of at least four *carabineros* and numerous assaults.

There was much debate about future policies on investigating human rights violations committed during the 16 years of military rule. Most of the thousands of cases submitted to the courts by human rights lawyers and others since 1973 remained unclarified. They included hundreds of "disappearances" and summary executions in the early years after the coup.

The opposition coalition stated that it would make every effort to establish the truth in such cases and that it would promote the repeal or annulment of the 1978 Amnesty Law. This law had been used to curtail investigations before the facts were fully established. The military warned, however, that no prosecutions against members of the armed forces accused of human rights violations before 1978 would be tolerated.

More than 100 of the approximately 700 "disappearance" cases before the courts were closed during 1989 through the application of the Amnesty Law. An August decision by the Supreme Court set a worrying precedent for future investigations into other cases. The Supreme Court confirmed the permanent archiving of the case of 10 Communist Party members who "disappeared" in 1976. It rejected two petitions against a 1986 Appeal Court decision to use the Amnesty Law to close the investigations before they had been completed (see *Amnesty International Report 1987* and *1988*). The decision meant that no further judicial investigations into this case were likely to take place.

64

In November two important investigations into "disappearances" were closed by a military judge on the basis of the Amnesty Law. One case stemmed from a criminal complaint presented in 1978 against General Manuel Contreras, former head of the *Dirección de Inteligencia Nacional* (DINA), Directorate of National Intelligence, and other senior members of the intelligence agency. They were accused of responsibility for the "disappearance" of 70 people between 1974 and 1976. This case was one of the most important legal actions to be taken against the DINA and included substantial evidence of illegal arrests, torture and "disappearances". The other investigation concerned the "disappearance" of 24 people — mainly peasants — from Paine in 1973. Lawyers submitted appeals against the decisions, which had not been ruled on by the end of the year.

On the basis of the Amnesty Law, the Military Court of Appeal confirmed in November a lower military court's ruling to close investigations into the "disappearance" of eight people arrested in Valparaíso in January 1975.

The impartiality of military courts in the prosecution of members of the security forces responsible for human rights violations continued to be called into question. One such case was that of Rodrigo Rojas and Carmen Quintana, who were set on fire by a military patrol in July 1986. Rodrigo Rojas died of his injuries (see *Amnesty International Report 1988*). In August a military judge gave Captain Fernández Dittus, head of the patrol, a 300-day suspended prison sentence for failing to ensure adequate treatment for the victims. The military judge accepted the patrol's version that the fire had been started accidentally, in spite of extensive evidence indicating that the two had been deliberately set alight.

By contrast, in November a military prosecutor recommended that Dr Ramiro Olivares and lawyer Gustavo Villalobos of the *Vicaría de la Solidaridad*, Vicariate of Solidarity, a church human rights organization, be sentenced to five years' imprisonment for "assisting terrorists" in 1986 (see *Amnesty International Report 1989*). Both men remained free on bail while legal proceedings continued. Amnesty International believed they were being prosecuted for their legitimate professional activities as human rights workers.

Approximately 450 political prisoners remained in prison. Most faced legal proceedings in military courts, the majority on charges of belonging to armed opposition groups or of armed offences. Irregularities, including long delays in trial proceedings and in access to trial dossiers, prompted complaints to higher courts. In February, for example, three political detainees accused of participating in the attempted assassination of General Pinochet in 1986 complained to the courts about extended delays in the pre-trial investigation (*sumario*). The *sumario* was not closed until November in these cases, three years after their arrest. Two political prisoners held since 1987 were released unconditionally in December after their cases were transferred to civilian courts. At least three others accused of politically motivated offences had charges against them revoked: the charges had been pending for several years.

There was concern for the health of Roberto Iko Andaur, a political prisoner who had been held in solitary confinement in Valparaíso prison since his arrest in May 1988 until December 1989, when the restriction was finally lifted.

A presidential pardon was granted to trade union leaders Manuel Bustos Huerta and Arturo Martínez Molina in October. They had served over 400 days of a 541-day internal banishment sentence for calling a work stoppage in October 1987 (see *Amnesty International Report 1989*). In addition, seven political prisoners serving 15-year sentences for illegal entry into the country were pardoned.

Some political detainees, though fewer than in previous years, said they had been tortured in police custody. Most of them were transferred to prison within five days or released. Among the cases reported was that of Julio Gerding Salas, who was arrested in August by members of the *investigaciones* (criminal investigations police). He said he was tortured with electric shocks before his release a week later. A number of others arrested during demonstrations reported being badly beaten after their arrest. For example, a number of political activists were kicked and beaten with rifle butts by *carabineros* in September. Some reports were also received of the torture of criminal suspects. José Miguel Donoso Muñoz, arrested by *investigaciones* in November and accused of robbery, alleged that he was given electric shocks and beaten.

Although most of those responsible for torture remained unpunished, in November the Supreme Court upheld a civilian court judge's decision to charge nine members of the *investigaciones* with the torture of two political detainees, Vasilly Carrillo and José Silva Hidalgo. In another case, five *carabineros* from a disbanded intelligence unit were sentenced in March to between two and six years' imprisonment for "unnecessary violence resulting in the death" of political detainee Carlos Godoy Echegoyen in 1985 (see *Amnesty International Report 1986*). At the end of the year the accused were still free on bail pending the completion of the legal proceedings.

There were fewer reports than in previous years of abduction and torture by clandestine groups believed to be linked to the security forces. However, the clandestine groups continued to harass opposition politicians, journalists, human rights lawyers and others. Their methods included death threats, surveillance and, in a few cases, assault and attacks on property. In September a group calling itself the *Comando 11 de Septiembre*, 11 September Command, said it had killed Jécar Neghme, leader of a political faction of the *Movimiento de la Izquierda Revolucionaria* (MIR), Movement of the Revolutionary Left. A few days later, Jaime Cavada, leader of the *Izquierda Cristiana*, Christian Left, was intercepted in the street by three civilians and beaten on the back and head. In November the house of journalist Juan Pablo Cárdenas, who had been subjected in previous years to political persecution including imprisonment, was burned down by unknown people. Allegations of the involvement of security force members in clandestine groups were given further weight in December when four plain-clothes men, who had attacked demonstrators in 1983 and who were later identified as members of the security forces, were convicted and given suspended prison sentences.

In February Juan Díaz Olea and Cristián Vargas Barahona were sentenced to death by a military court after being convicted of killing two police officers during an attack on a police station in 1984. The military judge who sentenced them was said to have discounted evidence that they were elsewhere at the time of the attack and to have ignored their allegations that they had been forced to sign confessions by being tortured. Two co-defendants were sentenced to long terms of imprisonment, while a third was acquitted after more than four years in prison. An appeal against the sentences was pending before the Military Court of Appeal at the end of the year.

In November the military prosecutor investigating the 1986 attack on General Pinochet's life and three attacks on members of the security forces recommended the death penalty for 15 political prisoners. In the same month, the death penalty was recommended for two men accused of killing a police officer during an attack on a shop in 1986.

In May Amnesty International published *Political Prisoners in Chile: Their Right to a Fair Trial.* This examined judicial procedures and highlighted numerous irregularities in legal proceedings against political prisoners. The organization called for a review of such cases by civilian courts under conditions that guaranteed a fair and impartial hearing. It repeated calls for full investigations into past human rights abuses and urged the authorities to introduce further measures to prevent the use of torture and to halt the activities of clandestine groups. Amnesty International also campaigned for death sentences to be commuted and for the death penalty to be abolished.

CHINA

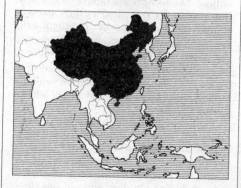

At least 1,000 people were killed and thousands more injured in the capital, Beijing, in early June when troops fired into crowds of unarmed protesters and bystanders to suppress pro-democracy protests. An atmosphere of terror made it impossible to determine the true death

66

toll. **Thousands of people were arrested throughout China in connection with the protests, including many prisoners of conscience, and held incommunicado. Some were reportedly severely beaten or tortured by soldiers or police. Dozens were publicly reported to have been sentenced to death or to terms of imprisonment after summary and unfair trials, and there were reports of secret executions. Earlier, over 1,000 people, including prisoners of conscience, were arrested after martial law was imposed in Lhasa, capital of the Tibet Autonomous Region (TAR), in March; some of them were also reportedly tortured, sentenced after unfair trials or summarily executed. Prisoners of conscience arrested in previous years continued to be held and further arrests for religious or political activities unrelated to the pro-democracy movement were also reported throughout the year. Torture and ill-treatment of criminal suspects remained common and the death penalty continued to be used extensively. At least 273 people were known to have been executed during the year.**

Student protests started in Beijing in mid-April and spread in May to most major cities, evoking wide popular support and developing into a pro-democracy movement. Several hundred students began a hunger-strike to demand political reform on 13 May, following which hundreds of thousands of people congregated to support them in Tiananmen Square in central Beijing. On 18 May an estimated one million people demonstrated in the capital in support of the students. On 20 May martial law was imposed in Beijing to "firmly stop the unrest", to safeguard public order and to "ensure the normal function" of government. On 23 May around one million people again took to the streets to protest the decision.

On the night of 3 to 4 June, hundreds of armoured military vehicles escorted by tens of thousands of troops moved into the centre of Beijing to enforce martial law. At least 1,000 people — mostly unarmed civilians, including children and old people — were killed and thousands were wounded by troops firing both at random and deliberately into the crowds. Further shootings of unarmed civilians occurred in the next few days.

Government reports said the aim was to "clear" Tiananmen Square of the thousands of students and workers occupying it, and to "restore order". It justified its use of lethal force by saying that a "counter-revolutionary rebellion" had occurred and that a "tiny handful" of people had exploited the student unrest with the aim of overthrowing the Chinese Communist Party and the socialist system in China.

In the following months at least 6,000 people were officially reported to have been arrested throughout the country in connection with the protests. The true number of those detained was believed to be much higher. Unofficial sources reported that in Beijing alone between 8,000 and 10,000 people had been arrested, and at least twice as many were believed to have been detained elsewhere. Some were held for questioning for a few days or weeks and released without being charged. Others were still detained without trial at the end of 1989 and some had been sentenced to imprisonment or death.

Those arrested included students, peasants, teachers, writers, journalists, artists, academics, military officers and unemployed people. Some charged with "counter-revolutionary" offences were believed to be prisoners of conscience, detained solely for the non-violent exercise of their fundamental rights.

Arbitrary detention or imprisonment is facilitated by provisions in Chinese law and by illegal practices which have become the norm, such as arbitrary detention for weeks or months without charge. There are also laws and regulations providing for various forms of administrative detention without charge or trial by the police, which were invoked to hold protesters. In Liaoning province alone, police said in June that they had imposed "administrative sanctions" on 1,000 people for "minor crimes" of "beating, smashing and looting" in connection with the protests.

People arrested for supporting the pro-democracy movement are believed to have been held incommunicado. Chinese law does not permit access to lawyers until a few days before trial — or in some cases until the trial starts. Eye-witnesses reported seeing detainees being severely beaten by soldiers or police. Some detainees were reported to have died as a result of torture.

Some of those arrested were sentenced to death or imprisonment after unfair trials. In June the authorities called on local courts to "try prisoners quickly and punish

[them] severely", using 1983 legislation that provides for swift and summary procedures with little opportunity for defence in the trials of "criminals who gravely endanger public security". There is no presumption of innocence in Chinese law and trials are often a mere formality, with the verdicts decided before the trial. The widespread practice of "verdict first, trial second" was openly criticized in 1988 by Chinese lawyers and acknowledged by senior members of the judiciary.

Xiao Bin, a worker from Dalian in northeast China, was the first person known to have been sentenced in connection with the protests for exercising freedom of speech. He was arrested on 11 June after being shown on Chinese television speaking to an American television crew in Beijing earlier that month. On 13 July the authorities said that he had been found guilty under Article 102 of the Criminal Law of "spreading rumours" and "vilifying the righteous act of the martial law troops". He was sentenced to 10 years' imprisonment for "counter-revolutionary propaganda and incitement".

In late August the first student known to have been tried in connection with the demonstrations was sentenced to nine years' imprisonment on the same charge. Zhang Weiping, an art student, was accused of telling Voice of America radio in June that students in Hangzhou had successfully asked provincial government officials to fly the national flag at half-mast to mourn those killed in Beijing.

Other protesters were charged with criminal offences such as blocking traffic, damaging vehicles, attacking soldiers or police, arson or looting. They faced summary trials and executions under the 1983 legislation. On 21 June three workers were shot in Shanghai after a "public sentencing rally" for allegedly setting fire to a train after it had ploughed through demonstrators blocking the track and killed at least six people. The next day seven "rioters" were executed in Beijing after being convicted of wounding troops and burning military vehicles in the capital on 4 June. In all, only a few dozen executions were reported publicly, but unofficial sources estimated that several hundred people were executed secretly in Beijing alone after 4 June. Various sources reported that, between June and August, groups of prisoners had been shot before dawn near the

Marco Polo Bridge in the southwest suburbs of Beijing. One report said that at least eight groups of up to 20 people had been shot there by mid-July. Executions were also said to have been carried out at other locations in Beijing.

In Tibet martial law was imposed in Lhasa on 7 March following two days of violent confrontations after police attempted to stop a peaceful demonstration by a small group of Tibetan monks and nuns calling for Tibet's independence. Eyewitnesses described "ill-organized" police savagely beating Tibetans and "firing indiscriminately". By 9 March the official death toll was 16, but Tibetan sources estimated that over 60 people had died and more than 200 had been injured.

Over 1,000 Tibetans were reportedly arrested although official sources acknowledged only a few hundred arrests. Arrests also continued during the following months. Tseten Norgye, a book-keeper, was reported to have been arrested in Lhasa in April or May after police found a mimeograph machine in his house which they alleged was used to print literature advocating Tibetan independence. He was held in Lhasa's Chakpori detention centre and reportedly suffered a severe eye injury as a result of torture. He is believed to have spent between 15 and 20 years in prison in the 1960s and 1970s. His situation was not clear at the end of 1989. There were fears that he might be at risk of summary execution as the authorities appeared to consider him a leading advocate of Tibetan independence. There were unconfirmed reports of summary executions after the March arrests.

Evidence of persistent human rights violations in Tibet continued to come to light in 1989, including reports of numerous arbitrary arrests, long-term detention without charge or trial, and torture. In January the official New China News Agency announced that 27 Tibetans had been publicly tried for offences related to demonstrations in 1987 and 1988. One of them — Yulo Dawa Tsering, a senior monk from Ganden monastery detained in December 1987 — was sentenced to 10 years' imprisonment and three years' deprivation of political rights in January on charges of "collaborating with foreign reactionary elements".

At least 16 Tibetan nuns were arrested for demonstrating in September and

October. Some were sent to labour camps without charge or trial, others sentenced to imprisonment on "counter-revolutionary" charges. Few details of these trials were given but they were not believed to have satisfied international fair trial standards. In August the *People's Daily* announced that 10 Tibetans accused of offences related to protests in Lhasa in March 1988 had been sentenced to imprisonment. Others were tried and sentenced during the following months. One, named as Passang, was sentenced to life imprisonment for taking part in the protests.

Evidence of torture and ill-treatment in Tibet included testimonies from detainees released in late 1988 and early 1989. Many detainees were reported to have been subjected to torture, including severe beatings, shocks with electric batons and prolonged suspension by the arms. Some detainees reportedly died as a result.

Many prisoners of conscience arrested in previous years remained in detention throughout 1989, despite an unprecedented appeal in February by 33 leading Chinese intellectuals. They urged the release of all political prisoners to mark the 40th anniversary of the foundation of the People's Republic of China. The authorities responded by criticizing sharply those who had initiated the appeal.

Xu Wenli was one of dozens of supporters of the democracy movement of the late 1970s who remained in prison. He was arrested in 1981 and later sentenced to 15 years' imprisonment for "counter-revolutionary activities". Since 1986 he has been held in solitary confinement in harsh conditions (see *Amnesty International Report 1989*). He was reportedly in poor health.

Song Yude was one of several Protestant evangelists who also remained in prison. He was sentenced to eight years' imprisonment in 1986 on charges of "counter-revolutionary propaganda and incitement".

Various church groups continued to be harassed and some of their members were arrested for carrying out religious activities without official approval. Among them were several Catholic priests and seminarians not affiliated to the officially recognized Patriotic Catholic Association. Three Catholic seminarians detained in Hebei province in January 1989 were reportedly stripped naked, beaten, forced to lie on cold concrete and burned with cigarettes

while in police custody.

In April several hundred Catholic villagers were severely beaten by police during a police raid on the village of Youtong, Hebei province. Two youths were reported to have died as a result and over 300 villagers, including old people and children, were reportedly injured, 88 seriously. Police took away 32 people.

The death penalty continued to be used extensively. During 1989 Amnesty International recorded 282 death sentences and 273 executions. The true totals were thought to be much higher.

In August Deng Anwei, an accountant, and Song Shunwen, a private businessman, were executed on charges of corruption, fraud and fleeing the country to avoid arrest. They were just two of the many executed in a continuing government "crackdown" on crime. Other executions were carried out in the suppression of the pro-democracy movement.

Throughout the year, Amnesty International sent numerous appeals and inquiries to the government about violations of human rights in China, but received no direct reply.

Following the imposition of martial law in Lhasa, Amnesty International urged the government to disclose the names of all those detained, to release prisoners of conscience and others not charged with a recognizably criminal offence, and to safeguard detainees against torture. After reports of summary executions, it also urged the government to cease executions. Amnesty International made further, urgent and intensive appeals in June after the killings in Beijing and urged the government to take immediate action to halt arbitrary arrests and detentions, torture, unfair trials and executions.

Amnesty International made an oral statement to the United Nations Commission on Human Rights (UNCHR) in February drawing attention to persistent reports of torture and ill-treatment of Tibetans. The Chinese delegation at the UNCHR denied that Tibetan detainees had been tortured and said some allegations had been investigated, but gave no details of such investigations.

Amnesty International also sent a report on the June events in Beijing to the UN. In August it made an oral statement to the UN Sub-Commission on Prevention of Discrimination and Protection of Minorities.

On 31 August the Sub-Commission adopted a resolution expressing concern about the events in China and, for the first time, asked the UN Secretary-General to transmit information about the situation in China to the UNCHR. The Chinese delegation rejected the resolution as "null and void" and with no "binding force on China whatsoever".

In a report published in January, *The Death Penalty in China*, Amnesty International said it had documented over 1,500 executions between 1983 and 1988 but that a comprehensive figure would be much higher. In April the organization published *The Death Penalty Debate*, which documented official Chinese views on the death penalty and the criticisms voiced by members of China's legal profession over the deficiencies of the judicial process in death penalty cases.

In February Amnesty International published a report, *Torture and Ill-treatment in Detention of Tibetans*, and submitted it to the Chinese Government, urging an impartial inquiry into the allegations and measures to allow all detainees and ex-detainees to testify about their treatment without risking reprisals.

In August Amnesty International published *Preliminary Findings on Killings of Unarmed Civilians, Arbitrary Arrests and Summary Executions since 3 June 1989*. This report concluded that many of the killings in Beijing were extrajudicial executions and the consequence of a deliberate decision to put a stop to peaceful protests even if this meant widespread killing. A government representative said on 31 August that the report constituted "interference" in its internal affairs and was "unreasonable and without foundation".

Before the 40th anniversary of the People's Republic of China on 1 October, Amnesty International again urged the government to release all prisoners of conscience, citing several cases, and to commute all death sentences.

COLOMBIA

Many hundreds of people, including judicial officials investigating human rights violations, were extrajudicially executed. Scores of other people "disappeared" after detention. Multiple killings of unarmed civilians, attributed to army **personnel, police and paramilitary groups under army or police command, continued. The government failed to disband paramilitary organizations, despite its introduction of decree laws outlawing such forces. Independent investigations uncovered further evidence of links between the regular armed forces and paramilitary groups. At least four prisoners of conscience were detained and charged under special decree laws ostensibly introduced to combat common criminals. Torture of political detainees, some of whom were prisoners of conscience, continued to be reported.**

Cease-fires declared by the major guerrilla groups at the beginning of the year led to a reduction in the number of direct confrontations with government forces. Negotiations between the government and the *Movimiento 19 de Abril* (M-19), 19 April Movement, led to the signing of a peace agreement in November, subject to ratification by Congress. Other guerrilla forces, however, rejected the peace proposal.

The *Ejército de Liberación Nacional* (ELN), National Liberation Army, continued its campaign of bombing oil pipelines and other economic targets. The ELN was also responsible for the execution-style killing of kidnapped victims. In October a 73-year-old Roman Catholic bishop, Jesús Emilio Jaramillo, was seized by gunmen who identified themselves as members of the ELN. The following day Bishop Jaramillo's body was found with gunshot wounds to the head. The ELN reportedly claimed that the bishop's efforts to mediate between the ELN and the government constituted "obstinate interference" in the ELN's "internal affairs".

70

The apparently drugs-related assassination of presidential aspirant Luis Carlos Galán in August heightened political tension and signalled a dramatic increase in criminal violence. The government of President Virgilio Barco Vargas decreed state of siege laws to combat the drugs trade. The legislation included Decree Law 1859, which empowered the armed forces to arrest and hold suspects incommunicado for up to seven working days in military installations. A wave of bombings in the principal cities and selective killings of politicians, journalists and judicial officials were attributed to drug-traffickers, apparently retaliating against renewal of an extradition treaty with the United States of America.

Against a background of continuing civil conflict and extensive drugs-related violence, government forces — sometimes operating in alliance with drug-traffickers — and paramilitary groups under their command committed widespread and systematic human rights violations. The abuses included extrajudicial executions and "disappearances". Members of legal left-wing parties such as the Communist Party and the political alliance *Unión Patriótica* (UP), Patriotic Union, continued to be targeted by paramilitary "death squads".

Luis Eduardo Yaya Cristancho, a UP town councillor in Villavicencio, Meta department, was shot dead by unidentified armed men in February. He reportedly had been subjected to death threats and given a police escort. On the morning of his death, however, the escort failed to appear. Within eight days of Luis Yaya's death, three members of the Communist Party's national executive were killed. Teófilo Forero, its National Secretary; Leonilde Mora, his wife; and José Antonio Sotelo, a Central Committee member, were killed in Bogotá when armed men opened fire on the car in which they were travelling. Four days later José Antequera, a member of the UP national coordinating committee and former general secretary of the Communist Youth, was shot dead by armed men at Bogotá's international airport. Senator Ernesto Samper Pizano, a senior member of the ruling Liberal Party, was seriously wounded in the attack.

Other killings of left-wing political leaders included the October shooting of Dr Gabriel Santamaría Montoya, a UP regional president in Antioquia department and a deputy in the departmental assembly. Dr Santamaría had recently returned to the country after recovering abroad from injuries received in an earlier attempt on his life. The four assailants, armed with submachine-guns, entered the departmental assembly building in Medellín unhindered, despite the presence of numerous police guards at the entrance to the building, and killed Dr Santamaría. Dr Santamaría's bodyguards killed one of the armed men as he attempted to leave the building.

"Disappearance" after detention by regular armed forces and paramilitary personnel continued to be reported, particularly from rural areas undergoing counter-insurgency operations. In February a military patrol detained Isidro Caballero Delgado, a teacher, and María del Carmen Santana, who was accompanying him, in Guaduas, department of Cesar. The patrol was believed to be from the Morrison military base in Líbano. Eye-witnesses testified before the regional Procurator that soldiers arrested the two, who were later taken away towards a mountainous area. Military authorities persistently refused to acknowledge their detention, and their whereabouts remained unknown.

In a report released in February, the United Nations (UN) Working Group on Enforced or Involuntary Disappearances found that the complexities of Colombian society made any comprehensive identification of those responsible for "disappearances" extremely difficult. It concluded, however, that "circumstantial evidence strongly suggests or precise information clearly demonstrates involvement of units of the armed forces or security services in enforced or involuntary disappearances".

The Colombian authorities made little progress in tracing the whereabouts of detainees who had "disappeared" or in bringing those responsible to justice. In February the Procurator General's Public Ministry ordered the 15-day suspension of an army captain for his part in the August 1986 arrest and "disappearance" of Alvaro Falla. In this case and all others, however, the military court system acquitted or dropped charges against members of the armed forces accused by the Public Ministry of responsibility for "disappearances".

Clear evidence of official responsibility

for abuses attributed to paramilitary forces emerged from investigations by the *Departamento Administrativo de Seguridad* (DAS), Administrative Security Department. DAS investigations identified a paramilitary network operating under the cover of ACDEGAM, a cattle ranchers' association based in Puerto Boyacá. The network was allegedly responsible for the torture, "disappearance" and killing of hundreds of peasant farmers, community leaders and members of left-wing political movements in the Magdalena Medio region of central Colombia. The investigations also found that the network operated in coordination with sectors of the Colombian armed forces and was financed by landowners, industrialists and drug-traffickers.

Colonel Luis Bohórquez Montoya, commander of the Bárbula Battalion based in Puerto Boyacá, Magdalena Medio, was removed from his post in April after DAS investigations revealed that the battalion's base had been used as a training centre for paramilitary groups. In a letter addressed to the Minister of Defence, Colonel Bohórquez claimed he had been made a "scapegoat" and insisted that "the military tasks were carried out in complete accordance with the strategy and orders from army high command".

In April and May President Barco decreed a series of laws designed to combat paramilitary forces. The new decree laws included the suspension of legislation which had empowered the armed forces to provide civilians with military weapons and introduced up to 15 years' imprisonment for membership of an illegal armed group. However, the Colombian Government failed to implement these measures effectively and paramilitary forces continued to commit extrajudicial executions and "disappearances" with virtual impunity.

Some civilian judicial authorities made significant progress in identifying those responsible for human rights violations, including several multiple killings reported in 1988. In April a civilian judge issued arrest warrants against an army captain and several subordinates attached to the XIV Brigade, based in Puerto Berrío, Magdalena Medio region. They were accused of abducting and murdering 17 miners from the Encenillo gold mine in San Rafael, Antioquia department, in June 1988. All of the victims, ranging in age from 17 to 64, were UP activists. They had apparently been hacked to death. According to the judge's ruling, the killings were reprisals for a left-wing guerrilla attack on an army convoy. It was not known at the end of the year whether the members of the armed forces implicated in the killings in San Rafael had been arrested.

The military justice system continued to reject the competence of civilian courts to investigate abuses attributed to army and police personnel, routinely claiming its own jurisdiction in such cases. Almost without exception, military courts failed to prosecute and convict those accused of committing human rights violations. In February arrest warrants were issued against army and police officers incriminated in the November 1988 attack on Segovia, Antioquia department. The military court system claimed jurisdiction to proceed with criminal investigation of the attack, in which 43 people were killed (see *Amnesty International Report 1989*). In a landmark decision, the Supreme Court of Justice awarded to civilian courts the jurisdiction to prosecute military personnel accused of human rights violations. The Supreme Court ruled that the "acts of terrorism" allegedly committed by two army officers and one police officer in Segovia were common-law crimes, not linked to their military duties and thus falling outside military jurisdiction. The then Minister of Defence stated that the armed forces would "respect the Supreme Court's ruling although we do not agree with it".

Some civilian members of paramilitary groups were convicted of political killings. In the vast majority of cases, however, members of the armed forces implicated by independent inquiries into human rights violations were shielded from prosecution by their superior officers. The officers repeatedly failed to comply with arrest warrants issued by the civilian courts.

The killings of civilian judicial officials investigating abuses attributed to members of the armed forces and paramilitary groups increased. In January, 12 members of a judicial commission of inquiry, including magistrates and detectives, were killed in La Rochela, Santander department. Although military authorities promptly attributed responsibility for the killings to guerrilla forces, judicial investigations soon established that army-linked paramilitary forces based in the region were responsible.

72

Two witnesses to the killings were themselves killed in March, apparently in reprisal for their cooperation with judicial authorities.

Some attacks on judicial officials were attributed to alleged drug-traffickers. Evidence emerged in other cases that judicial officials were threatened and killed because of their investigations into human rights violations. The judiciary's National Director of Criminal Investigation stated in February that investigations conducted by the judiciary increasingly uncovered army and police "complacency, toleration and sponsorship" of paramilitary groups. The director cited several cases in which armed forces personnel issued direct threats against judicial officials.

In July Dr María Elena Díaz Pérez, a judge, was shot dead by unidentified men in Medellín. Dr Díaz had replaced another civilian judge investigating the March 1988 massacre of 21 banana plantation workers (see *Amnesty International Report 1989*) and had confirmed warrants for the arrest of three army officers and two alleged drug-traffickers in connection with the killings. Several other judges, including the judge investigating the killings in Segovia, reported receiving warnings to halt their investigations or face the same fate as Dr Díaz.

In August and September the authorities arrested thousands of people under state of siege laws adopted to combat drug-trafficking. In Medellín the armed forces used their increased powers of arrest and incommunicado detention to suppress legal opposition movements and grassroots organizations. Military police in Medellín arrested Pablo Angarita Cañas, Luz Aurelia Puya Vasco, William Balbín Alvarez and Rodrigo Osorno Ospina in September. All were members of the legal educational organization *Instituto Popular de Capacitación* (IPC), Popular Training Institute. They were held incommunicado for four days in Military Police Battalion No. 4, where army personnel from the IV Brigade allegedly tortured them. In October a civilian court judge acquitted the IPC members of drug-trafficking offences and ordered their unconditional release.

On numerous occasions Amnesty International urged the government to implement independent and effective investigations into human rights violations and to ensure that those responsible were brought to justice. In October the organization published a report: *Colombia, Human Rights Developments: "Death Squads" on the Defensive?* It described the continuing pattern of gross and systematic human rights violations in Colombia and urged the authorities to take effective measures to halt the abuses. No response had been received from the Colombian Government by the end of the year.

In oral statements to the UN Commission on Human Rights and the UN Sub-Commission on Prevention of Discrimination and Protection of Minorities in March and August respectively, Amnesty International included references to its concerns in Colombia. In May Amnesty International submitted information about its concerns in Colombia for UN review under a procedure, established by Economic and Social Council Resolutions 728F/1503, for confidential consideration of communications about human rights violations.

COMOROS

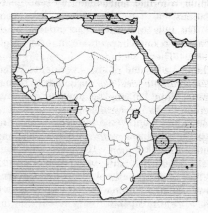

More than 70 people imprisoned for political reasons, including prisoners of conscience, were released in December after the Head of State was assassinated and a group of foreign mercenaries who had exercised considerable power left the country. Those freed included about 40 people who had been arrested in November for campaigning against changes to the Constitution, and others imprisoned since 1985 and 1987. However, up to 25 other people, who were reportedly arrested for political reasons in November 1987, were unaccounted for at the end of 1989.

In November a national referendum

approved a proposal that President Ahmed Abdallah should remain in office for a third six-year term although the Constitution provides for the president to retire after serving two terms. Opposition parties disputed the outcome of the referendum and claimed that it had been rigged by the government. On 26 November President Abdallah was assassinated, apparently by one of the foreign mercenaries serving as officers in the Presidential Guard. Saïd Mohamed Djohar, the President of the Supreme Court, was named as acting President Abdallah's successor under the terms of the Constitution. After the intervention of foreign governments, the mercenaries left the country in December.

Following the mercenaries' departure, the new authorities released about 40 people who had been arrested at the time of the referendum in November. The government had accused some of them of carrying out arson attacks on polling stations, but most appeared to have been detained for their non-violent criticism of the government. Those freed included Abdou Bakar Boina, a former ambassador to the United Nations.

The new authorities also released more than 30 people imprisoned since 1985 or 1987. They included Moustoifa Saïd Cheikh, a leader of the opposition *Front démocratique des Comores* (FDC), Democratic Front of the Comoros, who was sentenced to life imprisonment in 1985 in connection with an alleged conspiracy against the government (see *Amnesty International Report 1986*). He had been held in solitary confinement in a dimly lit cell at M'dé barracks before his release and was reported to have become seriously ill as a result of the harsh conditions of imprisonment. He was a prisoner of conscience. Sixteen former members of the Presidential Guard, who had been sentenced to life imprisonment in connection with the same alleged conspiracy, were also released.

Fourteen of those released had been held incommunicado without charge or trial since November 1987, when they and up to 25 others were arrested and accused of offences against state security and trespassing in a prohibited zone with criminal intent. At the time very little was known about these detainees and the authorities did not disclose how many were arrested or their identities. Reports suggested that three of them had died soon after arrest as a result of torture. By early 1989 only 14 of these detainees were reported to be still held incommunicado, without charge or trial, at Itsundzu Prison in a remote area of Grand Comore island. They included Moissi Moussa, a driver, Saïd Salim Chaufi, a civil servant, and Ali Boina, a former member of the Presidential Guard. It was not clear at the end of the year what had become of the others said to have been arrested in November 1987.

Amnesty International appealed for the release of Abdou Bakar Boina and others detained in November for their peaceful opposition to the government, and called for the release of Moustoifa Saïd Cheikh, who was adopted as a prisoner of conscience after the organization concluded that he had not been involved in a coup attempt or other acts of violence. Amnesty International also made inquiries about the detainees arrested in November 1987 and called for them to be released if they were not to be charged or tried.

CONGO

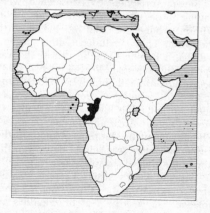

More than 40 suspected government opponents detained without charge or trial since 1987 and 1988 were released, but 26 other untried political detainees, including prisoners of conscience, were held throughout the year. Two journalists were briefly detained. At least two people were sentenced to death for criminal offences but no executions were reported.

At least 40 members of the Kouyou ethnic group who had been arrested in 1987 and 1988 and detained without

74

charge or trial were released in November. They included at least 10 people who had been arrested and held in the capital, Brazzaville. The remainder had been arrested in the Owando area of northern Congo. All the detentions were connected with an alleged conspiracy against the government of President Denis Sassou Nguesso led by Captain Pierre Anga, who was killed by security forces in July 1988 (see *Amnesty International Report 1989*), and other suspected Kouyou supporters of former president Joachim Yhomby-Opango.

Twenty-six others arrested in connection with the same alleged conspiracy remained in detention without charge or trial throughout 1989: in November the government announced that they would be brought to trial. They included people arrested in Owando, former president Yhomby-Opango and 11 civilians and former senior armed forces officers arrested in 1987 and 1988. All of them appeared to be imprisoned unlawfully: they continued to be held without charge or trial despite the requirement under Congolese law that all cases are referred to the procuracy within three days of arrest.

Several prisoners of conscience were among those who remained in detention without charge or trial at the end of the year. They included Father Joseph Ndinga, a Roman Catholic priest. He was apparently arrested in September 1987 because he ordered church bells to be rung in Owando when government troops were about to enter the town in an attempt to arrest Captain Anga and former president Yhomby-Opango. The reinstatement of the former president was said to have been the aim of the alleged conspirators.

Captain Anga's sister, Thérèse Okouli, also appeared to be a prisoner of conscience. She was held at Brazzaville's air force base, reportedly in ill-health, apparently because of her family connections. Three of Captain Anga's brothers and one of his half-brothers were also still detained at the end of the year.

Former president Yhomby-Opango also remained in detention without charge or trial throughout 1989. He was held at a government-owned villa on the *Cité des 17* estate. He was arrested in 1987. Other detainees included four military officers held without charge or trial since July 1987 as suspected supporters of the former president. One, Colonel Jean-Michel Ebaka,

went on hunger-strike in February in protest against the authorities' refusal to allow him relatives' visits, or to bring him to trial or release him. Following the hunger-strike he was reportedly allowed visits by relatives. At the end of the year he was held at the *Camp du 15 août* military camp in Brazzaville together with Colonel Henri Eboundit and Captain Lambert Emerson Elenga.

Lecas Atondi Monmondjo, a former director of the *Office national des librairies populaires* (ONLP), National Office of Peoples' Bookshops, was arrested in August 1987 and still detained without charge or trial at the end of 1989. After a hunger-strike in June he was moved from the Brazzaville headquarters of the Armoured Regiment to the *Plateau des 15 ans* military camp in Brazzaville, where his conditions reportedly improved. Damase Ikeye, a medical doctor arrested in Owando in 1987, was still detained without charge or trial at the end of 1989. It was not clear whether he and Lecas Atondi Monmondjo were imprisoned in connection with the alleged conspiracy on behalf of former president Yhomby-Opango.

In August, two journalists — Jean Baptiste Placca of the Paris-based *Jeune Afrique* magazine and Jacques Boy Buta Lumbwele, a Zairian refugee and an *Agence France Presse* (AFP), French News Agency, correspondent — were arrested after one of them received a letter smuggled out of prison by Lecas Atondi Monmondjo. Jean Baptiste Placca was held for one day's questioning and then expelled from Congo. Jacques Boy Buta Lumbwele was detained for two weeks and then released.

At least four death sentences were imposed by the courts: on two prisoners convicted in March of murder, and on two others convicted in November of armed robbery and murder. However, no executions were known to have been carried out.

Amnesty International urged the government to release Father Joseph Ndinga and other prisoners of conscience and to bring to trial promptly and fairly all other political detainees. Amnesty International also appealed for the commutation of all death sentences.

CÔTE D'IVOIRE

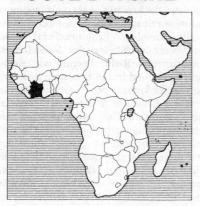

Five people were detained for short periods, apparently because of their political activities, and it appeared that a government opponent convicted on criminal charges may have been prosecuted for political reasons.

Bamba Moriféré, one of eight National Assembly Vice-Presidents, was arrested and placed under house arrest for a few days in April. Upon returning from abroad he had been found in possession of an opposition group manifesto. The ruling *Parti démocratique de Côte d'Ivoire*, Democratic Party of Côte d'Ivoire, of President Félix Houphouët-Boigny is the only officially recognized political party, although the Constitution does not prohibit other parties. He was not charged with any offence but was replaced as Vice-President a few weeks after his arrest. He retained his position as member of parliament.

Four other political arrests occurred in December. In Abidjan, security police detained two Togolese nationals, Têtevi Godwin Tété and Daniel Kuevi Akué, apparently because of their links with a Togolese political organization opposed to one-party rule in Togo. They were arrested when documents criticizing one-party rule in Togo were found in Têtevi Godwin Tété's possession after he arrived in Côte d'Ivoire from France. The documents did not advocate violence and both men appeared to be prisoners of conscience. After two weeks' detention without charge or trial, Têtevi Godwin Tété was expelled to France and Daniel Kuevi Akué to Senegal.

Mahan Gahe Basile and Kei Etienne,

both leading members of the *Fédération des syndicats libres de Côte d'Ivoire*, Federation of Free Trade Unions in Côte d'Ivoire, were also arrested in December. The federation is one of the few trade union organizations independent of the ruling party. Abidjan security police held the detainees for four days, questioned them about their trade union activities and released them without charge.

Innocent Kobena Anaky, managing director of a transit company and a leading member of the unauthorized party *Front populaire ivoirien*, Ivorian Popular Front, received a 20-year sentence in February for failing to pay taxes and customs fees on behalf of his company. These criminal charges may have been brought against him for political reasons. He had been arrested in November 1988 and initially held outside the framework of the law (see *Amnesty International Report 1989*). His lawyers were given little time to prepare his defence and left the court in protest. Innocent Kobena Anaky was reportedly convicted on the basis of answers he gave to an examining magistrate, despite his statement that he could not reply adequately to the charges without access to his company's accounts.

Amnesty International was concerned about the short-term detentions of trade unionists and others. In its appeal for the release of the two Togolese imprisoned in December, the organization urged that they not be repatriated to Togo, where it was believed they might be at risk of torture. Amnesty International sought information from the government about Innocent Kobena Anaky's imprisonment, noting indications that he may have been charged and convicted because of his non-violent political activities. In response, the Minister of Justice said that Innocent Kobena Anaky was an ordinary criminal prisoner.

CUBA

At least 60 government critics, many of them prisoners of conscience, were arrested and at least 33 of them remained in prison at the end of the year. The majority were sentenced to prison terms after trials which fell short of international standards for fairness. Some detainees were held for prolonged periods without access to

76

defence lawyers before they were charged and brought to trial. Several political prisoners, including at least two prisoners of conscience who had been detained in earlier years, were released. Four senior military officials convicted of drug-trafficking and corruption were executed in July. It was not known whether any other executions took place.

The majority of people detained were members of the growing number of small unofficial groups concerned with civil and political rights and environmental issues. The Cuban Government responded to the activities of such groups by increasingly repressing attempts to challenge the political monopoly of the Cuban Communist Party and public criticism of President Fidel Castro and his government.

Several members of the unofficial *Asociación Pro-Arte Libre* (APAL), Association for Free Art, were arrested. The association promotes creative work produced independently of governmental guidelines. In January Carlos Novoa Ponce and Jorge Luis Mari Becerra were arrested in Havana. They were initially held with five other members of APAL, who were arrested in October 1988 (see *Amnesty International Report 1989*), in the headquarters of the *Departamento de Seguridad del Estado* (DSE), Department of State Security Police. All seven were transferred in February from the DSE headquarters, also known as Villa Marista, to prison. During May and June Carlos Novoa Ponce, Jorge Luis Mari Becerra and one of the five other men, Lázaro Cabrera Puentes, staged hunger-strikes to protest their detention without charge or trial. Their detention appeared to contravene the Code of Penal Procedure, which provides that detainees should receive within 10 days of arrest formal notification of the charges against them. The seven APAL members were tried in September and received sentences of between nine and 21 months' imprisonment for offences including "illegal association". Six other APAL members arrested in October 1988 completed their sentences and were released during the year.

Nine members of the unofficial *Partido Pro Derechos Humanos en Cuba* (PPDHC), Cuban Human Rights Party, were arrested and imprisoned in the first four months of the year. In January police arrested Manuel González González and his wife, son and daughter-in-law. They were charged with illegally producing in their home the party bulletin *Franqueza, Openness*. Three days after their arrest they were tried before the *Tribunal Municipal Popular de Centro Habana*, Central Havana People's Municipal Court, reportedly without access to a defence lawyer. After a summary hearing Manuel González González was sentenced to one year's imprisonment. His wife, Lidia, was sentenced to nine months and his son to six months. His daughter-in-law was fined. His son and wife were released in July and October respectively.

In April five other PPDHC members were arrested after publicly announcing their intention to hold a "popular, peaceful" demonstration in Havana during the visit of Soviet leader Mikhail Gorbachev. The demonstration was reportedly planned to show support for Soviet reform policies. Those arrested included Dr Alfredo Samuel Martínez Lara, president of the PPDHC, David Moya Alfonso and Javier Roberto Bahamonde Masot. The three men, reportedly denied defence counsel, were tried before a municipal court on charges of illegal association. Dr Martínez Lara and David Moya were sentenced to nine months' imprisonment. Javier Roberto Bahamonde, initially sentenced to three months' imprisonment, was tried again in June and sentenced to an additional year's imprisonment for illegal economic activity because he had worked as a photographer without official authorization.

Dr Martínez Lara, David Moya and six other PPDHC members had been arrested in March while preparing an edition of *Franqueza* and charged with illegally producing an unauthorized publication. Dr Martínez Lara, David Moya and three other defendants were fined; the three others were acquitted. Other PPDHC members arrested during the year included Edita Esther Cruz Rodríguez, arrested by the *Policía Nacional Revolucionaria*, the

AMNESTY INTERNATIONAL REPORT 1990

national police, in November. Charges against her were apparently connected to her involvement in organizing a mass for a long-term political prisoner on hunger-strike. She had been among the PPDHC members arrested in April before the Soviet President's visit and had received at that time a suspended prison sentence of three months. After her arrest in November she was transferred to the *Centro de Reeducación para Mujeres del Occidente*, Havana's women's prison, where it is believed she was serving the three-month sentence previously imposed.

PPDHC members Guillermo Rivas Díaz and Aymé Llado, who were arrested in November 1988, were released in January and allowed to leave the country. They had received prison sentences of one year and three months respectively. The former Human Rights Party president, Tania Díaz Castro, was arrested in 1988 and sentenced to one year's imprisonment. She was released in November on completion of her sentence (see *Amnesty International Report 1989*).

State security agents arrested three leading human rights activists in August: Elizardo Sánchez Santa Cruz, president of the *Comisión Cubana de Derechos Humanos y Reconciliación Nacional* (CCDHRN), Cuban Commission of Human Rights and National Reconciliation; Hiram Abi Cobas Núñez, acting president of the PPDHC; and Hubert Jérez Mariño, president of the *Comité Martiano por los Derechos del Hombre* (CMPDH), "Martí" Committee for the Rights of Man. The three men, representatives of the recently formed *Coordinadora de Derechos Humanos de Cuba* (CODEHU), Coordinating Body of Cuban Human Rights Groups, were charged under Article 115 of the Penal Code with "spreading false news with the aim of endangering the prestige or standing of the Cuban State". The charges apparently stemmed from an interview they gave to foreign journalists about the trial and execution in July of four senior army and Interior Ministry officials. During the interview the three men reportedly stated they had reason to believe that the defendants were being subjected to "psychological pressure without legal protection which was tantamount to torture under international law".

The three men were held in Villa Marista until mid-September, then transferred to Combinado del Este prison in Havana. In Villa Marista they were reportedly held in cells with permanent artificial lighting and were denied fresh air, exercise and reading materials. The *Tribunal Popular Provincial de Habana*, People's Provincial Court of Havana, tried them in November and sentenced Elizardo Sánchez to two years' imprisonment and both Hiram Abi Cobas and Hubert Jérez to 18 months' imprisonment.

Hiram Abi Cobas had been arrested in January, apparently in connection with the publication of the PPDHC bulletin, and released the following day after paying a fine. He was also among the PPDHC members arrested in April and during that period of detention reportedly suffered a heart attack. He received a three-month suspended sentence, apparently on grounds of ill-health. Elizardo Sánchez had previously been imprisoned for political reasons on several occasions, most recently between September 1986 and May 1987 (see *Amnesty International Report 1987* and *1988*).

The release of long-term political prisoners continued, in accordance with a June 1987 agreement between the Cuban Government and the United States Catholic Conference. The agreement provided for the release of several hundred prisoners, including prisoners of conscience, and permission for travel to the United States of America (USA). In January the Cuban authorities announced expansion of the release program to include 44 prisoners whom it had previously described as too dangerous to release.

Two prisoners of conscience were released. Amado Rodríguez Fernández, who was serving a sentence imposed in 1985 of 15 years and six months, was released in April and Fernando Villalón Moreira, sentenced in 1986 to three years' imprisonment, was released in August (see *Amnesty International Report 1989*). The Cuban authorities gave no further information about the release program and the number of political prisoners released during the year was unclear. At least three so-called "*plantados históricos*", or political prisoners held since the 1960s and 1970s who refused to take part in prison rehabilitation programs or to obey certain prison regulations, remained in detention at the end of the year.

At least four prisoners were sentenced to death and executed in 1989. Division

78

General Arnaldo Ochoa Sánchez, Interior Ministry intelligence official Colonel Antonio de la Guardia Font, Captain Jorge Martínez Valdés, Major Amado Padrón Trujillo and 10 other armed forces and Interior Ministry officials were court-martialled before a Special Military Tribunal. Charges against them included hostile acts towards a foreign state, drug-trafficking and abuse of their official positions. They had allegedly assisted Colombian drug-traffickers in exporting cocaine to the USA via Cuba and engaged in illicit economic activities on the Angolan black market. A military honour tribunal preceding the court-martial had recommended that a Special Military Tribunal should try General Ochoa for high treason. At the end of the four-day court-martial, Justice Minister Juan Escalona, acting as State Prosecutor, requested the death penalty for seven of the 14 defendants. He argued that the incidents in which the accused were involved put in "imminent danger the security, prestige and honour" of the country. The defendants, while accepting responsibility for the charges against them, denied that their actions were politically motivated. State-appointed military defence lawyers confined their role to pleading for clemency on the grounds of extenuating circumstances.

Arnaldo Ochoa Sánchez and the other three defendants sentenced to death were executed by firing-squad in July, after the *Tribunal Supremo Popular*, People's Supreme Tribunal, and the *Consejo de Estado*, Council of State, confirmed the sentences. The 10 other defendants were sentenced to prison terms ranging from 10 to 30 years.

Amnesty International was concerned that although the alleged criminal offences were committed without apparent political motivation, the prosecution may have introduced political charges to permit the application of the death penalty. Under the revised 1987 Penal Code, the maximum sentence applicable for drug-trafficking offences is 15 years' imprisonment. Under Article 110 of the Penal Code, however, "hostile actions against a foreign state" resulting in reprisals against Cuba, alteration of diplomatic relations or war, may be punished by 10 to 20 years' imprisonment or death. Charges against the defendants included offences proscribed in Article 110.

Amnesty International appealed to the Council of State for commutation of the death sentences against Arnaldo Ochoa Sánchez, Antonio de la Guardia Font, Jorge Martínez Valdés and Amado Padrón Trujillo. The organization also continued to appeal for the release of prisoners of conscience and sought information from the Cuban authorities about the legal status of political prisoners. It urged the Cuban Government to implement judicial reviews of the cases of political prisoners whose trials had not conformed to internationally recognized standards. No substantive response to these communications was received during the year. Amnesty International expressed to the Cuban authorities its interest in attending the trial of Elizardo Sánchez, Hiram Abi Cobas and Hubert Jérez. The government responded that, although the trial was public, it was not willing to admit international observers.

CYPRUS

Two conscientious objectors to military service were imprisoned and were considered to be prisoners of conscience.

In April the government ratified the European Convention for the Prevention of Torture and Inhuman or Degrading Treatment or Punishment.

Cypriot law makes no provision for alternative civilian service for conscientious objectors to either military service or reservist exercises. A draft law providing for unarmed and civilian service, announced in 1988, had not been debated in parliament by the end of the year. The proposed duration of the civilian service was almost double that of military service. The draft law only made provision for religious objectors and did not take into account those who declare their conscientious objection after conscription.

Stelios Papadopoulos, a Jehovah's Witness, was detained from 11 January to 18 February following his refusal on conscientious grounds to participate in reservist exercises. He was held in a cell without a bed, lighting or heating.

Yannis Parpas, the first person in Cyprus to refuse to serve in the armed forces on solely pacifist grounds, was repeatedly charged for refusing to comply each time he was called up for reservist exercises. His trials were postponed until 8 June, when he was sentenced to four months' imprisonment by Nicosia Central Court. On 18 August he was sentenced to a further six months' imprisonment by the same court. His appeal against the second sentence was rejected in October and he was still in prison at the end of the year.

In July Amnesty International received a response from the Turkish Cypriot leader, Rauf Denktas, to an inquiry it had addressed to the Turkish Prime Minister, Turgut Özal, about three Greek Cypriots missing since the 1974 hostilities in Cyprus. In August Amnesty International addressed further inquiries concerning the cases to Mr Denktas and in November received a response stating that the Turkish Cypriot authorities believed that two of the missing had been killed in Cyprus in 1974 and that they had no information about the third. In August the organization published a report — *Missing Persons in Cyprus: Amnesty International's Actions 1974-89.*

Amnesty International appealed for the release of Stelios Papadopoulos and Yannis Parpas. The government responded by referring to the existence of the draft law and stated that no provision for conscientious objectors to reservist exercises was envisaged.

In February an Amnesty International delegate travelled to Cyprus to observe one of Yannis Parpas' trials, but the trial was postponed.

In March Amnesty International wrote to the Minister of Defence welcoming the proposed introduction of a civilian alternative to military service but urging that the length of civilian service should not be punitive, that the grounds for objection should be widened and that provision should be made for objection which develops after conscription into the armed forces. In August the organization wrote to President George Vassiliou, again raising its concerns about the shortcomings of the draft law. No reply had been received to either letter by the end of the year.

CZECHOSLOVAKIA

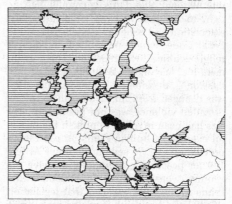

All known prisoners of conscience imprisoned under the former government of President Gustav Husak were released towards the end of the year, and criminal charges against those who might have become prisoners of conscience were dropped. Until the change of government there had been at least 36 known prisoners of conscience, while many more may have been held under laws restricting the peaceful exercise of human rights. Hundreds of people who peacefully exercised the rights to free expression and association were detained, charged and freed, then prosecuted while at liberty. Some detainees reported that they had been ill-treated in police custody. At least one person was sentenced to death.

In mid-November major political changes led to the resignation of the entire Communist Party leadership and the introduction of non-communists, including former prisoners of conscience, into government posts. On 29 December Vaclav Havel, a former prisoner of conscience, was sworn in as President.

At least 16 prisoners of conscience were released within two weeks of the Communist Party leadership's resignation. An amnesty announced in December freed an unknown number of people imprisoned on

80

all the charges usually brought against prisoners of conscience in the past.

The Penal Code review, which took place throughout 1989, was accelerated by the new government. On 13 December the Federal Assembly approved legislation proposed by First Deputy Prime Minister Jan Carnogursky, a former prisoner of conscience. The new laws were intended to strengthen the independence of the judiciary and bring the penal law into line with international standards guaranteeing the right to freedom of expression, assembly, association and religion. Article 101 of the Penal Code, which prohibited "misuse of religious office", was repealed. The punishment for "leaving the republic without permission", an offence under Article 109, was changed from imprisonment to a fine, provided violence was not used. Both articles had been invoked to punish the peaceful exercise of human rights. In contrast to previous years, no sentences under Article 109 for peacefully attempting to leave the country were reported. In December the Prime Minister announced that legislation to abolish the death penalty was being prepared.

There remained no legal provision for a civilian alternative to military service. In July Vladan Koci (see *Amnesty International Report 1989*) was sentenced to 16 months' imprisonment for refusing conscription. Vladan Koci, a Christian, objected to military service on religious grounds. He had received a 15-month sentence in 1988 on the same charge and was released that year under an amnesty. When he was called up again in May 1989, he refused to respond and was rearrested. He was pardoned and released in December.

Until December the state had a monopoly on publishing and prisoners of conscience detained during the year included people held for producing unofficial printed, audio or visual material politically unacceptable to the government. For example, Frantisek Starek was convicted of "incitement" under Article 100 of the Penal Code for producing an unofficial cultural journal and video magazine. He was sentenced in June to 30 months' imprisonment. Petr Cibulka, a worker from Brno who circulated unofficial literature and music cassettes, spent 13 months in pretrial detention on charges of "incitement", "speculation" prohibited under Article 117 and "unauthorized business enterprise"

prohibited under Article 118. Both prisoners were released in November.

Hana Marvanova and Tomas Dvorak (see *Amnesty International Report 1989*), who edited the bulletin of the unofficial Independent Peace Movement, were released in May after six months' detention. They had been given suspended sentences for "incitement" under Article 100 in April, but were held for a further month because the prosecutor objected to their release. In May an appeal court in Prague upheld the original sentence. In the amnesty announced in December these sentences were revoked, and the same charge of "incitement" against Lubomir Vydra, who had been arrested with the two editors but released in December 1988, was dropped.

Those distributing leaflets faced increased penalties after the maximum sanction for "violating public order", an offence proscribed under Section 6 of the Law on Misdemeanours, was doubled in February to six months' imprisonment. Jaroslav Popelka, a worker from Brno, was sentenced in April to four months' imprisonment for distributing leaflets. The leaflets called for a public meeting to discuss the Communist Party leadership's retirement and the formation of a Green Party. He had been convicted and imprisoned five times in 12 months for distributing such material, and he spent several weeks in custody later in the year before acquittal on the same charge.

Many people were detained without charge for up to 48 hours to prevent the exercise of their rights to free expression and association. Until mid-November the authorities rarely gave unofficial groups permission to hold public meetings. Criminal proceedings were initiated against hundreds of people who took part in peaceful, unsanctioned gatherings and who were usually at liberty during the prosecution. Those arrested at the beginning of a week-long wave of demonstrations in January included Jana Petrova and Otakar Veverka, members of unofficial peace groups, and playwright Vaclav Havel. Together with other human rights activists, they had tried to lay flowers in Prague in memory of Jan Palach, a student who set fire to himself in 1969 to protest the effects of the 1968 Warsaw Pact invasion of the country. The three were charged with public order offences. Vaclav Havel was sentenced to nine months' imprisonment and Jana Petrova to eight months. Both were paroled after serving half their sentences. Otakar Veverka, sentenced to 12 months' imprisonment, was pardoned at the end of November.

Dozens of people reported that they had been beaten and otherwise ill-treated by police who detained them following unsanctioned demonstrations. David Kabzan, for example, alleged that on 17 January he received some 20 truncheon blows to the head, back and arms at a police station in Prague. The blows followed his objection to officers inserting false information into his testimony.

In January Jaroslav Maly was sentenced to death by a court in Prague for the murder of three people. He remained under sentence of death at the end of the year.

Throughout the year Amnesty International called for the release of all prisoners of conscience and sought information on others thought likely to be prisoners of conscience. The organization appealed for commutation of Jaroslav Maly's death sentence and for the abolition of the death penalty. In June Amnesty International wrote to the Procurator General of Czechoslovakia concerning allegations that detainees were ill-treated in police custody following the January demonstrations. In July the organization wrote to the Ministers of Justice in the Czech and Slovak Republics, commenting on certain laws within the context of the Penal Code review.

Amnesty International representatives raised the organization's concerns during a visit in September to officials at the Ministry of Foreign Affairs and the Procurator General's Office. The representatives also met members of the officially registered Committee of the Czechoslovak Public for Human Rights and Humanitarian Cooperation, formed in December 1988.

For the first time, Amnesty International delegates were granted access to courtrooms during the year to observe proceedings. In October a delegate attended a hearing in Brno, where Stanislav Devaty was to appeal against his 20-month sentence for organizing petitions. The defendant, however, failed to appear and the hearing was adjourned. Stanislav Devaty was one of numerous people who received an amnesty in December. In November an Amnesty International delegate attended

the trial of prisoner of conscience Jan Carnogursky, which took place in Bratislava. The defendant, charged with "incitement" and, under Article 98, with "subversion", had criticized the Warsaw Pact invasion and published an unofficial journal. He was acquitted.

DJIBOUTI

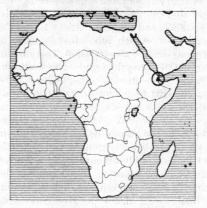

Six people were detained for several months for criticizing the government: they appeared to be prisoners of conscience. A seventh died in custody, possibly as a result of torture. Other government critics were detained for short periods. Prison conditions were harsh. A number of asylum-seekers from Somalia were forcibly returned to Somalia.

On 20 April several people were arrested in Tadjourah after a meeting with the Minister of the Interior. They were protesting against what they claimed to be the authorities' misappropriation of food supplies intended for flood victims. One of those arrested, Abdulqadir Daoud "Harbi", a former police officer, died in Gabode prison in the town of Djibouti on 2 May. There were claims that he had died as a result of torture. Two others, Houmed Dini "Lakisso" and Ali Mohamed "Faroura", were taken to court in June. A charge against them of contempt was withdrawn, but they were immediately rearrested. They went on hunger-strike in early July to protest their continuing detention. At the end of August they were tried and convicted of spreading false information, but were freed with suspended six-month prison sentences.

Four other people, including Mohamed Ali "Digdig", a journalist, were arrested in late June for making similar criticisms of the Tadjourah authorities and calling for a boycott of Independence Day celebrations. They too were tried in August on a charge of spreading false information and received short suspended prison sentences.

It was unclear whether a number of political prisoners arrested in 1987 and 1988 were still in custody in 1989 (see Amnesty International Report 1989). There were no reports of their being brought to trial during the year.

Conditions in Nagad prison near the town of Djibouti, where the people arrested in Tadjourah in April and Somali asylum-seekers were held, were reported to be harsh. Many prisoners were beaten and ill-treated, apparently as a matter of routine.

New information was received in 1989 about dozens of Somali asylum-seekers, members of the Issaq clan, who had been arrested and returned to Somalia in 1988 as a result of the Djibouti Government's policy not to grant asylum to refugees from Somalia. They had been detained on their return and ill-treated. In 1989 the same policy also led to scores of Somali asylum-seekers being forcibly returned to Somalia, but it was not possible to establish what happened to them.

Amnesty International wrote to the Minister of the Interior in May about the death in custody of Abdulqadir Daoud and the legal status of those arrested with him. The Minister replied that Abdulqadir Daoud had not been tortured, but had died in hospital after a heart attack. Amnesty International requested further details and urged an investigation, but no reply was received. Amnesty International also expressed concern that the six other prisoners then held were prisoners of conscience and called for their release.

DOMINICAN REPUBLIC

Short-term arrests of demonstrators and trade unionists were reported in the context of labour unrest. As in previous years there were violent clashes between the police and demonstrators, resulting in the death of three demonstrators and the

injury of many others. Several people were reported to have been threatened in detention and to have been kept in police custody in spite of a judicial order for their release. The government failed to clarify the fate of two people who had "disappeared" in previous years.

Arrests of demonstrators and trade unionists were reported in the context of a general strike on 19 and 20 June to protest against the economic policies of the government of President Joaquín Balaguer. Violent confrontations between the police and demonstrators resulted in the death of three demonstrators and the injury of many others. On 30 June Rafael Santo, the Secretary-General of the Dominican Teachers' Association, was detained with other teachers during a march held in Santo Domingo in support of higher salaries and other demands.

On 7 May police detained Roberto Duvergé Mejía, an elderly university professor; Fernando Peña Segura, a politics graduate; and Luis Lizardo, a mechanic, accusing them of responsibility for a series of bomb explosions. They were reportedly threatened while held in custody. The release of Roberto Duvergé and Fernando Peña, ordered by a judge and regional attorney owing to lack of evidence but ignored by the police for at least three weeks, did not take place until 17 June. Luis Lizardo continued to await trial in La Victoria prison.

No further information was received on the fate of Pablo Liberato Rodríguez or Luis Samuel Roche, who "disappeared" in 1974 and 1982 respectively (see Amnesty International Report 1979, 1983 and 1985 to 1989).

In June Amnesty International appealed on behalf of Roberto Duvergé, Fernando Peña and Luis Lizardo, requesting clarification of their exact legal situation.

ECUADOR

The use of torture and ill-treatment by police forces continued to be reported throughout the country. Of the 10 or more deaths in police or security force custody, five reportedly resulted from torture or ill-treatment. A congressional committee concluded that the victim of a "disappearance" in 1985 had in fact been killed by naval and police officers while in detention. The government failed to clarify other "disappearances" reported in previous years. Army and police officers allegedly ill-treated many indigenous people and peasants in the context of land disputes.

Police forces reportedly continued to inflict torture and ill-treatment on detainees. Héctor Vinicio Arteaga Carpio was detained on 8 June and taken to the *Servicio de Investigaciones Criminales* (SIC), the Criminal Investigation Service, in Azuay, where he was interrogated for two days. He alleged that SIC agents tied his hands behind his back, placed a club between his arms and then repeatedly submerged his head in water causing semi-asphyxia. He stated that he was forced to do exercises and that he was kicked in the face. On 19 June Héctor Mejía, a truck driver, and four colleagues were detained in Quito by agents of the SIC based in Pichincha. The detainees were reportedly interrogated under torture, including being hanged from their thumbs and having gas hoods placed over their heads.

Of the 10 or more people who died while in police or SIC custody, five showed clear medical signs of torture or ill-treatment. Selfido Ilves Camacho was detained in May in Caluma, Bolívar

province, accused of stealing two mules. A medical certificate indicated that he died as a result of an electric shock. An investigation into his death was initiated by a police tribunal. Gonzalo Quintero Mina was detained in July in Nueva Loja, Sucumbios province, by members of the national police. Witnesses said that he was beaten by the police on arrest, apparently to force him to divulge the name of a prisoner who had reportedly escaped: he was then taken to a police station. Three days later his relatives were told that his body was in the morgue of the local hospital.

A multi-party congressional committee which had been investigating the "disappearance" of teacher Consuelo Benavides Cevallos in 1985 (see *Amnesty International Report 1987*) concluded its investigation in early January. The committee, formed in September 1988, interviewed a large number of witnesses, including several members of the navy and the police. The committee's report concluded that Consuelo Benavides was killed in custody after having been subjected to torture. It named several high-ranking officers of the navy and the police as responsible for illegal and arbitrary arrest, torture, murder, document forgery and perjury. It was left to the Supreme Court to initiate judicial proceedings against those implicated, but this had not been done by the end of 1989.

No further information emerged about other people who "disappeared" after being taken into custody in 1985 and 1986. The government also failed to account for the whereabouts of Manuel García Franco, a car park attendant detained in 1987 by a member of the navy. His detention had followed a complaint from a navy officer's wife about the theft of her car.

Army and police officers, sometimes operating in conjunction with armed groups paid by landowners, allegedly ill-treated many members of indigenous and peasant communities. On 13 January combined army and police forces entered a peasant community in Baba, Los Ríos, where there was a dispute over land tenure. Many members of the community, including children, were reportedly beaten and received death threats. Eleven days later the same people and their families had their crops destroyed and were forcibly evicted by 80 armed men who had landed in helicopters. On 14 and 16 July some 150 police officers reportedly entered the Pijal

84   community in Imbabura province. They allegedly beat peasants, including children, while evicting them from the land.

In November Amnesty International wrote to President Rodrigo Borja expressing concern about reports of torture and ill-treatment, in some cases leading to deaths in custody, and asking for a full and impartial investigation. No reply had been received by the end of the year.

EGYPT

More than 8,000 political prisoners, including many prisoners of conscience, were detained for periods of one to three months without charge or trial, some repeatedly. At least 14 prisoners of conscience were imprisoned following the enforcement of a 1986 emergency court verdict. Five people were apparently imprisoned because of their religious beliefs. Torture and ill-treatment of political detainees, particularly supporters of Islamic groups opposing the government, were widely reported. At least five people, including for the first time a convicted drug-trafficker, were executed. At least 56 other people, including 40 convicted drug-traffickers, were sentenced to death.

A state of emergency, declared in 1981, remained in force. Under Article 3 of the Emergency Law, the Minister of the Interior has the power to "arrest and detain suspected persons or those who endanger public order or security". After 30 days in custody, detainees may petition the (Emergency) Supreme State Security Court, which can order their release. However, the Minister of the Interior can contest the Court's decision to release a detainee and the case then passes to a second court for a binding decision. The process permits administrative detention of up to 90 days without approval by any judicial authority. In security-related criminal cases, detainees may be held for up to 60 days before their first court appearance. The Minister of the Interior may prolong detention even if the court orders release.

The authorities used their wide-ranging powers under state of emergency legislation to quell opposition from left-wing groups, trade unionists and, especially, Islamic groups. There were a number of clashes between the security forces and Islamic opponents of the government of President Husni Mubarak. Some government opponents were involved in political violence, including the unsuccessful attempt in December to assassinate the Minister of the Interior.

At least 8,000 supporters or alleged supporters of the Islamic opposition were reportedly detained during the year. Several hundred trade unionists and other critics and opponents of the government were also detained. A great majority of detainees were apparently held under state of emergency provisions and released without charge or trial after periods of imprisonment ranging from a few days to three months. A few people were repeatedly imprisoned under consecutive detention orders. Consequently, they spent long periods in detention with only short intervals, or even no interval at all, between detention orders. Many detainees appeared to be victims of arbitrary arrest and some were prisoners of conscience.

Mass arrests occurred, particularly at times of political tension. For example, at the beginning of the year more than 300 suspected supporters of Islamic groups were in detention following violent clashes with the security forces in December 1988 in the Ain Shams district of Cairo (see *Amnesty International Report 1989*).

In April the newspaper *Al Ahram* reported that the Minister of the Interior had said that 1,500 "religious extremists" had been arrested in the previous two weeks. Nearly all were released within two to three months. These arrests followed protests against the imprisonment of Sheikh Omar Abdul Rahman, a leading figure in the Islamic opposition. He had been detained in April, at the beginning of the fasting month of *Ramadan*, after a clash between the security forces and supporters of Islamic groups in Fayoum. He was released, pending trial, in August.

During the weeks leading up to parliamentary elections in June, hundreds of opposition political activists were detained without charge for periods ranging from several days to several weeks.

EGYPT

85

In early August armed police broke up a steelworkers' sit-in protest at the Helwan Iron and Steelworks southwest of Cairo. More than 600 workers were detained. In late August about 60 people who had been active on behalf of the jailed steelworkers were arrested and accused of forming an illegal communist organization. Among those arrested were lawyers, human rights activists, journalists and others, including two leading members of the Egyptian Organization for Human Rights. The detainees were released without charge during September.

About 500 people were detained without charge in December after clashes took place between the security forces and student supporters of Islamic groups at Asyut University. The students had reportedly been involved in violent protests against a university outing planned to include both male and female students. Many were still held at the end of the year.

Only a small proportion of those detained during the year were charged with an offence. Thirteen defendants were brought to trial in September on charges connected with the Ain Shams disturbances in December 1988. The trial had not concluded by the end of the year. Fifty-five defendants, including Sheikh Omar Abdul Rahman, were charged in connection with the Fayoum disturbances. Their trial also had not concluded by the end of 1989. None of the 600 steelworkers arrested in August was brought to trial. Three of them remained in administrative detention at the end of the year, despite repeated court decisions that they should be released. Eight textile workers arrested in 1988 (see Amnesty International Report 1989) were released without charge in early 1989, after more than three months in detention.

A number of people who had converted to Christianity from Islam were detained without charge or trial under emergency legislation. Dr Ibrahim As-Sayyeh was detained between July and November, apparently because of his religious activities. At least four other Christians reportedly suffered months of detention because of their religious beliefs.

At least 14 prisoners of conscience were imprisoned after the government decided in September to enforce their sentences. An (Emergency) Supreme State Security Court had passed the sentences in 1986. Seven others were evading arrest at the end of the

year and another had died in the intervening period. Proceedings against the 22 began in 1981. They were prosecuted for membership of the banned Egyptian Communist Party and acquitted of this charge, although they were convicted of producing and possessing publications said to undermine basic constitutional and political principles (see Amnesty International Report 1987). They had no right to appeal against their sentences, which ranged between one and three years' imprisonment.

Torture and ill-treatment of detainees held under emergency provisions were reportedly widespread. People caught in waves of mass arrests were routinely beaten. Many others were systematically tortured in efforts to extract confessions of illegal activity or to obtain information. Defendants in the Egypt Revolution Organization trial (see Amnesty International Report 1988), which continued throughout the year, were held in solitary confinement between court appearances.

Police reportedly beat Sheikh Omar Abdul Rahman, who is blind and diabetic, and dragged him along the ground soon after they detained him in Fayoum. The authorities allegedly prevented him from receiving necessary medication during his detention.

Some steelworkers arrested in August were reportedly tortured. Muhammad Mustafa and Mustafa Nayed were said to have been beaten and tortured with electric shocks in order to force them to state that an illegal communist organization had orchestrated the steelworkers' protest. Sixty people apparently detained for protesting against the treatment of the steelworkers were themselves detained and beaten in August, before being released without charge.

While investigating the activities of suspected opposition groups, State Security Intelligence Police reportedly subjected dozens of detainees to systematic torture. Many of the victims were subsequently released without charge in the absence of evidence against them to warrant charges. For example, Dr Muhammad Abdul Latif, a physician, was held for six weeks beginning in late June, apparently because the authorities suspected him of belonging to an illegal Muslim Brotherhood cell. He claimed after he was released without charge that he had been beaten with sticks

86

and that electric shocks had been applied to his nipples and genitals.

Dr Fahmy Shinnawi, a 67-year-old urologist, was reportedly forced to stand continuously for 14 hours, beaten and tortured with electric shocks, because he was suspected of belonging to an illegal Shi'a organization. Forty people were arrested in August and held in connection with the investigation into this alleged organization. All were subsequently released and dozens submitted official complaints of torture and ill-treatment to the procuracy for investigation. Reports from official forensic medical doctors substantiated complaints in this and dozens of other cases. Little progress was apparent in investigations of these complaints or of torture alleged in previous years.

Anwar Hossein Kassar Hossein, a Pakistani national, was hanged in July for drug-trafficking. At least four other people, all convicted of murder, were also executed. At least 56 people were sentenced to death, six *in absentia*. Forty of these death sentences were imposed for drug-trafficking, including 19 death sentences handed down in June in a single court case. The other 16 death sentences were imposed for murder.

Amnesty International repeatedly appealed to the government to bring its detention laws into line with internationally recognized human rights standards. The organization also appealed to the authorities to discontinue practices facilitating arbitrary detention and torture and called for the release of all prisoners of conscience.

Amnesty International urged the government on numerous occasions to take effective action against the widespread torture of political detainees. It called for allegations of torture to be thoroughly investigated, the findings to be made public and the perpetrators to be brought to justice. The organization called on the government to permit detainees held under emergency laws to challenge the legality of their detention before a judicial authority within a few days of detention, as required by international standards, rather than after weeks or months.

In May Amnesty International published *Egypt: Arbitrary Detention and Torture Under Emergency Powers*, a report detailing human rights concerns under the state of emergency and containing the

text of a memorandum submitted to the government in June 1988.

Amnesty International also expressed concern about the rapidly increasing number of death sentences. The organization appealed against the execution in July of a convicted drug-trafficker, the first execution for this offence, and urged commutation of all death sentences.

In an oral statement delivered in August to the United Nations Sub-Commission on Prevention of Discrimination and Protection of Minorities, Amnesty International included reference to the torture and ill-treatment of detainees held in Egypt under emergency legislation.

EL SALVADOR

Trade union leaders and prominent academics were among scores of civilians who allegedly "disappeared" or were killed by military personnel often acting in the guise of "death squads". Many were killed in bomb attacks and raids by the security forces on trade union and university premises. The authorities said they would investigate these abuses, but in most cases little action was taken to bring those responsible to justice. Throughout the year there were large-scale arrests of suspected government opponents, including church workers, students and trade unionists. Torture and ill-treatment were routinely used to extract "confessions" from political detainees.

Following the victory of the right-wing *Alianza Republicana Nacionalista* (ARENA), the Nationalist Republican Alliance, in the general elections in March 1989, the government of President Alfredo Cristiani took office on 1 June. The elections took place amid a renewed wave of guerrilla activity by the *Frente Farabundo Martí de Liberación Nacional* (FMLN), the Farabundo Martí National Liberation Front.

The government's refusal to postpone the elections to allow the FMLN's participation as a political party was followed by a spate of killings of high-level government and military officials attributed to the FMLN.

On 11 November, after the breakdown of talks between the government and the FMLN initiated in September under the terms of the 1987 Central American Peace Agreement, the rebels launched a major military offensive. The following day the government declared a state of siege and launched a counter-attack which included heavy aerial bombardment of densely populated areas of San Salvador and San Miguel, leaving thousands of civilians dead, injured or displaced. The state of siege, which was extended in December, suspended certain constitutional guarantees. In November the National Assembly approved reforms to the Penal Code which would criminalize certain forms of peaceful opposition activity. At the end of the year President Cristiani returned the proposed legislation to the National Assembly for further discussion.

A renewed clampdown on members of pressure groups and suspected government opponents followed the coming-to-power of the new government in March. There were numerous incidents involving the mass arrest, short-term detention and torture of members of trade unions and humanitarian organizations. On 19 April riot police arrested 85 people during raids on the offices of the *Comité Cristiano Pro-Desplazados de El Salvador* (CRIPDES), the Christian Committee for the Displaced of El Salvador, and of two trade union organizations. Although most of those arrested were released within three days, eight were held in prison until 8 and 9 August, when they were released owing to lack of evidence. All eight alleged they were subjected to severe beatings and near-asphyxiation with the *capucha*, a rubber hood impregnated with lime, during detention at Treasury Police headquarters.

The National Police detained 64 trade unionists on 18 September during a demonstration organized by the *Federación Nacional Sindical de Trabajadores Salvadoreños* (FENASTRAS), the National Trade Union Federation of Salvadorian Workers. Many of those detained were reportedly tortured with the *capucha* and electric shocks; seven women and one man said they had been raped. Although most

were released within 72 hours, 18 were still in prison in December.

The number of politically related arrests escalated following the imposition of the state of siege in November. Members of trade unions, political parties, church and humanitarian aid organizations were persistently accused of supporting the FMLN offensive in the government-controlled media. Among the scores arrested were more than 50 Salvadorian and foreign church workers, detained after the police and army raided and ransacked some 60 church buildings and refuges. Although most were released shortly after arrest, at least 12 were still detained without charge at the end of the year. Under state of siege legislation, the period for which detainees could be held in police custody before being taken before a judge was increased from 72 hours to 15 days, during which time they were frequently denied access to family or lawyers. Reports of torture increased following the state of siege.

At the end of the year around 500 political prisoners were facing charges involving alleged links with the armed opposition. In many cases it was alleged that the charges were based on confessions obtained under torture. One detainee allegedly signed five statements saying that she was a member of the FMLN after being raped and repeatedly beaten. In some cases trial proceedings appeared not to have been completed within the time limits specified by Salvadorian law. There was no progress in proceedings against Jorge Alberto Miranda Arévalo, detained in December 1987 and accused of involvement in the murder of Herbert Anaya Sanabria (see *Amnesty International Report 1989*). Fresh evidence emerged that his confession had been obtained under torture. Other political detainees were repeatedly transferred from one prison to another, often to remote parts of the country, making access difficult for families and lawyers.

The security forces, acting in uniform or in the guise of "death squads", were allegedly responsible for dozens of "disappearances" throughout the year. Among the few to have survived "disappearance" and denounced their treatment were five students and staff from the University of El Salvador, abducted in July and August by armed men in civilian clothing. They were allegedly tortured in clandestine detention centres believed to be private houses. The

88

five were released in September. All reportedly recognized their captors as members of the *Segunda Brigada de Infantería*, the Second Infantry Brigade. They said that during interrogation they were accused of involvement in guerrilla activity and tortured with electric shocks and cigarette burns.

Juan Francisco Massi Chávez, a union member at the Lido factory in Soyapango, San Salvador, and Sara Cristina Chan Chan, a photographer for FENASTRAS, "disappeared" following their alleged detention on 19 August by uniformed members of the air force. No unit of the security forces acknowledged holding them and they remained "disappeared".

Amnesty International documented over 60 killings, allegedly carried out by government forces or "death squads" closely linked to them. Those killed included trade unionists, academics, members of political parties, and others apparently targeted on account of their opposition to government policies. The authorities claimed that some of the dead had been killed in armed confrontations with military personnel but in many of these cases the evidence suggested that the victims were unarmed civilians summarily executed by members of the armed forces.

Ten people were killed and 36 others injured in a bomb attack on the offices of FENASTRAS on 31 October. Febe Elisabeth Velásquez, former general secretary of FENASTRAS, was one of several prominent trade union leaders killed in the blast. The FENASTRAS offices had suffered three bomb attacks and repeated raids by the security forces earlier in the year. Hours before the FENASTRAS bombing, four people were injured in a bomb explosion at the offices of COMADRES, the organization of relatives of the "disappeared".

Human rights workers in El Salvador claimed that the bombings were carried out by members of the military in retaliation for a mortar attack by the FMLN on 30 October on the Armed Forces' Joint Chiefs of Staff, in which one person was killed and 15 injured. Whereas nine church workers were being held at the end of the year accused of involvement in the FMLN attack, no arrests had been made in connection with the FENASTRAS and COMADRES bombings despite government assurances of an exhaustive investigation.

Witnesses reported the abduction on 6 November of Cecilio Rivera Rodríguez and Apolinario Miranda, both members of the *Movimiento Popular Social Cristiano* (MPSC), the Popular Social Christian Movement, by armed men in plain clothes recognized as members of the *Destacamento Militar No. 6*, Military Detachment No. 6. Their bodies were found on wasteland the next morning.

On 16 November six Jesuit priests, their cook and her 15-year-old daughter were murdered at the *Universidad Centroamericana "José Simeón Cañas"* (UCA), the Jesuit-run Central American University in San Salvador. The six priests were prominent academics and included the rector of the university, Ignacio Ellacuría, and Segundo Montes, director of the university's human rights institute. The attack took place while a curfew was in force, in an area patrolled by troops. The priests' residence had been raided two days earlier by members of the Atlacatl battalion, an élite counter-insurgency unit. Death threats had been broadcast against Ignacio Ellacuría on the army-controlled radio days before the killings.

The government announced that it would investigate the killings and bring to justice those responsible, even if they were found to be members of the military. President Cristiani invited detectives from the Spanish, British, Canadian and United States (US) police forces to assist the governmental special investigative commission.

A report on these killings published by *Tutela Legal del Arzobispado*, the Legal Aid Office of the Archdiocese, concluded that members of the military had been responsible, basing its conclusions on the testimony of the housekeeper, who witnessed the killings, and on other circumstantial evidence. By the end of the year the government investigation had not yet resulted in arrests.

The majority of extrajudicial killings and other human rights abuses allegedly committed by the military in the past remained uninvestigated. Only in isolated cases were military personnel prosecuted. The investigation into the killing of 10 peasants in San Francisco in September 1988 (see *Amnesty International Report 1989*) was resumed following statements by the US Government that military aid would be reduced if no progress was made in the case. Within a month of these statements nine members of the Fifth Infantry Brigade were arrested, including the head of military intelligence of the brigade, Major Mauricio Beltrán Granados.

The suspects testified they had been ordered by Major Beltrán to execute the captured peasants by detonating several mines seized from a guerrilla store. Those still alive after the explosions were shot at point-blank range. Trial proceedings against the nine had not been concluded by the end of the year.

Throughout the year Amnesty International appealed to the government to investigate the numerous reports of extrajudicial killing and "disappearance". The organization sent repeated appeals urging that detainees in the custody of the security forces be treated in accordance with international standards. In September Amnesty International representatives met President Alfredo Cristiani and Dr José Manuel Pacas Castro, the Minister of Foreign Affairs, in London. Amnesty International expressed its concern about the continuing pattern of human rights violations. President Cristiani stated that the human rights situation would only improve with the termination of the armed conflict and that the abuses that had occurred were isolated cases which did not reflect government policy. Amnesty International urged President Cristiani to implement recommendations made by the organization to previous Salvadorian governments.

In an oral statement delivered in March to the United Nations Commission on Human Rights, Amnesty International drew attention to abductions, "disappearances" and politically motivated killings in El Salvador by "death squads" composed of police and military personnel.

EQUATORIAL GUINEA

At least one prisoner of conscience and about a dozen other political prisoners continued to serve sentences imposed after unfair trials by military courts in 1983, 1986 and 1988. One prisoner of conscience was released in January. Fifteen political prisoners were released after the sentences of all political prisoners were reduced in a clemency measure in August. Details emerged of the torture of prisoners arrested in August 1988.

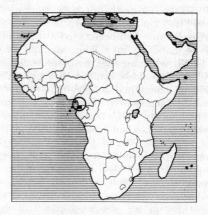

President Teodoro Obiang Nguema Mbasogo, leader of the only legal political party — *Partido Democrático de Guinea Ecuatorial*, Democratic Party of Equatorial Guinea — was returned to office in June in the first election since the country's independence in 1969. No information was available to indicate that the government had made progress in drafting new penal and procedural codes containing adequate human rights safeguards. Such reforms had been proposed under a plan of action drawn up in 1980 by an expert appointed by the United Nations Commission on Human Rights.

Primo José Esono Miká, a prisoner of conscience, remained in prison throughout the year. He was sentenced to 30 years' imprisonment in September 1988 after being convicted of conspiring to overthrow the government (see *Amnesty International Report 1989*). However, his arrest appeared to have been due to his opposition to one-party rule and his membership of a Spanish-based opposition party, *Partido del Progreso*, Progress Party. His sentence was reduced to 15 years' imprisonment in August, the 10th anniversary of the overthrow of the former head of state. Another defendant at the same trial, José Luis Jones Dougan, Secretary-General of the Progress Party, who was serving a 16-year prison sentence, was released in January shortly before President Obiang Nguema visited Spain: José Luis Jones Dougan has Spanish as well as Equatorial Guinean nationality. Neither he nor Primo José Esono Miká had used or advocated violence.

In the clemency measure announced in August, over 25 other political prisoners serving sentences imposed by military courts after unfair trials in 1983, 1986 and 1988 (see *Amnesty International Report 1989*) had their sentences reduced. Fifteen prisoners who had been convicted in 1983 of participating in a coup attempt were released while another, Sergeant Venancio Mikó, whose death sentence had previously been commuted to life imprisonment, had his sentence reduced to six years' imprisonment. Two other prisoners, whose death sentences had been commuted to life imprisonment after they were convicted of conspiring to overthrow the government in September 1988 (see *Amnesty International Report 1989*), had their sentences reduced to 20 years' imprisonment. The sentences of six others convicted at the same trial were halved and one of them, Metódio Esono Andong Mba, was released in September, apparently on humanitarian grounds.

There were reports that detainees suspected of criminal offences were tortured on at least two occasions. The methods used included severe beatings and electric shocks. In October two police officers were convicted of torturing prisoners and sentenced to several months' imprisonment.

Further information was received in 1989 about the torture and ill-treatment of those people arrested prior to the September 1988 trial. A total of about 40 people were arrested in August 1988 on suspicion of plotting to overthrow the government; all but nine were released before the trial. Most of those arrested were interrogated at Bata, the capital of the mainland province of Rio Muni. They were said to have been tortured by Equatorial Guinean soldiers acting under the supervision of Moroccan security personnel seconded to Equatorial Guinea under the terms of a bilateral military cooperation agreement. The detainees were apparently taken from prison at night for interrogation and severely tortured and ill-treated. Primo José Esono Miká was said to have had his arms and legs tied together behind him, causing his back to arch painfully, and then to have been suspended by a rope. As a result he temporarily lost the use of his limbs. Other prisoners were subjected to similar forms of torture, sometimes with a heavy stone placed on the arched back of the

suspended victim. Prisoners were also said to have been hung by the feet and to have had their heads immersed in a bucket of dirty water, partially suffocating them, and to have been tortured with electric shocks.

During their trial in September 1988, two of the nine defendants told the court that statements they had made in pre-trial custody had been extracted under torture. However, the court apparently took no steps to investigate the allegations. All nine were said to have been convicted largely on the basis of confessions.

Amnesty International expressed concern to the government about the alleged torture of detainees in late 1988 and continued to urge a review of the cases of prisoners convicted in September 1988. It called for the immediate and unconditional release of Primo José Esono Miká and expressed concern that his seven co-defendants who continued to be held might be prisoners of conscience. Amnesty International welcomed the releases and reductions in prison sentences announced in August. The government did not acknowledge or respond to a memorandum which Amnesty International had submitted in November 1988. This detailed the organization's concerns about a series of unfair military trials and called for procedural safeguards to ensure that prisoners' human rights are respected and that Equatorial Guinea fulfils its obligations under the various international human rights instruments it has ratified.

ETHIOPIA

Detention without trial of government opponents, including prisoners of conscience, continued. Over 170 people were arrested and held incommunicado after an unsuccessful coup attempt in May: the trial of 14 of them began in December but it was feared that some others might have died or been executed in custody. Over 900 prisoners were released in September: these included over 300 political detainees, many of whom were prisoners of conscience. As in previous years, the security forces were reported to have tortured or ill-treated political prisoners and to have extrajudicially executed some political prisoners and many unarmed civilians

as fighting continued between government troops and opposition forces in several parts of the country.

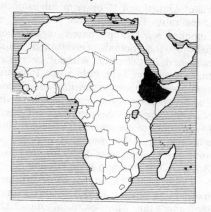

A state of emergency imposed in 1988 remained in force in Eritrea and Tigray, where opposition forces held or gained control of substantial territory. There was also fighting in other regions, including Gojjam, Wollega and Hararghe. Peace talks between the government and the Eritrean People's Liberation Front (EPLF) began in September, and for several months there was a *de facto* cease-fire in Eritrea. However, intensified fighting continued in the second half of the year in the Wollo, Gondar and Shoa regions of central Ethiopia, as the Tigray People's Liberation Front (TPLF) and an allied group extended their control and captured several towns. Incidents were reported of the EPLF and TPLF imprisoning or executing political opponents.

In an abortive coup attempt on 16 May by members of the armed forces, led by the army chief of staff and air force commander, government opponents shot dead the Minister of Defence. Soldiers in the Eritrean capital of Asmara mutinied and called for peace negotiations with opposition forces. They also demanded constitutional changes to permit freedom of expression. The coup attempt was put down after three days of fighting in the capital, Addis Ababa, Asmara and other military centres. The government reported that 44 coup supporters had been killed, including the army chief of staff and air force commander. It was impossible to evaluate claims by unofficial sources that several people arrested in connection with the coup attempt had been executed extra-judicially.

It remained difficult to obtain information about political prisoners and was frequently impossible to corroborate reports of abuses committed in areas affected by armed conflict. Intimidation by the security authorities of suspected opponents, relatives of political prisoners and released political prisoners added to the problems of accurately assessing the human rights situation, and made it impossible to determine the precise number of political prisoners held in 1989. However, at least several hundred were believed to be still held at the end of the year, including prisoners of conscience, despite the major releases.

After the May coup attempt, large numbers of armed forces personnel were arrested, in addition to those captured in the fighting. The government announced that 176 members of the armed forces were being held, but unofficial sources reported that several civilians had also been detained including the wives of three of the coup leaders. Among the civilians arrested were Teferra Wonde, former deputy prime minister, and Genet Mebratu, a World Health Organization employee and widow of one of the coup leaders. Some of those arrested were later released uncharged, including two other wives of coup leaders, but Genet Mebratu remained in detention. The detainees were held incommunicado and there were unconfirmed reports that at least one detainee "disappeared" while in custody. The authorities announced in September that a special military court was being set up to try the detainees and on 19 December the joint trial began of 13 army generals and the navy commander on a charge of treason. The trial was continuing at the end of the year.

Other arrests of alleged government opponents were reported during the year, particularly in Addis Ababa and areas where opposition forces were active. Prisoners often appeared to be held on suspicion of supporting insurgents from their home areas solely on the basis of their ethnic or regional origin. Members of several Protestant churches were reportedly detained for short periods in western Ethiopia and accused of "anti-revolutionary activities". Arrests of people trying to evade conscription were also reported.

On 2 September the government announced an amnesty to mark the 15th anniversary of the revolution which over-

92

threw Emperor Haile Selassie's government in 1974. In all, 907 prisoners were reportedly released, including 87 political prisoners. Many prisoners of conscience were freed, including Bede-Mariam, Michael and Wossen-Seged Mekonnen, three grandsons of the late Emperor Haile Selassie who had been held without charge since 1974. Also released were Tsehai Tolessa, wife of the Reverend Gudina Tumsa of the Ethiopian Evangelical Mekane Yesus Church who "disappeared" in 1979; Martha Kumsa, a journalist; and Zegeye Asfaw, a former Minister of Justice. They were among dozens of members of the Oromo ethnic group, held since 1980 on account of their alleged links with the Oromo Liberation Front (OLF), who were freed. Berhanu Dinka, Ethiopia's former representative to the United Nations (UN) in New York, who had been detained since 1986, was also freed. Over 30 long-term untried detainees who had been held as suspected supporters of Eritrean and Tigrayan opposition groups were released, as were seven suspected members of the opposition Ethiopian People's Democratic Alliance who had been detained without charge or trial since 1985.

A few days after the amnesty, a further 231 prisoners were released in Asmara. Most appeared to be political prisoners. Other political prisoners were also reported to have been released during 1989. One, Shimelis Teklu, a UN employee imprisoned since 1984, was freed in mid-1989 when the Supreme Court upheld his appeal against conviction for espionage. Amnesty International had been investigating his case as a possible prisoner of conscience.

Despite these releases, several hundred political prisoners remained in detention without charge or trial at the end of 1989, including some held since the early 1980s. In all cases they were held unlawfully: the Constitution requires that all detainees are brought before a court within 48 hours of arrest but the authorities have consistently failed to comply with this provision. Those who remained in detention included Dagne Bayissa, a development officer of the Ethiopian Evangelical Mekane Yesus Church, and Demissie Kebede, a trade unionist. Both had been held since 1980, apparently because of suspected links with the OLF. Berhanu Mamo, a former mayor of Mekelle, and Amare Dori, a district administrator in Adua, were also believed to be

still held. They were among hundreds of Tigrayans arrested in 1984 and accused of links with the TPLF. Colonel Abdullahi Yusuf Ahmed and 17 other members of the Democratic Front for the Salvation of Somalia, an Ethiopia-based organization fighting the Somali Government, also remained in detention without charge or trial. They have been held since 1985 and 1986 (see *Amnesty International Report 1989*). There was no news about Tesfa-Mariam Zeggai, a UN employee and possible prisoner of conscience arrested in 1982 and serving a life sentence imposed in 1987 for alleged links with the EPLF (see *Amnesty International Report 1989*).

There were new reports of torture, particularly in relation to the prisoners arrested after the May coup attempt. The prisoners were held incommunicado and some allegedly died under torture, although this could not be confirmed. The conditions under which prisoners were held for investigation – particularly in state security police centres – were harsh and amounted to cruel, inhuman or degrading treatment.

There were reports of extrajudicial executions of civilians by government security forces operating in Eritrea. Some of those detained in connection with the May coup attempt were said to have been summarily killed in custody. There were also reports that several airport employees were executed extrajudicially in Addis Ababa in October after being accused of sabotage.

Armed opposition organizations were also reported to have executed prisoners and committed other abuses. In May an EPLF group was said to have killed up to 200 members of the Afar ethnic group who refused to join their organization. The TPLF was reported to have executed two people – Teklu Hawaz, a former TPLF central committee member, and Alula Tadesse, a journalist. The TPLF was also reported to be holding prisoners in territory under its control, including Esteda Hadush, the wife of a former TPLF military commander who had criticized the organization, and Hagos Atsbeha, the commander's brother, who had been abducted by the TPLF in 1988 from Sudan, where he was a recognized refugee.

Amnesty International continued to appeal to President Mengistu Haile-Mariam for the release of prisoners of conscience and for other political prisoners to be brought to trial fairly and promptly, or released. The organization also expressed concern to the government about the incommunicado detention and reported torture of those arrested after the May coup attempt, but no reply was received.

In March, in an oral statement to the UN Commission on Human Rights, Amnesty International drew attention to the government's attempt to cover up a pattern of serious human rights violations.

In April Amnesty International submitted information about its concerns in Ethiopia for UN review under a procedure, established by Economic and Social Council Resolutions 728F/1503, for confidential consideration of communications about human rights violations. The submission was also sent to the government, together with recommendations for measures to halt abuses, but no response was received.

In August Amnesty International published a report, *Political Imprisonment in Ethiopia*, which detailed the cases of many prisoners of conscience and other political prisoners. The report criticized the absence of effective safeguards against arbitrary and illegal detention. It concluded that persistent reports of torture indicated that the law prohibiting and penalizing torture was rarely applied. The government made no comment on the report, nor did it reply to other appeals or inquiries by Amnesty International. However, many of the prisoners mentioned in the report were among those released in September.

Amnesty International welcomed the releases of prisoners of conscience in September and informed the authorities of its wish to send a delegation to visit Ethiopia to discuss human rights. However, no reply had been received by the end of the year.

FIJI

At least five critics of the government were briefly detained. The trials of other government opponents arrested but released on bail in 1988 were completed; some were convicted of sedition and others of unlawful assembly, but none was imprisoned. There were numerous reports of torture and ill-treatment of detainees.

A draft constitution published by the government in 1988 included provisions for "positive discrimination" in favour of ethnic Fijians over Fijian citizens of Indian origin. Human rights activists and the former Prime Minister, Dr Timoci Bavadra, who died in October, said the proposed constitution would infringe fundamental human rights. In September the government-appointed Constitution Inquiry and Advisory Committee issued a report which accepted the principle of "positive discrimination" and endorsed the draft constitution with minor revisions. There was speculation that Major-General Sitiveni Rabuka, who led two coups in 1987 and subsequently became Commander of the Armed Forces and Minister of Home Affairs, might stage a third coup in the face of mounting opposition to the draft constitution. Such speculation increased when a confidential military document detailing plans for the "neutralization" of civilian opposition leaders was leaked to the press. In October the Prime Minister announced that he would remain in office beyond December, when his interim government was due to complete its term, and Major-General Rabuka agreed to resign his civilian cabinet post.

In October at least five staff and students from the University of the South Pacific were detained for up to 24 hours by police and military officers and reportedly ill-treated by being kicked and beaten. Vijay Naidu, a Fijian citizen of Indian origin and a leading anti-nuclear activist, was arrested on 11 October and questioned about his political views and activities. He was reportedly denied access to a lawyer and subjected to racial taunts. He was released after several hours but was charged with illegal possession of a knife.

Dozens of people arrested on political grounds and released on bail in 1988 were

94 brought to trial on charges such as unlawful assembly, arms-smuggling and sedition (see *Amnesty International Report 1989*). In January, 18 anti-coup protesters who had been arrested in May 1988 were convicted of unlawful assembly but not imprisoned. In November eight chiefs from the island of Rotuma were found guilty of sedition and fined. The trial of 21 people detained in 1988 on suspicion of arms-smuggling was continuing at the end of the year, but treason charges against some of the defendants had been dropped.

There were numerous reports alleging torture and ill-treatment of criminal suspects. In January four men on trial for robbery testified that they had been assaulted in police custody and that their request for medical attention had been refused. One of the four appeared in court with blood stains on his shirt. While hearing this case, Chief Justice Apaitia Seru expressed concern about the frequency of "deliberate police assault" on suspects and called for an official inquiry. In September eight warders from Naboro Prison were convicted and sentenced to nine months' imprisonment for assaulting two escaped prisoners during their recapture in 1987 (see *Amnesty International Report 1988*). The judge reportedly described the assault as savage, brutal and "a flagrant violation of human rights". A prison official charged with murdering one of the escaped prisoners was acquitted.

Amnesty International wrote to the Fijian Government expressing concern about the detention of prisoners of conscience and the ill-treatment of both political detainees and criminal suspects. It urged the government to ensure that all detainees were humanely treated and that all reports of torture or ill-treatment were impartially investigated. The government replied in December saying that the allegations of torture and ill-treatment would be investigated by the Ministry of Justice.

FINLAND

Three conscientious objectors to military service began serving prison sentences; six others were released on completion of their sentences. All nine were considered prisoners of conscience.

In May Finland became the 23rd member state of the Council of Europe. On 5 May Finland signed the European Convention on Human Rights and its Protocol No. 6 concerning the abolition of the death penalty. It had not ratified these instruments by the end of the year. In August Finland ratified the United Nations Convention against Torture and Other Cruel, Inhuman or Degrading Treatment or Punishment.

Finnish law on unarmed and civilian service was last amended in 1987, extending the right to perform alternative civilian service to every applicant objecting to military conscription on ethical or religious grounds. However, the 1987 law also increased the length of alternative service from 12 to 16 months: twice as long as military service.

Three conscientious objectors began serving 12-month sentences in June: Karri Dyrendahl-Nyblin and Tomi Saarinen, both painters; and Juha Kanerva, a student. They had refused to perform alternative service partly on the grounds that the length was punitive.

Six conscientious objectors previously adopted as prisoners of conscience were released after serving their sentences: Markku Tattari in February, Jarmo Kaarlela in April, Raimo Rautiainen in June, Harri Mäkelä and Pekka Ylönen in July, and Jukka Seppälä in November (see *Amnesty International Report 1989*).

Amnesty International considered that because of its punitive length civilian service did not provide an acceptable alternative to military service and sought the release of conscientious objectors it considered prisoners of conscience.

FRANCE

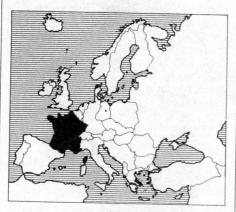

Hundreds of conscientious objectors to the national service laws, the vast majority of them Jehovah's Witnesses, were considered prisoners of conscience. There were several allegations of ill-treatment in police custody and reports that convicted criminals had been ill-treated in one prison.

A number of conscientious objectors benefited from a law introduced in July granting an amnesty to people who had failed to report for or deserted from national service before 22 May 1988. The amnesty also applied to certain politically motivated offences committed before 14 July 1988 by separatists in Corsica and the overseas departments of Guadeloupe and Martinique.

In December parliament adopted a law extending the scope of an amnesty, introduced in November 1988 as part of the Matignon Agreement on the future of the overseas territory of New Caledonia, to cover certain crimes of premeditated murder committed before 20 August 1988 (see *Amnesty International Report 1989*). The Ministry of Justice indicated that this would involve the halting of nine judicial proceedings. These included the cases of Kanak separatists accused of murdering four *gendarmes* in April 1988, an inquiry into allegations that members of the French security forces carried out extrajudicial executions of three Kanaks in Ouvéa in May 1988, and inquiries into the killing in previous years of important Kanak political activists (see *Amnesty International Reports 1987* to *1989*).

In January France ratified the European Convention for the Prevention of Torture and Inhuman or Degrading Treatment or Punishment.

Conscientious objectors who refused to conform to the national service laws continued to receive sentences of up to 15 months' imprisonment. Alternative civilian service is twice the length of ordinary military service. Amnesty International considers that it is therefore not an acceptable alternative and that those imprisoned for refusing to undertake it are prisoners of conscience.

Bruno Guilloré, a teacher, was granted conscientious objector status in 1983 but refused to carry out civilian service because, among other objections, he considered its length to be punitive. He was imprisoned in May 1989 when the Supreme Court confirmed a 12-month prison sentence which had been passed by lower courts in 1988. He was released in July under the provisions of the amnesty law.

At least two imprisoned conscientious objectors had been refused conscientious objector status because their applications had been made after their call-up orders were issued. Patrick Odent-Allet and Christophe Albouy were adopted as prisoners of conscience on the grounds that individuals should be able to seek conscientious objector status at any time.

Allegations of ill-treatment in police custody often concerned immigrants and French citizens of African origin. Lucien Djossouvi, from Benin, claimed that he was ill-treated by three plainclothes police officers on 5 September. One of them asked to see his identity papers, then insulted him and refused to show proof that he was a police officer. Lucien Djossouvi alleged that shortly afterwards the three officers handcuffed him and beat him to the ground with truncheons. They threw away his papers then dragged him to the entrance of a nearby building and beat him again. He was reportedly threatened with deportation if he made any official complaint and was then abandoned. He was admitted to hospital later that day to receive emergency treatment for serious head and facial injuries. On 12 September he made a judicial complaint, which was under investigation at the end of the year.

There were allegations that on 12 June prison guards ill-treated inmates of Clairvaux prison who had refused to leave

96

the exercise yard after three of them had reportedly attacked a guard. Eight prisoners claimed that, on returning to the prison building, they were stripped and hand-cuffed for body searches. They said they were then made to pass about 30 guards who beat them with fists and truncheons and, in some instances, threw them down a staircase. The prison doctor examined the eight prisoners within hours of the alleged incidents and issued medical certificates recording various cuts and bruises. One prisoner's relative obtained a copy of a cer-tificate describing a wound near the prison-er's left hip requiring three stitches, cuts and bruises to the head and face, and a pos-sible cracked rib. An administrative inquiry was immediately opened.

Amnesty International wrote to the Minister of Justice welcoming the admin-istrative inquiry into allegations of ill-treatment at Clairvaux prison. It asked to be informed of the inquiry's findings and of any disciplinary or judicial proceedings that might result. In September the Minister replied that a reasonable degree of force had been necessary to make a group of approximately 30 prisoners return to their cells and submit to body searches. The administrative inquiry had established that in eight cases "acts of violence were indeed committed...beyond the necessary use of force". In these cases, the injuries had been found to consist primarily of bruises arising from blows to the face or body. The Minister informed Amnesty International that at his request the Public Prosecutor of Troyes had opened a judicial inquiry. The administrative inquiry had failed to identify the guards responsible for the ill-treatment. According to press ar-ticles, apparently quoting the administra-tive inquiry's report, the guards were unwilling to incriminate each other and the prisoners were unwilling to identify the perpetrators "for reasons which are easy to understand". In December the Ministry of Justice informed Amnesty International that the Public Prosecutor of Troyes had carried out an inquiry to identify the perpe-trators of the ill-treatment but that this had also been unsuccessful.

Throughout the year Amnesty International appealed for the release of conscientious objectors considered to be prisoners of conscience.

GABON

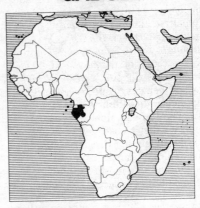

At least 20 people arrested in connection with an alleged plot against the govern-ment were still detained without charge or trial at the end of the year. Two others died in detention. Another government opponent was held for a few days in February and seven others were arrested in December. At least three people were sentenced to death, two of them in their absence, but no executions were reported.

At least 20 government employees and members of the security forces, together with two French nationals, were arrested in September and October and publicly accused by the government of conspiring to assassinate President Omar Bongo and overthrow the government. They included Commander Mathias Boussougou, head of the presidential guard, and Lieutenant-Colonel Georges Moubandjo. A government spokesperson claimed in November that the conspiracy had been planned by a gov-ernment opponent living in France, who had contacted members of the security forces in Libreville and sent the two French nationals to Gabon to examine ways of carrying out a coup. The spokesperson said that the basic rights of those in custody were being respected and that they would be brought to trial. However, no trial had started by the end of the year and it appeared that those arrested had not been formally charged. Furthermore, they had been denied access to visits by their relatives and legal counsel, and no information was available about their health or conditions of detention.

Two prisoners arrested in connection with the conspiracy died in custody. Both deaths were attributed to natural causes, but there was concern that the two may have been ill-treated or denied adequate medical treatment. Richard Anton, a French national, reportedly died from malaria in October. His relatives objected to an autopsy and independent confirmation of the cause of death was not available. Doukakas Nziengui, a director of a state-owned energy and water company, reportedly died from high blood pressure. His family was not represented at the autopsy: they subsequently challenged its findings, claiming that death had not been due to natural causes.

Antoine Meyo-Mendoutoume, an Air Gabon pilot, was arrested in February and held for six days by the national security service, *Centre de documentation* (CEDOC), Documentation Centre, apparently for being a member of the opposition *Mouvement de redressement national* (MORENA), Movement for National Recovery. He had been detained in 1987 for a similar reason. MORENA is an illegal organization: under the Constitution, Gabon is a one-party state ruled by the *Parti démocratique gabonais* (PDG), Gabonese Democratic Party. In November Louis Obame Biyoghe was detained for two days, apparently on suspicion of having links with MORENA. He was released uncharged but redetained in early December. At the end of December six other people suspected of distributing MORENA leaflets were arrested. All seven were still held without charge or trial at the end of the year.

Two Nigerian nationals were sentenced to death in their absence in June on charges of attempted murder. In addition, Théophile Mba-Ntem, a leading member of the religious cult *Alane Mvo'Ening*, was sentenced to death in November by Libreville High Court. He was convicted of murdering and eating the corpse of one of the cult's members and practising sorcery. No executions were reported.

Amnesty International called on the government to allow the prisoners held in connection with the conspiracy to receive visits by their relatives and legal counsel. The organization also appealed for the death sentence imposed in November to be commuted.

GERMAN DEMOCRATIC REPUBLIC

At the end of the year a new government announced its intention of revising the laws used to imprison prisoners of conscience. Two amnesties were declared under which any remaining prisoners of conscience should have been released. During most of the year thousands of prisoners of conscience were detained under laws greatly restricting freedom of expression, association, assembly and movement. Many of the prisoners were convicted in unfair trials. Detained demonstrators were ill-treated by the security forces.

Throughout the year increasingly large demonstrations took place on a variety of issues, such as restrictions on free expression, association, assembly and movement; the alleged falsification of election results; and allegations of official corruption.

A new Head of State, Egon Krenz, was appointed in October. The appointment occurred shortly after former head of state Erich Honecker resigned amid large-scale protests against government policies and a wave of emigration. Egon Krenz resigned on 6 December and Manfred Gerlach, leader of the Liberal Democratic Party, became acting Head of State.

On 27 October the Council of State declared an amnesty in which most non-violent political prisoners should have been released. A second amnesty was announced on 6 December. The amnesties and other measures suggested that any remaining prisoners of conscience would be released by the end of the year.

98

On 7 November the government resigned and a committee of the People's Chamber (parliament) rejected a draft law to ease foreign travel restrictions on the grounds that it failed to meet citizens' expectations. On 8 November the ruling Socialist Unity Party (SED) elected a new Politburo; on 9 November nearly all restrictions on foreign travel were lifted pending new foreign travel legislation. A new government was formed under Prime Minister Hans Modrow on 17 November. Announcements of this government included a plan to prepare new laws on foreign travel and freedom of association and assembly, and to provide a civilian alternative to military service. On 1 December the Interior Minister submitted to the People's Chamber a revised draft law which would grant every citizen of the German Democratic Republic (GDR) the right to travel abroad at any time without an exit visa. The draft was referred to parliamentary committees for further discussion. On 5 December a Justice Ministry spokesperson announced that the Penal Code and Code of Penal Procedure would be revised to conform to international instruments ratified by the GDR and to decriminalize non-violent political activity.

On 3 December the SED Politburo and Central Committee resigned. By 9 December an Extraordinary Congress of the SED had elected Gregor Gysi, the Chairman of the GDR Council of Lawyers' Associations, as its new leader. In the past Gregor Gysi had acted as defence counsel in some political trials.

Before the events of October and November, it was impossible in practice to gain official approval for associations and demonstrations opposing government policy. Afterwards, unofficial demonstrations were allowed and at least one hitherto unofficial political association, New Forum, received official recognition.

At least 232 prisoners of conscience or possible prisoners of conscience, including 102 convicted in 1989, served sentences during the year. Information about individual prisoners was restricted by the secrecy which surrounded political imprisonment and the real number of convicted prisoners of conscience was probably much higher. No convictions of prisoners of conscience were reported after the October amnesty.

As in previous years restrictions on freedom of movement were a major factor contributing to the convictions of prisoners of conscience. For example, Thomas Schütt was detained in March and sentenced to 30 months' imprisonment under Article 219 of the Penal Code for "making illegal contacts" and under Article 100 for "treasonable activity as an agent". In August 1988 he reportedly applied to emigrate. The authorities rejected his application and he filed an objection. When this was overruled, he protested again. In February 1989 he approached a member of a government delegation from the Federal Republic of Germany, seeking help to emigrate. Articles 219 and 100 were frequently used against would-be emigrants who turned to individuals or organizations outside the GDR for help. Thomas Schütt was released in November, following the October amnesty.

Throughout the year thousands of peaceful demonstrators were detained for supporting views contrary to official policies. Although the vast majority were released within 24 hours, some peaceful demonstrators were sentenced to prison terms and some were sentenced without trial. On 11 September, for example, the police reportedly detained more than 100 people who had gathered for a "Service for Peace" at St Nicholas Church in Leipzig. Although most were released within 24 hours, at least 16 demonstrators received prison sentences of between four and six months for "riotous assembly" (Article 217 of the Penal Code). Article 270 of the Code of Penal Procedure empowers judges to impose such sentences without trial if the accused pleads guilty. No evidence suggested that any of the 16 had advocated violence: all 16 were released on 13 October.

Unofficial demonstrations took place in several cities on the weekend beginning 7 October, the 40th anniversary of the founding of the GDR. According to an 18 November report by the General State Procurator, 3,456 demonstrators and bystanders were detained and all but those suspected of using violence were released by 15 October. The Berlin Police stated that on 13 October no demonstrators detained in Berlin remained in custody. On 17 October the General State Procurator said that only 11 people in the GDR continued to be held on suspicion of having committed violent acts during demonstrations. Therefore, the overwhelming majority of demonstrators arrested between 7 and 8

October were detained for exercising non-violently their right to free expression and assembly.

In November the General State Procurator informed a meeting of the SED Central Committee: "During the events surrounding 7 October, the security forces used excessive force.... Individuals were beaten [on arrest and while in custody], made to stand for long periods, sometimes in physically painful positions, and also subjected to degrading treatment." He informed the People's Chamber on 18 November that of the complaints received, 480 indicated that security forces may have committed criminal offences in their treatment of demonstrators and bystanders. He said 76 investigations had begun and four indictments had been prepared. One indicted police officer was sentenced by a Berlin court on 24 November to 14 months' imprisonment for pushing a detained demonstrator down a flight of stairs. On 21 December the Berlin Municipal Court which heard the police officer's appeal sent the case back for retrial, requesting clarification of whether the police officer had acted deliberately or negligently.

Before the events of October reports continued to indicate secret and summary proceedings in political cases. Political trials were routinely conducted *in camera*, with defendants' families and friends excluded and access to a lawyer severely restricted. Sylke Glaser, for example, was tried *in camera* and sentenced in June 1988 to 15 months' imprisonment by a court in Rostock. She had been convicted of "public vilification" under Article 220 of the Penal Code after distributing leaflets calling on participants in the official May Day demonstrations to reject official slogans and to write their own. She reported that she was allowed to look at relevant legal provisions for only 15 minutes and to speak to her lawyer for only 15 minutes before her trial. She served six months of her sentence.

During the year Amnesty International worked for the release of all detainees whom it could identify as prisoners of conscience and sought information from the authorities on others whom it believed might be prisoners of conscience.

In January Amnesty International published *GDR: Sweeping Laws — Secret Justice*, a report detailing its concerns in recent years. The concerns included the imprisonment of prisoners of conscience, laws used to imprison them and the secrecy surrounding political imprisonment.

In April and June Amnesty International submitted information about its concerns in the GDR for United Nations review under a procedure, established by Economic and Social Council Resolutions 728F/1503, for confidential consideration of communications about human rights violations.

In November Amnesty International wrote to Head of State Egon Krenz and to the GDR Ambassador in London to welcome the October amnesty and the lifting of restrictions on freedom of movement. It urged revision of the Penal Code articles used to imprison prisoners of conscience, in conformity with the GDR's obligations under the International Covenant on Civil and Political Rights, and requested the results of inquiries into allegations that security forces ill-treated detainees.

GERMANY, FEDERAL REPUBLIC OF

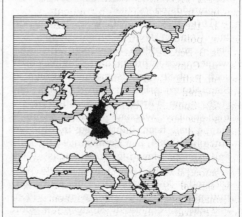

Prisoners detained under anti-terrorist legislation continued to be held in isolation. Allegations of gratuitous strip-searching of such prisoners were also received.

In July the FRG ratified Protocol No. 6 to the European Convention on Human Rights (concerning the abolition of the death penalty).

Prolonged isolation can have serious physical and psychological effects on prisoners and may constitute cruel, inhuman or degrading treatment. The authorities claimed that prisoners held in isolation under anti-terrorist legislation were in self-

AMNESTY INTERNATIONAL REPORT 1990

100

imposed isolation because they refused to be included in the general prison population and wished only to be accommodated with like-minded prisoners. The prisoners argued that the conditions attached by the authorities to association with other (non-political) prisoners were too onerous, for them and for the other prisoners. They also argued that political prisoners should be accommodated together. Most prisoners detained under anti-terrorist legislation (mainly Article 129a of the Penal Code) were not allowed to associate with each other.

In February 45 such prisoners, mainly members of the Red Army Faction (RAF) or its sympathizers, began a hunger-strike throughout the country. One of their demands was that the prisoners should be accommodated together in one or two large groups. The hunger-strike ended in May.

In November Alfred Herrhausen, the President of the Deutsche Bank, was killed by a bomb. In a letter claiming responsibility for the attack, members of the RAF demanded *inter alia* that prisoners held under anti-terrorist legislation should be accommodated together.

Three prisoners who were held in virtual isolation were Manuela Happe, Eva Haule and Andrea Sievering. The three women were imprisoned in a high-security section of Stuttgart (sometimes known as Stammheim) prison, a men's prison. The state, Baden-Württemberg, does not have a high-security women's prison. Manuela Happe had been imprisoned in Stuttgart since June 1984, Eva Haule since July 1987 and Andrea Sievering since August 1988. They were not allowed to associate with each other and reportedly only had intermittent contact with other women prisoners who were held in Stuttgart for short periods pending transfer to other prisons. The number of other women held in the prison was said to vary between one and nine. At the end of the year Manuela Happe and Eva Haule were transferred to prisons in other states.

One reason given by prisoners held under anti-terrorist legislation for refusing to associate with other prisoners was that this would involve repeated and gratuitous strip-searching. Amnesty International objects to strip-searching if it is undertaken with the deliberate intention of degrading or humiliating the prisoner.

In March Stuttgart regional court lifted a long-standing requirement that Christian Klar, detained under Article 129a in Stuttgart, be strip-searched before and after contact with other prisoners. The court stated that other less intrusive means of security control were available, such as frisking or the use of a metal detector. As such methods of security control had been available for a number of years, the court's decision raised questions about the claim by the federal and state authorities that strip-searching was conducted solely for security purposes without any intent to degrade or humiliate.

Prisoners held under anti-terrorist legislation complained that the prison authorities increased their isolation by means such as conspicuously noting down which non-political prisoners associated regularly with them, and by warning non-political prisoners that they would suffer if they had too much contact with prisoners held for terrorist offences.

During the year Amnesty International had extensive contact and correspondence with the authorities on the issue of isolation. In April, during meetings with a representative of Amnesty International, officials from the Baden-Württemberg and Bavarian Ministries of Justice denied that special note was made of contacts between prisoners held under Article 129a and other prisoners. They also denied that any prisoner would be disadvantaged in any way as a result of such contact. The Baden-Württemberg officials said that they expressly welcomed such contact and that any special measures were for security reasons only. At the end of the year the Baden-Württemberg Justice Ministry stated that Manuela Happe and Eva Haule had been transferred because Stuttgart prison was not suitable for the long-term detention of women prisoners.

In its letters Amnesty International said that, in most cases, it was not in a position to assess the conflicting claims as to whether the isolation of prisoners held under anti-terrorist legislation was voluntary or involuntary, or the extent to which the conditions attached to association with other prisoners were justified on security grounds. However, the organization believed that the evidence required it to take seriously allegations that offers of increased contact with other prisoners were accompanied by unreasonable conditions. Amnesty International called for prisoners deemed to warrant stringent security measures to be transferred to prisons where the security arrangements would allow them to associate more freely and permanently with other prisoners. At the end of the year the correspondence was continuing.

In February the West Berlin Interior Minister replied to Amnesty International's letter of December 1988 which had expressed concern over arrests and reported ill-treatment of demonstrators and bystanders during the anti-IMF/World Bank protests in September 1988 (see *Amnesty International Report 1989*). The Interior Minister said that Amnesty International's concerns were unfounded. In February the organization published its concerns and the Interior Minister's reply in a document entitled *West Berlin: The anti-IMF/World Bank Protests.*

GHANA

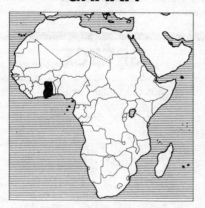

Two prisoners of conscience were released and two others briefly detained without charge or trial. At least 50 political detainees, mostly military personnel arrested following alleged coup attempts between 1982 and 1985, continued to be held without charge or trial throughout the year. At least seven other members of the security forces were detained without charge on suspicion of conspiring to overthrow the government: one committed suicide in detention, according to the authorities. At least 11 death sentences were passed but no executions were known to have been carried out.

Akwasi Adu-Amankwah, a Trades Union Congress official, and Yaw Tony Akoto-Ampaw, a former student leader, were released in May. Leading members of the New Democratic Movement, they had been held without charge or trial since 1987 when they were among at least eight prisoners of conscience who were detained. The others were freed before the end of 1988.

In June two leading officials of the Ghana Bar Association, Peter Adjetey and Nutifafa Kuenyehia, were arrested and held without charge for two and three weeks respectively. A Supreme Court judge was also reportedly held for a few hours. The Ghana Bar Association had planned to hold lectures to commemorate the murder of three judges in June 1982. The murders remain a sensitive subject with the military government, the Provisional National Defence Council (PNDC), headed by Flight-Lieutenant J.J. Rawlings. An inquiry recommended that 10 people be prosecuted for the crime: several were, but two members of the PNDC among the 10, including the head of the security services, were not charged or brought to trial (see *Amnesty International Report 1984*).

In early October the government announced that five members of the security forces had been detained following allegations that they had "compromised" the security of the state. Despite persistent rumours that one of the detainees was already dead, possibly as a result of torture, no mention was made of any death in the announcement. A further official statement in November said that one of the detainees, Flight-Lieutenant William Kofi Domie, had hanged himself on 29 September after confessing to an active role in a conspiracy to overthrow the government. It also said that a pathologist's report and an inquiry by senior armed forces and police officers had "confirmed that he had taken his life". The statement did not indicate whether there was to be an inquest into the circumstances of his death or the reasons why he might have committed suicide.

The November statement summarized the findings of an inquiry by military and security officers into the alleged conspiracy and revealed that at least seven members of the security forces had been detained, one of whom had subsequently been released for lack of evidence. According to the statement, one of the leaders of the alleged conspiracy, Major Courage E.K. Quarshigah, told the inquiry that Flight-Lieutenant

AMNESTY INTERNATIONAL REPORT 1990

102

Domie had appeared to be mentally unstable. None of the detainees had been charged with any offence or released by the end of the year.

There have been several attempts to overthrow the PNDC, which itself seized power in a coup in 1981. In 1989 at least 50 people, mostly members of the armed forces arrested in previous years following alleged coup attempts or conspiracies against the government, remained in detention without charge or trial. They were reported to include Warrant Officer Joseph Mensah, said to be suspected of involvement in a coup attempt in June 1983; Sergeant George Aza Adongo and Corporal Abraham Kweku Botchwey, allegedly involved in a coup attempt in February 1985; and Lieutenant-Colonel Thomas Theophilus Kutin, held since 1986 apparently on suspicion of involvement in a conspiracy against the government. Others reported to be held without charge or trial for political reasons included Narh Tetteh, who was detained in 1983 or 1984; George Darkoh, who was detained in 1984; and Martin Kwaku Ababio Owusu, a naval seaman held since 1985.

None of those detained for political reasons during the year was charged with any offence or brought to trial. The Preventive Custody Law, PNDC Law 4 of 1982, provides for the administrative detention without trial of any person suspected of threatening the security of the state. There has been no legal recourse against such detentions since the right to *habeas corpus* in these cases was removed in 1984.

Although no executions were known to have taken place during the year, 11 people were sentenced to death, one of them *in absentia*, following convictions for murder and armed robbery. Most had been convicted by Public Tribunals — special courts which may impose death sentences for offences including those which in law do not carry the death penalty, such as armed robbery. Under the Public Tribunal Law, PNDC Law 24 of 1982, a Public Tribunal may impose the death sentence for any crime specified a capital offence by the PNDC or if the court considers that it is merited in a particular case. The offence of robbery, defined as stealing with force or threat of force, carries a maximum sentence of life imprisonment under the amended Criminal Code of 1960. However, more

than 20 prisoners are believed to have been executed for robbery since 1982.

During 1989 Amnesty International pressed for the release of the two New Democratic Movement leaders and the Ghana Bar Association officials, and urged the government to ensure that all other political detainees were either brought to trial promptly and fairly, or released. The organization appealed for those arrested on suspicion of threatening state security to be safeguarded against ill-treatment while in detention and inquired into the circumstances of Flight-Lieutenant Domie's death. Amnesty International also appealed for the abolition of the death penalty and for the commutation of individual death sentences. In September the government denied an Amnesty International staff member a visa to visit Ghana for research. A government-owned newspaper subsequently accused the organization of conspiring with the Ghana Bar Association to destabilize the government, an allegation which Amnesty International totally rejected.

GREECE

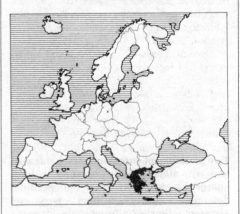

Some 400 prisoners of conscience, all conscientious objectors to military service, were in prison. The vast majority of them were Jehovah's Witnesses. Most were serving sentences of four years' imprisonment. Several detainees alleged they had been ill-treated in police custody.

A draft law drawn up in 1988, providing for an alternative civilian service double the length of military service, had still not been debated in parliament by the end of the year (see *Amnesty International*

Report 1989).

The majority of conscientious objectors continued to be sentenced to four-year prison terms. However, about 50 were serving sentences of up to five years' imprisonment.

Three conscientious objectors who had been sentenced in October 1988 to longer terms of imprisonment — two to 12 years and one to 13 years — had their sentences reduced to four years' imprisonment on appeal in February (see *Amnesty International Report 1989*).

Thanasis Makris, who had refused to perform military service on non-religious pacifist grounds, was sentenced in January to a further four months' imprisonment on charges of insulting a prison officer. In July he was released after serving 15 months of his 22-month sentence (see *Amnesty International Report 1989*).

One conscientious objector, Daniel Kokkalis, recognized by the Ministry for the Interior as a religious minister for Jehovah's Witnesses, was sentenced to four years' imprisonment in July despite the existence of Law 1763/88 exempting religious ministers and monks of a "known religion" from performing military service. In October his appeal against this sentence was rejected on the grounds that the Jehovah's Witness faith was not a "known religion".

Several detainees alleged that they had been ill-treated in police custody. For example Dimitris Voglis said that in May he had been beaten on the street by police after challenging them for assaulting an unconscious man. He was then taken to the Third Police Station in Thessaloniki where the police continued to beat him. Dimitris Voglis alleged that the police used wooden batons. A medical report certified bruising on various parts of his body, including the face and head. An investigation was ordered by the Public Prosecutor.

In November Amnesty International wrote to President Christos Sartzetakis requesting to be informed of the outcome of the investigation into Dimitris Voglis' allegations of ill-treatment. A response to letters concerning torture and ill-treatment sent to the authorities in previous years was also requested. By the end of the year no reply had been received.

Throughout the year Amnesty International appealed for the release of all imprisoned conscientious objectors. The organization urged the government to introduce alternative civilian service and to amend the draft law so that alternative service would not be of punitive length.

GRENADA

The Grenada Court of Appeal continued hearing the case of 17 former members of the People's Revolutionary Government (PRG), convicted in 1986 for the 1983 murders of Prime Minister Maurice Bishop and others. Fourteen of the defendants had been sentenced to death (see *Amnesty International Report 1987*). A total of 22 people were under sentence of death at the end of the year, but no executions had been carried out since 1978.

Prime Minister Herbert Blaize died on 19 December. The Governor General appointed Deputy Prime Minister Ben Jones in his place and a general election was due to take place by March 1990.

An inquiry by the Prison Department into allegations that prisoners had been ill-treated in 1988 found that "the degree of restraint by prison staff was consistent with the defiance and resistance offered by the prisoners". Some of the imprisoned former PRG members alleged that guards had severely beaten them at Richmond Hill Prison in November 1988. The incident occurred after one of the prisoners, Leon Cornwall, protested that he had been denied a bath and change of clothes for several weeks (see *Amnesty International Report 1989*). According to the inquiry findings, guards had restrained prisoners who wilfully disobeyed an order, defied prison staff and struggled with officers. The inquiry found no evidence to support Leon Cornwall's claims, and stated that the injury he suffered was "minimal" and consistent with the inquiry's conclusion that there had been a struggle.

104

The officers accused of ill-treatment belonged to the same agency that conducted the inquiry. The report of the inquiry did not indicate the composition, terms of reference or procedures of the investigating body. It also failed to indicate who had been interviewed and whether evidence was obtained from both prisoners and prison officers. It gave no details of the circumstances in which force was used, the number of officers involved, the nature of force used, the injuries found or the treatment given for injuries.

In November and December an Amnesty International delegate observed part of the appeal proceedings in the Maurice Bishop murder case.

GUATEMALA

The security forces and the "death squads" linked to them were reportedly implicated in hundreds of extrajudicial executions and "disappearances". When bodies were found they often bore marks of torture. People detained for short periods and the few survivors of unacknowledged kidnap-style arrests also reported having been tortured. Scores of real or suspected government opponents faced harassment and assault by the security forces, acting clandestinely or in uniform.

In most cases known to Amnesty International in recent years, real or suspected government opponents were not imprisoned: they "disappeared" or were extrajudicially executed. However, in August at least 60 teachers and 10 students were detained for short periods in connection with a strike by teachers. Some reported being ill-treated in custody. In October two former military officers were sentenced to seven years' imprisonment for their part in an attempted coup in May. Ordinary criminal prisoners protested that condi-

tions in Guatemala's largest prison were severely sub-standard.

Reports of human rights violations escalated sharply in 1989, having initially decreased after President Vinicio Cerezo came to office in 1986 (see *Amnesty International Report 1989*). Most violations were reported in the context of the ongoing guerrilla insurgency in a number of departments. The government attributed responsibility to forces they claimed were beyond their control, citing the military factions responsible for several attempted coups or the armed opposition. The abuses were frequently carried out by heavily armed men in plain clothes who used unlicensed vehicles with darkened windows, making attribution difficult. In many cases, however, there was evidence of official complicity. The choice of victims (often government opponents and dissidents or their families), the information to which their assailants had access, the armaments and vehicles used, and the fact that some of the victims were assaulted and seized in full view of uniformed security force personnel, all suggested that those responsible were serving members of the security forces, acting as "death squads". Amnesties declared immediately before and during President Cerezo's administration effectively granted immunity from prosecution to perpetrators of human rights violations under previous military governments. This created a climate conducive to further violations.

The consultative process known as the *Diálogo Nacional,* National Dialogue, which was set up under the terms of the 1987 Central American Peace Agreement, seemed to have little effect on the resurgence of human rights violations. A number of non-governmental participants in the dialogue were themselves the victims of abuses in 1989. Marcos Juan Baltazar, representing Guatemala's displaced people in the National Dialogue, was killed in August in circumstances suggesting that the official security forces were responsible. Exiled opposition leaders who had returned to participate in the dialogue left the country in May after repeatedly receiving anonymous death threats.

On 2 July men in plain clothes abducted José Rolando Pantaleón, a member of trade union theatre and music groups at the Guatemala City Coca-Cola bottling plant. His tortured body was found hours later.

Government authorities maintained that he was murdered for private motives. However, he and other theatre group members had been repeatedly threatened by heavily armed men in plain clothes after the group staged a satirical play lampooning the military. In February his brother had been shot and wounded by gunmen as police stood by.

Between 9 August and 11 September at least 12 students, all either former or current student leaders at the state University of San Carlos (USAC), a long-term target of human rights violations, were abducted, tortured, and either "disappeared" or were extrajudicially executed. They included Victor Hugo Rodríguez Jaramillo and his wife Silvia María Azurdia Utrera, abducted in Guatemala City in view of passing police cars on 23 August. The witnesses said the abductors' cars had been parked outside the couple's home for several hours, with heavily armed men clearly visible inside, but police nearby had made no effort to question them. The victims' car was seen later that morning outside a police station. The police first denied a car had been parked there, then claimed that it had been another, identical car. The couple's bodies were found on 10 September near the university, with those of two former USAC leaders abducted earlier. One of the latter, Carlos Humberto Cabrera Rivera, had returned from exile in 1986 and was in the leadership of the teachers' strike. All bore marks of torture. The tortured bodies of three more missing students were recovered later. Five remained missing, two of whom had been named on "death squad" death lists in a leaflet bomb which exploded at the university in February. Those named were warned to cease "subversive intervention" and abandon leadership of the USAC students' association. Government officials variously attributed responsibility to factional fighting in the student association, "terrorists", and "crazy members of the far right working in league with army dissidents".

Leaders and members of the *Consejo de Comunidades Etnicas*, "*Runujel Junam*" (CERJ), Council of Indigenous Communities "We are all Equal", "disappeared" and were threatened, intimidated and extrajudicially executed. CERJ was formed in 1988 to campaign for the human rights of Guatemala's indigenous peoples. In April four peasants, Luis Ruiz, Macario Pu Chivalán, Agapito Pérez and Nicolás Mateo, "disappeared" after being abducted from an estate in Suchitepéquez department by soldiers. Before the peasants "disappeared" the army had organized national press conferences at which they produced people they described as guerrilla defectors who accused CERJ of links with the armed opposition. Videos of the statements were then shown throughout the areas where CERJ is active and the army warned Indian villagers that they would be killed unless they denounced CERJ organizers. In May President Cerezo met CERJ President Amílcar Méndez Urízar concerning the four abducted in April. The President promised a response within the month but it had not been received by the year's end. Amílcar Méndez had received repeated death threats, some delivered anonymously, others made by army personnel.

Leaders and members of the *Grupo de Apoyo Mutuo* (GAM), Mutual Support Group — the relatives' group campaigning for information about the "disappeared" — were reportedly harassed and threatened by the military both in the capital and in departments where GAM was pressing for exhumation of victims of extrajudicial executions. One GAM member was abducted and murdered in July. In August heavily armed men in plain clothes seized another GAM member, who remained "disappeared". Also in August the group's headquarters were bombed.

Diana Ortiz, a United States (US) Ursuline nun, was one of the few survivors of abduction in recent years. She was seized on 2 November by men in plain clothes, after receiving death threats apparently related to her work with Indian children in Huehuetenango department. She later stated that she was handed over to uniformed police officers driving an official police car. She said they blindfolded her and took her to a warehouse, where she was asked to identify photographs of people she did not know, and then sexually abused, beaten and burned with cigarette butts by three interrogators. A fourth man arrived, said that the television news had identified her as North American and that her captors had made a "stupid mistake", and returned her to Guatemala City.

In August Maritza Hurtarte Guillén de Ruiz reportedly suffered a fractured vertebra after being beaten by the police while in short-term detention in the Antigua

106

Guatemala prison. She had been arrested on a demonstration in support of the teachers' strike. Other demonstrators were threatened, beaten and fired upon by police and military units.

In March prisoners took control of Guatemala's largest prison, Pavón, for four days in protest at alleged brutal treatment by prison guards, severe overcrowding, and inadequate sanitation and nutrition. The rebels seized warders' weapons and took over 500 hostages including children. Some 12 people were reportedly killed in crossfire during the takeover and 50 to 60 were injured, but the incident ended without further casualties when the government agreed that no reprisals would be taken against the rebels. However, in April it was reported that inmate Juan Carlos Tejeda Tórtola was beaten and deprived of food and water because of his leading role in the rebellion.

The government has periodically announced the formation of human rights investigatory bodies but these appear to have made little progress in investigating abuses; some apparently never began to function. New initiatives were often announced immediately before international bodies, such as the United Nations Commission on Human Rights (UNCHR), were to consider Guatemala's human rights record, or when President Cerezo faced national pressure on human rights issues. In October Gonzalo Menéndez de la Riva, who had been appointed to the constitutionally established office of Human Rights Attorney in August 1987, resigned, giving ill health as the reason. However, the Guatemalan press reported that he resigned because the Human Rights Attorney's office was ineffective.

The police and judiciary appeared unwilling or unable to investigate abuses and bring the perpetrators to justice, particularly when the military were implicated. In the few cases where inquiries were announced, the investigations foundered when evidence pointed to army involvement (see *Amnesty International Report 1989*). In other cases, families of the dead and "disappeared" were either too frightened to seek redress or were offered bribes by the security forces to abandon their efforts.

The case of student Luis Fernando de la Roca Elías, who "disappeared" in 1985, remained closed despite admissions by Guatemalan officials that evidence pointed clearly to military responsibility. Inquiries into the 1988 "death van" murder and "disappearance" cases also appeared to have stalled although the Treasury Police agents initially arrested for the abuses had alleged that the military were responsible. There was apparently no official effort to determine how extrajudicial execution victims exhumed in 1988 had died (see *Amnesty International Report 1989*). Similarly, no information was available regarding the investigation which San Marcos departmental police claimed had been undertaken into the "disappearance" of local social democratic leader Eladio Ambrosio, abducted in Tres Cruces on 16 June by men in plain clothes. His son pursued the car to a military base, but the commander denied Eladio Ambrosio was there. Local residents told foreign human rights workers investigating the case that five other people had been abducted from Tres Cruces since 1984, apparently by the military, but that families had been too frightened to report these "disappearances".

Six police officers sentenced to 30 years' imprisonment in 1988 for the murder of two USAC student leaders in Quetzaltenango the previous year continued to appeal against their convictions, charging that their claims that members of the Quetzaltenango military brigade were involved had not been investigated. Journalists and human rights investigators were denied access to the police officers. It was also reported that the six had offered the victims' families payments to drop the case.

There was continuing controversy over the highly publicized killing of 22 peasants in November 1988 in El Aguacate, Chimaltenango department. In December 1988 the Guatemalan Government flew two villagers to the United States of America (USA) where they declared at press conferences and public meetings that the armed opposition had carried out the killings. However, evidence compiled by Guatemalan and international human rights groups suggested that their testimony was false and that the army was responsible for the killings and had intimidated genuine witnesses. In January Assistant Human Rights Attorney Arturo Martínez Gálvez resigned, saying information about the case had been withheld from the Human Rights Attorney. In June the Human

Rights Attorney's office said inquiries had been hampered by lack of cooperation from the Attorney General and the judge handling the case. The same month Alberto Callejas, the father of one of the villagers taken to the USA, "disappeared". He had reportedly told human rights investigators that the military had coerced his son into giving false testimony and that they both believed the army had killed the villagers. Days later the military arrested another peasant and brought him before local villagers to confess that he was a member of an armed opposition group responsible for both the killings and the "disappearance" of Alberto Callejas. His family insisted that he had confessed after being drugged and beaten. Charges relating to the "disappearance" were later dropped, and he was sentenced to two years' imprisonment for stealing a weapon.

Amnesty International repeatedly asked the government to investigate reported abuses. Official human rights bodies replied that the government was committed to protecting human rights and that official agents were not responsible for the abuses. In April Amnesty International detailed its concerns in a memorandum to the government. No response was received, and in June the organization published *Guatemala: Human Rights Violations under the Civilian Government*, which launched an international action to press the government to take urgent steps to reverse the rapidly deteriorating human rights situation. In July the government gave Amnesty International materials described as the results of official inquiries into cases of "disappearances" and feared extrajudicial executions that the organization had raised, the first case-specific response Amnesty International had received from Guatemala since it began raising cases with the authorities in the 1960s. However, in many cases there was insufficient information to confirm the government's claim that a "disappeared" person had reappeared; in other cases the government's information clearly referred to people other than those on whose behalf Amnesty International had appealed.

In August the President of Congress and a member of Guatemala's Congressional Human Rights Commission met Amnesty International in London to discuss the organization's human rights concerns in Guatemala. In an oral statement delivered in February to the UNCHR, Amnesty International included reference to the Guatemalan authorities' failure to investigate effectively reported cases of "disappearances" and extrajudicial executions. In August the organization drew attention to abuses directed at Guatemala's indigenous people, particularly CERJ members, in an oral statement to the UN Sub-Commission on Prevention of Discrimination and Protection of Minorities.

GUINEA

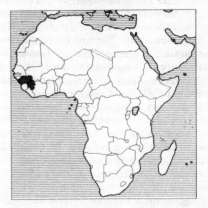

At least six suspected opponents of the government were arrested, all of whom appeared to be prisoners of conscience. They were reportedly tortured. Five were released in December; the sixth was still held at the end of the year. No new information was received about people arrested in October 1988, and the fate of 63 prisoners convicted in 1986 also remained unclear. One death occurred apparently under torture in police custody and several people were shot dead during a subsequent protest.

In October President Lansana Conté announced government plans for political change and a transfer of power from the military to a civilian government. He said that two political parties would be allowed and that these would compete for national assembly and presidential elections by 1994. The government appointed a commission to draft a new constitution, which was to provide for a clear separation of executive, judicial and legislative powers, and for the existence of a one-chamber national assembly. Although no political parties were specifically banned in 1989, in

108

practice the suspension of the constitution in 1984 was interpreted to mean that party politics were prohibited: supporters of the *Rassemblement du peuple guinéen* (RPG), Guinean People's Organization, were arrested.

In October Guinea ratified the United Nations Convention against Torture and Other Cruel, Inhuman or Degrading Treatment or Punishment.

Mohamed Ali Bangoura, a newspaper distributor, was arrested in November on suspicion of being a member of the RPG. Police had found a copy of *Malanyi* (Unity), an RPG newspaper, in his possession. At least five other suspected RPG members were subsequently detained in Conakry, including Bernard Bangoura, who worked at Pharmaguinée, a state-owned distributor of medicines, and Hassane François Bangoura, a lecturer at Conakry University. All those detained were reportedly tortured. All but one of the detainees were released in December after being held in police custody without charge or trial and without being referred to a judicial authority. Mohamed Ali Bangoura was believed to be still held at the end of the year.

At the end of October, 17-year-old Issaka Condé, known as "Memba", died in police custody at Labé, apparently as a result of torture. He had been arrested for damaging the headlamp of a motorcycle. Soon after he died, his relatives and other protesters were involved in a violent demonstration at the police station. Army troops called in to restore order opened fire on the demonstrators, reportedly killing six. Government officials from Conakry were sent to Labé, but it was not clear if they were to carry out an investigation into the circumstances of Issaka Condé's death or the subsequent killings.

No new information was received about Kabinet Kaba and others arrested in Conakry and the Kankan area in October 1988 after an incident during independence day celebrations (see *Amnesty International Report 1989*). Some were reported to be still imprisoned at the beginning of the year, but it was not known if they were subsequently released. The fate and whereabouts of 63 people convicted in secret and unfair trials in 1986 also remained unclear. In 1988, the government said they were no longer imprisoned, but it was not known at the end of 1989 whether they had been released (see *Amnesty International Report 1989*). There were consistent reports that a number of them had been executed secretly. Others were said to have died in custody, including Major Abraham Kabassan Keïta, a former government minister, and El Hadj Sory Sidibé, a relative of the former head of state, Ahmed Sékou Touré.

Amnesty International expressed concern to the government about the arrest of Mohamed Ali Bangoura and other suspected RPG supporters as possible prisoners of conscience and urged that they be charged and promptly tried for a recognizably criminal offence, or released. Government officials denied the arrests of the six men and said they were unknown to the prison authorities: they claimed that there had been no political prisoners in Guinea since 1985. The organization also made inquiries about prisoners arrested in October 1988, but received no response. Amnesty International urged the authorities to set up a full judicial inquiry to investigate the circumstances in which a prisoner and others had died in Labé in October.

GUINEA-BISSAU

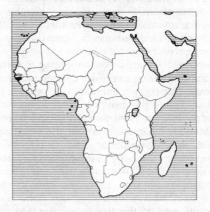

Eight political prisoners sentenced after an unfair trial in July 1986 were released in November but 24 others convicted in the same trial were still held at the end of the year. Some reports suggested that 11 other political prisoners might still be held despite completing their sentences.

Thirty-two prisoners convicted of plotting against the government were still held at the beginning of the year, serving sentences of between six and 15 years' imprisonment. They had been sentenced after an unfair trial before the Higher Military Court in July 1986: the court reportedly admitted as evidence statements which had been made under duress while the defendants were held in pre-trial custody. The defendants were also denied proper access to defence counsel (see *Amnesty International Report 1989*). In November, eight of these prisoners were released and 11 others had their sentences halved by the Higher Military Court. Those freed included Tué Nam Bagna, an army officer, who had been serving an eight-year sentence. He was reported to have been severely tortured following his arrest in October 1985 and forced to make a confession which was broadcast over the national radio a few weeks later, before he and his co-defendants were brought to trial.

The 11 whose sentences were reduced were all serving 12 or 13-year prison terms. They included Raul Tcham Namã, a military doctor, sentenced to 12 years' imprisonment in connection with an alleged plot to free detainees arrested in 1985 after he learned that one had died in custody. In all, six of those arrested as suspects in the alleged plot against the government died in custody between November 1985 and July 1986 (see *Amnesty International Reports 1987* to *1989*).

Reports received in 1989 suggested that 11 of the defendants at the July 1986 trial were still being held although they had been due for release: some had completed their sentences and the release of four of them had been announced by the government in December 1988 to mark the 40th anniversary of the Universal Declaration of Human Rights. Amnesty International sought clarification of these reports from the government of President João Bernardo Vieira but had not received a response by the end of the year.

The 24 prisoners still known to be held at the end of the year were restricted to islands in the Bijagos Archipelago, where they were required to undertake agricultural work. Although their families were permitted to live with them or visit them, transport difficulties and the scarcity of food and medical supplies made this difficult in practice.

Amnesty International continued to investigate the cases of some of those sentenced as a result of the July 1986 trial as they appeared possibly to have been imprisoned because of their association with leaders of the alleged conspiracy against the government rather than because of any real involvement in a plot.

GUYANA

Over 200 strike supporters were arrested during peaceful demonstrations or activities. Three people were awaiting trial at the end of the year charged with treason, which carries a mandatory death sentence. One execution was carried out and at least two people were sentenced to hang for murder. A bill was passed extending the use of the death penalty to some drug offences.

The imposition of stringent economic measures resulted in a strike by workers in the sugar and bauxite industries, Guyana's main sources of income. The strike started in April and lasted for over a month. More than 200 people were arrested during peaceful demonstrations in support of the strike or while involved in strike-relief activities. They were held for up to a few days and released without charges. During the strike there were acts of violence and arson, which the government attributed to two opposition parties — the People's Progressive Party (PPP) and the Working People's Alliance (WPA). Both organizations denied the allegation.

Bhoj Pertab Singh, Karran Persaud Deokarran and Neville Wordsworth, all PPP activists, were arrested by uniformed and plainclothes police officers between 3am and 4am on 28 April at their homes, according to eye-witnesses. They were held in unacknowledged detention for nearly eight days. They were not allowed to see

110 lawyers until 5 May and did not appear before a magistrate until 9 May. They were charged with treason for allegedly conspiring to overthrow the government. Their lawyers claimed at pre-trial proceedings that alleged confession statements taken during their unacknowledged detention had been obtained through police torture and inhuman treatment. Karran Deokarran collapsed in court on 1 August during pre-trial proceedings; he was taken to hospital for alleged head injuries and was reportedly kept chained to his bed. The trial of the three men had not started by the end of the year.

Abdool Shameer Hack was executed on 31 January. He had been convicted of murder and sentenced to death in May 1987. The National Assembly approved a bill in July extending the use of the death penalty to cases where death occurs as a result of supplying or administering narcotics to anyone under the age of 18. The President had not signed the bill into law by the end of the year.

There were no developments in the libel case against members of the executive of the Guyana Human Rights Association stemming from the publication in July 1988 of a report on police violence (see *Amnesty International Report 1989*).

Amnesty International expressed concern to the government in February about the execution of Abdool Shameer Hack and inquired whether he had had the opportunity to communicate with lawyers after the death warrant had been issued. No reply had been received by the end of the year. Amnesty International wrote to President Desmond Hoyte in December expressing concern about the new legislation expanding the use of the death penalty and urging him not to give his assent to the bill.

HAITI

Scores of people were arrested without warrant and detained without charge or trial for short periods. Those held included peasants and members of grassroots organizations apparently arrested for their peaceful activities or criticism of the authorities. Many detainees were reportedly tortured or ill-treated. Prison conditions continued to be harsh.

In March the 1987 Constitution, revoked in June 1988, was restored by presidential decree with the exclusion of 37 articles. Among the excluded articles was the provision stating that military personnel responsible for common crimes should be tried by civilian courts.

In April officers from the *Léopards* battalion, a special military unit, staged an uprising against President Prosper Avril. The insurgents were overpowered by troops loyal to the President, and their leaders were arrested and deported. A second uprising took place three days later in the Dessalines barracks in Port-au-Prince to protest the deportations and the dismissal of other officers, and to demand President Avril's resignation. Troops loyal to the President, however, regained control. The *Léopards* battalion was dissolved and the Dessalines barracks closed.

In September the government announced the creation of the *Office pour la protection des citoyens*, Office for the Protection of Citizens, to document and investigate human rights violations. No information about its activities had been received by Amnesty International by the end of the year.

The level of street crime and violence increased after the April uprisings. Members of the security forces were reportedly involved in a number of crimes, including robberies, assaults and murders. Although some officers were said to have been prosecuted for these offences, security forces' involvement in such incidents continued to be reported throughout the year in many parts of the country.

In the countryside, there were frequent reports that members of the security forces and *chefs de section* (rural police chiefs) intimidated, arbitrarily arrested and ill-treated peasants in the context of conflicts over land ownership, particularly in the Artibonite area in central Haiti. At least six peasants were reported to have been killed by local authorities in such disputes.

Scores of political and common-law prisoners were detained for several months without charge or trial and were denied access to relatives or legal counsel. The reasons for detention were often unknown to the detainees.

Scores of members of grassroots organizations throughout the country, and journalists sympathetic to them, were subjected to intimidation and arbitrary short-term arrest. In January two members of the *Assemblée nationale des organisations populaires* (ANOP), National Assembly of Popular Organizations, were arrested in Port-au-Prince as they distributed pamphlets protesting the high cost of living. They were held without charge and released after three days.

Rock Mondésir, a member of the *Coordination des associations de la Cité Soleil* (CASS), Coordination of Associations of Cité Soleil, arrested in November 1988 and held without charge (see *Amnesty International Report 1989*), was released in January. However, 23 members of a neighbourhood vigilance brigade linked to CASS were arrested in late April and early May and detained without charge for about one month.

In May Jean-Claude Duperval was arrested by the police in Port-au-Prince, following the killing of two of his brothers by armed robbers. He was reportedly arrested at the scene of the crime after he criticized the inability of the police to end the ongoing wave of violent crime. He was allegedly beaten, handcuffed and taken to the headquarters of the *Service d'investigation et de recherches anti-gang*, Anti-gang Investigation Service, where he remained in incommunicado detention without charge until his release in September. He was reportedly ill-treated during the initial days of his detention.

Another organization whose members came under attack was the *Mouvement des jeunes de Labadie* (MJL), Labadie Youth Movement, a peasant development organization and repeated target of human rights violations (see *Amnesty International Report 1989*). At least 13 of its members were arrested in the Artibonite department in July and August and reportedly ill-treated. They had all been released by the end of August. Throughout the year MJL members were harassed and threatened

with beatings by local officials if they continued their activities.

Also in July, 10 members of *Tèt Kole*, Heads Together, a grassroots peasant group, were arrested and reportedly ill-treated in the Jean-Rabel area apparently because they were putting up posters or wearing T-shirts commemorating the second anniversary of a peasant massacre (see *Amnesty International Report 1988*). They had all been released by the end of August.

In November Evans Paul, Jean-Auguste Meyzieux and Etienne Marineau, well-known political leaders, were arrested, allegedly severely ill-treated, and charged with plotting against the security of the state and illegal possession of firearms. After the arrests, the government issued a list of other people accused of plotting against the government, including former army sergeant Patrick Frantz Beauchard, who was arrested in December and reportedly ill-treated.

Torture and ill-treatment of political and common-law prisoners were widespread. Among the methods used were repeated beatings with fists and sticks and the technique known as the *djak* — a baton is wedged under the thighs and over the arms of the victim who is then beaten repeatedly. Jean-Robert Lalane, a member of the *Assemblée populaire nationale* (APN), Popular National Assembly, arrested in Cap-Haïtien in early August after he criticized the government on local radio, said he was subjected to severe beatings and to the *djak*. He was released the day after his arrest, but was taken to hospital because of the injuries he sustained in detention.

Extremely poor conditions continued to be reported in detention centres and prisons throughout the country. Many inmates were reported to be in bad health owing to malnutrition and poor hygiene conditions. Medical treatment was practically non-existent in detention centres and prisons.

In June the government informed Amnesty International that it had dismissed from the army two soldiers found responsible for the death of Jacques Fabien in April 1988 as a result of ill-treatment during his detention at the barracks in Petit-Goâve. Also in June, the government announced that disciplinary sanctions had been imposed on two soldiers found responsible for the ill-treatment of Ernst Louisdor in Port-au-Prince in January 1988. In March the government set up a

112

commission of inquiry to investigate the killing of four MJL members in August 1988. However, the commission included local officials whom the MJL had identified as responsible for abuses against its members. Shortly after the commission's visit to the Artibonite area, threats were issued against MJL members by local officials. Details of the inquiry had not emerged by the end of the year.

Amnesty International was not aware of any progress in the announced investigations into the 1988 killing of human rights lawyer Lafontant Joseph, the 1988 massacre at St Jean Bosco church apparently carried out by official forces, or the 29 November 1987 election day killings (see *Amnesty International Report 1988* and *1989*).

Throughout the year Amnesty International called for people who appeared to have been arbitrarily arrested to be released if not charged with a recognizably criminal offence. The organization called on the authorities to treat detainees humanely.

In April Amnesty International wrote to President Avril raising cases of human rights abuses since he took power in September 1988, requesting details of any inquiries and expressing concern at the apparent absence of progress in investigations of past human rights violations. No response was received.

HONDURAS

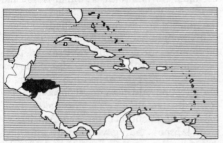

Torture of detainees being held incommunicado after arrest by the police and army was frequently reported. The fate of two people who "disappeared" was unknown at the end of the year. A student leader, a trade unionist and a university director were murdered; two of them had reportedly been under police surveillance, and the killings coincided with death threats against other leaders of trade unions and popular organizations, and human rights workers. Government opponents and human rights workers were frequently intimidated and harassed, allegedly by military intelligence agencies acting as civilian political groups. Extrajudicial executions of some criminal supects by the police continued to be reported.

National elections were held on 26 November. Rafael Leonardo Callejas, the opposition National Party presidential candidate, won just over 50 per cent of the vote. He was due to succeed President José Azcona in January 1990.

Armed anti-government activity was reported occasionally. Armed opposition groups claimed at least one political killing. In January Gustavo Alvarez Martínez, former commander-in-chief of the armed forces, was shot dead outside his home in Tegucigalpa by gunmen who ambushed his car. His driver was also killed. The *Movimiento Popular de Liberación — Cinchoneros* (MPL-C), Popular Liberation Movement — Cinchoneros, claimed responsibility. In July the same group was believed responsible for the killing of Pablo Flores García, reportedly a former member of the group who had turned informer. There were several bomb attacks on United States (US) armed forces personnel and other US targets. Responsibility for some of these attacks was claimed by previously little-known left-wing armed opposition groups, including the *Frente Patriótico Morazanista* (FPM), Morazanist Patriotic Front and the *Movimiento Revolucionario Hondureño* (MRH), Honduran Revolutionary Movement.

Political detainees were frequently held incommunicado for days and sometimes weeks despite constitutional provisions that all detainees be brought before a court within 24 hours of arrest. Torture and ill-treatment of detainees held in these circumstances were reported persistently. Student Mario Roberto Martínez Ortíz was arrested near Las Manos on the Nicaraguan border on 12 January. He was reportedly detained at the headquarters of the *Dirección National de Investigaciones* (DNI), National Directorate of Investigations, in Danlí and at the Ninth Infantry battalion barracks before being released without charge on 23 January. He was allegedly tortured, including being beaten, hooded, repeatedly kicked and threatened with death, while being questioned about his previous political activity as a student. Víctor Manuel Meza Elvir, a business student and member of an agricultural co-operative who was detained by the DNI on 31 July, was allegedly held incommunicado in clandestine detention centres for five days. He was brought to court on 4 August, then transferred to the National Penitentiary in Tegucigalpa on arms-trafficking charges. He alleged that during the first five days after arrest he was repeatedly beaten on the head and on the soles of the feet with a rubber truncheon, punched in the chest and stomach, and given electric shocks. He was in prison awaiting trial at the end of the year.

On 2 February José Leonel Suazo Castillo, a student of physical education, "disappeared" after reportedly being detained in Tegucigalpa. A work colleague who was accompanying him testified that he was being followed at the time by several people in a white van without number plates and with tinted windows. Leonel Suazo was said to have had a dispute a few days earlier with a police officer, who threatened reprisals. Both the *Fuerza de Seguridad Pública* (FSP), the police force, and the DNI denied having detained him. Three *habeas corpus* writs were filed on behalf of Leonel Suazo; a lawyer appointed by the courts inspected the headquarters of the FSP and the DNI in Tegucigalpa, but did not find him. There were unconfirmed reports that he had been seen in FSP custody in early May, but his whereabouts were unknown at the end of the year. José Alfredo Díaz Amaya, a Salvadorian, was detained on 7 September at his home in La Esperanza, department of Intibucá, by army intelligence agents from the Tenth Infantry Battalion. He was apparently suspected of being a member of the Salvadorian armed opposition group, the *Frente Farabundo Martí de Liberación Nacional* (FMLN), Farabundo Martí National Liberation Front. He was held at the battalion's base and was visited by his wife, who alleged that he had been tortured. However, on 9 November his wife was told by an officer of the battalion that he was no longer there. Despite repeated inquiries by human rights workers, José Díaz' wife was not informed of his whereabouts until December, when it was revealed that he had been deported to El Salvador on 19 October and released shortly afterwards.

A series of political killings occurred in July in the city of San Pedro Sula. On 4 July Edgardo Herrera, a leader of the *Frente de Reforma Universitaria* (FRU), Front for University Reform, was shot dead by two men in plain clothes while a third man waited in a white pick-up truck. Salomón Vallecillo Andrade, President of the Honduran Tobacco Workers' Union, was killed two days later. He was shot while waiting for a bus, reportedly by two men who drove off in a white pick-up truck. Both Edgardo Herrera and Salomón Vallecillo were reported to have been under police surveillance and to have previously received death threats. On 11 July Roberto Ramón Garay, director of the extramural studies department of the Regional University Centre of the North was killed in similar circumstances outside his home. None of those responsible for these crimes had been brought to justice by the end of the year.

In August it was reported that the Supreme Court had ordered a review of the investigation into the murder in January 1988 of human rights leader Miguel Angel Pavón and union official Moisés Landaverde (see *Amnesty International Report 1989*), in view of the lack of progress in establishing the identity of the killers. No results of the investigation or of the findings of the Supreme Court review were known at the end of the year.

Honduran human rights groups claimed that criminal suspects were killed by the police in circumstances which suggested the impermissible use of lethal force or summary execution. Those killed included Norberto Flores Flores, a tailor who had previously served a prison term. He was detained on 28 March near his home in Tegucigalpa, apparently on suspicion of robbery, and taken to the DNI headquarters. According to reports, he was taken from his cell during the night of 2 April. Two days later his body was found with bullet wounds on a road on the outskirts of Tegucigalpa. Police reportedly maintained he was shot attempting to escape while being taken to identify a hideout. However, friends said that they had taken him to hospital on the night of 3 April after he had survived an execution attempt and that DNI agents had taken him away the next morning. His common-law wife was reportedly accosted and threatened by people in civilian clothes after she had registered a

114

complaint before a criminal court against the director of the DNI and two DNI officers.

A campaign of defamation, harassment and intimidation of leading trade unionists and human rights workers, alleged by human rights groups to be instigated by the armed forces, persisted throughout the year (see *Amnesty International Report 1989*). Following the assassination of General Alvarez in January, Dr Ramón Custodio López, President of the Committee for the Defence of Human Rights in Honduras, Oscar Aníbal Puerto, its Vice-President, and three other prominent government critics were threatened with execution in a message broadcast on radio by a group calling itself the Alliance for Anti-communist Action (AAA). The group was one of several clandestine right-wing groups, believed to be linked to the armed forces, which mounted poster and graffiti campaigns slandering and threatening leading left-wing leaders and human rights activists. In July Gladys Lanza, President of the Electrical Workers' Union, and five other trade unionists and human rights workers reportedly received death threats by telephone. Further threats were said to have been made to the same people in November. Gladys Lanza escaped with minor injuries when a bomb exploded in her home on 15 November.

In January the Inter-American Court of Human Rights published its second decision on a Honduran "disappearance" case — that of Saúl Godínez Cruz, who "disappeared" in July 1982 reportedly after having been captured by a soldier and two men in plain clothes on the road between Choluteca and Monjarás. As in the case of Angel Manfredo Velásquez, the court found that the "disappearance" of Saúl Godínez was part of a systematic and selective practice of kidnappings and "disappearances" in Honduras from 1981 to 1984 (see *Amnesty International Reports 1982* to *1985* and *1989*). It held the government responsible for violation of his rights to life, personal freedom and humane treatment, and ordered it to pay fair compensation to his family. In July the court set compensation for the dependants of the two victims at a total of 1,400,000 lempiras (approximately US$700,000). The Inter-American Court also published its decision on the case of Costa Ricans Francisco Fairén Garbi, an economics student, and Yolanda Solís Corrales, a teacher, who allegedly "disappeared" in Honduras in December 1981 (see *Amnesty International Report 1989*). The court concluded that "numerous and insoluble difficulties" had prevented it from establishing whether the pair had "disappeared" in Honduras and whether the Honduran Government was responsible.

Amnesty International issued urgent appeals to the Honduran Government following reports of detentions, torture, alleged extrajudicial killings, "disappearances" and death threats. It called on the government to guarantee the safety of prisoners, to carry out prompt and thorough investigations into reports of killings and "disappearances", and to bring to justice those responsible. It also urged that measures be taken to prevent further intimidation of members of opposition groups and human rights workers, and to ensure their safety.

HONG KONG

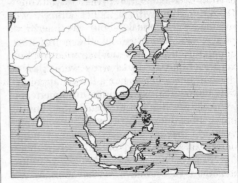

Eight people were arrested for demonstrating in support of China's pro-democracy movement and charged with unlawful assembly. Four of them were allegedly ill-treated by police. Seven were acquitted of the charges. Detained Vietnamese asylum-seekers were reportedly ill-treated. At least 10 people were sentenced to death for murder. No executions were carried out.

A second draft of the Basic Law of the Hong Kong Special Administrative Region (see *Amnesty International Report 1989*) was published in February for consideration by the people of Hong Kong. A final text was to be published in 1990 after approval by the National People's Congress, China's parliament, in Beijing.

Vietnamese asylum-seekers continued to arrive in large numbers, swelling the total arrivals during recent years to over 53,000.

Four members of a group formed to support the pro-democracy movement in China were arrested in September. They had protested against a National Day celebration organized by China's official New China News Agency (NCNA), which represents China's interests in Hong Kong. Police reportedly beat them and one protester apparently sustained a severe eye injury. Along with four other members of the group later arrested, they were charged with unlawful assembly under the Public Order Ordinance. One of them reportedly pleaded guilty. The other seven were acquitted in December. Hong Kong's Political Adviser reported the arrests to the NCNA in October, stating that the government "had no intention of allowing Hong Kong to be used as a base for subversive activities against China".

In July more than 100 Vietnamese asylum-seekers held at the Shek Kong Detention Centre, including children, were reportedly injured during beatings by police; one man died later. The incident apparently began when police tried to prevent asylum-seekers from receiving goods thrown over a fence to them from outside the centre. The government initiated an inquiry into the beatings but its outcome had not been made public by the end of the year. A separate investigation into the death was in progress.

Disturbances and instances of ill-treatment by police in other camps for Vietnamese asylum-seekers were also reported. Tension grew in some camps during the year amid overcrowding, poor sanitation and fears of forcible repatriation to Viet Nam. The screening procedure instituted in 1988 to evaluate individual claims for refugee status was seriously flawed. In mid-1989 the government said it would proceed with mandatory repatriation of people "screened out", or denied refugee status. A first group of 51 Vietnamese was forcibly returned to Viet Nam on 12 December.

At least 10 people were sentenced to death for murder, which carries a mandatory death penalty. No executions have been carried out since November 1966, following abolition of the death penalty in the United Kingdom (UK). The Governor of Hong Kong has commuted most death sentences imposed since that time. Amnesty International urged the government to adopt legislation abolishing the death penalty.

In a memorandum to the Basic Law Drafting Committee, Amnesty International called for further changes in the Basic Law to ensure human rights protection. The organization urged guarantees that Hong Kong will remain bound, after it comes under Chinese rule in 1997, to international human rights treaties to which it is now party through ratification by the UK. Amnesty International also called for explicit guarantees in the Basic Law of the rights to life and protection from cruel, inhuman or degrading treatment or punishment. It recommended adoption of a requirement that no legislation applied in Hong Kong after 1997, particularly during a state of emergency, may contravene the provisions of the International Covenant on Civil and Political Rights. Amnesty International published its comments on the Basic Law in November.

Amnesty International also expressed concern to the Governor about the prosecution of protesters for unlawful assembly and about the alleged ill-treatment of some of them. The authorities replied in December that they could not comment on the ill-treatment allegations but that the defendants, who were on trial at the time, could present their allegations to the court hearing their cases.

An Amnesty International delegation visited Hong Kong in November to examine the situation of Vietnamese asylum-seekers. Delegates witnessed screening interviews, visited detention centres and talked both to Hong Kong officials and individual Vietnamese asylum-seekers. In December Amnesty International expressed concern to the authorities about flaws in the screening procedure and called for suspension of plans for the forcible repatriation of Vietnamese asylum-seekers until these flaws had been remedied. The organization cited the possibility that forcible repatriation could place individuals at risk of arbitrary imprisonment, torture or execution.

In addition, Amnesty International expressed concern about reports that detained asylum-seekers had been assaulted and ill-treated, and called for impartial investigations into all such allegations.

HUNGARY

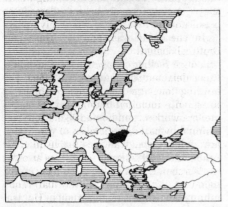

At least 70 prisoners of conscience imprisoned for conscientious objection to military service were released. A civilian alternative to military service was introduced. The number of offences punishable by death was reduced and it became constitutionally impossible to implement the death penalty while the role of the body which hears requests for commutation of death sentences was under review.

Political changes continued throughout the year under Prime Minister Miklós Németh, who replaced Károly Grósz as premier at the end of 1988. In October the ruling Hungarian Socialist Workers Party voted itself out of existence and a new party, the Hungarian Socialist Party, was set up in its place under the chairmanship of Rezsö Nyers.

The Ministry of Justice stated in March that all imprisoned conscientious objectors had been released pending legislation which would allow a civilian alternative to military service. In June the Hungarian Parliament passed legislation to allow conscientious objectors to perform alternative service in non-military institutions. The alternative service will be for 10 months longer than military service, but those undertaking it will not be confined to barracks or be called up for subsequent reserve service. In July legislation was adopted abolishing the death penalty for crimes against the state.

Amnesty International welcomed the release of imprisoned conscientious objectors, on whose behalf it had been appealing. The organization also urged the Hungarian Government to abolish the death penalty. In September Prime Minister Miklós Németh informed Amnesty International that it was constitutionally impossible to carry out the death penalty as the role of the Presidential Council — the body which hears requests for commutation of death sentences — was under review.

INDIA

Several thousand political prisoners, among them prisoners of conscience, were held without charge or trial under "anti-terrorist" or preventive detention laws. Other prisoners of conscience were detained for peaceful political activities but faced false criminal charges under the Penal Code. Torture and ill-treatment were widespread. Over 50 people reportedly died after torture in police custody. Several people "disappeared" after arrest and several hundred may have been extrajudicially executed. About a dozen people were believed to have been executed, at least one of whom may have been wrongly convicted.

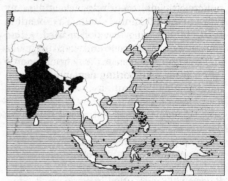

The Congress Party of Prime Minister Rajiv Gandhi, which lost its majority in the November general elections, was replaced by the minority government of Prime Minister V.P. Singh. The new National Front coalition government pledged "institutional accountability and human rights" and review of thousands of political prisoner cases in Punjab. In December it repealed the 59th Amendment to the Constitution, which permitted suspension of the right to life in Punjab.

In September, before the change of government, the authorities introduced the Scheduled Castes and Scheduled Tribes (Prevention of Atrocities) Act, which increases protection for members of the scheduled castes (formerly "untouchables") and tribes against torture and other abuses. It defines a range of offences as "atrocities", including wrongfully occupying land allocated to these groups or dispossessing them, forcing them to eat obnoxious substances, and fabricating or destroying evidence in certain types of criminal cases involving members of these groups. People charged under the Act are to be tried by special courts. State governments are required to implement specific measures to prevent "atrocities" and to provide legal aid and expenses for witnesses testifying about alleged abuses. No information on how the new Act was being applied was available.

Direct rule of the state of Punjab from Delhi was extended in October for a further six months. Both opposition groups and the security forces resorted to widespread violence throughout the year. According to official figures, police killed 495 "terrorists" in the first nine months of the year and Sikh groups demanding a separate state called "Khalistan" killed 764 people. The victims included government and police officials, their relatives and many other Sikh and Hindu civilians. In Andhra Pradesh left-wing revolutionaries killed several police officers and local officials, and held others hostage. Violence by opposition groups supporting demands for independence in Kashmir increased. Violence also increased in Assam, where Bodo tribal people sought a separate state on the north bank of the Brahmaputra.

In March the remaining 188 of the estimated 366 Sikhs detained since 1984 in Jodhpur jail (see *Amnesty International Report 1988* and *1989*) were released. Most were prisoners of conscience. Upon arrival in Punjab, 84 of them were rearrested. An official commission reviewed their cases and by the end of the year four of them remained in custody on criminal charges. Although the government stated in March that prisoners held in Punjab because of their speeches or writings would be released, several continued to be held without trial until early December. They included Prakash Singh Badal and Gurcharan Singh Tohra, two leaders of the Akali Dal party. Simranjit Singh Mann, arrested in November 1984, was charged in April with two Bombay professors, Jagmohan Singh and Dalip Singh, and a fourth defendant, Atinder Pal Singh, with

conspiracy to kill the former prime minister, Indira Gandhi, and faced the death penalty if convicted. Before leaving office, the Congress government ordered the release of the first three without giving reasons. The fourth was kept in prison facing criminal charges.

Police seeking suspects in Punjab sometimes detained relatives instead, effectively holding them hostage. Other prisoners of conscience included trade unionists, social welfare workers and human rights activists. Bhimrao Mhaske, a member of the Mahar scheduled caste, who was active in trade union and civil liberties work, was arrested in March for, among other things, urging members of the "adivasi" (tribal) community to exercise their rights. He was charged, under Section 151(3) of the Code of Criminal Procedure, with inciting the commission of an offence, but a High Court judge ordered his release after two weeks.

Eighteen environmentalists, lawyers and others involved in peaceful protests against the Narmada dam-building project and allegedly unfair local labour practices were arrested in Gujarat in January and February. They were charged with "spying" under the 1923 Official Secrets Act but released on bail several days later. In September the President of the Ladakh Buddhist Organization was detained for several weeks after calling for special protection of Buddhists' rights in Ladakh, part of the state of Jammu and Kashmir.

In May the Terrorist and Disruptive Activities (Prevention) Act, which provides for special courts to try people *in camera* and suspends important legal safeguards against arbitrary detention (see *Amnesty International Report 1988*), was extended for another two years. The Act, which severely limits release on bail, continued to be used extensively to detain thousands of political prisoners. Most were held without charge or trial. They included more than 1,000 suspected supporters of an autonomous Sikh state; dozens of tribal people in the Bastar district, Madhya Pradesh; and tribal people suspected of helping "naxalites" (Maoist revolutionaries) in Andhra Pradesh. Others detained under the Act included a newspaper editor in Manipur and her five-month-old baby; several hundred members of the All Bodo Students Union, which has pressed for a separate Bodoland; and hundreds of people suspected of political violence in Kashmir.

118

The National Security Act (NSA) was also used to detain political prisoners without charge or trial. The Act permits such detention for up to one year. Section 14(a) of the Act, a provision which lapsed in June, permitted such detention for two years in Punjab. Some detainees were denied the opportunity to request review by an advisory board which is empowered to order release from detention.

The extreme prolongation of some political trials has raised questions about protection of the right to fair and prompt trial. For example, 20 prisoners acquitted by a Hyderabad court in February had been among 40 people charged in 1974 with a "naxalite" conspiracy to overthrow the government. At least 12 different judges had presided over the trial since it began in 1977.

Torture remained widespread, particularly in states with armed opposition to the government. In Punjab suspects under interrogation were said to be routinely tortured. Many of the 780 untried political detainees held in Amritsar Central Jail complained to a judge in February that they had been tortured during several weeks of illegal detention in previous months before their arrest was formally acknowledged. Torture was also frequently alleged in Kashmir, and women belonging to tribal groups or scheduled castes in Bihar, Madhya Pradesh and Assam were reportedly raped while in police custody.

In February, 20 members of the Pardhi tribal community in Maharashtra were severely beaten during several weeks of unacknowledged detention — one victim died. As in other cases, a local magistrate apparently refused to register their complaints of torture. Such complaints have rarely been investigated, although some officials have acknowledged that torture occurs.

In Manipur witnesses testifying about torture allegedly committed by soldiers of the Assam Rifles in Oinam in 1987 have themselves reportedly been tortured (see *Amnesty International Report 1988*). One report received during the year described abuses suffered by a witness who testified in court in December 1988. He said he was beaten and given electric shocks, apparently because he brought witnesses to court who testified that Assam Rifles troops had raped them. He complained that a doctor examining him in an Assam

Rifles camp where he was detained refused to register his complaint of torture.

At least 50 prisoners died in police custody, nearly all of them shortly after arrest. Many were allegedly tortured, although the police often attributed deaths to natural causes or suicide. Few of these deaths were officially investigated. Some police officers were suspended or arrested on charges of murder, but none was known to have been brought to trial and convicted during the year for causing the death of a prisoner.

At least 11 political prisoners and criminal suspects "disappeared" after arrest in Punjab, Uttar Pradesh, Karnataka and Bihar. The police denied the arrests or claimed the "disappeared" person had "run away" from custody. Two of those who had "disappeared" were located after several months in unacknowledged detention. Others were feared to have been killed in custody. No further information was available about the fate of 32 men who "disappeared" in Meerut in 1987 (see *Amnesty International Report 1989*). The report of an official inquiry into their "disappearance" had still not been published by the end of 1989.

Scores, possibly hundreds, of suspected government opponents were reportedly executed extrajudicially by police in Andhra Pradesh and Punjab. The police said all killings occurred during "encounters" with armed opponents or during escape attempts by prisoners — but evidence suggested that some suspects were killed after arrest in "encounters" staged by the police. The Punjab police reported that in the two years up to June 1989, 808 suspected "terrorists" and 208 police officers were killed in 907 "encounters". It was impossible to verify independently the circumstances in which they had occurred.

In July members of the Central Reserve Police entered houses in Kashmir and shot four unarmed bystanders, apparently in retaliation for the killing of two police officers by suspected Kashmiri secessionists. In October police in Bihar reportedly failed to intervene when dozens of Muslims were killed by Hindus in the village of Chandheri.

In January Satwant Singh and Kehar Singh, two Sikhs sentenced to death for the murder of former prime minister Indira Gandhi, were hanged at Tihar Jail. Kehar Singh's conviction appeared to be based on unconvincing circumstantial evidence. An average of about a dozen people a year have been executed in recent years, according to estimates — official figures giving numbers of executions carried out annually have not been made available.

The government refused in May Amnesty International's request for discussions on its human rights concerns in India. In December Amnesty International was again denied permission to attend a non-governmental human rights conference in Bombay.

During the year Amnesty International worked for the release of prisoners of conscience and for the fair trial of other political prisoners. It took urgent action to clarify several "disappearances" and to prevent executions. It also published reports on the use of the death penalty, on "disappearances" and on human rights violations against underprivileged groups in Bihar and Maharashtra. In a February statement to the United Nations Commission on Human Rights, Amnesty International drew attention to attempts by security forces to sabotage judicial investigations into abuses in Manipur. In an August submission to the Working Group on Indigenous Populations of the United Nations, Amnesty International expressed concern that police had raped women belonging to underprivileged groups.

Allegations of human rights abuse by the Indian Peace Keeping Force in Sri Lanka are described under that country.

INDONESIA/ EAST TIMOR

More than 100 opponents or suspected opponents or critics of the government were prisoners of conscience. At least 60 of them were sentenced to prison terms during the year in a series of trials for subversion. At least 18 political prisoners were released, some of them after more than 20 years in prison. In East Timor at least 200 people, including prisoners of conscience, were arrested for political reasons. The majority were released without charge, but some remained in detention at the end of the year. There were serious doubts about the fairness of political trials; in some cases the courts accepted as evidence statements allegedly

obtained under duress during pre-trial custody. Political detainees and criminal suspects were reportedly tortured and ill-treated and a number of victims died in custody. At least 20 people were reported to have been unlawfully executed by members of the security forces in East Timor. President Suharto acknowledged that the deliberate killings of some 5,000 alleged petty criminals between 1983 and 1986 had been sanctioned by the government. Seven people were sentenced to death during the year and one execution was reported.

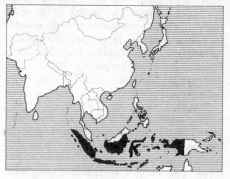

A clash between Islamic activists and security forces in February resulted in more than 100 deaths, according to unofficial sources. A crackdown on several Islamic groups ensued and the authorities arrested scores of suspected advocates of an Islamic state. Some of those arrested were tried on charges of subversion, which carries a maximum penalty of death. Armed riot police and military forces dispersed peaceful student demonstrations in April, July and August. Numerous arrests and injuries accompanied the dispersals. Most of those held were released within a few days. At least 11 people remained in custody for more than four months, six of whom faced up to seven years in prison on charges of insulting a government official. Regional autonomy or independence continued to be an issue in Irian Jaya, where dozens of supporters of secession who staged a public ceremony in December 1988 were charged with subversion. Hundreds suspected of sympathizing with secession were reportedly detained briefly during the year.

In January the Indonesian Government announced the official "opening" of East Timor to tourism and commerce. However, serious human rights violations continued to be reported there. People who disseminated human rights information and suspected members or supporters of the *Frente Revolucionaria de Timor Leste* (Fretilin), which has been waging a guerrilla war for independence since 1975, were among the reported victims of these abuses. Bishop Carlos Ximenes Belo, the Apostolic Administrator of Dili, criticized Indonesia's human rights record in the territory and called for a United Nations-supervised referendum on the political future of the territory. In October Pope John Paul II visited Indonesia and East Timor and appealed publicly for the protection of human rights.

Under a Ministry of Justice order of 15 April, certain categories of prisoners, including political prisoners convicted of subversion, were denied entitlement to benefits such as temporary home leave and parole normally granted for good behaviour.

At least 24 of the dozens of Islamic activists detained after February were convicted of subversion in trials in Lampung, Jakarta, Bandung, Bogor, Bima, Aceh and Madura. Seven received life sentences and three, including a 16-year-old boy, were sentenced to 20 years' imprisonment: the rest were sentenced to terms of between three and 17 years. More than 20 others were being tried at the end of the year. Most were charged with subversion through undermining the state ideology, *Pancasila*, and attempting to establish an Islamic state. Some were also accused of isolated acts of violence, but the majority of those sentenced appeared to be prisoners of conscience.

Emeng Abdurachman, an Islamic activist tried in Bandung, was accused of giving lectures which criticized the government and *Pancasila*, and of attempting to set up an Islamic state. In September he was found guilty of subversion and sentenced to five years in prison. The court acknowledged that his activities had been non-violent but found that his aims were subversive.

In December Haji Abdul Ghani Masykur received an 11-year prison sentence in Bima, West Nusa Tenggara province. He was accused of attending a meeting in February where there were discussions on the establishment of an Islamic state, and of contacting other Islamic activists. Zainal Arifin, who was said to have attended the same meeting and to have given lectures criticizing the government's birth control program, was sentenced to nine years' imprisonment.

Despite an official policy of religious tolerance, people were arrested and sentenced to prison terms for practising their faith. A court in Wonogiri convicted two elderly Jehovah's Witnesses, Suyadi and Sukasmin, of undermining public order by disseminating the teachings of an illegal organization. At least 22 other followers of the faith, which was banned in 1976, were reportedly detained in other parts of the country. In East Timor eight members of the Association of Santo Antonio, a Christian sect, were convicted of belonging to an illegal organization. The eight were among the thousands of East Timorese reportedly arrested in November 1988, most of whom were released without charge (see *Amnesty International Report 1989*).

Bambang "Isti" Nugroho, the coordinator of the Palagan Study Group at Gajah Mada University, Yogyakarta, and Bambang Subono, a student there, were both convicted of subversion and sentenced to eight and seven years' imprisonment respectively. Charges against them included holding illegal discussion meetings, possessing banned literature and criticizing government policies (see *Amnesty International Report 1989*). A third man, Bonar Tigor Naipospos, was arrested in Jakarta in June on related charges. He had not been brought to trial by the end of the year.

In Irian Jaya, 37 people were convicted of subversion for taking part in a peaceful flag-raising ceremony in December 1988 to proclaim the independent state of "West Melanesia"; all were believed to be prisoners of conscience. In September the leader of the group, Dr Thomas Wainggai, was sentenced to 20 years' imprisonment. Other members received terms of between four and eight years' imprisonment. This brought the number of political prisoners in Irian Jaya to over 100.

At least 300 Islamic activists imprisoned for subversion in previous years remained in custody throughout the year. At least 40 were prisoners of conscience, convicted of involvement with *usroh* groups, which advocate closer ties among Muslims and a stricter adherence to Muslim teachings (see *Amnesty International Report 1988* and *1989*).

More than 50 prisoners detained in the late 1960s were still held for alleged involvement in a 1965 coup attempt which the authorities attributed to the Indonesian Communist Party (PKI). A massive purge of the formerly legal party and its affiliated organizations resulted in an estimated 500,000 deaths and about one million arrests after the coup attempt. The majority of those still in detention may be prisoners of conscience, held for their lawful left-wing political activities. Thousands of former "PKI" prisoners were required to report regularly to local military authorities and suffered officially sanctioned discrimination in employment, and political and other fields.

At least 18 political prisoners were released. Pudji Aswati, aged 60, and Kartini, aged 65, were released in January after 20 years' imprisonment for their alleged involvement in the 1965 coup attempt. Sundari Abdulrachman, a former member of parliament imprisoned on similar charges, was released in August after serving over 20 years in prison. In addition to these three women who were "PKI" prisoners, those released included two Islamic activists and three suspected members of the Free Papua Movement (OPM), and at least 10 East Timorese political prisoners.

An estimated 200 people, including students and human rights activists, were arrested in East Timor on suspicion of sympathizing with Fretilin or other opponents of Indonesian rule in the territory. Most were held without charge or trial, reportedly tortured and ill-treated and subsequently released. At least 25 people were detained in October and November for their part in an apparently peaceful pro-independence demonstration during the visit of Pope John Paul II to East Timor in October. Some detainees were reportedly tortured with electric shocks and beaten while in detention. Unofficial sources reported that at least 10 untried detainees, most of them students, remained in custody in December.

Six university students arrested after a demonstration at the Bandung Institute of Technology in August were charged with expressing "feelings of hostility, hatred or contempt toward the Indonesian Government". They faced a maximum penalty of seven years in prison. Five other students arrested for their alleged part in the demonstration were temporarily released in December. The lawyers of the students still held reportedly received death threats, which they attributed to military sources, after publicly stating that some of their clients had been illegally detained and ill-treated in custody.

Serious doubts remained about the fairness of political trials conducted in 1989 and in previous years, particularly those held under the sweeping Anti-Subversion Law of 1963. Proceedings against alleged Islamic militants and student activists appeared to be political show-trials aimed at intimidating critics of the government. The legal basis and factual evidence for prosecutions were frequently obscure and a number of political prisoners were apparently convicted on the basis of uncorroborated statements obtained under duress. In July Husni bin Muhamad was tried without the benefit of legal counsel and sentenced to three years' imprisonment for subversion. Human rights lawyers said that he and two others arrested on similar charges in December 1988 had declined legal counsel after they were beaten and held in isolation cells at Bogor jail.

Torture and ill-treatment of both criminal suspects and political detainees were frequently reported, and some victims allegedly died as a result. Bishop Belo of Dili said that the torture and ill-treatment of detainees was commonplace in East Timor and condemned government denials of the practice. Three men involved in compiling information about human rights violations — Filomeno Gomes, Lazaro Ribeiro and Jaime dos Santos — were among dozens of political detainees reportedly tortured while held without charge. Detainees were subjected to electric shocks, beatings, burnings with lighted cigarettes, and several hours' immersion in water tanks.

Prisoners' relatives frequently alleged that deaths resulted from torture or ill-treatment, although police usually claimed that the prisoners had committed suicide, suffered accidents or died of sudden illness. In April Iwan Nirwana, a criminal suspect, died in police custody in Cianjur. Police suspected of torturing him reportedly offered his family unofficial financial compensation and a truck-load of vegetables. Another criminal suspect, Didin Tajudin, died in police custody in September. His corpse was reportedly covered with open wounds and bruises. Relatives said that he had complained of beatings by police; the police alleged that

122

he had committed suicide. No official inquiries into these deaths were known to have been conducted.

Dozens of police and military officers were tried for allegedly torturing or ill-treating prisoners. At least five were convicted of causing prisoners' deaths, but most received short prison sentences. In September two police officers were jailed for seven and 10 months for beating to death a prisoner called Sutaji. In June two others convicted of beating to death 17-year-old Bakri Budi Santoso received sentences of two and a half and three and a half years.

Some prisoners died in custody as a direct result of prison conditions which appeared to constitute cruel, inhuman or degrading treatment. Gustav Tanawani, a political prisoner convicted of subversion in 1984, died in custody at Madiun jail in January. Prison officials had denied his repeated requests for medical treatment. Government authorities failed to provide his family with a death certificate, a post-mortem report or the opportunity to view the corpse before burial. According to reports received in September, two prisoners had died and 15 were chronically ill because of harsh conditions at the Kalimantan Timur prison. A Ministry of Justice official said that the prison, designed to hold 500 inmates, held 800 people and lacked both a resident doctor and sufficient financial resources to feed prisoners properly.

At least 20 people were reportedly extrajudicially executed by members of the security forces in East Timor in late 1988 and 1989. Josefina Facundo was reportedly bound, raped and killed by army troops near Poros in January. Soldiers ostensibly searching for her husband, an alleged Fretilin supporter, had forced her to accompany them into the jungle. Parts of her mutilated body were later reportedly dropped at her village. In June three unarmed young men cutting wood outside the permitted timbering area near Ossu were reportedly killed by government forces. Soldiers apparently accused the three of being Fretilin spies, tied them together and immediately shot them. Their decaying bodies were discovered, still bound, several days later.

In an autobiography published in January, President Suharto said that the so-called "mysterious killings" of some 5,000 people during the "anti-crime" campaigns of 1983 to 1986 were officially sanctioned summary executions of suspected criminals (see *Amnesty International Report 1984, 1985* and *1986*).

Seven people convicted of murder were sentenced to death, bringing the total number on death row to at least 31. They included 13 people convicted of involvement in the 1965 coup attempt or of PKI membership and believed to be in imminent danger of execution. Azhar bin Mohammad Safar, an Islamic activist convicted in 1982 of subversion and illegal firearms possession, received a temporary reprieve 10 hours before his scheduled execution in December 1988. The other 17 known to be held on death row were convicted of murder or drugs-related offences. Bambang Sispoyo, an Islamic activist accused of subversion and murder and sentenced to death in 1985, was reportedly executed in July.

Amnesty International appealed for the release of prisoners of conscience and for a review of other political cases involving unfair trials. The organization expressed concern about reports of torture and ill-treatment in both Indonesia and East Timor, and appealed for the commutation of death sentences and an end to executions. The Indonesian Government provided no substantive response to the organization's appeals.

Following a meeting with representatives of the Indonesian Government in February, Amnesty International submitted a formal proposal for a visit to Indonesia and East Timor later in the year. Despite assurances that the proposal was under consideration, no official reply had been received by the end of the year.

In August Amnesty International submitted information about human rights violations in East Timor to the United Nations Special Committee on Decolonization. It noted that despite the official "opening" of East Timor in January, there were still reports of serious human rights violations in the territory.

IRAN

Over 1,500 executions for criminal offences were announced in the official press, more than 1,000 of them for drug-trafficking. Some of those executed as

alleged drug-traffickers may have been political prisoners. Hundreds of political prisoners arrested in previous years, including prisoners of conscience, remained imprisoned throughout 1989 although there were some releases. New arrests of alleged opponents of the government were also reported. Hundreds of people were sentenced to death or imprisoned after unfair trials before Islamic Revolutionary Courts. Over 40 of those executed were stoned to death, and people convicted of criminal offences were subjected to other cruel, inhuman or degrading punishments: floggings were common and at least nine people had fingers or a hand amputated. The government endorsed a death threat against a British author and, in at least three cases, exiled opponents of the government were killed in circumstances suggesting that they may have been the victims of extrajudicial executions.

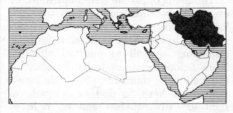

Ayatollah Ruhollah Khomeini, the leader of the Islamic Republic of Iran, died on 3 June and was succeeded by the then President, Seyed Ali Khamenei. In July Ali Akbar Hashemi Rafsanjani, Speaker of the *Majlis* (Islamic Consultative Assembly), was elected President with increased executive powers. The office of prime minister was abolished. The judiciary was restructured: the Supreme Judicial Council was abolished and replaced by a Head of the Judiciary, Ayatollah Mohamed Yazdi.

The full scale of the mass killings of political prisoners after the July 1988 cease-fire in the war with Iraq emerged more clearly during the course of 1989. It became evident that at least 2,000 prisoners had been summarily killed between August 1988 and January 1989, and that the true figure was probably far higher (see *Amnesty International Report 1989*). Many families had still not been officially notified by the end of 1989 that their relatives had been executed. Those that were notified were often not told where their relatives had been buried. This lack of official

information about the fate of political prisoners created a climate of rumour and uncertainty which hampered the gathering of information about the remaining political prisoners.

On 23 January a new law came into force imposing mandatory death sentences on those found in possession of specified quantities of heroin, opium or other proscribed drugs (see *Amnesty International Report 1989*). By the end of the year over 1,000 people had been executed for drugs-related offences. On 5 April the Prosecutor General was reported by Tehran Radio to have said that 313 smugglers had been executed so far, that 65 more were due to be hanged the following day, and that he hoped executions would continue until the last smuggler in the country was eliminated.

Multiple executions of up to 80 victims in a single day, in different towns, took place on many occasions. Some executions, particularly of women, took place inside prisons, but hundreds of people were hanged in public, often in groups. In some cases, several nooses were attached to a horizontal bar which was then raised, so that the victims were hauled up by the neck in a row to die of slow strangulation. Bodies were frequently left on display for hours, and in at least one instance in January a gibbet was mounted on a lorry and driven through the streets of Tehran with bodies still hanging from it.

In January the judicial authorities called for crimes to be punished more speedily. The result was that executions for offences such as murder, rape, armed robbery and prostitution increased dramatically. Over 250 such executions were announced between January and the end of May and more than 400 by the end of the year. Most victims were hanged, but at least 43 sentenced for adultery, prostitution or pimping were stoned to death. According to official reports, thousands of people witnessed such stonings and members of the public participated directly in some of them. In one incident in April, 12 women and three men were stoned to death in a football stadium in Bushehr.

Mass executions of political prisoners such as those in 1988 were not reported in 1989, although opposition sources claimed that some political prisoners were among those ostensibly executed for drug-trafficking. About a dozen people, according to the government, were executed on charges of spying, sabotage or armed insurgency. According to unconfirmed reports, three senior naval officers were executed in April and other military officers were among 30 people executed in July. Officials did confirm the execution in April of Fatemeh Moddares Tehrani, a political prisoner serving a seven-year sentence imposed after her arrest in 1982. It was not clear whether any judicial process preceded her execution.

The number of prisoners of conscience who continued to be held was not known. However, among them were about 10 women members or supporters of the Tudeh Party, who were arrested in 1982 before the party was banned. Some of them had been sentenced to prison after summary trials, but some were held without charge or trial and others were kept in prison after their sentences had expired. They were held throughout 1989 in Evin Prison in Tehran, together with about 90 other women political prisoners, some of whom may also have been prisoners of conscience.

The number of political prisoners still held at the end of the year was also unclear. At least 2,000 had been killed in the second half of 1988, hundreds were moved from one prison to another and an unknown number had been released after agreeing to "repent" and sign guarantees of future good conduct. Former prisoners who broke such guarantees – for example, by leaving the country – risked their relatives being fined or imprisoned.

In February amnesties were announced to mark the 10th anniversary of the revolution which brought the Islamic Republic into being. The authorities said that 2,600 out of a total of 3,500 political prisoners were to be released. Hundreds of political prisoners do appear to have been freed, but it was impossible to verify official figures. Subsequent amnesties specifically excluded "non-repentant" political prisoners. By the end of the year Ghasr and Ghezel-Hesar prisons, which had been used to hold political prisoners, were reported to have been closed down. Evin Prison was said by prisoners' relatives to be far less crowded than before.

Among the prisoners of conscience known to have been released were six supporters of the Association for the Defence of Freedom and Sovereignty of the Iranian Nation, who had been arrested in May 1988 (see *Amnesty International Report 1989*).

There were new arrests in September when relatives of prisoners and some former inmates reportedly held demonstrations in Behesht-e Zahra and Khavaran Cemeteries in Tehran to demand information about the fate of prisoners. Dozens of demonstrators were arrested but most were released by the end of the year. In December students were reportedly detained after clashes with security forces at a demonstration about student accommodation.

There were also periodic reports of political arrests in the Kurdish area of Iran where armed opposition to the government continued. However, details of those held, or what became of them, were impossible to obtain. It was also not possible to confirm reports received in the last quarter of 1989 of people being arrested for protesting about food shortages and other economic hardships.

Hundreds of people were imprisoned or executed after unfair trials before Islamic Revolutionary Courts, which are responsible for trying those charged with drug-trafficking as well as political offences. Trials before these courts fall far short of international standards for fair trial. Defendants have no defence counsel, no right to call witnesses and no right of appeal.

Amnesty International recorded nine cases where people convicted of repeated theft had four fingers of the right hand amputated, or the whole hand. Hundreds of people were also sentenced to floggings, which are imposed for a variety of offences, sometimes together with other punishments. For example, in one case in Varamin in May, three men convicted of rape received 80 lashes before being executed. A fourth man was sentenced to 129 lashes plus nine years' imprisonment.

In February Ayatollah Khomeini issued a *fatwa* (religious edict) to the effect that it was the duty of all Muslims to kill the British novelist, Salman Rushdie, for writing an allegedly blasphemous novel, *The Satanic Verses*. This *fatwa* continued to be endorsed by the Iranian Government throughout the year.

Leading members of opposition groups abroad were killed in at least three separate incidents in circumstances which suggested the complicity of the Iranian authorities. In June Atayollah Byahmadi, a former colonel in the Shah's Intelligence Service, was shot dead in his hotel room in Dubai. In July Abdul Rahman Ghassemlou, leader of the Kurdish Democratic Party of Iran (KDPI), was killed in a Vienna apartment together with two companions while taking part in negotiations with Iranian Government representatives. In November the Austrian authorities issued arrest warrants for three suspects in connection with the KDPI killings. The suspects included Iranian Government agents who had left Austria or gone into hiding in the Iranian Embassy in Vienna after the killings. In August Bahman Javadi, a member of the Central Committee of the Communist Party of Iran, was killed and a companion seriously wounded when unidentified gunmen attacked them in a Cyprus street.

In January Amnesty International submitted a written statement to the United Nations (UN) Commission on Human Rights summarizing the organization's concerns in Iran. In August Amnesty International delivered an oral statement to the UN Sub-Commission on the Prevention of Discrimination and Protection of Minorities, drawing attention to the execution of people under 18 years of age when the offence was committed. In December the government agreed for the first time to allow access to Iran by the UN Special Representative on the situation of human rights in the Islamic Republic of Iran.

Amnesty International campaigned throughout the year for an end to executions and in January published *Iran: The Death Penalty*, a short survey of the death penalty since the 1979 revolution. In February it urged the government to withdraw death threats against Salman Rushdie. In June it published *Iran: Over 900 Executions Announced in Five Months*, which documented recent executions for drug-trafficking. It also described the new directives issued by the judicial authorities to speed up the punishment of crime, which appear to have exacerbated the arbitrary and summary nature of arrests, trials and executions in Iran. Following the shootings of opposition activists in Dubai, Austria and Cyprus, Amnesty International called on the government to condemn such political killings and to make it clear to all its representatives that such actions would not be tolerated.

The Iranian Government continued to deny that mass killings of political prisoners had been carried out in 1988, despite mounting evidence to the contrary. This included letters of protest apparently written by Ayatollah Montazeri before his resignation as designated successor to Ayatollah Khomeini. In a response to Amnesty International's appeals, the authorities issued a document through the United Nations which maintained that only a small number of people had been executed; that they had taken part in, or collaborated with, an armed incursion into Iran by the opposition National Liberation Army in 1988 (see *Amnesty International Report 1989*); and that the government had the right to punish those who took up arms against it. The authorities failed to respond to repeated requests from Amnesty International for details of any charges brought against political prisoners executed in prison in 1988 and for information about the procedures followed at their trials.

The authorities responded to repeated calls from Amnesty International for an end to mass executions of drug-traffickers and other criminals by affirming their belief that the death penalty was an appropriate response to serious crime and an effective deterrent. They failed to respond to Amnesty International's concerns about the summary nature of the trials of many of those executed.

IRAQ

Thousands of political prisoners, among them prisoners of conscience, continued to be detained without charge or trial or imprisoned after trials which reportedly did not satisfy international fair trial standards. Torture of political prisoners remained widespread. "Disappearances" were reported and the government did not clarify the fate and whereabouts of thousands who "disappeared" in previous years. Many of the "disappeared" were believed to have been killed. Executions

were also reported. Some of those executed apparently had sought from the authorities benefits announced under official amnesties. In most cases it was unclear whether they had received any form of trial.

In February the government of President Saddam Hussein announced plans to draft a new constitution and to promulgate laws authorizing new political parties and introducing press freedoms. The government also stated that the possibility of holding Iraq's first presidential elections was under discussion. Elections were held in April for the National Assembly and in September for the Kurdistan Autonomous Region's Legislative Council. By the end of the year the planned political reforms had not been introduced and reports of widespread abuses continued to be received.

In February a general amnesty was declared for Iraqis abroad accused or convicted of political offences, provided they returned to Iraq between 1 and 30 April. Under the terms of the amnesty, all legal proceedings against them would be dropped. Those considered "agents of the Iranian regime" were excluded from the amnesty. In April the terms of the amnesty were amended, allowing Iraqis to postpone their return if they informed the authorities of their wish to benefit from the amnesty. Some 60 Iraqi Kurds reportedly returned from Turkey in April. They were among tens of thousands of Kurds who fled Iraq following chemical weapon attacks by government forces in the northern Kurdish region in August 1988 (see *Amnesty International Report 1989*). Some of the Kurds may have been returned to Iraq involuntarily, according to reports.

A number of people who returned to Iraq following amnesty announcements in 1988 were reportedly arrested, tortured or executed in 1988 and early 1989. Some returnees "disappeared". It was not possible to confirm government claims that 92,000 people had returned to Iraq by March as a result of the amnesties.

Thousands of political prisoners, including people who may have been prisoners of conscience, continued to be detained without charge or trial, or after summary trials. They included suspected members of prohibited political parties such as the Kurdistan Popular Democratic Party (KPDP), the Kurdistan Democratic Party (KDP), the Patriotic Union of Kurdistan (PUK); the Kurdistan Socialist Party-Iraq (KSP-I), the Iraqi Communist Party (ICP) and *al-Da'wa al-Islamiyya*, Islamic Call. Relatives of such suspects, including children, remained imprisoned while the authorities sought the suspects.

Political detainees held during the year included Mulla Muhammad Dalgayi, the Imam of the town of Qal'a Diza in Sulaimaniya Province. He was arrested in April soon after he and other Kurds met officials to appeal against government plans for forcibly resettling hundreds of thousands of Kurds and destroying Kurdish towns. There was no word of his fate or whereabouts until he was released without charge in August.

In September a British-based Iranian journalist, Farzad Bazoft, and a British nurse, Daphne Parish, were arrested in Baghdad on espionage charges. The arrests took place after Farzad Bazoft began investigating reports that hundreds of people had been killed in August in an explosion at a military plant south of Baghdad. The two detainees were held incommunicado for over six weeks and denied access to both consular representatives and legal counsel, giving rise to fears that they might be tortured. In October Farzad Bazoft appeared on Iraqi television and "confessed" to being an Israeli spy. Neither he nor Daphne Parish, who was said to be his accomplice, had been formally charged or tried by the end of the year.

Eight suspected members of the ICP, most of them engineers or students from Baghdad and Mosul, were reportedly arrested in late 1988 and in January. They included Athir Korkis, a graduate of al-Mustansariyya University, and Kifah Muhammad Kadhim, a social worker. Their fate and whereabouts remained unknown. The fate of some 200 military personnel and Ba'th Party officials arrested in December 1988 also remained unknown. They were arrested in Baghdad and Mosul on suspicion of plotting a coup. According to unconfirmed reports, 18 of them had been executed. There was no news of other former Ba'th Party officials reportedly arrested in the same period in Samarra'. 'Abdallah Sallum al-Samarra'i, a former government minister, was among these detainees.

Routine torture and ill-treatment of prisoners reportedly continued. Information was received during the year about the alleged torture of children and others arrested in previous years for political reasons. For example, eight school students aged between 13 and 16 were arrested in Sulaimaniya Province in May 1987 and reportedly tortured. They were detained without charge or trial for over 15 months, most of that time in Sulaimaniya Security Directorate. They allegedly suffered *falaqa* (beatings on the soles of the feet), beatings with metal cables while naked and suspended by the wrists from the ceiling, burnings with cigarettes, extraction of their finger-nails and electric shocks. In August 1988 they were brought before the Revolutionary Court and accused of anti-government activities, then released without conviction in September 1988. Unconfirmed reports said that four of them had been rearrested in April.

Among those reportedly tortured in 1989 was a member of the KSP-I's *Pesh Merga* forces or armed Kurdish units. He was arrested in February after giving himself up to the authorities in order to benefit from the 30 November 1988 amnesty (see *Amnesty International Report 1989*). He alleged after his release that he was held without charge or trial for 37 days, initially in the Military Intelligence Directorate in Baghdad and then in Prison No. 1 in the al-Harithiyya District of the city. He and 22 others shared a cell in Prison No. 1 measuring 12 metres by 12 metres. They were repeatedly beaten by their guards, who denied one prisoner medical treatment when he suffered a broken wrist from the beatings.

"Disappearances" were reported during the year and thousands of prisoners who "disappeared" in previous years, including 178 members of Shi'a families and some 8,000 Barzani Kurds (see *Amnesty International Report 1989*), remained unaccounted for. In October Amnesty International received information that 353 Kurds arrested in August 1988 subsequently "disappeared" in custody. They were arrested in 'Amadiyya, Duhok Province, following chemical weapons attacks in the area by Iraqi government forces. Among them were 33 members of the KDP's *Pesh Merga* forces. The others were civilians, most of them farmers. They also included 52 children aged 11 to 17. They were initially held at the Qal'a, the "castle", in Duhok and apparently "disappeared" in early September 1988.

Thirty-three Assyrians who returned from Turkey and Iran in late 1988 and early 1989 to benefit from government amnesties also reportedly "disappeared". They included whole families from Duhok Province. A number of Kurds from Bahark resettlement camp outside Arbil city, who had been among some 2,000 Kurds who returned to Iraq from Turkey in 1988 following the 6 September 1988 amnesty, were said to have "disappeared" in custody. They included Arjan Mari Hassan, Mari Mari Hassan and Khalid Khudaida, all alleged KPDP supporters.

Hundreds of people were reportedly executed; in most cases it was difficult to ascertain whether they had received any form of trial. Reports received in March stated that at least 11 army deserters had been executed in the town of al-'Amara in July 1988 and that 83 deserters had been executed in December 1988. In January, 14 army personnel and Ba'th Party officials arrested in December 1988 on suspicion of plotting a coup were reportedly executed. They included two brigadier-generals, 'Ala'uddin Hussain and 'Abd al-Ghani Shahin, and one general, Taleb 'Ali al-Sa'dun. Four others from this group were reportedly executed in July in Baghdad, among them Brigadier-General 'Abd al-Qader al-Shalawi and Lieutenant-Colonel Samir Sa'dallah.

Information received in February indicated that four members of an Assyrian family from 'Ain Kawa village in Arbil province had been killed between early September and mid-October 1988. The victims were Polous 'Aziz Sheba and Meska Wardina, husband and wife, and their two daughters, Hamama and Sabiha. They had lived in hiding after the execution of another member of their family, according to reports, but surrendered to the authorities shortly after the 6 September 1988 amnesty was announced. They were allegedly beheaded and their bodies, bearing marks of torture, were found in October 1988 on the Arbil-Mosul road.

Seven Kurds who sought to benefit from government amnesties were also executed in April in Dibs garrison near Kirkuk, apparently because of their past links with the *Pesh Merga* forces. They included Saber and Qader Sa'di, two brothers from the Qaradagh region in Sulaimaniya Province. Four other suspected Kurdish opponents of the government arrested in

128

1988 were executed in either March or April, three of them in Abu Ghraib Prison near Baghdad and one in Kirkuk following his trial by a military court. In January the government confirmed the execution in 1988 of two doctors, Isma'il Hassan al-Tatar and Hisham Maher al-Salman. It said they had been sentenced to death under Article 393/2/D of the Penal Code for "the crime of raping patients inside their clinics while practising their medical profession". They were allegedly arrested after they made remarks regarding President Hussain at a private gathering in Baghdad. Their comments apparently had been tape recorded.

Amnesty International continued to express its concern throughout the year about use of the death penalty and about allegations that some of those executed had been tortured.

Amnesty International also expressed its concern about mass political killing in previous years, including the killing of minors. In February it appealed to the government to halt the politically motivated brutal treatment of children and young people. The organization published in February the names of 396 minors, both Arabs and Kurds, who had been detained without trial, imprisoned following summary trials, tortured, executed or had been the victims of extrajudicial executions since 1980. Among those cited in the publication, *Children: Innocent Victims of Political Repression,* were the cases of 21 youths who were aged between 14 and 17 when executed and at least 351 youths who "disappeared" while in detention. In March the government denied allegations of these abuses, including the execution in 1987 of 16-year-old Ribwar Muhammad Karim 'Aziz. The government had previously confirmed his execution (see *Amnesty International Report 1989*). The government also denied in March reports that some 200 army personnel and Ba'th Party officials had been arrested in 1988 and that 14 of them had been executed in January.

In September and November Amnesty International appealed to the government to grant Farzad Bazoft and Daphne Parish legal and consular access and to ensure that they were protected from ill-treatment. It urged their immediate release unless they received a fair and prompt trial on recognizably criminal charges. By the end of the year no response had been received.

In an oral statement delivered to the United Nations Commission on Human Rights in March, Amnesty International drew attention to continuing human rights abuses, including deliberate killings and the torture and execution of political opponents and minors. An Iraqi Government representative said Amnesty International had launched a "premeditated endeavour...to deviate...world public opinion against Iraq". Amnesty International said in March that it was "deeply disturbed at the decision of the [Commission]...to take no action on the systematic and wide-ranging abuses in Iraq".

In an oral statement delivered in August to the United Nations Sub-Commission on Prevention of Discrimination and Protection of Minorities, Amnesty International expressed concern about the continued detention of Mulla Muhammad Dalgayi and the execution of Kurdish political opponents who had sought from the government benefits announced under official amnesties. An Iraqi Government representative responded by saying that Mulla Muhammad Dalgayi had been released and by denying that anyone had been executed after seeking benefits from an amnesty. Mulla Muhammad Dalgayi's release, which took place a few days before the government's response, was subsequently confirmed.

IRELAND
(REPUBLIC OF)

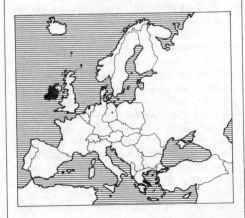

Two former prisoners pursued civil actions against the state claiming damages in connection with their imprisonment.

They had been convicted in 1978 solely on the basis of confessions allegedly obtained by ill-treatment during incommunicado detention. They were not allowed to raise their allegations of police assault in the civil proceedings on the basis that the trial court in 1978 had rejected the allegations.

On 8 December the Republic of Ireland ratified the International Covenant on Civil and Political Rights along with its Optional Protocol, and the International Covenant on Economic, Social and Cultural Rights.

Osgur Breatnach, Brian McNally and Nicky Kelly, Irish Republican Socialist Party members, had been arrested in 1976 for alleged involvement in the Sallins mail train robbery. During their 1978 trial they had claimed that their confessions were the result of ill-treatment during prolonged incommunicado detention in police custody in April 1976. The Special Criminal Court ruled that they had suffered injuries in custody, but that these had been self-inflicted. They were convicted solely on the basis of their confessions. In 1980, after they had served 17 months of their sentences, the Court of Criminal Appeal held that Osgur Breatnach and Brian McNally had been interrogated in a "possibly menacing environment" while being denied access to a lawyer. The court ruled that their confessions had been involuntary and quashed their sentences (see Amnesty International Report 1980 and 1981). In July 1984 Nicky Kelly was released on "humanitarian grounds" after serving four years of his sentence (see Amnesty International Reports 1981 to 1985).

Nicky Kelly and Osgur Breatnach subsequently brought separate civil proceedings against the state in connection with their imprisonment. However, in January 1986 and July 1989 respectively, courts ruled that their claims for damages on the grounds of police assault would not be allowed to proceed because the Special Criminal Court's 1978 judgment had found allegations of ill-treatment to be without merit. In the July 1989 ruling, the judge allowed Osgur Breatnach to proceed only with his other claims of malicious prosecution, false imprisonment and failure to vindicate constitutional rights. These proceedings opened in December 1989, but were adjourned after one day and scheduled to continue in 1990.

An Amnesty International delegate observed the December civil proceedings in the case of Osgur Breatnach. The organization's concerns relating to these cases dated back to 1977 when it sent a delegation to Dublin to investigate persistent allegations of ill-treatment in police custody following the introduction of emergency anti-terrorist legislation in 1976 (see Amnesty International Reports 1977 to 1979). An Amnesty International representative had observed the 1980 Court of Criminal Appeal proceedings. The organization had expressed concern about the Special Criminal Court's 1978 ruling in the light of numerous injuries which the accused had sustained in custody: some of these, according to expert witnesses at the 1978 trial, were incapable of being self-inflicted and were consistent with the allegations of assault (see Amnesty International Report 1980 and 1981).

129

ISRAEL AND THE OCCUPIED TERRITORIES

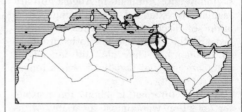

About 25,000 Palestinians, including prisoners of conscience, were arrested in connection with the *intifada* (uprising) in the Occupied Territories. Over 4,000 served periods in administrative detention without charge or trial. Several thousand others were tried by military courts. By the end of the year over 13,000 people were still in prisons or detention centres. At least 45 Israeli prisoners of conscience were held, most of whom were conscientious objectors to military service. Thousands of Palestinians were beaten while in the hands of Israeli forces or were tortured or ill-treated in detention centres. At least eight were reported to have died as a result. Over 260 unarmed Palestinian civilians, including children, were shot dead by Israeli forces, often in circumstances suggesting excessive use of force or deliberate killings. Others died in incidents where tear-gas was possibly

130

AMNESTY INTERNATIONAL REPORT 1990

deliberately misused. Official investigations into abuses appeared inadequate. One person remained under sentence of death.

Palestinians continued to protest against the Israeli occupation of the West Bank and Gaza Strip with strikes, tax boycotts and demonstrations in which stones, petrol bombs and other missiles were thrown. Palestinians also killed over 130 people, most of whom were suspected of collaborating with Israeli security services. The authorities responded to the unrest with mass arrests, restrictions of movement, deportations and a use of force which was often excessive or indiscriminate. They also demolished or sealed up to 200 homes of alleged Palestinian activists, imposed possibly punitive curfews, and closed off areas as military zones, thus preventing access by independent observers.

Over 4,000 Palestinians, including prisoners of conscience, were administratively detained without charge or trial. Most administrative detention orders were imposed for periods of six months and several hundred were renewed, prolonging the period of imprisonment. In August military regulations extended the maximum duration of each administrative detention order in the Occupied Territories from six to 12 months. They also introduced an automatic judicial review of orders longer than six months.

Crucial information about the reasons for detention was almost invariably withheld by the authorities from administrative detainees and their lawyers. This seriously impeded any meaningful exercise of the right to challenge the detention. Appeals by detainees were heard weeks or months after arrest, and most resulted in confirmation or only slight reductions in detention periods.

Prisoners of conscience held in administrative detention included Sami al-Kilani, a writer and poet detained between April and October, and Faisal al-Husseini, a leading Palestinian political figure, who was released in January after 18 months' detention. Other administrative detainees included Badran Jaber, a teacher held under consecutive detention orders since March 1988 and Ribhi Haddad, a labourer held since March 1988 and released in November 1989.

Among the Israeli prisoners of conscience held during the year were four editors of the newspaper *Derech Hanitzoz*, who were convicted in January of offences including membership of the Democratic Front for the Liberation of Palestine. Three served their sentences in full and were released during the year; Yacov Ben Efrat remained imprisoned serving an effective prison sentence of 30 months. Amnesty International believed they had not used or advocated violence. In October, Abie Nathan, a well-known Israeli peace campaigner, received an effective six-month jail sentence for having breached legislation forbidding unauthorized contacts between Israelis and the Palestine Liberation Organization (PLO). During the year eight other Israelis were charged with similar offences and a further four were awaiting appeal hearings.

At least 41 Israelis were sentenced to one or more periods of up to 56 days' imprisonment for refusing on grounds of conscience to undertake certain types of military service, such as duties in the Occupied Territories. Rami Hasson, a reservist, spent a total of 140 days in prison between 1988 and 1989. Amit Lewenhoff, a conscript, was imprisoned for a total of 103 days in 1989. Amnesty International considers such selective objectors to be prisoners of conscience.

Thousands of Palestinians were tried by military courts in the Occupied Territories. Some reportedly received sentences of up to five years' imprisonment for stone-throwing and up to nine years for throwing petrol bombs. Lawyers repeatedly went on strike to protest against aspects of the legal process. Their complaints included failure to inform detainees promptly about the reasons for their arrest; frequent and prolonged adjournments of hearings; remand hearings held without defence lawyers; and lack of adequate investigations into complaints of ill-treatment. A military court of appeal was introduced in the Occupied Territories in April.

Thousands of Palestinians were beaten by Israeli forces during the year. Many were punitively kicked or struck with clubs or rifle butts. The victims included people who refused to clear road-blocks or delete graffiti, or who were suspected of having thrown stones. Many suffered severe injuries, particularly fractures, and at least six reportedly died. Fares Salha, a tailor, died in hospital in April three weeks after soldiers reportedly assaulted him in his home in Jabalya refugee camp. The soldiers apparently hit him with a hoe and rifle butts and threw him down a staircase after he tried to stop them beating his sons.

There were reports of torture and systematic ill-treatment of political detainees, including beatings on various parts of the body, hooding, prolonged standing, sleep deprivation and confinement in coffin-sized cells. In October Sha'wan Jabarin — a human rights worker held in administrative detention — said in an affidavit that he had been severely beaten, burned with cigarettes, and jumped on several times by a soldier while he lay on the floor in a detention centre in Hebron.

Mahmud al-Masri died of a perforated stomach ulcer in Gaza Prison in March, while being held for interrogation by the General Security Service. An independent pathologist stated that the stress caused by the interrogation, including physical violence, and inadequate medical attention were contributory factors. Khaled Shaikh 'Ali died in the same prison in December. A second independent pathologist found that he died from internal bleeding from blows to the abdomen.

Conditions in the Ketziot detention centre in the Negev Desert remained harsh. About 4,000 prisoners, including the vast majority of administrative detainees, were held there by the end of the year. None received family visits and access to lawyers was inadequate. Detainees went on repeated hunger-strikes during the year to protest against conditions.

More than 260 unarmed Palestinian civilians were shot dead by Israeli forces using live ammunition and special types of plastic and other bullets. Several were also killed by settlers or Palestinians believed to be collaborating with the Israeli authorities. Almost half the victims were aged 18 or below and about 20 were aged 12 or below.

Although most killings appear to have taken place during demonstrations or riots, in many cases the victims did not appear to have been involved in life-threatening or even violent activities when they were shot. Unarmed Palestinians were also killed by soldiers or Israeli plainclothes personnel during operations ostensibly aimed at arresting them. After some shooting incidents, Israeli forces obstructed emergency medical care for the casualties.

Milad Shahin, aged 12, was shot dead in Bethlehem in May by a soldier at a look-out post. The boy had apparently moved out from behind a wall to throw a stone. Yaser Abu Ghawsh, aged 17, was shot dead at close range in August in Ramallah by plainclothes men after a brief street chase. The men also reportedly prevented a doctor who arrived at the scene from administering first aid.

At least seven people reportedly died in incidents in which tear-gas was used, possibly deliberately, in confined spaces where it could be lethal. In January a three-week-old baby, Islam Abu Dalfah, died reportedly after inhaling tear-gas from a canister thrown into her home by Israeli forces.

During the year two soldiers were convicted and jailed after courts-martial for fatal shootings in 1988. One received an effective jail sentence of three months. The other was sentenced to an effective jail sentence of two years, under appeal at the end of the year. In May four other soldiers received effective jail sentences of up to nine months for beating a man in 1988. The man subsequently died in custody, apparently after further beatings by other soldiers. The sentences on the four were later reduced and all were released by September. No prosecutions were known to have taken place in relation to allegations of deliberate and lethal misuse of tear-gas or allegations of torture and ill-treatment of detainees. However, several hundred officers and soldiers were officially said to have been disciplined for various abuses. In September the Chief of Staff reminded soldiers that force should not be used as a punishment and directed them not to hinder medical assistance to casualties.

Mordechai Vanunu, an Israeli former nuclear technician, continued to be held in solitary confinement with severely restricted access to visitors. Arrested in late 1986, he was serving a sentence of 18 years' imprisonment for offences including treason. His appeal was heard by the Supreme Court in May, but the verdict had not been announced by the end of the year. An Amnesty International delegate was refused access to the appeal proceedings.

John Demjanjuk, convicted in 1988 of offences including crimes against humanity, remained under sentence of death. His appeal to the Supreme Court was rescheduled for 1990.

Amnesty International appealed for the release of prisoners of conscience and published a report detailing its concerns about

132

the use of administrative detention. It also expressed concern to the authorities about alleged torture and ill-treatment of prisoners and possible extrajudicial executions.

The organization was particularly concerned that guidelines on opening fire may have permitted unjustifiable killings. Further, although in practice these guidelines were reportedly often disregarded, the authorities did not appear to investigate fatal shootings adequately and to bring to justice those found responsible for abuses.

In January Amnesty International delivered an oral statement to the United Nations Commission on Human Rights about human rights violations during the period of the *intifada*.

The Israeli authorities, in correspondence and discussions with Amnesty International representatives, argued that administrative detention was necessary because of the security situation and that its use was in accordance with international law. They said that selective conscientious objection to military service was unacceptable. With regard to the editors of *Derech Hanitzoz*, they reiterated the view that "any form of membership in a terrorist organization constitutes, at the least, advocacy of the use of violence against the State". The authorities also responded to a 1988 Amnesty International report on the misuse of tear-gas by arguing that the organization's concerns in the matter "were without any basis". No substantive response was received on specific cases of alleged torture or extrajudicial execution.

In view of the close cooperation between Israel and the South Lebanon Army (SLA), Amnesty International also sought assurances from the Israeli authorities about the treatment of Suha Beshara, a Lebanese woman believed to be held by the SLA. The Israeli authorities replied that this was "strictly an internal Lebanese matter".

ITALY

Hundreds of prisoners of conscience, all conscientious objectors to the national service laws, were in prison. Unreasonable delays continued to be reported in judicial proceedings in political cases. There were allegations of ill-treatment in police custody and prisons: some of these were not adequately investigated. Several judicial inquiries which had been opened into alleged ill-treatment in previous years remained unresolved.

In April the Defence Committee of the Chamber of Deputies (lower house of parliament) finalized a new draft law on conscientious objection (see *Amnesty International Report 1989*). Its proposals included widening the grounds on which conscientious objector status might be granted and reducing the length of civilian service from 20 to 15 months, three months longer than military service. In July the Constitutional Court ruled that the existing eight-month difference between military and alternative service was punitive to conscientious objectors. From 9 August recognized conscientious objectors were allowed to terminate their civilian service after 12 months. The draft law on conscientious objection was still awaiting parliamentary discussion at the end of the year.

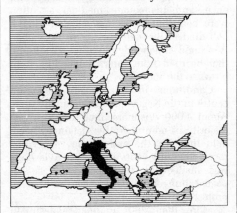

A new Code of Penal Procedure came into force on 24 October, replacing the inquisitorial system of criminal justice with a system containing many features of an accusatorial system (see *Amnesty International Report 1989*). The slow functioning of the criminal justice process, which frequently contributed to excessive delays in judicial proceedings in political cases, had been widely criticized for many years. In some cases, international standards relating to fair trial within a reasonable time had been breached (see *Amnesty International Reports 1987* to *1989*). The new code aims to simplify and speed up judicial procedures and strengthen the rights of the defence. However, judges' and lawyers' associations repeatedly alleged that the structural and administrative reforms necessary for the efficient functioning of the new code were incomplete and that this would exacerbate delays in judicial proceedings. Many judges and lawyers also called on the government to introduce an amnesty law to reduce substantially the massive backlog of proceedings; they considered this essential for the successful application of the new code. On 27 October the government presented a draft amnesty law applicable to numerous minor offences committed before 28 July 1989, which proposed that conscientious objectors sentenced for refusing military service should not be liable for further call-up. It was still awaiting parliamentary discussion at the end of the year.

In August the Chamber of Deputies asked the government to prepare legislation abolishing the death penalty from the Wartime Military Penal Code: this would abolish the penalty for all offences under Italian law. By the end of the year such legislation had not been introduced.

In January Italy ratified the United Nations Convention against Torture and Other Cruel, Inhuman or Degrading Treatment or Punishment.

In July the Ministry of Defence stated that there were 532 conscientious objectors held in military prisons, of whom 90 per cent were Jehovah's Witnesses. The law requires recognized conscientious objectors to perform civilian service but many objectors refused this option either on conscientious grounds or because they considered its length to be punitive. Until the Constitutional Court's July ruling effectively reduced the length of civilian service, Amnesty International considered that it was not an acceptable alternative to military service owing to its punitive length. It therefore considered those imprisoned for refusing to undertake civilian service to be prisoners of conscience.

The length of precautionary detention (the period between the moment of arrest and the passing of a definitive sentence by the final court of appeal) that is allowed by Italian law has repeatedly been criticized by legal experts. Although the new Code of Penal Procedure reduced the maximum permitted length of precautionary detention from six to four years, it allowed suspension of this limit in "particularly complex court hearings". A decree law passed in September also extended the permitted length of precautionary detention for people sentenced by first instance courts for serious offences relating to terrorism and organized crime.

During the 1980s there was widespread legal concern over the practice of filing multiple charges in political cases in order to extend the permissible limits of precautionary detention. The problems caused by this practice were evident in 1989 in proceedings against 421 defendants charged with promoting armed insurrection against the state and committing acts aimed at provoking civil war. They had been committed for trial in July 1983. Many of them had already been accused of and, in some cases, convicted of being members of the Red Brigades and frequently of having been involved in specific violent acts carried out by the Red Brigades. The new charges made possible a further period of precautionary detention. As a result, some defendants who had been on the point of release on the original charges spent up to four more years in prison in precautionary detention. In October 1989 Rome Assize Court fully acquitted the first 253 defendants; their trial had opened in March. The trial of the remaining defendants opened in November and ended with their acquittal two weeks later. No judicial justification was ever given for the delay of about six years between the committal order and the opening of the trials.

Reports of the alleged ill-treatment of criminal suspects in police custody continued throughout the year; some of the allegations related to 1988. There were also claims that there was an increase in the number of charges of calumny brought against detainees who had alleged ill-treatment by law enforcement agents. In some cases the judicial authorities appeared to have made little effort to investigate formal complaints of ill-treatment.

On 9 August 1988 Domenico Garzon submitted a complaint to the Verona Public Prosecutor's office. He alleged that he had been repeatedly ill-treated by law enforcement officers in San Bonifacio *carabinieri* station during the night of 26 May 1988. He claimed that they had punched and kicked his head and body and had beaten him with a wooden broom handle. He alleged that he was then made to kneel, handcuffed, for nine hours, facing the wall in an unlit cell and kicked and punched regularly. A medical report issued by Verona district prison immediately after his transfer on 27 May recorded numerous cuts and

134

bruises which appeared to be consistent with his allegations. No investigation was apparently carried out by the responsible judge of instruction and the original complaint was archived on 17 January 1989.

Little progress appeared to have been made in several judicial inquiries opened in previous years into allegations of ill-treatment in police custody. In July the Italian Interministerial Committee on Human Rights reported that judicial inquiries into the alleged ill-treatment of approximately 47 detainees in Milan in early 1988 and of Francesco Badano in Padua in May 1988 were still continuing. It added that criminal proceedings had been instituted against a *carabinieri* officer who had shot Antonio Leone in a Naples police station in July 1988 (see *Amnesty International Report 1989*). Two people, whose cases were included in an investigation into approximately 30 cases of alleged ill-treatment opened by the Naples Public Procurator in 1986, were awaiting trial on charges of calumny against the police. No progress was reported in the remaining cases in the Naples investigation (see *Amnesty International Reports 1987* to *1989*).

The trial of 15 law enforcement agents, in connection with Salvatore Marino's death in custody in Palermo in August 1985 (see *Amnesty International Reports 1986* to *1989*), opened in May but was immediately adjourned on the grounds that two defendants were absent from court. No date had been fixed for reopening the hearing by the end of the year.

Allegations of ill-treatment were also made by prison inmates. Pietro Barberino alleged that he and about 20 non-Italian prisoners were regularly beaten by prison guards in Pianosa Island prison between August 1985 and August 1988. He also claimed that two senior guards regularly entered the cells of foreign prisoners at night, forcing them to strip naked and then punching and kicking them. As a result, a number of these prisoners apparently suffered burst eardrums, broken teeth and numerous cuts and bruises. Pietro Barberino alleged that he was often beaten after he had intervened to stop the ill-treatment of fellow prisoners. He reportedly suffered numerous minor injuries, including broken teeth, and underwent an emergency eye operation as a result of blows inflicted by prison guards. He sent written complaints to the judicial authori-

ties in August and December 1988. He was interrogated by a Public Prosecutor in February 1989 but had apparently received no further news regarding the judicial investigation of his allegations by the end of the year.

Amnesty International appealed for the release of conscientious objectors considered to be prisoners of conscience. It welcomed the new Code of Penal Procedure insofar as it aimed at reducing the length of judicial proceedings, but was concerned that delays would persist owing to inadequate provision for the necessary structural reforms. It asked to be informed of the steps taken to investigate allegations of ill-treatment and monitored the progress of judicial inquiries opened into such allegations in previous years. The organization also investigated cases where charges of calumny were brought against detainees, apparently without full investigation of their original complaints.

JAMAICA

At least 27 death sentences were imposed for murder but no executions were carried out during the year. Some 230 prisoners were under sentence of death. The United Nations Human Rights Committee (HRC) adopted the view that there had been violations of the International Covenant on Civil and Political Rights (ICCPR) in the cases of two prisoners under sentence of death. The Judicial Committee of the Privy Council (JCPC) in London annulled the convictions of 10 prisoners under sentence of death. There were further reports of ill-treatment of prisoners. Prisoners reportedly died after incidents in which the authorities used force. There were allegations that several people who could have been arrested were shot dead by the police.

The People's National Party (PNP) won the February general election and Michael Manley was sworn in as the new Prime Minister on 13 February.

At least 27 people were sentenced to death for murder during the year but no executions took place. Some 230 prisoners were on death row. Earl Pratt and Ivan Morgan (see *Amnesty International Report 1989*), sentenced to death in 1979, were still on death row at the end of the year despite the fact that in April the HRC, which supervises the implementation of the ICCPR, adopted the view that Jamaica had violated its treaty obligations under the Covenant in their cases and that their death sentences should be commuted. The HRC found a violation of ICCPR Article 14 (the right to a fair trial) because the Court of Appeal had delayed issuing a written judgment for three years and nine months after hearing the appeal. This delay had prevented Earl Pratt and Ivan Morgan from appealing to the JCPC, the final court of appeal for Jamaica. It also found violations of Article 7 (the prohibition of torture or other cruel, inhuman or degrading treatment or punishment) because the two men had been notified of a stay of execution granted to them on 23 February 1987 only 45 minutes before their execution was due to be carried out, despite the stay being formally granted about 20 hours earlier. The HRC's view was that the two men were entitled to a remedy for the violations of the ICCPR and that "the necessary prerequisite...is the commutation of the sentence".

In decisions delivered in March and July the JCPC quashed the convictions of 10 prisoners under sentence of death. The JCPC found that the trial judges had failed to warn the jury adequately about the danger of convicting on the basis of uncorroborated identification testimony. The 10 men, who were released in March and September, had spent between four and 11 years under sentence of death. The JCPC had previously allowed only one appeal in a Jamaican death penalty case since 1980.

In early July some 380 prisoners at the General Penitentiary in Kingston started a hunger-strike to protest long delays in their court cases. Two days after starting their action, the prisoners refused to return to their cells unless they received assurances that their demands would be acted on. Prison warders, aided by police officers, used force and tear-gas to restore order reportedly after prisoners became aggressive to prison personnel. As a result one prisoner died, three were admitted to hospital — one of whom died a month later — and a large number sustained injuries and were not given medical attention. Some of them appeared in court on 10 July still showing serious injuries: the presiding judge ordered that all be afforded medical attention. The Minister of National Security agreed to investigate the incident but it is not known whether an investigation took place.

In September another prisoner, Phillip Leslie, died at St Catherine's Adult Correctional Centre allegedly after being beaten by warders when he refused to return to his cell. He reportedly sustained a broken leg and multiple head blows which resulted in a fractured skull; he died the same day. He had been among the prisoners injured in an incident in July 1988 at St Catherine's Adult Correctional Centre (see *Amnesty International Report 1989*). It was alleged that he had also been beaten on other occasions, which once resulted in his being sent to hospital with a fractured elbow.

There were reports that several people who could have been arrested were shot dead deliberately by police officers. The killings occurred in a context of widespread criminal violence in which over 100 people were killed in confrontations with the police.

David Wellington, aged 17, was allegedly shot dead at point-blank range by the police in July. A police report said that he had been killed when police officers returned fire from him and five other gunmen during a raid. However, witnesses claimed that armed police entered David Wellington's house, took him to the back of the building, pushed him under a staircase and shot him. Witnesses also said that there was no provocation, resistance or attack on the police. It was not known whether a police investigation said to have been initiated into the matter had been completed. Among other people reportedly killed by police in circumstances suggesting that they may have been unlawfully killed were Cedric Blake, Fitzroy Taylor, Paul Dawkins, Texton Bailey and George Barrington Miller. The police officers implicated in the death of Cedric Blake were to be charged. Amnesty International was seeking further information about all of

136

these cases, and any investigations of them, to determine whether they were extra-judicial executions.

In February the Minister of Justice replied to Amnesty International's inquiry about reports in July 1988 of ill-treatment of prisoners at St Catherine's Adult Correctional Centre and of the beating of four inmates in the Gun Court Rehabilitation Centre which resulted in the death of one inmate (see *Amnesty International Report 1989*). The Minister said that the Department of Corrections and the Jamaica Defence Force had been asked to carry out an investigation into the incident at St Catherine's. He said a police investigation of the Gun Court incident had been concluded and eight warders were to be charged with murder. Seven had been charged by the end of the year.

In March Amnesty International published *Jamaica — the Death Penalty*. The report raised serious concerns about the fairness in practice of capital trials despite guarantees in the Constitution. It examined the adequacy of legal representation, delays in the judicial process and the failure of the Court of Appeals to issue written judgments in many cases. The report also pointed to weaknesses in the use of uncorroborated identification evidence on which many convictions are based. Amnesty International urged the Prime Minister to commute existing death sentences and called on the government to take steps to abolish the death penalty in law. In November Amnesty International representatives discussed the organization's concerns relating to the death penalty with government officials and local organizations. Amnesty International delegates observed the appeal hearings before the JCPC which resulted in the convictions of 10 prisoners under sentence of death being quashed. The organization welcomed the decisions which could have implications for other Jamaican prisoners under sentence of death.

JAPAN

A prisoner sentenced to death in 1958 was acquitted and released, and another sentenced to death in 1975 was granted a retrial. One person was executed.

Emperor Hirohito died on 7 January and was succeeded by his son, who became Emperor Akihito. An amnesty granted in February in honour of the late Emperor did not affect prisoners under sentence of death.

An estimated 90 prisoners convicted of murder were believed to be under sentence of death. The Supreme Court had confirmed around 35 of these sentences, three of them in 1989. Takekazu Kondo was executed in November at the Fukuoka Detention Centre. He had been sentenced to death in 1972 on charges that included murder and arson.

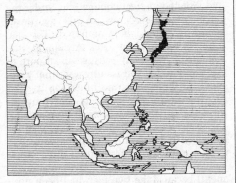

In January the Supreme Court upheld the acquittal of Masao Akahori on a charge of murder. At his retrial, the court ruled that his confession lacked credibility and that no other evidence linked him to the crime (see *Amnesty International Report 1989*). He was the fourth prisoner sentenced to death to be acquitted in a retrial since 1983.

In June the Supreme Court ordered the retrial of Norio Shimogami, who was sentenced to death in 1975 for murder. The court ruled that his conviction was based on the unreliable confession of an alleged accomplice and was contradicted by material evidence. The first hearing of the retrial took place in December.

An Amnesty International delegation visited Japan during February and March and met senior officials of the Ministry of Justice, judiciary and police. The delegates expressed concern about the use of the death penalty, sought information about detention procedures and emphasized the importance of effective safeguards against ill-treatment.

Amnesty International continued to press for the commutation of all death sentences and to urge the authorities to abolish the death penalty.

JORDAN

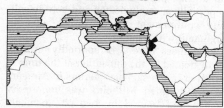

Over 100 suspected opponents of the government, including many prisoners of conscience, were arrested during the year. Most were detained without charge or trial following riots in April, held for several months, and then released before the end of the year. About 20 political prisoners were tried before the Martial Law Court whose procedures did not satisfy international standards for fair trial. About 60 political prisoners sentenced in previous years by this court remained in prison at the end of the year. Torture and ill-treatment of political prisoners were reported. At least three prisoners were executed for murder.

In April riots broke out in the south of the country in protest against economic measures introduced by the government. Twelve people were reported to have died and hundreds were injured. Hundreds of protesters were arrested, but most were released in May, with the exception of alleged political activists. Following the riots and widespread demands for economic and political reform, national elections for an 80-member Lower House of Parliament took place in November and King Hussein bin Talal appointed a 40-member Senate and a new government under Prime Minister Mudar Badran.

The authorities continued throughout 1989 to imprison people considered a threat to security using emergency powers provided by the Defence Law, in force since 1939, and martial law, in force since 1967. Some prisoners were administratively detained without charge, trial or judicial review. Others were prosecuted before the Martial Law Court. In December the new government announced that it would lift martial law within four to six months and "freeze" its use in the meantime. It also stated that it would review the cases of prisoners sentenced under emergency legislation.

Over 70 suspected opponents of the government were arrested in April in connection with the riots. They were detained without charge or trial under emergency legislation in Swaqa Prison, south of the capital, Amman. All the detainees were believed to be prisoners of conscience or possible prisoners of conscience. They included writers and journalists, engineers, students, lawyers, doctors and trade unionists. Many were alleged members of banned political organizations such as the Jordanian Communist Party, the Organization of the Popular Front in Jordan (OPFJ), and the Organization of the Democratic Front in Jordan (ODFJ). Some were former prisoners of conscience. For example, 'Imad Milhelm, Hashem Gharaybah and 'Ali Hamdan Zuyud had all previously served sentences of up to 10 years' imprisonment. Salem al-Nahhas, who was deputy president of the Jordanian Writers' Association when it was dissolved by the government in 1987, had previously been detained without charge or trial several times. Most of those detained without charge or trial in connection with the April riots were released in September; the remainder were freed by the end of 1989.

Among the other political prisoners arrested during the year were at least 15 alleged members of the OPFJ arrested between June and November and detained without charge or trial in the headquarters of the General Intelligence Department (GID) in Amman. Nine of them were arrested in October, apparently in reprisal for armed attacks against Israel carried out in September across the Jordanian border by the Popular Front for the Liberation of Palestine. The nine included Hamdi Matar and Ahmad Saleh Musleh, who were also members of the Palestine National Council (the Palestine Liberation Organization parliament in exile). All 15 were released in December.

Hundreds of prisoners were released during the year. In February about 900 prisoners were freed. They included about 50 political prisoners, over 30 of whom had been held without charge or trial on suspicion of belonging to banned organizations. Ahmad Fares al-Khatib had been detained without charge or trial since August 1983; at least 25 suspected members of al-Fatah and the OPFJ had been similarly detained since 1987. Forty-eight untried political detainees were released in December. Among them were a number of long-term detainees, some of whom may have been prisoners of conscience. They included Ziad 'Ali Qasem, detained since October 1984 and Rasem al-Hindi, detained since January 1988. Also released were two brothers detained as alleged members of the Islamic Liberation Party (ILP), Muhammad Yasin Zallum and 'Abd al-Halim Zallum, who had been arrested in October 1987 and June 1988 respectively.

About 20 people were reportedly tried on political charges before the Martial Law Court. In September Kamal Khalil, a musician, and Hasan Shahin, an academic researcher, were sentenced to four years' imprisonment after being convicted of membership of an illegal organization. They were reported to have been tortured in the custody of the GID following their arrest in November 1988. Munir 'Akrush, a student arrested in August, was tried under the 1953 Law of Resistance to Communism and sentenced in December to four years' imprisonment for possession of banned literature. In November Muhammad Jarrad, Jamal Shaker and Muhammad Khattab, three alleged members of the ILP who were arrested in April, were reportedly sentenced to three years' imprisonment. They, like others sentenced by the Martial Law Court, may have been imprisoned solely for the non-violent expression of their beliefs. Moreover, their trials did not satisfy international standards of fair trial. They had no right of appeal and the court was not bound by the code of criminal procedure or the law on evidence applicable in other Jordanian courts.

There were new reports of torture and ill-treatment of prisoners. In January between 12 and 18 political prisoners in Swaqa Prison were reportedly beaten and held in solitary confinement. They had been protesting against prison conditions, including restrictions on visits by relatives, and had tried to publicize their grievances. Majed al-Khawaja, an accountant serving a four-year sentence for membership of an illegal organization, was allegedly handcuffed to a prison gate (a method commonly called *shabah*), beaten and held in solitary confinement for over two weeks. In February Adib 'Afnan, an untried political detainee held since January 1987, was reportedly subjected to *shabah*, flogged with electric wires and whips, kicked and punched in the head. He allegedly lost consciousness and suffered severe bruising,

impaired mobility and apparent neurological damage. In June or July, Yaser Qubaylat, an untried political detainee aged 17, was reportedly severely beaten and held in solitary confinement for one week after an argument with a guard.

Detainees were also reportedly tortured or ill-treated by the GID, either at the time of arrest or in the GID headquarters in Amman. In April 'Imad Milhelm was reportedly beaten and injured by two GID members who arrested him in an Amman street. 'Akram Salamah, a student, was said to have had several of his fingers broken as a result of beatings by GID members in Irbid in April. In June 'Abd al-'Aziz Khadr, an engineer, was allegedly subjected to beatings on the soles of the feet. At least one person held in the Military Intelligence headquarters in Amman was allegedly tortured, including with electric shocks.

Three prisoners were executed in October for premeditated murder. Other executions may have been carried out during the year. Three prisoners reportedly convicted between 1978 and 1982 of politically motivated offences remained under sentence of death.

Amnesty International repeatedly appealed to the government to release prisoners of conscience and to ensure that all other political detainees received a prompt and fair trial on recognizably criminal charges, or were released. It continued to be concerned that trials of political prisoners by the Martial Law Court failed to meet international standards of fair trial. Amnesty International welcomed the releases of prisoners during the year.

Amnesty International urged the authorities to ensure respect for the United Nations Standard Minimum Rules for the Treatment of Prisoners and to investigate all allegations of ill-treatment of prisoners, bring to justice those found responsible and grant redress to the victims. The organization also appealed for clemency for prisoners sentenced to death.

In January the government responded to Amnesty International's 1988 call for Jordan to ratify the Optional Protocol to the International Covenant on Civil and Political Rights and the Convention against Torture and Other Cruel, Inhuman or Degrading Treatment or Punishment. The government said it was studying the matter but did not envisage an early decision. In March a senior Public Security Department official told Amnesty International that prison regulations, including those providing for corporal punishment, were being reviewed. In May the government denied holding prisoners of conscience and stated that all reports received by Amnesty International concerning torture and ill-treatment were "groundless and mere fabrications". However, the authorities had not responded to a memorandum on torture submitted by Amnesty International in 1987 nor had they provided specific information in response to inquiries about individual cases since 1987.

KENYA

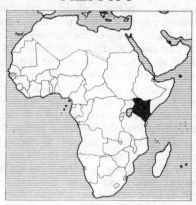

Seven political detainees held without trial, including prisoners of conscience, were released in June. Other prisoners of conscience and people who may have been prisoners of conscience were among 34 political prisoners released after completing prison sentences imposed in previous years. At least 24 political prisoners were still serving prison sentences at the end of the year. Three of these prisoners were sentenced during the year. Several other short-term political arrests occurred. Over 36 death sentences were imposed, and up to 200 people were reportedly under sentence of death. No executions were known to have taken place. Asylum-seekers from Uganda and Somalia were forcibly returned to their countries of origin. Some of those returned to Somalia were subsequently killed there.

All seven political detainees held in administrative detention without charge or trial under the Public Security Regulations

were released in June. Wanyiri Kihoro, a lawyer, and Mukaru Ng'ang'a, a historian, were prisoners of conscience held since 1986. Raila Odinga, son of former vice-president Oginga Odinga, and Samuel Okumu Okwany, a former air force member, had been detained since 1988. Mirugi Kariuki, a lawyer and prisoner of conscience, had been detained since 1986. The two other administrative detainees had been held since September 1988 (see Amnesty International Report 1989).

Forty-seven political prisoners were still detained at the beginning of the year. They had been convicted between 1986 and 1988 in connection with a clandestine opposition group, Mwakenya (Muungano wa Wazalendo wa Kukomboa Kenya, Union of Patriots for the Liberation of Kenya). Charges against them included possessing or distributing seditious publications and taking an unlawful oath to join Mwakenya. Some of those convicted were prisoners of conscience and others may have been prisoners of conscience. Thirty-four of the prisoners received one-third remission of their sentences during the year and were released. At least three of those freed were prisoners of conscience: Odhiambo Olel, a medical doctor who reportedly was suffering from injuries caused by torture; Kimani wa Nyoike, a former member of parliament; and Julius Mwandawiro Mghanga, a student leader. Harris Okong'a Arara, another prisoner of conscience arrested in connection with seditious publications, remained in prison. Formerly a member of the air force, he was serving a 10-year sentence for possessing publications of the clandestine opposition groups, the Kenya Patriotic Front and the Kenya Revolutionary Movement, a charge he denied.

Most convicted political prisoners were held illegally for long periods before being brought to court. They were denied legal representation and access to their families before their trials, and were subjected to torture or duress to make them plead guilty to the charges.

During 1989 several suspected opponents of the government were also subjected to arrest and detention. Most of them were released without charge after two or three weeks in the custody of the police Special Branch. At least five were brought to trial on sedition charges: two were acquitted on charges of possessing seditious publications and released, three were

140

convicted and imprisoned. Daniel Mwangi Theuri, who was unemployed, was sentenced in March to 20 months' imprisonment for failing to report the existence of a seditious organization. Dixon Jowe Alieth, a teacher, received a six-year sentence in October for possessing seditious publications. Wilson Awuor Ang'ong'a, a prison guard, pleaded guilty to joining *Mwakenya* and was sentenced to four and a half years' imprisonment.

In addition, three prisoners of conscience were charged with possessing the Protestant church magazine *Beyond*, which was banned in 1988 after criticizing the government's election procedures. Justin Kiborus Ngetich, a teacher, and his two sons, both school students, were arrested in October 1988. The three remained in custody throughout 1989, except for a short period when they were freed on bail. None of them had been brought to trial at the end of the year.

The editor of *Beyond*, Bedan Mbugua, was acquitted by the Appeal Court in August. He had been charged in 1988 with failing to submit an annual business report to the Registrar of Books and Newspapers, an offence for which he had received a nine-month prison sentence. Amnesty International believed his arrest had been politically motivated (see *Amnesty International Report 1989*). He had served two weeks of the sentence in August 1988, before his release on bail pending hearing of his appeal.

Despite a public statement by President Daniel arap Moi in February that torture was not permitted, reports were received about political prisoners who were tortured or threatened with torture. However, four police officers were imprisoned in February after they were found guilty of causing the death of Taalu Kotela Kiombwe. The victim, a Zairian musician tortured on suspicion of committing a criminal offence, died in custody in Mombasa early in 1988. No further developments were reported in the case of Peter Karanja, a political detainee who died in custody in 1987, although an inquest judge had concluded in 1988 that he had been tortured (see *Amnesty International Report 1989*).

Conditions of political imprisonment were harsh. Prisoners were held in solitary confinement and permitted to leave their cells for only one hour a day. Medical treatment and hygiene were poor and access to reading material was limited. Visits and correspondence from relatives were also severely restricted.

Courts imposed over 36 death sentences for robbery with violence or murder. While the government disclosed no information about the number of prisoners under sentence of death, up to 200 people reportedly remained on death row. Most had apparently filed judicial appeals or petitions for presidential clemency. No executions were announced and it was not known whether death sentences were carried out in 1989.

In February more than 200 Ugandan asylum-seekers were forcibly returned to Uganda, despite fears that they would be subjected to human rights violations there. Ugandan security officials reportedly detained some of them upon their return. In September some 60 asylum-seekers from Somalia were forcibly repatriated, 18 of whom were said to have been extrajudicially executed by Somali soldiers and the rest detained. Hundreds of others were forcibly returned to Somalia in November after over 3,500 people attempted to escape fighting by entering northeast Kenya. The Kenyan authorities refused to allow the Office of the United Nations High Commissioner for Refugees to assist these asylum-seekers, and more were detained and deported in December. Some Kenyan nationals of Somali origin were also arrested and forcibly sent to Somalia in December, according to reports, including at least one opponent of the Somali Government believed to be at risk of human rights violations in Somalia.

Amnesty International welcomed the release of the seven people from administrative detention and pressed for the release of all prisoners of conscience. It also continued to investigate cases of possible prisoners of conscience. The organization appealed to the government in November for adherence to international standards in its treatment of Somali asylum-seekers. It urged the government to give all asylum-seekers access to international procedures for the protection of refugees. Amnesty International protested when the government forcibly returned hundreds of asylum-seekers to Somalia.

Amnesty International also appealed for the commutation of all death sentences and for measures towards abolition of the death penalty.

KOREA
(DEMOCRATIC PEOPLE'S REPUBLIC OF)

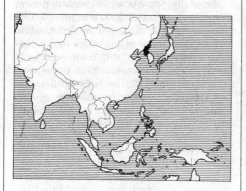

Two Japanese nationals, who may be prisoners of conscience, were held throughout the year. About 40 university staff and students reportedly detained in 1988 were possibly still held. Some sources suggested there were thousands of political prisoners but this could not be confirmed as it remained extremely difficult to obtain detailed information about human rights. The Democratic People's Republic of Korea (DPRK) authorities maintained strict censorship and the authorities and media rarely provided information about arrests, political trials or the death penalty.

Unofficial reports suggested that imprisonment is used extensively to curtail rights to freedom of expression and association guaranteed under the International Covenant on Civil and Political Rights (ICCPR), to which the DPRK acceded in 1981. Individuals who criticize President Kim Il Sung, his son and political successor Kim Jong Il or the policies of the ruling Korean Workers' Party are liable to lengthy terms of imprisonment.

Isamu Beniko and Yoshio Kuriura, two Japanese seafarers who were both sentenced in December 1987 to 15 years' "reformation through labour", continued to be held throughout 1989. They were possibly prisoners of conscience (see *Amnesty International Report 1989*).

It was not clear by the end of 1989 whether the authorities had released about 40 staff and students of the University of Pyongyang and the Kim Chaek University of Technology, who were reportedly detained in mid-1988 following the appear-

ance of wall posters criticizing the government's economic policies (see *Amnesty International Report 1989*). There was no new information about their cases.

An apparently authoritative report received by Amnesty International in 1988, based on information from visitors to the DPRK, suggested that in April 1987 tens of thousands of people were being held for political reasons at corrective labour camps throughout the country. Major camps were said to be located in Chongpyong, Hoenyong, Kyongsong, Onsong, Sariwon, Yodok, Yongpyon and Yongang, with at least four smaller camps near Pyongyang and Onsong town. It was not possible to obtain further information about these camps and the prisoners held in them during 1989.

Amnesty International continued to seek information about the trial, treatment and conditions of Isamu Beniko and Yoshio Kuriura. In May Amnesty International published a short report on its concerns in the DPRK. It contained information about trial proceedings, prison camps and the death penalty.

Amnesty International representatives were invited to the World Festival of Youth and Students in Pyongyang in July, but were unable to attend as the DPRK authorities failed to issue entry visas in time. At the inaugural ceremony, several delegates carrying a banner of support for Amnesty International were attacked by security personnel and the banner was snatched away. However, others carrying placards advocating observance of human rights in the DPRK and in the People's Republic of China were not disturbed.

KOREA
(REPUBLIC OF)

About 800 people were imprisoned for opposition activities, including at least 100 prisoners of conscience. Thousands more were held briefly for trade union activities, street demonstrations or for seeking contact with or expressing views sympathetic to North Korea. Six long-term prisoners of conscience were still imprisoned, one of them after 18 years. All prisoners held in administrative detention without charge or trial under the Public Security Law were released after its

142

repeal in May. Measures introduced in the previous two years to safeguard against incommunicado detention and torture were often disregarded and several political prisoners complained that they had been tortured. Two criminal suspects died in police custody, apparently as a result of beatings. Seven people sentenced to death on criminal charges were executed in August, after two years when no executions had been carried out.

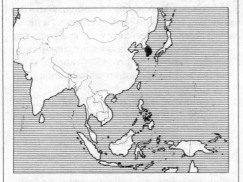

A wave of political arrests followed attempts by dissidents to have direct contact with North Korea outside Republic of Korea government channels, prolonged strikes in key industries and a campaign by opposition groups to force President Roh Tae-woo to resign. On 3 April a Joint Public Security Investigation Headquarters was set up to link the police, prosecution authorities, the Agency for National Security Planning and the Defence Security Command. The headquarters had acknowledged the arrest of 317 people on political charges and had charged 126 others without detaining them by the time it was disbanded on 19 June. Thousands of other people were detained briefly. Arrests continued in the second half of the year, but were fewer in number.

In April a new Law on Assemblies and Demonstrations was introduced to replace a similarly named law which banned "demonstrations likely to cause social unrest" and under which prisoners of conscience had been imprisoned in the past. The new law provides for demonstrations to be held so long as "public order and security are protected". In May the National Assembly repealed the Public Security Law of 1975, under which the Minister of Justice had been able to order the administrative detention without

charge or trial of prisoners who had completed sentences under the National Security Law if he did not consider them "thoroughly anti-communist". It was replaced by the Social Surveillance Law, introduced in June, which also provides for restrictions to be imposed on the freedom of association, expression and movement of former National Security Law offenders: breaking such restrictions is punishable with imprisonment. The National Security Law remained in force, although all the main political parties had agreed in 1988 that it should be amended. No changes were made to reduce the role of military and civilian security agencies in the investigation of political offences.

Most political arrests, including those of prisoners of conscience, were carried out under laws relating to North Korea or restricting freedom of expression, peaceful assembly and trade union activity. According to unofficial reports, those arrested in the first eight months of the year included almost 300 workers arrested in connection with strikes (some of which involved violence); over 270 students, most of them arrested for participating in violent demonstrations or for "supporting North Korea"; around 60 teachers who had set up a trade union (thousands more were briefly detained); and dozens of members of dissident political groups, publishers and artists, street vendors and people who resisted evictions from urban areas due for redevelopment.

Five prisoners of conscience were tried under the National Security Law for visiting North Korea. Dozens of others were charged under the same law with assisting them, failing to report them to the authorities, or because they advocated or attempted themselves to establish direct contact with North Koreans. In April the Reverend Moon Ik-hwan and Yu Won-ho, a businessman, were arrested when they returned from a visit to North Korea, during which they had discussed Korean reunification with government officials. Both were sentenced to 10 years' imprisonment in October. Lee Yong-hee, a journalism professor and editor of the opposition newspaper, *The Hankyoreh Shinmun*, was also arrested in April for planning to send a team of journalists to North Korea and to visit the country himself. He was convicted in September and received a suspended sentence of 18 months' imprisonment. Three co-chairpersons of *Chonminnyon*, the National Coalition for a Democratic Movement — Lee Bu-yong, Lee Chang-bok and Lee Jae-oh — were arrested in April. They were tried on charges relating to a *Chonminnyon* proposal for a conference where representatives of both Koreas would discuss reunification, and for supporting illegal demonstrations and workers on strike. They were each sentenced to one to two years' imprisonment.

In June Suh Kyung-won, an opposition member of the National Assembly, was arrested and charged with espionage and a foreign exchange offence, after he told the authorities that he had visited North Korea in 1988 and discussed reunification with officials. At his trial, which started in September, he denied espionage and said that he had been tortured to make him confess to this charge during pre-trial interrogation. In December Suh Kyung-won was convicted and sentenced to 15 years' imprisonment, although the court accepted that he had not divulged state secrets. Pang Yang-kyun, his secretary, was sentenced to seven years' imprisonment for committing similar offences under Suh Kyung-won's orders on the occasion of a visit to the Federal Republic of Germany. Nine other people, who were also tried for failing to report the member of parliament's visit to North Korea, were released on probation or on suspended sentences.

In August Im Su-kyong and Father Moon Kyu-hyun were arrested as they crossed the border with North Korea. Im Su-kyong had defied a government ban by attending the World Festival of Youth and Students in Pyongyang, North Korea, as a representative of *Chondaehyop*, the National Council of Student Representatives. Father Moon Kyu-hyun had joined her to support her attempt to return across the border. Their trial began in November and was still in progress at the end of the year. Around 20 people, mostly students, were arrested for helping to arrange the visit, as were three members of the Catholic Priests Association for Justice who had helped to send Father Moon to North Korea. The three priests were released on suspended sentences in December. More students had been arrested after participating in events to support *Chondaehyop's* participation in the youth festival. Four artists whose painting had been reproduced and displayed at the festival were

also arrested in July and August: three were released on suspended sentences in December but the trial of the fourth was still in progress at the end of the year.

Several dozen people were arrested for possessing or reproducing North Korean publications, which are prohibited to all but officially authorized scholars. Cho Song-u, director of the Peace Research Institute, was sentenced to 18 months' imprisonment in September for possessing books from the North Korean Social Academy. The authorities had denied him a licence to have North Korean material. Dozens of publishers were arrested but most were released almost immediately. However, some were held for a few months before being tried and released with suspended sentences. Dozens of students who wrote articles supporting North Korean ideology were also arrested, but the outcome of their trials was not known.

Hundreds of workers and labour activists were arrested for taking part in strikes, some of which involved violence, but little information was available on individual cases. Eight members of *Sonohyop*, Seoul Labour Council, a federation of 59 independent unions in the Seoul area, were arrested in April for illegal third-party involvement in strikes. Dan Byung-ho, the head of *Sonohyop*, was released on a suspended sentence in August, but it was not clear whether the others were also released.

Between mid-May and August thousands of teachers were arrested for participating in peaceful rallies and other activities to support their right to set up a trade union. The authorities declared *Chonkyojo*, the National Teachers' Union, illegal and accused its organizers of trying to introduce "leftist" ideology into schools and to seek to "change the country's democratic system". Although most were released without charge, around 60 teachers were tried for violating the Civil Service Law or the Private Schools Law. All except Yun Yong-kyu, the union's chairman, were released on suspended sentences. Yun Yong-kyu was sentenced to one year's imprisonment.

Over 200 people continued to be imprisoned for national security offences. Thirty-five were held without charge or trial under the Public Security Law because they had refused to "convert" to "anti-communism". Most had been held for between 10 and 13 years (see *Amnesty*

144

International Report 1989), but all were released by the end of October, following the repeal of the law in May. The others were serving long prison sentences: they had been convicted of being North Korean "spies" or "agents". Little was known about these long-term prisoners. Some were arrested in the 1950s and 1960s, and others were arrested in the 1970s or 1980s after a period abroad when they were alleged to have contacted supporters of North Korea. A few were considered prisoners of conscience.

The practice of interrogation during incommunicado detention was renewed. The Bar Association complained about restrictions on lawyers meeting their clients. Lawyers defending Reverend Moon Ik-hwan and Professor Lee Yong-hee were only allowed to meet them eight or nine days after their arrests after filing a complaint with the Prosecutor General. Lawyers representing Im Su-kyong could not see her until three weeks after her arrest, after securing a court order.

Several political prisoners alleged that they had been deprived of sleep and beaten while detained incommunicado by the Agency for National Security Planning. Hong Song-dam, one of the four artists arrested after their painting had been displayed in North Korea, said he was deprived of sleep, beaten about the face and otherwise ill-treated. A subsequent examination carried out at the request of the court trying Hong Song-dam concluded that injuries to his right leg and left ear had been inflicted while he was held by the Agency for National Security Planning.

Similar allegations of abuse were made by Suh Kyung-won, Pang Yang-kyun and Yu Won-ho, who stated that they had been beaten and denied sleep while in pre-trial detention. The court reportedly said that "overnight interrogation [of Suh Kyung-won] was inevitable because of the importance of the case" and that "in Pang Yang-kyun's case, the court cannot rule out the possibility that he was tortured...by the Agency for National Security Planning".

The body of Lee Chol-kyu, a student activist in Kwangju wanted by the police because of an article he had written, was found in a reservoir on 10 May. Unofficial sources claimed that he had been tortured to death. An official autopsy concluded that he had died of accidental drowning. In June two criminal suspects died from police beatings. Seven police officers were prosecuted for causing their deaths, but Amnesty International did not know the outcome of the trial by the end of 1989. The trial began of four other police officers accused of torturing Kim Keun-tae, a former prisoner of conscience, in 1985. It had not been completed by the end of the year.

Korean newspapers seldom report death sentences imposed by the courts. In April, however, there was wide publicity about the imposition of the death penalty on Kim Hyun-hui, a North Korean. She was convicted of planting the bomb which blew up a Korean Airlines aircraft in November 1987, causing 115 deaths. Her death sentence was upheld by the Seoul High Court in July.

Seven prisoners were executed on 4 August. They had been convicted of murder, aggravated in some cases by rape, kidnapping or robbery. A Ministry of Justice official said the executions had been carried out in an effort to stem an increase in violent crime.

Amnesty International called for the release of prisoners of conscience and investigated the cases of possible prisoners of conscience. It called for the trial or release of prisoners detained without charge under the Public Security Law, all of whom were released by the end of October. Amnesty International also asked for information about prisoners serving long prison terms for allegedly being "spies" or "agents" for North Korea. The organization was concerned about their cases because the definition of espionage was broad and ambiguous and because in some well-documented cases prisoners of conscience had been convicted after unfair trials. Amnesty International called on the authorities to investigate all allegations of torture and expressed its concern about the seven executions in August.

The authorities informed Amnesty International in October that all prisoners held under the Public Security Law had been released and that six other prisoners of conscience — three publishers, one writer, one journalism professor and one labour activist — had been released on bail or on suspended sentences at the end of 1988 or in 1989.

KUWAIT

At least 20 suspected opponents of the government, including possible prisoners of conscience, were arrested. Of these, five were still detained without charge or trial at the end of the year. Twenty-two other suspected government opponents were sentenced to prison terms by the State Security Court after an unfair trial. Some of these political detainees were reportedly tortured. Seven other political prisoners sentenced after unfair trials in previous years were still held. The death sentence was imposed on at least one person and there was one known execution.

At least 20 suspected opponents of the government, all Shi'a Muslims, were arrested following the execution of 16 Kuwaiti Shi'a pilgrims in Saudi Arabia on 21 September (see Saudi Arabia). Saleh Jawhar, Imam of the Imam al-Hussein mosque in al-Kuwait, was arrested on 21 September, apparently to prevent him from delivering a sermon the next day. He was released uncharged several days later. On 23 September, four sisters of Hani al-Misri, one of those executed in Saudi Arabia, were detained briefly for demonstrating against the executions outside the Saudi Arabian embassy. Sayyid Muhammad Baqir al-Musawi, a prominent religious scholar and Imam of the Imam 'Ali Mosque in al-Kuwait, was arrested the same day. He was detained by *Mabahith Amn al-Dawla*, State Security Intelligence, reportedly in connection with bomb attacks in Mecca, Saudi Arabia, but no charges had been brought against him by the end of the year. He was permitted one family visit shortly after his arrest, but was then held incommunicado at Amn al-Dawla Prison in al-Kuwait. His mother was assaulted by a prison official when she inquired about him and there were reports in November that he had been tortured and threatened with extradition to Saudi Arabia, where he might face execution.

Fourteen other Shi'a were arrested by *Mabahith Amn al-Dawla* in November, also apparently in connection with the September executions in Saudi Arabia. They included Faisal 'Abd al-Hadi al-Mahmid, an entrepreneur, who had delivered sermons in the Imam al-Hussein mosque after al-Haj Saleh Jawhar was arrested. He was reported to have been kicked and beaten during interrogation, as were several of the other detainees. Khalil Musa al-Musa, a teacher and former director of *Jam'iyyat al-Thaqafa al-Ijtima'iyya*, Social Culture Society, the only official Shi'a charitable society in Kuwait, was also arrested. Another detainee, 'Abd al-Hamid al-Saffar, was also reportedly tortured and told that his daughter would be assaulted in his presence if he refused to "confess". Four of those arrested were still held without charge or trial at the end of 1989.

In May, 33 people, all Shi'a, were tried by the State Security Court on various charges, including "belonging to banned groups aiming to destroy the basic structures of Kuwait by illegal means, and publicly defaming the Amir". Thirteen were tried in their absence. The 20 who appeared in court, who included Iraqi, Iranian and Lebanese nationals as well as Kuwaitis, had all apparently been detained by *Mabahith Amn al-Dawla* at the end of 1988. Twenty-two of the defendants, including nine of those tried in their absence, were convicted and sentenced to between five and 15 years' imprisonment; the 11 others were acquitted. The trial was conducted almost entirely *in camera*, despite a request by some defence lawyers that it be conducted in open court. The defendants also had no right of appeal to a higher tribunal, contrary to international fair trial standards. Those tried in their absence had no legal representation. In view of the secrecy of much of the proceedings, it was not clear on what evidence the defendants were convicted or whether any of them were prisoners of conscience.

In October four actors appeared before the Court of Misdemeanours charged with staging a play allegedly offensive to Islam. They reportedly faced between three months and seven years' imprisonment if convicted. The play, entitled *Hadha Saifu*, This is Saifu, had opened in May 1988 but was stopped after 36 performances following complaints to the state prosecutor that it insulted Islam. In November Sa'ad Faraj,

AMNESTY INTERNATIONAL REPORT 1990

146

Khalid al-Nafisi and Muhammad al-Sari' were acquitted. No sentence was passed on the fourth defendant, 'Abd al-Hussain 'Abd al-Ridha, on condition that he pledge to pay bail of 500 Kuwaiti dinars and pledge "good behaviour" for one year.

Seven Shi'a political prisoners tried between 1985 and 1987 continued to serve prison sentences ranging from three to 10 years. The seven, among them possible prisoners of conscience, had been convicted by the State Security Court on charges including the distribution of leaflets inciting violence, and membership of illegal groups. They had been tried almost entirely *in camera* and had no right of appeal (see *Amnesty International Report 1989*).

One person was sentenced to death for murder in December, but the sentence had not been carried out by the end of the year. There was at least one execution: an Indian national convicted of murder in 1988 was hanged in August. It was not known whether three other prisoners sentenced to death for murder in 1988 were executed (see *Amnesty International Report 1989*).

Amnesty International continued to seek information about the cases of the seven Shi'a prisoners tried by the State Security Court between 1985 and 1987 in order to establish whether any were prisoners of conscience. During the year the government told Amnesty International that four of them had been imprisoned for distributing leaflets "inciting the overthrow of the government . . . by using force, violence and terrorism [and which] contained a clear sign to murder", but copies of the leaflets were not made available.

Amnesty International expressed concern to the government about the detention without charge or trial and the reported torture of Sayyid Muhammad Baqir al-Musawi and other Shi'a detainees. In response, the authorities said he was being held for investigation in accordance with Kuwaiti law and was permitted family visits. Other reports received by Amnesty International, however, indicated that he continued to be held incommunicado.

In September the government also told Amnesty International that the 22 people convicted by the State Security Court in June included some who were found to be "members of extremist terrorist organizations", and convicted on the basis of "conclusive evidence as to their involvement in the crimes . . . including the confes-

sions made against each other and against themselves . . . and the seizure of leaflets". The authorities said the trial had been held *in camera* for reasons of state security.

Amnesty International appealed for the commutation of the death sentence passed in December, and expressed regret about the execution carried out in August.

LAOS

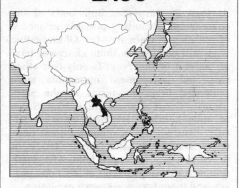

At least 37 suspected opponents of the government, including four known to be prisoners of conscience, remained under restrictions without charge or trial for "re-education" in Houa Phanh province. An unknown number of others were under restrictions for "re-education" in Attapeu province. Several political arrests were reported.

The first elections to a national parliament since the People's Democratic Republic of Laos was established in 1975 were held in March. All 121 candidates for seats on the 79-member Supreme People's Council were approved by the authorities and all but a few were members of the ruling Lao People's Revolutionary Party. The committee appointed in August to draft a constitution had not completed its work by the end of the year although the promulgation of a constitution was officially described as a "main task" of the newly elected assembly.

In November the Supreme People's Council adopted a criminal law and a criminal procedure law which replaced and expanded on regulations previously issued by various ministries. Legislation also established the People's Judiciary Institute for public prosecution and the Supreme People's Court. The death penalty apparently remained in force under the new legislation but no death sentences or judicial executions were reported.

At least 34 people associated with the pre-1975 government were reportedly still held without charge or trial for "re-education" in the northeastern province of Houa Phanh. Four of those known to be held were prisoners of conscience, detained for their non-violent opposition to the government, and others may have been prisoners of conscience.

The 34 were held at a small camp near the village of Sop Pan, formerly the main "re-education" centre in Houa Phanh, where improved conditions were reported. People held there included Khamphan Pradith, a Christian poet; Tiao Sisoumang Sisaleumsak, a 72-year-old doctor; Salat Rajasak, a former member of parliament; and 62-year-old Houmphanh Norasing, also a former member of parliament. All 34 were reportedly permitted to move somewhat more freely than in previous years in the area around Sop Pan. They were also permitted to send and receive letters. It appeared that most of them were no longer required to perform manual labour. Instead, they were employed in administrative or professional work. However, most of those restricted were said to be in poor health resulting from the conditions of imprisonment and restriction to which they have been subjected for 14 years.

Three other prisoners, Khamtou Sackda, Sisavanh Bannavong and Khamphan Thammakhanty, were reportedly released from a high-security detention centre, designated 07, at Sop Hao in northeastern Houa Phanh where they had been held for allegedly violating "re-education" regulations. They apparently had been held in isolation under harsh conditions.

No further information became available about 185 people previously reported to be held without charge or trial for "re-education" at various places in Attapeu province. Sisanone Khamphanh and several others were said to be restricted to the provincial capital, Samakhixai-ville, where they were employed in skilled jobs. Others apparently continued to work in labour gangs building and repairing roads.

The official news media continued to report arrests of alleged subversives. Early in the year the media reported that in 1988 public security officials in Bolikhamsai province arrested "12 enemies in various localities who were hiding among the people". The official report suggested that the 12 had been detained for spreading "false propaganda" and circulating leaflets that "tried to tarnish the reputations" of government leaders. No further details about their cases were known to have appeared in the official media, and there was no indication whether they were charged or brought to trial. In August official sources reported the arrest of 38 Vietnamese "reactionaries" who had entered Laos from Thailand. The 38 were to be tried in January 1990 by the Supreme People's Court.

In February Amnesty International wrote to Kaysone Phomvihan, Chairman of the Council of Ministers, to welcome the release of political prisoners in late 1988, to express concern about those still held and to inquire about three people reportedly arrested in 1988 and accused of spying in Vientiane province. The letter also proposed that an Amnesty International delegation visit Laos to discuss human rights and possibilities for incorporating international standards for human rights protection in the Constitution and other national law. Amnesty International received no response to the letter during the year. However, a delegation from Amnesty International met a senior government official in December and outlined the organization's concerns. The same month Amnesty International wrote again to inquire about human rights protection in the new legislation adopted in November.

LEBANON

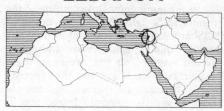

Government forces and armed militias carried out hundreds of arbitrary arrests of suspected political opponents, some of whom may have been prisoners of conscience. In most cases their fate and whereabouts remained unknown, but a small number were released in prisoner exchanges. A number of people were

148

killed outside the immediate context of armed conflict in what appeared to be extrajudicial executions.

Lack of central governmental control and armed conflicts between rival governmental and non-governmental forces posed considerable problems for obtaining and assessing accurately information about human rights violations. However, all sides were believed to have perpetrated some abuses.

A Charter for National Reconciliation, proposed by the Arab League, was endorsed by Lebanese deputies meeting in Ta'if, Saudi Arabia, in October. It proposed a series of political reforms, including the transfer of executive power from the president to the prime minister and dividing an increased number of parliamentary seats equally between Muslims and Christians. On 5 November Lebanese deputies elected René Mu'awad as President of the Republic, a post which had been vacant since September 1988. He was assassinated 17 days later in West Beirut and was succeeded by Elias Hrawi, who was elected on 24 November. However, by the end of 1989 General Michel 'Aoun, appointed as interim prime minister in September 1988 by the outgoing president Amin Gemayel, continued to challenge the legitimacy of the elections and President Hrawi's cabinet. He remained head of an interim military cabinet based in East Beirut.

Syrian government forces maintained control of northern Lebanon, the Beka' Valley, West and southern Beirut, and the coastal road towards Sidon. Israeli government forces maintained control of the so-called "security zone" along the Lebanon/Israel border.

The predominantly Druze militia of the Progressive Socialist Party (PSP) controlled the Shouf mountains south of Beirut. The mainly Shi'a Muslim Amal Movement retained control over territory in southern Lebanon between Sidon and the "security zone". The Lebanese Forces (LF), a mainly Christian militia, controlled territory in East Beirut and neighbouring coastal and mountain regions north and east of the city. The South Lebanon Army (SLA), a Christian militia, controlled an area along the southern Lebanese border, in conjunction with Israeli Defence Force (IDF) units. The PSP, Amal, the LF and the SLA, although not governments, all exercised effective control over particular areas and their populations,

and thus had the means and responsibility to respect human rights. Other non-governmental groups committed human rights abuses but lacked such extensive or effective territorial control. They included Hizbullah (Party of God), Islamic Jihad and various Palestinian factions.

Both government and non-government forces reportedly arrested combatants and civilians. Syrian government forces carried out arrests of suspected opponents. Some were held in Lebanon in detention centres under Syrian jurisdiction, while others were transferred to Syria. At least 160 detainees who had been arrested by Syrian forces in Lebanon in previous years, and then held without charge or trial in Syria, were released during the year (see Syria). In July Shaikh 'Abd al-Karim 'Ubaid, a prominent member of Hizbullah, was abducted by Israeli forces from southern Lebanon and placed under administrative detention in Israel.

In January it was reported that 15 detainees held by the LF on charges of sabotage and espionage had been released in December 1988. In February predominantly Christian units of the Lebanese Army clashed with the LF for control of parts of East Beirut and its suburbs. During two weeks of hostilities, the army reportedly arrested 148 members of the LF militia, some of whom were said to have been taken to the Defence Ministry in Yarzé, northeast of Beirut. The LF reportedly arrested some 100 army personnel. At the end of February leading members of the Maronite church reportedly mediated between the army and the LF to secure the release of the detainees, but it was not clear whether any were released. In November two Amal members previously arrested by the LF in Byblos were released in a prisoner exchange with Amal.

In January a cease-fire agreement was concluded in Damascus between Amal and Hizbullah, which provided for the release of prisoners held by both sides. The following month, a total of 32 prisoners held in southern Lebanon were exchanged, but others reportedly remained in detention. Hizbullah said that Amal still held about 500 people arrested in Tyre, Nabatiye, Jibchit and other areas, but it was not possible to verify this or obtain further information. In September Amal announced that it had detained a number of people in southern Lebanon who were intending to launch rocket attacks on Israel. It was not clear what had become of them by the end of the year. It was also not possible to obtain further information about 125 people reportedly detained by Amal in Ghazieh and Tyre in December 1988. However, two Palestinians detained by Amal in 1988 were reported to have been released in January, and two LF members arrested earlier in the year were known to have been released by Amal in the prisoner exchange with the LF in November.

The SLA continued to hold an estimated 300 people in Khiam detention centre in southern Lebanon, some of whom were arrested during 1989. In January, 19 people from 'Ain Qunya, Khiam, Hasbayya, Habbariyya and Markaba were arrested. One was released in February but the fate of the others remained unknown. In May several people were arrested in Jezzine, reportedly for refusing to join the SLA. About 50 people, most of whom were arrested in previous years, were said to be held for refusing to join the SLA. In October the SLA was reported to have detained 22 people from the villages of 'Aytaroun, Kfartebnit, Kfarhouna and Sha'ba. Nine were later released but the situation of the others was unclear at the end of the year. Among them were five villagers from Sha'ba in the district of Hasbayya. They were arrested on 17 October, apparently for resisting efforts by Israeli forces to establish a civil administration in the "security zone" in place of the existing Lebanese administration. Other detainees included Suha Beshara, who apparently remained in untried detention. She had been arrested while reportedly trying to assassinate General Antoine Lahad, the leader of the SLA, in November 1988.

Fourteen detainees were reportedly released from Khiam detention centre in January, nine others in February and a further nine in November: some of the last group had reportedly been held without charge or trial for over two years.

Information was received during 1989 about the torture in previous years of detainees held by Syrian forces in Lebanon (see Syria).

A number of people were apparently deliberately killed for political reasons outside the immediate context of the armed conflict. They included Shaikh Hassan Khaled, the Mufti of Lebanon and the country's highest Sunni Muslim authority,

who was killed on 16 May; Nazem Qadiri, a Sunni member of parliament killed on 20 September; and President René Mu'awad, who was killed in a bomb blast on 22 November. All three were killed in West Beirut. There was insufficient information to attribute responsibility for these and other apparent extrajudicial executions. In late November, two Shi'a Muslim detainees were killed during riots by prisoners in Khiam detention centre. Some reports suggested that they died from inhaling tear-gas used by guards to quell the riots, but other reports alleged that they were shot by guards. General Lahad reportedly ordered an investigation into the incident.

Amnesty International wrote to the LF in January to respond to its offer to hold talks with the organization (see *Amnesty International Report 1989*). Amnesty International asked for information from the LF in response to its previous inquiries as a basis for discussions. However, this was not forthcoming by the end of the year. In December Amnesty International wrote to the SLA expressing concern about the reported killing of two detainees in Khiam detention centre the previous month. The organization requested the names and details of the detainees and asked to be informed of the results of any investigation into the incident.

LESOTHO

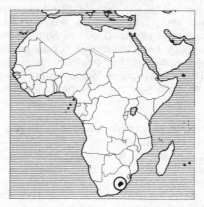

Two people who criticized the government were detained without trial for two weeks. The circumstances in which two prisoners died in custody and another reportedly "disappeared" in 1988 remained unclarified. An inquest into the killings in 1986

150

of two former government ministers and their wives began on 15 November, but was adjourned until January 1990.

The state of emergency declared in 1988 continued throughout 1989. Under emergency regulations, the police are empowered to arrest without a warrant people suspected of certain criminal offences and to detain them incommunicado for up to 14 days. Police have immunity against prosecution for any acts committed during the exercise of emergency powers. In September the head of the ruling Military Council, Major-General Justin Lekhanya, admitted at an inquest that he had shot dead a student in December 1988. On 5 October the inquest ruled that the killing constituted justifiable homicide.

Two people were briefly imprisoned and appeared to be prisoners of conscience. Joel Moitse, a university lecturer, was detained under the Internal Security Act in May, apparently on account of a letter he had written to a newspaper criticizing the Military Council. A former Cabinet minister in the government of Chief Leabua Jonathan, overthrown in a military coup in January 1986, he was released without charge after 14 days. Majara Jonathan Molapo, a nephew of the late Chief Jonathan and a leader of the Basutoland National Party, forbidden to operate owing to the ban on political activities, was also detained under the act for the same two weeks. Joel Moitse complained of "rough treatment" in the initial days of detention, when he was also denied access to a lawyer and doctor. Police were said to have threatened to deport him to South Africa although he is a Lesotho citizen, and to have harassed his relatives. Both Joel Moitse and Majara Molapo were issued with restriction orders at the time of their release in June, but these were rescinded within a week.

No inquests had been held by the end of the year into two deaths in custody in 1988: those of Samuel Hlapo, a bus hijacker who died in suspicious circumstances, and Mazizi Maqekeza, a wounded South African member of the banned African National Congress (ANC) who was shot dead while in hospital under police guard. No further information was received about Mbulelo Ngono, an ANC member who was reported to have "disappeared" from police custody in 1988 (see *Amnesty International Report 1989*). An inquest

began in November into the cases of two former government ministers and their wives who were killed in 1986 (see *Amnesty International Report 1987* and *1988*), but it was adjourned until January 1990.

In July the death sentences imposed on Tseliso Mona and Khopiso Mona in 1987 after they were convicted of murder were commuted to 20 years' imprisonment by King Moshoeshoe II. No new death sentences were imposed in 1989. One prisoner, Naso Letaso, convicted of murder, was reportedly awaiting execution.

In June Amnesty International urged the government to release Joel Moitse and Majara Molapo.

LIBERIA

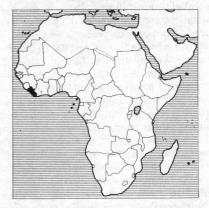

Ten prisoners of conscience arrested in 1988 remained in prison and three others were held for two weeks. Two prisoners charged with involvement in a politically motivated murder died in detention, apparently as a result of torture, illtreatment or medical neglect. Two other murder suspects and a prisoner under sentence of death also died in detention, apparently because of poor prison conditions. Government forces were reported to have extrajudicially executed unarmed civilians following an attempted invasion by exiled government opponents who also killed many civilians. Death sentences were passed on 20 people but no executions were reported.

Gabriel William Kpoleh and nine other prisoners of conscience sentenced to 10 years' imprisonment for treason in October

1988 (see *Amnesty International Report 1989*) remained in prison throughout the year. It appeared that they had been convicted after an unfair trial either because of their non-violent opposition to the government or in order to give credibility to the authorities' allegation of an attempted armed coup. The 10 prisoners were reportedly held in poor conditions at the Central Prison in the capital, Monrovia. In December the Supreme Court heard their appeal for a retrial but had not given a decision by the end of the year.

Momodu Lavala and two other University of Liberia students were detained illegally and without charge for two weeks in October; they were apparently suspected of contravening a ban on student political activities imposed by President Samuel Doe under an executive order in 1988. Momodu Lavala and another student had been suspended from the university after they re-established a student political party, citing a 1974 Supreme Court ruling that executive orders lapsed after one year if not ratified by the legislature.

In October two murder suspects died at Monrovia Central Prison, apparently as a result of torture, ill-treatment or medical neglect. The prison's superintendent told the court before which they had been indicted that they had been transferred from military custody in very poor health in September. Following their arrest, thought to have been in April or May, they had been held illegally and incommunicado in the Post Stockade, a military detention centre where political detainees have been tortured in the past. They and eight others were charged in August with conspiracy to commit a ritual murder — murder committed in the context of magical or religious beliefs — which was intended to assist in overthrowing President Doe. A former government minister, Major-General Gray Dioh Allison, had already been sentenced to death for the same ritual murder (see below), following a trial in which one of the two prisoners who died had testified for the prosecution. It appeared that the two may have been put under duress to induce them to testify for the state in a second trial; three of the others accused were released after apparently being offered immunity from prosecution if they agreed to turn state's evidence in the second trial. No inquest is known to have been held into the two deaths in prison.

Three other prisoners — suspected or convicted of criminal offences — died in custody, reportedly as a result of harsh conditions. A suspected murderer and another man sentenced to death for murder in February both died at Buchanan Central Prison in mid-1989; in October another murder suspect died at Monrovia Central Prison. The authorities did not reveal the cause of these deaths and no inquests were reported. However, the deaths were said to have been due to inadequate diet and poor conditions, particularly at Buchanan prison where there were no sanitary, washing or medical facilities. The authorities and voluntary bodies subsequently took steps to install toilets and improve the prisoners' diet at this prison.

Hundreds of unarmed civilians were killed after an estimated 100 exiled government opponents entered Nimba County in northeast Liberia on 24 December with the aim of overthrowing the government of President Doe. According to the authorities, the rebels initially attacked the villages of Butuo and Karnplay and killed some 16 officials and over 200 unarmed civilians. Refugees and other unofficial sources reported that the rebels killed dozens of people and that government forces retaliated by burning villages and killing large numbers of unarmed civilians who were unconnected with the rebels. Thousands of refugees fled to neighbouring Côte d'Ivoire and Guinea.

The chief of Butuo claimed that the armed forces which recaptured the village burned it down and shot dead the village commissioner, David Boley, and his wife on 29 December. After being questioned about the rebels, he and the Boleys were allegedly stripped, made to lie down and then shot; the chief of Butuo apparently survived because he was left for dead.

Following searches by the armed forces in Monrovia in late December, some 12 people suspected of supporting the invasion were reportedly arrested.

Twenty prisoners were known to have been sentenced to death following convictions for murder. Seventeen prisoners were sentenced in July after two trials in Voinjama, Lofa County. No executions were reported. Major-General Gray Dioh Allison, formerly minister of national defence, was sentenced to death in August for allegedly ordering a ritual murder intended to help him overthrow President Doe. He was

152 convicted following a trial *in camera* before a military court which allowed no right of appeal to a higher court. Excerpts of his trial were shown on government-owned television, but the international and local independent press were not allowed to attend the trial. It appeared that prosecution witnesses, many of them arrested as suspects weeks before Major-General Allison, may have been led to testify by torture, ill-treatment or illegal inducements. When Major-General Allison's civilian lawyers sought a review of the trial on the grounds that the court's judgment had not been consistent with the evidence and that it had overlooked inconsistencies in witness testimonies, they were refused a review, convicted of contempt of court and fined. Major-General Allison was transferred to a remote prison camp at Belle Yellah where prisoners have died in recent years from ill-treatment, malnutrition and medical neglect (see *Amnesty International Report 1989*). No decision on his petition for presidential clemency was known to have been made by the end of the year.

Amnesty International published a report in May which called for the release of the 10 prisoners of conscience convicted in the 1988 treason trial and described ways in which the trial was unfair. Amnesty International also inquired into the causes of deaths in detention and appealed against the use of the death penalty.

LIBYA

Five prisoners of conscience and 51 untried political detainees arrested in previous years were held throughout 1989. At least 60, but possibly many more, suspected critics or opponents of the government arrested in 1989 were detained incommunicado and without charge or trial at the end of the year. At least one political prisoner was reportedly kept in detention despite having been acquitted and at least 15 were serving sentences imposed after unfair trials. There was new information indicating that a prisoner of conscience had been executed in 1984.

In March the General People's Congress (GPC) discussed and promulgated a draft Law on the Consolidation of Liberty. This retained the ban on certain political and religious activities, but called for guarantees to protect the independence of the courts. It also called for the use of the death penalty to be restricted as a step towards its ultimate abolition.

On 16 May Libya became a State Party to the United Nations Convention against Torture and Other Cruel, Inhuman or Degrading Treatment or Punishment, and to the Optional Protocol to the International Covenant on Civil and Political Rights.

Five prisoners of conscience remained in Abu Salim Prison in Tripoli throughout the year. All of them had been arrested in 1973 and convicted of membership of the Islamic Liberation Party (ILP). A sixth alleged ILP member, 'Abd al-Qader al-Ya'qubi, was said to have become insane and to have died at the end of 1988 (see *Amnesty International Report 1989*).

At least 51 other political detainees arrested between 1980 and 1986 remained in detention without charge or trial throughout 1989. They included Rashid al-'Urfiyah, a law graduate, and 'Umran 'Umar al-Turbi, a dentist, who were suspected of belonging to illegal opposition groups and were arrested in 1982 and 1984 respectively. Most of these prisoners were held in Abu Salim Prison where many were apparently allowed family visits.

Hundreds of arrests were reported during 1989, particularly following violent clashes in January and April between religious activists and members of the security forces and Revolutionary Committees (local political groups set up to support official policies). At least 60, but possibly many more, of those arrested were reported to be still detained without charge or trial at the end of the year. They were held incommunicado and their whereabouts were unknown. They included Abu Bakr al-Sadiq Mahmud, an engineer arrested in January, and Muhammad al-Furtiya, who is regarded as a religious leader by some followers of the *Wahabiyya* Islamic doctrine in Libya and was arrested in February.

Further arrests were reported in October, following clashes between religious activists and members of the security forces and Revolutionary Committees. In a speech to the GPC in October, Libyan leader Colonel Mu'ammar Gaddafi described those involved as worse than "cancer" and "Aids", and stated that they should be "crushed". Following this speech hundreds of religious activists were said to have been arrested by members of the Revolutionary Committees. However, no details were available by the end of the year.

At least one political prisoner, 'Abdullah Menina, was reportedly kept in detention despite having been acquitted. Arrested in 1984, he was said to have been tried in 1985 and acquitted on charges related to illegal political activities.

At least 15 political prisoners were serving prison terms imposed after unfair trials. Twelve were Islamic activists reportedly arrested in 1983 and convicted of belonging to an illegal organization by a court set up by the Revolutionary Committees. Their whereabouts remained unknown. Another Islamic activist, Hussayn Hadiya Suwayd, sentenced to life imprisonment in 1983, was reported to have died in 1986 but this had not been officially confirmed. Three political prisoners were military officers convicted of attempted coups and sentenced to death in two separate military trials in 1970 and 1985. Their sentences were not carried out and were commuted by Colonel Gaddafi in June 1988. In all these trials the defendants were reportedly denied legal counsel and the right of appeal.

New information received during 1989 suggested that Muhammad Hilal, a prisoner of conscience held since 1980, had been executed in 1984. He was sentenced to death in 1983 by the Permanent Revolutionary Court, which convicted him of membership of the pro-Iraqi wing of the Ba'th Party. An ordinary criminal court had reportedly acquitted him of the same charges in 1982. Reports of his execution had not been confirmed by the government.

Amnesty International continued to appeal for the release of all prisoners of conscience and for clarification of the cases of other political prisoners. In 1988 the Libyan authorities undertook to review the cases of all remaining political prisoners after 400 were released in an amnesty (see *Amnesty International Report 1989*). To Amnesty International's knowledge, no such review had taken place by the end of 1989.

The organization expressed concern about the secret detention of the 60 or more religious activists arrested in early 1989 and reportedly still held at the end of the year. It called for them to be treated humanely and given access to relatives, lawyers and medical attention. Amnesty International also requested information about other arrests during the year, and about the reported deaths in custody, including that of Muhammad Hilal. No substantive responses were received.

MADAGASCAR

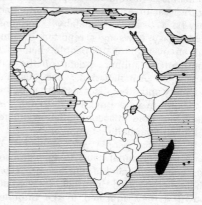

The government failed to investigate reports that hundreds of people in rural areas were extrajudicially executed by government forces in 1988. Over 100 prisoners were reported to have died as a result of harsh prison conditions. Two people were sentenced to death but there were no executions.

President Didier Ratsiraka was re-elected for a third seven-year term of office in March. The ruling *L'Avant-garde de la révolution malgache* (AREMA), The Vanguard of the Malagasy Revolution, increased its majority in the National People's Assembly following legislative elections in May. Both elections led to opposition allegations of fraud; in April clashes between police and demonstrators protesting against the outcome of the presidential election resulted in five deaths and at least 50 arrests.

No action was taken by the government to investigate summary killings of civilians by government security forces in 1988 or to punish those responsible. Several hundred farmers and villagers had been rounded up

154 and summarily executed in the course of operations against bandits and cattle thieves (see *Amnesty International Report 1989*). Some opponents of the government alleged in 1989 that the killings had been carried out to intimidate the rural population and stifle opposition in advance of presidential, legislative and local elections in 1989.

There appeared to be no improvement in the harsh conditions in prisons throughout the country (see *Amnesty International Report 1988*). Severe overcrowding, poor hygiene, malnutrition and inadequate medical facilities resulted in the deaths of more than 100 prisoners during the year in Antanimora, Arivonimamo, Nosy-Lava and Tsiafahy prisons. A Malagasy newspaper reported in June that an average of 10 people died each month in Antanimora prison on the outskirts of Antananarivo, the capital. Dysentery and other diseases were endemic in the prison where more than 2,500 prisoners were held in accommodation intended for less than half that number.

In July two people were sentenced to death by a criminal court in Fianarantsoa after being convicted of murder and armed robbery committed in 1988. It was not known if they appealed to the Supreme Court or petitioned the President for clemency, but no executions were reported during the year. Since independence in 1960 it appears that all death sentences have been commuted.

Amnesty International continued to urge the government to establish an inquiry into extrajudicial executions in 1988 and to identify those responsible and bring them to justice.

MALAWI

Dozens of people from the Northern Region, including at least 16 prisoners of conscience, were arrested between February and May after the Head of State publicly accused northerners of undermining the state. Most were still detained without charge or trial at the end of the year. At least 12 other prisoners of conscience arrested in previous years were also still held: two were sentenced after a grossly unfair trial and others were detained without charge or trial. In addition, there were said to be hundreds of other political prisoners whose identities were not known. There were reports of torture and ill-treatment of prisoners and one political detainee was alleged to have died as a result of torture. An exiled government opponent and nine of his relatives were alleged to have been extrajudicially executed.

In February Life-President Dr Hastings Kamuzu Banda publicly alleged that people from the Northern Region were seeking to undermine the economy and secede from the country. He said that northerners who were civil servants had acted irresponsibly and that those who were teachers deliberately taught badly when posted to the Central and Southern Regions. Dr George Mtafu, Malawi's only neurosurgeon, challenged the Life-President's claims and was arrested in February when he refused to apologize. No charges were brought against him and the authorities did not give reasons for his arrest or clarify the legal basis for his detention. However, he was believed to be held under the Public Security Regulations of 1965, which permit indefinite detention without charge or trial. He was held in Blantyre Central Prison at first but by the end of the year had been transferred to Mikuyu Prison near Zomba.

Thoza Khonje, a northerner working for the Sugar Company of Malawi, was also arrested in February. He had apparently been overheard criticizing an order by Life-President Banda that teachers should be transferred to their areas of origin. He and two others arrested with him were still detained without charge or trial at the end of the year and were considered to be prisoners of conscience.

Other northerners were arrested during

the first half of 1989 and also remained in detention without charge at the end of the year. They included civil servants and employees of state-owned companies, a teacher and a student. They were all held incommunicado in Mikuyu Prison and had no effective means to challenge the reasons or legal basis for their imprisonment.

At least 10 prisoners of conscience remained in detention without charge or trial throughout 1989. They included L.E. Chalodewa, held since 1977 apparently because of his friendship with a relative of Life-President Banda who was regarded as an opponent of the government. Kalusa Chimombo had been held since March 1978, apparently because of a speech in which he referred to Life-President Banda by name but not by official title, which was interpreted as indicating opposition to the Head of State.

Other prisoners of conscience in detention without charge or trial throughout 1989 included Jack Mapanje, an internationally renowned poet, held since September 1987; Goodluck Mhango, a veterinary surgeon detained in September 1987 after his brother, Mkwapatira Mhango (see below), published an article critical of the government in a foreign magazine; and John Malesa, held since December 1987 as a suspected supporter of Orton Chirwa, the imprisoned former cabinet minister and founder of the opposition Malawi Freedom Movement (MAFREMO).

Orton and Vera Chirwa, two prisoners of conscience serving life sentences imposed after a grossly unfair trial in 1983 (see Amnesty International Reports 1983 to 1989), were held at Zomba Central Prison, where the conditions were reported to be harsh.

Some prisoners of conscience were reported to be in poor health as a result of harsh prison conditions and deliberate medical neglect. Blaise Machira, a university lecturer detained without charge or trial since April 1988, was said to have been held in chains in Mikuyu Prison and to be suffering from schizophrenia. Margaret Banda, a leading member of a women's organization who had been detained without charge or trial since mid-1988, was reportedly denied medical treatment for hypertension and diabetes.

New information was received in 1989 about the torture of both political and criminal detainees. Prisoners were reported to have been beaten with hosepipes, wooden sticks and fists. At least one prisoner, Fred Sikwese, an employee of the Ministry of External Affairs, died reportedly as a result of torture in Lilongwe Prison. He had been arrested in February on suspicion of passing confidential government information to foreigners. There was no inquest or official investigation into his death and the government did not clarify the circumstances. Fred Sikwese was buried in the prison grounds after the authorities reportedly refused to release his body for burial by his relatives.

An exiled government opponent and nine of his relatives were killed in October, apparently the victims of extrajudicial executions. Mkwapatira Mhango and his relatives died when his home in Lusaka, Zambia, was attacked with a fire-bomb. Subsequently, the Zambian authorities detained four men who they alleged were security and intelligence agents employed by the Malawian Government to assassinate government opponents both inside Malawi and abroad. One of the four subsequently died in custody (see Zambia).

Amnesty International continued throughout 1989 to appeal for the release of Orton and Vera Chirwa, Jack Mapanje and all other prisoners of conscience. It also called for the prompt, fair trial, or release, of other political detainees. In November Amnesty International publicized its concerns in a report, Malawi: Human Rights Violations 25 Years After Independence, which also criticized harsh prison conditions and called for impartial investigations into allegations of torture and into the death in custody of Fred Sikwese. The government responded to the report by denying that torture had occurred but made no other comment. Amnesty International also expressed concern about the alleged extrajudicial executions of Mkwapatira Mhango and nine others. It called for an impartial inquiry to establish the extent of official accountability for these and other possible killings, and for those involved in such human rights violations to be brought to justice.

156

MALAYSIA

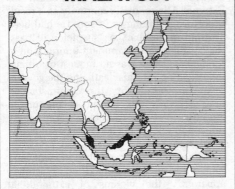

Sixteen prisoners of conscience, held without charge or trial, were released. Restrictions on others released from detention in 1988 were lifted. Three long-term political detainees who had been held without charge or trial since the 1970s were also released but placed under restrictions of movement, association and expression. Allegations of ill-treatment in detention continued and the national press reported that four people died in police custody. At least 71 death sentences were imposed, and at least 16 people were executed. Most of those executed had been convicted on drugs charges.

In June the Malaysian Parliament passed an amendment to the Internal Security Act (ISA) which reduced the power of the courts to challenge administrative detention orders. As a result, detainees held without trial and allegedly posing a threat to national security may challenge their detentions only on procedural grounds. The courts cannot rule on the validity of the reasons given by the Minister of Home Affairs for their detention. Prime Minister Dr Mahathir Mohamad, who is also Minister of Home Affairs, said the amendment was needed to prevent courts from overturning executive decisions.

At the beginning of the year 16 prisoners of conscience were held under the ISA. This act empowers the Minister of Home Affairs to authorize the detention, without charge or trial, of anyone suspected of acting "in a manner prejudicial to the security of Malaysia". Detention orders may be renewed for periods of up to two years. The 16 had been held since late 1987. They were among 106 critics and opponents of

the government arrested in late 1987 during what the authorities termed "Operation Lallang" (see *Amnesty International Report 1988* and *1989*). The other 90 detainees had been released before the end of 1988, although some had been placed under restriction orders.

The 16 still held included Karpal Singh and Lim Kit Siang, both leading members of the opposition Democratic Action Party; Dr Tuang Pik King, a Chinese educationalist; and Arokia Dass, a trade union official. All 16 were released before the end of April. Some of them, however, had restrictions imposed on their freedom of movement and association. In June the government lifted all restrictions placed on former "Operation Lallang" detainees.

Three other political detainees held without trial were also released between January and April. Teo Leong Hock, Heng Boon Lean and Cheah Swee Sam had been detained under the ISA since the late 1970s for alleged communist activities. Under the conditions of their release, their freedom of movement, association and expression were restricted. They were required to report regularly to the police and to refrain from making statements to the press.

Police brutality against prisoners continued to be reported. Abdul Rahman Hamzah, a former political secretary to the Chief Minister of the East Malaysian state of Sarawak, filed an affidavit in the High Court in January claiming ill-treatment during interrogation by police officers in 1988. He had been detained under the ISA and accused of involvement in a plot to assassinate the Prime Minister. He said that police had subjected him to threats, physical abuse and humiliating acts, some of a sexual nature. He was released unconditionally in July 1989. In December a statement issued by the Attorney General's Chambers said there was insufficient evidence to prosecute the police officers accused of ill-treating him and no action would be taken against them.

Defendants in several criminal cases testified in court that they had been forced to make false confessions during interrogation as a result of assaults by police. Disciplinary action against two police officers for such assaults was reported in January and February. The Deputy Minister of Home Affairs told Parliament in March that his ministry monitored all reports alleging the use of force by police personnel and would not hesitate to take appropriate action against those found guilty.

At least four people reportedly died in police custody during the year. A forensic consultant giving evidence at a coroner's inquest said that since 1979 he had examined up to 17 cases annually of death in police custody in the Kuala Lumpur area. He stated that a small number of these deaths had resulted from "foul play". The consultant provided this information at the inquest into the death of D. Anthonysamy, who had been detained under the ISA on a charge of armed robbery and died in police custody in October. An inadequately detailed post-mortem report led the coroner to return an open verdict.

At least 71 people received mandatory death sentences. Sixty of these sentences were imposed for drugs offences, seven for possession of firearms and four for murder. The Supreme Court confirmed the death sentences imposed on 33 people, who are permitted to file a final appeal with the Pardons Board of the state where the offence was committed.

At least 16 executions were carried out. Thirteen people were hanged for drugs offences, two for murder and one for a firearms offence.

Amnesty International appealed for the unconditional release of prisoners of conscience and for the commutation of all death sentences.

MALDIVES

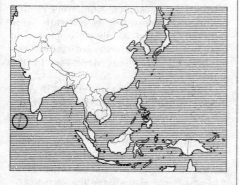

Sixteen people convicted of involvement in an attempted coup in 1988 were sentenced to death. The sentences were later commuted to life imprisonment.

The trial of over 70 people involved in an unsuccessful attempt to overthrow the government of President Maumoon Abdul Gayoom in November 1988 (see *Amnesty International Report 1989*) ended in August. Four Maldivians and 12 Sri Lankan nationals were sentenced to death. The remaining defendants — all Sri Lankan nationals — received prison sentences of between 17 and 38 years.

The sentences were passed by the High Court of the Maldives in the capital, Male. The defendants did not have access to a lawyer and there is no higher court of appeal. However, President Gayoom commuted all 16 death sentences to life imprisonment in October.

Amnesty International, which had appealed for the death sentences to be commuted, was informed by President Gayoom in October that he had granted clemency "considering the best interests of the country and, in particular, the importance of adhering to a long-standing tradition of not carrying out death sentences". He said the decision was made "purely on humanitarian and nationalistic grounds in an effort to ensure a climate of peace and stability for future generations".

MALI

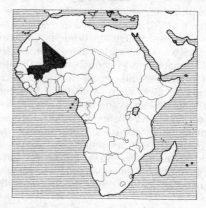

Nine prisoners of conscience were detained for two months and two of them were allegedly tortured. Four people were sentenced to death but no executions were carried out.

In June four students from the *Ecole nationale des ingénieurs*, National School of Engineers, were arrested. They were held illegally and incommunicado for about six weeks, two in security police custody and two in military custody. By

158

law, they should have been referred to the procuracy and formally remanded or released within 48 hours of arrest. The two held in military custody, Adama Bantjini Coulibaly and Souleymane Yaya Dembélé, were reported to have been tortured in the barracks of a parachute regiment in Djikoroni, near the capital, Bamako. Adama Bantjini Coulibaly was allegedly suspended by his wrists while being tortured. Large numbers of students and teachers were tortured and ill-treated there in 1980, including a student leader, Abdoul Karim Camara, who died in detention as a result of torture.

Five other students were arrested in early August, one of whom, Oumar Coulibaly, was later released without charge. The four others, together with the four arrested in June, were charged with distributing false information which might disturb public order, an offence punishable by up to three years' imprisonment. The charges related to the distribution of a leaflet by an unofficial student organization. The leaflet protested against difficulties experienced by students, including delays in the payment of grants, and called for students to be allowed to associate freely. In late August Souleymane Dembélé was convicted and given a suspended one-month prison sentence and the others were acquitted. All were released immediately.

The government of President Moussa Traoré was reported to have stated in May that it intended to abolish the death penalty. This announcement was apparently made in response to a call from the International Red Cross and Red Crescent Movement for governments to make a special humanitarian gesture to commemorate the movement's 125th anniversary. However, no formal moves were known to have been taken by the government to remove provisions for the death penalty from the law.

Four people were sentenced to death in June but no executions were carried out. The four were convicted of embezzling public funds by the Special Court of State Security, a special court in which military officers may sit as assessors to assist the court's civilian judges. It was established in 1976 with the power to impose the death penalty for offences against the security of the state and for embezzlement of state funds or property worth more than 10 million CFA francs (about US$34,000). Those convicted have no general right of appeal, although they may appeal on procedural irregularities to the Supreme Court.

Amnesty International appealed for the release of prisoners of conscience and called for an inquiry into allegations that detainees had been tortured or ill-treated in military custody. The organization also appealed for the commutation of death sentences.

MAURITANIA

At least 200 people, including prisoners of conscience, were detained without charge or trial for over four months in the wake of intercommunal violence in April. Other prisoners of conscience were among at least 60 political prisoners serving sentences imposed in previous years, mostly after unfair trials: 19 of these were released in December. Numerous reports of torture, some resulting in death, were received. At least 30 people appeared to have been victims of extrajudicial killings by government forces deployed in the south.

Hundreds of people were killed in April during intercommunal violence which affected both Mauritania and Senegal. Most of the victims in Mauritania were Senegalese nationals. Black Mauritanians belonging to ethnic groups from the south of the country, as well as other black Africans, were also among the victims. As tension between Mauritania and Senegal rose in response to the killings, Senegalese living in Mauritania were repatriated and thousands of Beïdanes and Haratines living in Senegal were returned to Mauritania. The Mauritanian Government also expelled more than 50,000 black Mauritanians between May and September, claiming they were Senegalese. During this mass expulsion, government forces committed extensive abuses, including arbitrary arrests and detentions, torture and extrajudicial executions. Following the mass expulsions, some deportees returned to Mauritania to collect their cattle and belongings. They admitted responsibility for committing violent acts against security forces and others who had expropriated their property.

Most of those detained belonged to the black Halpulaar ethnic group. The authorities apparently considered members of this group to be the main critics of the Beïdane community's predominant role in the government. Farmers and cattle-herders in the south who opposed the expulsions or the expropriation of their property were among those detained. At least 60 state employees were also arrested. Oumar Tall, a manager in a state company, and Diop Mamoudou, the deputy governor of Aïoun El Atrouss region, were arrested in the capital, Nouakchott, because of their suspected political activities.

Numerous detainees were held without charge or trial for periods ranging from a few days to more than four months, apparently because they were suspected of involvement with the opposition *Forces de libération africaine de Mauritanie* (FLAM), Mauritanian African Liberation Forces. FLAM, which opposes the predominant role in government of the Beïdane community, had not appeared to be active since the imprisonment of FLAM supporters in 1986 and 1987.

Most of the detainees appeared to be held unlawfully. Detainees in Nouakchott were held in "safehouses" rather than regular prisons or police stations. Most arrests in the south were carried out by the National Guard, a paramilitary force responsible for guarding the country's borders. Many of those arrested were summarily expelled from Mauritania at the time of their release. Kane Lamine was among six people arrested in the southern town of Jeder-El-Mohguène during late May; it was not known whether he had been freed by the end of the year. The other five were detained for several weeks and summarily expelled to Senegal upon their release.

Numerous arrests took place after protests against the expulsions and other abuses. Most arrests occurred between May and July, and most detainees were freed when the rate of expulsions fell in September. Abdallahi Ould Bah Nagi Ould Kebd, a student leader and member of the Beïdane community who had been detained without charge or trial from December 1988 to January 1989, was arrested again in late May. He was apparently suspected of writing a leaflet which criticized the expulsions. The authorities released him without charge in early September. Forty-four villagers were arrested in Fondou at the end of July, following a protest against abuses committed by the National Guard. The detainees, including Deputy Chairman Mamadou Yéro War of Bagodine rural area, were taken to Aleg prison and held without charge until October. Members of Maghama Town Council, including Isma Abdoul Kane, were among at least 30 people arrested in May in Maghama. These arrests followed protests against abuses committed by the gendarmerie. The detainees were released without charge in October.

Suspected black activists, virtually all of them Halpulaar, were arrested in October and November, mostly in Nouakchott or the southern town of Kaédi. It appeared that those arrested were suspected of links with either FLAM or another group composed of both Beïdanes and black Mauritanians which criticized the mass expulsions. At least 30 people were still held at the end of 1989, including Ladji Traoré, a former prisoner of conscience from Nouakchott, and Oumou Kalsoum Barro, a school teacher in Kaédi.

In contrast to previous years, none of those detained for political reasons in 1989 was brought to trial. The security forces appeared to have powers of detention and imprisonment without reference to the courts.

More than 60 people sentenced after a series of political trials in the previous three years, including at least six prisoners of conscience, remained in prison at the beginning of the year (see *Amnesty International Report 1987, 1988* and *1989*). Most of them were black civil servants, academics, students, or armed forces personnel. In December President Maaouiya Ould Sid' Ahmed Taya ordered the reduction of all convicted political prisoners' sentences by one year. As a result, the six prisoners of conscience and 13 others were freed.

Trials held between 1986 and 1988 were

160

unfair by international standards: defendants were convicted primarily on the basis of statements made under duress and their lawyers were not given sufficient time to prepare their defence (see *Amnesty International Report 1987, 1988* and *1989*).

Thirty-three political prisoners who had been serving their sentences at Oualata prison, where four prisoners died in 1988 because of harsh conditions, were moved to Aïoun El Atrouss barracks in February. This transfer improved their conditions of imprisonment and they were allowed to receive family visits. Seven of a group of eight political prisoners, who were supporters of the Ba'th Arab Socialist Party convicted on political charges in 1988, were transferred during the latter half of the year from Tichitt prison to improved conditions at Tidjikdja. The eighth prisoner, former government minister Mohamed Yehdih Ould Breidelleil, was released in December.

Numerous reports alleged the torture of detainees, particularly black Mauritanians held in the south. Five students detained from December 1988 to January 1989, among them Béchir El Hassen and Mohamed Mahmoud Ould Hamakttar, were also reportedly tortured. The torture methods reported included burning with hot coals and the "Jaguar", during which a detainee is suspended upside-down and beaten on the soles of the feet. Prisoners were also reportedly beaten and deprived of food, drink and sleep for long periods. Mohamed Yéro Bâ, a headmaster and member of Kaédi Town Council, was arrested in June and, according to reports, suspended above a fire and beaten in detention. Eye-witnesses said that his body was covered with burns. It was not known whether an official inquiry into his death in police custody took place. At least nine other people died as a result of torture.

Although Mauritanian law prohibits the use of torture, the authorities took no known action to investigate torture allegations or to prosecute alleged torturers.

At least 30 people, most of them Halpulaar herders, appeared to have been extrajudicially executed in the south by government forces. Some reports suggested that troops had adopted a policy of shooting on sight in the vicinity of the border with Senegal, although no such policy was officially announced. Most killings were attributed to the National Guard but few details were available about individual cases. The victims of apparent extrajudicial executions included two boys, 10-year-old Abdoulaye Bâ and 12-year-old Mamadou Bâ, whose throats were reportedly cut in June by members of the National Guard. The boys were herding in the Pattoucone area when they were killed. An eye-witness reported that Abdramane Lam, a cattle-herder from Mbout area, was killed in June by gendarmes who then attempted to hide his body. Members of the National Guard killed Hadiya Bâ, a teacher and member of the Boully Town Council, in October. In November three members of the National Guard fired on a group of six women and children outside their village of Néré-Walo, near Kaédi. Three people were killed: Houlèye Baïdi Bâ, a young woman, and two children aged 13 and four. The judicial authorities and government were not known to have investigated any of these killings.

Amnesty International expressed concern to the government about reports of arbitrary arrests, torture and killings following the disturbances in April. In July the organization publicly urged the authorities to prevent further human rights violations. The government responded by denying that abuses had occurred and accusing Amnesty International of favouring Senegal in the dispute between Mauritania and Senegal.

In November Amnesty International published a report, *Mauritania 1986-1989, Background to a Crisis*, which described human rights violations such as the torture and unfair trials of political prisoners and the jailing of prisoners of conscience. Earlier, the organization had submitted to the government detailed information about the use of torture and recommendations for steps to end torture, including investigation of torture reports and prosecution of alleged torturers. Amnesty International continued to investigate the cases of political prisoners sentenced after unfair trials in previous years.

MAURITIUS

Nine possible prisoners of conscience were briefly detained during the year. One man was sentenced to be hanged for

drug-trafficking, bringing the number of prisoners under sentence of death to six. There were no executions.

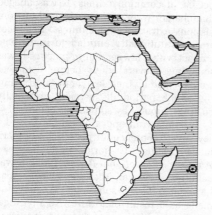

In January Harish Boodhoo, leader of the *Parti socialiste mauricien* (PSM), Mauritian Socialist Party, was arrested after calling for an inquiry into the alleged involvement of government ministers in the sale of Mauritian passports. Vedi Ballah, editor of the PSM newspaper, *Le Socialiste*, The Socialist, was also arrested after he published Harish Boodhoo's allegations. Both men were charged under the Public Order Act with giving out false information that could cause disturbances. Vedi Ballah was released on bail after one week, but Harish Boodhoo remained in custody for three weeks until bail was granted. The trial of the two men had not begun by the end of the year.

In August six trade unionists including Ravin Ramasawmy, President of the *Fédération des syndicats progressistes* (FSP), Federation of Progressive Trade Unions, and one journalist were arrested as police broke up a peaceful demonstration in support of a sacked trade union official. The seven were accused of participating in an illegal demonstration and were freed on bail. It emerged in a court hearing in November that the authorities had still not prepared the precise charges against the seven. Their trial had not begun by the end of the year.

In August Radha Krishna Kunnath, an Indian national, was sentenced to death in the Court of Assizes after being convicted under the Dangerous Drugs Act. He had an automatic right of appeal to the Supreme Court, but this had not been heard by the end of the year.

In June the Supreme Court turned down the appeal of Steven Francis, an Indian national sentenced to death in October 1988 for drug-trafficking (see *Amnesty International Report 1989*). The court granted him permission to appeal to the Judicial Committee of the Privy Council (JCPC) in the United Kingdom, the highest court of appeal for Mauritius. Four other prisoners under sentence of death, two for drug-trafficking and two for murder, continued to wait for their appeals to be heard by the JCPC.

Amnesty International appealed to the Mauritian Government to commute the sentences of those facing execution. It also urged the government to abolish the death penalty and called for the penalty to be removed from the Dangerous Drugs Act as an important step towards abolition.

MEXICO

Numerous prisoners were released following a series of pardons including two political activists who had been held on allegedly fabricated charges. Reports of torture or ill-treatment, leading in at least three cases to death in custody, were received, although the authorities denied that ill-treatment was systematic. The new government said it was investigating individual "disappearance" cases which occurred during the 1970s and early 1980s but no progress had been reported by the end of the year. A special commission was set up to investigate the "disappearance" of José García in 1988 but his case remained unclarified. Killings were reported in rural areas, some of which may have been carried out by landowners or *pistoleros* (gunmen) acting with the acquiescence of local authorities. In a few

162 | cases, investigations into these killings and other human rights abuses resulted in charges being brought against those allegedly responsible, but many cases remained unresolved.

The new administration of President Salinas de Gortari, who assumed office in December 1988, embarked on a series of measures with the stated intention of "modernizing" the country. Some of these related to human rights. In February President Salinas announced the first in a series of pardons for certain prisoners detained for "socially and politically motivated offences" as a step towards "national reconciliation". Among the first prisoners to be released were Israel Gutiérrez and Francisco Urbina Hernández, who had been arrested in 1984 (see *Amnesty International Report 1989*). Although they were charged with criminal offences, Amnesty International believed they might have been arrested for their non-violent political activities. By November several hundred prisoners had been released, many of them indigenous people thought to have been arrested in the context of land disputes, as well as other long-term prisoners held for politically motivated offences.

In February a Directorate of Human Rights was set up within the Interior Ministry. One of its main functions was to receive complaints of human rights abuses. The head of the Directorate, Luis Ortíz Monasterio, stated that cases of detainees alleged to have "disappeared" in the 1970s and early 1980s would be "analysed on a case-by-case basis, in an attempt to resolve the matter to the satisfaction of all parties involved". He and several other officials — including a state attorney general — acknowledged that torture occurred although they denied that it was deliberate policy. They criticized the use of initial statements taken by police as the "queen of proofs" (compelling evidence) against suspects because of the risk that it may have been obtained through coercion. In November torture was made a state crime in Chihuahua, punishable with between two and 10 years' imprisonment. Local bishops and other human rights activists had reported numerous cases of torture in the state, and by the end of the year several police agents had been detained and accused of killing two men in September and October allegedly through torture.

New reports from several states accused judicial police, and on occasion military personnel, of torture and ill-treatment of detainees. Most of those affected were suspected of common crimes. It was alleged that charges were sometimes based on confessions extracted under duress. Detainees are constitutionally entitled to immediate contact with a lawyer, but in practice it was sometimes several days before detainees were located by their lawyer or family, during which period ill-treatment, especially beatings, reportedly sometimes occurred.

In January an appeal court confirmed a seven-year sentence for possession of marijuana against Gregorio Castañón (see *Amnesty International Report 1989*). It was believed, however, that the charges may have been based solely on a confession made as a result of torture. An investigation by the Ministry of Defence dismissed the torture allegations as unfounded but details of the inquiry were not known. Gregorio Castañón's retraction of his confession — on the grounds that he had been forced to ratify it under the effects of torture — was reportedly dismissed by the courts *inter alia* because he had not submitted a formal complaint.

In March eight women, some pregnant, who were arrested and accused of crimes related to abortion, said they were held incommunicado for almost 20 hours by members of the since disbanded Intelligence Directorate in Tlaxcoaque, Mexico City. Two of them alleged that the group were threatened with death, stripped, kicked and beaten. Only days before, an agreement had been published in the government's *Official Gazette* which included the stipulation that individuals in police custody were not to be held incommunicado and that detainees should be treated "with the greatest respect and dignity".

A few detainees, such as Communist Party member Antonio Orozco arrested by judicial police in March, alleged they were tortured with electric shocks. Juan Alvarez Rosales, arrested in March in Veracruz, said he had to be taken to hospital after police beat, kicked and punched him, and on two occasions forced him to swallow pieces of glass with carbonated mineral water containing chilli. In August Eleazar Beltrán from Chihuahua state registered a formal complaint declaring he was held blindfold in a military barracks, stripped naked and beaten. He said soldiers repeatedly threw cold water on him, placed a plastic bag over his head, tied a rope round his neck and kept tightening it, strung him up by his arms and told him he was going to die. After two days they took him away in a truck, and eventually abandoned him.

In April the Attorney General's Office of the Federal District asked the courts to issue arrest warrants against five judicial police agents accused of causing the death in custody of Octavio Hernández Pérez the same month. Reports indicated that he had died as a result of blows to the head and other parts of the body. The outcome of the investigations into his death was not known. The head of the Federal District Judicial Police acknowledged initially that the police "went too far" during the interrogation.

In May the president of the Mexican Bar Association called on the judicial police in Mexico state to end the use of torture and the practice of holding detainees incommunicado. The Attorney General of the Republic was reported as saying in September that an investigation would be carried out into the ill-treatment of detainees and that anyone found responsible would be brought to justice.

Although the authorities promised to investigate cases of "disappearances" from the 1970s and early 1980s, no progress was reported by the end of the year. In July members of the *Comité Eureka*, an organization which campaigns for clarification of "disappearance" cases, submitted a formal complaint to the Attorney General's Office requesting that José Zorrillo Pérez, former head of the Federal Security Directorate (see below), and other former security agents should be interrogated about a number of "disappearance" cases in which they allegedly participated. The "disappearance" of José Ramón García, a member of the *Partido Revolucionario de los Trabajadores*, Revolutionary Workers' Party, also remained unclarified. He "disappeared" in December 1988 in Cuautla, Morelos, on the way to a meeting. A commission was set up by the authorities to monitor investigations, but by the end of the year little progress had been reported.

Reports of killings, mostly in the context of land disputes, were received from the states of Michoacán, Puebla, Oaxaca, Veracruz, Hidalgo, Chiapas and Chihuahua. The problems in obtaining information from remote rural areas meant that it was difficult to ascertain the full circumstances of many of the killings and subsequent investigations. Amnesty International sought information to determine whether, as in the past, local authorities had colluded with local landowners and *pistoleros* to cover up the crimes.

In February, eight peasants were killed in Pijijiapan, Chiapas, when, according to witnesses, about 50 men — landowners and *pistoleros* — opened fire on peasants who had gathered to meet landowners and local agents of the Public Ministry to discuss land issues. The agents of the Public Ministry are reported to have fled when the shooting started. Four people were reportedly arrested shortly afterwards, but the current state of investigations was not known at the end of the year.

In June Pedro Hernández Hernández was murdered in Embocadero, Veracruz. He had been active, together with former prisoner Zózimo Hernández, in publicizing abuses against his community including numerous killings as a result of land disputes. The two men had been warned earlier by an agrarian reform official that they would be killed if they returned to Embocadero. In November a member of a peasants' union was arrested without warrant and charged with the murder of Pedro Hernández, and the killing of three landowners in 1984. However, it was alleged that his confession had been extracted as a result of beatings and near-asphyxiation. Lawyers appealed for the charges to be revoked against seven other men from Embocadero arrested in November and also charged with the murder of the three landowners. At least three said that police coerced them into confessing by beating and almost drowning them.

In a few other cases investigations into killings led to the imprisonment of those allegedly responsible, although most cases remained unclarified. At least eight rural police officers were arrested in Xoxocotla, Mexico state, in January in connection with the killing in the same month of four people and the injuring of numerous others: they had shot at a crowd gathered to protest against alleged fraud during local elections. In August landowner Roberto Zenteno finally gave himself up to the courts to face charges of shooting dead indigenous peasant leader Sebastian Pérez in Chiapas in December 1988. An arrest warrant had been issued in January.

The arrest in June of José Zorrillo Pérez,

164

on charges of ordering the murder of a journalist, set an important precedent. Manuel Buendía, one of numerous journalists killed in unclarified circumstances during the past few years, was shot in Mexico City in 1984. At the time of his death he had been investigating allegations of police and government involvement in drug-trafficking. Delays in investigations under previous administrations had called into question the willingness of the authorities to clarify the case.

Amnesty International welcomed the new measures taken by the government concerning the release of prisoners and the announcement that "disappearances" would be investigated on a case by case basis, but continued to press for information about the outcome of the investigations. It sought further information about reports of torture and of killings, particularly in rural areas. In July the organization sent a document to President Salinas outlining cases of torture, killings, political prisoners and "disappearances" which had been submitted to previous administrations and which in many cases had not been satisfactorily resolved. In October a response was received from the Foreign Ministry informing Amnesty International of steps taken by the government regarding human rights and stating its intention to respond at a later date to the specific issues raised in the letter.

MOROCCO AND WESTERN SAHARA

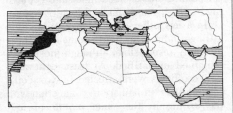

Over 300 political prisoners, including prisoners of conscience, were held during the year. Fifty were pardoned in May, 31 of whom were prisoners of conscience. Many of the remaining prisoners were serving sentences imposed after trials which fell short of internationally recognized standards for fair trial. Reports of torture and ill-treatment, mainly in *garde*

à vue (incommunicado) detention, continued. Sixteen people died in custody under suspicious circumstances. Some prison conditions amounted to cruel, inhuman or degrading treatment and one of several prisoners on hunger-strike protesting against these conditions died. The fate of about 100 former military personnel imprisoned since the early 1970s was still unknown, as were the whereabouts of people of Saharan origin arrested by Moroccan security forces since the mid-1970s. Three death sentences were passed, but no executions were carried out.

Fifty political prisoners, including 31 prisoners of conscience, were released after King Hassan II granted them a royal pardon on 6 May. Those freed included Allal El Azhar, a teacher, and Driss Rekab Bouissef, a university lecturer. Both had been among a group of prisoners tried in 1977; they had been sentenced to 30 and 20 years' imprisonment respectively.

Eight other prisoners of conscience, sentenced to long prison terms in 1977 on charges of plotting against the state and membership of clandestine Marxist-Leninist groups, did not benefit from the royal pardon. They remained in Kenitra Central Prison throughout the year. Among them were Driss Benzekri and Mohamed Srifi, two students serving 30-year terms. Another prisoner of conscience, Ali Idrissi Kaitouni, a painter and poet, was also held in Kenitra Central Prison. He was sentenced to 15 years' imprisonment in May 1982 on account of his writings.

The widow, a cousin and six children of General Mohamed Oufkir, who died in dubious circumstances after a 1972 coup attempt, remained under house arrest near Marrakech. They had been held incommunicado and without charge or trial in prison camps for 15 years, apparently because of their family links with General Oufkir. They were considered prisoners of conscience. Four of the children escaped in April 1987, contacted lawyers and made a public appeal, but they were rearrested after several days.

Over 120 students were arrested and imprisoned for up to three years following widespread student demonstrations in May. The students were calling for improved facilities and recognition of the *Union nationale des étudiants marocains* (UNEM), Moroccan National Students' Union, as their official negotiating body. At least 85 students from universities at Fes, Meknes and other cities were tried and convicted on charges which included disturbing public order, demonstrating on the university campus, causing damage to property, and membership of unauthorized political organizations.

Many of the students were held in *garde à vue* detention for prolonged periods after arrest. In some cases, official records were falsified by police to conceal this. In one case, the police stated that 24 students had been arrested in Fes on 8 July when they had actually been arrested on 23 and 24 June. All 24 were held in *garde à vue* detention until 13 July. They subsequently received six-month prison sentences, which were suspended in the cases of three women. They were convicted on charges of belonging to an illegal organization and disturbing public order. All these students claimed to have been ill-treated or tortured. One of them, Boudra Boussa, who had been taken to Derb Moulay Cherif, a detention centre in Casablanca, did not appear in court with the others. He was in hospital with a broken hand, reportedly as a result of torture. He was later tried separately and was also sentenced to six months' imprisonment.

Seventeen alleged supporters of an Islamic movement, 14 of them teachers, were sentenced in Taroudant in December to prison terms of between one month and one year. They were charged with belonging to an unauthorized organization, possessing documents liable to cause a breach of the peace and holding unauthorized meetings. They appeared to be prisoners of conscience.

In November Mohamed Idrissi Kaitouni, the director of *L'Opinion*, an opposition party newspaper, was sentenced to two years' imprisonment for publishing a joint statement by two human rights organizations. The *Association marocaine des droits de l'homme* and the *Ligue marocaine de défense des droits de l'homme* issued a statement about four deaths in custody in August in "suspicious circumstances". Mohamed Idrissi Kaitouni was subsequently pardoned by King Hassan II on 12 November. The government refused entry into the country to two Amnesty International delegates seeking to observe the trial.

At least 112 political prisoners sentenced after apparently unfair trials in pre-vious years were still held at the end of the year. Among them were 19 students of a left-wing tendency within the UNEM, convicted in 1984 of conspiring to overthrow the government, and 70 alleged supporters of an Islamic movement, convicted in 1984 of plotting against the monarchy, planning to set up an Islamic republic and threatening state security.

Twenty-three other prisoners, mostly members of the UNEM and the *Syndicat national des enseignants* (SNE), National Teachers' Union, were serving sentences of between six and 20 years' imprisonment in Casablanca, Tangiers, Safi and Kenitra prisons. They were convicted in Casablanca in 1986 of membership of the clandestine *Ila al-Amam* (Forward) movement, and of conspiring against the government (see *Amnesty International Report 1987*).

All three groups of prisoners were sentenced after trials in which proceedings did not appear to satisfy internationally recognized standards for fair trial. In particular, defendants were convicted on the basis of confessions allegedly obtained under torture or threat of torture during prolonged pre-trial detention.

There were new reports of torture and ill-treatment of people in *garde à vue* detention. In May the trial of Ali Belmeziane and five other students opened in Fes in the absence of the defendants — apparently because they still bore signs of torture. In August six students on trial in Meknes on charges arising from disturbances at the university alleged that they had been tortured at Derb Moulay Cherif detention centre. Others said that they were threatened with rape in police custody in order to force them to sign confessions. Detainees were said to have been tortured by being beaten while suspended in contorted positions, beaten on the soles of the feet, and partially suffocated with rugs drenched with urine or detergent.

Sixteen people died in police custody, leading to further allegations of torture and ill-treatment. Two of these deaths reportedly resulted in police officers being prosecuted for assaulting prisoners. In another case, the Minister of Justice was reported to have ordered an official inquiry into the death in February of Abdeljalil Yakouti who police said had hanged himself. The outcome of the inquiry was not known to Amnesty International. Eye-witnesses were said to have seen signs of torture on

166

the dead man's body. In August Larbi Charrat, a welder and member of the *Parti du progrès et du socialisme* (PPS), Party of Progress and Socialism, died in custody. The police said he had committed suicide by hanging himself in the headquarters of the gendarmerie at Sidi Slimane. He had been arrested two days earlier for participating in protests against the destruction of shanty towns in Dar Bel Amri, near Kenitra. However, unconfirmed reports suggested that his death was the result of torture.

Prison conditions were reported to be harsh. Conditions in a number of prisons appeared to constitute cruel, inhuman or degrading treatment. At Laalou Prison in Rabat, for example, prisoners who protested against inadequate medical care were reportedly beaten and chained in *"cachots"* (small, windowless, underground punishment cells). In April four political prisoners in Laalou Prison went on hunger-strike for improved conditions and an investigation into their long-standing torture allegations. They broke off the hunger-strike for a time, but renewed it on 17 June. They were transferred at the end of July to Avicennes Hospital in Rabat where one, Abdelhaq Chbada, died on 19 August. The three others were still in hospital, where they were being force-fed, at the end of the year.

Hassan Aharrat and Noureddine Jouhari, two political prisoners who were among a group of six who went on hunger-strike in June 1985, also remained in hospital at the end of the year. Three others had been released in 1988 and 1989 after completing their sentences. The fourth, Moulay Tahar Douraidi, was said to have ended his hunger-strike in August. He was seen by his mother for the first time in five years in December and soon after resumed his hunger-strike. The six began intermittent hunger-strikes in 1984 in protest against torture during *garde à vue* detention and inhumane prison conditions, including insufficient medical care. They were reportedly kept bound to their beds in a basement room. Guards forcibly fed them through gastric tubes and their clothes were changed only every four to six months. For the last four years in hospital, with the exception of the one visit which Moulay Tahar Douraidi received in December, they had not been permitted to see lawyers or relatives.

No new information was received about approximately 100 military personnel who were sentenced to prison terms following attempts on the life of King Hassan II in 1971 and 1972. They were believed to be still held incommunicado and at a secret location. Some of them were still held although their sentences had expired.

There was also continuing uncertainty about the fate of hundreds of Sahrawis reported to have "disappeared" in the custody of Moroccan security forces since the mid-1970s. They included Fatma el-Ghalia Ment Moulay Ahmed Ould Leili, an administrator from Tan Tan, who was arrested in January 1976, and Sidati Ould Selami Ould Lehbib, a blind radio announcer, arrested in November 1987 in Laayoune. According to the government, inquiries had revealed no trace of those alleged to have been arrested and to have "disappeared".

Three people were sentenced to death for murder in March and death sentences imposed in 1988 on two Italian nationals convicted of drug-trafficking and murder were confirmed on appeal. There were no executions.

Amnesty International welcomed the release of prisoners of conscience in May and pressed for the release of other prisoners of conscience. It sought information about possible prisoners of conscience. Amnesty International also expressed concern to the authorities about reports of torture and ill-treatment of detainees in *garde à vue* detention and urged thorough and impartial investigations of all torture allegations and deaths in custody. Amnesty International also sought further information about Sahrawi prisoners alleged to have "disappeared" in the custody of Moroccan security forces. No response was received to the memorandum submitted to the government in July 1988 following the January 1988 visit of an Amnesty International delegation to Morocco.

MOZAMBIQUE

More than 750 untried political prisoners arrested in previous years and 37 sentenced after unfair trials by the Revolutionary Military Tribunal were released. The tribunal itself was abolished. About 140 other untried detainees arrested in previous years and accused of crimes against the security of the state

remained in custody while the authorities considered whether to prosecute them. There were at least 300 new arrests of people suspected of violent opposition to the government. Judicial flogging was abolished and no one was sentenced to flogging by the courts: however, some prisoners were reported to have been flogged unlawfully or tortured or ill-treated in other ways. No progress was made in clarifying the fate of dozens of prisoners who "disappeared" in the 1970s.

The government took important steps to increase protection for human rights in a continuing program of legal reform. The Revolutionary Military Tribunal was abolished in March following the establishment of the Supreme People's Court and the Procurator General's Office in December 1988 (see *Amnesty International Report 1989*). The Revolutionary Military Tribunal had been set up in 1979 as an interim measure pending the establishment of the Supreme Court. It tried political prisoners using summary procedures and there was no right of appeal against its decisions. Flogging, a punishment which could be imposed by all courts, was abolished in September.

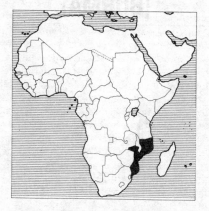

Fighting between government troops and the *Resistência Nacional Moçambicana* (RENAMO or RNM), Mozambique National Resistance, continued throughout the year. Talks between government representatives and RENAMO leaders were held to seek an end to the conflict but no agreement was reached by the end of 1989. Millions of civilians were affected by the fighting. RENAMO reportedly abducted hundreds of civilians, some of whom it tortured and killed. In an attack on Massinga in southern Mozambique in May, a RENAMO

unit reportedly cut off the genitals of seven men, raped and then killed three women and abducted 50 civilians. In Gaza Province in August, dozens of civilian prisoners were reportedly axed or clubbed to death by RENAMO guerrillas after their hands had been tied behind them.

There were also claims that civilians had been tortured and killed by government troops during counter-insurgency operations, but it was impossible to corroborate these independently. The authorities acknowledged some abuses and several soldiers and militia members were arrested and prosecuted. Three soldiers were arrested in May and charged with torturing a radio journalist they had accused of trespassing on military property. They had not been tried by the end of the year. In October, two militiamen were each sentenced to 20 years' imprisonment for killing a school teacher in Niassa Province.

Over 750 long-term political detainees, most of them suspected of committing crimes on behalf of RENAMO, were released in late 1988 and in 1989 under Laws of Pardon passed in December 1987 (see *Amnesty International Report 1988*) and July 1989. About 140 others remained in custody: their cases were referred to the procuracy to consider whether they should be brought to trial. One such prisoner was tried in the Maputo City Provincial Court in October and sentenced to 18 years' imprisonment for spying on behalf of RENAMO.

At least 300 suspected members or supporters of RENAMO were arrested or captured by the army in areas of conflict during the year but few details emerged about individual cases. One man arrested in Tete Province in March was reported in the press to have admitted ordering the killing of 80 civilians captured by RENAMO. Some of those held were reportedly kept incommunicado in military custody for long periods although the law requires that prisoners held by the army are handed over to the security or criminal police immediately after questioning. None of those arrested was brought to trial.

At least a few prisoners were also held incommunicado for several months in the custody of the *Serviço Nacional de Segurança Popular* (SNASP), People's National Security Service. They included three businessmen from South Africa and a Mozambican colleague who were arrested in Maputo in January, apparently for political reasons. They were denied access to lawyers, relatives or consular officials until shortly before they were released uncharged in May and June.

All 37 prisoners serving sentences imposed after unfair trials by the Revolutionary Military Tribunal in previous years were released in August under a Law of Pardon passed in July. They included Carlos Gamboa Lopes Valerio, Pedro José Gonçalves and Ian Douglas Grey (see *Amnesty International Report 1988* and *1989*). Another, Tomás Mukoe Simango, who received a 15-year sentence in 1986 for armed rebellion and kidnapping civilians on behalf of RENAMO, had lost full use of his legs as a result of being kept tightly tied for many hours after his arrest. All 37 had been convicted by the Revolutionary Military Tribunal of crimes against the security of the state.

There were several reports of torture or ill-treatment inflicted by police, soldiers and prison warders. Eight people, who were subsequently sentenced to between three and 14 years' imprisonment for fraud, told the Maputo City Court in September that criminal investigation police had tortured them to extract confessions. The court ordered an inquiry into the torture allegations, which was continuing at the end of 1989.

No flogging sentences were imposed by the courts between January and September, when the punishment was abolished by law. However, several people were unlawfully whipped on the orders of soldiers and prison guards. For example, a militia commander in Cabo Delgado Province ordered two militiamen to be given 13 lashes each for firing their guns without permission. Six common-law prisoners were flogged in March when they were recaptured after escaping from a prison in Maputo. Prisoners were unlawfully whipped for disciplinary offences in the security and civil prisons at Machava on the outskirts of Maputo.

There was no news of dozens of detainees who had been arrested in the mid-1970s and subsequently "disappeared" in custody (see previous *Amnesty International Reports*).

Although Mozambique retained the death penalty, no death sentences were passed in 1989. The last executions took place in May 1986.

In September Amnesty International published *Mozambique: the Human Rights Record, 1975-1989 – Recent Government Measures*. The report surveyed human rights in Mozambique since independence in 1975 and described changes introduced since the mid-1980s to improve the protection of human rights. It recommended the restriction of the SNASP's powers of incommunicado and indefinite detention, the investigation of cases of prisoners who "disappeared" in the mid-1970s and the abolition of the death penalty. At the same time as the report, Amnesty International published a letter from the Minister of Justice. This acknowledged that abuses had occurred, but explained the government's policy to protect human rights in the face of destruction and gross abuses by RENAMO. Amnesty International welcomed the release of political prisoners and made inquiries about others, including untried detainees and prisoners who were reportedly flogged or otherwise ill-treated.

MYANMAR (BURMA)

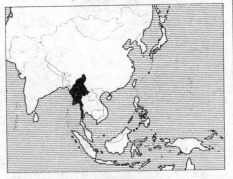

Many hundreds, possibly thousands, of suspected government opponents, including prisoners of conscience, were detained without charge or trial or sentenced to prison terms after unfair trials before military tribunals. Torture was widely reported as were extrajudicial executions by government troops combating long-standing insurgencies in ethnic minority areas. The authorities failed to investigate thousands of killings of pro-democracy demonstrators by government troops in 1988. At least 100 people were sentenced to death, although it was not known whether any such sentences had been carried out. All death sentences for crimes committed before the military coup of 18 September 1988 were commuted.

Martial law orders introduced after the State Law and Order Restoration Council (SLORC), headed by General Saw Maung, took power in a military coup in September 1988 remained in force throughout 1989. These severely restricted the scope of political activity, making participation in gatherings of more than four people (Martial Law Order 2/88) and public criticism of the armed forces (Notification 8/88) punishable by imprisonment. Further restrictions on freedom of expression and association were in force under legislation passed in years previous to the military coup. On 17 and 18 July martial law orders 1/89 and 2/89 declared that people who opposed martial law by "violation or defiance of the orders issued by the SLORC, the government or (military) commanders" would be tried summarily and only by military tribunals.

The full number of prisoners of conscience and other political prisoners held in Myanmar is believed to have run into thousands. At the end of the year Amnesty International had detailed information about more than 200 prisoners of conscience and possible prisoners of conscience, but these constituted only a small proportion of those reportedly arrested for political reasons. By mid-August, according to some estimates, 3,000 people had been arrested, and there were many further arrests before the end of the year.

Many prisoners of conscience were critics and opponents of the government detained for campaigning peacefully against martial law restrictions on freedom of expression. Arrests were reported throughout the year. Those held included Aung Din, the acting Chairman of the All-Burma Federation of Student Unions (ABSFU), who was arrested in the capital, Yangon, on 24 April. He had publicly criticized the SLORC in speeches and organized public meetings in defiance of the authorities. He was still believed detained without charge or trial at the end of the year. Other government opponents were arrested during the Burmese new year festival in April: they included Pa Du, a National League for Democracy (NLD) activist who had led a troupe of young actors whose performances were interpreted as criticizing the armed forces. Pa Du also was still reportedly held without charge or trial at the end of 1989.

Widespread arrests of political party leaders and activists in Yangon, Mandalay and other principal towns began on 17 July and continued at least until the end of the month. Those held included Moe Hein, leader of the Democratic Party for a New Society (DPNS), who appeared to be a prisoner of conscience. It was not known if he was charged or tried. Ten people were arrested during an illegal gathering of monks at Shwedagon Pagoda, Yangon. On 28 July, after a single morning session, a military tribunal sentenced seven of them to five years' hard labour for violating Order 2/88: the status of the other three was not known.

On 20 July troops arrested five members of the NLD executive committee and placed its principal leaders under house arrest. Aung San Suu Kyi, the daughter of Aung San, an independence hero, was still under house arrest at the end of the year. Tin U, a retired army general and NLD chairman, was also put under house arrest in July; in December he was sentenced to three years' imprisonment for "creating public disturbances". Those arrested in July included 38 other NLD supporters who were seized at the NLD headquarters: some of them were then reportedly interrogated under torture at Ye Kyi Aing detention centre. Most were believed to remain in custody at Yangon's Insein Prison at the end of the year. Details of charges against them were not known.

Leaders of other legally registered political parties also among those detained in July included Aye Lwin, Chairman of the Students' Revolutionary Party for Democracy, Ko Aung Win (also known as U Aung Win), General Secretary of the Youth and Students' Union Association, and Daw Cho Cho Than, General Secretary of the Patriotic League for Peace.

U Nu, an 82-year-old former prime minister, and 13 of his supporters were placed under house arrest on 29 December for refusing to repudiate a symbolic "parallel government" proposed to act under his authority.

Some government opponents arrested in 1988 remained prisoners of conscience. Nay Min, a lawyer arrested in October 1988, was sentenced to 14 years' imprisonment in October 1989 for having provided information to the foreign news media. Two prominent ethnic Kachin lawyers,

170

both of whom were detained in September 1988 in Myitkyina, were also still held. One, Bawk La, a Baptist preacher, was detained after making a series of speeches during demonstrations. He was reportedly beaten and given electric shocks during interrogation and to have suffered some memory loss as a consequence: his legal status was not known. Nan Zing La, also a Baptist, was tried and sentenced to five years' imprisonment reportedly as a consequence of two speeches he had made in September 1988. Neither of them was known to have advocated violence.

Trials for offences under martial law were held in accordance with the special norms and summary procedures established in July by Order 2/89. This stipulates that military tribunals are to "waive unnecessary witnesses" and not recall those "who have already testified". It requires tribunals to punish offenders with "(a) the death sentence; (b) life imprisonment; or (c) a jail term of not less than three years with hard labour", with death penalties to be imposed "regardless of the provisions under existing laws". Order 2/89 also stipulates that "decisions and judgments passed by a military tribunal shall be final". No judicial appeal is allowed. Death sentences must be ratified only by the area military commander and the sole recourse of the condemned is to ask the army Commander-in-Chief within 30 days to "review" the sentence.

There were new reports of torture and ill-treatment of prisoners during interrogation, in some cases leading to death. Torture methods reportedly included electric shocks, burns by cigarettes, superficial cuts with knives, near-drowning, hanging by the arms and the rolling of iron bars along the shin bones. Prisoners were often kept blindfold; forced to stand for long periods, to kneel on sharp stones, and to do callisthenics; and were denied food, water and sleep for extended periods.

Allegations of torture were received from many parts of the country and involved at least six distinct security agencies: the regular forces of the military (Tatmadaw) and the People's Police Force, and specialized agencies; the Military Intelligence Services (MIS); the Special Branch or political police; the police Criminal Investigation Department (CID); and the Bureau of Special Investigation Department (BSI), responsible for dealing with "economic crimes". NLD youth leader Myo Thein, a student and ethnic Mon, was detained in Yangon by the MIS in July. He was reportedly beaten and had his head plunged repeatedly into water during interrogation. He was said to be held in Ye Kyi Aing detention centre at the end of the year. U Soe Myint, the DPNS secretary for Ayeyarwady, was reportedly arrested at his home by troops in May and interrogated at the MIS headquarters in Pathein. According to other prisoners he was hooded with a rice bag, beaten and kicked, had his head held under water and was badly injured when an iron bar was rolled forcefully along his shins, removing much of the skin. He reportedly remained in detention at Pathein Prison at the end of 1989.

Torture as well as extrajudicial executions reportedly continued in ethnic minority areas where government forces were in conflict with armed opposition groups (see *Amnesty International Report 1989*). One former detainee, held from February to April as a suspected collaborator of Kachin insurgents, said he had been tortured at the army's Northern Military Command Headquarters at Myitkyina: he said that after "ordinary beatings" he was subjected to the "helicopter" (being spun around while hung from the ceiling) and beaten while in "the motorcycle" position (crouching down in a rider's position). He said he was partially suffocated with a plastic bag and subjected to the "iron road" (the rolling of an iron bar along his shins).

Government soldiers reportedly forced civilian villagers in minority areas to act as porters for them (see *Amnesty International Report 1989*) and frequently ill-treated or even killed them. One Kayin villager said soldiers had repeatedly kicked him while he was a porter in June because he had fallen and was "unable to stand back up quickly". A former soldier alleged that ethnic minority porters were sometimes killed for fear that they might reveal the whereabouts of government troops to opposition forces. This occurred, he said, when porters become too exhausted to proceed.

Those required to serve as military porters reportedly included people arrested in urban areas for protesting against the government. In August, shortly after the SLORC announced the imminent release of 1,500 prisoners from Insein prison, up to 500 political prisoners — mostly students

— were said to have been taken by the army at night from the prison and sent by train to the northern Shan state town of Nong Cho. In September one group of about 48 students was reportedly seen in the Shan village of Human, Nam Hsan township, having been assigned to food and ammunition porterage duties for army counter-insurgency units. Soldiers allegedly beat five other students to death in the nearby Nam Tu township.

Extrajudicial executions were also reported in the course of military operations in communities alleged to support ethnic insurgents. On 1 December troops reportedly fired indiscriminately on the inhabitants of the Kayin village of Thetkaya when most of them were assembled to watch a film. Three young girls, two older women and a 15-year-old monk at the village monastery were reportedly shot dead without warning or provocation. Many of the villagers subsequently sought refuge in Thailand. No official inquiry was known to have been held into the shootings.

No official inquiry was known to have been carried out into the killings of demonstrators by government forces in 1988. Amnesty International had urged such an inquiry at the end of 1988 and had pressed the government to introduce safeguards limiting the use of lethal force by government forces (see *Amnesty International Report 1989*).

At least 100 people were sentenced to death but it was not known if there were any executions. A military tribunal sentenced three young NLD activists to death in July for alleged involvement in a bombing, in a trial completed in a single morning. Moe Kyaw Thu, aged 17, Zaw Zaw Gyi and Nyi Nyi U were still under sentence of death at the end of the year. They alleged that false charges had been brought against them in an attempt to discredit the NLD. The SLORC said in October that 100 people had been sentenced to death in the previous three months: 76 by civilian courts and 24 by military tribunals. All death sentences for crimes committed before the military coup of September 1988 were commuted. Amnesty International was unable to confirm whether any executions had been carried out by the end of the year.

Amnesty International urged the government to release prisoners of conscience and to ensure that all other political detainees were either tried fairly and

promptly on recognizably criminal charges, or released.

The government informed Amnesty International in February that people detained in the course of demonstrations in late 1988 were being held for contravening Order 2/88 and the 1950 Emergency Provisions Act. The government said they were "unscrupulous instigators" who intended to create "confusion and chaos" and could not be considered non-violent.

Amnesty International expressed particular concern about the introduction of summary trials before military tribunals, which appeared grossly unfair and were empowered to hand down death sentences without effective appeal. The organization also urged the commutation of all death sentences and called for impartial investigation of all allegations of torture and of unlawful killings in the Kayin state.

Amnesty International wrote to the government several times to propose that a delegation from the organization should visit Myanmar to discuss human rights, but there was no response.

In May Amnesty International submitted information about its concerns in Myanmar for United Nations review under a procedure, established by Economic and Social Council Resolutions 728F/1503, for confidential consideration of communications about human rights violations.

In August Amnesty International published a report on torture, ill-treatment and killings of civilians in the Kayin state and in November published a report, *Myanmar (Burma): Prisoners of Conscience*, detailing arrests since September 1988.

NAMIBIA

Political prisoners were released and legislation permitting detention without trial was abolished, in accordance with a United Nations (UN) plan for Namibia's independence from South Africa. As well as the political prisoners released by the South African authorities, hundreds of prisoners who had been held outside Namibia by the armed opposition South West Africa People's Organisation (SWAPO) were freed and allowed to return to Namibia. However, hundreds of people detained in previous years either by the South African authorities in Namibia or

172

by SWAPO forces in Angola remained unaccounted for and had effectively "disappeared". There were new reports of torture and former prisoners held by both sides to the conflict said they had been tortured in previous years. Some prisoners were said to have been deliberately killed and several SWAPO supporters were allegedly executed extrajudicially. Four prisoners were sentenced to death but there were no executions.

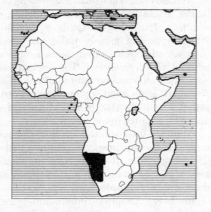

The UN plan, which came into effect on 1 April, involved a series of major political changes. The South African-appointed government was dissolved in March and Namibia was administered under a transitional arrangement by South Africa's Administrator-General. The UN Secretary-General's Special Representative for Namibia supervised the independence plan, with the assistance of the UN Transition Assistance Group (UNTAG), a military and civilian monitoring force drawn from various countries. Repressive or restrictive laws, including those that had permitted long-term and incommunicado detention, which had facilitated torture and other human rights violations in the past, were repealed. From April onwards political prisoners were released and Namibian exiles, particularly SWAPO supporters based in Angola, returned to Namibia. Most South African forces were withdrawn from Namibia or confined to base. Elections for a 72-member Constituent Assembly were held in November. SWAPO won 41 seats while the Democratic Turnhalle Alliance (DTA), which had dominated the previous government, won 21. The assembly began drafting a constitution (which required a two-thirds

majority) on the basis of principles drawn up by the UN Security Council in 1982. These included guarantees for civil liberties and an independent judiciary.

At the beginning of April there were major clashes in northern Namibia between South African forces and SWAPO guerrillas before UNTAG units arrived in the area. Some 300 SWAPO guerrillas were killed. SWAPO said that the guerrillas were already in Namibia while the South African authorities said they had crossed from Angola after 1 April, in violation of the UN plan. In subsequent months there were numerous politically motivated assaults on SWAPO supporters, including some killings. Many of these attacks were attributed to members or former members of the paramilitary Counter-Insurgency Unit (COIN) known as *Koevoet* (Crowbar).

Dozens of uncharged political detainees whose arrest had been acknowledged by the South African authorities were released between April and June. In July, 24 convicted political prisoners and one who was awaiting trial were freed. Another who was sentenced in August to nine years' imprisonment for a politically motivated murder was released in November.

The fate of many people who reportedly "disappeared" after being detained by the South African security forces in the 1970s and 1980s remained unknown. Reacting to lists of some 60 "disappearance" cases submitted by SWAPO and by Amnesty International, the South African authorities said that those named had either been released or were not known. However, further evidence emerged in 1989 about the absence of safeguards for detainees in the past, calling into question the reliability of the South African authorities' response to reported "disappearances". Dozens of SWAPO combatants captured in previous years had apparently been held in unacknowledged detention for up to five years on a farm run by police near Tsumeb. Seventeen left the farm in September after smuggling out a letter about their plight. A police commander subsequently claimed that they were paid labourers rather than prisoners.

In May SWAPO announced the release of 200 prisoners it had been holding in its military bases in Angola. It had previously admitted holding about 100 prisoners accused of spying for South Africa. Eventually over 500 were reported to have been released. Among them were Bience Gawanas, a London-based lawyer who had been arrested by SWAPO in Zambia in August 1988 and subsequently detained in Angola (see *Amnesty International Report 1989*).

Some of those released claimed that many other prisoners were still detained in SWAPO bases outside Namibia and that others had died or been killed in detention. These allegations, together with accounts of torture by those previously detained in Angola, received considerable publicity in Namibia. In September a UN delegation visited 30 SWAPO bases in Angola and Zambia to investigate the allegations but found no prisoners still in SWAPO's custody. The UN subsequently reported that some 1,100 names of alleged prisoners had been submitted to it. Of these, 163 names were either incomplete or duplications. A further 67 people had never been detained; 517 had been imprisoned and were known to have been released; 123 were reported to be dead (although the circumstances of their deaths were not noted) and 263 could not be accounted for. Among those named were two prominent SWAPO members who had been imprisoned in Namibia before rejoining SWAPO in exile. Bernardus Petrus was reported to have died in 1986 and Victor Nkandi's fate was said not to be known (see *Amnesty International Report 1987*). The UN said it would continue to investigate the outstanding 263 cases.

A civil court action to secure the release of six people reportedly detained by SWAPO in Angola was initiated in the Windhoek Supreme Court in May by relatives of the six and the Parents' Committee, an organization set up to press for the release of detainees held by SWAPO. In November the court ruled that five of the six had been unlawfully detained by SWAPO until at least May 1989, but that there was insufficient evidence to prove that the sixth had been detained. Although it lacked the power to order the release of prisoners held in Angola, the court instructed SWAPO to account for the five, if they had been released since May.

Convicted political prisoners who were released from Windhoek Central Prison in July said that they had been tortured by South African security forces following their arrest in previous years and had witnessed other prisoners being tortured. They described severe beatings, electric shocks,

suspension by the feet and partial suffocation as among the methods of torture which had been used.

Prisoners released from SWAPO custody in Angola also said they had been tortured. The methods they cited included severe beatings, being suspended by the wrists or ankles, being burned, and being partially buried. They said they had been held in large pits roofed with zinc sheets or tree-trunks. SWAPO representatives acknowledged that prisoners had been tortured.

There were also new reports of torture and ill-treatment in custody. A commission of inquiry heard that two suspected criminals, Josiah Pineas and Paulus Ndume, had been blindfolded and bound, suspended on a bar and subjected to electric shocks during interrogation in a Windhoek police station in June. The commission instructed the police authorities to investigate the case with a view to prosecuting those responsible. Two leading SWAPO members laid charges against police after they were apparently assaulted by police in Oshakati police station in November. One of them, Maxuilili Nathaniel, a former acting president of SWAPO's internal wing, sustained a deep cut in his head.

There were allegations that South African police and security forces had deliberately killed prisoners. Among the 300 SWAPO guerrillas killed in April, at least 18 were apparently shot in the back of the head at close range after they were captured. In August police shot a former *Koevoet* member dead at his home in Rundu, claiming he had resisted arrest. Petrus Joseph had joined SWAPO after leaving *Koevoet* and in March had testified in court that *Koevoet* personnel had been ordered to arrest and intimidate suspected SWAPO supporters. In September the murder of Anton Lubowski, a prominent lawyer and SWAPO member, fuelled speculation that the South African authorities might be implicated. A police investigation into the murder was announced and was still continuing at the end of the year.

In March the Supreme Court ruled that the immunity from prosecution granted by South Africa's State President in 1988 to six soldiers suspected of killing a SWAPO supporter should be withdrawn. However, the authorities were granted leave to appeal against the court's ruling. By the end of the year there had been no decision concerning a similar appeal on behalf of four soldiers

174

who beat a political detainee to death in 1985 (see *Amnesty International Report 1989*). In November the Administrator-General granted an amnesty to two members of the South African security forces accused of murders committed during counter-insurgency operations in 1985.

Four people were sentenced to death. Leonard Sheehama, a SWAPO member, was sentenced to death in April for a bomb explosion which killed five people in Walvis Bay, a South African enclave in Namibia. He was tried in Walvis Bay by a South African court. Three other men convicted of murder were sentenced to death in Windhoek in June. A stay of execution was granted in favour of Lukas Matsuib shortly before he was due to be hanged on 9 June. He had been convicted of murder in 1988. There were no executions.

In March Amnesty International submitted to the UN lists of political prisoners reportedly held by the South African authorities in Namibia including convicted prisoners, untried detainees and prisoners feared to have "disappeared" in custody. It also submitted a list of prisoners reportedly detained by SWAPO in Angola. It made inquiries about prisoners who were believed to have "disappeared" in custody, both in Namibia and in SWAPO's bases in Angola. Amnesty International called for strong human rights guarantees to be included in Namibia's new constitution. It appealed against the use of the death penalty.

NEPAL

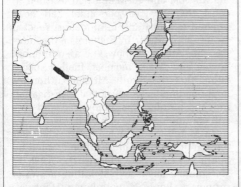

Hundreds of political prisoners including journalists, students, teachers, members of political groups and human rights activists were detained during the year under legislation allowing detention without charge or trial. Some were prisoners of conscience. Thousands of people were held briefly for participating in peaceful demonstrations. There were persistent reports that political prisoners were tortured.

In March a trade agreement with India dating from 1950 lapsed, resulting in the imposition of trade and transit restrictions by India on land-locked Nepal. Nepal suffered shortages of essential supplies and tension mounted between the two countries. Although all political activities remained officially banned under Nepal's non-party *panchayat* (assembly) system, the main opposition party, Nepali Congress, other political parties, students and journalists publicly criticized the government's handling of negotiations with India.

Two journalists, Gopal Gurung and Balaram Sharma, both prisoners of conscience arrested in mid-1988 for publishing material the authorities considered offensive, remained in prison throughout the year. They were held under the Treason Act and the Public Security Act (PSA) respectively.

During April and May a dozen other journalists were arrested and detained for up to four months for writing critically about the government's handling of the trade dispute. All were reportedly released without being brought to trial.

In April hundreds of students were arrested during peaceful demonstrations about the trade dispute and the government's closure of university campuses. Most were released after a few days, but others, including Ghanshyam Bhusal and Vijaya Subedi, were detained without charge or trial for several months under the PSA.

At least 22 prisoners of conscience were sentenced to between eight months' and six years' imprisonment for converting to Christianity or proselytizing. Both are offences under Nepal's legal code. For example, Krishna Bahadur Rai from Solukhumbu district in eastern Nepal was sentenced in February to six years' imprisonment for proselytizing.

In August at least 10 peaceful demonstrators, including Nepalese members of Amnesty International, were detained for several hours in Biratnagar during a march opposing the worldwide use of the death penalty.

In September, according to Nepali Congress, around 3,000 of its members and supporters were detained nationwide. Most were freed without charge within a week, but 21 were charged with disturbing the peace and security for political gain. They were released on bail.

Hundreds of political prisoners were detained during 1989 and about 100 were in detention without having been tried at the end of the year. Many were detained under the Treason (Crime and Punishment) Act and the Organizations and Associations (Control) Act for criticizing or encouraging criticism of the monarchy or the non-party system. Some had been held for several years without trial. Others were held under the PSA's provisions for detention without charge or trial for up to three years on broadly defined grounds of national security.

The PSA was amended in August; the maximum period of detention was halved to 18 months and the powers of local officials to detain people were brought further under the control of local courts and the central government. An advisory board must now review cases after nine months' detention, but prisoners still have no access to legal representation at these boards and there is no judicial scrutiny of PSA detentions. In the past, several people had been held for longer than the legally permitted three years. For example, Bhola Bohra, a student arrested in January 1984, was not released until May 1989. In September the Home Minister said that 19 people remained in detention under the PSA. By the end of the year most of these had been released.

Torture was reported from several police stations and prisons, including severe beatings, insertion of pins under finger and toenails and sleep deprivation. In October a student who had been severely beaten by police was taken unconscious to hospital. Some detainees were reportedly tortured while held for up to three months in unacknowledged detention. Some unacknowledged detainees were reportedly released by order of the Supreme Court, but the police appear to have flouted other release orders and transferred detainees to other police stations. The health of many prisoners was reportedly jeopardized by overcrowding, inadequate sanitation, the prolonged use of fetters and the lack of medical facilities in many police stations and prisons.

In August an amendment to the Treason (Crime and Punishment) Act abolished the death penalty for crimes against the state. It remains a punishment for attacking the royal family. No executions had taken place in Nepal since 1979.

Amnesty International urged the government to release prisoners of conscience and to release or charge and try more than 60 other political prisoners whose cases it was investigating. It also requested information about changes to the laws under which political prisoners are held. No response was received from the government.

NICARAGUA

Army troops reportedly killed at least 12 peasants suspected of collaborating with armed opposition groups known as the *contras* in some of the zones affected by armed conflict. In March the government initiated investigations into some of these cases and others dating from earlier years. Some soldiers and security personnel found responsible for abuses were convicted and sentenced to prison by military courts. The government failed to clarify the whereabouts or fate of several prisoners alleged to have "disappeared" in 1987 and 1988. Six prisoners of conscience or possible prisoners of conscience were released after appeal hearings by civilian courts or government pardons. In March the government pardoned and released 1,649 alleged former members of the National Guard of the previous government of Anastasio Somoza Debayle; they had been convicted by special courts, many of them for gross human rights abuses. The procedures of these courts had been subject to serious irregularities. Thirty-nine alleged former guardsmen

176 were excluded from the pardon and continued to serve their sentences. The government continued to hold 1,268 other prisoners alleged to be members or supporters of the *contras*. Most had also been convicted by special courts whose procedures failed to guarantee a fair trial. There were isolated but serious reports of ill-treatment of prisoners.

The human rights situation in Nicaragua was influenced by agreements reached between the presidents of Costa Rica, El Salvador, Guatemala, Honduras and Nicaragua on measures to find peaceful settlements to the armed conflicts in the Central American region. In February, at a meeting of the presidents in Costa Del Sol, El Salvador, Nicaragua's President Daniel Ortega agreed to hold elections no later than 25 February 1990 and to invite international observers, including representatives of the United Nations (UN) and the Organization of American States (OAS). The presidents agreed to draw up a joint plan for the demobilization of *contra* forces which were based in Honduras and supported by "humanitarian" aid from the United States (US) Government. The *contra* combatants and their families were to be repatriated to Nicaragua or relocated in third countries. In August, pursuant to a further agreement at Tela, Honduras, an International Commission of Support and Verification was established under the auspices of the UN and the OAS to supervise the demobilization. A few days before the Tela meeting, the Nicaraguan Government reached an agreement with opposition parties on reforms of electoral procedures, media laws and penal legislation. It also agreed to a broad and unconditional amnesty for political prisoners, to be put into effect when the demobilization plan had been implemented. Although the plan was scheduled to be completed in December, by the end of the year few *contras* had taken up the demobilization offer and it was extended into 1990.

Contra activity in rural areas continued to be reported throughout the year despite assurances by *contra* commanders that they would respect the cease-fire regularly and unilaterally renewed by the government since April 1988. On 1 November President Ortega announced that, in response to mounting *contra* attacks during October, the government would not renew the cease-fire unless the US Government ceased all further support for the *contra* forces. Given the continuation of such assistance, the cease-fire was not renewed and military activity subsequently intensified. Reported killings and summary executions of civilians by *contra* units became more frequent in the last months of the year.

At least 12 peasants were reportedly killed by soldiers or security officers in circumstances suggesting that they had been summarily executed as suspected *contras* collaborators. They included Sergio Molina Monge, an evangelical preacher, alleged by the government to be a messenger for the *contras*. He was reportedly abducted by soldiers from his home in Uló, Matagalpa department, in February. Witnesses to his arrest heard shots fired and the next day his body was found nearby with the throat slit. The *Comisión Nacional de Promoción y Protección de los Derechos Humanos* (CNPPDH), National Commission for the Promotion and Protection of Human Rights, the government-sponsored human rights organization, reported in August that two soldiers had been sentenced to 16 years' imprisonment for the murder. Two other soldiers and two civilians were sentenced to eight years' imprisonment as accomplices. Adolfo Chavarría Blandón, said to be a former *contra* who had been granted a government amnesty in November 1987, was killed in June allegedly while in the custody of the police or the *Dirección General de Seguridad del Estado* (DGSE), General Directorate of State Security. He was arrested by police officers in Esquipulas, Matagalpa department, on 2 June and his body was found on 14 June, reportedly bearing signs of beating. There was no information as to whether the case had been investigated by the government. Eight soldiers were tried and sentenced to imprisonment in connection with the killing of six civilians in La Gateada, Chontales department, in January. In two further cases, the government said that those responsible were civilians.

In March military prosecutors initiated a series of investigations into killings of civilians reportedly carried out by government troops since 1987, particularly in the departments of Matagalpa, Jinotega, Zelaya and Chontales. Celso del Socorro Herrera Carvallo was allegedly captured and killed by army troops on 11 July 1988 near El Ventarrón, Pantasma, Jinotega department (see *Amnesty International Report 1989*). In July a military court concluded that he had been killed in cross-fire during a combat. However, it was unclear from court records provided by the government on what evidence this conclusion was reached. Information published by the CNPPDH in August indicated that soldiers and DGSE officials had been sentenced to prison by military courts for the killing of five civilians in 1988. In three other cases, the CNPPDH said that although military suspects had been identified, those alleged responsible had evaded arrest. In December the government informed Amnesty International that investigations into four of 11 killings in Ubú, Zelaya department, in 1987 had been closed owing to insufficient evidence. In only one of the remaining cases was a military suspect identified, and he was said to be in hiding.

Government investigations failed to clarify the whereabouts or fate of at least five people who are alleged to have "disappeared" after their arrest in 1987 and 1988. They included Félix Pedro Herrera Carvallo, the younger brother of Celso del Socorro Herrera Carvallo. He was reportedly detained in El Ventarrón, Jinotega department, on the day that his brother was killed (see *Amnesty International Report 1989*). Trial proceedings were opened in April against the officer allegedly responsible for the "disappearance" of José Francisco Martínez Murillo in Chontales in 1987.

Prisoner of conscience Mario Baldizón Avilés, a former government employee who had been sentenced by a military court in 1986 to 10 years' imprisonment for treason, was released on parole in March and officially pardoned in April. He had been accused of helping his brother, Alvaro Baldizón Avilés, a former employee of the Ministry of the Interior, to leave Nicaragua and seek asylum in the United States of America (USA— see *Amnesty International Report 1988*). The government submitted his case for review by the CNPPDH, which found his conviction to have been unsound. The government also pardoned María Auxiliadora Rivas Urbina, who had been sentenced by a *Tribunal Popular Antisomocista* (TPA), Popular Antisomocista Tribunal, to seven years' imprisonment in March 1986 for recruiting for the *contras*. She appeared to have been convicted on the basis of a fabricated confes-

sion (see *Amnesty International Report 1988*). She was allowed home on parole in February and pardoned in April. Economists Mario Alegría Castillo and Nora Aldana Centeno were released in April. They had been sentenced by an ordinary court in June 1988 to 16 years' imprisonment for allegedly passing "secret" economic data to officials of the US Embassy (see *Amnesty International Report 1989*). They and the two other defendants in the case, José Adrian Espinales Rodríguez and Pedro Pablo Su Olivas, were released after the Third Region Appeals Court upheld their appeal and urged the government to introduce legislation regulating the definition of official secrets. Thirteen government opponents, including opposition party leaders Agustín Jarquín Anaya, Myriam Arguello Morales, Róger Guevara Mena and Carlos Huembes Trejos, who had been given suspended prison sentences in December 1988, had their sentences revoked in April by the Fourth Region Appeals Court. In a highly publicized case, the lower court had held them responsible for an outbreak of violence during an opposition protest rally in Nandaime on 10 July 1988 (see *Amnesty International Report 1989*). There appeared to be no evidence that the convicted leaders had themselves participated in or instigated violence. The Appeals Court concluded that the charges could not be sustained.

On 14 March the National Assembly passed a decree pardoning 1,894 prisoners who had been convicted by special courts between 1979 and 1981 for crimes allegedly committed by them as members of the National Guard under the previous government of Anastasio Somoza Debayle. The procedures of the special courts had involved serious irregularities which had aroused international concern (see *Amnesty International Report 1981* and *1982*). The government pardon, which followed a review of the trials by the Inter-American Commission of Human Rights (IACHR), was agreed by President Ortega at the summit meeting of Central American presidents in February. On 16 March, 1,649 prisoners, all but 39 of the alleged National Guard still in prison (some 245 had already been allowed home under the prison rehabilitation program), were released. Some of the released prisoners were reportedly subsequently harassed and threatened by

178

government security officers.

There was concern that the exclusion of the 39 prisoners from the pardon was based on factors other than an objective and impartial assessment of the fairness of their trials. In its 1988 to 1989 report, the IACHR published a list of the excluded prisoners, all of whom were said to be suffering from illnesses. It considered that there was no valid evidence that any of them had committed atrocious crimes, and reiterated its hope that the 39 would be pardoned and released.

In August the government acknowledged holding 1,268 other prisoners who had been convicted for belonging to or supporting the *contras*. Most had been tried by TPAs, special government-appointed courts whose structure and procedures were inconsistent with international standards of fairness and impartiality. They severely restricted the time available for defence and appeals against verdicts could be made only to the TPAs' own appeals court. The TPAs were dissolved in January 1988. Although more than 230 alleged *contra* collaborators were reportedly released in August, the block release of most of the remaining prisoners, which President Ortega had stated would be carried out in early September, had not been implemented by the end of the year.

A group of more than 20 prisoners were reportedly ill-treated in El Chipote, the DGSE detention centre in Managua, after prison authorities suppressed a hunger-strike at the Model Prison in Tipitapa in February. Several prisoners alleged that after being transferred to El Chipote they were kept handcuffed and naked for five days, given no water and made to sleep on a cement floor without a mattress. Other prisoners who were not transferred were alleged to have been beaten by guards and prison officials and forced to maintain painful positions for long periods. The prison authorities denied any ill-treatment had occurred.

In October the National Assembly repealed the Law for the Maintenance of Public Order and Security, which had been in force since 1981, and under which the majority of political prisoners had been tried, including some prisoners of conscience or possible prisoners of conscience (see *Amnesty International Report 1982*). The National Assembly also passed amendments to the Law of Jurisdictional Func-

tions of the Sandinista Police, ending police powers to use summary procedures to impose prison sentences for minor offences, without trial or rights of defence or appeal. During 1988 numerous opposition party members had been sent to prison for short periods by police magistrates for public order offences during protest demonstrations (see *Amnesty International Report 1989*). Both reforms were a result of the agreement reached in August between the government and opposition parties.

Amnesty International received no reply to a memorandum which it had submitted to the government in July 1988, summarizing its concerns under the state of emergency. However, cases raised in that document and Amnesty International's current concerns were discussed with government authorities in February and March 1989, when Amnesty International representatives visited Nicaragua. In May Amnesty International met President Ortega and Foreign Minister Miguel D'Escoto in London. President Ortega took note of Amnesty International's concerns and promised that they would be promptly investigated. In the following months Amnesty International received detailed information from the government on the results of official inquiries into several of the cases it had raised. It was also informed that following representations from Amnesty International, cubicle-sized cells, known colloquially as *chiquitas* (the small ones), had been dismantled in DGSE detention centres in two regions. Persistent reports had been received that cells of this type, which were dark, unventilated and too small to sit down in, had been used to hold prisoners for days while they were undergoing interrogation (see *Amnesty International Report 1988* and *1989*).

In November Amnesty International published a report, *Nicaragua: the Human Rights Record 1986-1989*. It welcomed progress in several areas of human rights protection, including the release of prisoners who had received unfair trials, greater legal protection for detainees, and the identifying and bringing to justice of those responsible in some cases of human rights violations. However, Amnesty International expressed concern about persisting reports of killings of non-combatants by army troops and of "disappearances". It urged the government to take further measures to halt these abuses. A letter was received in response to the report from the President of the CNPPDH, on behalf of the government. The letter welcomed the positive effort made by Amnesty International to analyse the human rights situation objectively, but considered that the report did not give due weight in its conclusions to government efforts to bring those responsible for human rights violations to justice.

NIGER

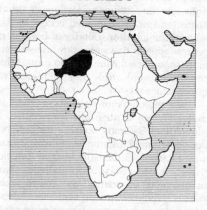

All the remaining 12 political prisoners sentenced after unfair trials were released on the Head of State's orders in April and December. Two people were sentenced to death after being convicted of murder.

In September a new constitution was approved by referendum to make Niger a one-party state ruled by the *Mouvement national de la société de développement*, the National Movement for the Society of Development. Presidential and national assembly elections took place in December.

In April, on the 15th anniversary of the coup which brought the armed forces to power in 1974, President Ali Saïbou ordered the release of 10 prisoners convicted of politically motivated offences after unfair trials. Seven of them, including Mohamed Mohamed Abdoulahi, known as "Billa", had been sentenced to death in 1985 in connection with an attack that year on government buildings in Tchin Tabaraden. When he was appointed Head of State in 1987, President Ali Saïbou had commuted their death sentences to life imprisonment and later reduced these to 30 years (see *Amnesty International Report 1988*). The three others freed in April were

two army officers and a journalist convicted in 1988 in connection with an unsuccessful coup attempt in 1983 and sentenced to between seven and nine years' imprisonment. The two freed in December were also army officers convicted in connection with the same coup attempt and sentenced to 10 and 20 years' imprisonment. They had been among 28 people tried in 1988 by the State Security Court. After these releases no other political prisoners were known to be held in the country.

In March two people were sentenced to death in Zinder after being convicted of murder. It was not clear whether they exercised their right of appeal but they had not been executed by the end of the year.

An Amnesty International delegation visited Niger in March and met the Minister of Justice, the Minister of the Interior and several other officials from the two ministries. Ministers told the delegates that the government had resolved not to tolerate human rights violations and was prepared to take legal steps to ensure that human rights were respected.

Amnesty International asked about the whereabouts of five people arrested and sentenced after the attack on government buildings in Tchin Tabaraden in 1985 who had not been released. It was informed that four of them had died in 1985 of gastroenteritis in Birni-Nkonni New Prison, and that the fifth had died during the attack on the government building.

NIGERIA

At least 30 critics of the government, all prisoners of conscience, were detained without charge or trial, most for brief periods but some for several months. Eleven trade union leaders who were arrested after a strike had their life sentences reduced to 10 years' imprisonment. Harsh prison and detention conditions continued to be reported. The number of known executions dropped sharply to 12 during the year, but this may have been because the authorities halted executions in public and did not announce the number carried out inside prisons.

The ban on political parties, in force since the armed forces took power in 1983, was lifted in May as a step towards the

180

restoration of civilian rule planned for 1992. However, after criticizing the 13 parties which sought registration, the President, General Ibrahim Babangida, reimposed the ban in October. In December the government established two new political parties — one of the right and one of the left — which alone can contest forthcoming elections.

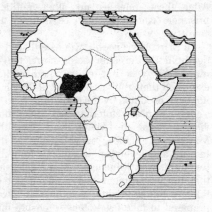

At least 30 prisoners of conscience, many of them journalists, were detained without charge, most for periods of less than one week, but in some cases for up to eight months. They were held under the State Security (Detention of Persons) Decree, No. 2 of 1984, which provides for the indefinite administrative detention without charge or trial of any person suspected of threatening the economy or the security of the state.

Journalists who wrote articles critical of the government were routinely questioned by the security police, the State Security Service (SSS), and sometimes detained for short periods. Following an article in *The Republic* newspaper in June about a court action against the government, the police sought to arrest the editor, Paxton Olu-Idowu, and four of his staff. When he could not be found, armed police arrested his wife, Florence Olu-Idowu. Although eight months pregnant, she was held with a male suspect in a police cell without food, water or toilet facilities until her husband reported to the police the following day. He and four colleagues were subsequently detained for a week before being freed without charge.

Other journalists were held for longer periods. Anthony Ukpong, a reporter with the *Weekly Metropolitan* newspaper, was arrested in December 1988 and held without charge until July when he was released before a legal action challenging his detention came to court. He had written an article speculating that the head of the police force was to be dismissed. Femi Aborisade, editor of *Labour Militant*, was detained without charge from February to September. He said he was questioned only about why he had continued to publish the newspaper after he had been detained for two weeks in 1988. Both complained of being held almost naked in cramped conditions at the SSS interrogation centre in Lagos, and of being denied access to their lawyers or families. Detainees held at the centre apparently went on hunger-strike more than once during 1989 to protest their conditions but did not achieve any improvements.

Two prisoners of conscience detained under Decree 2 were also prosecuted. In May Alhaji Balarabe Musa, a former civilian governor of Kaduna State, was arrested and charged with launching a political party while being disqualified from involvement in politics, an offence which carries a five-year prison sentence. Anyone who held office in any former government is banned from holding government office or a post in a political party until 1992; officials who have been convicted of any offence are banned for life. Although a court ordered Alhaji Balarabe Musa's release on bail two days after his arrest, he was immediately redetained under Decree 2. His trial was adjourned in August and he was released in October; the trial had not resumed by the end of the year.

In June Gani Fawehinmi, a lawyer and prominent government critic, was arrested in Lagos during a public meeting about the government's economic policies. He was detained in harsh conditions in northeast Nigeria, over 1,500 kilometres from his home in Lagos. He required hospital treatment a week later because he had not been given medication required for high blood pressure. In July the High Court in Lagos awarded him damages for unlawful arrest but ruled that it did not have jurisdiction to question his administrative detention. In September he was charged with obstructing the political transition program, an offence punishable by five years' imprisonment, for criticizing the government in a magazine interview. The courts agreed to his release on bail, but he was immediately redetained under Decree 2 and held until October when he was released after widespread protests. His trial had not resumed by the end of the year.

Hundreds of students were arrested in May and June during countrywide demonstrations and riots against the government's economic policies. According to official statements, 22 people died in the disturbances, but unofficial sources put the death toll as high as 100. Six universities were closed and several student leaders were detained without charge under security legislation. The President of the National Association of Nigerian Students (NANS), Salihu Mohammed Lukman, was detained without charge throughout August and released after the High Court ordered the SSS to justify his detention. Gbenga Olawepo and Gbenga Komolafe, also leading officials of NANS, were arrested in September and October respectively. The Lagos High Court ruled in November that it had no jurisdiction to order their release, but a judge at a subsequent hearing ruled that the conditions for detention required by Decree 2 had not been met. This rendered the detention orders unlawful and they were released.

Eleven senior employees of the National Electric Power Authority (NEPA), sentenced to life imprisonment in December 1988 after organizing a strike which cut power supplies, remained imprisoned although their sentences were reduced. They were convicted by the Miscellaneous Offences Tribunal, a special military court, of conspiracy to interfere unlawfully with NEPA equipment and of inducing others to do so (see *Amnesty International Report 1989*). In April they withdrew their appeal to the Special Appeals Tribunal in the hope of clemency from the President; in August he reduced their sentences to 10 years' imprisonment.

In September it was reported that restrictions had been lifted on the movement of Major-General Muhammadu Buhari, the former head of state whose military government was overthrown in 1985, and Major-General Tunde Idiagbon, his former chief of staff. Following their release from detention in December 1988 (see *Amnesty International Report 1989*), they were apparently confined to their home districts.

Although the number of reported executions dropped sharply, from at least 85 in 1988 to at least 12 in 1989, the real figure for 1989 was believed to be considerably higher. In September the Chief Justice of Nigeria stated that executions in public had been stopped. It appeared that executions by firing-squad, formerly carried out in public, might be taking place out of public view. As with hangings, which take place inside prisons, they were not officially announced. The government did not state how many executions had been carried out in the year.

The last public executions known to Amnesty International were of three prisoners shot by firing-squad in February in Abuja, the new federal capital, before a crowd of thousands. They were convicted by a Robbery and Firearms Tribunal, a special court which allows no right of appeal to a higher court. One of those executed, Matthew Anu, was reported to have been aged 18 at the time of the execution and to have been a minor at the time of the offence.

Amnesty International appealed for the release of prisoners of conscience, for other political detainees to be either charged or released and for the repeal of legislation permitting the imprisonment of prisoners of conscience. The organization investigated whether power workers serving long prison sentences were prisoners of conscience and called for improvements in prison conditions. Amnesty International also expressed concern that prisoners, including at least one minor, continued to be executed after trials before special courts which allowed no right of appeal. In response to calls for the abolition of the death penalty, the government informed Amnesty International in July that a human rights department was to be established under ministerial control; no further information about it had been received by the end of the year.

PAKISTAN

At least 100 prisoners of conscience were detained for non-violent political or religious activities, but most were only held for short periods. They included members of the Ahmadiyya community who were arrested for expressing their faith. Torture in police custody was widespread, sometimes resulting in death. Two public

lashings were reported. At least 60 people were sentenced to death but there were no executions.

Prime Minister Benazir Bhutto's Pakistan People's Party (PPP) controlled the federal government and the provincial governments of Sind and North West Frontier Province. However, the PPP was in opposition in Punjab and, from February, in Baluchistan. The Punjab Government was controlled by the Islamic Democratic Alliance, and from February the Baluchistan provincial government was controlled by an alliance of the Baluchistan National Alliance, the Islamic Democratic Alliance and the Islamic *Jamiatul-Ulema-e-Islam.*

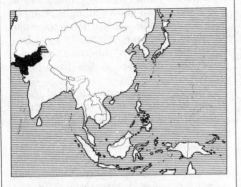

Violence between different ethnic communities continued in Sind province. Ahmadis — a religious group whose members consider themselves Muslims but whose Islamic status is denied under Pakistani law — were victims of sectarian violence in Punjab province in April and July.

The majority of political prisoners who had been convicted in unfair trials by special military courts under the previous government were released in an amnesty in December 1988 (see *Amnesty International Report 1989*). However, several hundred prisoners convicted of serious criminal offences by these courts were excluded from the amnesty, including some allegedly convicted on false criminal charges brought against them for political reasons. The prisoners were barred from judicial appeal, except on limited procedural grounds, by amendments to the Constitution made before the lifting of martial law. By August about 700 of these cases had been examined by a review board, which recommended the release of 69 prisoners.

Several politicians and scores of party workers were arrested during 1989. Some were administratively detained, others were held on a range of criminal and political charges. A tour of Sind by G.M. Syed, the 87-year-old leader of the Sind National Alliance (SNA), was halted when he was put under house arrest in October on a 30-day detention order and charged with sedition. The detention order, imposed by the Sind provincial authorities under the Maintenance of Public Order Ordinance (MPO), was extended for a further 30 days in November and again in December. He and about 30 SNA supporters were arrrested after the Pakistani flag was allegedly burned by a group who had gathered to greet him at Sukkur airport. At the end of the year G.M. Syed and about 12 of his supporters were awaiting trial by a special court under the 1974 Suppression of Terrorist Activities (Special Courts) Act on charges of sedition and desecration of the national flag.

The MPO permits an initial period of up to three months' detention without trial to be imposed on anyone considered to be "acting in any manner prejudicial to public safety or the maintenance of public order". Section 16 provides for up to three years' imprisonment for anyone whose speeches or statements are considered to cause "fear or alarm" to "any section of the public" or to promote "any activity prejudicial to public safety or the maintenance of public order".

Salman Taseer, deputy leader of the opposition PPP in the Punjab Assembly, was arrested in August under a detention order issued by the Punjab provincial authorities under Section 16 of the MPO and charged with sedition for a speech he had made in January. He had already been granted bail on other charges, and was released on bail on the sedition charge early the next day.

Members of the Ahmadiyya community — whose claims to be Muslim are punishable by imprisonment under Pakistani law — continued to be arrested for practising their faith. They were detained as prisoners of conscience for periods ranging from a few days to three months. Mirza Mubarak Ahmad Nusrat was arrested at Mirpurkhas, Sind province, in January and charged with defiling the name of the Prophet Muhammad, an offence which can carry the death penalty. He had included blessings to the Prophet Muhammad, as well as to the founder of the Ahmadiyya movement, in a letter. He was released on bail after three months. In March the Ahmadiyya centenary celebrations were banned in Punjab province. In the same month 24 Ahmadis were arrested at Rabwah, the Ahmadiyya community headquarters, in connection with the celebrations. Four were charged with violating the banning order. The others were charged with offences relating to the practice of their faith. All were released on bail. In October four Ahmadis, including two senior leaders, were arrested at Rabwah after the authorities withdrew permission for an annual Ahmadiyya conference after it had already begun. They were released on bail two days later.

Scores of people were reportedly tortured in police custody. In some cases police officers were charged following investigations, but no trials of police officers on charges relating to torture were reported. At least eight women were allegedly raped by police while in custody. In July two women were reportedly beaten with leather thongs in Mandi Bahauddin Saddar police station, Punjab province. They were then reportedly stripped and raped by six or seven police officers in turn, who also thrust sticks into their vaginas. After a protest demonstration, charges were brought against the police officers allegedly involved but it was not known whether they were taken into custody. In Sind province an inquiry was called into the alleged rape of Saima Anjum, a 16-year-old criminal suspect, by police at Landhi in December 1988. Police officers were said to have beaten and raped her, and forced chillies into her uterus. The police officers charged with the rape of three women in Nawan Kot police station, Lahore, Punjab province, had still not been arrested by the end of 1989 (see *Amnesty International Report 1989*). In July a Lahore High Court judge directed that women should only be detained in judicial custody and not in police stations, as a protective measure.

Dozens of people reportedly died in custody, in many cases following alleged torture. In one case, medical officials were alleged to have falsified post-mortem reports to cover up the death from torture of Basir Ahmed, who died in Bahlak police station, Faisalabad, Punjab province, in July. The report of a first post-mortem said that he had died from natural causes but a subsequent examination found that his death had been due to torture. The police officers allegedly involved were charged with murder and suspended, but it was not known whether they were taken into custody or brought to trial.

The Sind provincial authorities informed Amnesty International that they had investigated the alleged torture in 1987 of Wazir Leghari, which had resulted in the amputation of both his legs below the knee (see *Amnesty International Report 1988*). They found that he had been "severely beaten and maltreated" in Dadu District Jail, and beaten again after his transfer to Hyderabad Central Jail. On admission to hospital "he had been beaten so severely that both his feet had badly swollen" and had had to be amputated. The investigation led to two prison officers being charged with causing grievous harm and suspended from service. However, the officers were subsequently reinstated without being brought to trial.

An unknown number of people were sentenced to lashing for sexual offences and drug-trafficking. In April Farida Bano was sentenced to four years' imprisonment and five lashes for adultery. In November Mohammad Sarwar Siddiqi and Mohammad Amin Bhatti were each sentenced to 30 lashes for rape. The sentences were passed under the *Hudood* laws, introduced in 1979 as part of former President Zia ul-Haq's "Islamization" program. Sentences of lashing are usually carried out at the end of the prison sentence but it was not known in how many cases this occurred. In January Fateh Mohammad, known as Fatto, reportedly received 30 lashes in public at Haroonabad, Punjab province, after having served a prison sentence for kidnapping and rape. In December a public lashing was reported in Rawalpindi, Punjab province.

Three Ahmadis were shot dead in a sectarian attack by Muslims at Chak Sikander, Punjab province, in July. One of the attackers was also reportedly shot dead. Police were alleged to have been present but not to have taken any action to protect the Ahmadiyya minority. However, to Amnesty International's knowledge, no independent inquiry was held into the incident. The attack apparently intended to drive Ahmadis from the locality and by the end of the year, Ahmadis who had fled from Chak Sikander were still being prevented from returning.

At least 60 people were sentenced to death but there were no executions. Special Courts for Speedy Trials (see *Amnesty International Report 1988* and *1989*) imposed at least 12 death sentences. As the federal government did not place the ordinance extending their duration before the National Assembly for approval, it lapsed in February. These courts then ceased functioning in all provinces except Punjab, where the authorities argued that they could continue to sit until November. The Lahore High Court ruled in September that the continuation of speedy courts after February had been illegal. However, the implementation of this judgment was suspended in October by the Supreme Court, which granted leave to the Punjab Government to appeal.

At least eight people were sentenced to death by stoning under the *Hudood* laws. In April Munir Ahmed and Parveen Akhtar were sentenced for adultery in Bahawalnagar, Punjab province. In June one woman and five men were sentenced to death by stoning in Khairpur, Sind province. The woman's first husband alleged she had remarried without being divorced. She and her second husband were sentenced for adultery; the four other men were sentenced as accomplices to the second marriage. The Governor of Sind quickly announced a stay of execution. The appeals to the Federal *Shari'a* Court — which hears appeals in cases brought under Islamic law — had not been heard by the end of the year.

An Amnesty International delegation visited Pakistan in August for talks with Prime Minister Bhutto and other members of the federal government and provincial administrations. Amnesty International pressed for the repeal or amendment of laws permitting the arrest and detention of prisoners of conscience. It called for a review of the remaining cases of prisoners convicted after unfair trials by special military courts. It urged the government to ratify international human rights standards, to introduce procedures to ensure prompt and thorough investigations into allegations of human rights abuse and to provide improved safeguards against torture in police custody and jails. It also asked that the use of fetters on prisoners be abolished.

Amnesty International later requested information on the precise grounds of detention of G.M. Syed and other SNA supporters.

PANAMA

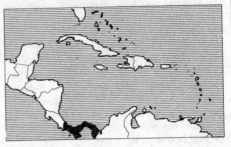

Several hundred political prisoners were released in December. Their release followed the entry of United States (US) armed forces into the country on 20 December and the overthrow of Panama's *de facto* ruler, Defence Forces' Chief Brigadier General Manuel Noriega. Several thousand supporters of General Noriega were briefly detained by US troops during the intervention. Before the US action, hundreds of critics and opponents of General Noriega's government had been held, mostly for short periods, without trial or after summary proceedings. Many said they had been tortured or ill-treated while held in sub-standard prison conditions. Some detainees were deported upon release. Other Panamanians were refused entry to the country; some were detained at the airport and tortured. A number of Defence Forces' officers arrested after a March 1988 coup attempt were held in detention without trial until they were released following the US action. At least three people were allegedly extrajudicially executed by the Defence Forces in the context of elections in May. Thirteen Defence Forces' officers were reportedly summarily executed without trial following a failed military uprising in October. Some were said to have been tortured.

The US action followed the declaration of war by Panama on the United States of America (USA) on 15 December; among the US' stated purposes were to protect US lives and to detain General Noriega on drug charges filed against him in the US. Following the US intervention, the Defence

Forces were disbanded. Guillermo Endara Galimany, the apparent victor in May elections which had been annulled by General Noriega's government, was sworn in as Panama's new president. General Noriega took refuge in the residence of the Papal Nuncio, where he remained at year's end.

Following the US action, several thousand supporters and suspected supporters of General Noriega were reportedly detained on US army bases in the Canal Zone or in temporary holding camps constructed by US forces. Many were members of the Defence Forces or the paramilitary civilian Dignity Battalions linked to them. At the end of the year several hundred remained in detention.

The human rights violations which preceded General Noriega's overthrow took place in a context of political instability and unrest. Continued efforts by the opposition to remove General Noriega from power were met with abuses by the Defence Forces and the Dignity Battalions. Political tensions were exacerbated by the annulment of the May elections, by the October military uprising which General Noriega's supporters said was part of a US effort to bring down his government, and by steps taken by General Noriega to make himself the country's *de jure* leader.

General Noriega's administration said it annulled the May elections because of fraud, violence, and what it described as US-organized interference. However, international observers and local and foreign journalists said the opposition was in the lead when the government-controlled electoral tribunal stopped the count. Journalists reported and filmed widespread harassment and intimidation of the opposition by Defence Forces' personnel and Dignity Battalions. Opposition presidential candidate Guillermo Endara was beaten unconscious on 10 May when men wearing Dignity Battalion T-shirts attacked opposition demonstrators in the capital with clubs and iron bars as uniformed soldiers stood by. Vice-presidential candidate Guillermo Ford was also brutally beaten and then held overnight in military custody. Hundreds of opposition supporters were brought before night courts and sentenced to imprisonment or fines, without being legally represented. Night courts, from which there is no right of appeal, are meant to deal only with infringements of the administrative code such as

theft and embezzlement.

Most people arrested in connection with the elections were released by December. Seventy-one were freed after an intercession by European Community ambassadors in June. Some said that after their release they had immediately been deported against their will.

Among those not released until the US action was Humberto Montenegro, bodyguard to Guillermo Ford. He had been arrested in May and charged with killing fellow bodyguard Alexis Guerra during the 10 May incident, in which he was himself gravely wounded. The opposition maintained that both bodyguards were shot by members of the Dignity Battalions. Initially, his detention was denied and it was feared that he had "disappeared". His detention in Modelo prison in the capital was later confirmed. He was reported to have been denied adequate medical attention for serious bullet wounds sustained on 10 May. Legal proceedings against him had stalled.

In the aftermath of the October military uprising, the government acknowledged the detention of 37 members of the Defence Forces. However, the local and foreign press reported that scores of others had gone missing after the rebellion, and were believed to be held in unacknowledged custody. Among the civilians arrested was radio journalist and opposition party member Senén Alfonso Briceño, who was arrested without warrant on 3 October, and allegedly beaten after Defence Forces' personnel overheard him express support for the uprising. His brother, Mario Briceño, who had publicly objected to Senén Briceño's detention, was himself arrested the following day as he left a supermarket. He was found to be carrying a banknote on which a derogatory name for General Noriega had been written. He was held for several weeks on charges of insulting the Panamanian state; Senén Briceño was held until late November. Opposition presidential candidate Guillermo Endara was briefly taken into custody on 5 October when the Dignity Battalions attacked the opposition's headquarters with firearms, clubs and teargas as uniformed Defence Forces' personnel stood by.

Guillermo Márquez Amado was detained by men believed to be from army intelligence when he arrived at Panama City's airport on 8 November. They interrogated him about a Christian Democrat meeting he had attended abroad and his supposed links with exiled Panamanians. His captors reportedly hooded him, cocked their guns and threatened to shoot. He said that after threats to rape his wife in his presence and to kill his daughters, he signed a statement that he had cooperated with US attempts to overthrow General Noriega and was released.

Twenty Defence Forces' officers detained and reportedly tortured after a failed coup in March 1988 (see *Amnesty International Report 1989*) remained in custody until their release following the US intervention. Their continued detention had been permitted by military law, under which military personnel could be transferred to civilian jurisdiction after one year in detention without trial, the maximum permissible under military law. At the time of the US action, pre-trial investigatory procedures initiated by the civilian courts had not been completed. Following the officers' release, tiny punishment cells where some said they had been held were displayed to the public and then destroyed.

Both military and civilian prisoners who had been held in Modelo prison, in El Renacer prison in Gamboa, and in the offshore penal colony of Coiba complained about conditions. They said they had been overcrowded, that food, water, health care and sanitary facilities were inadequate or non-existent, and that access to legal counsel and their families had been severely limited or prohibited. A number of prisoners were reportedly subjected to beatings, burning, and disfigurement with razor blades and knives.

Election-related abuses included at least three apparent extrajudicial executions. One victim was Father Nicolás Van Kleef, a paralysed Dutch priest. Soldiers commandeered his car on election day as he announced mass times by loudspeaker, and shot him in the back of the neck. The following day government supporters led by riot police attacked an apparently peaceful crowd of opposition supporters. Three journalists were apparently singled out for attack and suffered serious injuries.

Following the October coup attempt, the Defence Forces announced in an official war communique that 10 rebel officers had died in the fighting. The opposition claimed that they, as well as three others originally listed as detained, had been summarily executed without trial immediately after they surrendered. The body of one, Captain Nicasio Lorenzo Tuñón, was returned to his relatives for burial; they rejected official explanations that he had hanged himself in his cell. Families of some of the dead officers alleged they had been tortured before being shot.

There was no news under General Noriega's administration of any official efforts to establish responsibility for the mutilation and murder in 1985 of an outspoken opposition leader, Dr Hugo Spadafora, a former Panamanian vice-minister of health. Much evidence had emerged over the years to link the Defence Forces to Dr Spadafora's murder and decapitation, but the perpetrators had not been brought to justice (see *Amnesty International Report 1988*).

Amnesty International repeatedly called on General Noriega's government to investigate reported abuses and bring those responsible to justice. The organization asked the government to take steps to ensure the safety of detainees and to charge or release them. Letters were sent in May and November, asking the government to ensure that full and impartial inquiries were conducted into the human rights violations which took place in the context of the May elections and the October coup attempt. They were unanswered at the time of the change of government at the end of the year.

In November Amnesty International expressed concern about reported torture in Panama to the Organization of American States.

PAPUA NEW GUINEA

Scores of people suspected of supporting or sympathizing with an armed opposition group on the island of Bougainville were detained without charge or trial for periods of up to one month. Some of the detainees were tortured or ill-treated by government security forces. At least five people appeared to have been extrajudicially executed, some after torture by government forces.

On Bougainville, which forms part of North Solomons Province (NSP), the government faced armed opposition from the Bougainville Revolutionary Army (BRA).

The BRA, which has been active since late 1988, sought additional compensation for land occupied by the large Bougainville Copper Limited (BCL) mine and for resulting environmental damage. In 1989 the BRA began to advocate Bougainville's secession from Papua New Guinea. The BRA committed acts of violence, including murder and possibly torture of civilians suspected of informing on BRA activists. Security forces subjected suspected BRA sympathizers, including entire communities in areas of alleged BRA activity, to intimidation and random beatings, death threats, sexual harassment, house burnings and destruction of other property.

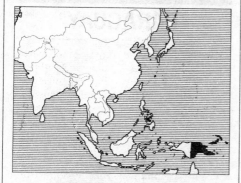

On 26 June the government of Prime Minister Rabbie Namaliu imposed a state of emergency on the island. The decree, which remained in force at the end of the year, gave security forces increased powers of arrest, detention and seizure. In practice, security forces often exceeded these powers. In late October the Parliamentary State of Emergency Committee recommended the passage of a new Internment Law, which would permit the detention of suspected BRA members or sympathizers for up to two months without charge or trial. The legislation had not been passed by the end of the year.

Despite the government's assurances that it was committed to protecting human rights guaranteed by the Constitution, reported human rights violations by members of the security forces were seldom investigated and those allegedly responsible were not known to have been prosecuted. In December a retiring National Court Judge, Mr Justice Tos Barnett, expressed concern over the failure of the government and the courts to investigate numerous allegations of human rights abuse. He said that if the situation was not remedied,

"official violence and extra-legal punishments would be legitimised in the minds of the security forces and of the public".

Police and Defence Force soldiers beat dozens of people on Bougainville, including political leaders, local government workers, medical professionals and villagers. They also threatened some of these people with death. The victims included Joseph Kabui, the Premier of NSP, and Michael Laimo, the NSP Minister for Agriculture. Both men had actively sought a peaceful solution to the Bougainville crisis. They were severely beaten by police in separate incidents in July. Michael Laimo lost an eye when members of the Police Riot Squad stopped his car, beat him and struck him with the barrel of a gun. Police dragged Premier Kabui from his car as he returned from church with his elderly mother, punched and hit him with a rifle butt, and forced him to lick the blood of a slain police officer from the side of a police vehicle.

In December Edmond Benny and seven young men travelling by truck to Arawa were stopped by Defence Force soldiers who accused them of making "bad signs" at soldiers manning a roadblock. Troops ordered the eight to drive to Army Camp 10 at Panguna, where a group of soldiers dragged them from the truck and beat them with gun butts, fists and boots. Edmond Benny and one other man were reportedly beaten until unconscious and the others sustained bruises and cuts. The military authorities subsequently acknowledged that the detainees were not rebels and the soldier who led the assault apologized for the "error".

At least one person reportedly died in detention after being tortured. Aloysius Minitong, an outspoken critic of environmental destruction in the area of the BCL mine, was said to have been tortured following his arrest in December. He was apparently suspected of being a member of the BRA, although no charges were brought against him. According to reports he was first held at Boku police station, where he sustained knife wounds requiring stitches and knee injuries so severe that he could not walk. He was then transferred to Army Camp 10, where he was beaten and kicked about the head and body until he lost consciousness. He was taken to a hospital and eye-witnesses there said he was unable to stand and his face was severely swollen.

188

After only one day in hospital he was removed against medical advice to the Joint Forces Headquarters in Arawa, where he received further beatings. He was then moved to Arawa police station, denied medical attention and bedding, and reportedly died in his cell three weeks after his arrest.

Security forces were believed to have deliberately killed at least five people in their custody. The government claimed that they had died in combat with government troops. Autopsies indicated that some of the victims had been tortured. In August it was reported that three corpses had arrived at Arawa General Hospital with visible signs of torture. Attached to the body of one victim, Ambrose Leo, was a note saying "This is the first billion of your ten billion", evidently a reference to the BRA's demand for 10 billion Kina (US$7.2 billion) in compensation for land and environmental damage. Doctors who examined Ambrose Leo's body said that he had been kicked and beaten before being shot at close range. Another victim, Peter Tarupiu, had multiple bruises to his face, neck and chest. He was bleeding from both ears and one of his cervical vertebrae was completely severed. The cause of death was said to be neck and spinal column damage resulting from a heavy blow.

In November Defence Force soldiers detained Vincent Onari, a maintenance worker at the BCL mine, and another man suspected of BRA membership. Soldiers beat the two before taking them to Army Camp 10. According to eye-witness accounts, Vincent Onari was semi-conscious when thrown out of a military vehicle outside the army camp, kicked and beaten with rifle butts and then shot four times in the head.

Scores of people were detained without charge or trial on suspicion of supporting the BRA. Some were held for up to one month, although the law requires that detainees be charged soon after arrest, normally within a few hours. Paul Minnou, a community youth worker, was detained without charge for 30 days following his arrest in November. Police interrogators reportedly accused him of supporting the BRA, threatened him with death and held him handcuffed and without food and water for one night at Hutjena police station. He was then transferred to custody elsewhere before his release.

In October Amnesty International sent a memorandum to Prime Minister Rabbie Namaliu detailing reports of arbitrary arrests, beatings and alleged extrajudicial executions in Bougainville and expressing interest in meeting officials in Papua New Guinea. By the end of the year the government had not provided any substantive reply. In December Amnesty International called for an impartial investigation into the reported torture and extrajudicial killing of Vincent Onari. In the same month the organization wrote to the government concerning the deteriorating human rights situation in Bougainville, and reiterated its interest in visiting Papua New Guinea.

PARAGUAY

An improvement in human rights protection followed a change of government in February. Two long-term political prisoners were released. Judicial investigations were initiated to establish criminal liability for some past human rights violations, including the torture and deaths in custody of prisoners of conscience. However, the short-term arrest and ill-treatment of detainees who may have been prisoners of conscience continued to be reported, particularly in the context of land disputes and labour conflicts.

In February General Andrés Rodríguez led a military coup in which at least 30 people, including two civilians, reportedly died. General Alfredo Stroessner, who had ruled Paraguay for 34 years, resigned and sought asylum in Brazil. The provisional government headed by General Rodríguez immediately undertook a purge of the armed forces, and at least 10 civilian members of the previous administration were arrested and charged with economic crimes.

The new and largely civilian government pledged to respect human rights and took important steps for their protection. Restrictions on trade unions, political parties and news media were lifted and political exiles were allowed to return. In May presidential and congressional elections were held with the participation of the principal opposition parties. The *Asociación Nacional Republicana, Partido Colorado*, National Republican Association, Colorado Party, won the election amid claims by opposition parties and international observers of widespread irregularities. General Rodríguez was elected president by a large majority.

In August the government ratified the American Convention on Human Rights. In October it signed the United Nations Convention against Torture and Other Cruel, Inhuman or Degrading Treatment or Punishment and the Inter-American Convention to Prevent and Punish Torture, but it had not ratified these by the end of the year.

In August Congress repealed two penal code laws against subversion. The previous government had frequently used Law 209, "Defence of Public Peace and Liberty of Persons", and Law 294, "Defence of Democracy", to detain prisoners of conscience. Legislators also created a Congressional Human Rights Commission mandated to oversee judicial investigations into alleged abuses and considered a draft bill which would penalize those responsible for illegal detentions and for torturing or ill-treating detainees.

Two long-term political prisoners were released. Alejandro Mella Latorre, a Chilean national convicted of participating in the assassination of former Nicaraguan president Anastasio Somoza, was released in February and expelled to Chile in March. Remigio Gímenez Gamarra was released in August (see *Amnesty International Report 1986* and *1987*).

Judicial authorities opened over 30 criminal investigations into cases of arbitrary arrest, torture, death in custody and "disappearance" which allegedly occurred under the previous government. In several of these cases victims or their relatives lodged criminal complaints against senior members of the former administration, including President Alfredo Stroessner, chief of police General Francisco Brítez Borges, Minister of the Interior Sabino

Augusto Montanaro and Pastor Milciades Coronel, who directed the *Departamento de Investigaciones de la Policía* (DIPC), Police Investigations Department.

In April the widow of Mario Raul Schaerer Prono formally accused Pastor Coronel and three of his subordinates of direct responsibility for her husband's death. Mario Schaerer, a student, died in the DIPC headquarters in April 1976, allegedly as a result of torture. Police authorities had claimed that he died from injuries sustained while resisting arrest. Witnesses, including a Catholic priest and a police officer, testified before judicial authorities in 1989 that Mario Schaerer was slightly wounded in one foot but otherwise in good physical condition when arrested and handed over to DIPC officials. Other students arrested at the time, in a police operation against an alleged fledgling armed opposition movement, testified that Mario Schaerer was severely tortured in the DIPC headquarters over a two-day period and was killed by a blow to the back of his neck with an iron bar. In April judicial authorities ordered the pre-trial detention of Pastor Coronel and his subordinates implicated in the case.

Prolonged delays or obstruction by the authorities marked some judicial inquiries into past human rights violations. In April the *Comité de Iglesias*, Interchurch Committee, presented a formal complaint to judicial authorities on behalf of a former political prisoner who alleged that during the 1970s at least six political prisoners had been executed and secretly buried in a police barracks on the outskirts of Asunción. The *Agrupación Especializada*, formerly known as *Guardia de Seguridad*, had been used as a high-security detention centre. Ignacio Duarte, detained in the *Agrupación Especializada* between 1972 and 1976, stated that he had been ordered on several occasions to spray water on newly dug graves in the grounds of the barracks to ensure that the earth settled. A criminal court judge's inspection of the site was suspended when the *Agrupación Especializada*'s commander refused to allow Ignacio Duarte access to the barracks. By the end of the year no inspection had been carried out and the investigation had not progressed.

The majority of reported arbitrary arrests and short-term detentions targeting people who may have been prisoners of

190

conscience took place in the context of land conflicts. Leaders and members of peasant organizations attempting to establish peasants' land claims were reportedly detained arbitrarily and, in some cases, subjected to ill-treatment by the security forces.

In early November soldiers from the 3rd Cavalry Division reportedly arrested, without judicial authorization, more than 150 peasant farmers. The military operation was an attempt to expel farmers from land they had recently occupied in Co'eti and Siete Monte-i localities in Curuguaty, San Pedro department, which was owned by a leading member of the ruling Colorado Party. Soldiers allegedly beat 10 peasants at the time of the arrests and released the majority of those detained only after holding them incommunicado for three days in the Curuguaty army base. Two of the peasant leaders reportedly beaten, Vidal Quintana and Brigido Paredes, were transferred to the 1st Army Corps in Asunción. They were held incommunicado for a further three days before being released without charge. Several peasants alleged after their release that soldiers in Curuguaty had denied them food. Some peasants said they had been beaten in custody.

Trade union leaders were reportedly arrested amid increasing numbers of labour disputes. Carlos Fillizola and Silvio Ferreira, leaders of the newly created labour confederation *Central Unica de Trabajadores* (CUT), and Pedro Salcedo, General-Secretary of the *Sindicato de Obreros de CAPSA*, CAPSA workers' union, were detained in October. Police allegedly beat and arrested the three union leaders after they delivered a petition to the presidential palace in Asunción. The petition called for the reinstatement of factory workers thought to have been dismissed for attempting to organize trade unions. The three men were released, without charge, the day after their arrest.

In December two workers at the Itaipú hydroelectric dam project on the Paraguayan/Brazilian border were killed and several others were injured when soldiers opened fire on striking workers. Soldiers from the border battalion based in Ciudad del Este, Alto Paraná department, were apparently attempting to break a picket line at the dam entrance. The circumstances of the shootings remain unclear. Army spokesmen claimed that the

strikers had fired on soldiers who had then responded in self-defence. Independent witnesses to the incident alleged that although some workers threw stones at the soldiers, strikers fired no shots. The government ordered a commission of inquiry to investigate the incident.

In February Amnesty International wrote to General Rodríguez welcoming the new government's stated commitment to uphold human rights. The organization also urged in its letter a judicial review of the two remaining political prisoner cases; investigation of "disappearance" cases attributed to the previous government; repeal of "subversion" Laws 209 and 294; and the adherence to international human rights instruments.

PERU

At least 503 people, including 69 children and young people, "disappeared" and hundreds more were victims of extrajudicial execution. They included human rights lawyers, teachers, trade unionists and peasant community leaders. Prisoners of conscience were held on false charges of "terrorism". Torture by the military and police, including rape, continued to be reported throughout the country.

A campaign of assaults, sabotage and execution-style killings by clandestine opposition groups, a high incidence of narcotics-related crime and a severe economic crisis provided the backdrop to gross human rights abuses as President Alan García approached the end of his six-year term. Campaigning began for national elections scheduled for April 1990. The government responded to proliferating political violence by continuing to renew states of emergency restricting civil rights: by the end of the year 67 of Peru's 181 provinces were under emergency measures. Political and military authority in these areas was delegated to the Armed Forces Joint Command, with all but the provinces of Lima and Callao administered by the armed forces. These political-military commands were able to assume virtual autonomy from civil authority under Law 24,150 of 1985. In practice they had the authority to carry out detentions without notifying civil authorities or accounting for the fate of prisoners. Military courts exercised jurisdiction over police and military personnel nationwide but were not known to have punished such personnel for recent human rights abuses in the emergency zones.

The legal means of redressing human rights abuses became increasingly inoperative in the emergency zones. The courts did not generally implement *habeas corpus:* even had attempts been made to do so, the armed forces continually denied the judiciary and public prosecutors access to military camps and bases where prisoners were known to be held incommunicado. The Public Ministry, headed by the Attorney General, increasingly failed to discharge its constitutional responsibility to defend human rights. This had been fulfilled in the past largely through its public prosecutors who received complaints and were empowered to take steps to remedy abuses. Since 1988 two successive Attorneys General have withdrawn resources and political support for investigations in the emergency zones and transferred or dismissed prosecutors who have brought criminal charges against army officers (see below and *Amnesty International Report 1989*). In January the United Nations Special Rapporteur on torture observed that in areas administered by the military the machinery of the law "had ground to a halt". Access to the emergency zones was increasingly denied and the work of human rights groups based within the zones was obstructed by arrests, death threats, bombings and, in two cases, extrajudicial executions.

The clandestine *Partido Comunista del Perú "Sendero Luminoso"*, Communist Party of Peru "Shining Path", remained active throughout most of the country. Its forces continued regularly to murder cap-

tives in summary, execution-style killings, sometimes after torture and mock trials. Most of its victims were civilians but others killed included police and military personnel who were captured or incapacitated by wounds. Shining Path demanded a boycott of November's municipal elections and threatened to murder candidates and voters: they killed over 350 people in October alone. The Senate Commission on National Pacification reported 243 police and 105 military personnel killed in 1989 and said the Ministry of the Interior had estimated the killing of between 3,000 and 5,000 "subversives", although some may have been non-combatant civilians.

In July Peru ratified the two Protocols additional to the Geneva Conventions which relate to the protection of victims of international (Protocol I) and non-international (Protocol II) armed conflicts.

Of 503 people who were known to have "disappeared" after arrests during 1989, 92 were subsequently released or found dead; the others remained unaccounted for. Amnesty International had records of 2,761 prisoners reported to have "disappeared" and who remained unaccounted for since this phenomenon was first reported in January 1983; the true number of "disappearances" may be much higher. A commission formed by the Peruvian Congress in 1988 to investigate "disappearances" announced in September that 5,877 people had "disappeared" over the previous nine years. The former special commissioner for the investigation of "disappearances", prosecutor Carlos Escobar Pineda, told the press that his team had proof of army responsibility for some 500 cases of "disappearance" in 1987 and 1988 and had prepared charges against army commanders which had been stopped by higher civilian authorities. Carlos Escobar Pineda had been removed from his post in November 1988 and in August 1989 he was dismissed by the Attorney General.

"Disappearances" were in part a consequence of the armed forces' policy to deny holding prisoners. The majority of the "disappeared" were members of isolated peasant communities. Scores of children and young people — the age groups from which Shining Path is known to concentrate its recruiting — "disappeared" after detention during army raids. In May soldiers raided communities in Santo Tomás de Pata, Huancavelíca department, and detained

192

schoolboy Sergio Huamancusi Ramos and four others who subsequently "disappeared". Ten-year-old Juan Carlos Pocco Contreras was detained by troops in July in Pachaconas in Apurímac's Antabamba province. Although reportedly seen in army custody at the Santa Rosa *Base Contra-Subversivo*, Counter-Subversive Base, his fate was not known.

"Disappearance" was often reported in conjunction with extrajudicial execution. Walter Wilfredo Valer Munalla "disappeared" after detention by troops on 29 September but his body, marked by torture, was found dumped at the door of his place of employment in Ayacucho on 7 October. His sister, 14-year-old Rita Marlene Valer Munalla, was detained in Ayacucho city by the army on 11 October. Another schoolgirl saw her being forced into an army vehicle but her detention was denied and she remained "disappeared".

Often whole communities appeared to be collectively punished. On 17 May troops of the army's Ollantaytambo Battalion reportedly detained 20 residents of the peasant community of Calabaza in Junín's Satipo province. The following day the bodies of 11 of them were found on the banks of the Calabaza river. On 13 June, according to local sources, troops raided the Santa Ana community in Ayacucho's Lucanas province but found that all but the elderly had fled into the heights: they killed Natividad Quispe, aged 90, and three others. On 26 June troops reportedly returned in a night raid before residents could escape, illuminating the village with flares. Three men were killed and young women were reportedly taken into the church and raped. Fourteen-year-old Casimira Quispe Condori was reportedly raped and then severely wounded in the back with a bayonet. The following day troops moved into the nearby community of Pampamarca, and established a temporary military headquarters in the church while residents were screened as potential "subversives"; eye-witnesses reported that 10 people were killed on the spot. No investigations were known to have begun into these cases.

Others believed to have been targeted for extrajudicial execution included journalists, lawyers, human rights activists, leaders of women's groups, trade unionists and political opposition leaders. Some were killed — others were only threatened

or were victims of bomb attacks on homes and offices.

Human rights lawyer Fernando Mejía Egocheaga was taken barefoot from his home in Oxapampa by uniformed troops of the local garrison on 15 June; his wife, who subsequently fled the country, was reportedly raped after the arrest and threatened with death should she make a formal complaint. The same night the head of the Oxapampa branch of the national teachers' union, Aladino Melgarejo Ponce, was seized by troops. The bodies of the two men were found a day later bearing marks suggesting they had been tortured. Investigations into the killings were not known to have taken place.

Other attacks and apparent extrajudicial executions followed threats made anonymously or in the name of shadowy "revenge" groups, but believed to originate with the military and police and with gunmen working with the ruling party, the *Alianza Popular Revolucionaria Americana* (APRA), American Popular Revolutionary Alliance. A communique of July 1988 had announced the creation of the *Comando Democrático Rodrigo Franco* (CRF), Rodrigo Franco Democratic Command, saying that "to defend Peru" it would take reprisals for every "mayor, soldier or police officer killed". Actions attributed to CRF proliferated in 1989, although different forces appeared to be responsible. In Ayacucho and San Martín departments, the evidence suggested that the political-military commands were directly responsible for attacks. In cities elsewhere, information based on dozens of case studies suggested that responsibility lay with military and police units as well as gunmen of the ruling party, apparently operating with the sanction of some high authorities. Some attackers operating in CRF's name in the capital, Lima, were identified as cadres of APRA after capture by police, but all were released rapidly without charge.

Other possible extrajudicial executions occurred in the context of trade union activity. On 9 February police of the Special Operations Division, who were uniformed but disguised with hoods and camouflage paint, opened fire on several thousand demonstrating farmers as they approached the town square of Pucallpa, in Ucayali department. In September a provincial prosecutor told the press he had brought charges against police for the murder of 23 farmers in Pucallpa but protested that none had been detained and the case had not progressed.

Cases of mass killings by military personnel in past years had not resulted in convictions by the end of the year. Military trials were not known to have been held in relation to the 1985 detention and murder by troops of 69 people — 26 of them under the age of 15 — in the Ayacucho hamlet Accomarca (see *Amnesty International Report 1986*). An army lieutenant, who had told a Senate Commission that even Accomarca's infants had been "dangerous" and that he took the decision to eliminate the villagers because "they have an ideological tendency", was promoted. Two officers of the Republican Guard (a paramilitary police force), charged with responsibility for the extrajudicial executions of 124 prisoners at Lurigancho Prison in 1986 (see *Amnesty International Report 1987* and *1988*), were sentenced to 15 and seven years' imprisonment by a military court. Both men planned to appeal. Seventy-five police and army personnel involved in the same operation — including the army general who commanded it — were acquitted. Prosecutions for the 31 or more killings by the army at Cayara, Ayacucho, in May 1988 (see *Amnesty International Report 1989*) continued to be frozen by the office of the Attorney General, and obstructed through death threats and the murder of witnesses. A ninth witness who had testified to army atrocities in Cayara, Marta Crisostomo, was murdered in September. In November prosecutor Carlos Escobar Pineda — who investigated the Cayara case — fled the country after further threats to his life.

Almost all political prisoners acknowledged to be in detention have been accused of "terrorism". They have included prisoners of conscience who were falsely charged, among them trade unionists, community leaders and members of legal opposition parties, although these prisoners have generally been released after short periods. Two prisoners of conscience held for longer periods were released. Agripino Quispe Hilario (see *Amnesty International Report 1989*), a Presbyterian pastor, was released in October after more than four years' imprisonment. Porfirio Suni Quispe, the head of the Aricoma Peasants' Federation who had been detained in May 1988, was released in March when a "terrorism" charge was dropped. Other prisoners of conscience who remained in custody included Carmela Ferro Estrada, detained in September 1988 for travelling to Abancay, Apurímac, to seek information about the fate of her husband, Anacleto Lliulli, who had "disappeared" following his arrest by troops in Huayrapampa in July 1988. She was awaiting trial, charged with "terrorism", in the Abancay prison.

Abusive treatment continued and was reportedly common practice during criminal and political investigations in both rural and urban areas. Torture, including rape, was widespread during army operations in rural areas, with frequent reports of systematic beatings, near-drowning, hanging by the arms and threats of mutilation or death. Sexual abuse by troops of women in Quechua-speaking peasant communities was reportedly routine — but other women also reported rape during periods in army custody. No army personnel stationed in the emergency zones were known to have been prosecuted for the rape of women in their custody and effective investigations into charges of torture were not known to have taken place.

Amnesty International appealed for the release of prisoners of conscience and investigated the cases of possible prisoners of conscience. It pressed the authorities to account for prisoners detained during the year and in previous years who had "disappeared", to investigate reported extrajudicial executions, and to bring the perpetrators to justice. These appeals received no formal response from the government, although some Peruvian embassies acknowledged the receipt of copies of letters sent to the authorities.

In August Amnesty International published a report entitled *Peru: Human Rights in a State of Emergency* and in September a report on the army massacre at Cayara was published. In November the organization published *Peru Briefing: 'Caught between two fires'*, and launched an international campaign aimed at bringing the pattern of gross human rights abuse to the attention of responsible Peruvian authorities and international public opinion.

In oral statements to the United Nations (UN) Commission on Human Rights and the UN Sub-Commission on Prevention of Discrimination and Protection of Minorities in March and August respectively,

194 Amnesty International included reference to its concerns in Peru.

In May the organization submitted information about its concerns in Peru for UN review under a procedure, established by Economic and Social Council Resolutions 728F/1503, for confidential consideration of communications about human rights violations.

PHILIPPINES

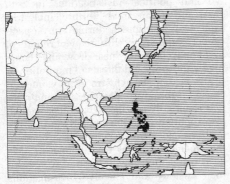

More than 200 people, including human rights activists, church workers, trade unionists and peasants, were killed in apparent extrajudicial executions. Dozens of others reportedly "disappeared". At least 29 prisoners of conscience remained in custody at the end of the year, and some of the estimated 600 other political prisoners were also believed to be prisoners of conscience. Political detainees were allegedly tortured under interrogation to extract confessions. Legislation introduced in the Senate to restore the death penalty had not been passed by the end of the year.

In December President Corazon Aquino imposed a national state of emergency and Congress enacted legislation granting the President broad powers for a six-month period. The measures followed an attempted military coup, the sixth and most serious since President Aquino came to power in 1986. The President ordered that the captured coup leaders be tried swiftly by military tribunal and Defense Secretary Fidel Ramos urged that the death penalty be restored for rebellion.

Armed conflict between government forces and the New People's Army (NPA), the armed wing of the outlawed Communist Party of the Philippines (CPP), continued throughout the year. The authorities frequently labelled non-governmental organizations, including human rights groups, as "fronts" for the CPP or the NPA. Armed actions by the Moro National Liberation Front (MNLF), which seeks the independence of predominantly Muslim areas in the south, escalated towards the end of the year.

The government's counter-insurgency campaign used regular armed forces, official paramilitary forces known as the Citizens' Armed Forces Geographical Units (CAFGUs), and armed groups known as "vigilantes" which have no legal status. The CAFGUs, with some 62,000 members by the end of the year, were intended to replace the "vigilante" groups and the Civilian Home Defense Forces (CHDF), a paramilitary force established under former President Marcos. Both the CHDF and "vigilantes" were officially disbanded in 1988 because of their poor human rights record. However, in many areas "vigilante" groups continued to operate with the consent and cooperation of local military commanders, or their members were recruited into the new CAFGU units. CAFGU forces were reportedly responsible for extrajudicial executions, torture and "disappearances".

The bombing and strafing of villages suspected of harbouring NPA and MNLF guerrillas resulted in the evacuation of tens of thousands of people. Conditions in many of the evacuation centres were poor and hundreds of people, most of them children, died of disease. Harassment, ill-treatment and killing of evacuees by anti-communist paramilitary forces were frequently reported.

The NPA was responsible for killing a large number of soldiers, police and non-combatant civilians. NPA "sparrow" units – urban-based assassination squads – killed more than 60 soldiers, police officers and government officials during the year in Manila. The NPA was thought to be responsible for the killing in April of United States Army Colonel James Rowe, a counter-insurgency expert. Government authorities claimed discovery of hundreds of bodies, allegedly people killed during an NPA internal purge of military spies. In June, 37 adults and children belonging to the anti-communist Itoman religious sect in Digos, Davao del Sur, were killed in an NPA guerrilla attack on a church.

The government took a number of measures to promote and protect human rights, including the creation of a special task force to investigate "disappearances" and the establishment of a Human Rights Committee to advise the President on the human rights situation. In December 1988 the Defense Secretary announced a new policy that would punish senior military commanders for the human rights violations committed by their subordinates. In August 1989 the government ratified the Optional Protocol to the International Covenant on Civil and Political Rights.

However, several factors impeded the investigation of violations and the prosecution of suspects. These included a lack of cooperation from local military authorities, long delays in the judicial process, witnesses' refusal to testify for fear of reprisals and limitations on the autonomy and effectiveness of the government-appointed Philippines Commission on Human Rights (PCHR). Of 2,694 cases of human rights violations filed with the PCHR between 1986 and August 1989, only 276 were resolved. The government claimed that some military officers had been punished for human rights-related offences, but it appeared that the stiffest punishment in practice was discharge from military service and that only three officers had received this under President Aquino's administration. In December President Aquino vetoed congressional legislation to repeal Presidential Decree 1850, promulgated under the administration of President Marcos, which protects members of the armed forces from prosecution in civilian courts.

Several military officers were tried during the year for human rights-related offences, but none was found guilty. In July, 23 soldiers charged with the February 1987 massacre of 17 villagers in Lupao, including six children and a couple in their eighties (see *Amnesty International Report 1988* and *1989*), were acquitted by a military tribunal. The tribunal reportedly ruled that the soldiers had "no criminal intent" when they fired on the villagers. In June a military investigating team cleared 28 Marines accused of torturing and killing nine Paombong fishery workers in April. The investigators said that the victims had been caught in the crossfire of an armed encounter: human rights groups and medical professionals claimed that some of the bodies showed visible signs of torture. The victims included a man in his seventies and a girl aged 13.

More than 200 critics, opponents or suspected opponents of the government appeared to be victims of extrajudicial executions committed by government or government-backed forces. The dead included church workers, trade unionists, human rights activists and members of various lawful non-governmental organizations accused of being fronts for the CPP or NPA. Dozens of villagers living in areas where the NPA was active were deliberately killed by military and paramilitary forces. The authorities often claimed that the victims were NPA members who died in "legitimate encounters", although the victims included elderly people and very young children killed in their homes.

In February Pedro and Encarnacion Pagao and their two children, 11-year-old Eduardo and seven-year-old Rosalia, were shot dead by troops of the 62nd Infantry Battalion in *barangay* (the village of) Carayman, Calbayog City, Western Samar. Four unidentified people were also killed at the time. The military claimed that the eight were NPA rebels killed in an armed encounter. In its case report, the PCHR said that there was "no doubt" that 62nd Infantry Battalion personnel were responsible for the killings. It concluded that the Pagao family members were civilians and that the killing incident was "not an encounter but rather a strafing and massacre committed by military soldiers". Although the PCHR recommended further investigations with a view to prosecutions, it was not known whether charges had been filed by the end of the year.

In March a joint counter-insurgency force of CAFGUs and the Philippine Constabulary (PC) in *barangay* Buena Vista, Santa Catalina, Negros Occidental, detained and killed three farmers and two young children. The children's father, Nicosio Opiar, was among the farmers killed. A fourth detained adult was wounded but escaped and reported that the others had been stabbed and shot in a military "safe-house". The farmers' wives witnessed the arrests and identified five of the perpetrators by name, but it was not known by the end of the year whether any of the suspects had been charged or tried.

At least six church workers known for their social and human rights work were killed by military or paramilitary forces.

196

They included the Reverend Vizminda Gran, killed with her husband in Baliangao, Misamis Occidental in May. The killings occurred shortly after her name appeared on a "hit list" apparently prepared by the 44th Infantry Battalion.

Oscar Tonog, a human rights lawyer, was shot by unidentified armed men in March in Poblacion, Catarman, Northern Samar province. He died of his wounds the following day, becoming the sixth human rights lawyer killed since late 1987 in circumstances suggesting extrajudicial execution by military or paramilitary personnel. He had worked since 1980 for the Free Legal Assistance Group (FLAG), a network of lawyers which provides free legal aid to political prisoners and disadvantaged groups. According to his family, he had received death threats which he attributed to members of the military.

Other human rights lawyers and activists, trade unionists, church workers and journalists were also subjected to anonymous death threats and named on "hit lists" circulated by anti-communist "vigilantes" and CAFGUs, apparently with the consent and cooperation of local military commanders. In Negros Occidental province two "hit lists" labelled 25 people as "communist dogs" and "traitors". The lists called on the local population to kill those named, including Antonio Fortich, the then Bishop of Bacolod and a well-known human rights advocate. Several other church workers, radio broadcasters, lawyers and labour leaders were also named on the lists.

Dozens of people active in civil rights and social welfare organizations, which the military and some government officials described as fronts for the CPP or the NPA, reportedly "disappeared" during the year. According to the PCHR, 37 people "disappeared" between January and August, but independent human rights groups in the Philippines placed the figure somewhat higher. The military and the government questioned the authenticity of "disappearance" reports, claiming that many of the "disappeared" were voluntarily in hiding or were victims of CPP or NPA purges. The authorities produced little evidence, however, to support these allegations.

Those who "disappeared" in 1989 included Maria Nonna Santa Clara, a social worker in the Legaspi area, and Angelina Llenaresas, a co-worker. They were last seen on 26 April in the custody of military and CAFGU personnel and were thought to be detained at the Headquarters of Regional Command 5 at Camp Bagong Ibalon in Legaspi City. The military denied holding them. Those who filed a *habeas corpus* petition on the women's behalf in June and witnesses who testified at the subsequent hearings received death threats which they believed came from members of the military.

Felix Cardano and Rodolfo Ubusan, both trade union leaders, reportedly "disappeared" following the dispersal of a May Day rally in Manila by security forces. Their legal trade union federation, the Malabon Labour Alliance-Kilusang Mayo Uno (KMU), was accused by the authorities of being a front organization for the CPP or the NPA. Dozens of KMU members were victims of arbitrary arrest, ill-treatment and apparent extrajudicial execution.

Twenty-seven prisoners of conscience were released in September and October, but at least 29 remained in custody. An estimated 600 other people were believed to be held for political reasons, some of whom may be prisoners of conscience. Most were accused of supporting the insurgency and charged under Presidential Decree 1866 with illegal possession of firearms in furtherance of rebellion, but some were apparently arrested for their non-violent activities in lawful non-governmental organizations. Many suspects alleged that they were detained without warrant and ill-treated or tortured to extract confessions.

Eighteen people attending a meeting in Pampanga province at an office of the Alliance of Farmers of Central Luzon (AMGL), a peasant organization critical of the government's land reform program, were arrested in March and charged with illegal possession of firearms in furtherance of rebellion. Six months later they were acquitted for lack of evidence and released. They denied possessing firearms and said that any weapons found must have been "planted" by those who arrested them. The "subversive literature" which they were accused of possessing consisted of pamphlets on agrarian reform and political literature available in shops and libraries. On 2 January 1990 two of the 18 reportedly "disappeared" after being detained by an armed group, including a man identified by witnesses as a PC sergeant.

Thirteen farmers active in the AMGL in Nueva Ecija province, who were arrested in

June 1988 on charges of subversion and believed to be prisoners of conscience, were still being tried at the end of the year. In October nine of the 13 were granted bail and conditionally released, but four remained in detention.

A 12-month trial of 25 farmers from Leyte province, charged with rebellion and other acts of violence, ended in February. However, no verdict had been delivered by the end of the year. The defendants, believed to have been arrested for publicizing human rights violations by "vigilante" groups, remained in prison. At least three of the farmers claimed that police beat them during interrogation. Several people closely associated with the case were subjected to threats or acts of violence. One of the defence lawyers, Attorney Alfonso Surigao, was shot dead in June 1988 (see *Amnesty International Report 1989*) and in 1989 a PC major was charged with the murder.

Torture and ill-treatment of political detainees during interrogation by police and military personnel were frequently reported. Military officials denied allegations of torture, labelling them as part of the CPP's "propaganda war". Government officials admitted "isolated" instances of torture but denied that its use was government policy.

Raphael Olite was arrested in April in Pasay City on suspicion of belonging to an NPA "sparrow" unit which had killed a police officer. He was reportedly taken to a military "safe-house" and tortured for 12 hours. He said that he had been stripped and that various parts of his body, including his genitals, had been rubbed with ice and then given electric shocks. He also said that a hose with running water was placed alternately in his nostrils and his mouth.

Medical professionals stated that at least 21 of 25 people detained by the military in July on suspicion of belonging to NPA "sparrow" units had injuries and symptoms consistent with their allegations of "physical and mental torture". The detainees, held at Camp Bagong Diwa, the Capital Regional Command (CAPCOM) headquarters, claimed that they were subjected to death threats, the "wet submarine" torture involving submersion of the head in water, burning with lighted cigarettes and beatings.

At least three new bills to reinstate the death penalty, provisionally abolished

under the 1987 Constitution, were introduced in the Senate (see *Amnesty International Report 1989*) but were not debated before the end of the year. Both President Aquino and the Defense Secretary urged Congress to restore the penalty for certain "heinous crimes", including rebellion and murder.

Amnesty International appealed for the release of prisoners of conscience, and called for independent and impartial investigations into reports of extrajudicial executions, "disappearances" and torture by members of government and government-backed forces. It urged the government to review the use of civilian paramilitary forces in the counter-insurgency campaign.

Amnesty International urged the government not to restore the death penalty. In April it published a report *Philippines: Case Studies in the Use of the Death Penalty* and in November testified at Senate hearings on the death penalty.

POLAND

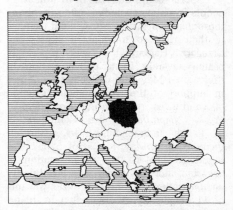

One prisoner of conscience was sentenced to a suspended term of imprisonment for evading military service. In the first half of 1989 many people were detained for short periods for the non-violent exercise of their right to freedom of expression. There were continued reports of ill-treatment of people in police custody. Three people under sentence of death had their sentences commuted to 25 years' imprisonment.

A framework for political reform, including legislative changes, was put together during the Round Table talks between the government and opposition

198

groups in February, March and April. As a result of decisions made during the negotiations, partially free elections were held in June. The formerly banned trade union *Solidarnosc,* Solidarity, won 99 per cent of the seats in the newly formed Senate and all 35 per cent of the seats allocated to it in the *Sejm,* the Polish Parliament, under the terms of the Round Table Accord. In September a new government was formed under Prime Minister Tadeusz Mazowiecki, a member of Solidarity. The Penal Code and Petty Offences Code were under review throughout the year. In July Poland ratified the Convention against Torture and Other Cruel, Inhuman or Degrading Treatment or Punishment.

Prisoner of conscience Jan Tomasiewicz, detained in December 1988 for conscientious objection to military service, was released on 25 January after a military court in Warsaw imposed a two-year suspended prison sentence for evading military service. He was ordered to do alternative service (see *Amnesty International Report 1989*).

Reports continued of ill-treatment of people in police custody – often involving those detained for the non-violent exercise of their right to freedom of expression. Grzegorz Hajdarowicz was reportedly beaten severely in a police station in Kielce on 1 May after collecting signatures in support of the parliamentary election of candidates representing *Konfederacja Polski Niepodleglej,* the Confederation of Polish Independence. In a further incident on 1 May, Krzysztof Szpak was reportedly beaten at a police station in Szczecin after participating in a Solidarity demonstration. Zygmunt Miszczak was one of 11 people reportedly beaten by plainclothes police officers on 4 July after being arrested at a peaceful picket outside the parliament building in Warsaw.

On 29 May the *Sejm* passed legislation abolishing Article 282a of the Penal Code and amending Article 52a of the Petty Offences Code. The articles had been introduced in 1982 and 1986 respectively (see *Amnesty International Report 1983, 1984* and *1987*) and many prisoners of conscience had been imprisoned under their provisions. Article 282a carried a sentence of up to three years' imprisonment for inciting public unrest or organizing a protest meeting. Article 52a of the Petty Offences Code carried a sentence of a

heavy fine or three months' imprisonment for actions designed to foster public disquiet, unauthorized publishing activity or membership of unauthorized organizations. In future Article 52a will apply only to those who publicly advocate a crime or forcible resistance to obeying a law or lawful order of a state organ.

In August the *Sejm* set up a special commission to investigate past alleged murders of opposition activists by the authorities. In September the newly formed Senate established the *Biuro Interwencji Komisji Praw Czlowieka i Praworzadnosci,* the Intervention Office of the Commission on Human Rights and Rule of Law, headed by former prisoner of conscience Zbigniew Romaszewski. Among other activities, the office initiated an investigation into reports of ill-treatment, including torture, in Raciborz prison.

Three people under sentence of death had their sentences commuted to 25 years' imprisonment under the terms of an amnesty in November, which also freed around 17,000 minor offenders.

At the beginning of the year Amnesty International called for the release of Jan Tomasiewicz. An Amnesty International delegation visited Poland in January for discussions about its concerns with officials from the Ministries of Justice and the Interior, and others.

PORTUGAL

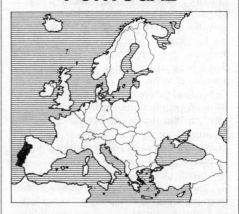

Ill-treatment in police custody and prisons was reported. It was alleged that ill-treatment contributed to the death of one prisoner.

In February Portugal ratified the United

Nations Convention against Torture and Other Cruel, Inhuman or Degrading Treatment or Punishment.

Some of the allegations of ill-treatment in police custody referred to 1988 or earlier years. Ill-treatment was reportedly often inflicted with a view to extracting confessions or other information from criminal suspects. It was claimed that many detainees were reluctant to make an official complaint of ill-treatment when they appeared before a judge because police officers had threatened them with further ill-treatment or longer prison sentences.

Daniel Rodríguez Perez, a Spanish citizen, was arrested in April 1988. He alleged that officers of the Public Security Police punched and kicked him in Santo Tirso police station and struck his head with a pistol. Eight days later, after his transfer to Chaves prison, he was taken to a local police station for further questioning by officers of the Judicial Police. He claimed he was beaten with truncheons and punched and kicked until he lost consciousness. He alleged that when he regained consciousness, he was bleeding from his mouth and ears but that his requests for medical assistance were refused, as were his requests to contact a lawyer, his family or the Spanish consul. A week later he was apparently taken back to the police station, again beaten with truncheons, and physically forced to sign various papers. He alleged that he was threatened with a longer prison sentence if, during his trial, he complained to the judge about his treatment.

He sent written complaints to the judicial authorities in August and November 1988 and described his treatment to the Santo Tirso court, which sentenced him in October 1988 to seven and a half years' imprisonment on various criminal charges. On 30 November 1988 he was summoned before a court in Matosinhos to make a statement and answer questions about his allegations of ill-treatment. He had received no further information regarding the court's action and the investigation of his complaints by the end of 1989.

Mário Manuel da Luz, from the Republic of Cape Verde, died in June while serving a 17-year prison sentence for murder and robbery. Before his death he had been held in a punishment cell in Linhó prison, undergoing a one-month disciplinary term for seriously wounding a prison guard. On 21 June, the day before this punishment was to expire, he was reportedly found unconscious on his bed. He was taken to Caxias prison hospital where he died a few hours later. A number of fellow prisoners alleged that, during his month in the punishment cell, he had been kept almost constantly handcuffed to the cell window, subjected to severe daily beatings by prison guards, often after immobilizing sprays had been used against him, and fed on a soup containing large quantities of a sedative drug. Some inmates of Caxias prison hospital alleged that they had observed marks on his body suggesting that he had been beaten.

In July the Director of Prison Services stated publicly that the Linhó prison authorities had reported that nothing irregular had occurred. He added that there was no reason to doubt this information but that if the autopsy raised any doubts, an inquiry would be opened. In October the Procurator General's office reported that judicial and administrative inquiries were under way.

Amnesty International expressed concern about the alleged ill-treatment of detainees, particularly Daniel Rodríguez and Mário Manuel da Luz, and sought information from the authorities about the steps taken to investigate such allegations.

ROMANIA

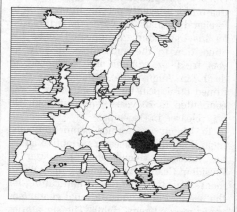

All prisoners of conscience imprisoned under the former government of President Nicolae Ceausescu were reportedly released in December. Before the change of government there were at least 27 known prisoners of conscience, and

AMNESTY INTERNATIONAL REPORT 1990

dozens of possible prisoners of conscience were imprisoned or under house arrest, often without charge or trial. Reports of ill-treatment in police custody included at least one case which allegedly resulted in death. Hundreds of people died during the overthrow of President Ceausescu's government at the end of the year. Many were killed indiscriminately or summarily executed by the security forces. Former President Ceausescu and his wife, Elena, were executed after a summary trial. Special military tribunals with emergency powers were set up under the new government.

Following the overthrow of President Ceausescu in December the new authorities, the National Salvation Front headed by President Ion Iliescu, announced the release of all political prisoners imprisoned under the former government, the abolition of the death penalty, and the repeal of some laws restricting human rights.

In March the United Nations Commission on Human Rights voted to appoint a Special Rapporteur to examine the human rights situation in Romania.

Censorship under the Ceausescu government severely restricted information about political trials; consequently both the total number of prisoners of conscience and statistics on the death penalty were not known.

Mircea Raceanu, a senior official in the Ministry of Foreign Affairs, was arrested in January and charged with espionage and treason for allegedly passing information to foreign diplomats. However, the real reason for his imprisonment appeared to be his opposition to the authorities. In July he was tried *in camera* and sentenced to death. In August the sentence was confirmed on appeal but in September it was commuted to 20 years' imprisonment. He was released in December.

In March six former senior officials, including Mircea Raceanu's adoptive father Ion Raceanu, signed an open letter to President Ceausescu criticizing the government's human rights record and calling for the restoration of constitutional guarantees concerning citizens' rights. The signatories of the letter were subjected to various restrictions on their freedom of movement. For example, former foreign minister Corneliu Manescu, aged 73, was placed under house arrest and in May was forcibly moved to another residence in Bucharest,

where he remained confined under constant surveillance until December.

Many other people who openly criticized the Ceausescu government were reportedly placed under house arrest, often without any formal charges being brought against them. Doina Cornea, a former university lecturer from Cluj, remained under virtual house arrest for her human rights activities until December, apart from a few days of relative liberty in January following international pressure (see *Amnesty International Report 1989*). In an open letter to President Ceausescu in April, in which she queried the legal basis for her treatment, she stated that security agents were placed at her door, that she was not allowed visitors, that her telephone had been cut off and her mail withheld. She reportedly received a number of death threats and was twice beaten by the police. Mircea Dinescu, editor of the literary review *Romania Literatura*, was placed under virtual house arrest in March after giving an interview to the French newspaper, *Libération*, in which he stated that the judicial system, the press and the police force had become instruments of "intimidation and terror". All restrictions on him were lifted in December.

Petre Mihai Bacanu, a journalist for the newspaper *Romania Libera*, was arrested in January at the state publishing house *Scinteia* in Bucharest. He was apparently suspected of being one of the authors of a pamphlet entitled *The Disease of Power*, which allegedly called for peaceful opposition to the administration of President Ceausescu. In June he was reportedly tried *in camera* and sentenced to six years' imprisonment for illegal trading in cars, coffee and other commodities. Amnesty International believed he may have been imprisoned for his non-violent exercise of the right to free expression. He was released in December.

Prisoner of conscience Dumitru Iuga was released in September after serving six years of a 12-year prison sentence for "propaganda against the state". Werner Sommerauer, sentenced to three years' corrective labour in 1987 following a demonstration, was freed in December (see *Amnesty International Report 1989*).

Reports of torture and ill-treatment of people in police custody included the case of Janos Tamas, an ethnic Hungarian from Balan, Harghita County. He was taken into custody in May on suspicion of obtaining meat illegally. He was allegedly suspended by his wrists and beaten by four police officers until he died of liver failure on 26 May. On 2 October Ana Ciherean was found dead in a park: she had been detained by police officers at a hotel in Timisoara the previous evening. She had reportedly been raped and her arms and legs were broken. Bela Sepsey, an ethnic Hungarian, reportedly suffered serious head injuries while in police detention in Timisoara on 15 October after being detained on suspicion of possessing foreign currency. His arrest may have been related to his membership of the Reformed Church in Timisoara, which had been in conflict with the authorities. On 2 November the pastor of this church, Laszlo Tokes, an outspoken critic of both the government and church leadership, was reportedly beaten by "unknown assailants" who broke down the door of his apartment. He was apparently under constant police surveillance at the time of the attack but the police did not intervene.

Hundreds of people died, many killed indiscriminately or summarily executed by the security forces, during a period of unrest leading up to and following the overthrow of President Ceausescu's government. On 17 December demonstrations began in Timisoara after the authorities forcibly evicted Laszlo Tokes from his church in the city and transported him to the remote parish of Mineu in the north of the country. A large crowd gathered in the centre of Timisoara and some demonstrators began to attack police buildings. Troops and tanks were brought in and security forces opened fire indiscriminately, killing large numbers of demonstrators, including children. It was reported that the security forces hunted down people known to have participated in the demonstrations, and summarily executed them. Violent clashes also took place in other towns throughout the country, including Bucharest, Arad, Sibiu and Brasov.

President Ceausescu and his wife, Elena, were executed on 25 December after a summary trial. On 26 December the newly established National Salvation Front announced the creation of special military tribunals with emergency powers to summarily try and execute those still fighting the new authorities. However, no further executions took place and at the end of December the death penalty was abolished.

During the year Amnesty International urged the authorities to release prisoners of conscience and to provide further information about other people imprisoned or under house arrest who were possible prisoners of conscience. The organization urged the authorities to institute full and impartial investigations into the deaths of Janos Tamas and Ana Ciherean, and into the alleged ill-treatment of Bela Sepsey and Laszlo Tokes. In December it called for a full and impartial investigation into the killings and reported summary executions of demonstrators by security forces. The organization urged the new authorities to abolish the death penalty and expressed regret at the execution of Nicolae and Elena Ceausescu. It also called on them to bring to justice those responsible for past human rights abuses, but urged that this should be done in accordance with internationally recognized requirements for fair trials.

RWANDA

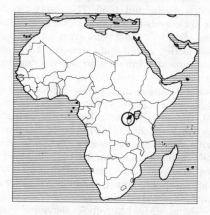

One prisoner of conscience serving a 10-year sentence and at least three political prisoners held without charge or trial remained in detention throughout the year. At least 76 death sentences were commuted by the Head of State; no executions were reported.

In October the Minister of Justice ordered the procuracy to charge or release 1,900 prisoners held without charge or trial in Kigali prison for periods ranging from a few months to several years. It was reported that most of them had been arrested without warrants. It was not clear whether any of those affected by the order had been detained for political reasons. There was no subsequent information to indicate how many prisoners were released.

Donat Murego, a prisoner of conscience, continued to serve his 10-year sentence at Ruhengeri Prison in northern Rwanda (see *Amnesty International Report 1989*). He was convicted in 1981 by the State Security Court of distributing seditious documents. He was due for release in April 1990.

Innocent Ndayambaye, a student who was arrested in October 1986, continued to be held at the central prison in the capital, Kigali. He was reported to have been accused of writing and distributing leaflets criticizing the government of President Juvénal Habyarimana. His case was reportedly referred to the procuracy for investigation and possible prosecution, but no date was set for his trial and the authorities offered no explanation for his lengthy detention without trial. He appeared to be held for exercising his right to freedom of expression.

Claude Bahintasi and Callixte Sinaruhamagaye remained in detention without charge or trial at Kigali central prison throughout 1989. They were arrested in December 1987 apparently because of their family connections with an opposition leader, Alexis Kanyarengwe, a former government minister who left the country in 1980 to avoid arrest (see *Amnesty International Report 1989*). In May, Aloys Sebiziga, a medical doctor at Kigali hospital, was also arrested, apparently because he was suspected of having been in contact with Alexis Kanyarengwe. He was still held without charge or trial at the end of the year and, like Claude Bahintasi and Callixte Sinaruhamagaye, appeared to be a prisoner of conscience.

Donat Muvananyabo remained in Ruhengeri Prison's high security unit serving a life sentence imposed in 1983 following his forcible repatriation from Uganda in 1981. He was convicted by the State Security Court of having had contact with opponents of the Rwandese Government while in Uganda, founding an opposition group and writing insulting remarks in his diary about President Habyarimana (see *Amnesty International Report 1984*). However, it was not clear that his activities involved the use or advocacy of violence and it appeared that he might be a prisoner of conscience.

Seventy-six prisoners had their death sentences commuted to life imprisonment by President Habyarimana in March, at the beginning of a new session of the national assembly, but many other prisoners reportedly remained under sentence of death. In mid-1988 there were said to be about 200 prisoners under sentence of death at Kigali prison alone (see *Amnesty International Report 1989*). Five others, including Théonèste Lizinde, a former head of the security service, continued to be held incommunicado and in harsh conditions in Ruhengeri Prison's high security unit. All five, who were sentenced to death in 1985 on charges of secret and unlawful killings of political prisoners in the mid-1970s, were still awaiting a review of their cases by the Appeal Court (see *Amnesty International Report 1989*).

Amnesty International continued to appeal for the release of Donat Murego and investigated the case of Donat Muvananyabo as a possible prisoner of conscience. Amnesty International also pressed for other political detainees to be released if they were not to be charged or brought to trial on recognizably criminal charges. The organization welcomed the commutation in March of 76 death sentences and appealed to the government to commute all death sentences, to reduce the number of offences punishable by death as a step towards abolition of the death penalty, and to ensure that all prisoners facing possible death sentences are provided with automatic access to legal counsel.

SÃO TOMÉ AND PRÍNCIPE

Thirty-nine members of an opposition organization were sentenced to prison terms for seeking to overthrow the government. The prisoners' trial fell short of international standards as they had no right of appeal.

The Special Court for Counter-Revolutionary Acts was abolished in February. It was created in 1975, soon after the country became independent, to try political cases. It used summary procedures and defendants had no right of appeal. After its abolition, jurisdiction over political cases passed to the ordinary courts.

Forty-three members of the *Frente da*

Resistência Nacional de São Tomé e Príncipe-Reformada (FRNSTP-R), Reformed São Tomé and Príncipe National Resistance Front, were brought to trial in August before the Higher Court of Appeal for allegedly attempting to overthrow the government of President Manuel Pinto da Costa (see *Amnesty International Report 1989*). There is no right of appeal from this court, the highest in the country. FRNSTP-R leader Manuel Afonso do Rosario dos Santos, known as Afonso Santos, and his companions were arrested in March 1988 when they entered the country illegally.

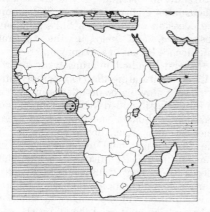

The defendants were charged with treason, armed rebellion and other offences including "mercenarism". Both foreign mercenary activities and use of foreign money to take up arms against the government are covered under "mercenarism", which is the only crime punishable by death in São Tomé. Afonso Santos allegedly received money from an unspecified foreign source and, with his supporters, attempted to capture the Head of State and the Minister of Defence. A Portuguese lawyer represented Afonso Santos, while two court-appointed defence lawyers represented the other 42 defendants.

All but four of the accused were found guilty in September on some of the charges. Although none was convicted of "mercenarism", the court found that the group had endangered the sovereignty of the state by accepting money from a foreign source. The court recognized that the defendants had been armed only with four unloaded pistols, but judged that the group's actions constituted an attempt against the life of the President and Defence Minister. Afonso Santos was sentenced to 22 years' impris-

onment and ordered to pay compensation to the families of three of his supporters. The three had been killed in March 1988 when security forces captured the group. Thirty-four defendants were sentenced to between 16 and 21 years' imprisonment and four received two-year sentences.

Amnesty International welcomed the abolition of the Special Court for Counter-Revolutionary Acts. It expressed concern that those sentenced in September had no right of appeal against their convictions or sentences. The organization also urged the authorities to investigate allegations that some of the defendants had been ill-treated during interrogation and that one had been shot after his arrest. There was no reply from the government.

SAUDI ARABIA

At least 27 prisoners of conscience were imprisoned and other prisoners of conscience may have been among more than 70 detainees held without charge or trial. Some political detainees were held without trial in prolonged incommunicado detention. Torture was reportedly common and one death in custody may have been caused by torture or ill-treatment. Sentences of amputation and flogging continued to be imposed and carried out. At least 111 people were executed, 16 of them for political offences.

Information about political prisoners was limited because of strict official censorship and restrictions on freedom of movement within the country and access from abroad.

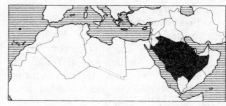

Suspected opponents of the government, including prisoners of conscience, were arrested by *al-Mabahith al-'Amma*, General Intelligence, and detained without trial. Most were Shi'a Muslims from the Eastern Province. Among them were suspected members or supporters of *Munadhamat al-Thawra al-Islamiyya fil Jazira al-'Arabiyya*, the Organization of

204

Islamic Revolution in the Arabian Peninsula (OIRAP); *Hizbul 'Amal al-Ishtiraki al-'Arabi-al-Jazira al-'Arabiyya*, the Arab Socialist Action Party-the Arabian Peninsula (ASAP-AP); and *Hizbullah fil Hijaz*, the Party of God in Hijaz.

At least 27 suspected OIRAP members or supporters were held without charge or trial at the General Intelligence Prison in al-Dammam. All were prisoners of conscience. Five of them were arrested in 1988 and the others between January and September 1989, principally in al-'Awamiyya, Senabes, al-Awjam, Safwa and Saihat in the Eastern Province. Among them were religious scholars, shopkeepers, company employees and university students. Sayyid Fadhil al-Sadda, a student, was arrested in Riyadh in January. He had been previously arrested in November 1979, at the age of 14, and held without charge or trial for a year. He was among 25 of the 27 detainees still held at the end of the year. The two released detainees were Sheikh Hassan Makki al-Khuwaildi, freed in April, and Sheikh Muhammad al-Silebi, released in September.

In March, six suspected members or supporters of ASAP-AP, who may have been prisoners of conscience, were arrested in Safwa and Riyadh. They too were detained without charge or trial in the General Intelligence Prison in al-Dammam. One was released in June, while the others remained in detention at the end of the year. Those still detained included 'Adil Salman 'Abdul-Hadi, a bank worker, and three employees of Saudi Arabian American Oil Company (Saudi ARAMCO).

Four alleged members or supporters of *Hizbullah fil Hijaz* were also detained without charge or trial. They were arrested in al-Ihsa', Saihat and al-Qatif in July and October and held in General Intelligence prisons in al-Ihsa' and al-Dammam. Sayyid 'Adnan Sayyid Muhammad al-Yusuf was one of these detainees. He was arrested when he returned to Saudi Arabia from Syria, reportedly after receiving an assurance from the Saudi Arabian embassy in Syria that he would not be arrested. He had also been detained without charge or trial in 1982 and in 1986.

Thirty-six other alleged *Hizbullah* supporters were in detention at the beginning of the year. They were arrested in April and August 1988 following explosions in al-Jubail petro-chemical complex and held at the General Intelligence Prison in Riyadh (see *Amnesty International Report 1989*). Twenty of them were released in the first half of the year, while the others were still held without charge or trial at the end of 1989.

At least 28 other suspected opponents of the government were arrested and held without trial in Riyadh, al-Dammam and al-Ihsa'. They may have been prisoners of conscience. Twelve of them were released in October, while the others remained in detention. They included Ahmad Hassan al-Mutawa', a lecturer at King Fahd University in Dhahran. He was arrested in August after giving a lecture on Shi'ism on the occasion of *'Ashura*, a Shi'a religious observance, and held in the General Intelligence Prison in al-Dammam.

Several hundred pilgrims were reportedly arrested during the *Hajj*, or holy pilgrimage, following bomb attacks in Mecca in July. They included Kuwaiti, Omani and Pakistani nationals, most of whom were released after brief detention. Some of the 29 Kuwaitis held incommunicado in General Intelligence prisons in Jeddah and Mecca were later transferred to Riyadh. During their detention some were reportedly tortured. In September a *Shari'a* (Islamic law) court tried the 29 on charges of sabotage. The proceedings failed to meet international standards of fair trial. The defendants were not allowed legal representation and were convicted on the basis of "confessions" reportedly extracted under torture. Nine of the Kuwaitis were acquitted, four were sentenced to between 15 and 20 years' imprisonment in addition to flogging, and 16 were sentenced to death.

Torture of political detainees, both during the year and in previous years, was reported. Former detainees alleged that the most commonly used methods included *falaqa* (beating on the soles of the feet), *ta'liq* (suspension by the wrists from the ceiling or a high window), *tas-hir* (sleep deprivation), electric shocks and beatings all over the body. Detainees were usually held in solitary confinement until interrogation ended, in some cases for over six months.

Sheikh Muhammad al-Silebi, a religious scholar arrested in March on suspicion of links with the OIRAP, was held in solitary confinement for three months by General Intelligence in al-Dammam. In June he was moved to hospital for a week, apparently after being tortured, then returned to solitary confinement in al-Dammam. In August his health deteriorated further and he reportedly lost cognitive abilities. He was released in September.

In July 'Abdul-'Aziz al-Faris, 'Ali al-Lail and Salah Nisfan, three university students, were reportedly tortured by members of the General Intelligence. Interrogators allegedly attempted to force them to confess to starting fires in the students' residence at King Saud University in Riyadh by subjecting them to *falaqa* and *tas-hir*. At the end of the year they remained in detention without charge or trial at the General Intelligence Prison in Riyadh, where they were denied access to legal counsel.

One death in custody was said to have been caused by torture. Zahra' Habib Mansur al-Nasser from al-Awjam in the Eastern Province died in police custody three days after she and her husband were arrested in July at al-Hudaitha checkpoint on the border between Saudi Arabia and Jordan. She was apparently arrested because she possessed a photograph of Ayatollah Khomeini and a Shi'a prayer book. She was reportedly tortured at al-Hudaitha detention centre and her body allegedly bore marks of torture when returned to her family. Her husband was later released from custody.

Yasser 'Ali Muhammad al-Faraj, who was detained four times between April 1986 and December 1988, alleged he was tortured and ill-treated while in the custody of General Intelligence in al-Dammam. He said he was suspended by the wrists with chains and severely beaten, subjected to electric shocks and *falaqa*, burned with cigarettes and deprived of sleep for nine days. He was interrogated continuously for two months in 1986 and needed treatment for 15 days at al-Dammam Central Hospital.

Fourteen people convicted of repeated theft, including 11 Yemeni nationals, were punished by amputation of their right hands. At least 11 others were sentenced to floggings of between 150 and 900 lashes following conviction for theft and complicity in theft. Four Kuwaiti nationals arrested in July in connection with bomb attacks in Mecca were sentenced in September to floggings of between 1,000 and 1,500 lashes.

In September, 16 Kuwaiti nationals were executed. The 16 had been on a pilgrimage to Mecca and were convicted of planting bombs there in July.

Between February and December, 95 Saudi and foreign nationals were executed for criminal offences, including murder and drug-trafficking. Among those executed were two brothers sentenced to death in 1970 for murder. They had remained on death row until their victim's eldest son, one month old at the time of the murder, reached the legal age of consent. Under Islamic law as practised in Saudi Arabia, the relatives of the murder victim may demand *qisas* (retribution) in the form of the death penalty or may waive such a claim freely or by financial settlement.

All executions were carried out publicly by beheading, except that of a Filipino housemaid who was publicly shot in Riyadh in March following her conviction for murder.

Amnesty International pressed for the release of prisoners of conscience, investigated the cases of people who may have been prisoners of conscience, and expressed concern to the government about the continued pattern of detaining political suspects without trial. The organization urged the authorities to investigate reports that political detainees were tortured and to establish an impartial inquiry into Zahra al-Nasser's death in custody. It urged that all sentences of flogging and amputation be commuted.

Amnesty International also informed the government of its concern about the dramatic rise in the number of executions carried out, reiterated its unconditional opposition to the death penalty and urged the commutation of all death sentences. No responses were received.

In March Amnesty International wrote to the government proposing that a delegation from the organization visit Saudi Arabia to discuss human rights concerns. No response had been received by the end of the year.

SENEGAL

A journalist arrested in October appeared to be a prisoner of conscience. Five supporters of independence for Casamance region who had been arrested in 1988 were detained without trial throughout the year. Other suspected Casamance activists were arrested, one of whom reportedly died as a result of torture.

206

Intercommunal disturbances broke out in April, when mobs in several towns attacked people of Mauritanian origin. Most of those attacked were from Mauritania's Beïdane (Moors) and Haratine (former slaves speaking the same language as the Beïdanes) communities, including many who were born in Senegal or were long-term residents in the country. Several dozen people were deliberately killed. Mob violence also occurred in Mauritania, where Senegalese and black Mauritanians from southern Mauritania were attacked. Relations between Senegal and Mauritania deteriorated rapidly, leading to the repatriation of Beïdanes and Haratines to Mauritania. Thousands of Senegalese living in Mauritania were also repatriated. After abuses committed by the Mauritanian security forces received international publicity, the Mauritanian Government claimed that thousands of Mauritanians were imprisoned unlawfully in Senegal. There was, however, no evidence that this was so.

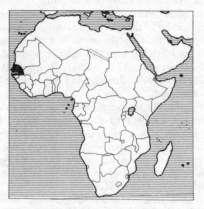

The government continued to face opposition in Casamance region, where separatists called for greater autonomy or independence. Most reports of torture in past years were received from this region.

The authorities brought criminal charges against several journalists associated with a leading opposition party, the *Parti démocratique sénégalais* (PDS), Senegalese Democratic Party. Cheikh Koureyssi Bâ, editor of the PDS-owned newspaper *Sopi*, was tried and convicted in November in connection with the newspaper's claims that the PDS presidential candidate had received more votes in 1988 than President Abdou Diouf. The editor was sentenced to six months' imprisonment but remained free after filing an appeal.

Madior Sokhna N'Diaye, a journalist working for *Sopi*, was arrested in October on a charge of complicity in "spreading false news". He had dealt with a reader's letter which, after publication, turned out to be a forgery. The letter had apparently been designed to damage the reputation of the person whose name had been forged, although it was not clear whether Madior Sokhna N'Diaye was aware of the forgery. He was released in December to await trial.

Throughout the year the authorities banned several meetings and demonstrations planned by opposition parties. Members of *And-Jëf*, an opposition party, were convicted in December of conducting a "banned demonstration which caused damage" and were sentenced to prison terms. Three people received one-month sentences. Ousmane Sané, a student whose arm was broken during arrest, was among these three. Awa Diop Fall, a teacher, was sentenced to 15 days' imprisonment. The arrests took place in mid-December as riot police known as the *Groupement mobile d'intervention* (GMI), Mobile Intervention Unit, reportedly used tear-gas to disperse a demonstration against the banning of a meeting organized by *And-Jëf*.

Mamadou Sané, "N'Krumah", an advocate of Casamance independence, and four others arrested with him remained in custody. They were awaiting trial on charges of plotting against the internal and external security of the state and of forming an unlawful association. They had been arrested in February 1988 in Guinea-Bissau and then handed over to the Senegalese authorities. Their trial before the State Security Court, which has jurisdiction over all alleged offences against the security of the state, had not begun by the end of 1989. Mamadou Sané was imprisoned from 1982 to 1987 on charges relating to political activism in Casamance (see *Amnesty International Report 1989*).

In April Jean-Pascal Badji, a religious songwriter for a group of singers in Balandine, in Casamance's Bignona district, was arrested by the army near the Guinea-Bissau border. He was apparently suspected of being a member of the Casamance independence movement. He died soon after his arrest, allegedly as a result of torture during detention. Although there appeared to be no judicial investigation at the end of year into the circumstances of his death, the Minister of Justice told Amnesty International that an inquiry would be initiated into its causes.

Two leading PDS members, Cheikh Touré and Papa Samba M'Boup, and four former police officers were arrested in December 1988 in connection with a car bombing in Dakar. They were all released in January to await trial (*liberté provisoire*) following the arrest at the end of December 1988 of three other suspects. These three were charged in January: Amadou Clédor Sène was charged with threatening the internal security of the state and destroying vehicles, the other two with complicity. They remained in custody and had not been tried by the end of the year.

Ansoumane Bodian, a teacher and former political prisoner from Casamance who was released in 1985 after serving three years' imprisonment, was arrested in Bouloulou in June. The authorities held him at the Gendarmerie station in Ziguinchor before releasing him without charge in July.

In May Amnesty International sent the government a memorandum detailing evidence of torture in Casamance between 1983 and 1987. It included testimonies from former prisoners, observations by people who had examined prisoners and an extract from an official document from the prison service complaining about ill-treatment of prisoners in police custody. All of the victims had been held incommunicado at the time of their alleged torture. Amnesty International urged the authorities to investigate the allegations and to take steps to prevent torture. The organization recommended, in particular, reducing the eight-day period during which political detainees may be held legally in police custody.

An Amnesty International delegation visited Senegal in October and met President Abdou Diouf, government ministers and judicial officials, as well as security officials in Ziguinchor, the capital of Casamance. The President and other authorities reaffirmed the government's opposition to torture and commitment to its prevention. However, the authorities said that no official investigation into allegations of torture in Casamance had taken place because no formal complaints had been received. They rejected Amnesty International's call for an official inquiry, referring to the June 1988 amnesty which led to the release of prisoners from Casamance. Those freed had been convicted of offences committed before July 1987. The authorities said that the amnesty also covered offences possibly committed by security forces, such as torture. They said, however, that in the future representatives of the procuracy would check regularly on the well-being of individuals in detention.

Amnesty International expressed concern that a journalist imprisoned in October might be a prisoner of conscience. The organization also sought details about Jean-Pascal Badji's death in detention and urged an official investigation. The government replied that an inquiry would be initiated into his death.

SIERRA LEONE

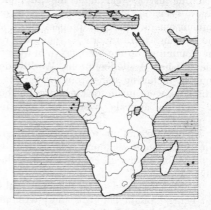

A former deputy head of state and five others were executed in October, the first executions in Sierra Leone since 1975. Two prisoners of conscience were detained for two weeks without charge. Three other political detainees, arrested in 1987 and held without charge or trial, were released. A commission of inquiry set up in 1987 after criticism of high prison mortality rates reported to the government, but no planned improvements in prison conditions were announced.

In June the President, Major-General Joseph Saidu Momoh, announced an end to the state of "economic emergency" which had been in force since November 1987. This removed any provision in law for the administrative detention without charge or trial of those suspected of harming public safety.

In September, 12 prisoners sentenced to

208

death for their involvement in an attempted coup in 1987 (see *Amnesty International Report 1988* and *1989*) had their appeals dismissed by the Supreme Court. In early October Francis Mischeck Minah, former First Vice-President and a former Attorney General and Minister of Justice, and Gabriel Mohamed Tennyson Kai Kai, a former Assistant Superintendent of Police, both convicted of treason, were executed. Also hanged were four soldiers convicted of both treason and murder. The six others sentenced to death for treason were granted presidential clemency. Two prisoners sentenced to terms of imprisonment for misprision of treason also had their appeals dismissed. The decision not to grant presidential clemency to six of the prisoners under sentence of death was taken with great haste and their executions were carried out just a week after the Supreme Court decision and without any prior announcement. Practical preparations for the hangings were reportedly made before the Committee on the Prerogative of Mercy had finished its deliberations. Worldwide appeals, including some from foreign governments, were made for clemency for the 12 whose appeals were rejected in September.

No other executions took place although one other death sentence was passed in April following a murder conviction in the High Court.

People continued to be detained without being brought before a court without delay as specified in law. Kalilu Totangay and Emmanuel Moigua were detained for nearly two weeks in September by the security police in the capital, Freetown, before being released without charge. Both were members of the Pan-African Union, an organization opposed to Israeli or South African commercial interests in Sierra Leone. They were arrested in Kenema in eastern Sierra Leone after distributing documents criticizing the presence in Sierra Leone of an Israeli-owned diamond company.

Joseph Coker was released in April after being detained without charge or trial for two years. Reportedly, he was arrested after he accused a senior government official of involvement in a ritual murder. His arrest appeared to have been ordered by the official concerned and therefore to have been an abuse of power.

Two detainees, Mary Amara and Sulley Kamara, apparently held without charge or trial since the coup attempt in March 1987, were released in November after the High Court granted a writ of *habeas corpus* on their behalf. It appeared that Mary Amara may have been detained simply because of her family relationship to defendants in the 1987 treason trial.

A commission of inquiry into the administration of prisons, appointed in 1987, reported its findings to the government in December but the report was not made public. The inquiry, chaired by Mr Justice M.E. Tolle Thompson, was established following criticism of the high rate of prison deaths in the mid-1980s (see *Amnesty International Reports 1984* to *1989*). Although it ordered 16 former prison officials to repay more than 1,170,000 Leones (about US $19,000) that they had allegedly embezzled, there did not appear to be any recommendation that they be prosecuted. Reports continued to be received of poor prison conditions; however, no reforms of prison administration or planned improvements in prison conditions were announced by the government during the year.

Amnesty International appealed for the commutation of individual death sentences and protested against the executions in October. It requested further information about the detention without charge of Mary Amara. In November an Amnesty International delegate visited Sierra Leone as part of the organization's worldwide campaign against the death penalty and appealed to President Momoh to abolish the death penalty.

SINGAPORE

Six prisoners of conscience were granted conditional release, one after almost 23 years in untried detention under the Internal Security Act (ISA). Two remained in detention without charge or trial under the act. A mandatory punishment of caning was introduced for further criminal offences and the death penalty was extended to cover certain drugs offences. Two people were sentenced to death and five executions were carried out.

In January the government amended the ISA and the Constitution to restrict *habeas corpus* in cases involving administrative detention. The ISA permits the President and the Minister of Home Affairs to order detention of indefinite duration without charge or trial. Following the amendment detainees held under such orders can no longer submit their case for judicial review and court powers are limited to verifying that procedural requirements have been complied with. The amendment also abolished the right of appeal to the Privy Council in the United Kingdom, Singapore's highest appellate court for ISA detainees. An amendment to the Constitution validated the ISA changes.

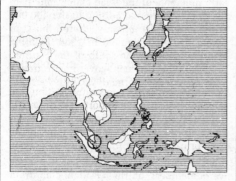

Chia Thye Poh, a former opposition member of parliament detained since October 1966 under the ISA, was released conditionally in May into internal exile. His freedom of movement and association remained severely restricted. Previously, the government had insisted that he publicly renounce his alleged membership of the proscribed Communist Party of Malaya (CPM) as a condition of his release. He maintained that such a renunciation would imply that he was a CPM member, an allegation he has consistently denied, and that his arrest was justified. At the time of his conditional release, the government said that the CPM had been sufficiently weakened and disrupted to prevent him from posing a "security problem".

Teo Soh Lung, a lawyer, and Vincent Cheng, the former secretary of Singapore's Catholic Archdiocesan Justice and Peace Commission, remained in detention without charge or trial under the ISA and in solitary confinement throughout the year. Vincent Cheng, held continuously since May 1987, was served in June with an order for a further year's detention. He and Teo Soh Lung were among 22 people arrested in connection with an alleged "Marxist conspiracy to subvert the existing

social and political system". Except for Vincent Cheng, all of the other detainees had been released before the end of 1987, although 20 of them were placed under restriction orders. During April and May 1988, Teo Soh Lung and eight others were rearrested after they alleged publicly that they had been ill-treated in detention (see *Amnesty International Report 1989*). Teo Soh Lung and three others brought *habeas corpus* actions to contest their detentions. The courts ruled in their favour and ordered their release in December 1988. However, all four were immediately rearrested and served with new detention orders. Teo Soh Lung's detention order was renewed in June for a further year. The three others — Kevin Desmond de Souza, Chng Suan Tze and Wong Souk Yee — were released under restriction in March. Their restriction orders limited their freedom of movement and association. Both Teo Soh Lung and Vincent Cheng brought *habeas corpus* actions in the High Court challenging their most recent detention orders. Teo Soh Lung's action was dismissed in April and a Court of Appeal had not ruled on her case at the end of the year. Vincent Cheng's application was heard in September, although the presiding judge barred his appearance in court. Vincent Cheng alleged in written testimony that he had been struck repeatedly by security officers and forced to sign under duress prepared statements admitting the existence of a Marxist conspiracy. He also claimed that he had been threatened with prolonged incommunicado detention. No judgment had been delivered by the end of the year.

Caning has been a mandatory punishment for about 30 offences since 1973. Amendments to the immigration law took effect on 31 March and 31 August, under which illegal immigrant workers and people who knowingly hire more than five of them face mandatory caning and imprisonment upon conviction. Before the end of the year more than 20 immigrant workers had reportedly been caned for overstaying their visas.

In November Parliament passed an amendment to the Misuse of Drugs Act (1973), which made the death penalty mandatory for those convicted of possessing specified quantities of cocaine, cannabis and opium. Since 1975 the death penalty has been mandatory only for possession of and unauthorized trafficking in

210

specified amounts of heroin and morphine.

Two people were sentenced to death following conviction for drug-trafficking. Five people convicted of drug-trafficking were executed, four in May and one in November, bringing the number of people hanged for drugs offences since 1975 to 25. The appeals of nine others against death sentences were pending. No death sentences or executions for offences not related to drugs were reported.

Amnesty International continued to appeal for the unconditional release of Teo Soh Lung and Vincent Cheng, and for the lifting of restrictions imposed on Chia Thye Poh and other former ISA detainees. It also urged commutation of all death sentences and an end to further executions.

SOMALIA

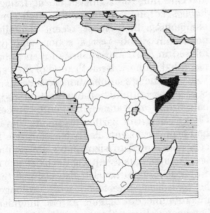

Over 50 prisoners of conscience – one of them held for almost 20 years – and hundreds of other political prisoners were released under a general amnesty for political prisoners announced in January. A human rights lawyer and several Islamic leaders were among prisoners of conscience arrested in mid-1989, but most were freed within a few months. Hundreds of other political prisoners arrested in 1988 remained in detention without trial, and more were arrested during the year and held for varying periods. Some were tortured or ill-treated in detention, and prison conditions were harsh. Over 200 people were reportedly shot dead by the security forces during anti-government demonstrations in Mogadishu in July. Amid mass arrests, 46 people

detained by military police were extra-judicially executed. In several parts of the country where insurgents were active, reprisal killings of civilian non-combatants were reported. Over 100 people were estimated to be under death sentences during 1989, although no official figures were available; several were executed.

There was fighting throughout the year in the north between the opposition Somali National Movement (SNM) and government forces. The latter committed numerous human rights violations against civilians suspected of supporting the SNM, particularly members of the Issaq clan. Many people fled to Ethiopia, adding to the 400,000 Somali refugees already there, most of whom had fled Somalia in 1988. Fighting also broke out in the south of the country, in particular between government troops and the newly formed Somali Patriotic Movement (SPM): here too there were reports of reprisals by government troops against unarmed civilians, thousands of whom fled to Kenya. The SNM also reportedly killed a number of unarmed government supporters in early 1989. The victims were members of the Ogaden clan from Ethiopia living in refugee camps in the north.

On 25 January the government announced a general amnesty for all political prisoners and government opponents living abroad. In the following months, hundreds of prisoners of conscience and other political prisoners were freed, and there was increasing public debate about human rights and political freedoms. An Amnesty International visit took place in June – the first time representatives from the organization had been allowed to visit during President Mohamed Siad Barre's 20-year rule. However, in a major setback for human rights, there were mass arrests and extrajudicial executions of suspected government opponents shortly afterwards. Some of those arrested were released in October. The government announced in August that political parties other than the ruling Somali Revolutionary Socialist Party would be permitted to contest the next parliamentary elections, postponed to December 1990.

Among the first to be freed under the general amnesty was Yusuf Osman Samantar, a lawyer and former member of parliament, detained continuously since 1975 and previously for several other periods since 1969. By March, over 50 prisoners of conscience and several hundred other political prisoners had been released. Among them were prisoners of conscience sentenced to death or long prison terms after unfair trials by the National Security Court. They included Aden Yusuf Abokor, medical director of Hargeisa hospital, and others jailed with him in 1982; Abdi Ismail Yunis, a former university dean, and Suleiman Nuh Ali, an architect, who were both serving 24-year prison terms after the commutation of death sentences imposed on them in early 1988; and nine Islamic leaders originally sentenced to death in 1986, whose sentences were commuted to life imprisonment. Also freed were Safia Hashi Madar, a relief agency employee sentenced to life imprisonment in 1985, and five military cadets detained without trial after being forcibly repatriated from Egypt in August 1988. One of the cadets had incorrectly been reported to have died in custody (see *Amnesty International Report 1989*).

Other prisoners of conscience were released later in the year. Fahima Dahir Jama, a school student, and four other women held in Hargeisa since 1986 were freed in August. However, hundreds of other political prisoners detained in 1988 after SNM attacks in the north were believed to be still imprisoned at the end of the year in Hargeisa, Berbera and Borama. Also still held were Hussein Mohamed Nur, an Ethiopian pilot detained without trial since 1976, and Ahmed Dhore Farah, a district judge detained without trial since 1979.

There were numerous new arrests of critics and suspected opponents of the government. Some were held for only a few days, but over 20 were detained without trial for several months. Ismail Jumaale Ossobleh, a prominent lawyer who had defended many political prisoners in the previous decade, was arrested in Mogadishu on 13 July. Others detained at the same time were Abdulkadir Aden Abdullah Osman, an engineer and son of a former president of Somalia; Abdirashid Sheikh Ali Sufi, *Imam* of Casa Populare mosque in Mogadishu; and several other religious leaders.

On 14 July there were mass arrests after anti-government demonstrations at the main mosques in Mogadishu. The demonstrators were protesting at the arrests of religious leaders who had criticized the government's handling of investigations into the murder the previous week of the Roman Catholic Bishop of Mogadishu, Monsignor Salvatore Colombo. Some of the protesters attacked members of the security forces, several of whom were killed. Troops retaliated by shooting demonstrators and other suspected government opponents. In three days, over 200 people were reportedly killed, although the government only acknowledged 28 deaths. Hundreds of other suspected government opponents were arrested, including many who had not taken part in the demonstrations. They were held in National Security Service or army detention centres, such as Danane army camp, 50 kilometres southwest of Mogadishu. Most were released uncharged after a few days or weeks. However, some were still detained without trial at the end of the year, or were unaccounted for and feared killed.

On 16 July soldiers made over 100 arrests in the Medina district of Mogadishu. Forty-seven of those arrested, of whom all except two were members of the Issaq clan, were separated from the rest and taken in army trucks to Jezira, 30 kilometres on the way to Danane army camp. On the beach, soldiers shot them, killing all but one who survived with injuries. President Siad Barre ordered an inquiry into the incident, to be headed by the Chairman of the Defence Committee of the National Assembly. The result of the inquiry had not been disclosed by the end of the year.

On 24 July security forces arrested Major General Aden Abdullahi Nur, a former defence minister, and General Mohamed Abdullah Ba'adleh, a former interior minister. They were accused of inciting opposition to the government – the former in connection with an army mutiny in Kismayu, and the latter in connection with the July demonstrations. Both were members of the National Assembly and ministers in the President's office: they were still detained without trial at the end of 1989.

Despite the constitutional and legal requirements that prisoners should be referred to a court within 48 hours of arrest, Ismail Jumaale Ossobleh, other prisoners of conscience and other political detainees were not taken to court or charged with any offence. The government alleged that Ismail Jumaale Ossobleh was

212

"mobilizing an illegal assembly, holding secret meetings to overthrow the government, inciting trouble, and in possession of seditious and anti-government publications". He was also questioned about his meetings with Amnesty International delegates in June, although the government denied that this was the reason for his arrest.

Ismail Jumaale Ossobleh and Abdulkadir Aden Abdullah Osman were released on 21 October in an amnesty to mark the 20th anniversary of President Siad Barre's accession to power. A total of 1,168 other prisoners were freed in the amnesty, but their identities and the reasons for their imprisonment were not made public, so it was not clear if any were political prisoners. Several religious leaders were freed on 1 November, but Abdirashid Sheikh Ali Sufi was still detained without charge or trial at the end of the year.

Abukar Hassan Ahmed, known as "Yare", a law lecturer arrested in Mogadishu in November 1988, was tried by the National Security Court in March 1989, after spending four months in pre-trial detention on charges of possessing seditious publications. One of these was an Amnesty International report, *Somalia: A Long-Term Human Rights Crisis*, published in September 1988. He pleaded not guilty and complained that he had been tortured by National Security Service officers. The judges did not order any investigation of his torture allegations and he was convicted. He was freed on payment of a fine and later fled the country to avoid rearrest.

Some reports were received of torture or ill-treatment of people arrested during the year for political reasons, particularly after the July demonstrations. Prison conditions were harsh and dozens of criminal prisoners in Mogadishu central prison reportedly died owing to poor conditions and medical neglect. Eleven port employees in Mogadishu died on 16 October after military police arrested them and imprisoned them in an arms store, where they died from suffocation. Eight police officers were later arrested and charged with responsibility for their deaths.

Hundreds of extrajudicial executions were reported in areas where insurgents were active. For example, over 200 civilians were killed by government troops in Erigavo, the capital of Sanag region in the north, soon after SNM forces withdrew after

capturing the town for some hours on 16 March. Killings of civilians by soldiers were also reported near Belet Wein in central Somalia and around the southern port of Kismayu after armed opposition activity by the United Somali Congress (USC) and mutinous soldiers in mid-1989. Dozens of civilians were killed by soldiers in Dobleh, on the Kenyan border, on 20 September, after fighting with SPM forces in the area. Others fled to Kenya, but 18 of them were forcibly returned to Somalia by the Kenyan authorities a few days later and were reportedly killed by Somali soldiers. In villages near Galkayo in central Somalia, over 120 civilians were reportedly killed by troops on 24 November for allegedly providing assistance to the USC or to soldiers who had mutinied.

Some 100 or more people were believed to be under sentence of death during the year in prisons throughout the country. Several executions were reported in Mogadishu central prison.

Amnesty International welcomed the release in early 1989 of many prisoners of conscience for whose release it had been appealing for many years. It continued to work for some prisoners who had not been released, some of whom were freed later in the year.

In February Amnesty International drew attention to its concerns about torture in an oral statement delivered to the United Nations Commission on Human Rights. In May the organization submitted further information about its concerns in Somalia for United Nations review under a procedure, established by Economic and Social Council Resolutions 728F/1503, for confidential consideration of communications about human rights violations. The submission was also sent to the government, together with recommendations for measures to halt abuses, but no response was received.

An Amnesty International delegation visited Somalia in June for talks with the government at the President's invitation. The delegates met President Siad Barre, relevant government ministers and officials, and received assurances that the government would cooperate with Amnesty International in the protection of human rights in Somalia.

In July, deeply concerned at new human rights abuses so soon after its visit, Amnesty International appealed for the release of Ismail Jumaale Ossobleh and other prisoners of conscience arrested with him, and for an impartial investigation into the extrajudicial executions at Jezira. In October Amnesty International submitted to the government a series of recommendations for measures to guarantee protection of human rights and published details of its current human rights concerns. The following month it sent the government a full report of its visit, as the basis for further talks requested for early 1990. It urged the government to amend national security laws which were incompatible with international human rights standards and to adopt safeguards to protect people from torture or extrajudicial execution.

SOUTH AFRICA

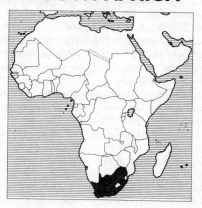

Scores of people, including prisoners of conscience, were detained without charge or trial under state of emergency regulations. Hundreds of others were released following a wave of hunger-strikes, but most of them had their freedom of movement, association and expression restricted. Five prisoners of conscience who had been in custody since late 1984 or early 1985 were freed by the Appeal Court. Allegations continued to be received that political detainees, including some held in the nominally independent "homelands", were tortured. Three former security police officers said they had been part of a "death squad" which had murdered government opponents in South Africa and abroad. At least 60 people were hanged at Pretoria Central Prison and further executions were believed to have been carried

out in the "homelands". However, the authorities in the Transkei "homeland" announced a moratorium on executions.

P.W. Botha resigned as State President and was replaced in July by F.W. de Klerk. The National Party was returned to power in September with a reduced majority following a general election, from which the majority black population was excluded. The election took place in the face of a defiance campaign organized by the Mass Democratic Movement (MDM), a broad coalition of anti-*apartheid* groups. During the campaign the number of arrests and allegations of police brutality increased.

The newly elected administration relaxed controls on demonstrations and released eight long-term political prisoners, including Walter Sisulu, former Secretary-General of the banned African National Congress (ANC). These government measures coincided with a reduction in violent activities by the ANC. However, the high level of violence continued in Natal between supporters of Chief Gatsha Buthelezi's Inkatha movement, a conservative KwaZulu "homeland"-based organization, and supporters of the United Democratic Front (UDF), a broad coalition of anti-*apartheid* organizations.

In June the government renewed for a further year the nationwide state of emergency which had been continuously in force since June 1986. Emergency regulations continued to be used by the authorities to ban political meetings, demonstrations and politically sensitive funeral processions. The activities of certain organizations, including human rights groups, were prohibited under the regulations. All members of the police and security forces retained immunity from prosecution for acts committed in "good faith" during the exercise of their emergency powers. They also retained powers to arrest people considered a "threat to public safety" and to detain them incommunicado, without charge or trial, for up to 30 days. The Minister of Law and Order held powers to prolong such detentions indefinitely by administrative order.

At the beginning of the year, at least 1,000 critics and opponents of the government were held without charge or trial under the emergency regulations. Many prisoners of conscience were among them, including the leading UDF member Mutile Henry Fazzie and his wife, Ethesia

Buyiswa Fazzie. Like many others, the couple had been held continuously since 1986. Most of these detainees were released in the first half of the year following a wave of hunger-strikes by emergency detainees protesting their continued imprisonment. Mutile Henry Fazzie and Ethesia Buyiswa Fazzie were among those released in May.

Some emergency detainees, however, were released conditionally. At least 650 of them had their freedom of movement, association and expression restricted. Contravention of the restrictions was punishable by imprisonment. Godfrey Molekwa, a prisoner of conscience held since June 1986, was restricted to Mokorong District upon his release from detention in March. He was prohibited from participating in the activities of the Mapela Youth Congress and from attending any meeting involving criticism of the government. He was also required to report twice daily to a police station about 65 kilometres from his home, and was prohibited from entering the school where he formerly taught.

A leading journalist, Zwelakhe Sisulu, remained under overnight house arrest and had been prohibited since his release from detention in December 1988 from writing for publication (see Amnesty International Report 1988).

Children and young people were among those detained without charge or trial under the emergency regulations. Between June 1988 and June 1989 over 200 children were reportedly detained. April Mohau, a 17-year-old boy, was detained in April and Petrus Labasi, aged 16, in June. Both youths had been placed in emergency detention twice previously. At least 39 young people released from detention were placed under restriction orders.

Over 80 suspected government opponents were detained for interrogation under Section 29 of the Internal Security Act (ISA) of 1982, which permits the security police to hold detainees indefinitely incommunicado and in solitary confinement, without charge, for interrogation. Similar provisions were used to detain political suspects in the nominally independent "homelands". Ngconde Balfour, a leading activist in the Western Cape, was held incommunicado under Section 29 for almost six months before he was released without charge in July. Law and Order Minister Adriaan Vlok said in April that 82 people were in detention under Section 29 provisions.

Five prisoners of conscience sentenced at the end of the so-called Delmas Treason Trial in 1988 (see Amnesty International Report 1989) were released in December when the Appeal Court overturned their convictions. Among them were Mosioua "Terror" Lekota, Popo Molefe and "Moss" Chikane who had been in custody continuously since early 1985.

Political detainees held without trial were reportedly tortured, although official restrictions on media coverage of detention and prison conditions obscured the extent to which torture occurred. In March a witness at an inquest in the case of Caiphus Nyoka, a student leader who died in 1987 after being shot by police during his arrest, described being tortured by police at Daveytown police station. Exodus Guguletu Nyakane, who was with Caiphus Nyoka when the police arrested him at Caiphus Nyoka's home, said he had been shut in a locker containing tear-gas, been partially suffocated with a cloth, had boiling water poured down his back and been given electric shocks. The inquest court rejected his testimony. It also ruled that the police, who had shot Caiphus Nyoka nine times after bursting into the bedroom where he was sleeping, had acted in self-defence and were not criminally liable for his death. The police told the court that they had believed Caiphus Nyoka to be armed. No substantial evidence was produced in court to support this claim.

In another case, however, the Pietermaritzburg Supreme Court issued a restraining order against four police officers accused of torture and vigilante action. One of the applicants in the case, Imbali youth activist Nonginkosi Zondi, alleged in a sworn statement to the court in November that the police had detained him three times and tortured him with electric shocks, beatings, near asphyxiation with a plastic tube placed over his head and threats to kill him. After each detention he was released without charge. His allegations were supported by a medical report and the sworn statements of other community activists who alleged they had been tortured by the police.

Torture in Bophuthatswana and other "homelands" was also reported during the year.

In April it was reported that emergency

detainees in Johannesburg and other centres who required treatment after going on hunger-strike had been shackled to their beds with leg-irons. The authorities said they had used shackles to prevent escape. Hunger-striking detainees in the Transkei "homeland" were also reported to have been shackled to hospital beds.

An inquest into the murder of Mathew Goniwe and three other community activists from Cradock (see *Amnesty International Report 1986*) concluded in February without identifying those responsible for the deaths. In March, however, six police officers in the Ciskei "homeland" were convicted of culpable homicide in connection with the death in 1987 of another black activist, Eric Mntonga (see *Amnesty International Report 1988* and *1989*).

In the Venda "homeland", hundreds of people were arrested in July and August, apparently in efforts to pre-empt protests against official celebrations of the 10th anniversary of Venda's "independence". At least a dozen detainees required hospital treatment after having been assaulted, kept in unhygienic cells, and given food of poor quality. The younger detainees appear to have borne the brunt of police violence. Among them was Michael Nevari, aged 17, detained and assaulted until he lost consciousness at Thohoyandou police station in July.

Political detainees in both Venda and Transkei said after their release that they had been held in harsh conditions. Many were held incommunicado in unhygienic conditions and reportedly denied adequate medical treatment. Misile Stemele, a church worker detained in Transkei from November 1988 until late 1989, said he and others had been given rags to serve as blankets during the winter months and dirty food, and had been forbidden to receive food parcels and clothing from outside the detention centre.

There was renewed concern that opponents of the government might have been victims of extrajudicial executions, particularly following the murder in May of prominent human rights activist David Webster. The concern increased in October and November, when three former members of the security police admitted in separate accounts that they had been involved in the early 1980s in at least nine "death squad" murders. The victims were govern-

ment opponents living in South Africa and in neighbouring states. Butana Almond Nofomela, scheduled to be hanged in October for a murder unrelated to "death squad" activity, was granted a stay of execution after he had alleged in a sworn statement that he was one of four security police involved in the 1981 murder of Griffiths Mxenge, a lawyer and former political prisoner.

Butana Nofomela named senior police officers who he said had organized the "death squad" unit and had paid him and his fellow assassins to murder Griffiths Mxenge. His allegations were corroborated by both his former commanding officer, Dirk Johannes Coetzee, and a former member of the unit, David Tshikalange. Dirk Coetzee said he had knowledge of, or had taken part in, the killings of several suspected ANC members inside and outside South Africa. He said victims' bodies had been burned to conceal the murders. He also stated that the security police had sent parcel bombs to kill government opponents, including Ruth First, who was killed in Mozambique in 1982.

An inquiry into the allegations of "death squad" activity was established under the direction of the Attorney General of the Orange Free State but the government rejected appeals for a judicial commission of inquiry. Butana Nofomela was charged with the murder of Griffiths Mxenge. His trial was adjourned until 1990. The Minister of Justice announced that Dirk Coetzee and David Tshikalange would also be prosecuted, although both had fled the country.

The death penalty continued to be used extensively, although the number of executions declined significantly from previous years. At least 60 people were hanged at Pretoria Central Prison. An unknown number of executions were also carried out in the nominally independent "homelands". In October the authorities in the Transkei "homeland" announced a moratorium on executions, pending consideration of abolishing the death penalty.

In May, 14 of the 26 defendants tried in connection with a politically motivated killing at Upington were sentenced to death. Like 12 people sentenced to death in June in connection with a similar case in Ciskei, the defendants were convicted and sentenced on the basis of the "common purpose" doctrine. This maintains that

216

people present at the time of a killing may be considered culpable even without proof of their direct participation in the crime. Appeals were pending in both cases at the end of 1989.

In November the Appeal Court set aside the death sentences of five people from Queenstown convicted on the basis of "common purpose". After retrial before the Supreme Court they received prison terms ranging up to 20 months. The court ruled that a process of "deindividuation" could occur whereby members of a highly aroused crowd lost their individual sense of identity and could therefore be held only partially responsible for the actions of the group.

Amnesty International continued throughout the year to press for the release of prisoners of conscience and to express concern about the detention without charge or trial of other political detainees. The organization made numerous appeals on behalf of individual detainees and people placed under restriction orders. It also called for impartial investigation of all torture allegations. After the "death squad" disclosures of Butana Nofomela, Amnesty International urged the government to establish an independent judicial inquiry into allegations of police complicity in unlawful killings and attacks on government opponents. In addition, it urged State President de Klerk to commute all death sentences.

In December two Amnesty International delegates preparing to attend an Appeal Court hearing were refused visas to enter South Africa. Amnesty International provided testimony of its concerns in South Africa to the United Nations on several occasions, addressing the *Ad Hoc* Working Group of Experts on Southern Africa, the 12 to 13 December Special Session of the United Nations (UN) General Assembly on *Apartheid*, and other UN bodies.

SPAIN

Allegations of ill-treatment were made by detainees held under anti-terrorist legislation and by criminal suspects in police custody. Numerous judicial proceedings involving members of the security forces were in progress in connection with allegations of torture and ill-treatment. There were also complaints of ill-treatment in prisons. A Galician nationalist was imprisoned for burning a Spanish flag during a political demonstration.

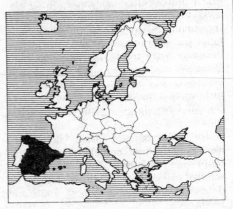

A three-month cease-fire observed by the armed Basque group *Euskadi Ta Askatasuna* (ETA) ended in April with a series of bomb attacks. By the end of the year 23 people, including members of the security forces and civilians, had been killed in violent actions reportedly carried out by ETA. A small number of killings and violent actions were attributed to other armed separatist groups and to armed political groups of the left and right.

In May Spain ratified the European Convention for the Prevention of Torture and Inhuman or Degrading Treatment or Punishment.

Many judicial inquiries opened in previous years into allegations of torture and ill-treatment remained unresolved, but several members of the security forces were found guilty of torturing and ill-treating detainees.

In October the Supreme Court issued a noteworthy ruling, overturning the Madrid Provincial Court's acquittal in 1985 of two police officers. They had been charged with allowing the torture of José Arregui, an alleged ETA member detained under their supervision. José Arregui died in hospital after nine days' incommunicado detention in Madrid in 1981 (see *Amnesty International Report 1981* and *1982*). The certified cause of death was pneumonia, but the autopsy also revealed injuries to his lungs and eyes, burns on his feet, bruises on his body and severe internal bleeding. The Supreme Court sentenced one officer to four months' suspended imprisonment and three years' suspension from duty. It sentenced the other to three months' suspended imprisonment and two years' suspension from duty.

There were sporadic reports of arrests under anti-terrorist legislation. Since May 1988 the maximum permitted period of incommunicado detention under this legislation has been five days. During 1989 most detainees were released before this limit. Detainees continued to allege ill-treatment, especially in the form of disorientation techniques such as hooding and deprivation of food and sleep during persistent interrogation.

During the last two weeks of September, at least 46 people suspected of collaborating with the Araba commando of ETA were arrested in the Basque country. Some were released without appearing in court, but most were brought before the National Court in Madrid. A number of detainees complained to the judges that they had been tortured and ill-treated while held incommunicado by the Civil Guard in the Basque country and in Madrid.

Relatives and lawyers who saw the detainees during and after their court appearance alleged that some of them displayed injuries resulting from ill-treatment. On 20 September Alejandro Ros declared to the court that he had been beaten and subjected to a mock hanging. José Antonio Mujika Huici claimed he was subjected to severe beatings and near-asphyxiation. When he appeared in court on 21 September, he was heavily bruised near his left eye and in the region of his kidneys. Nearly all the suspected Araba detainees reportedly complained of repeated insults, threats and psychological pressure such as hooding and blindfolding.

Several criminal suspects were reportedly ill-treated in police custody. Félix Rodríguez Santana was arrested in Las Palmas on 4 July, on suspicion of sexually assaulting two female minors. After an unknown period in police custody, he was transferred on remand to a local prison. Fifteen hours later, he was admitted to hospital for the treatment of serious injuries apparently incurred as a result of severe beatings. He died on 23 July. A judicial inquiry was opened after his sister complained to the local court that she had heard him screaming while police beat him. In a public statement the police denied all responsibility for Félix Rodríguez' injuries, speculating that he had probably been beaten by fellow prisoners after his admission to prison. The local prison director, however, stated that Félix Rodríguez had not been beaten while in prison and had been kept apart from other prisoners at all times. There was no news regarding the outcome of the judicial inquiry at the end of the year.

Incidents of ill-treatment were reported in several prisons during the year. There were reports that prisoners held at Alcalá-Meco maximum security prison were subjected to persistent physical ill-treatment by prison guards and that immobilizing sprays were sometimes used for punishment. It appeared that the alleged ill-treatment often occurred after prisoners had refused to stand for regular cell-checks, submit to strip-searches or comply with other orders given by prison guards.

The claims of ill-treatment were made by prisoners accused of common criminal offences as well as by alleged members of Basque, Catalan and Galician armed political groups. Some prisoners required medical assistance as a result of their ill-treatment and some allegations were supported by information from lawyers and national human rights groups.

Francisco Rodríguez Sánchez, a prominent member of the *Bloque Nacionalista Gallego* (BNG), a Galician nationalist party, was imprisoned in June. He had played a leading role in a demonstration organized by the BNG in June 1984 during which a Spanish flag was burned. Police arrested and detained him briefly three days later on suspicion of "committing an outrage against the Spanish nation by insulting the flag". He denied the charge, but in 1986 La Coruña Provincial Court sentenced him to two years, four months and one day's imprisonment. In March 1989 the Supreme Court rejected Francisco Rodríguez' appeal against the sentence and he was imprisoned on 21 June. He was granted provisional liberty on 18 July, pending the outcome of a further appeal to the Constitutional Court. The Constitutional Court had not ruled on his case by the end of the year.

Amnesty International expressed concern at the prosecution and detention of Francisco Rodríguez because there was no evidence of his use or advocacy of violence.

Amnesty International requested information on the steps taken to investigate ill-treatment alleged by detainees arrested

218

under anti-terrorist legislation and by criminal suspects held in police custody. It also monitored the progress of judicial inquiries into alleged ill-treatment opened in previous years. In November Amnesty International wrote to the Minister of the Interior expressing concern about reports suggesting systematic ill-treatment of prisoners in Alcalá-Meco prison. It urged a full and impartial investigation into the allegations and asked to be informed of developments in cases where formal complaints had been lodged with the judicial authorities.

SRI LANKA

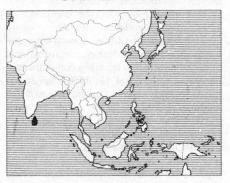

Thousands of people "disappeared", died in custody or were victims of extrajudicial executions carried out in the south by Sri Lankan security forces and "death squads" believed to be associated with them. The government failed to clarify the fate of 800 people who "disappeared" in previous years. Thousands were detained without trial under emergency regulations and there were widespread allegations of torture. The Indian Peace Keeping Force (IPKF) reportedly carried out extrajudicial executions in the northeast and numerous reports alleged torture of prisoners by IPKF personnel and Tamil groups allied to them.

In January President Ranasinghe Premadasa's interim government lifted the state of emergency which had been in force since May 1983 and released 1,519 people who had been detained without charge under emergency regulations. These regulations, including Regulation 55FF permitting police to dispose of bodies without postmortem or inquest, were reintroduced in June amid widespread violent strike action

and unrest instigated by the armed opposition group *Janatha Vimukthi Peramuna* (JVP), People's Liberation Front.

Parliamentary elections held in February were boycotted by the Liberation Tigers of Tamil Eelam (LTTE) in the northeast. The JVP, which threatened to kill participants, boycotted elections in the south. The ruling United National Party (UNP) was returned to power after a campaign marked by political violence. Fourteen opposition candidates and several hundred other people, including members of the UNP, were killed. Most of the attacks in the south were attributed to the JVP and in the northeast to the LTTE. Rivalries between parties contesting the elections may also have resulted in some killings.

The JVP and the associated *Deshapremi Janatha Viyaparaya*, Patriotic People's Movement, continued a campaign of violence and intimidation and were widely believed responsible for thousands of murders. The victims included people perceived as "traitors" to the groups, prisoners, security forces personnel and their families, members of the ruling UNP, senior public officials, broadcasters and left-wing opposition activists, including some Buddhist monks. Members of the two groups reinforced their calls to strike and to demonstrate against the government by threatening to murder those who refused to participate. They also destroyed government offices, post offices, tea plantations and other state property.

Rohana Wijeweera, the JVP leader, and his deputy, Upatissa Gamanayake, were reportedly killed in November in disputed circumstances. The government said that after Rohana Wijeweera's arrest he had taken security forces personnel to the JVP headquarters in Colombo and had been killed there in a shoot-out. Officials said Upatissa Gamanayake was shot dead soon afterwards while attempting to escape from custody. In addition, several other JVP leaders were reportedly killed.

The LTTE was also considered responsible for political murders. At least 38 people died in Trincomalee in April in a bomb explosion attributed to the LTTE. Other victims included about 100 Sinhalese villagers killed in the first four months of the year, a Tamil parliamentary candidate, the Government Agent of Jaffna, and two leaders of the Tamil United Liberation Front.

In April President Premadasa offered an

amnesty to Tamil militants and the JVP. The JVP did not respond but in June the LTTE announced a cessation of hostilities against the Sri Lankan Government. However, fighting continued between the LTTE and the IPKF together with allied Tamil groups.

The Indian Government agreed in September to withdraw the IPKF by the end of the year, provided that arrangements had been made for the safety of the Tamil community in the northeast. Apparently in anticipation of the withdrawal, the Eelam People's Revolutionary Liberation Front (EPRLF) and its allies abducted and detained thousands of young men and some women for training in a new Indian-backed defence force. Indian troops withdrew from Amparai District in October and the unofficial Tamil National Army (TNA), believed to have incorporated those abducted and trained, appeared in its place. By the end of the year an estimated 25,000 Indian troops remained in Jaffna and Trincomalee districts. As the Indian troops withdrew, heavy fighting was reported between the LTTE and the TNA, and between the LTTE and the armed Tamil groups allied with the Indian forces.

In October the government invited the International Committee of the Red Cross (ICRC) to Sri Lanka to trace missing people, visit places of detention and inform the parties to the conflict about the rules of war.

In the south extrajudicial executions were carried out by uniformed members of the security forces and by "death squads" believed to be associated with them. Many hundreds of people were killed, apparently because they were suspected of supporting or sympathizing with the JVP, but it was impossible to establish the true total. The identity of many victims was not known because bodies were mutilated beyond recognition, burned in heaps on tyres or thrown in rivers. Some bodies were dumped long distances from the scene of execution. The relatives of missing people were often too frightened to pursue inquiries. However, some people witnessed their relatives being taken into custody and later identified bodies. Some victims had been taken by uniformed police or army officers; others had been abducted by unknown armed men in civilian clothes, some of them travelling in unmarked vehicles. Security force spokespersons said many victims were JVP sympathizers or collaborators. Other people killed were from villages believed to be collectively sympathetic to the JVP.

In a new development, responsibility for many retaliatory killings following attacks by the JVP was claimed in the name of "vigilante" or paramilitary groups. The government claimed these groups operated independently and without official sanction. However, the security forces were widely believed to have been directly involved or to have acquiesced in these killings. Witnesses said some victims had been in security forces custody shortly before they were killed.

Reports of extrajudicial executions attributed to the security and paramilitary forces increased significantly after emergency regulations were reintroduced in June. These regulations permitted security forces to dispose of bodies without post-mortem or inquest. Reports of extra-legal killings increased again from August, when the JVP announced it would kill the families of personnel who did not resign from the security forces. Posters, some signed in the name of the Sri Lanka Army, then appeared in public places bearing threats that 10 or more relatives of JVP members would be killed for each killing of a security force member's relative.

Hundreds of demonstrators, many of them coerced into demonstrating by the JVP, were shot dead by security forces. In July hundreds of people, under pressure from the JVP, defied curfew regulations and demonstrated against the Indian military presence in Sri Lanka. About 150 peaceful demonstrators were reportedly shot dead by police at several locations in the south. Hundreds more deaths are believed to have remained unrecorded.

Lawyers pursuing human rights cases were among those who were apparently extrajudicially executed. Charitha Lankapura and Kanchana Abhayapala had filed hundreds of *habeas corpus* applications with the courts on behalf of "disappeared" prisoners and others arrested in the south. The former was killed by unknown armed men in July and the latter in August. At least 20 other lawyers were reportedly threatened with death in attempts to prevent them from working on such cases. Several people who complained of or witnessed human rights violations by the security forces were also reportedly killed.

220

By July over 400 *habeas corpus* petitions had been filed on behalf of people who had allegedly "disappeared" or been illegally arrested in the south. Very few petitions were filed after Charitha Lankapura's death because lawyers feared reprisals for taking on such cases.

Information was received during the year about over 2,000 "disappearances" after arrests by security forces in the south. Most victims were young men, many from socially depressed areas, but included some Buddhist monks and students. Some people who reportedly "disappeared" were later released after being held in unacknowledged detention by the authorities. Other "disappeared" people were believed to have been killed, and the fate of many remained unknown.

The authorities arbitrarily arrested thousands of people on the basis of anonymous denunciations and suspected links with the JVP. Some detainees were released after short periods. Others were detained under the Prevention of Terrorism Act (PTA), which permits up to 18 months' detention without charge or trial, or under the emergency regulations (reintroduced in June) which permit indefinite detention without charge or trial. Detainees were commonly held incommunicado. Many reportedly were tortured and died in custody. Relatives of suspects were also held as "hostages" in the absence of the wanted person. Many of the relatives were apparently beaten in custody and some were killed. The brother of an army deserter was reportedly arrested in Kandy district in place of his brother in July. Next day his body was found in a nearby reservoir.

The trial of three police officers accused of murdering Wijedasa Liyanarachchi in September 1988 (see *Amnesty International Report 1989*) was postponed until December because the defendants had difficulty retaining a lawyer. One lawyer who had been retained went into hiding after an attack on his home, presumed to have been carried out by the JVP, in which a member of his household was killed. The suspects charged with murdering three students in Ratnapura in October 1988 (see *Amnesty International Report 1989*) were released on bail in January. The suspects included the Chief Minister's son and several law enforcement officers. Their trial had not started by the end of the year.

In April the Supreme Court awarded damages to several torture victims and people who had been illegally detained. A lawyer received death threats after her client was awarded record damages for torture. A few days after a victim of wrongful detention was awarded damages, he was reportedly abducted and "disappeared".

Several trials for violent political offences in the south began during the year. Five people were charged under the PTA and emergency regulations for a grenade attack on the parliament building in August 1987 (see *Amnesty International Report 1988*) and for other offences. Their trial, which began in August, had not been completed by the end of the year. Four people suspected of murdering the UNP Chairman in December 1987 (see *Amnesty International Report 1988*) were put on trial in May. One of the defendants was shot dead in hospital by unidentified armed men in September — he had been admitted after suffering heart trouble in jail. He said he had been tortured during interrogation.

In the northeast hundreds of people were arrested by the IPKF and screened for links with the LTTE. Members of the EPRLF and allied Tamil groups aided the IPKF in identifying suspects. Relatives of LTTE suspects were also reportedly detained. The Indian authorities did not disclose whether these detainees were held under Sri Lankan or Indian legislation. There were no reports that detainees had been charged or tried. In August the Indian authorities reportedly said 5,489 prisoners were in IPKF custody. Members of the EPRLF and other Tamil groups also regularly arrested and detained LTTE suspects, according to reports, but no information was available on how many were detained.

Both the IPKF and groups allied with them reportedly tortured prisoners. Indian troops regularly beat prisoners and subjected them to electric shocks. Dozens of prisoners were reportedly killed in custody. There were dozens of cases in which arrests by the IPKF or EPRLF were witnessed and after the authorities said the detainees had been released, their bodies were found with gunshot wounds.

Several reprisal attacks by the IPKF after ambushes by the LTTE were reported. Up to 46 people were extrajudicially executed at Valvettiturai in August after the LTTE had ambushed an IPKF patrol there and killed six Indian soldiers. Among the reported victims was a one-year-old child.

Many extrajudicial executions in the northeast were reportedly committed by the EPRLF and their allies, acting with the backing or acquiescence of the IPKF. The EPRLF was allegedly responsible for scores of extrajudicial executions. Ahilan Thiruchelvam, the son of the editor of a Jaffna-based newspaper, was detained in May by armed men seeking his father. The son's body was found soon after with gunshot wounds.

Information was received during the year that at least two of six Tamil asylum-seekers who were forcibly returned to Sri Lanka from the United Kingdom in February 1988 had been tortured after their return. One of the victims was reportedly tortured by the IPKF in Jaffna, and the other by police in Colombo.

In January Amnesty International welcomed the lifting of the state of emergency and the release of prisoners detained under emergency regulations. It urged the government to repeal indemnity legislation passed in December 1988 (see *Amnesty International Report 1989*). The organization proposed a visit to Sri Lanka by an Amnesty International delegation to discuss human rights issues with the authorities.

Throughout the year Amnesty International urged the government to adopt effective safeguards to protect detainees from torture, death in custody and "disappearance". It recommended that the PTA and the reintroduced emergency regulations be amended to protect human rights. The organization expressed particular concern about increased reports of extrajudicial executions attributed to the security forces and to "death squads" apparently working with them. It urged the government to withdraw Emergency Regulation 55FF, to institute an independent commission of inquiry into extrajudicial executions and to clarify the fate of the "disappeared". Amnesty International also requested effective protection for people who had received death threats.

The government responded in July that Amnesty International's proposed visit should be "postponed for the time being". In August the Minister of Foreign Affairs informed Amnesty International that the "Sri Lanka Government has not repeat has not given orders to execute anybody", and that "subversives" had been killed by the security forces during exchanges of fire in combat.

Amnesty International urged the Indian Government to investigate reports of torture, deaths in custody and extrajudicial executions committed by the IPKF and allied Tamil groups in the northeast. The organization also called for safeguards to prevent such human rights violations. It appealed to the Northeastern Provincial Council to halt the abduction and forcible detention of "recruits" to an irregular security force and to release people held for training against their will. The council responded to Amnesty International that the recruitment was voluntary.

In May Amnesty International published a report, *Sri Lanka: Continuing Human Rights Violations*, which detailed its concerns in both southern and northeastern Sri Lanka. In December it published *Sri Lanka: Reports of Extrajudicial Executions*.

SUDAN

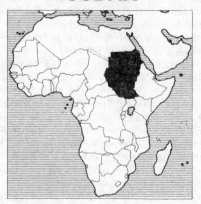

Several hundred prisoners of conscience were detained without charge or trial following a military coup in June. Some were subsequently released but at least 200 were still detained at the end of the year. Dozens of prisoners of southern origin were executed extrajudicially by soldiers and hundreds of civilian non-combatants were deliberately killed by pro-government militias in areas affected by armed conflict. Forty-two people of southern origin "disappeared" in custody. Dozens of prisoners were tortured in November and December. A prisoner of conscience and at least five other people were sentenced to death, and several

222

hundred other people were under death sentences for murder. At least four executions took place.

There was continuing armed conflict in the south between government forces and the armed opposition Sudan People's Liberation Army (SPLA). Both sides were alleged to have extrajudicially executed prisoners taken in the course of the fighting and to have committed other abuses. A cease-fire was announced in May but renewed fighting broke out in October following a change of government in Khartoum.

In February 150 senior army officers submitted a memorandum to Prime Minister Sadiq al-Mahdi calling for a new government, a peaceful solution to the armed conflict with the SPLA and major political and economic reform. This led to a new coalition government being formed in March, which included the Umma Party, the Democratic Unionist Party (DUP), representatives of political parties deriving their support largely from southerners, and the trade unions. The National Islamic Front (NIF) refused to join the coalition because of disagreements about the implementation of Islamic laws and the new government's intention to negotiate with the SPLA.

The coalition government led by Prime Minister Sadiq al-Mahdi was overthrown on 30 June in a military coup led by Lieutenant-General Omar Hassan al-Bashir, who became head of a new military governing body, the National Salvation Revolution Command Council (NSRCC). On 9 July the NSRCC appointed a cabinet of mainly civilian ministers, several of whom were believed to be NIF supporters.

Immediately after taking power on 30 June the NSRCC declared a nationwide state of emergency, banned all political parties and trade unions, dissolved the Constituent Assembly (parliament) and suspended the Constitution. All non-religious associations were suspended, including local human rights groups and the Sudan Bar Association. Under new state of emergency legislation, the security forces were empowered to arrest people without warrants and to detain them indefinitely without charge or trial. No provision was made for such untried detainees to challenge the grounds for their detention before the courts or for independent review of detention orders. Under an amendment to the state of emergency laws, organizing a strike became an offence punishable by death.

On 6 July the NSRCC created special military courts to try people arrested under the state of emergency laws and others. Defendants were not allowed full legal representation. On 27 September these courts were abolished and replaced by six new Revolutionary Security Courts and a high court. Defendants were then said to have been allowed the right to defence counsel. However, in December further special courts were created: in these, lawyers were allowed to give advice to their clients during the trial but were not allowed to address the court directly or to present arguments to the court in support of their client. Prisoners convicted by these courts were allowed to lodge an appeal to the Chief Justice but had no right of appeal to a higher court.

On 7 December a member of the NSRCC announced that the government would implement the "September laws" enacted in 1983 by the government of former President Gaafar Nimeiri, which had been partially suspended since that government's overthrow in 1985. These laws, based on an interpretation of Islamic law, provided for the judicial amputation of limbs, flogging as a penalty for numerous offences, and stoning and crucifixion as methods of execution.

Immediately after the June coup, some 80 leaders and officials of political parties and former government officials were arrested and held in detention without charge or trial at Kober prison in Khartoum. These included the deposed Prime Minister and leader of the Umma Party, Sadiq al-Mahdi; Dr Hassan al-Turabi, leader of the NIF; Mohamed Osman al-Mirghani, leader of the DUP; and Mohamed Ibrahim Nugud, General Secretary of the Sudan Communist Party. Some detainees were released uncharged after a few days; others were freed after several months. For example, 19 prisoners released uncharged on 16 November included former government minister Omar Nur al-Daiem and senior members of the Umma Party and the NIF. All those released were prohibited from leaving the country. Sadiq al-Mahdi and some 30 other former government officials and prominent politicians, including prisoners of conscience, remained in detention without charge or trial at the end of the year. Dr Hassan al-Turabi and Mohamed Osman al-Mirghani were released from prison and placed under house arrest at the end of November.

More than 150 trade union activists and dozens of others, including academics, lawyers and journalists, were also arrested and detained without charge or trial from August onwards, after a number of trade unions and professional associations presented the government with a memorandum on 31 July, protesting against new restrictions on trade union rights. Some of those arrested were detained at Kober prison, but most were transferred either to Shalla prison in western Sudan or to a prison in Port Sudan, in the northeast, after they complained about their conditions at Kober prison. However conditions at Shalla and in Port Sudan were said to be even harsher. Among those still detained at Shalla prison at the end of the year were Ahmed Mohamed Saleh, President of the Electrical Engineers' Union, and Omar Ahmed al-Amin, Secretary-General of the Sudanese Employees Union. In contrast to the detained former government officials and politicians, who were allowed family visits at Kober prison, the trade union prisoners were denied family visits or access to lawyers.

Two prominent human rights activists were among those detained. Ushari Ahmed Mahmoud, a lecturer at Khartoum University, was arrested on 8 July and detained at Kober prison. Amin Mekki Medani, a lawyer and founder member of the Sudanese Organization for Human Rights, was arrested in Khartoum on 7 September and detained in Port Sudan. Although no reason for their detention was divulged, it seemed that both were imprisoned because their past activities in defence of human rights in Sudan resulted in their being regarded as potential opponents by the new government. Other prominent lawyers and members of the Sudan Bar Association were arrested in early August. Some were released in November, including Sadiq al-Shami and Ishaq Shadad, but others, including two members of the Bar Association's Executive Committee, Kamal al-Jazuli and Gelal Eddine al-Sayed, were still detained without charge or trial at the end of the year.

A further wave of arrests in Khartoum in late November and December followed a week-long strike by medical doctors in protest at the arrest and dismissal by the authorities of some of their colleagues and the banning of the Sudan Doctors' Union. Dozens of doctors were arrested. Most were released a few days later, but more than 20 were believed to be still detained without charge or trial at the end of the year, including Dr Yahya Omar Hamza and Dr Mohamed Abdelgadir Hilal. The military authorities announced after the coup that all those arrested for political reasons would be tried fairly and promptly. However, by the end of the year only a few political prisoners had been charged and brought to trial. One of them, Idris al-Banna, a former deputy chairman of the Supreme Council of State, was convicted on 2 September by a special military court on corruption charges and sentenced to 40 years' imprisonment. His lawyer was present in court but was not allowed to defend him, and the hearing was reported to have lasted less than half an hour. Amnesty International was concerned that criminal charges may have been brought against him for political reasons and that his trial did not conform to internationally recognized standards of fairness.

In December, four doctors accused of organizing a strike in November were also tried by a special court. They were denied legal representation and the right to appeal to a higher court. One of them, Dr Maamun Mohamed Hussein, was sentenced to death on 10 October and another, Dr Sayed Mohamed Abdallah, was sentenced to 15 years' imprisonment. The other two were acquitted on the grounds of insufficient evidence.

Some doctors and others were reported to have been tortured and ill-treated by members of the security services following their arrest. Dozens of those arrested in November and December were held initially at "safe houses" in Khartoum and kept blindfold during their interrogation and tortured. Farouk Mohamed Ibrahim, a lecturer at Khartoum University who was arrested on 30 November, was kept in a secret interrogation centre for several days and reportedly severely beaten before being transferred to Kober prison. In another case, Buthina Douka, a nursing sister at a hospital in Khartoum, who was arrested soon after the coup, was reported to have been beaten, tied up with ropes and severely ill-treated while detained at Omdurman prison. She was released in early November. Sadiq al-Mahdi, the former prime minister, was reported to have

AMNESTY INTERNATIONAL REPORT 1990

224

been ill-treated by senior military officers. He said that on the night of 3 October he was taken out of prison, interrogated for some four hours by senior military officers, verbally abused and threatened with execution.

Suspected SPLA supporters arrested in areas of armed conflict were also reportedly tortured or ill-treated. In March three Dinka men were arrested at an army checkpoint on the outskirts of Meiram, in south Kordofan. They were then tightly bound and left lying in the sun for some seven hours, apparently to make them confess to membership of the SPLA. They were then released: however one, Manut Deng, died within a few hours and the other two were so seriously injured by the way they had been tied that they both later had both their arms amputated in Khartoum civil hospital. Despite widespread publicity about these cases, the authorities were not known to have taken any action against those responsible or to have instructed soldiers not to use this method of tying up prisoners.

There were reports of extrajudicial executions of civilians by members of progovernment militias and the armed forces both before and after the military coup. On 23 April troops and militias reportedly destroyed a number of villages near Abri in the Nuba mountains in apparent retaliation for the killing of soldiers in landmine explosions. On 19 July, at least 34 civilian prisoners were killed by soldiers in the town of Wau in the south. The killings occurred after a soldier was injured by a mine near the airport. Troops were reported to have arrested civilians in Zagalona and Grinti markets in Wau and to have opened fire on them shortly after dark.

In late October pro-government Murahaleen militia forces were reported to have raided Nuba villages in the Lagawa area of southern Kordofan and killed more than 100 people, injuring many others. Forty-two people from the Nuba and Dinka communities who had sought refuge from the fighting in the south by moving to Khartoum were arrested and subsequently "disappeared", including Mary Ajak, a nurse, and Joseph Madot, a trader. Unconfirmed reports suggested that military intelligence officers had taken them from police custody and extrajudicially executed them in al-Markhiat, near Omdurman.

Dr Maamun Mohamed Hussein, a pris-

oner of conscience, was sentenced to death by a special military court on 10 December. He was convicted of participating in and calling for a strike and of incitement to opposition against the government. He was denied full legal representation at his trial. Although the presiding judge at the court said that he had the right to appeal against his conviction, the Head of State, Lieutenant-General Omar Hassan al-Bashir, was reported to have said publicly that he considered the strike an act of treason, that Dr Maamun Mohamed Hussein deserved the death penalty, that he could not appeal to a higher court against his sentence and that he would not benefit from clemency. However, Dr Maamun Mohamed Hussein had not been executed by the end of the year.

Two people sentenced to death for murder by ordinary courts in previous years were executed in February. There were further death sentences and more executions in December of people convicted in unfair trials by special military courts. Magdi Mahgub, a businessman sentenced to death by a special court on 1 December for illegal possession of foreign currency, was executed on 17 December. He had not been allowed assistance from defence counsel. After the coup, the military authorities had ordered everyone in possession of foreign currency to declare the amounts in their possession to the government and threatened severe punishment, including the death penalty, for those contravening new currency regulations. Gergis al-Ghous Boutros, an assistant pilot working for Sudan Airways, was sentenced to death on 24 December by a special court in Khartoum on charges of attempting to smuggle foreign currency out of Sudan.

Sayed Ahmed Ali Gaballa was executed on 17 December in Khartoum. He had been sentenced to death for alleged drug dealing by a special court in Khartoum on 23 October.

Several hundred people convicted of murder in previous years were believed to be still under sentence of death. In late September the Supreme Court confirmed the death sentences on five Palestinians who were sentenced to death in October 1988 for killing several people in bomb and machine-gun attacks on a hotel and a club in Khartoum in May 1988. However, the Supreme Court modified the mandatory death sentences imposed on the five to allow the relatives of those killed to decide whether the five should be executed or not.

The SPLA was also reported to have killed members of the armed forces and pro-government militias captured in combat. Following the SPLA's capture in March, of Bor, in the Upper Nile region, several hundred captured government soldiers were reportedly executed and their bodies thrown into the Bahr al-Jabal river. Also in March, seven government soldiers were reported to have been extrajudicially executed soon after their surrender in the village of Lolyanga, a few miles south of Torit in Eastern Equatoria.

The SPLA was also reported to be holding former members of its own organization in detention, among them Joseph Oduhu, who had previously participated in SPLA delegations to other countries. In December Amnesty International wrote to SPLA leader John Garang detailing reports of alleged killings of prisoners by SPLA forces, urging that they be investigated and that steps be taken to prevent any recurrence of such abuses.

During the first half of the year, Amnesty International urged Prime Minister Sadiq al-Mahdi's government to investigate reports of extrajudicial executions and torture by the armed forces and militias.

Following the military coup, Amnesty International appealed for the release of prisoners of conscience and urged that all those detained be allowed to contest in court the reasons for their imprisonment.

An Amnesty International delegation visited Khartoum in November and met two members of the NSRCC responsible for areas of the south and other senior government officials. However, the delegation's requests for meetings with the Head of State and NSRCC members responsible for political prisoners were not granted. The delegates expressed concern about widespread violations of human rights in the context of the civil war in southern Sudan and the continuing detention without charge or trial of more than 150 prisoners of conscience arrested after the military coup. In December Amnesty International published a report, *Sudan: Human Rights Violations in the Context of Civil War*, which detailed human rights violations which had occurred in the context of the armed conflict in the south. Also in December it published a document detail-

ing the cases of prisoners of conscience detained without trial after the coup.

The organization called for the commutation of the death sentence imposed on Dr Maamun Mohamed Hussein, a prisoner of conscience, in December and the commutation of all other death sentences. It urged the military government to investigate reports of extrajudicial executions and to take action to prevent prisoners being killed by troops or militia.

SWAZILAND

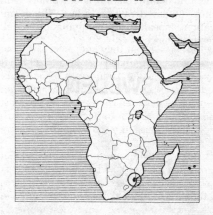

A trade union official held briefly under an administrative detention order appeared to be a prisoner of conscience. Nine other people were held under administrative detention orders, without charge or trial, in connection with an alleged plot against the government. Six people were under sentence of death but no executions were carried out.

David Mncina, Secretary-General of the Swaziland Union of Financial Institutions and Allied Workers, was arrested in June after calling for a bank workers' strike. He was placed under an administrative detention order signed by the Prime Minister which permitted 60 days' detention without charge or trial. However, he was released unconditionally after four days.

Nine other people, six senior prison guards and three civilians, were detained under 60-day orders in March. They were allegedly involved in a conspiracy to help Prince Mfanasibili Dlamini escape from prison, and to install him as Head of State in place of King Mswati III. The prince, a member of the royal family, was formerly a government minister.

226

In February a suspected member of the African National Congress of South Africa was removed at gunpoint by unidentified men from hospital in Mbabane. He had been held under police guard while recovering from injuries sustained in a car chase prior to his arrest by Swazi police. His fate and whereabouts were not known.

Six people convicted of criminal offences were under sentence of death. No executions were carried out.

Amnesty International was concerned about the detention of David Mncina, who appeared to be a prisoner of conscience, and sought information about others held under 60-day detention orders. The organization appealed for commutation of all death sentences.

SWEDEN

Seven Kurdish refugees from Turkey remained under town arrest for the entire year as a result of an administrative order imposed by the government in 1984.

Originally the restrictions on freedom of movement had been imposed on nine Kurdish refugees, who were suspected by the government of being terrorists (see *Amnesty International Report 1989*). The government had declared that they could not be deported to Turkey because they risked persecution there. Instead, the government imposed restrictions on their freedom of movement in accordance with anti-terrorist provisions in the Aliens Act. The Kurds had to report three times a week to the police and could not leave or change their town of residence without permission from the police. Breach of any of these regulations could result in imprisonment

for up to one year.

In August the government lifted the restrictions on two of the Kurdish refugees. It also eased restrictions on two of the others, although they remained under town arrest.

By the end of 1989 the government had not responded to a December 1988 letter from Amnesty International asking about the procedures used to impose restrictions on the Kurds and about review procedures. The organization was concerned that the authorities had not indicated when these restrictions might be lifted. It was also concerned that the restrictions had been administratively rather than judicially imposed and that the legality of the restrictions could not be challenged before a court. In October copies of the letter to the government were sent by Amnesty International to members of a parliamentary committee set up to review the antiterrorist provisions in the Aliens Act.

SWITZERLAND

A total of 534 people were sentenced to prison terms for refusing to perform military service. Of these, 261 based their refusal on religious, ethical or political grounds, according to statistics published by the Federal Military Department. However, as in previous years, there were claims that the total number of people who had refused on conscientious grounds was far higher than that reflected in the department's restricted categories. Many conscientious objectors served their sentences during 1989, including some who had been sentenced in previous years. All were considered prisoners of

conscience. **A large number had expressed their willingness to perform an alternative civilian service.**

Under Article 18 of the Constitution, there is a binding obligation to perform military service. Male citizens carry out a total of approximately 12 months' service between the ages of 20 and 50; there is no provision for alternative civilian service. Unarmed military service is available to conscripts able to prove that the use of arms would result in "a severe conflict of conscience" on religious or ethical grounds.

In a national referendum held in November, 64.4 per cent of those who voted were against a proposal to abolish the army. Parliament continued to examine a draft bill proposing changes in the penalties for certain categories of conscientious objection (see *Amnesty International Report 1989*). On 14 December the National Council approved the bill and passed it to the other chamber, the Council of States, for consideration. Under the bill, refusal to perform military service would remain a criminal offence. If a conscript were able to show that he could not reconcile military service with his conscience because of "fundamental ethical values", then he would be sentenced to a period of work in the public interest, ranging from one and a half times the total length of military service to two years. This would not result in a criminal record. Those objecting on other, unrecognized, grounds would continue to receive prison sentences and a criminal record.

Article 81 of the Military Penal Code allows military tribunals to sentence people refusing military service to up to three years' imprisonment. However, in practice sentences rarely exceed one year. Where a tribunal recognizes a conscript's "severe conflict of conscience" on religious or ethical grounds, a sentence of up to six months' imprisonment may be imposed. Such sentences are normally served in the form of *arrêts répressifs* or *semi-détention*, allowing prescribed or approved work outside the prison during the day.

Nils Phildius, a theology student, began a sentence of six months' *arrêts répressifs* in October after a military tribunal had recognized that his refusal of military service was motivated by sincere religious convictions and that he had suffered a "severe conflict of conscience". Denis

Laurent, a cook, served an eight-month prison sentence for refusal of military service and desertion. He had left barracks after his first shooting-practice, returning the next day to explain the moral and pacifist beliefs compelling him to refuse military service. He also informed the military tribunal hearing the case in November 1988 of his willingness to perform an alternative civilian service. The tribunal considered he had acted "for reasons of an essentially moral nature" but had not suffered a "severe conflict of conscience".

Amnesty International continued to appeal for the release of people imprisoned for refusing to perform military service on conscientious grounds. It pressed for the introduction of the right to refuse military service on such grounds and for the provision of a genuine alternative service outside the military system. The federal authorities replied that the introduction of such a service required an amendment to Article 18 of the Constitution and that national referendums in 1977 and 1984 had decisively rejected this.

SYRIA

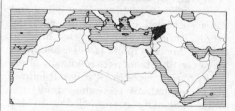

Thousands of political prisoners, including hundreds of prisoners of conscience, continued to be detained under state of emergency legislation in force since 1963. The majority were held without charge or trial. Some had been held for over 20 years. Others remained in prison after the expiry of their sentences. However, more than 320 untried political detainees, including three prisoners of conscience, were released during 1989. Torture of prisoners was said to be widespread and routine, and one "disappearance" was reported. One person was executed.

Thousands of suspected government opponents arrested in Syria and in Syrian-controlled areas of Lebanon continued to be detained without trial. At least 122 more were arrested during the year. Among those detained were 286 prisoners of conscience and 178 others who may have been prisoners of conscience. Many were suspected members of prohibited political parties or Palestinian groups, such as *Hizb al-'Amal al-Shuyu'i*, Party for Communist Action (PCA); *al-Hizb al-Shuyu'i al-Maktab al-Siyassi*, Communist Party Political Bureau (CPPB); *al-Ikhwan al-Muslimun*, Muslim Brotherhood; *al-Tanzim al-Sha'bi al-Nasiri*, Popular Nasserist Organization (PNO); Democratic Front for the Liberation of Palestine (DFLP); Popular Front for the Liberation of Palestine (PFLP); *Fatah*; Popular Front for the Liberation of Palestine-General Command (PFLP-GC); *Harakat al-Tawhid al-Islami*, Islamic Unification Movement (IUM); and the pro-Iraqi Arab Socialist Ba'th Party.

Fourteen CPPB members were arrested between February and June and held without charge or trial in Damascus, Saidnaya and Tartus. Four of them were released uncharged in September (see below). The 10 others were still in detention without charge or trial at the end of the year. They included Fawwaz Hammuda, a laboratory technician from Deir al-Zor, who was held in Saidnaya Prison.

In April Syrian forces reportedly arrested a number of people in West Beirut and Zahle suspected of cooperating with the mainly Christian army brigades loyal to General Michel 'Aoun (see Lebanon). In May over 100 others were reportedly arrested by Syrian forces in West Beirut following demonstrations protesting against the killing of Shaikh Hassan Khaled on 16 May (see Lebanon). It was not possible, however, to obtain further details of these arrests. Between April and August, Syrian forces arrested 14 suspected members of the pro-Iraqi Ba'th Party in Tripoli and the Beka' Valley, but it was not known where they were held. At least 69 Palestinians suspected of being members of *Fatah* or of supporting Yasser 'Arafat, Chairman of the Palestine Liberation Organization (PLO), were also reported to have been arrested during the year by Syrian security forces in Lebanon. Most were arrested near the Sabra, Chatila, Burj al-Barajneh, Mar Elias and Tal al-Za'tar refugee camps in Beirut, or near other Palestinian refugee camps in Sidon and Tyre in southern Lebanon.

Some of those detained were reportedly arrested by Amal, a predominantly Shi'a militia in Lebanon, and later handed over to Syrian troops. These included three brothers arrested in Tyre and Sidon on 27 October. Two of them, Khalil and Muhammad Khattab, were released two days later, but the fate of the third, Ibrahim Khattab, remained unknown. In November Amal reportedly arrested 25 PFLP-GC members in southern Lebanon on suspicion of cooperating with anti-Syrian Palestinian factions in the area. They were reportedly handed over to Syrian intelligence, and their fate remained unknown. Among them were Mahmud Musleh and Kamel al-Haj, leading PFLP-GC figures in southern Lebanon.

Political detainees arrested in previous years continued to be held without charge or trial. Some had been in detention for over 20 years. Ahmad Suwaidani, a former army officer, diplomat and member of the Ba'th Party's Regional Command, was arrested in 1969. He was held in al-Mezze Prison, Damascus. In July he went on hunger-strike to protest against his continued detention without charge or trial. Three members of the Jewish community arrested in 1987 and 1988 (see *Amnesty International Report 1989*) were also still held without charge or trial in 'Adra Civil Prison. The whereabouts of two of them, Eli and Selim Swed, remained unknown until October, when relatives were allowed to visit them.

Some 450 people arrested between August 1987 and March 1988 on suspicion of supporting the PCA were believed to have remained in detention without trial (see *Amnesty International Report 1989*). A further 111 CPPB members arrested between 1980 and 1988 were also among those who remained in detention without charge or trial throughout 1989. Among them was Ghassan Khouri, an architect and university lecturer from Deir 'Atiyya. Arrested in May 1988 by *Amn al-Dawla*, State Security, he was held in al-Sadat detention centre in Damascus. Jalal Khanji and Riad Bastati, who were among 80 members of the Syrian Engineers' Association arrested in 1980 after demanding political reforms, remained in detention without charge or trial in 'Adra Prison. The whereabouts of most of those arrested with them were unknown.

More than 320 untried political detainees, three of whom were prisoners of conscience, were released. Of these, about 160 had been arrested by Syrian forces in Lebanon. 'Issam 'Abd al-Latif, a member of the DFLP's Political Bureau, and Salah Salah, the PFLP's representative in Lebanon, were released in January. They had been held without charge or trial for 23 and 10 months respectively. Three lawyers, all prisoners of conscience, were released in April: Salim 'Aqil, Thuraya 'Abd al-Karim and 'Abd al-Majid Manjouneh had been detained since 1980. A member of the Syrian Engineers' Association also detained since 1980, 'Abd al-Majid Abu Sha'la, was released in May. In June 140 Palestinians, all said to be supporters of Yasser 'Arafat, were released, as were 45 IUM members or supporters. Many had been detained for over five years. Nineteen CPPB members were released between July and October; they had been detained for periods ranging between three and 18 months. In November, 117 IUM members or supporters were released. In December three members of the Jewish community were released from 'Adra Prison: Albert and Victor Laham and Zaki Mamroud had been held in detention without trial for two years. During the year information was also received of the release in late 1988 of two CPPB members held in detention without trial since May 1988, including Butros 'Abd al-Massih (see *Amnesty International Report 1989*).

The routine torture and ill-treatment of prisoners continued to be widely reported. Prisoners were also frequently reported to have been denied medical treatment. Among the victims were four Palestinians — Hassan Dib Khalil, Fayez 'Arafat, Diab Muhammad Mustafa and Muhammad Dawud. They were held without charge or trial in *Fara' al-Tahqiq al-'Askari*, Military Interrogation Branch, in Damascus. All were members of *Fatah* arrested in Lebanon in 1983 and 1985 and reportedly tortured on various occasions since then, including in 1989. In November they were reported to be in a critical condition after being denied medical treatment for injuries resulting from torture and for ailments contracted as a result of prolonged detention and poor prison conditions.

Testimonies alleging torture were also received from former detainees arrested in previous years in Syria and Lebanon. One was from a Palestinian released in late 1988 after being held for 21 months at 'Anjar detention centre in Lebanon and *Fara' Falastin*, Palestine Branch, in Damascus as a suspected PLO member. He said he had been tortured with electric shocks, beaten all over his body and partially asphyxiated by having his head immersed in water. Another was from a Lebanese member of the pro-Iraqi Ba'th Party arrested in June 1988 and held for 42 days at the *Madrasat al-Amrican*, American School, in Tripoli. He said he had been beaten and flogged for long periods, given electric shocks and hung by his wrists from the ceiling with nylon rope. He also said he was tied to a metal chair, the back of which was bent so as to put severe strain on his spine, neck and limbs, causing him to lose consciousness. Another Palestinian suspected of PLO membership arrested at Damascus airport in September 1988 and held for almost a month in *Fara' Falastin* was allegedly tortured both during and after interrogation. According to his testimony, he was flogged and beaten with metal cables while naked, and subjected to *falaqa* (beating on the soles of the feet) for prolonged periods.

Mudar al-Jundi, an engineer from Tartus arrested in September 1987 on suspicion of supporting the PCA, was held in *Fara' Falastin* in Damascus after his arrest. He was reportedly tortured during interrogation in 1987, denied medical treatment for acute asthma, and then "disappeared". His whereabouts remained unknown.

One execution was reported in 1989. Ahmad 'Abdallah Ahmad was publicly executed by hanging in Tartus in June after being convicted of murder and armed robbery.

Amnesty International repeatedly expressed concern to the government about the continued detention without trial of prisoners of conscience and other political prisoners, and about reports of torture and ill-treatment of detainees. In June an Amnesty International delegation attending an international meeting in Syria met Vice-President 'Abd al-Halim Khaddam and other government officials, the first such contact since 1978. The delegation urged the release of prisoners of conscience and the prompt, fair trial or release of other untried political detainees, the impartial investigation of torture allegations and deaths in custody, and abolition of the death penalty. Government officials said they would be prepared to establish contact with Amnesty International and in future would respond to its inquiries. The organization presented the names of over

230

400 untried political detainees, among them prisoners of conscience. The officials stated they would examine them and respond in detail. However, the government had provided no further information about these prisoners by the end of 1989.

In an oral statement delivered to the United Nations (UN) Commission on Human Rights in February, Amnesty International drew attention to reports of the routine torture of political detainees by Syrian security forces, consequent deaths in custody and the failure of the government to investigate complaints of torture. There was no response from Syrian Government representatives. On 8 March the Commission on Human Rights announced its decision to drop Syria from consideration by the UN under a procedure established by Economic and Social Council Resolutions 728F/1503. Amnesty International had made a submission to the UN under this procedure in April 1988, drawing attention to a consistent pattern of human rights violations in Syria and Syrian-controlled areas of Lebanon (see *Amnesty International Report 1989*).

TAIWAN

Five prisoners of conscience sentenced to prison terms in previous years were held throughout the year but two others were released. Two prisoners of conscience were newly imprisoned in 1989. Four other people, some of them possible prisoners of conscience, were put on trial but their trials had not been completed by the end of the year. Three police officers were prosecuted for torturing a criminal suspect. Sixty-nine people convicted of criminal offences were executed, over three times the number executed in 1988.

The Civic Organizations Law was amended in January, formally lifting a 40-year ban on the formation of political parties. However, the law requires that such parties should not violate the Constitution, or advocate communism or the division of the national territory. Taiwan is officially considered a province of China by the governments of both Taiwan and mainland China. By the end of the year there were some 40 political parties. Other new legislation provided for electoral reforms and for deputies elected on mainland China before 1949 to voluntarily retire.

Five prisoners of conscience continued to serve prison sentences imposed in previous years. Shih Ming-teh was imprisoned in 1980 and Tsai Yu-chuan and Hsu Tsao-teh in 1988 (see *Amnesty International Report 1989*). Chuang Kuo-ming and Dr Huang Kuang-hsiung were convicted in 1988 of having joined an organization advocating Taiwanese independence when they were living abroad.

Two prisoners of conscience were released. In April Cheung Ki-lok's 40-month sentence (see *Amnesty International Report 1989*) was quashed when the High Court acquitted him of sedition after his case was heard again. In September the Supreme Court ordered a further hearing of his case, but this had not started by the end of the year. Tsai Keh-tang was released in November on expiry of his reduced sentence (see *Amnesty International Report 1988*).

Chen Nan-jung, publisher and editor-in-chief of the opposition magazine *Freedom Era Weekly*, committed suicide by setting fire to himself on 7 April as police were forcing entry into his office to arrest him. He was facing charges of sedition for reproducing in his magazine the text of a constitution for an independent Taiwan.

There were several political trials. In June Chen Sheng-nan, a street vendor in Kaohsiung, was sentenced to seven years and two months' imprisonment for sedition. He was alleged to have spread propaganda for the People's Republic of China by showing and selling video films which apparently showed Chinese leader Deng Xiaoping calling for the reunification of Taiwan with mainland China. He was considered a prisoner of conscience.

Other trials involved dissidents who sought to return to Taiwan from abroad although the authorities had banned them from doing so on national security grounds. Some who entered Taiwan undetected were subsequently expelled, but three were tried under the National Security Law for entering the country without permission.

Chen Wan-chen, a journalist who returned secretly in May after spending 10 years in the United States of America (USA), was sentenced to five months' imprisonment in July. However, she was not imprisoned because the prosecution appealed against the sentence. Luo Yi-shih, the General Secretary of the World Federation of Taiwanese Associations, was sentenced to 10 months' imprisonment in December. Normally resident in Canada, he had returned to Taiwan to help the opposition's electoral campaign after previously being deported when he entered Taiwan legally in August. He was considered a prisoner of conscience.

Hsu Hsin-liang, a former commissioner of Taoyuan county, was arrested in September. He had twice previously been prevented from entering Taiwan, although he was wanted by the authorities on sedition charges. At his trial he was accused of planning to overthrow the government in 1979 together with others connected with the opposition *Formosa* magazine (see *Amnesty International Report 1980*) and of having made a number of statements opposing the Taiwanese authorities when he was in exile in the USA. He was sentenced in December to 10 years' imprisonment, reduced to six years and eight months under a 1988 presidential amnesty for offences committed before 1988. His trial was completed in one hearing and his conviction was in part based on confessions made by former *Formosa* magazine colleagues almost 10 years earlier which, they said, had been extracted under duress.

The trials of Hsieh Chang-ting, an opposition member of Taipei City Council, and Hong Chi-chang, an opposition member of the National Assembly, concluded in June and September respectively. They were both convicted on account of violence by others at a demonstration they had organized in June 1987 to oppose the National Security Law (see *Amnesty International Report 1988*). Hsieh Chang-ting was sentenced to 18 months' imprisonment. Hong Chi-chang was sentenced to 15 months' imprisonment and then in October to a further 18 months in connection with another protest demonstration in May 1988. Both

men — who were not detained — lodged appeals which had not been concluded by the end of 1989.

In October three police officers from Hoping West Road police station in Taipei were arrested and prosecuted for torturing a criminal suspect. One week earlier they had allegedly hit him on the head with a pistol, beaten him on the soles of his feet, dripped water into his nose and subjected him to other abuses. The result of the prosecution was not known.

According to the authorities, 69 prisoners were executed for crimes that included robbery, rape, murder and kidnapping — more than three times the number known to have been executed in 1988. According to press reports, district courts imposed over 75 death sentences for criminal offences.

Amnesty International continued to call for the release of prisoners of conscience and to investigate the cases of possible prisoners of conscience. Before his suicide, Amnesty International had urged the government not to arrest Chen Nan-jung but to respect his right to freedom of expression.

Amnesty International also expressed concern to the authorities about the rise in executions and called for the death penalty to be abolished. In May the Government Information Office replied that the death penalty was supported by the public and that it was necessary because of an increase in serious crimes.

TANZANIA

Two prisoners of conscience were released on the mainland. In Zanzibar non-violent critics or opponents of the government were among more than 100 people arrested and detained for short periods. Fifteen people jailed in Zanzibar in connection with a demonstration in 1988 may have been prisoners of conscience. Police on the mainland reportedly ill-treated criminal suspects, causing the death of at least one person. The High Court sentenced at least 18 people to death for murder. Fifteen Burundi refugees arrested in March for their non-violent political activities were still detained at the end of the year.

Opposition in Zanzibar to continued union with mainland Tanzania became

232

increasingly vocal. Political opponents of the union called for a referendum on its termination. In March former president Julius Nyerere, who heads the ruling *Chama Cha Mapinduzi*, Party of the Revolution, urged government officials in Zanzibar to arrest people who insulted national leaders or incited others to defy the country's sole legal party. He suggested that such people be held under renewable 48-hour detention orders, effectively without charge or trial.

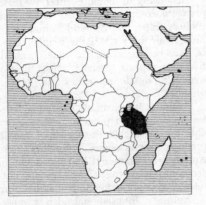

In April flogging was added to imprisonment as punishment for a range of offences, including robbery and assault committed with intention to steal. However, no reports of floggings were received.

The authorities released two prisoners of conscience in April. James Mapalala and Mwinyijuma Othman Upindo had been detained in 1986 and then banished to remote parts of the country in 1987 for circulating a petition calling for a multi-party system in Tanzania (see *Amnesty International Report 1989*).

In August K.L. Bazigiza, a student leader, was arrested after he publicly criticized the composition of a Tanzanian delegation sent to a youth festival in North Korea. He had been among the delegates and was considered to be a prisoner of conscience until his release, without charge, later in August.

At least 100 people were arrested in Zanzibar in connection with opposition to the union with mainland Tanzania. Many were released without charge after 48 hours' detention. Others were charged with attending illegal meetings or participating in proscribed political activities. In June, 35 people on the island of Pemba were charged with membership of an illegal

political party and with attending illegal meetings. They were released on bail and, like most others who faced such charges, had not been brought to trial by the end of the year.

Seif Shariff Hamad, a former chief minister of Zanzibar and a prominent critic of the union, was arrested in May shortly after he had called for a referendum on the union. He was initially charged with attending illegal meetings on Pemba. Following a search of his home, illegal possession of government documents was added to the charges against him. This offence is punishable by up to 12 years' imprisonment. In July the charges were changed on the grounds that some of the documents allegedly found addressed intelligence matters. Under the terms of a national security law he may now face up to 20 years' imprisonment. He was refused bail and remained in custody at the end of the year, awaiting the outcome of a preliminary inquiry into whether evidence against him warrants his prosecution. He may be a prisoner of conscience.

In June, 15 people held in Zanzibar who may be prisoners of conscience were sentenced to 18 months' imprisonment for participating in an illegal demonstration and destroying property. Three of them were also convicted of inciting others to breach the peace. The 15 were arrested after a demonstration held in May 1988 to protest against a speech by Sofia Kawawa, the head of the Tanzania Womens' Organization. She had criticized a number of Muslim practices on the grounds that they discriminate against women. As police broke up the demonstration, cars were damaged and stones were thrown at them. The police opened fire, killing two demonstrators and wounding several others. Official accounts of the demonstrations differed significantly from those of eye-witnesses. It was not clear that the 15 men convicted were involved in the violence which occurred at the end of the demonstration.

Several reports alleged that criminal suspects on the mainland had been ill-treated and tortured by the *sungusungu*, local police employed by traditional authorities, and the ordinary police. In at least two cases, the authorities arrested police officers accused of torturing or ill-treating prisoners. In July, 11 *sungusungu* were charged with torturing four criminal suspects whom they had allegedly beaten in Bukoba. In September Teretid David Nkunda died in Oysterbay Police Station in Dar es Salaam and two police officers were charged with his murder. Their trial had not begun by the end of the year.

The High Court sentenced at least 18 prisoners to death by hanging, all of them convicted of murder. There were no reports of executions.

Fifteen refugees from Burundi, who had lived in Tanzania for several years, were arrested in March at Mishamo refugee camp in Mpandi District. They included Remi Gahutu, President of a Burundi opposition movement, the *Parti pour la libration du peuple Hutu* (PALIPEHUTU), Hutu People's Liberation Party. The Tanzanian authorities accused the 15 of political activity which could be detrimental to Tanzania's relations with Burundi. The detainees were released shortly after arrest and ordered to leave the country. When they failed to depart they were rearrested and held in Keko Prison in Dar es Salaam, pending deportation to a third country.

In April at least 21 other Burundi refugees were reportedly arrested in Ulyankulu refugee camp, also for alleged political activities, and detained in Urambo Prison. It was not clear if they remained in detention at the end of the year. The arrests coincided with improved relations between Tanzania and Burundi.

Amnesty International welcomed the release of James Mapalala and Mwinyijuma Othman Upindo, while remaining concerned about the short-term detention of people arrested in Zanzibar on account of their peaceful political activities. The organization appealed for the release of K.L. Bazigiza and investigated the cases of Seif Shariff Hamid and 15 other people in Zanzibar who may have been prisoners of conscience. In September Amnesty International raised its concerns in Zanzibar when the organization's representatives met Dr Omar Ali Juma, the Chief Minister of Zanzibar, in London.

THAILAND

Three prisoners of conscience were serving sentences for distributing leaflets critical of the Royal Family. The leader of a Buddhist religious sect and over 70 of his followers, possible prisoners of con- science, were arrested but later released on bail. Seven people arrested for political offences were held without charge or trial. Twelve prisoners standing trial for alleged "communistic activities" were released as a result of a government-sponsored amnesty bill, but other political prisoners convicted previously after unfair trials were still held. At least two criminal suspects alleged that they had been tortured and new information was received about torture and ill-treatment of prisoners in previous years which, in many cases, had allegedly resulted in death in custody. At least 17 people were sentenced to death, but no executions were reported.

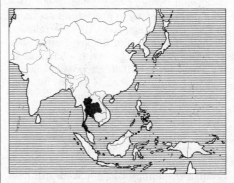

A government-sponsored amnesty bill was passed by parliament in July and came into effect at the end of August. The bill marked King Bhumibol Adulyadej having become the longest-reigning monarch in Thai history in July 1988. The amnesty applied to those accused, tried or imprisoned on communist charges, and people convicted of offences endangering national security, provided the offences were committed before July 1988. Members of parliament had submitted five other draft amnesty bills calling for a wider amnesty, but these were unsuccessful.

Montrii Aksorn-in, Chana Srikiatsak and Sanit Janduongsri remained in prison throughout the year. They had been arrested in July 1988 and sentenced to between four and a half and three and a half years' imprisonment in November 1988 after a trial held *in camera* (see *Amnesty International Report 1989*). They were convicted of "lese majesty" for producing and attempting to distribute leaflets critical of the Royal Family. All three were considered to be prisoners of conscience.

In June Rak Rakphong, known as Phra Bodhirak, leader of the Santi Asoke

234

congregation of Buddhist devotees, was arrested by police for defying an order from religious authorities that he cease his activities as a priest. He was charged with violations of the Ecclesiastical Act but released on bail. His trial had not been completed by the end of 1989. Santi Asoke devotees advocate what they consider to be a pure form of Buddhism. Since 1975 they have reportedly practised their beliefs outside the authority of the official Ecclesiastical Council, which has legal authority to govern the monastic orders of Buddhism in Thailand. In August, 79 Santi Asoke monks were arrested for allegedly violating the Penal Code by dressing as clergymen when they had not been ordained according to procedures set down in the Ecclesiastical Act. All were released on bail, but they and 20 lay Santi Asoke devotees were charged with violations of the Penal Code. All faced possible prison terms if convicted and would be considered prisoners of conscience.

Six alleged Muslim separatists, including Pariya Samor, Kuyayor Janae and Medor Bulasor, were reportedly arrested in Yalaa province in February by security forces from the 43rd Police-Military-Civilian Headquarters. They were still held without charge or trial at the end of 1989. Suwan Taphcheuy, known as Sor Pitak, an alleged communist insurgent, was reportedly arrested in Traang province in April by troops of the Fourth Army Region. He too was still held without charge or trial at the end of the year.

Twelve people charged with insurrection and involvement in insurgent "communistic activities" were released following the September amnesty bill. They included Phirun Chatwanitkun and Rangsan sae Sii, who had been held since April 1984; Suwat Mungchoetchuutham, who was arrested in September 1986; and Nop Prasertsom and Chitchanok Soophonpaan, who had been held since April 1987 (see *Amnesty International Report 1985, 1988* and *1989*). They were being tried before military courts, from which there is no right of appeal for such charges. Their trials had been repeatedly postponed because of the non-appearance of government officials called as prosecution witnesses.

Despite the amnesty measure, at least 22 political prisoners were believed to be still imprisoned at the end of 1989 under sentences imposed after unfair trials before military courts in previous years. They included Surachai sae Dan, Adun Bunreuang and at least three others convicted of "communistic activities" or politically motivated acts of violence in connection with them, and 17 Muslims from south Thailand convicted of acts of political violence in connection with separatist activities.

At least two criminal suspects alleged they were tortured or ill-treated during police interrogation. Charan Phanduingtri, a student arrested in January, said police officers had beaten him, forced his head into a sink of water and applied electric shocks to his genitals to force him to "confess". In August Samnao Khamthaawee alleged that a senior police officer and five other police interrogators had applied electric shocks to his genitals while questioning him in connection with a fraud case. It was not known whether any official investigation was carried out into these allegations.

In February a spokesperson for the Coordinating Group for Religion in Society, a local organization advocating human rights protection, reported that the group had collected information on 30 possible cases of death in detention due to ill-treatment since 1987. He cited details of two cases in 1987 in which warders or police officers allegedly beat prisoners to death. In June relatives of Charoen and Pan Wianglor alleged the brothers had been killed by the police. They said that Charoen Wianglor had been beaten to death in October 1988 by police interrogators who accused him of stealing a Buddha image from a village temple. Pan Wianglor had apparently also been beaten while being interrogated about the theft, but had been released when he promised not to reveal the cause of his brother's death. However, his family alleged he was shot dead in June after he asked the Police Department and Minister of the Interior to investigate it.

At least 17 people were reportedly sentenced to death for murder, and the death sentence of another, who had been convicted of a drug offence, was reportedly finalized by the Supreme Court. No executions were known to have taken place.

In September Amnesty International wrote to Prime Minister Chaatchai Chunhawan to welcome the release in December 1988 of Wimon Choertchuuchon,

Siifaa Sawaangyen, Wasuthii Sukkasang and the 12 other political prisoners freed as a result of the amnesty bill introduced in parliament by his government. The organization urged the immediate and unconditional release of Montrii Aksorn-in, Chana Srikiatsak and Sanit Janduongsri and the restoration of the right of appeal to political prisoners tried before military courts; including those already convicted. The letter called for the commutation of all death sentences.

TOGO

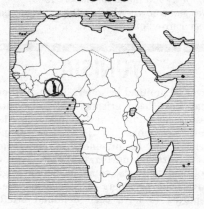

Three suspected government opponents were held incommunicado throughout the year. Fifteen political prisoners were held in harsh conditions and one case of torture was reported.

The National Commission for Human Rights in Togo, established by the government in 1987, continued to investigate alleged miscarriages of justice and human rights abuses: few of these cases involved political prisoners.

Three government opponents were held incommunicado throughout 1989 at Akodessewa police station in Lomé. They had been tried *in absentia* in December 1986 and convicted of plotting to overthrow the government of President Gnassingbé Eyadéma. Lawoé Folly Sossou and Kubah Otsiguey, who received eight-year prison sentences, were abducted from Ghana by Togolese security agents in 1987 (see *Amnesty International Report 1989*). Aballo Célestin Zekpa, sentenced to death *in absentia*, was abducted in February 1988 from Benin. The cases of Lawoé Folly Sossou and Kubah Otsiguey were referred

to the judicial authorities in October 1988, after they had been detained in secret for over a year. They were told they could accept their sentences or seek a retrial. Neither had been retried by the end of the year. Kubah Otsiguey reportedly requested a retrial. Aballo Célestin Zekpa's case was referred to the judicial authorities in October but the outcome was unclear at the end of the year. It was also unclear whether the President had commuted his death sentence, as other death sentences imposed at the same trial had been commuted. All three prisoners were said to have been tortured after abduction and detention.

Fifteen other defendants at the December 1986 trial, who were present in court at the December 1986 trial and convicted of plotting the violent overthrow of the government, were still serving prison sentences in military custody at the beginning of 1989. They were subject to particularly harsh conditions at Tokoin barracks in Lomé, where they remained handcuffed and were denied all visits. One of them, known as "Ali Baba", died in July, apparently as a result of illness. In September the prisoners were transferred to a civil prison in Lama-Kara, in northern Togo, and told they could receive visits. In October the President informed Amnesty International that he had ordered removal of their handcuffs.

Kwasikuma Kluga, a farmer from Akata Agame village in the Kpalime region, was reportedly tortured. Members of the Gendarmerie, the police force in rural areas, detained him for four days in mid-June in connection with inquiries about a missing farmer. He was allegedly subjected to severe beatings and other abuses while in custody, then released without charge. The National Commission for Human Rights' investigation into his reported torture had not been concluded by the end of the year.

An Amnesty International delegation visited Togo in October and met President Eyadéma, government ministers and other officials. The delegates were permitted access to the remaining 14 prisoners sentenced in December 1986 and the three held at Akodessewa police station. The President assured the delegation that the prisoners' conditions would be improved. He also told the delegates of his personal opposition to the death penalty and said the government would consider

236

steps to abolish it.

Amnesty International drew several cases to the attention of the National Commission for Human Rights, including the reported torture of Kwasikuma Kluga, and received replies to most of its inquiries.

TRINIDAD AND TOBAGO

At least 24 people were sentenced to death after being convicted of murder. This brought the total number of prisoners on death row to 94. There have been no executions for 10 years. Two prisoners under sentence of death were released during the year. A Commission of Inquiry into the effectiveness and status of the death penalty was established in March.

In February the Judicial Committee of the Privy Council (JCPC) in London, which acts as the final court of appeal for Trinidad and Tobago, quashed the murder conviction of Shabir Ali. He was released in March. The JCPC considered that inadmissible hearsay evidence presented at his trial may have influenced the jury and that therefore a miscarriage of justice may possibly have occurred. This was the first time since 1981 that the JCPC had allowed an appeal from a prisoner under sentence of death in Trinidad and Tobago.

James Scott, the longest serving death row prisoner, was granted a presidential pardon in August on the country's independence anniversary and was released from prison. He had been convicted of murder in 1974 and had exhausted all legal appeals.

The Commission of Inquiry approved by the Senate in April 1988 to examine the death penalty (see *Amnesty International Report 1989*) was appointed in March. Its task was to consider whether the penalty,

mandatory for murder and treason, should be retained. The three-member Commission invited the public to submit memoranda on the issue.

In April Amnesty International wrote to the government welcoming the appointment of the Commission and expressing the hope that this would lead to the abolition of the death penalty. In June the organization submitted to the Commission a detailed statement of the reasons why the death penalty should be abolished.

The government did not reply to a letter sent to it by Amnesty International in 1988 about a pending sentence of flogging (see *Amnesty International Report 1989*), and it was not known whether the sentence had been carried out.

TUNISIA

Over 90 political prisoners, some of whom may have been prisoners of conscience, were released in amnesties in March, May and November. At least five people believed to be prisoners of conscience were arrested during the year. Tens of political activists, some of whom might have been prisoners of conscience, were reported to have been detained briefly, tortured or ill-treated, and then released uncharged. Three people were sentenced to death but there were no executions. In November President Zine El-Abidine Ben Ali stated publicly that he would not sign any orders for execution.

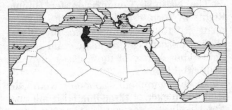

The first general elections were held since the change of government in November 1987. President Ben Ali's ruling *Rassemblement constitutionnel démocratique* (RCD), Constitutional Democratic Rally, was returned to power in April, winning all seats. Several parties which had applied for official registration had not been accorded legal status by the end of the year. They included the *Hizb al-Nahda*, Party of the Renaissance, (formerly the *Mouvement de la tendance islamique*, MTI,

Islamic Tendency Movement).

Following an amnesty in March, 35 supporters of an Islamic movement, some of whom were believed to be prisoners of conscience, were released. They had been detained without trial since November 1987. In May the remaining detainees from this group, including Professor Moncef Ben Salem and Sayyed Ben Burawi Ferjani, were among 52 political prisoners released in an amnesty to mark the end of Ramadan. Some of them, including Sayyed Ferjani, were ill after having allegedly been tortured in detention. Mohamed Chemmam and Ali al-Zraoui, who were imprisoned after an unfair trial in September 1987, were also among those released.

Under a general amnesty signed by the President in July, civil rights were restored to 5,416 former prisoners, including political prisoners. Further political prisoners were released in an amnesty on 7 November to mark the second anniversary of President Ben Ali's accession to power.

Jalloul Azzouna, a lecturer at the University of Tunis and leader of a faction of the *Parti de l'unité populaire* (PUP), Popular Unity Party, was arrested in July. In August he was sentenced to one year's imprisonment and a fine by the Tunis Court of First Instance, confirmed by the Court of Appeal in September. He was considered a prisoner of conscience. He was accused of libelling the Head of State and distributing unauthorized communiques. In one communique he claimed that "terror brigades" of plainclothes government security officers had slashed tyres and broken windows of the cars of nine PUP executive council members. He was among those released in the November amnesty.

Radhia Nasraoui, one of 20 lawyers defending Jalloul Azzouna, was arrested by plainclothes police immediately after the trial on charges of spreading false information likely to damage public order and defamation of the security forces. The charges arose out of statements she had made at the trial in which she described the police as aggressors and attacked the Press Law. She was released after four days.

Four members of the *Parti communiste des ouvriers tunisiens* (PCOT), Tunisian Workers' Communist Party, were possible prisoners of conscience. Afifa Hizem, Fethia Hizem, Hamdi Laabidi and Mortadha Laabidi were arrested in September in Gafsa for distributing leaflets. Their houses were searched at night by police without search warrants, although these are required by law. Mortadha Laabidi alleged that he was tortured. The four were convicted of various charges including belonging to an illegal organization and distributing illegal literature. They were sentenced in October to between eight and 18 months' imprisonment. Two others, Ammar Amroussia and Chafik Aijadi, who were tried *in absentia* on similar charges, were sentenced to 18 months' imprisonment. All those in custody were released on bail pending appeal.

Bechir Essid, a lawyer and founder of the *Union démocratique unioniste* (UDU), Democratic Unionist Union, was arrested in September. He was charged with defamation and libel of the President in connection with a communique he was said to have distributed. He was allegedly ill-treated and denied medicines while in detention. At the end of the year he was still being held without trial.

During the year tens of political activists, some of whom may have been prisoners of conscience, were arrested and briefly detained. Most were released without charge or trial. They included supporters and members of the national or local leadership of *Hizb al-Nahda*, the PCOT, and other unregistered organizations.

Four prisoners convicted after an unfair trial in September 1987 of participating in bomb explosions in tourist hotels or acid attacks remained in prison at the end of the year (see *Amnesty International Report 1988*).

There were new reports of torture and ill-treatment of prisoners. Many short-term political detainees said that they were ill-treated and beaten while in police custody. Mabrouk Abdeljaouad, Moncef Matalla, Moulidi Abassi, Mohamed al-Tahir Hamouda and Noureddine Brahimi, who were arrested in June and released four days later, claimed to have been severely tortured. They said they had been beaten, subjected to *falaqa* (beating on the soles of the feet), suspended in contorted positions, and had ether applied to their genitals. Medical certificates appeared to corroborate their allegations.

Three death sentences were passed. At least three sentences passed in 1987 and 1988 remained in force. There were no executions.

238

Amnesty International welcomed the amnesties of prisoners but expressed concern about the continued imprisonment of prisoners of conscience and other political prisoners sentenced after unfair trials. It also expressed concern about reports of torture and ill-treatment of prisoners. Amnesty International urged the Head of State to commute all death sentences and to abolish the death penalty. It had earlier welcomed President Ben Ali's personal opposition to the death penalty expressed publicly on several occasions, including to an Amnesty International delegation in April 1988.

TURKEY

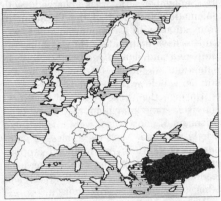

Thousands of people were imprisoned for political reasons, including hundreds of prisoners of conscience. Political trials in military and state security courts did not meet international standards of fair trial. The use of torture continued to be widespread and systematic, in some cases resulting in death. Civilian and military courts passed at least 10 death sentences. At the end of the year 255 people under sentence of death had exhausted all appeals and their sentences awaited ratification by parliament. Iranian asylum-seekers, including some recognized as refugees by the Office of the United Nations High Commissioner for Refugees (UNHCR), were forcibly returned to Iran.

In November Prime Minister Turgut Özal was elected President. At the end of the year a state of emergency was still in force in eight provinces in southeast Turkey where the security forces were engaged in counter-insurgency operations against Kurdish secessionist guerrillas. Many human rights

violations by the security forces were alleged to have taken place in the context of this conflict. The guerrillas were also reported to have carried out attacks on the civilian population, taking prisoners and torturing and killing some of them.

Draft amendments to the Penal Code to shorten the maximum detention period and grant lawyers access to detainees in police custody were announced by the cabinet in September. A prime-ministerial decree of the same month gave detainees access to their lawyers in some exceptional cases, but not to their families and doctors. The proposed measures fell short of internationally recognized standards and did not go before the Grand National Assembly during 1989.

The independent Human Rights Association estimated that there were approximately 5,000 political prisoners at the end of 1989. They included hundreds of prisoners of conscience, among them members of political organizations, trade unions and banned Kurdish groups, as well as journalists and religious activists.

Hundreds of people were prosecuted during 1989 for membership of banned non-violent political parties, under Article 141 of the Penal Code. Among them were some 20 people who returned to Turkey after years in exile. In September Hüseyin Hasançebi, S. Ekrem Çakiroglu and Tektas Agaoglu were detained on arrival in Istanbul. They were committed to Sagmalcilar Prison and charged with activities on behalf of the Turkish Socialist Workers' Party (TSIP). On 3 November they were released, but at the end of the year their trial continued in Istanbul State Security Court.

Another group of exiles who returned in September included Ahmet Kardam, Seref Yildiz and Mehmet Bozisik, who publicly announced that they were members of the Central Committee of the banned Turkish United Communist Party (TBKP). They were sent to prison and charged under Articles 141 and 142 ("making communist propaganda"). Their trial was due to start on 19 January 1990 in Istanbul State Security Court.

The trial of Haydar Kutlu and Nihat Sargin, leaders of the TBKP imprisoned since November 1987, which had started in mid-1988 in Ankara State Security Court, was still continuing at the end of 1989 (see *Amnesty International Report 1989*).

The sentences passed under Article 141 on Ali Ugur and six other alleged members of the Turkish Communist Party (TKP) in November 1988 by Izmir State Security Court were confirmed in May by the appeal court. The six, who had been released pending appeal, were reimprisoned (see *Amnesty International Report 1989*). Ali Ugur had been kept in detention since his arrest.

The Minister of the Interior stated that 4,426 people were detained between January and June in southeast Turkey where most of the population is of Kurdish origin. Of these, 1,558 had been charged. Most of the Kurdish political prisoners known to Amnesty International were charged with violent offences, but some were prisoners of conscience held for non-violent political or cultural activities.

In February six members of the Kayseri Branch of the legal Socialist Party (SP) were charged under Article 142 and taken to Kayseri Closed Prison. They had expressed hopes for the freedom and liberties of Kurdish and Turkish citizens and had condemned "state terror" in southeast Turkey in a telegram. In May they were convicted by Kayseri State Security Court and sentenced to 50 months' imprisonment. However, the verdict was quashed by the appeal court in October and the prisoners were released.

Trials of religious activists charged under Article 163 for "attempting to change the secular nature of the State" continued. Münip and Ömer Erdem had been imprisoned since mid-1988 on charges of leadership of the brotherhood of the *Nurcus*, an alleged anti-secular organization. In 1988 they were convicted by Izmir State Security Court but in June the appeal court quashed the sentence. They were retried by Izmir State Security Court in October on a fresh charge and sentenced to 50 months' imprisonment, but released pending further appeal.

Writers, publishers and journalists were imprisoned under various articles of the Penal Code, including Article 142, Article 159 ("insulting the State authorities") and Article 312 ("incitement to commit a crime"). Some of them were also charged under Article 141.

Celal Gül and Mehmet Bayrak, co-owners of a political journal, *Özgür Gelecek*, and Bekir Kesen, the editor-in-chief, were detained on 22 July in Ankara. Their jour-nal had reported a speech about the situation of Kurdish women, given at a women's congress in June by Nuray Özkan, a doctor. She was charged with making separatist propaganda. The other three were charged with membership of a banned Kurdish organization, *Özgürlük Yolu*, Path of Freedom. Nuray Özkan was released on 27 September, the others on 6 October, but the trial of all four was still in progress at the end of the year.

Many political prisoners have been sentenced to imprisonment or death after unfair trials. Although martial law was lifted in 1987, trials before military courts continued. Over 60,000 people were sentenced by military courts during the 1980s. Some defendants had been held in pre-trial detention for more than eight years. Since 1984 thousands of political prisoners have been tried before state security courts. Both military and state security courts have failed to investigate allegations of torture and in some cases have permitted statements extracted under torture to be used as evidence. In addition, most defendants have not been granted facilities for an adequate defence.

There were many new allegations of widespread and systematic torture of political and criminal detainees and prisoners. Even children were among the reported victims. The same methods of torture were reported by almost all detainees: blindfolding and being stripped naked, beatings on all parts of the body, particularly the soles of the feet (*falaqa*), hosing with ice-cold water and applying electric shocks.

In most cases the victims were held incommunicado in police stations, but allegations of torture and ill-treatment also came from high-security prisons for political prisoners, known as E- and L-type prisons.

One case was that of Salih Zeyrek, aged 19. In July he and seven villagers from Sirnak district were interrogated for over 10 days at the local rural police station. Salih Zeyrek said that he was confined in a closed barrel for 24 hours. In addition to the July heat, cotton wool was burned on the lid. The others were forced into the barrel in turn. Those not in the barrel were constantly beaten.

Oguz Yaman, a defendant accused of belonging to a banned organization, testified in court that in Mersin Police Headquarters he was stripped naked, his

240

legs and arms were tied to the ground and he was given electric shocks to his penis and other parts of his body. He said that he was then hosed with ice-cold water. This testimony was typical of hundreds received during the year.

Some prisoners were reported to have died following torture and ill-treatment. Mehmet Yalçinkaya and Hüseyin Hüsnü Eroglu, imprisoned for alleged membership of a banned Kurdish organization, died on 2 August. They had been on hunger-strike for 35 days in Eskisehir Prison. On 2 August they and 257 other hunger-striking prisoners were transferred to Aydin Prison in metal vans ventilated only by a small hole in the back, despite the heat. When the 15-hour journey was over, they were reportedly stripped naked, hosed with ice-cold water and beaten. The Public Prosecutor in Aydin announced that an autopsy had established that the two prisoners died of dehydration. However, a second autopsy on Hüseyin Hüsnü Eroglu reportedly also found bruises on his body.

At least 10 people were sentenced to death by military and civilian courts. Other death sentences were confirmed by appeal courts. By the end of the year the number of people under sentence of death who had exhausted all judicial appeals had reached 255. Draft amendments to the Penal Code announced by the cabinet in September would reduce the 29 offences carrying a mandatory death penalty by 13. However, the changes referred to provisions hardly ever used.

Hundreds of Iranians fleeing from persecution in Iran continued to seek refuge in Turkey. Those caught crossing the border without authorization were frequently denied access to the relevant Turkish officials or to the UNHCR to have their asylum claims assessed. Many were summarily returned, including some recognized as refugees by the UNHCR. It emerged that seven members of a Kurdish opposition group in Iran, two of whom had been recognized by the UNHCR, were executed in Iran shortly after being forcibly returned in November 1988.

Amnesty International continued throughout the year to call for the release of prisoners of conscience, for fair and prompt trials for all political prisoners, and for an end to torture and the death penalty. In April Amnesty International submitted to the government a revised list of 219 names of prisoners who reportedly had died in custody between December 1979 and March 1989, asking about the cause of death. At the end of the year replies on 174 cases had been received, acknowledging ill-treatment in 41 cases.

The Turkish authorities also responded to a number of specific torture allegations raised by Amnesty International. In some cases they stated that investigations were still in progress, in others that medical reports had shown that torture had not been inflicted.

In January Amnesty International published a report on the systematic abuse of human rights in Turkey, followed in October by a further report on torture and unfair trials of political prisoners.

In June Amnesty International wrote to the Prime Minister about three Greek Cypriots, missing since 1974 when they were reportedly taken prisoner by the Turkish Armed Forces (see *Amnesty International Report 1975, 1976* and *1978*). A reply was received in July from the Turkish Cypriot leader, Rauf Denktas (see Cyprus).

Amnesty International sought to prevent the *refoulement* of Iranian refugees. It appealed to the Turkish authorities on behalf of a number of individuals and continued to urge that all asylum-seekers be given access to fair procedures for assessing their asylum claims.

Amnesty International delegates observed the trial of 20 alleged members of the Turkish Communist Party/Union (TKP/B) in March in Malatya State Security Court. All 12 defendants present alleged that they had been tortured. In September Amnesty International delegates observed the trial before Izmir Criminal Court of Dr Alpaslan Berktay, President of Izmir Human Rights Association, charged with insulting the authorities for having called torturers "the devil in person". Dr Berktay was acquitted in October.

In February Amnesty International drew attention to its concerns about torture in an oral statement to the United Nations Commission on Human Rights and in May the organization submitted information about its concerns for United Nations review under a procedure, established by Economic and Social Council Resolutions 728F/1503, for confidential consideration of communications about human rights violations.

UGANDA

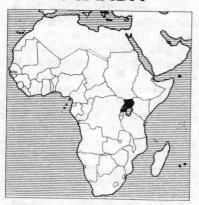

At least 2,300 political detainees held without trial were released but more than 1,000 political arrests occurred, mostly in areas of armed conflict. More than 2,000 people remained in detention without charge or trial at the end of 1989. Seventeen people faced trial on charges of treason, which carries the death penalty. Prisoners in military custody were reportedly tortured and ill-treated and government forces operating in the north and east reportedly killed civilians extrajudicially. At least 10 prisoners were executed, 23 others were facing execution after the Supreme Court rejected their appeals, and at least 35 people were sentenced to death.

Armed opposition to the government of President Yoweri Museveni continued in several areas. Government forces clashed in the north with groups belonging to the Holy Spirit Mobile Force and with a dissident faction of the Uganda People's Democratic Army (UPDA). In the east, the rebel Uganda People's Army (UPA) was active in Kumi and Soroti districts. A small rebel group, the Ruwenzururu, was active in Kasese District in the southwest. Villagers were killed by rebels in all three areas and prisoners were reportedly killed by the army in both the north and the east.

In June the National Resistance Council (NRC), Uganda's Parliament, passed the Magistrate's Courts (Criminal Procedure/ Special Provisions) Act. This permits Magistrate's Courts in areas of insurgency to try people on charges carrying the death penalty. It also empowers the Head of State to appoint anyone as a magistrate, irrespec-

tive of the person's legal qualifications. Such magistrates are to be assisted during trials by a soldier and a locally elected official. The act removes guarantees of fair trial by placing the burden of proof on the accused and by granting the courts discretion to convict on the basis of uncorroborated testimony. No trials under the new act were known to have taken place by the end of the year.

The National Resistance Army (NRA) continued to carry out police and military duties. In October President Museveni directed the army to shoot automobile robbers who resisted arrest, following a spate of car thefts in the capital, Kampala. The army was also responsible for virtually all political arrests. Many of the detainees, who were effectively held illegally and without referral to the courts, were kept in ordinary prisons, where they were known as "lodgers". Others, particularly people suspected of conspiring against the government, were held in military barracks by the army's military intelligence branch.

At least 2,300 political detainees, the overwhelming majority of them from northern and eastern Uganda, were released during the year. Most had been detained during counter-insurgency operations during the previous three years and were held without charge as "lodgers". Most of those released appear to have been civilians, rather than members of armed opposition groups, who had been suspected of supporting rebels. Some 600 detainees from Kitgum District were released during the first four months of the year. A further 1,075 from Kitgum, Lira and Apac districts were released in August. In October, 625 detainees, most of them from Kumi, Tororo and Soroti districts, were released: however, more than 300 of them were later rearrested in order to "protect" them, the government said, from mob justice.

At least 2,000 people remained in detention without charge or trial at the end of the year. More than 100 people suspected of armed opposition to the government were arrested in Gulu District in May and about 600 former soldiers were detained in July on suspicion of belonging to armed opposition groups. In September, 57 alleged NRA deserters and others suspected of involvement with the Ruwenzururu opposition group were arrested in Kasese District.

Among those held throughout the year

242

were people detained for allegedly plotting to overthrow the government. They included Major Fred Mpiso, who had been held without charge or trial at Luzira Prison since he was acquitted in March 1988 of treason. At least 28 people arrested in October 1988 in connection with an alleged coup attempt were also reportedly still held. Unconfirmed reports received in May indicated that two soldiers, Godfrey Kiyindire and Emazi Zzibu, and a civilian, Ssbuliba, had died in custody.

The courts ordered the release of some "lodgers" on writs of *habeas corpus*, but in some cases the authorities did not comply. In May a court order for the release of Stanley Owunu, a customs official arrested by the NRA in October 1988, was ignored by the Attorney General and prison authorities. A second release order issued in June was also ignored. The High Court then issued a third order for Stanley Owunu's release, but it was not known if he was freed.

Ten soldiers and civilians accused of conspiring against the government appeared before the High Court on charges of treason, a capital offence. Ben Masaba Mityero and three others accused of seeking to reinstate former president Milton Obote went on trial in June. They told the court that they had been tortured following their arrest in January 1987. Their trial was still continuing at the end of the year. The trial of Captain Frank Kibuuka and five others, which began in November, was also in progress at the end of the year. The defendants in this trial had been held since January 1987. Seven other people accused of committing political offences between August and October 1989 were also charged with treason and remanded in custody by the Jinja District Court in November.

The army reportedly tortured and ill-treated prisoners, particularly in areas of armed conflict. For example, villagers detained or questioned by soldiers were reportedly subjected to severe beatings in Gulu District in May and in Soroti District in July. The body of one man allegedly killed in July by NRA soldiers in Dakabela, Soroti District, was bound in the manner known as *kandooya* or "three-piece" tying, a practice officially outlawed within the NRA in 1987 (see *Amnesty International Report 1988*). The victim's elbows, wrists and ankles were tied together, then all of the bindings were knotted together behind his back. Ill-treatment was also reported from areas without armed conflict. In August Pampilio Elungat, the bursar of Wairaka College in Jinja, died in detention in Gadaffi Barracks, Jinja, shortly after his arrest. A post-mortem examination revealed that he had been whipped before death.

Government soldiers reportedly carried out numerous extrajudicial executions during counter-insurgency operations, but few details of individual cases emerged. In February soldiers reportedly killed two women and their eight children at Bwobo, Gulu District, and at least 35 people were said to have been extrajudicially executed in May in the Bobi area, Gulu District. The May killings may have been the subject of a NRA inquiry, but no findings had been made public.

In July, 69 people held in NRA custody at Mukuru, Soroti District, died. Most of the victims suffocated after they were locked in an abandoned train. Others were allegedly beaten to death or shot. The government said that those responsible for the deaths would face execution and 14 army officers were arrested. It was not known if the arrested soldiers had been brought to trial.

Firing squads executed at least seven soldiers convicted by military tribunals of murder, armed robbery or rape. Soldiers appearing before such tribunals had no guaranteed right to legal counsel or to appeal against sentence or conviction. Nine soldiers were known to have been sentenced to death in other military courts but it was not known if they were executed.

Kassim Obura, a former deputy director of the Public Safety Unit, a security force unit responsible for killing a number of political prisoners in the 1970s, and two other people convicted of murder were hanged in March. These executions were the first carried out following civilian court trials since 1977. The Supreme Court dismissed the appeals of 23 other prisoners, most of whom were sentenced to death in the early 1980s for murder or robbery. It was not known if other executions took place. The High Court sentenced to death at least 26 people convicted of murder or robbery. They included Ali Fadhul, who had been a government minister in the 1970s and was found guilty of a murder committed in 1972.

In January an Amnesty International

delegation visited Uganda to compile information and meet officials. The NRA prevented the delegates from carrying out inquiries in the town of Gulu and ordered them to return to Kampala. In March Amnesty International published a report, *Uganda: The Human Rights Record 1986-1989*, which summarized human rights developments since President Museveni took power. In response to a government invitation, an Amnesty International delegation visited Uganda in April to discuss the report's contents. The delegates met President Museveni, ministers and other officials. The government denied both the use of torture and extrajudicial executions described in Amnesty International's report and the practice of incommunicado detention. However, the authorities agreed to investigate specific reports of torture and killings by military intelligence which had occurred in 1988. The government responded to reports of extrajudicial executions in 1986 and 1987, denying that any of the incidents reported had been unlawful killings.

Amnesty International welcomed the release of political detainees held without charge or trial and urged that others in detention also be released or given an opportunity to challenge the reasons for their detention before a court.

At the beginning of the year Amnesty International welcomed the announcement that a commission composed of civilians and military personnel was to investigate reports of extrajudicial executions by soldiers in Gulu District in late 1988. Several months later the government told Amnesty International that the commission's findings would soon be made public, but no findings had been disclosed by the end of the year. Amnesty International later expressed concern at reports of further extrajudicial executions and, in particular, at the deaths of 69 prisoners in Soroti District. Amnesty International also appealed to the government to cease executions and to abolish the death penalty.

UNION OF SOVIET SOCIALIST REPUBLICS

243

A new parliament began reforms which brought some laws closer to international standards on human rights. About 50 prisoners of conscience benefited from early release, but others were arrested during the year, particularly conscientious objectors to military service and critics of official policy on nationality issues. The authorities made wide use of administrative measures to restrict human rights: more than 2,000 people seeking to exercise their human rights were put in prison or psychiatric hospitals under administrative procedures for short periods; 20 people were killed and many others injured when armed security troops broke up peaceful public meetings. At the end of the year at least 60 people prosecuted under criminal law were still imprisoned, or forcibly confined in psychiatric hospitals, for exercising their human rights. Proposals to restrict the death penalty were deferred. Thirty-one death sentences came to light and at least five people were executed.

In May Mikhail Gorbachov became President of a new parliament, the Congress of People's Deputies. Intense interest in the elections — which offered voters a choice of candidates for the first time — forced constitutional issues to the front of the political picture throughout the year. Mass rallies in some parts of the USSR called for alternatives to the Communist Party of the Soviet Union or increased sovereignty for certain republics or ethnic groups. Violence erupted between some national and ethnic groups in the southern republics; in some cases troops were deployed to restore order.

244

The USSR maintained a public commitment to international human rights standards. In February it recognized the role of the International Court of Justice in disputes arising from the interpretation or application of the Convention against Torture and Other Cruel, Inhuman or Degrading Treatment or Punishment, and five other conventions. The new parliament began to implement reforms promised since 1987 which were apparently intended to give Soviet citizens more of the human rights guaranteed by international standards. In July it abolished the laws against "anti-Soviet agitation and propaganda" and "circulating anti-Soviet slander". These had penalized free expression and had been used to imprison hundreds of people since the 1960s. They were replaced by a law which prohibits public incitement to violent overthrow of the state. There was no change in the legal status of religious believers; they are still required to register their congregations with the authorities, thereby giving up rights such as evangelizing and teaching religion to children. However, the authorities lifted an administrative ban on Jehovah's Witnesses and Ukrainian Greek Catholics and allowed them to seek official registration for the first time.

Legal changes introduced at the end of the year offered the prospect of fairer trials. Suspects now have the right to contact a lawyer from the moment they are detained, arrested or charged. Previously they could be held incommunicado for up to nine months and were allowed to contact a lawyer only when the investigation had been completed, shortly before trial. Reports of ill-treatment during incommunicado detention had been common. Trial by jury was also introduced for capital offences and other grave crimes. Formerly, defendants were convicted and sentenced to death by a panel of three judges, only one of whom was professionally trained. A new Law on the Status of Courts set up a "judicial collegium" which appeared to strengthen the independence of judges. Previously, they were elected by local officials and were vulnerable to their influence. Now judges cannot be appointed or dismissed without the consent of fellow judges.

The policy of granting early releases to political prisoners continued, but more slowly than before. At least 49 were freed,

bringing to 465 the total known to have been so released since the authorities announced in February 1987 that they were reviewing prisoner cases. The 49 included 16 people who had been confined against their will in psychiatric hospitals for up to 21 years. At the end of the year at least 60 people were believed still imprisoned, or forcibly confined in psychiatric hospitals, for exercising their human rights. One was Eduard Kritsky, a trawler worker imprisoned since 1980, when he was arrested for carrying a placard saying "meat for the workers and non-party unions!".

In a statement to the United Nations (UN) Human Rights Committee in October, the USSR Minister of Justice acknowledged that "in the past people had been imprisoned for rightly criticizing negative aspects of Soviet society". He was reporting on Soviet compliance with the provisions of the International Covenant on Civil and Political Rights. Nevertheless, the authorities did not restore full civil rights to released prisoners of conscience so that many still found it impossible to get jobs, housing and medical help.

Most prisoners of conscience imprisoned during the year were conscientious objectors to military service. Fifteen, mostly Jehovah's Witnesses, were sentenced to up to three years' imprisonment for "evading regular call-up to active military service". Reports also emerged of another 10 men serving sentences imposed before 1989: this suggested that the real number of conscientious objectors held at the end of 1989 was higher than the 32 known to Amnesty International. In November constitutional provision for a civilian alternative to military service for conscientious objectors was introduced in Latvia but no such provision was made in the other 14 republics.

As in 1988, no one was reported imprisoned under laws that restricted religious activity. However, Pavel Solovyov, a Pentecostalist who held an outdoor service, was sentenced in March to three years' imprisonment for "hooliganism" in the Ukrainian city of Slavyansk. Other prosecutions ran counter to the spirit of the legal reforms. In November a court in Sverdlovsk in the Russian Republic sentenced a journalist, Sergey Kuznetsov, to three years' imprisonment for "defamation", after he had criticized local officials. The conduct of his case aroused the public concern of

Soviet journalists and members of parliament as well as human rights organizations in the USSR and abroad. In March Oleg Pletnyov was given 18 months' imprisonment for "illegal exit abroad" by a court in the Ukrainian city of Simferopol, although shortly afterwards parliament approved proposals recognizing the right to leave the country. He had not been released by the end of the year.

Many arrests were reported in areas of ethnic conflict in the southern republics of the USSR. However, martial law, curfews and, in Azerbaidzhan, a state of emergency made it difficult to obtain corroborative information. While most of the arrests were apparently for violent crimes, it seemed that some people were imprisoned for questioning official policy on nationality issues. At least 40 people may have been arrested on these grounds and charged with inciting racial hatred, disturbing the peace or holding illegal meetings. After several months' imprisonment, most were given suspended sentences or released pending trial. They included several Moldavians, some supporters of the Popular Front of Azerbaidzhan and 14 members of an unofficial Armenian Karabakh Committee.

The authorities made wide use of administrative measures to restrict human rights. More than 2,000 people seeking to exercise their human rights were put into "preventive detention" or under "administrative arrest", sometimes repeatedly. "Preventive detention" could be imposed by the militia or riot troops, without the sanction of a court or procurator, for up to three hours. In areas where a curfew was in force, it could last for up to 30 days. "Administrative arrest" of up to 15 days could be imposed by a single judge without the right of appeal.

During the election campaign these measures were used widely against people supporting unofficial candidates or advocating electoral boycotts. Other victims included those demonstrating against the June massacre of students in the Chinese capital of Beijing; people displaying national symbols in the Ukraine; Jews staging vigils for the right to emigrate; and members of unofficial information agencies concerned with politics and human rights. Often detainees were beaten. At least one was reportedly sent to Chernobyl, the radioactive site of a nuclear reactor which exploded in 1986. He was Petro Zelenyukh,

a priest of the Ukrainian Greek Catholic Church.

Eight people were believed to have been forcibly confined in psychiatric hospitals on political grounds during the year despite appeal provisions introduced in 1988 ostensibly to reduce the risk of such wrongful confinement. Four of them had contested official candidates for the elections: Vladimir Chebanu, Mikhail Mikhailov, Andrey Sharonov and Fyodor Yadamenko. All eight were confined under administrative procedures and released shortly afterwards. Another eight people who were put in psychiatric hospitals on political grounds before 1989 were believed still to be confined at the end of the year. In June a leading Soviet newspaper acknowledged for the first time that Soviet psychiatry had been systematically perverted for political reasons. *Literaturnaya gazeta (The Literary Gazette)* condemned the 1988 appeal provisions as inadequate and joined numerous Soviet legal scholars in recommending the adoption of a comprehensive law to safeguard the rights of people confined in psychiatric hospitals, which would be enforceable by the procuracy and courts.

In several parts of the USSR security forces armed with truncheons and shields broke up meetings which appeared to be peaceful. In the Georgian capital of Tbilisi in April, 20 people were killed and up to 3,000 were said to have been injured when soldiers and riot troops dispersed a crowd demonstrating for Georgian independence. The troops allegedly used firearms, shovels and poisonous gas. In his statement to the UN Human Rights Committee in October, the Minister of Justice said that the procedures for holding public meetings and deploying riot troops needed prompt review. The procedures were regulated by statutes adopted without any public discussion (see *Amnesty International Report 1989*). In some reported cases officials used force to disperse people who were unaware that they were attending unauthorized meetings.

Throughout the year prisoners kept in pre-trial custody alleged that they had been ill-treated. They included prisoners of conscience such as Sergey Kuznetsov and members of the Armenian Karabakh Committee, who said they had been systematically beaten in the Butyrka investigation prison in Moscow. People awaiting trial for capital crimes also alleged ill-treatment. Dmitry Berman, convicted of murder in March by a court in the Ukrainian city of Nikolayev on the basis of a confession, told the court that his confession had been extracted through beatings. He had spent seven months in incommunicado detention. People at his trial said one of his arms appeared to be dislocated. No independent investigation of his allegations was known to have been carried out. All the allegations referred to beatings before November, when suspects were given the right to more prompt access to a defence lawyer.

The new parliament deferred discussion of the draft Principles of Criminal Law, which would significantly restrict the scope of the death penalty (see *Amnesty International Report 1989*), and in the meantime ordered no stay on death sentences or executions. At least 31 death sentences were reported, four of them on people who would have been exempt if the proposed changes to criminal law had been adopted. They were a woman, two men aged over 60, and a man convicted of embezzlement. Unusually, a death sentence for murder and rape was passed before a crowd of 5,000 in a stadium in Naberezhnye Chelny in the Tatar autonomous republic, which raised doubts about the fairness of the trial. Five people were known to have been executed, and the execution of four others was thought probable after their clemency petitions were rejected in August. Death penalty statistics remained secret and the real number of people sentenced to death and executed was probably much higher.

One death sentence was reported commuted. Amnesty International welcomed this and urged the authorities to commute every death sentence of which it learned. It also appealed for the immediate release of all prisoners of conscience and the restoration of their full civil rights. In March a delegation went to Moscow as guests of the USSR Academy of Sciences and met government officials and legal scholars, as well as former prisoners of conscience and unofficial advocates of human rights. The delegation explained Amnesty International's concerns and explored the aims and progress of the current legislative review. A report published by Amnesty International in October, USSR: *Human Rights in a Time of Change*, made 12 recommendations to the USSR Government. These included the

ratification of the Optional Protocol to the International Covenant on Civil and Political Rights; the introduction of a civilian alternative to military service and a fair procedure for applying it; and the requirement that any compulsory psychiatric confinement be judicially approved.

Following the killings in Tbilisi in April, Amnesty International urged the Procurator General to investigate all the alleged incidents resulting in death or injury and to make public the instructions given to the security troops and the precautionary measures they allegedly took. It also asked him to investigate whether any of those who died were deliberately killed, and to ensure the release of any individuals imprisoned for non-violent political activity. At the end of the year it was trying to obtain the report completed in December by the USSR parliamentary commission that investigated the killings.

UNITED ARAB EMIRATES

A 15-year-old possible prisoner of conscience continued to be detained without charge or trial. At least three people were lashed in public as a judicial punishment. The government failed to respond to requests for an investigation into detailed allegations of torture.

Mahmud Sulaiman 'Abdi, a 15-year-old Somali national who was arrested in December 1987 (see *Amnesty International Report 1989*), continued to be detained without charge or trial at al-Wathba Central Prison in Abu Dhabi throughout the year. There was no information to suggest he had been involved in any illegal activities in the United Arab Emirates (UAE) and his imprisonment appeared to be connected with his father's political activities as an exiled opponent of the Somali Government. No further information was available on the fate or whereabouts of Isma'il al-Nouri, an Iraqi national detained in 1988 (see *Amnesty International Report 1989*).

On 10 October an unidentified woman received 80 lashes of the whip in public in Ras Al Khaymah as punishment for being found drunk in public. Later in October two unnamed youths, aged 16 and 18, were each sentenced to 550 lashes for theft. The sentences were carried out in public with the youths receiving approximately 40 lashes every Friday for three months.

In January Amnesty International wrote to the UAE President, His Highness Shaikh Zayed Ibn Sultan al-Nahayyan, to urge an inquiry into allegations of torture and ill-treatment of prisoners in al-Wathba Central Prison in 1988 and previous years (see *Amnesty International Report 1989*). Ronald Startup, a British national who had been held in the prison without charge or trial between July and October 1988, testi-fied that several of his fellow prisoners had been beaten and tortured. The authorities did not respond to Amnesty International's letter and no inquiry was believed to have been instituted. There was also no response to other inquiries by the organization, for example in relation to Mahmud Sulaiman 'Abdi.

Amnesty International urged the author-ities to abolish judicial floggings which constitute a form of torture, or cruel, inhuman or degrading treatment or punishment. It also appealed to the author-ities on behalf of several Somali and Iranian nationals said to be at risk of forcible repatriation to their countries of origin, where it was believed they would be at risk of torture or execution. The orga-nization was not aware of any cases of forcible repatriation of refugees.

UNITED KINGDOM

An official investigation into complaints about police behaviour after disturbances in London in 1985 was completed, but its findings were not made public. Four pris-oners who had been convicted of murder in 1975 after bomb attacks in England had their convictions quashed as a result of evidence that police had lied in court about their alleged confessions. Six other people, also sentenced in 1975 on the basis of disputed evidence to life impris-onment for murder, remained imprisoned. Investigations into killings by the security

forces continued to be hampered by **247** delays and procedural constraints on inquests and by government refusals to make public the findings of police inquiries. The government continued to reject proposals for a judicial inquiry to examine disputed killings and re-evaluate the procedures under which investiga-tions and inquests are held in Northern Ireland. Nor would it consider a judicial examination of all the available evidence concerning the killings of three members of the Irish Republican Army (IRA) by British soldiers in Gibraltar in 1988. Evidence emerged of collusion between members of the security forces in Northern Ireland and loyalist armed groups. Asylum-seekers were expelled without being allowed an adequate oppor-tunity to present their cases. A court ruled that asylum-seekers who had been returned against their will to Sri Lanka in 1988 should be allowed to return to the United Kingdom (UK).

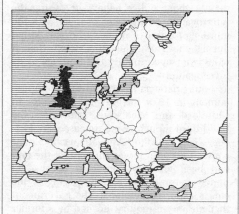

Armed groups from both the minority Catholic and the majority Protestant com-munities in Northern Ireland continued to resort to violence in support of their demands. Republican armed groups such as the IRA are opposed to the British pres-ence in Northern Ireland and fight for a united Ireland. Members of security forces, loyalist leaders and civilians have been killed as a result of IRA attacks, mainly in Northern Ireland but also in England and continental Europe. Loyalist armed groups, notably the Ulster Volunteer Force (UVF) and the Ulster Freedom Fighters, want Northern Ireland to remain a part of the UK. Their acts of violence are mainly directed against the Catholic population. It was reported that during 1989, 54 people were killed by the IRA, 19 by loyalist groups, and four by the security forces.

The government continued to derogate from those articles of the European Convention on Human Rights and the International Covenant on Civil and Political Rights which state that anyone arrested has the right to be brought promptly before a judge. This right was violated in cases where people had been arrested under the Prevention of Terrorism Act, which allows suspects to be held for up to seven days without judicial supervision (see Amnesty International Report 1989).

In September the Police Complaints Authority (PCA) brought disciplinary charges against the senior police officer who led inquiries into disturbances at London's Broadwater Farm estate in 1985 (see Amnesty International Report 1988 and 1989). The in camera disciplinary hearing had not taken place by the end of the year. The charges followed an investigation supervised by the PCA into complaints about police behaviour during the interrogation of juveniles charged with the murder of a police officer who was killed during the riot. The PCA stated that it would not make public the findings of its investigation.

Four prisoners sentenced to life imprisonment in 1975 for IRA pub bombings in Guildford and Woolwich, known as the "Guildford Four", were released in October. The Court of Appeal quashed their convictions after it was shown that the four had been wrongly convicted because of police malpractice, including lying to the courts about confessions. The government then set up an inquiry, headed by a former senior judge, into the circumstances of the convictions and into the reasons it took so long for crucial information to be disclosed. The inquiry was also to look into wider policy issues, such as the use of uncorroborated confessions as the basis for prosecution, the adequacy of safeguards for suspects in terrorist cases, and the procedures used to investigate possible miscarriages of justice.

Six people sentenced to life imprisonment in 1975 for IRA bombings in Birmingham, known as the "Birmingham Six", remained imprisoned. The six consistently claimed that their confessions resulted from ill-treatment and threats of violence while being held incommunicado (see Amnesty International Report 1988

and 1989). New information added to concern about the reliability of the convictions. The government's assertion that the prisoners' allegations of ill-treatment by police were groundless was undermined in June when the West Midlands Serious Crimes Squad, some of whose officers had interrogated the six in 1974, was disbanded. Some police officers from the squad had been involved in obtaining confessions subsequently found by courts to be unreliable. An investigation into the practices of the disbanded squad was opened, supervised by the PCA and carried out by a senior officer from another police force. The investigation, which covered only the cases handled by the squad since 1986, was continuing at the end of the year. Repeated requests for the investigation to include the cases of the "Birmingham Six" were rejected by the police. On 23 November the European Parliament voted to have the case of the six Birmingham prisoners investigated by its Legal Affairs Committee.

Inquests into the deaths of six unarmed people killed in 1982 by the security forces in Northern Ireland had still not been completed at the end of the year. Of these, the inquest into the deaths of Gervaise McKerr, Eugene Toman and Sean Burns, which began in November 1988, was adjourned because of an appeal to the Court of Appeal (see Amnesty International Report 1989). It was further postponed in January 1989 after the government appealed against the judgment of the Court of Appeal to the House of Lords. The appeal was not resolved during 1989, delaying inquests into some 17 killings by members of the security forces.

A police inquiry, carried out between 1984 and 1986 by senior police officers John Stalker and Colin Sampson, found evidence that police officers had conspired to pervert the course of justice after the 1982 killings. However, the report of the inquiry continued to be withheld from the public on grounds of "national security" (see Amnesty International Report 1989).

New reports suggested that evidence from Spanish police officers could be crucial in answering questions left unresolved by a coroner's inquest into the deaths of three unarmed IRA members in Gibraltar (see Amnesty International Report 1989). Mairead Farrell, Daniel McCann and Sean Savage had been shot dead in March 1988 in disputed circumstances by British soldiers. The UK Government said that the three had planned a bomb attack; explosives were later found in Spain. Some eyewitnesses testified at the inquest, held in Gibraltar in September 1988, that the three were shot without warning. They also stated that after the victims fell to the ground, they were shot again while lying incapacitated. The soldiers said that they had continued shooting until the three were dead because they believed — wrongly — that the three were carrying a device which could set off a bomb. The jury found that the three had been lawfully killed. British intelligence officers testified at the inquest that they had received no prior warning that the three suspects were going to enter Gibraltar on 6 March 1988. Some Spanish police officers reportedly contradicted this after the inquest. They stated that the British authorities had been notified that the three were heading towards Gibraltar on that day. Although the new reports did not provide a clear picture of what had happened between 4 and 6 March 1988 in Spain, they served to heighten concern about the Gibraltar inquest's failure to examine fully the circumstances of the killings, including evidence from Spanish surveillance teams.

Evidence emerged that intelligence files on republican suspects were being handed over by members of the security forces in Northern Ireland to members of loyalist armed groups. In some instances these files were used to target individuals and kill them. In August Loughlin Maginn was killed by the clandestine UVF, which claimed that he was a liaison officer of the IRA. When his family challenged this claim, the UVF revealed that they had obtained their information from police files which were in their possession. Earlier in the year two members of the security forces were given 18-month suspended sentences for passing confidential files and photographs of IRA suspects to loyalist organizations that carry out sectarian killings. After the convictions, one of them resigned from the Ulster Defence Regiment but the other remained a soldier in the British Army.

In mid-September the new Chief Constable of the Royal Ulster Constabulary, Hugh Annesley, appointed John Stevens, the Deputy Chief Constable of Cambridgeshire, to investigate the disappearance of security documents from police and army bases. By the end of September lists containing over 250 names of suspects had been given to the news media by members of the security forces or by loyalist groups. In October the authorities said they had revised procedures for the handling of intelligence information on suspects by members of the security forces.

A number of cases illustrated deficiencies in procedures for dealing with asylum applications. In July the High Court ruled that five Tamil asylum-seekers, whom the authorities had forcibly returned to Sri Lanka in 1988, should be allowed to return to the UK. The procedures had allowed the five no opportunity to appeal against refusal of asylum before being returned to Sri Lanka, where at least two of them were reportedly detained and tortured (see Sri Lanka).

The authorities returned a number of Turkish Kurds to Turkey, reportedly without fully examining their claims for asylum. A Turkish Kurd, who had been identified as a refugee by the Office of the United Nations High Commissioner for Refugees, was expelled. Selahattin Ozberk stated that he had recently been beaten during interrogation by the Turkish police. The authorities refused his application for asylum and expelled him, without giving him any opportunity for an appeal to be heard. He was, however, allowed to travel to Italy.

In March Amnesty International called on the government to investigate the overall pattern of police behaviour in the wake of the 1985 Broadwater Farm riot. It said that allegations made by detainees and rulings of trial court judges revealed evidence of police interrogation procedures which put at risk the fairness of subsequent trials. The organization therefore urged the government to review fully the cases of all those convicted of serious offences in connection with the disturbances on the basis of uncorroborated and contested confessions. The government replied that it had no role in the PCA investigation, although it believed that the issues raised by Amnesty International were being dealt with in the context of that investigation. The government stated that if the PCA investigation were to provide grounds for cases to be referred to the Court of Appeal, the Home Secretary would consider them.

Amnesty International sent an observer to the appeal hearing of the "Guildford

250

Four" in October, and welcomed their release. In the light of new information on the "Birmingham Six", Amnesty International urged the government to review their cases. The organization reiterated its concern that a considerable body of evidence existed that the six men had been ill-treated while in police custody and that their confessions could have been involuntary.

During a meeting held in April Amnesty International told the Secretary of State for Northern Ireland about its concern over the lack of thorough investigations into disputed killings by security forces in Northern Ireland and the fact that results of investigations were not made public. Amnesty International renewed its call for the government to establish a full judicial inquiry into disputed killings in Northern Ireland, focusing in particular on the procedures used to investigate such incidents and on legislation governing the use of lethal force. It also expressed concern that inquests into the disputed killings of 1982 had still not been completed.

In April Amnesty International published *Investigating Lethal Shootings: The Gibraltar Inquest*. This report outlined the organization's concerns relating to the 1988 shootings in Gibraltar and the coroner's inquest into the deaths. Amnesty International's delegates who observed the inquest found that the proceedings were conducted fairly but failed to bring out the full facts. They also found that the inquest failed to answer the main question raised by the Gibraltar killings: whether the three unarmed IRA members had been killed as a result of an official policy to eliminate or permit the elimination of specific individuals rather than to arrest them. The evidence was from the outset incomplete. Details of government policy, the planning of the operation, and the quality of the intelligence information were not revealed because the government blocked information. Crucial forensic evidence was lacking as well as testimonies from Spanish officers involved in the surveillance operation before the three were killed. The coroner had explicitly discouraged the jury from reaching an open verdict (one which does not reach a conclusion on how death occurred). Given the complex and contradictory evidence presented and the absence of crucial evidence, Amnesty International believed that it was wrong to discourage

such a verdict. The organization urged the government to establish a judicial examination of all the evidence in this case, including testimony by Spanish officers. Amnesty International considered that existing inquest procedures were inadequate for a full investigation of the circumstances surrounding disputed killings. It called on the government to ensure effective procedures for fully investigating and explaining disputed killings by its security forces.

UNITED STATES OF AMERICA

Sixteen prisoners were executed in 1989. At the end of the year more than 2,300 people were under sentence of death in 34 states and under US military law. The Supreme Court ruled that juvenile offenders as young as 16 and the mentally retarded could be executed. However, one state prohibited the execution of the mentally retarded. Federal legislation to reintroduce the death penalty and extend it to crimes to which it did not previously apply was pending before Congress at the end of the year. Amnesty International continued to investigate a number of criminal cases in which it was alleged that the prosecutions were politically motivated. There were concerns relating to the trial of a member of the Puerto Rican independence movement.

President George Bush called on Congress to introduce the death penalty under federal law for murder and drug-trafficking. Legislation pending before Congress at the end of 1989 sought to reintroduce the death penalty under federal law for a broad range of crimes including espionage, treason, assassination of the president and other offences involving murder. It would also extend the death penalty to offences to which it did not previously apply, such as attempted assassination of the president. Amnesty International appealed to members of Congress to oppose the reintroduction of the death penalty at federal level and its extension to new crimes. International human rights standards, including the American Convention on Human Rights (which the USA has signed but not ratified), state that the use of the death penalty should not be extended.

At least eight states passed legislation increasing the number of crimes punishable by death. However, proposals to reintroduce the death penalty in 11 abolitionist states failed.

In September a committee of federal judges recommended strict new limits on judicial review of capital cases, with the aim of reducing delay in carrying out the death penalty. The legislation was pending before Congress at the end of 1989. Amnesty International was concerned that the proposed changes would reduce the judicial scrutiny of capital cases, which could result in an increased number of executions, possibly based on miscarriages of justice. In a letter to the majority and minority leaders of the US Senate in November, it urged Congress to recognize current problems surrounding the death penalty's use, including race discrimination and the severe strain it places on the criminal justice system.

Death sentences continued to be imposed and carried out, especially in southern states. Sixteen prisoners were executed in 1989, bringing the number of executions since 1977 to 120. Four executions each were carried out in Alabama and in Texas; two in both Florida and Nevada and the others in Georgia, Mississippi, Missouri and Virginia. An estimated 300 new death sentences were imposed. Amnesty International appealed for clemency whenever it learned that an execution was imminent.

Despite judicial safeguards, evidence suggested that the death penalty continued to be applied in a racially discriminatory manner (see *Amnesty International Report 1988*). Although blacks and whites were the victims of homicide in almost equal numbers, death sentences were more often passed when the victim was white.

Between 1976 (when the death penalty was reinstated by the courts) and the end of 1989, 120 defendants were executed. They had been sentenced to death for the murder of 121 victims. Of these, 101 were white and 20 were black or from another ethnic minority group. No white offender was executed during this period for the murder of just one black victim.

State governments have maintained that these disparities are due to differences in the types of crime committed by or against members of different racial groups. However, research studies have isolated race as a key factor in death sentencing, after allowing for differences in the types of homicide.

Leo Edwards, convicted of murder in 1980, was executed in Mississippi on 21 June. Leo Edwards and the victim were black, as was about 30 per cent of the population in the county where the trial took place. But the case was heard by an all-white jury, after the prosecution excluded all seven black potential jurors. The Supreme Court had prohibited the exclusion of members of a defendant's own race from a trial jury solely on account of their race in 1986. However, this ruling was announced after Leo Edwards' conviction had been affirmed on direct appeal and was not applied retroactively to such cases.

On 26 June the Supreme Court ruled by five votes to four that the execution of juvenile offenders as young as 16 did not constitute "cruel and unusual" punishment (see *Amnesty International Report 1989*). The court said it had looked to the USA's standards, not the sentencing practices of other countries, in determining what constituted "evolving standards of decency". Amnesty International had submitted an *amicus curiae* (friend of the court) brief in September 1988 presenting evidence on international practice and standards prohibiting the execution of minors.

On 13 July the Indiana Supreme Court set aside the death sentence imposed on Paula Cooper, a 15-year-old offender. It held her death sentence to be "unique and disproportionate" in light of Indiana's 1987 law establishing 16 as the minimum age for the imposition of the death penalty. At the end of the year 28 juvenile offenders were under sentence of death in 12 states.

On 26 June the Supreme Court ruled by five votes to four that the execution of mentally retarded prisoners was not

252

categorically prohibited, provided those responsible for passing sentence took this factor into consideration. The appeal had been brought by John Paul Penry in Texas, who was found to have an intelligence quotient (IQ) of between 50 and 63 and a mental age of seven. He was sentenced to death for the rape and murder of a woman in 1979. The Supreme Court set aside his death sentence because the sentencing jury had not been instructed that it could consider his mental retardation as mitigating evidence (see *Amnesty International Report 1989*).

In May Maryland became the second state to enact legislation prohibiting the death penalty for defendants found to be mentally retarded. At least 10 per cent of prisoners under sentence of death nationwide are thought to be mentally retarded.

Horace Dunkins, a black, mentally retarded prisoner, was executed in Alabama on 14 July. He was sentenced to death by an all-white, all-female jury for the murder of a white woman in 1980. According to lawyers, Horace Dunkins had unknowingly waived his right to a lawyer before being interrogated by police after his arrest. They argued that the jury at his trial had not been told that he had an IQ of only 65 to 69. Despite its June ruling that mental retardation was a factor juries should consider in deciding whether to impose the death penalty, the US Supreme Court declined to stay the execution.

Horace Dunkins' execution by electrocution was protracted. The first jolt of electricity failed to kill him, apparently because the electric chair had been wired incorrectly. Doctors found he was unconscious but had a strong heartbeat. A second electric shock was administered nine minutes later after the chair had been reconnected. Amnesty International wrote to the Governor of Alabama expressing its deep concern with what had happened.

Two weeks before Ronald Monroe was to have been executed in August, the Governor of Louisiana commuted the death sentence. Ronald Monroe had been convicted in 1980 of murdering a neighbour. His lawyers presented evidence casting doubt on his guilt and pointing to a more likely suspect.

On 7 July the European Court of Human Rights ruled unanimously against the extradition of Jens Soering from the United Kingdom to Virginia to face trial for capital murder. The court held that if Jens Soering was extradited to Virginia he ran a considerable risk of being sentenced to death and that exposure to the "death row phenomenon" in Virginia would violate the European Convention's prohibition of inhuman or degrading treatment or punishment. The court took into account the six to eight-year period between sentence and execution in Virginia, Jens Soering's youth (he was 18 at the time of the offence) and the severity of conditions on death row.

On 30 March a federal court of appeal upheld the convictions of eight members of the church-based "Sanctuary Movement". The eight were convicted in May 1986 of violating US immigration laws by helping Salvadorians and Guatemalans to enter and obtain refuge in the USA. They were sentenced to probationary terms. Amnesty International believes the people assisted by the church risked human rights violations if returned to their countries of origin. It considers that the eight would be prisoners of conscience if imprisoned for the offences of which they were convicted (see *Amnesty International Report 1987* and *1988*).

Leonard Peltier, a leading member of the American Indian Movement, was denied leave to appeal against his extradition from Canada to the USA in 1976. The Supreme Court of Canada gave no reasons for its June decision not to hear the appeal. Leonard Peltier's lawyers had asked the court to rule the extradition invalid and to order his return for a new hearing. Following a gunfight in 1975, during which two Federal Bureau of Investigation (FBI) agents were killed, Leonard Peltier fled to Canada. He was extradited to the USA and convicted of murder in 1977. The FBI later admitted fabricating evidence in order to secure Leonard Peltier's extradition from Canada to stand trial in the USA. (This evidence was not used at the trial itself.) Amnesty International believes that the interests of justice would best be served by granting Leonard Peltier a new trial (see *Amnesty International Report 1985, 1986* and *1987*).

In July and August Filiberto Ojeda Ríos, a member of a Puerto Rican independence organization, was tried by a court in San Juan, Puerto Rico. He was charged with assaulting FBI agents and resisting arrest when being arrested for alleged armed robbery in August 1985 in San Juan. At the trial he maintained that he had acted in self-defence in view of previous threats to his life made by FBI agents and the large number of heavily armed agents surrounding his house. On 26 August he was found not guilty and was released after 12 months' detention. Following his original arrest in August 1985, he had been held in pre-trial detention in Connecticut for 32 months on charges of armed robbery. A federal court ordered his release on bail in May 1988 (see *Amnesty International Report 1989*), but he was rearrested in August 1988 on the assault charges. The trial on charges of armed robbery remained pending. Amnesty International sent a delegate to observe the trial in San Juan: his findings sustained the organization's concerns about the length of pre-trial detention and the delay in bringing charges relating to the 1985 arrest.

In December the Louisiana Pardons Board recommended to the state governor that Gary Tyler, convicted of murder in 1975, should have his sentence reduced from life to 60 years' imprisonment. Gary Tyler, who is black, had been sentenced to death as a 16-year-old student for the murder of a white youth during a racial incident in Louisiana in October 1974. His sentence was subsequently commuted to life imprisonment. A court of appeal found in 1980 that Gary Tyler's trial had been "fundamentally unfair", but upheld the conviction on technical grounds. Amnesty International's investigations since the trial led it to conclude that there were grounds to doubt the validity of the conviction (see *Amnesty International Report 1980*). In letters to the Louisiana Pardons Board and to the governor supporting Gary Tyler's petition, it expressed its belief that a miscarriage of justice had occurred and that racial prejudice had played a major part in the case. The governor's decision had not been announced by the end of the year.

In September a Federal Court of Appeal ruled that two women convicted of politically motivated criminal offences had not been placed in a maximum security unit because of their political beliefs. This reversed a lower court's ruling in 1988 that their transfer to a High Security Unit (HSU) in Lexington Federal Prison, Kentucky, had been unconstitutional. The conditions under which the women were held in the HSU, which closed in 1988, had at times "skirted elemental standards of human decency", according to the Federal District Court (see *Amnesty International Report 1988* and *1989*). In December Amnesty International wrote to the Federal Bureau of Prisons to reiterate its concern at the Bureau's rationale for placement in, and removal from, a maximum security unit such as the HSU. It urged that the conditions under which the women had been held in the HSU should not be replicated in other maximum security institutions.

URUGUAY

In April a national referendum resulted in the retention of the 1986 Expiry Law, which had ended state powers to prosecute military and police personnel for human rights violations committed under the military government. Official investigations into "disappearances" continued but failed to clarify any case. Three people died in disputed circumstances while in police custody or during arrest; official investigations were opened into these cases.

In elections in November, Luis Alberto Lacalle of the main opposition Blanco (National) Party was elected President. He was due to succeed President Julio María Sanguinetti on 1 March 1990.

On 16 April the electorate voted in a referendum not to repeal the 1986 Expiry Law which had ended the state's power to prosecute or punish military and police personnel for human rights violations committed during the period of military rule from 1973 to 1985; however, a strong minority (42 per cent) supported repeal. The referendum brought to a close a two-year campaign against the law by human rights

254

groups, relatives of victims and opposition politicians (see *Amnesty International Report 1989*).

Under the Expiry Law the government had responsibility for administrative investigations into "disappearances" during military rule. However, the investigations were entrusted to military prosecutors, leading to serious doubts regarding the impartiality of the investigations. In six cases the military prosecutor had concluded that the "disappeared" had never been detained, despite considerable evidence to the contrary presented to the courts by relatives and human rights groups (see *Amnesty International Report 1988* and *1989*). In January an official investigation into the fate of Juan Manuel Brieba, who "disappeared" in 1975, was closed. A carpenter and member of the Communist Party, Juan Manuel Brieba was detained with his mother in October 1975 at their home in Montevideo. His mother, who was released a few days later, claimed she had seen her son while in detention, but he was never seen again. The Montevideo police authorities failed to supply information about the ownership of a vehicle used in the detention, which was alleged to belong to the Ministry of Defence. The military prosecutor concluded that there was no evidence of the participation of the armed forces or police in the "disappearance". He drew similar conclusions in other cases and continued to investigate at least 10 others.

In June Sara Méndez presented a complaint to a civilian court stating that the adoptive parents of a child living in Montevideo, whom she believed to be her son, were concealing his true identity. Sara Méndez had been detained in 1976 in Buenos Aires during a clandestine operation carried out by Uruguayan and Argentinian security forces. On her detention her three-week-old son, Simón Antonio Riquelo, was taken from her and his whereabouts remained unknown. Sara Méndez was subsequently transferred to Uruguay and was released in March 1981. The magistrate investigating the case recommended referral to the Executive under the Expiry Law. However, the Expiry Law refers to the investigation of crimes committed by military or police personnel; lawyers representing Sara Méndez argued that the Simón Riquelo case related to a possible criminal offence, simulation of civil status committed by civilians, and the investigation of the identity of a minor. No decision had been reached by the end of the year and the adoptive parents continued to refuse blood tests on the child.

Two men died in police custody in disputed circumstances. Guillermo Machado, a construction worker, was arrested with a friend on 16 July while eating lunch in a Montevideo square. The friend was released shortly after arrest, but Guillermo Machado was kept in detention after an altercation with the officer in charge about the return of his personal belongings. That evening he was found unconscious in his cell, and taken to hospital where he died without regaining consciousness on 24 July. During an inquiry into the death, police officers testified that Guillermo Machado had attempted suicide by hanging himself with a sweater, a version which was denied by his relatives. The judge said he found insufficient evidence to sustain criminal charges in connection with the death, but ordered the police officer responsible to be tried on a charge of illegal arrest. The Machado case provoked questions in parliament and intense public debate. Large demonstrations were held in protest at powers exercised by the police to conduct *razzias* (sweeps) in poor neighbourhoods and to hold people detained for questioning. As a result of the controversy, the Minister of the Interior, Antonio Marchesano, resigned and police sweeps were suspended.

In August Jorge Ricardo Inciarte Castells, a trader, died in similar circumstances. He was arrested outside a bar in Montevideo and was taken to a police station where, according to a police statement, he hanged himself with his trousers from the bars of his cell window. He was taken to hospital but was dead on arrival. The owner of the bar reported that Jorge Inciarte was severely beaten on arrest, was bleeding profusely and that the police ignored his requests to be taken to hospital. An inquiry found that he had committed suicide but at the end of the year it was reported that new witnesses had come forward and the family was seeking to reopen the case.

Also in August, Néstor Castillo Romero, who suffered from psychiatric problems, was killed outside his home, a shack in a poor Montevideo neighbourhood. According to a police statement, he was shot in the leg after resisting arrest and firing a pistol at a police officer, and died after being taken to hospital. Neighbours, however, claimed they heard only one shot and that while Néstor Castillo lay wounded, a police officer had struck two heavy blows on his head with a truncheon. Investigations into the killing were continuing at the end of the year.

In February Amnesty International sent letters to leaders of the three major political parties outlining its concerns with regard to the Expiry Law. In not providing guarantees for full and impartial investigations of "disappearances" and extrajudicial executions, relatives of victims had been deprived of legal means to establish the fate and whereabouts of their loved ones. The law thus appeared to conflict with Uruguay's obligations under international human rights treaties.

VENEZUELA

Events surrounding protests and looting in February resulted in arbitrary killings reportedly committed by the security forces as well as the arrest and alleged torture of a group of political, student and community activists. Several other cases of torture or ill-treatment were reported during the year. Most prisoners held for several years for politically motivated offences were released. Investigations into alleged human rights abuses, which generally made little or no progress in the courts, had numerous shortcomings. In a few cases, however, charges were brought against police officers.

Carlos Andrés Pérez of the party *Acción Democrática*, Democratic Action, took office as President in February. He introduced a series of severe economic measures almost immediately, sparking off widespread protests, riots and looting on 27 February. The following day the army was deployed to restore order and a curfew was imposed. A wide range of constitutional guarantees, including the right to personal liberty, were suspended, and most were not restored until 22 March.

Official statements reported 276 deaths mostly between 27 February and 8 March, but the real number may have been much higher. Although many died in the context of looting and other violence, or in circumstances difficult to clarify, a number of deaths apparently resulted from the unnecessary use of lethal force by the police and military. Some people were killed in circumstances suggesting extrajudicial execution.

Crisanto Mederos, a poet and political activist, was reportedly shot and killed by soldiers who searched his home during the night of 3 March. In Petare, a Caracas working class neighbourhood, soldiers fired on unarmed civilians, including children, on 1 March. At least five people were killed.

As in previous instances of social disturbance, the security forces rounded up student, community and political activists. Thirteen men and women were arrested at the beginning of March and accused of "incitement to rebellion" and "military rebellion". Ten of the 13 said they were tortured during incommunicado detention at the headquarters of the *Dirección de Inteligencia Militar* (DIM), Military Intelligence Directorate. The Venezuelan Constitution prohibits incommunicado detention, even when constitutional guarantees have been suspended.

Beatings, electric shocks, near-asphyxiation with plastic bags placed over the head, and mock executions were among the methods of torture reported by the 10 people held in DIM custody. Some said that a man who appeared to be a doctor monitored their physical condition during torture and gave medical treatment. The head of the DIM denied that torture had taken place. However, a member of a presidential commission appointed to investigate the situation of these detainees and which visited them a week after their arrest told the press he believed their allegations. All of the 13 were acquitted by presidential decree, supporting allegations that they had been arbitrarily detained, and released by 22 March.

256

Some of approximately 80 students held for up to a week by the *Dirección de los Servicios de Inteligencia y Prevención* (DISIP), Directorate of Intelligence and Prevention Services, also said they were beaten or threatened. Security forces also raided the premises of a group of Jesuit priests working in a poor neighbourhood. They accused the priests of "subversion" and detained them for several hours. Several other activists, including a former political detainee, had their homes raided but were not arrested.

In the wake of the February protests, the Catholic Archbishop of Caracas announced the formation of a special vicariate, the first of its kind in Venezuela, to work for human rights protection. A second human rights vicariate was established in the diocese of Cumaná.

In January outgoing President Jaime Lusinchi ordered the release of nine of the remaining 10 political detainees. They had been accused of politically motivated offences and imprisoned for several years without conviction. Four of them had been held since 1980 or earlier (see *Amnesty International Report 1989*). Long delays and other irregularities in their trials had been reported. Amnesty International was seeking clarification of the legal status of the one political detainee who remained in custody. Poet and former prisoner of conscience Carlos Baez, released in 1988 after 10 years' imprisonment, was detained for short periods at least three times in early 1989. Although some reports indicated that he had been arrested because his name had not yet been removed from a computerized government list of "wanted" prisoners, he may have been harassed deliberately.

Attorney General Ramón Escovar Salom stated shortly after his appointment to the post in June that he was committed to defending human rights, which he acknowledged "are frequently violated" in Venezuela. The Attorney General's Office had often been criticized for failing to protect human rights and to ensure that those responsible for abuses were brought to justice.

In an important development in November, a judge and a state attorney visited six detainees accused of taking part in a bank robbery and who were held incommunicado by the *Policía Técnica Judicial* (PTJ), criminal investigations police. The detainees were in poor physical condition and given immediate medical examinations. Investigations into allegations that they had been tortured were also initiated. The judicial officials reportedly found instruments in the police station which had been used for torture, including batons and electrical cables. Four of the detainees were released a few days after their arrest and the remaining two were transferred to prison pending possible charges. The PTJ said that five of its agents had been suspended in connection with the case. Several other detainees suspected of common crimes were also reportedly tortured or ill-treated.

Numerous shortcomings, in particular long delays, were reported in investigations into complaints of arbitrary killings during previous years by police and military personnel. In January a military court closed the case of 16-year-old cadet José Palomares, despite strong evidence suggesting that he died in September 1987 as a result of severe beatings. Officials told the youth's relatives that the case was still under investigation and the family learned only several months later via a third party that the case had been closed (see *Amnesty International Report 1989*).

Some progress was made in a few investigations. A Metropolitan Police officer was arrested in connection with José Méndez Astudillo's death in custody. In August a judge sentenced four Metropolitan Police officers to 12 years' imprisonment for the murder of Elias Avila Bogado (see *Amnesty International Report 1989*).

In April a military court of appeal revoked charges of homicide and ordered the release of 19 members of a military and police patrol allegedly responsible for killing 14 fishermen in El Amparo in October 1988 (see *Amnesty International Report 1989*). The court based its decision on a technical irregularity, and doubts that the military courts offer sufficient guarantees of impartiality continued. The Supreme Court finally ruled in December that the military court of appeal should reverse its decision. However, by the end of the year the 19 men had not been re-arrested. (In August the Supreme Court had rejected a request by lawyers representing two survivors of the attack for *avocamiento*, a procedure by which the Supreme Court takes jurisdiction of a case. The lawyers had hoped to prevent protracted delays through this procedure.)

Most complaints of abuses committed during the February protests were before military courts and little or no progress was reported. However, civilian judges charged two police officers with the murder of two students, one killed in Caracas and the other in Maracay, and two other police agents with causing serious injuries to two people wrongly accused of violating the curfew. In November a civilian judge charged another police officer with firing buckshot in the face of a young man and blinding him during the period of suspended constitutional guarantees. Also in November a civilian judge rejected a request to exhume bodies buried in a common grave, among them those of several people believed to have been unlawfully killed by the security forces. The judge ruled on grounds of jurisdiction that the request should be handed over to the military courts. A state attorney contested the ruling and the Supreme Court had not ruled on the case by the end of the year.

Amnesty International informed President Carlos Andrés Pérez in March and April of its concerns about alleged abuses committed during the February protests. The President denied the allegations in his response, but offered the organization full facilities to do research into reported abuses. In May an Amnesty International delegation visited Caracas to interview relatives of people who died during the period of suspended constitutional guarantees. A medical doctor among the delegates examined individuals who said they had been tortured or ill-treated. The delegates also met the President, members of the Commission for Internal Political Affairs of the Chamber of Deputies, state attorneys and members of the judiciary.

An Amnesty International delegation met Dr Ramón Escovar Salom in July, before he assumed the post of Attorney General, to discuss the organization's concerns regarding the role of the Attorney General's Office in protecting human rights and in investigating human rights abuses.

In August Amnesty International published *Venezuela: Arbitrary Killings by Police and Military Personnel*, which described a pattern of killings and detailed 16 between 1983 and 1989. The authorities had failed to clarify the circumstances of most of these 16 killings. The report also reiterated Amnesty International's recommendations for better training of police, strict disciplinary measures to show that such killings will not be tolerated, and legal steps to ensure that cases are properly investigated.

VIET NAM

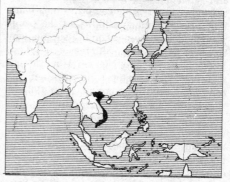

At least 15 prisoners of conscience and 24 people who may have been prisoners of conscience were held throughout the year. Many other people were also believed to be held because of their religious or cultural activities, their alleged political beliefs or their attempts to leave the country clandestinely. Some of those imprisoned had been sentenced after unfair trials; others had been detained since 1975 without charge or trial in "re-education" camps. Torture and ill-treatment in police custody and in "re-education" camps continued to be reported. At least four people were sentenced to death. It was not known whether any executions were carried out.

Legal and judicial reforms for safeguarding human rights continued to be enacted as part of the official *dôi moi*, "renovation", policy. A new Criminal Procedure Code came into force on 1 January. It affirms the presumption of innocence as the basis for administration of justice. It also sets out procedures governing arrest, investigation and the conduct of trials. While the new code appears to proscribe detention without trial, decrees and regulations providing for such detention apparently remained in force.

Several prisoners of conscience were transferred from prison to a "re-education" camp in Dong Nai Province, where conditions were reportedly less harsh and detainees were allowed to receive visitors and to correspond with relatives. Those transferred included Thich Tri Sieu and Thich Duc Nhuan, Buddhist monks sentenced in 1988; Dominic Tran Dinh Thu, a Roman Catholic priest, and some defendants tried with him in 1987; and Doan Quoc Sy and Hoang Hai Thuy, writers held since 1984. Thich Tue Sy, a Buddhist monk and scholar, was reportedly transferred in December to a remote camp in Phu Khanh Province. The inaccessibility of the camp prevented him from receiving supplementary food needed for health reasons.

Ho Hieu Ha and Nguyen Huu Cuong, two Protestant pastors and prisoners of conscience who were convicted in 1987 of "preaching against the revolution" (see *Amnesty International Report 1988*), were reportedly offered release in February on the condition that they would emigrate to the United States of America. Although officials said in May that the pastors had been released, it appeared that they remained in detention at the end of the year.

Phan Van Lam Binh, a writer who had been a prisoner of conscience since 1978, was reportedly released but placed under restrictions of movement. At least six people who may have been prisoners of conscience during detention without charge or trial since 1975 were also released. They included Phan Nhat Nam and Tran Duy Hinh, both of them writers, and Yoshida Ganshin, a Buddhist monk and military chaplain.

The situation of some 200 people was unknown and many of them, including possible prisoners of conscience, were believed to have remained in detention without trial. Some had been held for up to 14 years. They included Buddhist, Roman Catholic and Protestant clergy, former members of parliament, lawyers, teachers and students arrested on account of their political or religious beliefs and activities. Among them were Tran Xuan Tu, a Protestant pastor arrested in 1987; Nguyen Khac Chinh, a lawyer arrested in 1975; and Truong Tuy Ba, a 71-year-old business woman arrested in 1975.

Attempting to leave the country without official permission is a crime under Articles 85, 88 and 89 of the Criminal Code. People arrested for attempted "illegal departure" may be detained without trial or charged under the Criminal Code. At least 30 people were reportedly detained without trial for attempted "illegal departure",

and the actual number was believed to be much higher. Lam Thi Tuyet and her five children were reportedly arrested in February while trying to leave the country by boat. It was believed that they remained in detention without trial at the end of the year.

In August officials reportedly said that efforts to prevent clandestine departures had intensified during 1989. They stated that in two northern provinces, 413 people had been convicted of "illegal departure" between January and June. Those convicted received prison sentences of up to 12 years. According to one foreign press report, an official said that the authorities in his province had shot people attempting illegal emigration and that two people were executed for such attempts during the first half of the year.

The government said in May that no more than 130 former soldiers and officials of the previous Republic of Viet Nam (RVN) Government remained in "re-education" camps. However, the situation of several hundred former RVN military officers and a number of former civil servants, who had been held in camps, was not known. Among them were Truong Kim Cang, a former military attaché in Phnum Penh; Nguyen Van Hao, a pharmacist and lieutenant in the RVN medical corps; and RVN military chaplains Tran Ba Loc and Nguyen Khac Nghi. Some prisoners among this group of several hundred may have been released under government amnesties in 1987 and 1988. A further government amnesty was declared in September to mark the country's National Day, but the names of released prisoners were not made public.

Despite the introduction of the Criminal Procedure Code, political trials apparently still proceeded with restricted rights to defence. While little information about the trials was available, some details were received about a trial conducted before the Ho Chi Minh City People's Court on 31 December 1988. Three brothers were reportedly convicted on charges of "antigovernment" activities. Two of them, Tran Vong Quoc and Tran Tu Thanh, had been held since December 1984. The two were said to have been accused, in part, of compiling information for human rights organizations abroad about "reactionary activists" who were tried and executed for political crimes. Tran Tu Huyen, the third brother, was charged with failing to report his brothers' activities. The three were reportedly denied legal representation. Tran Vong Quoc received a 12-year sentence and remained in prison at the end of the year, Tran Tu Thanh received a five-year term and was released in September and Tran Tu Huyen was released on probation.

The official media continued to report torture and ill-treatment, although less frequently than in 1988. The Communist Party theoretical journal *Tap Chi Cong San* stated in February that "many of those responsible for upholding the laws...have tortured people themselves or ordered others to torture prisoners" and that "they [public security officers] can arrest, threaten and oppress anyone they want without fear of being brought to trial or punished".

In December legislation governing the Vietnamese media was introduced. A new law states that while the media is obliged to "struggle against acts of law-breaking" it requires official authorization and is subject to stringent controls by the central and local government. In addition, the judicial authorities "have the right not to supply information to the media".

Torture and ill-treatment of inmates was said to remain common in "re-education" camps. According to former detainees, each camp has a special "disciplinary" house for solitary confinement. Prisoners are reportedly held there in near total darkness for weeks or months at a time, often shackled, and on reduced food rations. Even minor infringements of camp rules can be punished with such imprisonment. Former prisoners also alleged that they had been beaten with rifle butts, rubber hoses and sticks for failing to meet required work quotas while detained for "re-education".

Mai Van Hanh, a dual French-Vietnamese national who was sentenced to death for treason in 1984, was released in January. His death sentence had been commuted in 1985.

At least four people were sentenced to death. It was not known whether there were any executions. In June the Vung Tau Con Dao People's Court sentenced Nguyen Nhu Binh to death on charges of "swindling, murder and robbery, and organizing illegal emigration". In September two people were sentenced to death for murder, attempted murder and armed robbery. In December Ha Van Hang was reportedly convicted of participating in "politically subversive activities" and sentenced to death by a people's court in Binh Duong.

In May an Amnesty International delegation visited Viet Nam for the first time in 10 years. The delegation met senior officials from the Interior, Justice and Foreign Affairs ministries, as well as senior members of the judiciary and the procuracy. The delegates visited one "re-education" camp in Thuan Hai Province, but requests to visit other camps were turned down. Officials stressed the government's commitment to the "renovation" process, to ensuring that arrest, imprisonment and trial procedures conform to the new Criminal Procedure Code, and to enforcing legislation prohibiting torture and ill-treatment.

Amnesty International urged the government to release all prisoners of conscience, to review the cases of all detainees held without charge or trial, to ensure that trials were conducted in accordance with international standards, to commute all death sentences and to take steps towards the abolition of the death penalty.

YEMEN
(ARAB REPUBLIC)

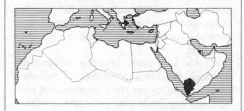

Over 100 political prisoners, including possible prisoners of conscience, were held without charge or trial during the year, some of whom were reportedly subjected to torture or ill-treatment. One detainee died in custody, allegedly as a result of torture. At least three judicial amputations were carried out. New information was received about 12 political prisoners alleged to have "disappeared" in previous years. Forty-eight people were executed for criminal offences, and eight death sentences imposed in 1985 were confirmed by the Ta'iz Court of Appeal.

In November the government approved a draft constitution for a unified state with the People's Democratic Republic of Yemen to be ratified by the legislative bodies in

260

both countries within six months. It was announced that a plebiscite on the draft constitution and the election of a single legislative body for the new Yemen Republic would then be held.

In May the Council of Ministers announced that the government would accede to the International Covenant on Civil and Political Rights (ICCPR), but it had not done so by the end of the year.

In January two students were reported to have been killed by security forces and 50 others arrested when they demonstrated in Ta'iz to protest against alleged killings and harassment of villagers by soldiers based at the town of al-Rahida. Most of those arrested were released soon after: it was not clear whether any were still held at the end of the year. Fourteen other people, mostly suspected members or supporters of the prohibited National Democratic Front (NDF), were arrested in Sufian, Sana'a Province, in August and September following further protests against alleged abuses by the armed forces. They were released uncharged in December. Among them was Muqbil Ahmad Sayfan, a farmer from Sufian. He was arrested on 30 August at Sa'da Central Hospital, where he was receiving treatment for a bullet wound sustained five days earlier while resisting a previous arrest attempt by members of al-Jihaz al-Markazi Lil-Amn al-Watani, Central Apparatus for National Security (CANS).

At the beginning of 1989, at least 26 political detainees arrested in previous years, including possible prisoners of conscience, remained in detention without charge or trial. All were suspected NDF members or sympathizers. Some had been held incommunicado for long periods: for example, 'Ali Muhammad Nu'man, a trade unionist arrested in Ta'iz in March 1983, was denied visits for six years while held without trial in Hadda detention centre, on the outskirts of the capital, Sana'a. He was released in November.

One of those held throughout the year was 14-year-old 'Ayesh 'Ali 'Ubad from al-Baydha province. He was arrested by members of the Seventh Armoured Brigade in December 1987 when only 12 years old, apparently because he is related to exiled opponents of the government. He was initially held for about 10 weeks in Qasr al-Basha'ir detention centre in Sana'a, where he is said to have been tortured. He was

then transferred to Sana'a Central Prison.

In November the government informed Amnesty International that seven people reportedly arrested in June 1987 for alleged sabotage had been brought to trial. Four were sentenced to prison terms ranging from seven to 10 years and three were acquitted (see *Amnesty International Report 1989*). The authorities did not indicate how the trial was conducted or when it took place.

Political detainees were reportedly subjected to torture or ill-treatment. This included the common use of iron shackles for long periods. One untried detainee died in al-Shabaka detention centre in Ta'iz on 1 April, allegedly as a result of torture. Qa'ed Qassem Sa'id, a member of the Central Committee of the opposition *Hizbul-Wahda al-Sha'biyya al-Yamani*, Yemeni Party of Popular Unity (YPPU), had been detained without charge or trial since February 1986 and had last been seen by his relatives in December 1987. In December the authorities confirmed his death in custody, but stated that it had been due to "physical and mental illness".

One former detainee, who had been held without charge or trial for more than 16 years prior to his release in 1989, told Amnesty International that during his detention he had been made to walk barefoot over nails and suspended for long periods from a metal bar inserted between his knees and elbows while his hands were tied — a form of torture known locally as "Kentucky chicken". He had also been forced to wear leg irons for over seven years.

At least three judicial amputations were carried out: in February, three people convicted of theft had their right hands amputated publicly in al-Tahrir Square in Sana'a.

Twelve people arrested for political reasons in previous years were reported in 1989 to have "disappeared" from custody. They included 'Ali 'Abdul Majid 'Abdul Qader, who was arrested by members of CANS in Sana'a in February 1983 as a suspected member of the YPPU. He was initially held at al-Hadda detention centre. Another case was that of Tawfiq Tahir al-'Ashawi, an electrical engineer from Ibb Province, arrested by members of the armed forces in January 1981 on suspicion of NDF membership. He was initially held for one month in Yarim detention centre in Radhma district, Ibb province. The fate of the 12 detainees and that of Colonel Sultan Amin al-Qirshi, who "disappeared" in 1978 (see *Amnesty International Report 1989*), remained unknown.

At least 48 people, all of whom had been convicted of murder, were publicly executed during the year. In March, the Ta'iz Court of Appeal confirmed the death sentences imposed in 1985 on eight NDF members, five of whom were in custody. The five had surrendered to the authorities following a general amnesty in 1982 but were subsequently arrested, tried and convicted of murder. The charges arose from alleged killings which occurred before 1982 as a result of clashes between the NDF and government forces. Their defence lawyer reportedly withdrew from the trial in protest against alleged procedural irregularities. Their sentences had not been ratified by the Supreme Judicial Council and they had not been executed by the end of the year.

Amnesty International sought information about prisoners detained without trial and expressed concern to the government about the increased use of the death penalty and the high number of executions carried out. It pressed for commutation of the death sentences outstanding against eight NDF members and for clemency for other prisoners under sentence of death. It also called for an end to judicial amputations. In March the government told Amnesty International that executions and amputations were carried out in accordance with the Shari'a (Islamic law), which "gives the detainee the right to defend himself by all appropriate means...including the non-admissibility as evidence of statements extracted from him under duress". The government also stated that the death sentences passed on eight NDF members were for criminal offences not covered by the 1982 general amnesty.

YEMEN
(PEOPLE'S DEMOCRATIC REPUBLIC OF)

At least 31 suspected opponents of the government were arrested and held without charge or trial, including possible prisoners of conscience. At least 17 other detainees arrested in previous years were held without trial throughout 1989, while 14 others were brought to trial in August.

Thirty-four political prisoners sentenced after trials in 1987 were released in an amnesty declared in March. Political detainees were reportedly tortured; one died in custody in suspicious circumstances. The fate of 16 detainees who "disappeared" in previous years remained unknown. Eight death sentences ratified by the Presidium of the Supreme People's Council were reportedly carried out.

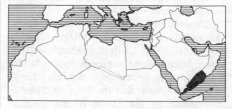

In July the government issued a draft Document for Comprehensive Political and Economic Reform as a basis for further discussion of reforms. In November the government approved a draft constitution for a unified state with the Yemen Arab Republic. The new constitution would take effect only if the legislatures of both countries ratify within six months, followed by plebiscite approval in both countries.

In December the Central Committee of the ruling Yemeni Socialist Party (YSP) announced that opposition groups would be legalized and that steps would be taken to publish new newspapers after a revision of the press and censorship law.

The government granted an amnesty in March to 36 political opponents who had been sentenced in 1987 to prison terms (see *Amnesty International Report 1988*). Two of the 36 had been tried in their absence; the others were released.

At least 31 suspected supporters of former president 'Ali Nasser Muhammad were arrested and all but three were still detained without charge or trial at the end of 1989. Seven of the detainees were arrested in Aden in March, including Hussein 'Umar Thiban, an aeronautical engineer, and Fatima Ahmad Muhammad, a former secretary to the Minister of Finance. The seven were first held at al-Fateh detention centre and later moved to al-Mansura prison. In May, 24 others were arrested in Shabwa. They included students, police officers, civil servants and labourers. Three of the 24 were released in August.

At least 17 suspected government opponents arrested in previous years remained

262

in detention without charge or trial. They included 11 suspected members of the banned *al-Ikhwan al-Muslimun*, Muslim Brothers, who were arrested in late 1987 and early 1988. Four suspected supporters of the former president who were arrested in Shabwa in May 1988 also remained in custody. Sa'id Aghbari (see *Amnesty International Report 1989*) and Muhammad Saleh al-Hammati, detained for political reasons since 1986, were still held at the end of the year.

Those freed during the year included 'Abdul Karim Shamsan, formerly a candidate of the YSP Central Committee, who was released without charge in April (see *Amnesty International Report 1989*). Information was also received in 1989 of the release in July 1988 of 38 political detainees held without trial. They had been among a group of 52 suspected supporters of the former president arrested in al-Mukalla in January 1988 (see *Amnesty International Report 1989*). In August the remaining 14 detainees were tried *in camera* by the Supreme Court of the Republic on charges of treason and membership of an illegal organization. Ahmad Nasser Salim al-Fadhli, a government employee, was among 11 defendants sentenced to between five and 15 years' imprisonment. The other three defendants were released. Another defendant in the case was tried *in absentia* and sentenced to 15 years' imprisonment. The secrecy of the trial prevented an independent assessment of the proceedings and some of the defendants may have been prisoners of conscience.

One detainee believed to have been arrested for political reasons died in suspicious circumstances in June. Farid 'Awadh Haidara was arrested in February 1988, shortly after returning to the country. Prior to his return, the Minister of State Security had reportedly promised him and his relatives a pardon for fleeing the country with the former president. Farid 'Awadh was placed in the custody of *Amn al-Dawla*, State Security, in 'Utaq Central Prison. Some reports suggested that he had been tortured. His body was handed over to his family for burial.

Information was received in 1989 about the torture of political detainees in previous years. 'Abdullah Salem Ba'um, a former deputy director of the Institute of Commerce in al-Mukalla, was reportedly beaten with cables and forced to stand for over 12 hours in al-Fateh detention centre in March 1988. 'Abdullah 'Abdo Bashr, a navy captain, was allegedly beaten with cables while suspended naked from a ceiling during his detention in 1987. He was also forced to stand in a heated metal barrel.

The fate of 16 political detainees who "disappeared" after arrest between 1967 and 1975 remained unknown. They included Tawfiq 'Azazi, a former chief magistrate at the Supreme Court, and 'Abdul-Hamid Ghanim, a restaurant owner (see *Amnesty International Report 1981, 1982* and *1983*).

Eight prisoners convicted of aggravated murder were believed to have been executed shortly after the Presidium of the Supreme People's Council ratified their death sentences in February. A bank manager convicted of embezzling public funds and sentenced to death by the Hadhramut Province Court in January had not been executed by the end of the year.

Amnesty International expressed concern about the detention without charge or trial of suspected government opponents, urging that all detainees be either promptly charged with recognizably criminal offences and fairly tried, or released. Amnesty International sought information about the circumstances of Farid 'Awadh Haidara's death and appealed for the commutation of all nine known death sentences. In response to an inquiry by Amnesty International, the government stated in January that the names of 16 "disappeared" detainees did not appear in prison records. The government also asserted that the 1987 trial of 138 people charged in connection with the violent events of January 1986 (see *Amnesty International Report 1988*) had been conducted in accordance with international standards for a fair trial. In April the government informed Amnesty International that the seven alleged supporters of the former president who were arrested in March were under investigation in connection with "a spy network operating on behalf of a foreign state". The government failed to confirm the reported death in custody or to explain the circumstances in which it occurred.

YUGOSLAVIA

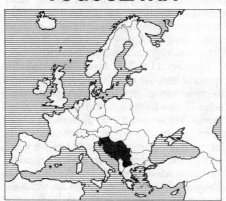

At least 4,500 people were detained for political reasons during 1989, the great majority of them ethnic Albanians. Of these, some 1,700 were prisoners of conscience, of whom about 1,000 were imprisoned for up to 60 days for taking part in non-violent protest strikes in Kosovo province in February. At least 27 people were killed and over 1,000 arrested during demonstrations in March, November and December by ethnic Albanians protesting against constitutional change. Political prisoners were often denied a fair trial and there were allegations that political detainees had been ill-treated during pre-trial detention. At least one person died in suspicious circumstances after being held for questioning by police. Ethnic Albanians who were arrested for political reasons in March and held in administrative detention reported that they were brutally beaten by prison staff. Conditions in some prisons where prisoners of conscience were detained were harsh. At least one person was sentenced to death and another was executed: both had been convicted of murder.

The political and economic crisis in the country deepened. In February there were widespread strikes by ethnic Albanians in Kosovo province in protest against proposed constitutional changes limiting the province's autonomy and giving greater powers to the republic of Serbia, which includes Kosovo. The changes followed complaints by the Serb and Montenegrin minorities in Kosovo that the local authorities failed to protect them from persecu-

tion by ethnic Albanians, the majority in the province. On 27 February the federal authorities introduced emergency measures in Kosovo and deployed federal security forces there. Shortly afterwards some 50 ethnic Albanian officials and industrialists were arrested in connection with the strikes and about 1,000 striking workers were sentenced to up to 60 days' imprisonment. The adoption of the constitutional changes on 23 March led to six days of demonstrations and riots by ethnic Albanians in which, according to official sources, 22 demonstrators and two police officers were killed. Yugoslav and foreign press reports estimated that over 100 people may have died. Subsequently about 900 demonstrators were sentenced to up to 60 days' imprisonment. In addition, 237 ethnic Albanians, including people who had signed a petition against the constitutional changes, were arrested and held without charge in administrative detention, known as "isolation". Some were held in administrative detention for over four months. Although the authorities stated that by mid-July no one was still held in "isolation", over 40 administrative detainees continued to be held for investigation on political charges.

The authorities stated that in the first six months of 1989 the police in Kosovo reported 614 people for political crimes, and 2,284 for minor political offences (punishable by up to 60 days' imprisonment). The corresponding figures for the country as a whole were 858 and 3,481. In November the trial began of Azem Vllasi, Kosovo's former Communist Party President, and 14 other ethnic Albanians. Strikes and demonstrations by ethnic Albanians resulted in further arrests and convictions. Three demonstrators died during conflicts with security forces. Among them was Bedri Sokoli, who, according to an official account, was shot by a police officer acting in self-defence. However, three eye-witnesses asserted that Bedri Sokoli was unarmed and was shot in the back while attempting to flee.

The number of political prisoners serving sentences was reduced to 232 from 436 in the period from January to November, according to official figures. This was partly due to the official pardoning of over 70 political prisoners. Of the 232, all but 22 were reportedly ethnic Albanians. However, this figure did not include the

AMNESTY INTERNATIONAL REPORT 1990

great majority of political prisoners who were awaiting trial or the results of appeal hearings, or those serving prison sentences of up to 60 days for minor political offences.

The death penalty was abolished in September under Slovenian law, but remained in force under the laws of Yugoslavia's other constituent republics. Draft amendments to the federal criminal code put before the Yugoslav Assembly at the end of November proposed a reduction in the number of capital offences.

On 18 April Yugoslavia signed the Convention against Torture and Other Cruel, Inhuman or Degrading Treatment or Punishment, but had not ratified this by the end of the year.

Among the prisoners of conscience convicted during the year were Liman Jashari and four other ethnic Albanians. In January they were sentenced by a court in Skopje, Macedonia, to between six and 10 years' imprisonment on charges under Article 134 of the federal criminal code of "inciting national hatred". They had allegedly expressed nationalist views and led demonstrations in August 1988 against the closing of classes in local schools with Albanian as the language of instruction. On appeal, Liman Jashari's prison sentence was reduced to nine years; the other prisoners' sentences were all reduced by three years.

In April Nexhat Maliqi and nine other ethnic Albanians were sentenced to between one and five years' imprisonment by a court in Pristina, Kosovo. They were convicted of being members of an illegal organization seeking republic status for Kosovo province and of distributing nationalist pamphlets. They were not accused of having used or advocated violence. Their sentences were confirmed on appeal.

In Kosovo people continued to be prosecuted for "hostile propaganda" under Article 133 of the federal criminal code, but this was rare elsewhere. In July Pristina district court sentenced Rexhep Bislimi to two years' imprisonment for having given to friends three books which in the court's view presented the situation in Yugoslavia in a "malicious and untrue way".

Scores of ethnic Albanians were charged with "counter-revolutionary undermining of the social order" under Article 114 of the federal criminal code, generally in connec-

tion with protests against constitutional change. Among them was Bajram Selmani, who was sentenced in July to six years' imprisonment. He was accused of organizing peaceful demonstrations in November 1988 and strikes in February 1989 by fellow-workers at a cement factory.

Article 114 had been contested frequently because of its broad formulation. It became the object of further controversy after its use in the much-publicized case of Azem Vllasi and 14 co-defendants. Apart from Azem Vllasi and one other, the accused were employees of Stari Trg mine. All 15 were charged with having organized or supported strikes at the mine in February, when miners called for the resignation of unpopular political leaders and expressed their opposition to constitutional changes. Azem Vllasi himself was accused of having visited the miners and thus of having encouraged them to persist in their demands. He was also said to have encouraged the demonstrations of November 1988. Although the accused were not charged with having used or advocated violence, the prosecution sought to hold them responsible for the events of March, including the deaths that occurred during demonstrations, at a time when they were in detention. These charges were punishable by prison sentences of between 10 and 20 years or the death penalty. The trial had not finished by the end of the year.

At least 20 prisoners of conscience were serving sentences for refusing to do military service, usually on religious grounds. Most were Jehovah's Witnesses from the republics of Slovenia and Croatia. In July new regulations were introduced providing for a 24-month period of unarmed military service (twice the length of armed military service) for religious conscientious objectors. The authorities stated that by the end of November all imprisoned conscientious objectors had been released.

Political prisoners often did not receive fair trials. At the trial of Ilir Nallbani and eight other soldiers accused of attempting to set fire to a hall at the Belgrade military academy in 1988, the Belgrade military court refused to hear witnesses and other evidence proposed by the defence. At this trial, as at many other political trials, public access was restricted, although the proceedings were formally open. Seven of the nine accused and two witnesses alleged in court that officials conducting investigation proceedings had forced them to make false statements. The court did not seek to investigate their allegations that threats and other psychological and physical pressures had been used. In June the accused were all convicted and sentenced to between three and 10 years' imprisonment.

Lawyers who have regularly defended ethnic Albanians accused of political offences said that many of their clients had stated in court that they had been forced by police or state security officers to make false self-incriminating statements, but that these complaints were almost always ignored. They nonetheless noted that on several occasions during 1989 courts in Kosovo had acquitted people charged with political offences. This had rarely happened in the past.

In May and June the Croatian press published accounts of ill-treatment by several ethnic Albanians. They were among 237 political detainees arrested following the introduction of emergency measures in Kosovo and held in "isolation" without charge or trial. One of them, Agim Vllasi, described how a doctor questioned him about his health in Leskovac prison on 28 March. He said he was then beaten by two prison staff and afterwards was twice forced to run the gauntlet of a group of prison officers, who beat him with truncheons and kicked and punched him. On the second occasion he was naked. He was beaten again on the second day. Another detainee, Bahri Osmani, described similar ill-treatment in Vranje prison. He said he was later transferred to Sabac prison where he was beaten unconscious by a police interrogator. Two days later he was taken to Belgrade prison hospital where he was allegedly held for five days in chains. Agim Vllasi and Bahri Osmani were released on 15 May. In October, 12 officers from Vranje prison were indicted on charges of having beaten and insulted 22 detainees. In December the trial began of nine guards, the director and the head of the security service at Leskovac prison on charges of ill-treating 41 detainees, including Agim Vllasi.

Xhemail Berisha from Prizren, Kosovo, died in custody on 6 April. According to an official statement, he died from injuries sustained after he threw himself from the second floor of a police station where he was being questioned by police, and there were no injuries on his body other than those caused by his fall. Unofficial sources alleged that he was a political detainee and had been physically and psychologically ill-treated before his death.

Prison conditions were reportedly harsh in Zenica, Bosnia-Hercegovina; in Lepoglava and Stara Gradiska, Croatia; in Idrizovo, Macedonia; and certain local prisons where some prisoners of conscience were held.

In August Laszlo Tubicak was executed and in November Tomislav Tomovski was sentenced to death. Both had been convicted of murder.

Throughout the year Amnesty International worked for the release of prisoners of conscience. It called on the authorities to end the practice of "isolation" and to institute an impartial investigation into allegations of ill-treatment of ethnic Albanians held in "isolation". Amnesty International also urged an impartial investigation into the death of Xhemail Berisha as well as the deaths that occurred during demonstrations by ethnic Albanians in March and November. The organization called for the commutation of death sentences.

In September Amnesty International delegates observed the trial of prisoners of conscience Jovan Opacic, a Serb, and Haxhi Maliqi, Xhemal Jashari and Fuat Jashari, ethnic Albanians. Jovan Opacic was acquitted by a court in Sibenik, Croatia, of the main charges against him, which included "inciting national hatred". He was released pending appeal against a conviction for "disturbing a public meeting". In Skopje, Haxhi Maliqi and his co-defendants were convicted of "inciting national hatred" and sentenced to between three and nine years' imprisonment. Amnesty International's delegate concluded that they had not incited violence.

Amnesty International delegates were denied access to three political trials in Kosovo: those of Avdullah Lohaj and 10 co-defendants in February; of Azem Vllasi and 14 co-defendants, which started on 30 October; and of Selim Vllasi in November. It considered all the defendants in these trials to be prisoners of conscience. In December Selim Vllasi was acquitted and released.

In December the organization received a letter from the state presidency stating its intention to bring Yugoslav legislation governing the rights of citizens "into accord with adopted international conventions".

ZAIRE

At least 100 people, many of them prisoners of conscience, were imprisoned on account of their political activities or religious beliefs. Few were brought to trial and most were freed without even being referred to the judicial authorities. Some were held incommunicado for a few weeks or months by the security forces. Some untried detainees, including two forcibly repatriated from a neighbouring country and held in secret, were still detained at the end of the year. Detainees were reportedly beaten, mostly at the time of arrest. More than 20 death sentences were imposed by the courts and eight executions were reported.

In February the government of President Mobutu Sese Seko announced its ratification of the United Nations (UN) Convention against Torture and Other Cruel, Inhuman or Degrading Treatment or Punishment, although by the end of the year the UN was unable to confirm that Zaire's instrument of ratification had been deposited. In September the government issued a decree which made the decisions of a government ministry – the Department for the Citizen's Rights and Freedoms – unchallengeable in the courts. In October the Department was empowered to refer any official accused of torture for prosecution.

A special minister, known as the State Commissioner for the Security of the Territory, was appointed to supervise the activities of the country's various police and security services. However, the security services continued to exercise extensive powers to detain political prisoners without following normal legal procedures,

which would entail referring them to the procuracy within a few days of their arrest. The only check on the security forces' imprisonment without charge or trial of political prisoners appeared to be the Department for the Citizen's Rights and Freedoms. The Department could investigate, but not challenge, cases of long-term detention.

Several students were killed, dozens injured and scores arrested by soldiers using guns and bayonets to disperse demonstrations in February over price rises. The demonstrations started in Kinshasa, after the government announced increases in fuel and transport prices. There were further demonstrations in Lubumbashi after the body of a student was discovered near a military barracks. The detained students were released in March when the President announced that no proceedings would be taken against them. An army officer in Lubumbashi was subsequently court-martialled and imprisoned for improperly ordering troops to fire on demonstrators.

Dozens of supporters of the *Union pour la démocratie et le progrès social* (UDPS), Union for Democracy and Social Progress, an opposition party which is illegal under Zaire's one-party constitution, were arrested during the year. Most were detained in either Kinshasa, the capital, or in the Kasaï Occidental or Kasaï Oriental regions, and were held for a few weeks or months before being released uncharged. In January soldiers belonging to the *Service d'action et de renseignements militaires* (SARM), Military Action and Intelligence Service, arrested at least 10 UDPS supporters, beat them severely and detained them overnight before releasing them. In March Tshisekedi wa Mulumba, a well-known UDPS leader, was placed under house arrest at his home in Kinshasa's Gombe district. The order keeping him under house arrest was apparently issued by the State Commissioner for the Security of the Territory, acting outside the law. In May he was allowed to move to a house in the Limete district of Kinshasa, but he remained under house arrest. In July, after he attempted to attend his brother's consecration as a bishop, he was detained for three days. Two members of his household were also arrested by the SARM: they were still detained without charge or trial at the end of the year. Tshisekedi wa Mulumba was not permitted visitors, although Amnesty International delegates visiting Zaire in November were allowed to see him. He was still under house arrest at the end of the year.

In May Kanana Tshiongo, a UDPS leader and former member of the National Assembly, was briefly detained and beaten by members of the national security service, the *Agence nationale de documentation* (AND), National Documentation Agency. Several people, including Luc Alingibala and Joseph Bula, were arrested in July for being in possession of a UDPS magazine, *Combat*. They were reportedly charged with possessing and distributing propaganda material and were still held in Kinshasa's Makala Prison at the end of the year.

In August seven other people, including UDPS members, were detained without charge or trial for political reasons. Three were held until October apparently because they were found in possession of a United States of America (USA) congressional resolution reducing military aid to Zaire. The four others were arrested because they had had contact with representatives of the New York-based Lawyers' Committee for Human Rights who were visiting Kinshasa. The four were kept blindfold for about two weeks in an unofficial military detention centre next to the army's Kinsuka firing range, west of Kinshasa. Three were then released. The fourth, Omene Samba, was freed in late October. All seven appeared to have been prisoners of conscience. After his release, one of the four, Mangala Ngolu Ndoki, a teacher, was taken by the government to the USA and France to deny that his detention had been politically motivated or related to his contact with the Lawyers' Committee for Human Rights. When he returned to Kinshasa, however, he was reportedly forced to stay in a hotel under guard and not allowed to resume his normal activities.

General Mukobo Mundende Popolo, a former army chief of staff, who was arrested in July 1987 and then banished, remained in internal exile (see *Amnesty International Report 1989*). His former Head of Operations Division, Major Kayembe Mbandokulu, who was also arrested in July 1987 and banished, continued to be subjected to similar administrative measures.

In Lubumbashi, the capital of the southern Shaba region, four people were reportedly imprisoned throughout the year on account of their alleged membership of the *Organisation démocratique katangaise*, Katanga Democratic Organization. The organization was not known to have used or advocated violence and its imprisoned members appeared to be prisoners of conscience. The four were among a group of more than 20 arrested in early 1988 and reportedly convicted during 1989 on charges of inciting tribal and regional hatred. Most were freed by mid-1989.

Arrests of Jehovah's Witnesses, whose religious sect was banned in 1986, continued during 1989. In July six Jehovah's Witnesses were tried in Mbanza Ngungu, a town in Bas-Zaire region, on charges of insulting the national flag by failing to salute it and insulting the nation's emblem by refusing to wear ruling party badges or to chant party slogans. They were acquitted, but were said in court to have been severely ill-treated in pre-trial detention. The court apparently took no action in response to their allegations.

Most of the students arrested in February were released in March. However, Fariala and Mwamba, two students who had unsuccessfully sought asylum in the Central African Republic and been forcibly repatriated, were arrested on their return in June. They were still detained without charge or trial at the end of 1989. Also detained after his forcible repatriation from Burundi in April was Kabongo Ntambwe, who had been recognized as a refugee by the Office of the UN High Commissioner for Refugees. The Zairian authorities did not acknowledge his detention. Although he was released in October, he was reportedly restricted to a hotel in Kinshasa.

Allegations of torture of detainees continued, although on a reduced scale by comparison with several years ago. Detainees were reportedly subjected to severe beatings, mostly at the time of arrest, as in the case of Kanana Tshiongo.

Twenty-one people were sentenced to death in September. They included 10 soldiers, five of whom were convicted in their absence. The 21 were convicted of armed robbery and murder by military and civilian courts in Kinshasa. The trials were widely publicized, and reports suggested that they might be executed in public if their appeals and petitions for clemency were rejected. Three other death sentences were imposed in October on people apparently convicted of murder. The same

268

month, eight prisoners sentenced to death in previous years were reported to have been executed in Likasi's Buluo Prison in Shaba, although the authorities did not confirm this. It was not known how many prisoners were under sentence of death or whether there were other executions.

Amnesty International appealed for the release of Tshisekedi wa Mulumba and other prisoners of conscience, sought information about other untried political detainees and urged the government to commute all death sentences. In May Amnesty International submitted a memorandum to the government, calling for the powers of detention of the security forces to be greatly reduced and for all detainees to have their cases referred to a judicial authority soon after arrest. In November an Amnesty International delegation visited Zaire and discussed human rights with several government ministers, the President of the Judicial Council, the Procurator General and officials of the Department for the Citizen's Rights and Freedoms.

ZAMBIA

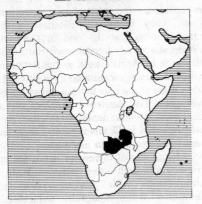

Three prisoners of conscience and six other long-term political prisoners were released from administrative detention without charge or trial, but at least one other long-term political detainee was still held without trial at the end of the year. Torture and ill-treatment of prisoners was reported, allegedly leading to at least two deaths. At least 18 prisoners were executed, the first executions reported since 1985, and the death penalty continued to be imposed on prisoners convicted of aggravated robbery or murder.

At the beginning of the year at least 13 political prisoners were held in administrative detention without charge or trial under the Preservation of Public Security Regulations, which allow the Head of State to authorize such detention indefinitely "for the purpose of preserving public security". The regulations require that detainees are told the reason for their detention within 14 days, and that their cases are reviewed periodically by a special tribunal empowered to recommend their release or continued detention. However, the tribunal sits *in camera* and the President is not obliged to implement its recommendations which are made confidentially.

Among those held in administrative detention at the beginning of 1989 were at least three prisoners of conscience who had been held since 1986 as suspected members of the illegal opposition Peoples' Redemption Organization (PRO): the ruling United National Independence Party is the only political party permitted under Zambia's constitution (see *Amnesty International Report 1989*). Peter Chiko Bwalya was freed in April and Henry Kalenga in November. The third, Joseph Chitalu, was arrested with them but was also charged with sedition in July 1987. However, this charge was dropped and he was also released in November.

At least three people, but probably many more, detained for alleged links with the South African Government were held without charge or trial. Two of these were released in 1989: James Gondwe, held since 1986; and James Kasamanda, an army captain held since March 1988. However, Hendrik Stephen du Plessis, a South African national held since December 1987 as an alleged spy, remained in detention throughout 1989.

Four other political detainees held since October 1988 — two civilians and two army officers — were released uncharged. However, four army officers arrested with them, including Lieutenant-General Christon Tembo, were charged with treason in August. They were alleged to have plotted to overthrow the government in 1988 (see *Amnesty International Report 1989*). Their trial was to take place in 1990.

There were reports of torture and ill-treatment of criminal prisoners by police and prison staff. In March a High Court judge expressed concern at the increase of such abuses. In September another judge instructed senior officers from Lusaka Central Prison to investigate an alleged assault by a team of warders on three criminal prisoners, causing injuries to their legs and arms. In October the Appeal Court awarded substantial damages to MacMillan Mhango for torture inflicted on him in police custody. The court had previously acquitted him of murder and aggravated robbery.

The deaths in custody of at least two prisoners were alleged to have resulted from police torture or ill-treatment. Abel Nyirenda, who died in police custody in April, was said to have been subjected to severe beatings. Ishmael Zimba, an alleged security agent for the Malawi Government, was also reported to have been tortured prior to his death in November in police custody in Lusaka. He was one of several Malawians arrested in October following the murder of Mkwapatira Mhango, an exiled opponent of the Malawi Government, and nine others in Lusaka. The police said Ishmael Zimba's death would be the subject of a judicial inquiry but it was not known if this had begun by the end of 1989.

At least 18 prisoners convicted of murder or aggravated robbery were hanged at Mukobeko Maximum Security Prison in Kabwe. These were the first known executions since 1985. In June, 11 prisoners under sentence of death had their sentences commuted to life imprisonment by President Kenneth Kaunda. At least six prisoners convicted of aggravated robbery or murder, both of which carry a mandatory death sentence, were sentenced to death. The Supreme Court overturned at least four death sentences passed in previous years, and upheld five others.

In August the African National Congress (ANC) of South Africa, whose headquarters is in Lusaka, unlawfully imprisoned four former ANC members suspected of involvement in bomb attacks against the organization. One, Sipho Hubert Mbeje, was reportedly beaten severely. The Zambian authorities intervened and the four were handed over to Zambian officials after two weeks in ANC custody. Three were later released but Sipho Hubert Mbeje was remanded in custody on unrelated criminal charges.

Amnesty International welcomed the releases of prisoners of conscience and other untried political detainees and called for other political detainees to be brought promptly to trial, or released. In June Amnesty International published a report on its concerns, *Zambia: Continuing Cases of Administrative Detention and Torture*. The Zambian authorities did not respond directly to Amnesty International but were reported in the Zambian press to have rejected the contents of the report. Amnesty International also expressed concern about the increase in executions and appealed for the commutation of all death sentences.

ZIMBABWE

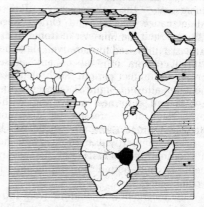

At least 15 people held without trial for periods varying from a few days to over a month appeared to be prisoners of conscience. Eight long-term untried political detainees were released, but at least four others were held throughout the year. It was reported that a suspected criminal was beaten and ill-treated by police officers, and new allegations were made about the torture of political prisoners by the Central Intelligence Organization (CIO) in 1987. Four people were sentenced to death but there were no reports of executions.

In accordance with an agreement reached in December 1987, the ruling Zimbabwe African National Union-Patriotic Front (ZANU-PF), headed by President Robert Mugabe, and the Zimbabwe African People's Union (ZAPU) merged at the end of 1989 to become one party. However, a new opposition party, the Zimbabwe Unity Movement (ZUM), was formed in April by Edgar Tekere, a former government minister.

The *Resistência Nacional Moçambicana* (RENAMO), Mozambique National Resistance, the armed opposition group fighting the Mozambican Government, made incursions into eastern Zimbabwe and killed a number of civilians. Zimbabwean troops have been deployed in Mozambique in support of the Mozambican Government since 1982. Some asylum-seekers who entered Zimbabwe were said to have been forcibly returned to Mozambique. Other Mozambicans were reportedly detained incommunicado by the army in Zimbabwe, although details were difficult to obtain.

The government renewed the state of emergency which has been continuously in force since 1965. Under the state of emergency, the Emergency Powers (Maintenance of Law and Order) Regulations permit the Minister of Home Affairs to order the administrative detention without charge or trial of any person for an unlimited period. Such detainees must be allowed immediate access to a lawyer and informed in writing within seven days of the reason for detention. Thereafter, their cases are considered by a review tribunal within 30 days and then at six-monthly intervals, but the government is not bound to implement its recommendations.

New emergency regulations were introduced in August, following a strike by some doctors in May. They made it an offence punishable by up to two years' imprisonment for workers in "essential services" to strike, or for others to incite them to strike. Essential services were defined to include finance, industry and commerce. The new regulations were used almost immediately against 116 striking employees of the Posts and Telecommunications Corporation (PTC), who were arrested in late August. However, they were held only briefly and charges against them were dropped in October.

In June the government amended the Prisons Act to abolish corporal punishment for adults, in accordance with a 1987 Supreme Court ruling that whippings were inhuman and degrading, and therefore unconstitutional. In 1989 the Supreme Court ruled that the whipping of juveniles was also unconstitutional.

In September the Protection of Wildlife (Indemnity) Act came into force. This granted indemnity to game-park rangers and scouts, the police, the security forces and others from criminal liability resulting from any act carried out "in good faith" in connection with the suppression of poaching. At least 15 poachers were killed by anti-poaching units during the course of the year, two of them within 14 days of the new law coming into force.

Two student leaders, Arthur Mutambara and Enock Chikweche, were arrested in a police raid in October at the University of Zimbabwe in Harare. The university's Students' Representative Council (SRC) had published a statement condemning an earlier police action which broke up a meeting on the university campus to commemorate anti-corruption demonstrations in 1988. There were further student protests after the arrests of the two SRC leaders, who were both placed under administrative detention orders and were prisoners of conscience. The university was closed. The two students successfully challenged their detention orders in the High Court, but they were then charged with issuing a subversive document. Nine other students were charged with the same offence. All 11, together with four other students charged with public order offences, were released on bail before the end of October by the High Court, which set aside an instruction from the Minister of Home Affairs to deny the students bail. They were still awaiting trial at the end of the year.

Morgan Tsvangirai, Secretary-General of the Zimbabwe Congress of Trade Unions (ZCTU), was also administratively detained without charge or trial after the ZCTU protested against the closure of the university. He too was a prisoner of conscience. He challenged his detention in the High Court, which twice ordered his release. However, each time he was immediately redetained by CIO officials who accused him of being a South African intelligence agent. In November he was released unconditionally, shortly before his detention was again to be challenged in the Supreme Court.

Cornelius Watama, the ZUM provincial secretary for Mashonaland West, was also administratively detained in October for alleged links with the South African Government. When he challenged this, the High Court ordered his release. He had been arrested with 10 other ZUM members while travelling to Kariba to campaign in a by-election. Eight were released after a few days, but Cornelius Watama and two others were held until the High Court ordered their release in late October.

At least 12 untried political detainees arrested in previous years were still held at the beginning of 1989 because of alleged links with South Africa or for involvement in acts of violence. Eight were released during the year, four in August and four in November. Those freed in August included Patricia Brown and Jack Lewis-Walker. In both their cases, the review tribunal had recommended their release on three separate occasions. Among those still held without charge or trial at the end of 1989 was Leslie Lesia, a South African national suspected of involvement in a bombing in Harare in May 1987 (see *Amnesty International Report 1989*).

Sheikh Dawood Parker, the representative in Zimbabwe of the Muslim organization *Qibla*, was also detained without charge or trial as an alleged South African spy. He was arrested in April after refusing to leave Zimbabwe on the orders of the police, but was released in June. He was then redetained by the CIO and was still held in administrative detention without charge or trial at the end of the year.

The alleged torture by police of a criminal suspect came to light at a trial in October. Veronica Matewere claimed that she had been forced to do physical exercises and had been beaten while under investigation by police in Harare for allegedly receiving stolen property. The Regional Magistrate hearing the case accepted her claims and warned the police against taking investigative "short cuts" through the use of torture. New claims that the CIO had used torture in 1987 were made during 1989. Velapi Mbiwa, who was sentenced in February to nine years' imprisonment for spying for South Africa, alleged that he had been beaten on the soles of his feet and that his head had been immersed in water while he was being interrogated by CIO officials.

Early in the year the police reported back to the High Court the results of their investigation into the "disappearance" of nine ZAPU supporters in 1985 (see *Amnesty International Report 1988* and *1989*), in accordance with a High Court ruling of June 1988. Their investigation did not clarify what had happened to the "disappeared" prisoners. The police officers conducting the investigation reportedly failed to interview all relevant witnesses or

to investigate the use of police and security force vehicles on the night the men "disappeared". In a separate case, the police acknowledged to the widow of Fraser Gibson Sibanda, who "disappeared" after his arrest by police in 1985, that he had been unlawfully killed. However, no action was known to have been taken against those responsible for his death. According to the Ministry of Home Affairs in July, the "disappearance" of Edward Moyo was also under investigation. He was one of two brothers who were not seen again after being taken into police custody in July 1985. However, neither the nature of the investigation nor its outcome had been disclosed by the end of the year.

Four people convicted of murder were sentenced to death in the High Court. Murder carries a mandatory death sentence unless there are mitigating circumstances. No executions were reported.

Amnesty International appealed for the release of Morgan Tsvangirai and other prisoners of conscience. It expressed concern about the continued detention of other political prisoners being held under administrative detention orders without being charged or given a prompt trial. Amnesty International also appealed to the government to abolish the death penalty.

APPENDICES

AMNESTY INTERNATIONAL VISITS BETWEEN 1 JANUARY 1989 AND 31 DECEMBER 1989

MONTH	COUNTRY	PURPOSE	DELEGATE(S)
January	Uganda	Research/Discuss Amnesty International's concerns with government authorities	— Two staff members of International Secretariat
January	Poland	Research/Discuss Amnesty International's concerns with government authorities	— Two staff members of International Secretariat
January	Jamaica	Observe appeal hearing by Privy Council in London	— Wesley Gryk (USA) — Staff member of International Secretariat
February	Egypt	Research	— Two staff members of International Secretariat
February	Cyprus	Research	— Alain Ottan (France)
February	Nicaragua	Research	— Yvon Le Bot (France) — Two staff members of International Secretariat
February	Yugoslavia	Trial observation	— Hans Rau (FRG) — Staff member of International Secretariat
February/March	Japan	Research/Discuss Amnesty International's concerns with government authorities	— Christian Tomuschat (FRG) — Staff member of International Secretariat
February/June	Israel & Occupied Territories	Research	— Curt Goering (USA)
March	Turkey	Trial observation	— Staff member of International Secretariat
March	Brazil	Research	— Miguel Angel Machin (Uruguay) — Susana Irin (Uruguay)
March/April	Nicaragua	Discuss Amnesty International's concerns with government authorities	— Sofía Macher (IEC) — Two staff members of International Secretariat
March/April	Mozambique	Research	— Staff member of International Secretariat
March/April	USSR	Discuss Amnesty International's concerns with government authorities	— Secretary General of Amnesty International — J. Herman Burgers (Netherlands) — Staff member of International Secretariat
March/April	Niger	Discuss Amnesty International's concerns with government authorities	— Bacre Waly Ndiaye (IEC) — Two staff members of International Secretariat
March/April	Federal Republic of Germany	Research	— Staff member of International Secretariat
April	Benin	Discuss Amnesty International's concerns with government authorities	— Bacre Waly Ndiaye (IEC) — Two staff members of International Secretariat
April	Argentina	Research	— Two staff members of International Secretariat
April	United Kingdom	Discuss Amnesty International's concerns with government authorities	— Deputy Secretary General of Amnesty International — Three staff members of International Secretariat

April/May	Bolivia	Research	— Two staff members of International Secretariat
April/May	Turkey	Research	— Staff member of International Secretariat
April/May	Uganda	Discuss Amnesty International's concerns with government authorities	— Secretary General of Amnesty International — Staff member of International Secretariat
May	Israel & Occupied Territories	Observe appeal hearing	— Menno Kamminga (Netherlands)
May	Viet Nam	Discuss Amnesty International's concerns with government authorities	— Deputy Secretary General of Amnesty International — Geoffrey Robertson (Australia) — Staff member of International Secretariat
May	Italy	Trial observation	— John Vervaele (Belgium) — Staff member of International Secretariat
May	Australia	Research/Discuss Amnesty International's concerns with government authorities	— Staff member of International Secretariat
May	Venezuela	Research	— Wilder Tayler (Uruguay) — Hans Draminsky Petessen (Denmark) — Two staff members of International Secretariat
June	Burundi	Discuss Amnesty International's concerns with government authorities	— Bacre Waly Ndiaye (IEC) — André Morel (Canada) — Two staff members of International Secretariat
June	Pakistan	Research	— Staff member of International Secretariat
June	Israel & Occupied Territories	Research	— Staff member of International Secretariat
June	Jamaica	Observe appeal hearing	— Wesley Gryk (USA)
June	Syria	Discuss Amnesty International's concerns with government authorities	— Secretary General of Amnesty International — Two staff members of International Secretariat
June/July	Somalia	Discuss Amnesty International's concerns with government authorities	— Kevin Boyle (Ireland) — Staff member of International Secretariat
June/July	Austria	Research	— Staff member of International Secretariat
July	Peru	Research	— Robin Kirk (USA) — Staff member of International Secretariat
July	Ecuador	Research	— Robin Kirk (USA) — Staff member of International Secretariat
July	United Kingdom	Research	— Staff member of International Secretariat
July/August	Puerto Rico	Trial observation	— David Matas (Canada)
July/August	Pakistan	Discuss Amnesty International's concerns with government authorities	— Secretary General of Amnesty International — Virginia Leary (USA) — Ghanim al-Najaar (Kuwait) — Staff member of International Secretariat

August	Colombia	Research	— Staff member of International Secretariat
August	Paraguay	Research	— Staff member of International Secretariat
September	Argentina	Trial observation	— Jorge Salazar (Peru) — Staff member of International Secretariat
September	Yugoslavia	Trial observation	— Staff member of International Secretariat
September	Turkey	Trial observation	— Wesley Gryk (USA) — Staff member of International Secretariat
September	Yugoslavia	Trial observation	— Staff member of International Secretariat
September/ October	Czechoslovakia	Research/Discuss Amnesty International's concerns with government authorities	— Two staff members of International Secretariat
October	Bolivia	Research	— Staff member of International Secretariat
October	Federal Republic of Germany	Research	— Tony Peters (Belgium) — Lyeven Dupoint (Belgium)
October	Turkey	Research	— Staff member of International Secretariat
October	Senegal	Discuss Amnesty International's concerns with government authorities	— Franca Sciuto (Italy) — Antoine Comte (France) — Staff member of International Secretariat
October	Norway	Trial observation	— Lars Adam Rehof (Denmark)
October	Argentina	Trial observation	— Jorge Salazar (Peru)
October	Czechoslovakia	Trial observation	— Wolfgang Rainer (Austria)
October	Yugoslavia	Trial observation	— Timothy Owen (United Kingdom) — Staff member of International Secretariat
October	Togo	Discuss Amnesty International's concerns with government authorities	— Peter Duffy (IEC) — Staff member of International Secretariat
October	United Kingdom	Trial observation	— Staff member of International Secretariat
October	German Democratic Republic	Trial observation	— Staff member of International Secretariat
October/ November	Tunisia	Research	— Staff member of International Secretariat
October/ November	United Kingdom	Research	— Staff member of International Secretariat
November	Zaire	Discuss Amnesty International's concerns with government authorities	— Bacre Waly Ndiaye (IEC) — Two staff members of International Secretariat
November	Egypt	Research	— Staff member of International Secretariat
November	Czechoslovakia	Trial observation	— Herbert Rainer (Austria)
November	Austria	Research	— Staff member of International Secretariat
November	Republic of Ireland	Observe court hearing	— Hanna Kolff (Netherlands)
November	Jamaica	Discuss Amnesty International's concerns with government authorities	— Magdaleno Rose-Avila (USA) — Ezzat Fattah (Egypt) — Staff member of International Secretariat

November	Czechoslovakia	Trial observation	— Herbert Rainer (Austria)
November	Sudan	Discuss Amnesty International's concerns with government authorities	— Secretary General of Amnesty International — Two staff members of International Secretariat
November	Greece	Trial observation	— Staff member of International Secretariat
November/ December	Grenada	Observe appeal hearing	— Lawrence Kershen (United Kingdom)
November/ December	Hong Kong	Research	— Wesley Gryk (USA) — Anita Klum (Sweden)
November/ December	Jordan	Research	— Lynn Welchman (United Kingdom) — Staff member of International Secretariat
December	Antigua and Barbuda	Observe court hearing	— Staff member of International Secretariat

STATUTE OF AMNESTY INTERNATIONAL
Articles 1 and 2

As amended by the 18th International Council meeting in Aguas de Lindóia, Brazil, 30 November — 6 December 1987

Object

1. CONSIDERING that every person has the right freely to hold and to express his or her convictions and the obligation to extend a like freedom to others, the object of AMNESTY INTERNATIONAL shall be to secure throughout the world the observance of the provisions of the Universal Declaration of Human Rights, by:

a. irrespective of political considerations working towards the release of and providing assistance to persons who in violation of the aforesaid provisions are imprisoned, detained or otherwise physically restricted by reason of their political, religious or other conscientiously held beliefs or by reason of their ethnic origin, sex, colour or language, provided that they have not used or advocated violence (hereinafter referred to as "prisoners of conscience");

b. opposing by all appropriate means the detention of any prisoners of conscience or any political prisoners without trial within a reasonable time or any trial procedures relating to such prisoners that do not conform to internationally recognized norms;

c. opposing by all appropriate means the imposition and infliction of death penalties and torture or other cruel, inhuman or degrading treatment or punishment of prisoners or other detained or restricted persons whether or not they have used or advocated violence.

Methods

2. In order to achieve the aforesaid object, AMNESTY INTERNATIONAL shall:

a. at all times maintain an overall balance between its activities in relation to countries adhering to the different world political ideologies and groupings;

b. promote as appears appropriate the adoption of constitutions, conventions, treaties and other measures which guarantee the rights

278

contained in the provisions referred to in Article 1 hereof;

c. support and publicize the activities of and cooperate with international organizations and agencies which work for the implementation of the aforesaid provisions;

d. take all necessary steps to establish an effective organization of sections, affiliated groups and individual members;

e. secure the adoption by groups of members or supporters of individual prisoners of conscience or entrust to such groups other tasks in support of the object set out in Article 1;

f. provide financial and other relief to prisoners of conscience and their dependants and to persons who have lately been prisoners of conscience or who might reasonably be expected to be prisoners of conscience or to become prisoners of conscience if convicted or if they were to return to their own countries, to the dependants of such persons and to victims of torture in need of medical care as a direct result thereof;

g. work for the improvement of conditions for prisoners of conscience and political prisoners;

h. provide legal aid, where necessary and possible, to prisoners of conscience and to persons who might reasonably be expected to be prisoners of conscience or to become prisoners of conscience if convicted or if they were to return to their own countries, and, where desirable, send observers to attend the trials of such persons;

i. publicize the cases of prisoners of conscience or persons who have otherwise been subjected to disabilities in violation of the aforesaid provisions;

j. investigate and publicize the disappearance of persons where there is reason to believe that they may be victims of violations of the rights set out in Article 1 hereof;

k. oppose the sending of persons from one country to another where they can reasonably be expected to become prisoners of conscience or to face torture or the death penalty;

l. send investigators, where appropriate, to investigate allegations that the rights of individuals under the aforesaid provisions have been violated or threatened;

m. make representations to international organizations and to governments whenever it appears that an individual is a prisoner of conscience or has otherwise been subjected to disabilities in violation of the aforesaid provisions;

n. promote and support the granting of general amnesties of which the beneficiaries will include prisoners of conscience;

o. adopt any other appropriate methods for the securing of its object.

The full text of the Statute of Amnesty International is available free upon request from: Amnesty International, International Secretariat, 1 Easton Street, London WC1X 8DJ, United Kingdom.

AMNESTY INTERNATIONAL NEWS RELEASES 1989

4 January
Turkish Government has taken no effective steps to improve "appalling" human rights record, charges Amnesty International

22 January
Brazil: Authorities fail to act against killings

25 January
Truth about human rights in **German Democratic Republic** shrouded in secrecy, Amnesty International says

30 January
New Amnesty International move on executions in **Iran**

10 February
Amnesty International appeals to all sides to protect political prisoners and non-combatants in **Afghanistan**

22 February
Ethnic Turks and **human rights activists** imprisoned in **Bulgaria**, says Amnesty International

28 February
Iraqi children victims of brutal abuse by security forces, Amnesty International charges

8 March
Amnesty International calls on new **Jamaican** Government to end executions and commute 200 death sentences

8 March
Amnesty International "deeply disturbed" by United Nations body's inaction over **Iraq** abuses

10 March
Amnesty International calls on **Venezuelan** Government to investigate reports of human rights violations during unrest

14 March
Amnesty International appeals to **Kampuchean** Government for information on political detainees

22 March
Amnesty International calls for investigation into increasing reports of killings and torture in **Uganda**

13 April
Amnesty International fears for safety of detained neurologist in **Malawi**

18 April
Gibraltar inquest did not answer fundamental question, Amnesty International observers conclude

18 April
Amnesty International calls for judicial inquiry into "wide-ranging" human rights abuses by **Israeli** forces

25 April
Amnesty International calls on 100 governments to end **"cold-blooded and premeditated" killings** worldwide

10 May
Amnesty International says **Egyptian** Government must end arbitrary detention and torture of political prisoners

19 May
Israel and the Occupied Territories: Fear of extrajudicial execution

1 June
Administrative detention violates fundamental human rights in **Israel and the Occupied Territories**, Amnesty International says

5 June
Killings in **China**: Amnesty International calls on governments worldwide to press for end to massacre

14 June
Human rights violations continue under civilian government in **Guatemala**, Amnesty International says

27 June
Supreme Court ruling on death penalty in **United States of America** is "retrograde step", says Amnesty International

29 June
Amnesty International fears for lives of hundreds of **Chinese** detainees in post-massacre round-ups

7 July
Amnesty International concerned about arrest of former political leaders in **Sudan**

19 July
Amnesty International calls on **Indian** Government to account for "disappeared" prisoners

25 July
Wave of human rights abuses in **Mauritania**, says Amnesty International

3 August
Human rights violations continue in **Ethiopia**, Amnesty International says

16 August
Amnesty International calls for **United Nations** action on human rights violations in **China**

17 August
Amnesty International calls on **Sri Lankan** Government to end rising tide of human rights violations

23 August
Pall of terror spreads over **Peru**, says Amnesty International

30 August
Amnesty International calls on **Chinese** Government to end use of judicial killing as "political tool"

1 September
Amnesty International stands by report on **China**, calls on government to respond adequately to charges of gross human rights violations

20 September
Amnesty International appeals for end to **"cruel and arbitrary" judicial executions**

21 September
Saudi Arabia: Amnesty International appalled at beheadings

29 September
China: Amnesty International appeals for release of prisoners of conscience and end to executions

October
Somalia: Amnesty International appeals for release of prisoners of conscience

11 October
Amnesty International says **Colombian** armed forces – often allied to drug-traffickers – committed "unprecedented" political killings in past 16 months

17 October
United Kingdom: Amnesty International welcomes announcement on "Guildford four" prisoners – and calls for further review of Birmingham pub bombing case

18 October
Dramatic shift in **Soviet** perspective on human rights, says Amnesty International

25 October
Amnesty International annual report cites **"killing grounds"** around the world

31 October
Unabated use of torture in **Turkey**, says Amnesty International

2 November
Amnesty International fears for safety of journalist and nurse detained in **Iraq**

6 November
El Salvador: Amnesty International calls for investigation into recent bomb attacks

6 November
Hong Kong needs "firm and precise" human rights guarantees, says Amnesty International

7 November
Amnesty International cites political imprisonment, torture and deaths in custody in **Malawi**

9 November
Amnesty International says **Nicaraguan** human rights record improves – but violations continue

14 November
Amnesty International calls on **Organization of American States** to act against wave of gross human rights violations in **Latin America**

15 November
Amnesty International appeals against death sentences and unfair trials in **Myanmar**

29 November
Children and young people targets in **Peruvian** armed forces' strategy of "terror to fight terror", says Amnesty International

30 November
Mauritanian security forces target black population for human rights abuses, Amnesty International says

11 December
Hong Kong refugee procedures "critically flawed" says Amnesty International – and calls for halt to repatriation plans

12 December
Sudan's military rulers hold political opponents in north while killing of unarmed civilians and captives continues in south, says Amnesty International

14 December
Hundreds of defenceless people have been deliberately killed in **Sri Lanka** during increased violence, says Amnesty International

28 December
Amnesty International appeals to new **Romanian** Government to protect political prisoners from summary trials and executions

AMNESTY INTERNATIONAL AROUND THE WORLD

There are now 4,149 local Amnesty International groups in over 60 countries around the world. In 46 countries these groups are coordinated by sections, whose addresses are given below. In addition, there are individual members, supporters and recipients of Amnesty International information (such as the monthly *Amnesty International Newsletter*) in more than 150 countries and territories.

SECTION ADDRESSES

Australia:
Amnesty International,
Australian Section,
Private Bag 23, Broadway,
New South Wales 2007

Austria:
Amnesty International,
Austrian Section,
Wiedner Gürtel 12/7, A-1040 Wien

Barbados:
Amnesty International, Barbados Section,
PO Box 872, Bridgetown

Belgium:
Amnesty International, Belgian Section
(*Flemish branch*), Kerkstraat 156,
2008 Antwerpen

Amnesty International, Belgian Section
(*francophone branch*), 9 rue Berckmans,
1060 Bruxelles

Bermuda:
Amnesty International,
Bermuda Section,
PO Box HM 2136,
Hamilton 5

Brazil:
Anistia Internacional,
Rua Harmonia 899,
05435 - São Paulo - SP

Canada:
Amnesty International, Canadian Section
(*English-speaking branch*),
130 Slater Street, Suite 900,
Ottawa, Ontario, K1P 6E2

Amnistie Internationale,
Section canadienne (*francophone*),
3516 ave du Parc, Montreal,
Quebec, H2X 2H7

Chile:
Señores, Casilla 4062, Santiago

Côte d'Ivoire:
Amnesty International,
Section de Côte d'Ivoire,
04 BP 895, Abidjan 04

Denmark:
Amnesty International, Danish Section,
Frederiksborggade 1, 1360 Copenhagen K

Ecuador:
Señores, Casilla 240,
Sucursal 15, Quito

282

Faroe Islands:
Amnesty International,
Faroe Islands Section,
PO Box 1075, FR-110 Torshavn

Finland:
Amnesty International, Finnish Section,
Ruoholahdenkatu 24,
SF-00180 Helsinki

France:
Amnesty International, French Section,
4 rue de la Pierre Levée,
75553 Paris Cedex 11

Federal Republic of Germany:
Amnesty International,
Section of the FRG,
Heerstrasse 178, 5300 Bonn 1

Ghana:
Amnesty International,
Ghanaian Section,
PO Box 1173, Koforidua E.R.

Greece:
Amnesty International, Greek Section,
30 Sina Street, 10672 Athens

Guyana:
Amnesty International, Guyana Section,
Palm Court Building, 35 Main Street,
Georgetown

Hong Kong:
Amnesty International,
Hong Kong Section,
216 Beverley Commercial Centre,
87-105 Chatham Road, Kowloon

Iceland:
Amnesty International,
Icelandic Section,
PO Box 618, 121 Reykjavík

India:
Amnesty International, Indian Section,
c/o Dateline Delhi,
21 North End Complex,
Panchkuin Road,
New Delhi 110001

Ireland:
Amnesty International, Irish Section,
8 Shaw Street, Dublin 2

Israel:
Amnesty International, Israel Section,
PO Box 23003, Tel Aviv 61230

Italy:
Amnesty International, Italian Section,
viale Mazzini 146, 00195 Rome

Japan:
Amnesty International, Japanese Section,
Daisan-Sanbu Building 2F/3F,
2-3-22 Nishi-Waseda, Shinjuku-ku,
Tokyo 169

Luxembourg:
Amnesty International,
Luxembourg Section,
Boîte Postale 1914,
1019 Luxembourg

Mexico:
Sección Mexicana de Amnistía
    Internacional,
Ap. Postal No. 20-217, San Angel,
CP 01000 Mexico DF

Netherlands:
Amnesty International, Dutch Section,
Keizersgracht 620, 1017 ER Amsterdam

New Zealand:
Amnesty International,
New Zealand Section,
PO Box 6647, Wellington 1

Nigeria:
Amnesty International, Nigerian Section,
PMB 59 Agodi, Ibadan, Oyo State

Norway:
Amnesty International,
Norwegian Section,
Maridalsveien 87, 0461 Oslo 4

Peru:
Señores, Casilla 581, Lima 18

Portugal:
Seccão Portuguesa AI,
Apartado 1642, 1016 Lisboa Codex

Puerto Rico:
Calle Cabo Alverio 562,
Ext. Roosevelt Hato Rey, San Juan 00918

Senegal:
Amnesty International,
Section Sénégalaise,
126 rue Joseph Gomis (ex rue de Bayeux),
B.P. 3813, Dakar

Spain:
Amnesty International,
Sección Española,
Paseo de Recoletos 18,
Piso 6, 28001 Madrid

Sweden:
Amnesty International,
Swedish Section,
Gyllenstiernsgatan 18,
S-115 26 Stockholm

Switzerland:
Amnesty International, Swiss Section,
PO Box 1051, CH-3001 Bern

Tanzania:
Amnesty International,
Tanzanian Section,
National Secretariat,
PO Box 4904, Dar es Salaam

Tunisia:
AI Section Tunisienne,
B.P. 256, 1002 Belvédère

United Kingdom:
Amnesty International,
British Section,
99-119 Rosebery Avenue,
London EC1R 4RE

United States of America:
Amnesty International of the USA
(AIUSA), 322 8th Ave,
New York, NY 10001

Uruguay:
Amnistía Internacional,
Sección Uruguaya,
Yi 1333 Apto. 305,
Montevideo

Venezuela:
Señores Amnistía Internacional,
Apartado 5110, Carmelitas,
Caracas 1010

COUNTRIES WITH LOCAL AMNESTY INTERNATIONAL GROUPS, BUT NO SECTION

Algeria	Egypt	Papua New Guinea
Aruba	Republic of Korea	Philippines
Argentina	Kuwait	Sierra Leone
Bangladesh	Macau	Sri Lanka
Colombia	Mauritius/Rodrigues	Taiwan
Costa Rica	Morocco	Thailand
Curaçao	Nepal	Yugoslavia
Dominican Republic	Pakistan	Zambia

INTERNATIONAL EXECUTIVE COMMITTEE

Stephen R. Abrams/United States of America
Peter R. Baehr/Netherlands
Peter Duffy/United Kingdom
Anette Fischer/Denmark
Charles Henry/United States of America
Sofía Macher/Peru
Ravi Nair/India
Bacre Waly Ndiaye/Senegal
Natasha Rogai/International Secretariat

284

SELECTED INTERNATIONAL HUMAN RIGHTS TREATIES

States which have ratified or acceded to a convention are party to the treaty and are bound to observe its provisions. States which have signed but not yet ratified have expressed their intention to become a party at some future date; meanwhile they are obliged to refrain from acts which would defeat the object and purpose of the treaty.

(AS OF 31 DECEMBER 1989)

	International Covenant on Civil and Political Rights (ICCPR)	Optional Protocol to ICCPR	International Covenant on Economic, Social and Cultural Rights (ICESCR)	Convention against Torture and Other Cruel, Inhuman or Degrading Treatment or Punishment
Afghanistan	X		X	x (28)
Albania				
Algeria	X	X	X	x (22)
Angola				
Antigua and Barbuda				
Argentina	X		X	x (22)
Australia	X		X	X
Austria	X	X	X	x (22)
Bahamas				
Bahrain				
Bangladesh				
Barbados	X	X	X	
Belgium	X		X	S
Belize				X
Benin				
Bhutan				
Bolivia	X	X	X	S
Botswana				
Brazil				X
Brunei				
Bulgaria	X		X	x (28)
Burkina Faso				
Burundi				
Byelorussian SSR	X		X	x (28)
Cameroon	X	X	X	X
Canada	X	X	X	x (22)
Cape Verde				
Central African Republic	X	X	X	
Chad				
Chile	X		X	x (28)
China				x (28)
Colombia	X	X	X	X
Comoros				
Congo	X	X	X	

	International Covenant on Civil and Political Rights (ICCPR)	Optional Protocol to ICCPR	International Covenant on Economic, Social and Cultural Rights (ICESCR)	Convention against Torture and Other Cruel, Inhuman or Degrading Treatment or Punishment
Costa Rica	X	X	X	S
Côte d'Ivoire				
Cuba				S
Cyprus	X	S	X	S
Czechoslovakia	X		X	X (28)
Denmark	X	X	X	X (22)
Djibouti				
Dominica				
Dominican Republic	X	X	X	S
Ecuador	X	X	X	X (22)
Egypt	X		X	X
El Salvador	X	S	X	
Equatorial Guinea	X	X	X	
Ethiopia				
Fiji				
Finland	X	X	X	X (22)
France	X	X	X	X (22)
Gabon	X		X	S
Gambia	X	X	X	S
German Democratic Republic	X		X	X (28)
Germany, Federal Republic of	X		X	S
Ghana				
Greece			X	X (22)
Grenada				
Guatemala			X	
Guinea	X	S	X	X
Guinea-Bissau				
Guyana	X		X	X
Haiti				
Holy See				
Honduras	S	S	X	
Hungary	X	X	X	X (22) (28)
Iceland	X	X	X	S
India	X		X	
Indonesia				S
Iran	X		X	
Iraq	X		X	

	International Covenant on Civil and Political Rights (ICCPR)	Optional Protocol to ICCPR	International Covenant on Economic, Social and Cultural Rights (ICESCR)	Convention against Torture and Other Cruel, Inhuman or Degrading Treatment or Punishment
Ireland	X	X	X	
Israel	S		S	S
Italy	X	X	X	x (22)
Jamaica	X	X	X	
Japan	X		X	
Jordan	X		X	
Kampuchea	S		S	
Kenya	X		X	
Kiribati				
Korea (Democratic People's Republic of)	X		X	
Korea (Republic of)				
Kuwait				
Lao People's Democratic Republic				
Lebanon	X		X	
Lesotho				
Liberia	S		S	
Libyan Arab Jamahiriya	X	X	X	X
Liechtenstein				S
Luxembourg	X	X	X	x (22)
Madagascar	X	X	X	
Malawi				
Malaysia				
Maldives				
Mali	X		X	
Malta			S	
Mauritania				
Mauritius	X	X	X	
Mexico	X		X	X
Monaco				
Mongolia	X		X	
Morocco	X		X	s (28)
Mozambique				
Myanmar (Burma)				
Nauru				
Nepal				
Netherlands	X	X	X	x (22)
New Zealand	X	X	X	X

	International Covenant on Civil and Political Rights (ICCPR)	Optional Protocol to ICCPR	International Covenant on Economic, Social and Cultural Rights (ICESCR)	Convention against Torture and Other Cruel, Inhuman or Degrading Treatment or Punishment
Nicaragua	x	x	x	s
Niger	x	x	x	
Nigeria				s
Norway	x	x	x	x (22)
Oman				
Pakistan				
Panama	x	x	x	x
Papua New Guinea				
Paraguay				s
Peru	x	x	x	x
Philippines	x	x	x	x
Poland	x		x	x (28)
Portugal	x	x	x	x (22)
Qatar				
Romania	x		x	
Rwanda	x		x	
St Lucia				
St Christopher and Nevis				
St Vincent and The Grenadines	x	x	x	
Samoa				
San Marino	x	x	x	
São Tomé and Príncipe				
Saudi Arabia				
Senegal	x	x	x	x
Seychelles				
Sierra Leone				s
Singapore				
Solomon Islands			x	
Somalia				
South Africa				
Spain	x	x	x	x (22)
Sri Lanka	x		x	
Sudan	x		x	s
Suriname	x	x	x	
Swaziland				
Sweden	x	x	x	x (22)
Switzerland				x (22)
Syria	x		x	

	International Covenant on Civil and Political Rights (ICCPR)	Optional Protocol to ICCPR	International Covenant on Economic, Social and Cultural Rights (ICESCR)	Convention against Torture and Other Cruel, Inhuman or Degrading Treatment or Punishment
Tanzania	X		X	
Thailand				
Togo	X	X	X	X (22)
Tonga				
Trinidad and Tobago	X	X	X	
Tunisia	X		X	X (22)
Turkey				X (22)
Tuvalu				
Uganda			X	X
Ukrainian SSR	X		X	X (28)
Union of Soviet Socialist Republics	X		X	X (28)
United Arab Emirates				
United Kingdom	X		X	X
United States of America	S		S	S
Uruguay	X	X	X	X (22)
Vanuatu				
Venezuela	X	X	X	S
Viet Nam	X		X	
Yemen (Arab Republic)				
Yemen (People's Democratic Republic)	X		X	
Yugoslavia	X		X	S
Zaire	X	X	X	
Zambia	X	X	X	
Zimbabwe				

s – denotes that country has signed but not yet ratified
x – denotes that country is a party, either through ratification or accession
(22) denotes Declaration under Article 22 recognizing the competence of the Committee against Torture to consider individual complaints of violations of the convention
(28) denotes that country has made a reservation under Article 28 that it does not recognize the competence of the Committee against Torture to examine reliable information which appears to indicate that torture is being systematically practised, and to undertake a confidential inquiry if warranted

The countries listed in this chart are those included in the official United Nations publication entitled *Human Rights International Instruments: Signatures, Ratifications, Accessions etc.*

SELECTED REGIONAL HUMAN RIGHTS TREATIES

(AS OF 31 DECEMBER 1989)

ORGANIZATION OF AFRICAN UNITY (OAU)
AFRICAN CHARTER ON HUMAN AND PEOPLES' RIGHTS (1981)

Algeria	x	Gabon	x	Rwanda	x
Angola		Gambia	x	Saharawi Arab	
Benin	x	Ghana	x	Democratic Republic	x
Botswana	x	Guinea	x	São Tomé y Príncipe	x
Burkina Faso	x	Guinea-Bissau	x	Senegal	x
Burundi	x	Kenya		Seychelles	
Cameroon	x	Lesotho	s	Sierra Leone	x
Cape Verde	x	Liberia	x	Somalia	x
Central African Republic	x	Libya	x	Sudan	x
Chad	x	Madagascar		Swaziland	
Comoros	x	Malawi		Tanzania	x
Congo	x	Mali	x	Togo	x
Côte d'Ivoire		Mauritania	x	Tunisia	x
Djibouti		Mauritius		Uganda	x
Egypt	x	Mozambique		Zaire	x
Equatorial Guinea	x	Niger	x	Zambia	x
Ethiopia		Nigeria	x	Zimbabwe	x

s – denotes country has signed but not yet ratified
x – denotes that a country is a party, either through ratification or accession

This chart lists countries which were members of the OAU at the end of 1989.

ORGANIZATION OF AMERICAN STATES (OAS)
AMERICAN CONVENTION ON HUMAN RIGHTS (1969)

Antigua and Barbuda		Ecuador	x (62)	St Christopher	
Argentina	x (62)	El Salvador	x	and Nevis	
Bahamas		Grenada	x	St Lucia	
Barbados	x	Guatemala	x (62)	St Vincent and	
Bolivia	x	Haiti	x	The Grenadines	
Brazil		Honduras	x (62)	Suriname	x (62)
Chile	s	Jamaica	x	Trinidad and	
Colombia	x (62)	Mexico	x	Tobago	
Costa Rica	x (62)	Nicaragua	x	United States of	
Cuba		Panama	x	America	s
Dominica		Paraguay	x	Uruguay	x (62)
Dominican Republic	x	Peru	x (62)	Venezuela	x (62)

s – denotes country has signed but not yet ratified
x – denotes that a country is a party, either through ratification or accession
(62) denotes Declaration under Article 62 recognizing as binding the jurisdiction of the
Inter-American Court of Human Rights (on all matters relating to the interpretation
or application of the American Convention)

This chart lists countries which were members of the OAS at the end of 1989.

	European Convention on Human Rights (1950)	Article 25	Article 46	Protocol No. 6*	European Convention for Prevention of Torture**
	COUNCIL OF EUROPE				
Austria	X	X	X	X	X
Belgium	X	X	X	S	S
Cyprus	X	X	X		X
Denmark	X	X	X	X	X
Finland	S			S	
France	X	X	X	X	X
Germany, Federal Republic of	X	X	X	X	S
Greece	X	X	X	S	S
Iceland	X	X	X	X	S
Ireland	X	X	X		X
Italy	X	X	X	X	X
Liechtenstein	X	X	X		S
Luxembourg	X	X	X	X	X
Malta	X	X	X		X
Netherlands	X	X	X	X	X
Norway	X	X	X	X	X
Portugal	X	X	X	X	S
San Marino	X	X	X		
Spain	X	X	X	X	X
Sweden	X	X	X	X	X
Switzerland	X		X	X	X
Turkey	X	X			X
United Kingdom	X	X	X		X

s – denotes country has signed but not yet ratified
x – denotes that a country is a party, either through ratification or accession
Article 25: denotes Declaration under Article 25 of the European Convention, recognizing the competence of the European Commission of Human Rights to consider individual complaints of violations of the Convention
Article 46: denotes Declaration under Article 46 of the European Convention, recognizing as compulsory the jurisdiction of the European Court of Human Rights in all matters concerning interpretation and application of the European Convention

* Protocol 6 to the European Convention on Human Rights (1983): concerning abolition of the death penalty
** European Convention for the Prevention of Torture and Inhuman or Degrading Treatment or Punishment (1987)

This chart lists countries which were members of the Council of Europe at the end of 1989.

OVERDUE REPORTS

BY STATES PARTIES TO THE INTERNATIONAL COVENANT ON CIVIL AND POLITICAL RIGHTS

Governments which have ratified or acceded to the International Covenant on Civil and Political Rights (ICCPR) are referred to as "States Parties" to that treaty. Article 40 of the ICCPR requires States Parties to submit reports to the United Nations "on the measures they have adopted which give effect to the rights recognized [in the ICCPR] and on the progress made in the enjoyment of those rights". The reports are supposed to "indicate the factors and difficulties, if any, affecting the implementation of the present Covenant".

The initial report is due within one year after the ICCPR enters into force for the particular state; subsequent reports are due every five years. They are reviewed by the Human Rights Committee, the body of 18 experts which monitors implementation of the ICCPR.

The Human Rights Committee has repeatedly expressed concern about the non-compliance of states with their reporting obligations.

The Committee noted that there may be various reasons for reports being overdue, including a shortage of resources, the assignment of insufficient priority, and in some cases the reluctance of states to expose themselves to scrutiny.

The UN General Assembly has urged States Parties to the ICCPR which have not yet done so "to submit their reports as speedily as possible".

As of 31 December 1989 the following states were at least one year late in submitting their initial, second or third periodic report.

INITIAL REPORTS

State Party	Date due	Number of reminders sent
Gabon	20 April 1984	11
Niger	6 June 1987	5
Sudan	17 June 1987	5
Equatorial Guinea	24 December 1988	2

SECOND PERIODIC REPORTS

State Party	Date due	Number of reminders sent
Libyan Arab Jamahiriya	4 February 1983	13
Iran (Islamic Republic of)	21 March 1983	13
Madagascar	3 August 1983	12
Bulgaria	28 April 1984	12
Cyprus	18 August 1984	12
Syrian Arab Republic	18 August 1984	12
Cook Islands (New Zealand)	27 March 1985	1
Gambia	21 June 1985	10
Suriname	2 August 1985	9
Venezuela	1 November 1985	9
Lebanon	21 March 1986	8
Kenya	11 April 1986	8
Mali	11 April 1986	8
United Republic of Tanzania	11 April 1986	8
Jamaica	1 August 1986	6
Sri Lanka	10 September 1986	6

Morocco	31 October 1986	6
Netherlands Antilles	31 October 1986	1
Guyana	10 April 1987	6
Iceland	30 October 1987	5
Democratic People's Republic of Korea	13 December 1987	4
St Vincent and The Grenadines	8 February 1988	–
Austria	9 April 1988	3
Peru	9 April 1988	3
Egypt	13 April 1988	3
Viet Nam	23 December 1988	–
El Salvador	31 December 1988	2

THIRD PERIODIC REPORTS

State Party	Date due	Number of reminders sent
Libyan Arab Jamahiriya	4 February 1988	3
Iran (Islamic Republic of)	21 March 1988	3
Lebanon	21 March 1988	3
Panama	6 June 1988	–
Madagascar	3 August 1988	3
Yugoslavia	3 August 1988	3
Byelorussian SSR	4 November 1988	3

OVERDUE REPORTS

BY STATES PARTIES TO THE CONVENTION AGAINST TORTURE AND OTHER CRUEL, INHUMAN OR DEGRADING TREATMENT OR PUNISHMENT

Governments which have ratified or acceded to the Convention against Torture and Other Cruel, Inhuman or Degrading Treatment or Punishment are referred to as "States Parties" to that treaty. Article 19 of the Convention against Torture requires States Parties to submit reports to the United Nations "on the measures they have taken to give effect to their undertakings [under the Convention against Torture]".

The initial report is due within one year after the Convention against Torture enters into force for the particular state; supplementary reports are due every four years and should cover "any new measures taken". The reports are reviewed by the Committee against Torture, the body of 10 experts which monitors implementation of the Convention against Torture.

As of 31 December 1989 the following states were at least one year late in submitting their initial reports.

INITIAL REPORTS

State Party	Date due	Number of reminders sent
Afghanistan	25 June 1988	2
Belize	25 June 1988	2
Bulgaria	25 June 1988	2
Uganda	25 June 1988	2
Ukrainian SSR	25 June 1988	2
Uruguay	25 June 1988	2
Panama	22 September 1988	2
Luxembourg	28 October 1988	2
Spain	19 November 1988	2
Togo	17 December 1988	2

SECOND OPTIONAL PROTOCOL TO THE INTERNATIONAL COVENANT ON CIVIL AND POLITICAL RIGHTS AIMING AT THE ABOLITION OF THE DEATH PENALTY

The United Nations General Assembly adopted the following instrument by Resolution 44/128 of 15 December 1989.

The States parties to the present Protocol,
Believing that abolition of the death penalty contributes to enhancement of human dignity and progressive development of human rights,
Recalling article 3 of the Universal Declaration of Human Rights adopted on 10 December 1948 and article 6 of the International Covenant on Civil and Political Rights adopted on 16 December 1966,
Noting that article 6 of the International Covenant on Civil and Political Rights refers to abolition of the death penalty in terms which strongly suggest that abolition is desirable,
Convinced that all measures of abolition of the death penalty should be considered as progress in the enjoyment of the right to life,
Desirous to undertake hereby an international commitment to abolish the death penalty,
Have agreed as follows:

Article 1
1. No one within the jurisdiction of a State party to the present Optional Protocol shall be executed.
2. Each State party shall take all necessary measures to abolish the death penalty within its jurisdiction.

Article 2
1. No reservation is admissible to the present Protocol except for a reservation made at the time of ratification or accession which provides for the application of the death penalty in time of war pursuant to a conviction for a most serious crime of a military nature committed during wartime.
2. The State party making such a reservation will at the time of ratification or accession communicate to the Secretary-General of the United Nations the relevant provisions of its national legislation applicable during wartime.

3. The State party having made such a reservation will notify the Secretary-General of the United Nations of any beginning or ending of a state of war applicable to its territory.

Article 3
The States parties to the present Protocol shall include in the reports they submit to the Human Rights Committee in accordance with article 40 of the Covenant information on the measures they have adopted to give effect to the present Protocol.

Article 4
With respect to the States parties to the Covenant which have made a declaration under article 41, the competence of the Human Rights Committee to receive and consider communications that a State party claims that another State party is not fulfilling its obligations shall extend to the provisions of the present Protocol, unless the State party concerned has made a statement to the contrary at the moment of ratification or accession.

Article 5
With respect to the States parties to the (First) Optional Protocol to the International Covenant on Civil and Political Rights adopted on 16 December 1966, the competence of the Human Rights Committee to receive and consider communications from individuals subject to its jurisdiction shall extend to the provisions of the present Protocol, unless the State party concerned has made a statement to the contrary at the moment of ratification or accession.

Article 6
1. The provisions of the present Protocol shall apply as additional provisions to the Covenant.
2. Without prejudice to the possibility of a

reservation under article 2 of the present Protocol, the right guaranteed in article 1, paragraph 1, of the present Protocol shall not be subject to any derogation under article 4 of the Covenant.

Article 7

1. The present Protocol is open for signature by any State which has signed the Covenant.

2. The present Protocol is subject to ratification by any State which has ratified the Covenant or acceded to it. Instruments of ratification shall be deposited with the Secretary-General of the United Nations.

3. The present Protocol shall be open to accession by any State which has ratified the Covenant or acceded to it.

4. Accession shall be effected by the deposit of an instrument of accession with the Secretary-General of the United Nations.

5. The Secretary-General of the United Nations shall inform all States which have signed the present Protocol or acceded to it of the deposit of each instrument of ratification or accession.

Article 8

1. The present Protocol shall enter into force three months after the date of the deposit with the Secretary-General of the United Nations of the tenth instrument of ratification or accession.

2. For each State ratifying the present Protocol or acceding to it after the deposit of the tenth instrument of ratification or accession, the present Protocol shall enter into force three months after the date of the deposit of its own instrument of ratification or accession.

Article 9

The provisions of the present Protocol shall extend to all parts of federal States without any limitations or exceptions.

Article 10

The Secretary-General of the United Nations shall inform all States referred to in article 48, paragraph 1, of the Covenant of the following particulars:

(a) Reservations, communications and notifications under article 2 of the present Protocol;

(b) Statements made under its articles 4 or 5;

(c) Signatures, ratifications and accessions under its article 7;

(d) The date of the entry into force of the present Protocol under its article 8.

Article 11

1. The present Protocol, of which the Arabic, Chinese, English, French, Russian and Spanish texts are equally authentic, shall be deposited in the archives of the United Nations.

2. The Secretary-General of the United Nations shall transmit certified copies of the present Protocol to all States referred to in article 48 of the Covenant.

PRINCIPLES ON THE EFFECTIVE PREVENTION AND INVESTIGATION OF EXTRA-LEGAL, ARBITRARY AND SUMMARY EXECUTIONS

At its 15th Plenary Meeting the United Nations Economic and Social Council (ECOSOC) by Resolution 1989/65 of 24 May 1989 recommended that the Principles on the Effective Prevention and Investigation of Extra-Legal, Arbitrary and Summary Executions annexed to the Resolution be taken into account and respected by governments. The United Nations General Assembly subsequently endorsed the Principles by Resolution 44/162 of 15 December 1989. The text of the Principles is given below.

Prevention

1. Governments shall prohibit by law all extra-legal, arbitrary and summary executions and shall ensure that any such executions are recognized as offences under their criminal laws, and are punishable by appropriate penalties which take into account the seriousness of such offences. Exceptional circumstances including a state of war or threat of war, internal political instability or any other public emergency may not be invoked as a justification of such executions. Such executions shall not be carried out under any circumstances including, but not limited to, situations of internal armed conflict, excessive or illegal use of force by a public official or other person acting in an official capacity or a person acting at the instigation, or with the consent or acquiescence of such person, and situations in which deaths occur in custody. This prohibition shall prevail over decrees issued by governmental authority.

2. In order to prevent extra-legal, arbitrary and summary executions, Governments shall ensure strict control, including a clear chain of command over all officials responsible for the apprehension, arrest, detention, custody and imprisonment as well as those officials authorized by law to use force and firearms.

3. Governments shall prohibit orders from superior officers or public authorities authorizing or inciting other persons to carry out any such extra-legal, arbitrary or summary executions. All persons shall have the right and the duty to defy such orders. Training of law enforcement officials shall emphasize the above provisions.

4. Effective protection through judicial or other means shall be guaranteed to individuals and groups who are in danger of extra-legal, arbitrary or summary executions, including those who receive death threats.

5. No one shall be involuntarily returned or extradited to a country where there are substantial grounds for believing that he or she may become a victim of extra-legal, arbitrary or summary execution in that country.

6. Governments shall ensure that persons deprived of their liberty are held in officially recognized places of custody, and that accurate information on their custody and whereabouts, including transfers, is made promptly available to their relatives and lawyer or other persons of confidence.

7. Qualified inspectors, including medical personnel, or an equivalent independent authority, shall conduct inspections in places of custody on a regular basis, and be empowered to undertake unannounced inspections on their own initiative, with full guarantees of independence in the exercise of this function. The inspectors shall have unrestricted access to all persons in such places of custody, as well as to all their records.

8. Governments shall make every effort to prevent extra-legal, arbitrary and summary executions through measures such as diplomatic intercession, improved access of complainants to intergovernmental and judicial bodies, and public denunciation. Intergovernmental mechanisms shall be used to investigate reports of any such executions and to take effective action against such practices. Governments,

including those of countries where extra-legal, arbitrary and summary executions are reasonably suspected to occur, shall co-operate fully in international investigations on the subject.

Investigation

9. There shall be a thorough, prompt and impartial investigation of all suspected cases of extra-legal, arbitrary and summary executions, including cases where complaints by relatives or other reliable reports suggest unnatural death in the above circumstances. Governments shall maintain investigative offices and procedures to undertake such inquiries. The purpose of the investigation shall be to determine the cause, manner and time of death, the person responsible, and any pattern or practice which may have brought about that death. It shall include an adequate autopsy, collection and analysis of all physical and documentary evidence, and statements from witnesses. The investigation shall distinguish between natural death, accidental death, suicide and homicide.

10. The investigative authority shall have the power to obtain all the information necessary to the inquiry. Those persons conducting the investigation shall have at their disposal all the necessary budgetary and technical resources for effective investigation. They shall also have the authority to oblige officials allegedly involved in any such executions to appear and testify. The same shall apply to any witness. To this end, they shall be entitled to issue summons to witnesses, including the officials allegedly involved, and to demand the production of evidence.

11. In cases in which the established investigative procedures are inadequate because of lack of expertise or impartiality, because of the importance of the matter or because of the apparent existence of a pattern of abuse, and in cases where there are complaints from the family of the victim about these inadequacies or other substantial reasons, Governments shall pursue investigations through an independent commission of inquiry or similar procedure. Members of such a commission shall be chosen for their recognized impartiality, competence and independence as individuals. In particular,

they shall be independent of any institution, agency or person that may be the subject of the inquiry. The commission shall have the authority to obtain all information necessary to the inquiry and shall conduct the inquiry as provided for under these Principles.

12. The body of the deceased person shall not be disposed of until an adequate autopsy is conducted by a physician, who shall, if possible, be an expert in forensic pathology. Those conducting the autopsy shall have the right of access to all investigative data, to the place where the body was discovered, and to the place where the death is thought to have occurred. If the body has been buried and it later appears that an investigation is required, the body shall be promptly and competently exhumed for an autopsy. If skeletal remains are discovered, they should be carefully exhumed and studied according to systematic anthropological techniques.

13. The body of the deceased shall be available to those conducting the autopsy for a sufficient amount of time to enable a thorough investigation to be carried out. The autopsy shall, at a minimum, attempt to establish the identity of the deceased and the cause and manner of death. The time and place of death shall also be determined to the extent possible. Detailed colour photographs of the deceased shall be included in the autopsy report in order to document and support the findings of the investigation. The autopsy report must describe any and all injuries to the deceased including any evidence of torture.

14. In order to ensure objective results, those conducting the autopsy must be able to function impartially and independently of any potentially implicated persons or organizations or entities.

15. Complainants, witnesses, those conducting the investigation and their families shall be protected from violence, threats of violence or any other form of intimidation. Those potentially implicated in extra-legal, arbitrary or summary executions shall be removed from any position of control or power, whether direct or indirect, over complainants, witnesses and their families, as well as over those conducting investigations.

16. Families of the deceased and their legal representatives shall be informed of, and have access to, any hearing as well as to all information relevant to the investigation, and shall be entitled to present other evidence. The family of the deceased shall have the right to insist that a medical or other qualified representative be present at the autopsy. When the identity of a deceased person has been determined, a notification of death shall be posted, and the family or relatives of the deceased immediately informed. The body of the deceased shall be returned to them upon completion of the investigation.

17. A written report shall be made within a reasonable period of time on the methods and findings of such investigations. The report shall be made public immediately and shall include the scope of the inquiry, procedures and methods used to evaluate evidence as well as conclusions and recommendations based on findings of fact and on applicable law. The report shall also describe in detail specific events that were found to have occurred, and the evidence upon which such findings were based, and list the names of witnesses who testified, with the exception of those whose identities have been withheld for their own protection. The Government shall, within a reasonable period of time, either reply to the report of the investigation, or indicate the steps to be taken in response to it.

Legal proceedings

18. Governments shall ensure that persons identified by the investigation as having participated in extra-legal, arbitrary or summary executions in any territory under their jurisdiction are brought to justice. Governments shall either bring such persons to justice or co-operate to extradite any such persons to other countries wishing to exercise jurisdiction. This principle shall apply irrespective of who and where the perpetrators or the victims are, their nationalities or where the offence was committed.

19. Without prejudice to Principle 3 above, an order from a superior officer or a public authority may not be invoked as a justification for extra-legal, arbitrary or summary executions. Superiors, officers or other public officials may be held responsible for acts committed by officials under their hierarchical authority if they had a reasonable opportunity to prevent such acts. In no circumstances, including a state of war, siege or other public emergency, shall blanket immunity from prosecution be granted to any person allegedly involved in extra-legal, arbitrary or summary executions.

20. The families and dependants of victims of extra-legal, arbitrary or summary executions shall be entitled to fair and adequate compensation within a reasonable period of time.

APPENDIX XI

297

UNITED NATIONS CONVENTION ON THE RIGHTS OF THE CHILD

On 20 November 1989, during its 44th session, the United Nations General Assembly by Resolution 44/25 formally adopted the Convention on the Rights of the Child. The Convention, which will come into force after ratification by 20 states, contains 54 articles covering the specific rights of children within the broad range of civil, economic, social, cultural and religious rights, for example rights in the fields of education, health, adoption, child labour and sexual exploitation. It also includes the provision, in Article 37(a), that "no child shall be subjected to torture or other cruel, inhuman or degrading treatment or punishment. Neither capital punishment nor life imprisonment without possibility of release shall be imposed for offences committed by persons below eighteen years of age." The monitoring body of the treaty — the Committee on the Rights of the Child — is to consist of 10 independent experts elected by the States Parties.

SELECTED STATISTICS

AMNESTY INTERNATIONAL
MEMBERSHIP

At the beginning of 1990 there were 4,149 local Amnesty International groups in over 60 countries. There were more than 700,000 members and subscribers in about 150 countries.

PRISONER CASES
AND RELEASES

In 1989 Amnesty International took up 3,376 cases involving the adoption of prisoners of conscience or those under investigation as possible prisoners of conscience. During the year, action began on 1,643 new prisoner cases. A total of 1,143 cases involving the release of prisoners of conscience or those under investigation as possible prisoners of conscience was recorded.

URGENT ACTION APPEALS

During 1989 Amnesty International initiated 577 Urgent Action appeals on behalf of 2,886 people in 87 countries. Of these appeals, 95 were prompted by reports of torture and 18 were made on behalf of prisoners in a critical state of health and urgently in need of medical treatment. Some 153 appeals were issued in cases of arbitrary arrest, prolonged incommunicado detention, detention without charge or trial or unfair trial. Some 133 appeals related to extrajudicial killings or "disappearances" and 125 were made on behalf of prisoners sentenced to death. Twenty-three appeals related to death threats and 15 to ill-treatment. Others were issued in cases of deaths in detention, risk of *refoulement*, amputation, hunger-strike and political executions.

REGIONAL ACTION NETWORKS

Amnesty International's Regional Action Networks deal with human rights abuses in almost all of the world's countries. During 1989 participants in these 19 networks remained ready to take action when abuses occurred in Africa, the Americas, Asia and the Pacific, Europe and the Middle East and North Africa. In 1989 the Regional Action Networks worked on the cases of thousands of victims of human rights violations.

AMNESTY INTERNATIONAL FUNDING

The budget adopted by Amnesty International for 1989 was £9,109,700. This sum represents approximately one third of the estimated income likely to be raised during the year by the movement's national sections. Amnesty International's national sections and local volunteer groups are responsible for funding the movement. There is no central fund-raising program and no money is sought or accepted from governments. The donations that sustain Amnesty International's work come from its members and the public.